Constitutional Interpretation in Singapore

At the heart of constitutional interpretation is the struggle between, on the one hand, fidelity to founding meanings, and, on the other hand, creative interpretation to suit the context and needs of an evolving society. This book considers the recent growth of constitutional cases in Singapore in the last ten years. It examines the underpinnings of Singapore's constitutional system, explores how Singapore courts have dealt with issues related to rights and power, and sets developments in Singapore in the wider context of new thinking and constitutional developments worldwide. It argues that Singapore is witnessing a shift in legal and political culture as both judges and citizens display an increasing willingness to engage with constitutional ideas and norms.

Jaclyn L Neo is an Assistant Professor in the Faculty of Law at the National University of Singapore.

Routledge Law in Asia
Series editors: Randall Peerenboom and Pip Nicholson

3 **Support for Victims of Crime in Asia**
Edited by Wing-Cheong Chan

4 **Administrative Law and Governance in Asia**
Comparative perspectives
Edited by Tom Ginsburg and Albert HY Chen

5 **Regulation in Asia**
Edited by John Gillespie and Randall Peerenboom

6 **New Courts in Asia**
Edited by Andrew Harding and Penelope (Pip) Nicholson

7 **Legal Education in Asia**
Edited by Stacey Steele and Kathryn Taylor

8 **Legal Reforms in China and Vietnam**
A comparison of Asian communist regimes
John Gillespie and Albert HY Chen

9 **Public Interest Litigation in Asia**
Po Jen Yap and Holning Lau

10 **Freedom of Information Reform in China**
Information flow analysis
Weibing Xiao

11 **Law and Development in Asia**
Edited by Gerald Paul McAlinn and Caslav Pejovic

12 **The Judicialization of Politics in Asia**
Edited by Bjorn Dressel

13 **Juries in the Japanese Legal System**
The continuing struggle for citizen participation and democracy
Dimitri Vanoverbeke

14 **Confucian Constitutionalism in East Asia**
Bui Ngoc Son

15 **Religion, Law and Intolerance in Indonesia**
Tim Lindsey and Helen Pausacker

16 **Constitutional Interpretation in Singapore**
Theory and practice
Edited by Jaclyn L Neo

Constitutional Interpretation in Singapore

Theory and practice

Edited by Jaclyn L Neo

Routledge
Taylor & Francis Group
LONDON AND NEW YORK

First published 2017 by Routledge

2 Park Square, Milton Park, Abingdon, Oxfordshire OX14 4RN
711 Third Avenue, New York, NY 10017

Routledge is an imprint of the Taylor & Francis Group, an informa business

First issued in paperback 2017

British Library Cataloging-in-Publication Data
A catalogue record for this book is available from the British Library

Library of Congress Cataloging-in-Publication Data
Names: Neo, Jaclyn L., editor.
Title: Constitutional interpretation in Singapore : theory and practice / Edited by Jaclyn L. Neo.
Description: New York, NY : Routledge, 2017. | Series: Routledge law in Asia ; 16 | Includes bibliographical references.
Identifiers: LCCN 2016000856| ISBN 9781138914483 (hardback) | ISBN 9781315690766 (ebook)
Subjects: LCSH: Constitutional law–Singapore.
Classification: LCC KPP171 .C66 2017 | DDC 342.95957–dc23LC record available at http://lccn.loc.gov/2016000856

ISBN: 978-1-138-91448-3 (hbk)
ISBN: 978-1-138-47775-9 (pbk)

Typeset in Times New Roman
by Wearset Ltd, Boldon, Tyne and Wear

Contents

Table of cases

Contributors

Michael W DOWDLE *BM (Kansas), MM (Johns Hopkins), MPhil (Columbia), JD (NYU)* is an Assistant Professor of Law at the National University of Singapore. He was formerly Chair in Globalization and Governance at the Institut d'Etudes Politiques de Paris (Sciences Po) where he taught graduate and undergraduate courses on comparative constitutionalism and comparative regulation. Prior to that, he held faculty positions at the University of Washington School of Law, Qinghua University Law School, the Australian National University and the New York University School of Law.

GOH Yihan *LLB (Hons) (NUS), LLM (Harvard)* is an Associate Professor of Law at the Singapore Management University since 2014. Before that, he was an Assistant Professor at the National University of Singapore, and an Assistant Registrar and the Senior Justices' Law Clerk at the Supreme Court of Singapore. Yihan is at present also a board member of the Singapore Institute of Legal Education and the Singapore Judicial College. He has written on various aspects of the Singapore legal system and specialises in the law of contract and torts. Among his many publications, he is a contributor to *The Law of Contract in Singapore* (2012) and a co-author of *Contract Law in Singapore* (2012). In 2013, he was awarded the Singapore Law Merit Award by the Singapore Academy of Law in recognition of his contributions to the development and advancement of Singapore law.

Andrew J HARDING *LLM (NUS), MA (Oxford), PhD (Monash)* is a Professor of Law at the National University of Singapore (NUS). He is a leading scholar in the fields of Asian legal studies and comparative constitutional law. He commenced his academic career at NUS before moving to SOAS, University of London, where he became Head of the Law School and Director of the Centre for South East Asian Studies. He joined NUS as Director of the Centre for Asian Legal Studies and Director of the Asian Law Institute, from the University of Victoria, BC Canada, where he was Professor of Asia-Pacific Legal Relations and Director of the Centre for Asia-Pacific Initiatives. Andrew has worked extensively on constitutional law in Malaysia and Thailand, and has made extensive contributions to scholarship in comparative law, and law and development, having published nine books as author or editor.

He is co-founding editor of Hart Publishing's book series 'Constitutional Systems of the World', a major resource for constitutional law in context, and has authored the books on Malaysia and Thailand in that series (2011, 2012).

Swati JHAVERI *BA (Oxon), BCL (Oxon)* joined the National University of Singapore's Law Faculty in August 2012. She previously taught at the Chinese University of Hong Kong's Faculty of Law. Her areas of research include public law and the law of torts. She has published in these areas in Public Law, the Tort Law Review and the International Journal of Constitutional Law. While at CUHK, she was awarded the Vice Chancellor's Exemplary Teaching Award. She was also awarded a competitive research grant from the General Research Fund of the Research Grants Council of Hong Kong to investigate the post-1997 impact of judicial review on legislative process and content. At NUS she was awarded the Faculty and University's Annual Teaching Excellence Awards for the 2013/2014 Academic Year. She is also co-author of *Hong Kong Administrative Law* (2016) and a forthcoming text on Administrative Law in Singapore with Jaclyn Neo and Lim Wei Lee.

Jack Tsen-Ta LEE *LLB (Hons) (NUS), LLM (London), PhD (Birmingham)* is an Assistant Professor of Law at the Singapore Management University (SMU). After his postgraduate studies at University College London on a British Chevening Scholarship, he returned to Singapore and worked as an Assistant Director for the Singapore Academy of Law, a professional association of judges, lawyers, government legal officers and law academics. His doctoral research at the University of Birmingham examined the interpretation of bills of rights from a comparative law perspective. Jack has published widely on constitutional law, human rights law, and cultural property and heritage law. Some of his recent publications include 'According to the Spirit and not to the Letter: Proportionality and the Singapore Constitution' 8(3) Vienna Journal on International Constitutional Law 276 (2014), 'The Text through Time' 31(3) Statute Law Review 217 (2010), and 'Interpreting Bills of Rights: The Value of a Comparative Approach' 5 International Journal of Constitutional Law 122 (2007).

Jaclyn L NEO *LLB (Hons) (NUS), LLM (Yale), JSD (Yale)* is an Assistant Professor of Law at the National University of Singapore (NUS). She specialises in constitutional and administrative law, as well as issues of migration and citizenship. Jaclyn received her Doctor of the Science of Law (JSD) from Yale, where she worked on a new constitutional theory on state and religion. She is the recipient of several academic scholarships, including the NUS Law Faculty scholarship and the NUS Overseas Graduate Scholarship. Jaclyn's recent work on constitutional and human rights law has been published in the International Journal of Constitutional Law (ICON), the Oxford Journal of Law and Religion, the Human Rights Quarterly and the Singapore Journal of Legal Studies. She is also a co-author of a forthcoming text on Administrative

Law in Singapore with Swati Jhaveri and Lim Wei Lee. Jaclyn has also been involved in various consulting projects for civil society organisations and presided over a research project on religious freedom in Southeast Asia commissioned by the Human Rights Resources Centre.

VK RAJAH, Senior Counsel *LLB (NUS), LLM (Cambridge)* is currently the Attorney-General of the Republic of Singapore. He was Managing Partner of Rajah & Tann from 1986 to 2003. VK was appointed Judicial Commissioner of the Supreme Court on 2 January 2004, and was subsequently appointed Supreme Court Judge on 1 November 2004. He was elevated to Judge of Appeal in April 2007 and assumed office as Attorney-General in June 2014. In November 2014, he was appointed an Honorary Bencher of the Honourable Society of the Middle Temple.

Victor V RAMRAJ *BA (Hons) (McGill), LLB (Toronto), MA (Toronto), LLM (Dist) (Queen's–Belfast), PhD (Toronto)* is the Chair in Asia-Pacific Legal Relations at the Centre for Asia-Pacific Initiatives (CAPI) and Professor of Law at the Faculty of Law at the University of Victoria in British Columbia, Canada. He has graduate degrees in law and philosophy and served as a judicial law clerk at the Federal Court of Appeal in Ottawa and as a litigation lawyer in Toronto. For sixteen years, Victor was based at the National University of Singapore where he served for five years as the NUS law faculty's Vice Dean for Academic Affairs. During his time in Singapore, he was seconded to London for a year as co-director of the Center for Transnational Legal Studies (CTLS). Victor has edited/co-edited many books, including *Emergency Powers in Asia: Exploring the Limits of Legality* (2010). His work on comparative constitutional law has been published in leading law journals on five continents. He is currently working on a book on the implications for public law of economic globalisation and transnational regulation.

David TAN *BCom (Melbourne), LLB (Hons), LLM (Harvard), PhD (Melbourne)* is an Associate Professor of Law and Vice Dean (Academic Affairs) at the National University of Singapore. He is also an accomplished fine art fashion photographer, having published a coffee-table book, *Visions of Beauty*, in association with Versace, and *Tainted Perfection* in collaboration with Cartier in Singapore. His most recent retrospective collection of photographs *David Tan: The First Decade* is exclusively distributed by PageOne/Kinokuniya bookstores. David was formerly with the Singapore Administrative Service, serving as Director of Sports at the Ministry of Community Development, Youth & Sports and as Director of International Talent at the Ministry of Manpower. In the area of law, he has published in a diverse range of journals such as the Harvard Journal of Sports & Entertainment Law, Cardozo Arts & Entertainment Law Journal, Yale Journal of International Law, Sydney Law Review, Australian Law Journal, Singapore Journal of Legal Studies and Law Quarterly Review.

Eugene KB TAN *LLB (Hons) (NUS), MSc Comparative Politics (LSE), JSM (Stanford)* is an Associate Professor of Law at the School of Law, Singapore Management University, where he teaches courses at the law, business and social sciences schools at the undergraduate, graduate and executive education levels. Eugene's inter-disciplinary research interests include constitutional and administrative law, law and public policy, the regulation of ethnic conflict, and the government and politics of Singapore. He has published in these areas in various edited volumes and peer-reviewed journals such as The China Quarterly, Ethnic and Racial Studies, Israel Law Review, as well as Law and Policy. Eugene served as a Nominated Member of Singapore's 12th Parliament between 2012 and 2014.

Kevin YL TAN *LLB (Hons) (NUS), LLM (Yale), JSD (Yale)* is Adjunct Professor at the Faculty of Law at the National University of Singapore (NUS) as well as at the S Rajaratnam School of International Studies at Nanyang Technological University (NTU). He is a leading scholar in constitutional law, the Singapore legal system, international human rights and legal history. Kevin has edited, co-edited and written over thirty books on the law, history and politics of Singapore, including *Managing Political Change in Singapore: The Elected Presidency* (1997), *Constitutional Law in Malaysia and Singapore* (2010) (with Thio Li-ann) and *Evolution of a Revolution: Forty Years of the Singapore Constitution* (2009). In addition, Kevin is currently a director of Equilibrium Consulting Pte Ltd, President of the Singapore Heritage Society, and Chairman of the Foundation for the Development of International Law in Asia (DILA).

THIO Li-ann *BA (Oxford) (Hons), LLM (Harvard), PhD (Cambridge), Barrister (GI, UK)* is Professor of Law (Provost's Chair) at the National University of Singapore. She teaches and has published widely in the fields of public international law, human rights law, constitutional law and administrative law. She is currently Chief Editor of the Singapore Journal of Legal Studies, and on the editorial board of the Journal of East Asia and International Law, and the National Taiwan University Law Review, and on the advisory board of the New Zealand Yearbook of International Law, the Australian Journal of Asian law and the Max Planck Encyclopedia of Comparative Constitutional Law. A leading Singapore constitutional scholar, she has authored many books, including *A Treatise on Singapore Constitutional Law* (2012). From 2007 to 2009, she was a Nominated Member of the Singapore Parliament and is currently a Senior Advisor to the Ministry of Foreign Affairs.

Arun K THIRUVENGADAM *LLB (Hons), BA, LLM (National Law School, Bangalore), LLM JSD (NYU School of Law)* is an Associate Professor at the School of Policy and Governance, Azim Premji University, Bengaluru, India. He is a lawyer by training, and has worked as a judicial law clerk and a practising lawyer before the High Courts of Madras and Delhi, and the Supreme Court of India. His doctoral research focused on comparative constitutional law and Indian public law. Prior to joining the School of Policy and Governance at Azim Premji University in July 2015, Arun spent a decade at the Faculty of Law, National University of Singapore, where he taught and researched on the legal systems of India and Singapore, comparative public law, legal theory, law and politics in South Asia and law and development. His published work in Singapore constitutional law has focused on historical trends of use of foreign law in constitutional adjudication, the evaluation of judicial reforms under Chief Justice Yong, and the practice of public interest law. He is the co-editor of two books: *Emergency Powers in Asia* (2010) and *Comparative Constitutionalism in South Asia* (2012).

YAP Po Jen *LLB (NUS), LLM (Harvard), LLM (London), PhD (Cantab)* is an Associate Professor at the University of Hong Kong, Faculty of Law, where he specialises in constitutional and administrative law. He graduated from the National University of Singapore with an LLB degree and he obtained LLM qualifications from both Harvard Law School and University College London. He also has a PhD degree from the University of Cambridge. He is an Advocate and Solicitor of the Supreme Court of Singapore and an Attorney at Law in the State of New York (USA). He has authored over fifty publications in law journals that include the Law Quarterly Review, Legal Studies, and Public Law, and he is the sole author of a monograph entitled *Constitutional Dialogue in Common Law Asia* (2015).

Acknowledgements

This edited volume is the culmination of a workshop and a conference titled 'Judging the Constitution: The Theory and Practice of Constitutional Interpretation in Singapore', which were held in January 2015 and May 2015 respectively. The funding for these events and the research project as a whole come from the Centre for Asian Legal Studies. In particular, I would like to thank Andrew J Harding, the Director for the Centre for Asian Legal Studies, for his unceasing support of Asian legal scholarship. Regana Zara Mydin and Haikel Rino Selamat at the Centre for Asian Legal Studies made the workshop and conference happen with much flourish and deserve the greatest praise for their dedication.

I would also like to thank Carolyn Oei of *The Creative Voice* for her excellent work in copyediting this volume. She made sure we dotted the i's and crossed our t's.

Furthermore, this research project and edited volume would not have been possible without the help of my student assistants at the National University of Singapore's Faculty of Law: Sri Balan s/o Krishnan, Preston Wong, John Cheah Ren Zhi, Lai Jian Qin, Tham Shen Hong, Felicia Chew Li Ying, and Rachel Tan Xi'En.

I would like to thank the contributors for their support of this project.

Finally, this volume is dedicated to my husband, Markus K Labude, without whom *leaning in* would not be possible.

Introduction

Judging the Singapore Constitution

*Jaclyn L Neo**

I Interpreting the Constitution: context and disagreement

> In the ideal world, the process of interpretation should begin and end with the legal text alone. Such a process would obviate concerns over uncertainty or cost, because the text would always mean what it said and say just what the drafter meant. Unfortunately, the world in which we construct and interpret legal texts is far from ideal. There will inevitably be a mismatch between the position of a drafter, who operates afflicted with imperfect knowledge and endowed with limited linguistic tools, and the position of an interpreter, who operates blessed with perfect hindsight. Unsurprisingly then, the interpreters will find from time to time that legal texts do not say what they were meant to say.[1]

This observation about interpretation by Chief Justice Sundaresh Menon, while applied specifically by him to statutes and contracts, is also broadly applicable to constitutional interpretation. As he points out, '[t]he subject of interpretation has attracted considerable debate through the years, with judges, practitioners, academics and jurists each offering different perspectives'.[2] Indeed, most, if not all, of a judge's work involves the element of interpretation.[3]

Constitutional interpretation introduces additional factors for consideration, as compared to the interpretation of statutes and contracts. The constitution often purports to be a legal document, but it is more than that; it can also be seen as a political document. The written constitution, as most constitutions today are, not only prescribes legal rules giving rise to rights and obligations, it also embodies the political, and sometimes social, aspirations of the people it purports to govern. It is often regarded as or at least proclaimed to be the primary source of legal authority within a state.[4] In this regard, the constitution also contains provisions allocating powers to different institutions in accordance with the theory of separation of powers. The constitution thus seeks to make legal and legitimate political and social choices. In doing so, the written provisions become the focal point of legal, political, and social disagreement. Ascertaining what these provisions mean becomes an integral exercise in resolving disagreement and conflict. This is where interpretation comes in.

Interpretation is necessary not least because the written constitution is apt to contain ambiguity or even gaps. After all, it is well-nigh impossible to draft a perfectly clear and perfectly complete legal text, especially one that is meant to endure over time. Moreover, constitutions contain provisions with varying degrees of specificity. Some provisions are very specific and rule-like; these are the least likely to give rise to interpretive difficulties. However, most provisions are drafted at a higher level of generality and interpreting these principles and standards may not be so easy. This interpretive difficulty is further complicated by the fact that constitutions are often multifaceted and highly complex documents; not all the provisions are perfectly compatible with one another, and may conflict at times. Furthermore, constitutions sometimes inadequately deal with or even foresee developments, some of which may threaten the principles the constitution was intended to safeguard.[5]

Debates about how to interpret the constitution therefore, understandably, occupy a central space in the intellectual discourse of many constitutional systems. These debates revolve around a multitude of questions about the sources of meaning as well as the degree of authoritativeness of these various sources. Commonly accepted primary sources include the text, structure, context, norms and theories of the constitution. But even if we can identify the source of meaning, can we determine which should have primary weight in ascertaining the meaning of a constitutional provision? Is the text controlling, and if so, does it always carry a fixed meaning? If it does not, thereby accepting that texts do not inexorably lead to one interpretation, how should we legitimately choose between conflicting meanings? Can we look further afield to the historical context within which the text was drafted or should we look to the contemporary social and/or political context against which the text should currently be understood? Moreover, how much weight should the purpose of the text have, and should we focus on the general or the specific purpose?

Scholars, lawyers and judges grappling with these questions have come up with a range of theories and modalities to try to explain the way constitutional interpretation takes place. This orbit of constitutional interpretation contains a few commonly used theories and modalities. Textualism, originalism, purposivism (purposive interpretation) and living constitutionalism are some commonly used interpretive theories (although some may consider them modalities rather than theories). Within each theory, there are variations. Nonetheless, there is some basic agreement on the primary focus of interpretation. Thus, textualism places primacy on the text. Judges 'interpret' the constitution by deriving meaning from the language of the text, employing accepted canons of interpretation.[6] On the other hand, originalism valorises the original intent of the drafters. It takes the position that the 'content of a constitution is determined partly by the intentions or purposes of its founders, or the understandings of the founding generation'.[7] Purposivism or purposive interpretation focuses on the purpose of the constitutional provision, whereas living constitutionalism advocates interpreting the constitution to meet the evolving needs and to suit the evolving norms of society, which are considered to be of principal value in the constitutional exercise.[8] As would be understandable, there is considerable disagreement among supporters of each of these theories, and no clear consensus on how to decide which of these differing approaches should be applied. Furthermore, different jurisdictions prioritise different interpretive theories. Debates as to which theory should be preferred or otherwise also differ.[9]

In Singapore, constitutional interpretation has similarly revolved around this orbit of theories and modalities. It may be said that there is evidence for textualism, originalism and purposivism being used in the courts, although not much living constitutionalism. However, a critical examination of how judges interpret the constitution, specifically what sources, methods, and theories they consider authoritative, had for a long time been limited by the paucity of constitutional cases. In a recent study of constitutional cases between 1963 (when Singapore became a self-governing state) and 2013, Jack Lee notes that there were only a total of 153 cases decided during this period, which averages out to about three cases per year.[10] This number of constitutional law cases is extremely low. For instance, in another Commonwealth jurisdiction, Australia, the High Court there decided 193 constitutional cases (21.44 cases per year) between 2000 and 2008 alone (a nine-year period).[11] Furthermore, Singapore's annual average drops markedly if one were to take 2006 as the cut-off point because a significant number of cases (around 25 per cent) were decided in the last eight years alone (between 2006 and 2013).[12] Notably, the numbers may vary depending on the methodology one adopts. However, what is clear is that there has been a significant increase in the number of cases in the last ten years. Between 2006 and 2015, in my estimation, there were about fifty reported cases where constitutional issues were raised. This is an average of about five cases per year. In 2015 alone, between January and October, about fourteen cases decided by the courts raised constitutional matters.[13] During this time, constitutional issues raised included whether the right to life and personal liberty included the right not to be tortured (Article 9(1) of the Singapore Constitution),[14] the scope of religious freedom,[15] freedom of speech,[16] as well as judicial independence.[17]

II Constitutional culture and constitutional law

The initial slow growth of constitutional law is perhaps attributable to Singapore's hitherto fledgling democratic and constitutional culture. In a handbook published in 2015, Kevin Tan defines constitutional culture as 'the agglomeration of beliefs and attitudes that the people, judges, lawyers and the state hold towards the Constitution and constitutional law in general'.[18] He points out that for some time the Singaporean public had not had 'much of an opportunity to develop its own unique constitutional ethos'.[19] The public was barely involved in Singapore's constitution-making, both before and after independence. This was exacerbated by the dire social and economic conditions during the early years of independence that led to the over-emphasis on what are known as bread-and-butter issues. The political philosophy of the dominant ruling party (the People's Action Party (PAP)) saw government as an elite representative enterprise,[20] which further fuelled a passive citizenry.[21] The PAP's dominance and the relatively restrictive climate for freedom of speech and political opposition have led to Singapore being characterised as an authoritarian or semi-authoritarian state. For instance, in a 2015 article, Mark Tushnet employs Singapore as his prime case study of authoritarian constitutionalism, where 'liberal freedoms are protected at an intermediate level, and elections are reasonably free and fair'.[22]

However, this has arguably started to change. In the past decade, Singapore has witnessed a relatively significant expansion in political space for debate and opposition.[23] At the very least, the political rhetoric has changed from a top-down approach to a more consultative one.[24] This change in political culture correlates with the exponential increase in the number of constitutional law cases before the Singapore courts. It also suggests a shift in constitutional culture whereby citizens are increasingly aware of their rights and are more willing to pursue them in court. This development was noted not least by the Attorney-General VK Rajah in a 2015 speech made at the annual Opening of the Legal Year. As he notes, there has been an 'increase in civil litigation between the public and the state in administrative and constitutional law issues' in recent years. This is partly attributable to the 'rise of an educated class with more awareness of their civil and constitutional rights.'[25] Crucially, the Attorney-General stresses that this is 'not a negative development' because 'judicial review is the hallmark of the judicial enforcement of the rule of law, in relations between the state and its people.' Indeed, judicial review is 'essential to the rule of law' and 'the Government is subject to the rule of law as much as the least of us members of the public are'.[26] It is perhaps too early at this stage to ascertain whether this shift in constitutional culture will continue in its current trajectory, or whether it is merely an exceptional and temporary phase created by the presence of a maverick lawyer on the constitutional law scene. Indeed, this is the question that Rajah and Thiruvengadam emphasise in their article on cause lawyering, which, among others, examines the role that lawyer M Ravi plays in advancing constitutional law in Singapore.[27]

Nonetheless, there are factors suggesting that this change in constitutional culture is likely to continue. This is because this change is not primarily civil society driven, but is also facilitated by the political elite. In other words, it is not only a bottom-up initiative but is also encouraged (however passively and indirectly) top-down. Thus, besides the government's repeated emphasis on a more consultative and responsive style of government under current Prime Minister Lee Hsien Loong, judges have also displayed an increasing willingness to engage with constitutional ideas and norms in their judgments, as well as take creative positions in adjudicating between citizens and the state. Indeed, one might discern a shift in judicial attitude and engagement with constitutional cases in the past decade. The first constitutional case where the court engaged in close and judicious interpretation of the Constitution is the 2006 case of *Chee Siok Chin v Minister for Home Affairs*.[28] In deciding whether the provisions of the Miscellaneous Offences (Public Order and Nuisance) Act violated the constitutional guarantee of free speech and assembly under Article 14, the High Court issued an extensive judgment noting that '[t]he threshold for legitimacy in relation to any legislative fetter of rights as spelt out in Art 14(2) of the Constitution is whether the curtailment is "necessary or expedient", inter alia, in the interest of security or public order'.[29] Furthermore, the court interpreted the phrase 'necessary or expedient' as conferring on Parliament 'an extremely wide discretionary power and remit that permits a multifarious and multifaceted approach towards achieving any of the purposes specified in Art 14(2) of the Constitution'.[30] This thus left the court to interpret Article 14 as imposing on it the 'sole task' of ascertaining whether an impugned law is 'within the purview of any of the permissible restrictions'.[31] It concluded that the Act was 'necessary or expedient' in the interest of public order.

While this interpretation and indeed the outcome may appear unremarkable, even disappointing, to many constitutional scholars, the significance of this case can be better discerned by contrasting it to another earlier case addressing the same issue of whether a law restricting freedom of speech and assembly is unconstitutional under Article 14 of the Constitution. This earlier case, very much representative of the judicial attitude towards constitutional cases at that time, is *Chee Soon Juan v Public Prosecutor* and the impugned law was the Public Entertainments and Meetings Act ('PEMA'). Here, in coming to the conclusion that the law is constitutional, the High Court merely asserted that free speech is not absolute, but must be balanced against '[b]roader societal concerns such as public peace and order'. The court opined that this was 'embodied in art 14(2)(a) [of the Constitution]'. What is perhaps unsatisfactory is the leap to the conclusion that the court 'did not find the provisions of PEMA to be in any way contrary to our Constitution' and that 'it seemed eminently clear that the enactment of PEMA was fully within the power of the legislature pursuant to the power granted to it by art 14(2)(a)'.[32] There was little attempt to explain or give reasons for this interpretation of Article 14 of the Constitution.

There is, therefore, cause to find some of the earlier constitutional cases unsatisfactory because of this apparent lack of engagement in constitutional interpretation. Interpretation is an integral part of the reason-giving process, which in turn is a key judicial function. Bosland and Gill highlight that the giving of reasons 'demonstrates "an absence of arbitrariness", and promotes "good decision making". It acts as an important check on the exercise of judicial power'[33] as well as 'work[ing] to encourage the acceptance of decisions and to reinforce confidence in the administration of justice'.[34] The giving of reasons thus enhances judicial legitimacy. The maxim that 'justice should not only be done, but should manifestly and undoubtedly be seen to be done'[35] is after all a central feature of the administration of justice.[36]

Consequently, some scholars like Thio Li-ann and David Chong see the enhanced engagement in constitutional interpretation as significant. Thio and Chong noted in 2012, in a chapter for a festschrift written in honour of the third post-independence Chief Justice, Chan Sek Keong, that:

> the judicial trajectory under the Chan Court has been oriented towards greater and more nuanced engagement with academic ideas, foreign cases and international law, accompanied by more elaborated reason-giving by way of appeal to text, original intent, local particularities, with attention to foreign and international developments and first principles.[37]

While the trend may have started before Justice Chan took over as Chief Justice – the case of *Chee Siok Chin* was decided before that – it is fair to say that the trend towards greater engagement in interpretation and reason-giving accelerated during his time as Chief Justice.

Indeed, Thio Li-ann explicates further her observation of this 'sea change' in her chapter in this book (Chapter 4), arguing that there have been 'three waves of interpretive approaches' and that the current wave (associated with the court under former Chief Justice Chan Sek Keong and current Chief Justice Sundaresh Menon) is characterised by 'principled pragmatism'. She particularly notes the court's now regular engagement with foreign case law and international legal arguments, and reference to academic opinion, as well as more elaborate expositions of judicial reasoning, which she contrasts with the statist, cursory judgments that particularly characterised the second wave of interpretive approach. Similarly, discussing this issue more specifically in relation to the use of foreign constitutional law in Singapore, Eugene KB Tan in his chapter in this book (Chapter 11) also notes an important shift in judicial engagement and reason-giving. However, although others may acknowledge this change in judicial engagement, they would point out that this engagement is not sufficiently robust. Indeed, Arun K Thiruvengam argues along these lines in his chapter (Chapter 12) with regards to the use of foreign precedent. Ultimately, how one interprets these developments appears to very much depend on one's measure of change. If one's measure is the frequency and perhaps depth of judicial reasoning, then there has been a discernible change. However, if one looks towards openness to foreign jurisprudence or even at its actual impact, then the change may not be very significant.

III Fifty years of the Singapore Constitution: is this the next phase?

There is therefore some disagreement and debate about these recent constitutional developments, which deserve closer study. The chapters in this book use constitutional interpretation as the focal point from which to analyse and theorise about these developments in Singapore. The book focuses on judicial interpretation, thereby taking a court-centric, rather than an institutional, approach to constitutional law. This distinguishes this book from Li-ann Thio and Kevin YL Tan's 2009 *Evolution of a Revolution: Forty Years of the Singapore Constitution.* The book, commemorating forty years as a significant milestone for the Singapore Constitution, took a more institutional and political perspective of constitutional law. This may be because that phase of constitutional development was characterised by constitutional remodelling during which the Constitution was amended extensively to modify existing institutions and schemes to tailor-make the constitutional system to Singapore's conditions and requirements.[38] This period of remaking intensified during the 1980s and early 1990s with several new innovations: the Non-Constituency Member of Parliament and Nominated Member of Parliament schemes changed the fully elected nature of Parliament; the introduction of Group Representation Constituencies changed the electoral system from the purely single-member constituency voting arrangement in 1988; and finally, the ceremonial office of the President was changed into an elected one with custodial powers over financial reserves and key civil service appointments. These changes were implemented through extensive constitutional amendments and introduced measured political plurality to serve the ultimate purpose of political stability.[39]

As Thio points out in the concluding chapter of *Evolution of a Revolution*, '40 years marks the passing of a generation' as well as 'the attainment of maturity and coming of age' in the Hebrew tradition.[40] How constitutional law has developed in this era of having come of age (or not) is the focus of this current volume. Indeed, it is this work's primary claim that interpretation typifies this next phase of constitutional evolution. Interpretation is the dominant, though not sole, domain of the judiciary. In this regard, the Singapore courts appear to accept (although one can debate upon the degree of acceptance) the prevailing constitutional tradition rooted in US Chief Justice John Marshall's exposition in *Marbury v Madison* that:

> [i]t is emphatically the province and duty of the judicial department to say what the law is. Those who apply the rule to particular cases must of necessity expound and interpret that rule. If two laws conflict with each other, the courts must decide on the operation of each.[41]

Indeed, while judicial review powers were not explicitly provided in the constitution, it has always been asserted, within the tradition of *Marbury v Madison* and without much controversy, as part of judicial power.[42] For instance, in 2011 the Court of Appeal affirmed that it has 'jurisdiction to adjudicate on every legal dispute on a subject matter in respect of which Parliament has conferred jurisdiction on it, including any constitutional dispute between the State and an individual'.[43] This gives effect to Article 4 of the Constitution, which asserts the supremacy of the Constitution over all laws. Indeed, the role of the judiciary in interpreting and upholding the Constitution as an independent institution has been closely tied to the rule of law. Even in overturning a High Court decision that a law was unconstitutional, the Court of Appeal affirmed in the 1998 case of *Public Prosecutor v Taw Cheng Kong*: 'The courts, in upholding the *rule of law* in Singapore, will no doubt readily invalidate laws that derogate from the Constitution which is the supreme law of our land.'[44] Similarly, speaking extra-judicially, then Chief Justice Chan Sek Keong observed in 2012:

> It is the role of the Judiciary which claims the ultimate capacity to decide what the law is and to apply the law impartially and equally to all. No powers are above the law and no person or institution is beyond the reach of the courts.[45]

Interestingly, however, then Chief Justice Chan followed this assertion with a deferential tone. He stated:

> The Judiciary has a duty to check all unlawful legislative or executive acts, but it also has the responsibility not to interfere with or obstruct the lawful policies of an elected government.[46]

This begs the question of what is 'lawful'. The statement, however, reveals a persistent attitude of deference towards the political branches. While there is an increasing assertion of the rightful role of the judiciary in upholding the Constitution, this is nonetheless constrained by an attitude of self-restraint, which presumably stems from the judiciary's perception of its role within the democratic system. The counter-majoritarian difficulty remains very much alive in Singapore.[47] Singapore's political context, where only one political party has formed the government since independence, presumably shapes the judiciary's self-perception of its role within the constitutional system. This manifests itself in the acceptance that the government should be given the broadest benefit of the doubt, which is reflected in the doctrine of the presumption of constitutionality, as discussed by Jack Lee in his chapter (Chapter 6), as well as in how judges use certain interpretive techniques such as balancing to legitimise taking into account competing interests, as I discuss in my chapter (Chapter 7). Consequently, although the courts are playing a far more prominent role in this phase of constitutional development, it must be noted that the institutional and political contexts are never entirely outside the parameters of the enquiries engaged in this volume, since the division between law and politics is not always so neatly defined.

Indeed, Singapore's constitutional jurisprudence is by no means at a stage of mature development from the perspective of constitutional review. It remains the case that except for one early High Court case (*Taw Cheng Kong v Public Prosecutor*[48]), which was later overturned by the Court of Appeal, the Singapore courts have never struck down a law as being unconstitutional. However, there is now a discernible shift from strong judicial deference to Parliament and the executive, towards an increasing openness to creating a real conversation on the proper scope and limits of their constitutional powers. Thus, in *Review Publishing Co Ltd and Another v Lee Hsien Loong & Anor*,[49] the Court of Appeal refrained from deciding whether to adopt the *Reynolds* test of responsible journalism but signalled to Parliament and even future judges that there should be scope for reconsideration in future cases. There have also been other cases where the courts have taken a more assertive approach in interpreting the Constitution in favour of limiting executive powers. For instance, in the case of *Vellama d/o*

Marie Muthu v Attorney-General,[50] the Court of Appeal held that the Prime Minister's constitutional right to call for a by-election when a seat falls vacant is not unlimited. There, the court relied on the text of the Constitution as well as the unwritten principle of the rule of law. Therefore, while the judicial attitude in these cases remains persistently restrained and deferential, there are tentative but real overtures towards more respectful engagement in constitutional law.

IV The chapters: an organisational overview

The chapters in this volume address these changes, focusing on constitutional interpretation, from a variety of perspectives and approaches. I have organised the chapters into three broad sections. The first section contains chapters that take a broad theoretical perspective of constitutional interpretation. They focus on interpretive theories and doctrines that influence the interpretive exercise in Singapore. Thus, in providing a comprehensive examination of constitutional cases in Singapore, the Honourable Attorney-General VK Rajah's chapter takes as its starting point the desirability of the textualist approach. Kevin Tan's chapter identifies Westminster constitutionalism as an interpretive framework in Singapore. Andrew Harding's chapter engages with another interpretive doctrine that has been proposed, rejected and reignited in recent constitutional discourse – the basic features doctrine (Kevin Tan) or basic structure doctrine (Andrew Harding). In its original conception, the basic structure or features doctrine, originating in the famous Indian case of *Kesavananda Bharati v State of Kerala* ('*Kesavananda*'),[51] refers to certain basic features in the Constitution that judges have identified as being non-amendable. This is a serious restriction on the legislature's constituent power and has not been accepted in Singapore. Nonetheless, as both Kevin Tan and Andrew Harding discuss in their chapters, there has been an attempt to reformulate this doctrine into an interpretive tool, repackaged as the basic *structure* doctrine (in the looser sense of basic structure as simply a tool of interpretation as opposed to a limitation on the power of constitutional amendment).[52] This discussion reflects an ongoing engagement with the history and origins of Singapore's Constitution. Thio Li-ann's chapter takes a long view of constitutional interpretation, proposing principled pragmatism as the animating theory *about* constitutional adjudication in Singapore. As she puts it, this consists of 'principled' judicial impulses to intervene and 'pragmatic' impulses to refrain or to practice restrained review. On the other hand, Yap Po Jen's chapter examines originalism and textualism, the two dominant theories of constitutional interpretation in Singapore. He takes an anti-formalistic approach in 'uncovering' the use of these theories of interpretation.

The second section of this book consists of chapters that interrogate modalities and canons of interpretation, particularly examining how they have been employed over time and the philosophy undergirding their use. Jack Tsen-Ta Lee's chapter examines the presumption of constitutionality in constitutional cases. He argues that the presumption should not be invoked to impose a substantial evidential burden but should be reinterpreted as a mere reminder that an applicant must establish a prima facie case, or better still, should be done away with entirely. My chapter examines the use of the balancing metaphor in constitutional cases and traces its evolution as an interpretive tool for judicial deference and its emerging use in constitutional dialogue. Swati Jhaveri's chapter capably identifies the many iterations of the fundamental rules of natural justice as an interpretive device since it was first introduced by the Privy Council in the case of *Ong Ah Chuan v Public Prosecutor*. David Tan's chapter takes a serious look at what it means to have an autochthonous reading of the Constitution by focusing on free speech jurisprudence that has arisen in the context of political defamation and contempt of court cases.

The book's third section challenges us to rethink the boundaries of constitutional interpretation. Goh Yihan's chapter questions whether the conventional wisdom that the Constitution should be treated *sui generis* and interpreted differently from statutes and even contracts is justifiable. Eugene Tan's chapter argues that the commitment to the four walls doctrine is more apparent than real, and that legal autochthony does not mean becoming insular but striking a balance between local context and global connections. In his chapter, Arun K Thiruvengadam analyses the courts' engagement with foreign law and identifies different levels of resistance in constitutional cases. Victor V Ramraj's chapter is forward-looking in that he asks how constitutional interpretation should evolve to meet new challenges arising from the blurring of the public–private divide, particularly in the transnational regulatory space. Finally, in an unconventional chapter, Michael Dowdle and Kevin Tan engage in a dialogue about political and juridical constitutionalism as ways to understand constitutional changes.

V Constitutional debates and themes

There is clearly debate and disagreement among the chapters in this book. Some chapters view the constitutional developments more favourably while others consider the changes significant but insufficiently robust. This disagreement reflects a healthy state of constitutional scholarship in Singapore. Among the chapters I have identified five issues, and disagreement on some of them, that various chapters have sought to grapple with. First, there is an issue of how the lack of a momentous constitutional founding impacts constitutional interpretation. The presence of a founding moment, and indeed other discernible constitutional moments, undergirds Ackerman's defence of constitutional review as not counter-majoritarian or anti-democratic but as preservationist.[53] In interpreting the Constitution to control legislative and executive acts, the court is merely preserving solutions reached by 'the People' during discernible constitutional moments against their easy erosion by politicians.[54] Thus, in striking down legislative and executive acts as unconstitutional, judges are merely performing their obligation to enforce constitutional principles that were adopted by the People.[55]

The lack of a founding constitutional moment in Singapore's founding appears to continue to influence constitutional interpretation and encumber the development of a more robust form of constitutional review. Indeed, Attorney-General VK

Rajah's chapter begins by reminding us: 'Our Constitution did not have a storied birth. There were no grand speeches by founding fathers at constitutional conventions. We came into nationhood suddenly, and needed a working constitution in short order.' This unremarkable starting point appears to dampen any argument for more robust constitutional review based on broader constitutional norms and doctrines. Indeed, Rajah's argument for a textualist approach to constitutional interpretation appears very much rooted in the need to temper constitutional supremacy against the lack of a founding moment. Without the force of a discernible voice of the People, judges are therefore wise to rely on the text of the constitution. As Rajah puts it: 'Fidelity to the idea of a written constitution must mean fidelity to its text.' Similarly, Andrew Harding's argument against the basic structure doctrine places much weight on the lack of a founding moment (Chapter 2). He argues: 'There was no constitutional moment in which Singapore's Constitution was created, and therefore no process whereby constitution-makers expressly or impliedly laid down a basic structure for Singapore's Constitution which could not be destroyed by constitutional amendment.'

The lack of a constitutional moment could indeed cast doubt upon the legitimacy of an originalist approach to constitutional interpretation. After all, originalism presumes that there is something significant about the drafting moment that constrains interpretation. Yap Po Jen's chapter argues against an originalist understanding of the Singapore Constitution (see Chapter 5). Originalism presents constitutional interpretation as the enunciation and implementation of the text as originally meant by the drafters. Indeed, originalism 'presents itself as a resolution to the tension between constitutionalism and democracy' because judges are portrayed as 'merely enforcing the original meaning of the constitutional text that was duly enacted by the people via their representatives'. However, the lack of a discernible founding moment and thereby an identifiable drafting body imbued with the legitimacy of an independent people, Yap argues, makes it difficult to defend an originalist approach to constitutional interpretation. As he explains: 'The constitutional text of Singapore's Fundamental Liberties Clauses, of which the due process clause is one of them, was not deliberated upon by a Constituent Assembly.' Instead, 'the Singapore legislature simply made most Fundamental Liberties provisions found in the Malaysia Federal Constitution applicable to Singapore via the Republic of Singapore Independence Act'. While there was conscious adoption of these provisions, 'Singapore's constitutional framers did not deliberate upon the phraseology of the Fundamental Liberties Clauses, but merely imported them as a matter of expedience from Malaysia' and therefore 'one does wonder whether it is even possible to discern at all what original meaning they attached to those provisions adopted from Malaysia'. He further argues that:

> [a]t best, one can try to discern the original intent of the framers (and, indeed, the members of the Reid Commission) when the Malaysian Constitution was drafted and adopted, but it would be a very curious state of affairs for Singapore judges in modern independent Singapore to give effect to and

be fettered by the original intent of another nation-state's constitutional framers.[56]

A second underlying debate concerns the foundational principles and norms that can and should govern constitutional interpretation. Except for the most ardent supporter of textualism, most constitutional scholars and judges recognise that the text sometimes (or oftentimes) does not inexorably lead to only one interpretation. While some constitutional provisions necessarily point to a single interpretation, most constitutional provisions could be subject to various interpretations. As has been pointed out, this stems simply from the inherently imprecise nature of language. A literal-textualist approach whereby one attempts to ascertain meaning by simply looking at the text, even by relying on dictionaries, is often not satisfactory.[57] In this regard, there can be no doubt that some other sources of interpretation, beyond the text, would be required. Indeed, while eschewing 'non-textual approaches' which he says have no basis on or resemblance to the text of the Constitution, Attorney-General VK Rajah, nonetheless points out in his chapter notes that 'fidelity to the constitutional text does not stop at giving effect to the literal meaning of the text' and that '[s]ometimes, value judgments have to be made in interpreting and applying the Constitution'. This, however, argues Rajah, remains rooted in the text in that 'judges must reach their decisions guided only by considerations that flow from the text and the structure of the Constitution, and the principles that undergird the text and the Constitution'.

But, what are some of these principles undergirding the Constitution that could legitimately inform constitutional interpretation? In Chapter 3, Kevin Tan points to one interpretive doctrine: Westminster constitutionalism. Tan argues that 'despite having been independent for half a century, Singapore courts still assiduously adopt the Westminster model and its attendant matrix, and that this directly impacts the way in which judges interpret the Constitution'. Surveying early Privy Council cases and the Singapore courts' revitalisation of the characterisation of Singapore's Constitution as a 'Westminster constitution', Kevin Tan emphasises that this is significant for constitutional interpretation because 'Westminster style constitutions are necessarily imbued with a particular structural form and suffused with the substantive rules of the common law, including the so-called "fundamental rules of natural justice"'. Thus, while he does not disagree with VK Rajah and Andrew Harding's stance that Singapore should not adopt the basic features doctrine in the form crafted by the Indian Supreme Court in *Kesavananda*, Kevin Tan nonetheless argues that the Westminster constitution is a useful interpretive doctrine that has been effectively employed by the Singapore courts (see *Law Society of Singapore v Phyllis Tan*,[58] *Mohammad Faizal bin Sabtu v Public Prosecutor*[59] and *Vellama d/o Marie Muthu v Attorney-General*[60]). That said, the legal effect of this Westminster constitutionalism and the basic structure which it apparently provides is not entirely clear. Kevin Tan further states the 'basic structure', which he distinguishes from the basic features doctrine, does put 'minimal constraints on Parliament's constitution amending powers'. This is the part of his argument that pushes the basic structure of the Westminster constitution doctrine closer to the basic features doctrine's underlying motivation, which is to impose extra-constitutional constraints on Parliament's amendment powers. However, his argument remains a modest one as he appears to suggest that interpretation aside, the only extra-constitutional constraint on Parliament is that it cannot fundamentally change the basic structure of the Constitution in violation of the separation of powers.

Third, there is an implicit debate among the chapters as to the legitimate role of the judiciary when it comes to constitutional interpretation. Many chapters appear to accept the distinction between constitutional *interpretation* (a legitimate judicial function) and constitutional *change* (not a legitimate judicial function), albeit to varying degrees. VK Rajah (Chapter 1) and Thio Li-ann (Chapter 4) rely heavily on this distinction in their chapters. Rajah's strong emphasis on the text is underpinned by his conviction that 'interpretation' beyond the text is tantamount to constitutional change and is not properly a legitimate judicial function. Indeed, he argues: 'To venture beyond the text of the Constitution and enunciate a meaning that reflects what the law should be, is to disrespect the principle of separation of powers – this is an exercise that violates rather than upholds the Constitution.' Furthermore, for Thio, this distinction between interpretation and change partly explains the judges' principled pragmatism. She points to Singapore's fairly accessible amendment procedure, concluding that '[c]onstitutional fossilisation is thus unlikely and judicial activism is not an imperative'. Furthermore, the rejection of the Indian basic features doctrine by Andrew Harding and Kevin Tan points to an underlying commitment to this distinction (Chapters 2 and 3 respectively). While interpretation is within the legitimate role of the judge, restricting constitutional change oversteps the boundaries of interpretation and itself is tantamount to the judiciary engaging in constitutional change.

However, even accepting the distinction between constitutional interpretation and change, some authors argue that the current judicial approach may be too restrictive. Yap Po Jen's critique of the use of originalism and textualism in Singapore (Chapter 5) suggests that the interpretive exercise has been overly restrained and is subject to the criticism of inconsistency, among other criticisms. Swati Jhaveri's survey of the interpretation of Article 9 of the Constitution (Chapter 8) suggests some judicial ambivalence to the concept of fundamental rules of natural justice, which could benefit from a more rigorous and structured proportionality-type adjudication. In my chapter, I note the shift towards a slightly more robust form of balancing as indicative of judicial engagement with the political branches as part of an emerging constitutional dialogue (Chapter 7). This could be seen as the judiciary coming into its role as a co-equal, rather than a subsidiary, branch of government, which is its rightful role in a constitutional system committed to judicial review, constitutional supremacy and the separation of powers.

Fourth, the authors are generally in agreement that the Singapore courts take a deferential stance towards the political branches of government, and that this significantly impacts constitutional interpretation. This deference manifests itself in several interpretive doctrines, methods, and theories: the presumption of constitutionality (Jack Lee, Chapter 6), balancing (Jaclyn Neo, Chapter 7), originalism and textualism (Yap Po Jen, Chapter 5), purposive interpretation (Goh Yihan, Chapter 10), and resistance towards foreign law (Arun K Thiruvengadam, Chapter 12). Furthermore, deference accounts for the rejection of the basic features doctrine (Andrew Harding, Chapter 2), as well as the rejection of substantive and procedural rights as part of the fundamental rules of natural justice (Swati Jhaveri, Chapter 8). It further explains the embrace of a pragmatist, albeit principled pragmatist, approach to constitutional interpretation (Thio Li-ann, Chapter 4) and a neo-Confucianist approach to free speech jurisprudence (David Tan, Chapter 9). But, deference has differing levels and the authors differ in their assessment as to the extent and appropriate levels of deference. For instance, Jack Lee argues (in Chapter 6) that the courts' deferential attitude underlying the presumption of constitutionality should be revised as it makes certain assumptions about parliamentary conduct and the supposed undemocratic nature of judicial review. His view is that 'the presumption is better treated as a technique for reading down potentially unconstitutional statutes, and as a reminder that claimants must discharge their ordinary evidential burden of raising a *prima facie* claim against the Government'. Indeed, to do so would require a shift from strong deference to a modest form of deference, which he does not suggest has taken place. I, on the other hand, argue in my chapter (Chapter 7) that there appears to be a shift from strong deference in some of the earlier cases to a more modest form of deference in the later cases, and this can be discerned from the way the balancing metaphor has been used in Singapore.

Lastly, one can discern an acceptance among many of the chapters of the embedded nature of the judiciary and thus constitutional interpretation as part of a larger political context. In this regard, the authors explicitly or implicitly agree with the claim for an autochthonous constitution. What this means, however, varies. David Tan's chapter for instance accepts that the courts have developed a neo-Confucianist ethos to interpret the free speech clause under Article 14 in relation to defamation and contempt of court cases. However, he argues that, even accepting this autochthonous narrative, it does not mean that the current laws on defamation and contempt should not be interpreted to expand freedom of speech protection. Indeed, he argues that even in 'an Asian system of government of "good men", the behaviour of these men should still be subject to appropriate scrutiny by the citizens of Singapore to ensure that they remain "good"'. Consequently, '[r]obust debate and rigorous scrutiny should not be confined only to the hallowed chambers of Parliament House'. Accountability remains key, and '[a] well-informed and well-educated citizenry that can more freely discuss and debate matters of public interest relating to government and governance will more intelligently and effectively supervise the organs of the state'. Tan's argument is refreshing as it goes beyond the usual equation of Asian constitutionalism with authoritarianism. Instead, he argues from within the Confucianist tradition for governmental accountability and increased protection for free political speech. In comparison, other authors engage with this question of embeddedness by highlighting ways in which judicial reasoning and case outcomes respond to the political dominance of the ruling party in government. Arun K Thiruvengadam suggests in his chapter that 'it is often the political choices of judges that help explain some of their legal choices, especially in relation to whether and which comparative law to engage with.'

Victor V Ramraj's chapter also contextualises constitutional interpretation but within the wider context of its political–economic situation. In discussing recent cases expanding the scope of judicial review in administrative law, he suggests some 'openness to paradigmatic change', including 'a recognition in public law jurisprudence that some forms of private power are amenable to judicial review on public law principles'. Indeed, he argues that as the Singapore government continues to legislate extraterritorially and engage with global governance bodies, Singapore judges will need to reconsider their approaches to public law, including constitutional law. While constitutional law had previously been conceptualised primarily as a territorially bound area of law, this extra-territorial expansion as a response to globalisation may challenge judges to go beyond the existing understanding of constitutionalism as a legal device for regulating and moderating power.

VI Conclusion

At the end of the day, constitutional interpretation is about sources of authority. The theories of interpretation that judges adopt appeal to different sources of authority.[61] This could be the authority of the constitution as law, as a social contract, or as embodying the national ethos. Where the constitution predominates because it is the highest law, then there is a tendency to focus on doctrines and precedents since these promote a stable and consistent approach to constitutional interpretation. The law in this regard tends to be treated in a fairly formalistic fashion. In comparison, where the constitution is regarded as a social contract, strong emphasis is placed on its underlying history and historical narrative in constitutional interpretation. Where the authority of the constitution is based on its embodying the national ethos, constitutional interpretation has to reflect the living experience and norms of the nation.[62]

Consequently, when judges invoke different interpretive modalities in deciding these cases, they are in fact engaging in a broader conversation about the nature of the constitution's authority – whether it is rooted in the idea of the constitution as law whereby the text tends to be primary, or the authority of the constitution as embodying consent whereby historical understandings become most important, or the idea of the constitution as a manifestation of the nation's identity or values. Constitutional interpretation is therefore part of a process of grappling with the past, the present, and the future. In examining the theory and practice of constitutional interpretation, the essays in this book seek to contribute to this process by offering critical reflections of the various interpretive doctrines and principles, and identifying the underlying assumptions concerning the authority of the constitution. This volume is particularly timely as it marks fifty years of Singapore's independence, a significant half-century mark which is an appropriate time for critical reflection and self-reflection. It is hoped, therefore, that the essays in this volume will trigger further debate and reflections on the trajectory of constitutional development in Singapore in years to come. Indeed, the last chapter of this book by Michael Dowdle and Kevin Tan is deliberately left open-ended to signify the book's commitment to contribute to but not conclude the conversation on constitutionalism in Singapore.

Notes

* I am grateful to Kevin Y: Tan, Swati Jhaveri, Jack Tsen-Ta Lee, and Arun K. Thiruvengadam for their helpful comments on previous drafts of this Introduction.

1 Sundaresh Menon, 'The Interpretation of Documents: Saying What They Mean or Meaning What They Say' (2014) 32 Singapore Law Review 3, 30.

2 ibid 4.

3 ibid.

4 SA de Smith, *Constitutional and Administrative Law* (Harry Street and Rodney Brazier (eds), 5th edn, Penguin Books 1986) 75.

5 Jeffrey Goldsworthy, 'Introduction' in Jeffrey Goldsworthy (ed), *Interpreting Constitutions: A Comparative Study* (Oxford University Press 2007), 1.

6 Antonin Scalia and Bryan A Garner, *Reading Law: The Interpretation of Legal Texts* (Thomson/West 2012), Preface xxx.

7 Jeffrey Goldsworthy, 'Constitutional Interpretation', in Michel Rosenfeld and András Sajó (eds), *The Oxford Handbook of Comparative Constitutional Law* (Oxford University Press 2012) 689, 691.

8 In a stronger version of living constitutionalism, proponents have gone so far as to suggest that the judiciary is able to adapt the Constitution to new circumstances without formal amendment, presumably even to the point of 'rewriting' of the constitution. See Bruce Ackerman, *The Holmes Lectures: The Living Constitution*, (2007) 120(7) Harvard Law Review 1737. For a critique, see William H Rehnquist, 'The Notion of a Living Constitution' (2006) 29 Harvard Journal of Law & Public Policy 401.

9 For instance, the debate in the United States has largely centred upon the disagreement between originalism and living constitutionalism. However, in recent times, scholars like Balkin have attempted to synthesise the approaches, specifically originalism and living constitutionalism. In Balkin's constitutional theory of 'living originalism', he marries text and principle to propose a theory of interpretation where judges interpret the Constitution in a way that best applies the original meaning of the constitutional text as well as the principles that underlie the text. He explains:

> The method of text and principle requires fidelity to the original meaning of the Constitution, and in particular, to the rules, standards, and principles stated by the Constitution's text. It also requires us to ascertain and to be faithful to the principles that underlie the text, and to build out constitutional constructions that best apply the constitutional text and its associated principles in current circumstances.
>
> Jack M Balkin, *Living Originalism* (The Belknap Press of Harvard University Press 2011) 1

10 Jack Lee explains: 'Cases were regarded as "constitutional" if they involved the application of provisions of the Constitution': Jack Tsen-Ta Lee, 'Foreign Precedents in Constitutional Adjudication by the Supreme Court of Singapore, 1963–2013' (2015) 24(2) Washington International Law Journal 253, 260.

11 ibid.

12 This is only an estimation as Lee did not include a full list for his numbers and one can only surmise the difference since differences in methodologies and identification may give rise to differing statistics.

13 At least four other cases mentioned the Constitution but the constitutional discussion was not integral to the case. See *Ang Pek San Lawrence v Singapore Medical Council* [2015] 2 SLR 1179 (Singapore High Court); *ANB v ANC* [2015] SGCA 43 (Singapore Court of Appeal (Sing CA)); *Re Rogers, Heather QC* [2015] 4 SLR 1064 (Singapore High Court); *TBC v TBD* [2015] 4 SLR 59 (Singapore High Court).

14 *Yong Vui Kong v Public Prosecutor* [2015] 2 SLR 1129 (Singapore Court of Appeal [Sing CA]).

15 *Madan Mohan Singh v Attorney-General* [2015] 2 SLR 1085 (Singapore High Court); *Vijaya Kumar s/o Rajendran and others v Attorney-General* [2015] SGHC 244.

16 *Attorney-General v Au Wai Pang* [2015] 2 SLR 352 (Singapore High Court) (with regards to contempt of court); and *Attorney-General v Lee Kwai Hou Howard, Xu Yuen Chen, Loh Hong Puey Andrew, Choo Zheng Xi, Lee Song Kwang and Ting Choon Meng* [2015] SGDC 114 (with regards to the Protection from Harassment Act 2014).

17 *AHQ v Attorney-General and another appeal* [2015] 4 SLR 760.

18 Kevin YL Tan, *The Constitution of Singapore: A Contextual Analysis* (Bloomsbury 2015) 58.

19 ibid 61.

20 Drawing from Glenn Patmore's three models of representative democracy, one can squarely place the ruling party's conception of representative democracy, at least until recent times, as conforming to the elite model, where democracy is, at best, considered a means of choosing decision-makers and curbing their excesses. See Glenn Patmore, 'Making Sense of Representative Democracy and the Implied Freedom of Political Communication in the High Court of Australia' (1998) 7(1) Griffith Law Review 97, 99.

21 Some may also argue that the political apathy was the result of the PAP's deliberate suppression of dissent and opposition through the use of defamation laws and preventive detention laws. This is a criticism particularly targeted at governmental action in the 1980s and 1990s. See Jothie Rajah, *Authoritarian Rule of Law: Legislation, Discourse and Legitimacy in Singapore* (Cambridge University Press 2010).

22 Mark Tushnet, 'Authoritarian Constitutionalism' (2015) 100 Cornell Law Review 391, 396.

23 See Thio Li-ann, 'Singapore: Regulating Political Speech and the Commitment "to Build a Democratic Society"', (2003) 1(3) International Journal of Constitutional Law 516. cf Derek da Cunha's critique that this opening up of space may be more apparent than real: Derek da Cunha, *Singapore in the New Millennium: Challenges Facing the City-State* (Institute of Southeast Asian Studies 2002) 271–74. Nonetheless, this shift may have become more significant after the 2011 General Elections where the opposition made significant gains, winning six parliamentary seats for the first time since independence in 1965: 'Singapore Opposition Make "Landmark" Election Gains' (BBC News, 9 May 2011) www.bbc.com/news/world-asia-pacific-13313695 accessed 21 September 2015.

24 For instance, in his National Day speech in 2006, Prime Minister Lee Hsien Loong explicitly stated that the Government would build a more open society and encourage freer debate. See Lee Hsien Loong, 'National Day Message 2006' www.mfa.gov.sg/content/mfa/overseasmission/washington/newsroom/press_statements/2006/200608/press_200608_01.html accessed 21 September 2015.

25 VK Rajah, 'The Rule of Law', Speech at the Opening of the Legal Year 2015, edited excerpt *The Straits Times* (Singapore, 7 January 2015) www.agc.gov.sg/DATA/0/Docs/NewsFiles/OPENING%20OF%20LEGAL%20YEAR%202015_ATTORNEY-

GENERAL%20V%20K%20RAJAH'S%20SPEECH_5%20JAN_checked%20against %20delivery.pdf accessed 21 September 2015.
26 ibid.
27 Jothie Rajah and Arun Thiruvengadam, 'Of Absences, Masks and Exceptions: Cause Lawyering in Singapore' (2014) 31(3) Wisconsin International Law Journal 646.
28 *Chee Siok Chin v Minister for Home Affairs* [2005] SGHC 216 (Singapore High Court [Sing HC]) ('*Chee Siok Chin*').
29 ibid [44].
30 ibid [49].
31 ibid [49].
32 *Chee Soon Juan v Public Prosecutor* [2003] SGHC 122 (Sing HC).
33 See Jason Bosland and Jonathan Gill, 'The Principle of Open Justice and the Judicial Duty to Give Public Reasons' (2014) 38(2) Melbourne University Law Review 1, 7.
34 ibid.
35 *R v Sussex Justices, ex p McCarthy* [1924] KB 256, 259 (Lord Heward CJ).
36 Bosland and Gill (n 33) 2.
37 Thio Li-ann and David Chong, 'The Chan Court and Constitutional Adjudication: "A Sea Change into Something Rich and Strange?"' in Chao, Phang, Rajah and Yeo (eds), *The Law in His Hands: A Tribute to Chief Justice Chan Sek Keong* (Academy Publishing 2012) 88, 118.
38 See Thio Li-ann, 'The Right to Political Participation in Singapore: Tailor-making a Westminster-modelled Constitution to Fit the Imperatives of "Asian" Democracy' (2002) 6 Singapore Journal of International & Comparative Law 181.
39 Critics have argued that political stability has been conflated with maintaining the political dominance of the People's Action Party (PAP), which has been the ruling party since independence. See Li-ann Thio, 'In Search of the Singapore Constitution: Retrospect and Prospect' in Li-ann Thio and Kevin YL Tan (eds), *Evolution of a Revolution: Forty Years of the Singapore Constitution* (Routledge-Cavendish 2009) 323, 328. For a critical examination of constitutional law in Singapore, see Rajah (n 21).
40 Li-ann Thio, 'In Search of the Singapore Constitution: Retrospect and Prospect' in Li-ann Thio and Kevin YL Tan (eds), *Evolution of a Revolution: Forty Years of the Singapore Constitution* (Routledge-Cavendish 2009) 323.
41 *Marbury v Madison* 5 US 137 (1803).
42 Jack Lee notes that this power of judicial review is confined to the Supreme Court (comprising the Court of Appeal and the High Court). The State Courts, which are lower courts in Singapore, have no power to exercise supervisory jurisdiction over tribunals or public authorities, judicially review the acts or decisions of any persons or authorities, or issue prerogative orders. The State Courts can, however, apply the Constitution in some uncontroversial circumstances: Jack Lee (n 10) 257.
43 *Yong Vui Kong v Attorney-General* [2011] 2 SLR 1189 (Sing CA) [31]. Earlier pronouncements in similar a vein were made in *Chan Hiang Leng Colin v Public Prosecutor* [1994] 3 SLR(R) 209 (Sing HC) [50]; *Public Prosecutor v Taw Cheng Kong* [1998] 2 SLR(R) 410 (Sing CA) [89]; *Mohammad Faizal bin Sabtu v Public Prosecutor* [2012] 4 SLR 947 (Sing CA) [14].
44 *Taw Cheng Kong*, ibid (Sing CA) [89].
45 Reproduced as Chan Sek Keong, 'The Courts and the "Rule of Law" in Singapore' (2012) Singapore Journal of Legal Studies 209–31.
46 ibid.
47 Alexander M Bickel, *The Least Dangerous Branch* (2nd edn, Yale University Press 1986).
48 [1998] 1 SLR(R) 78.
49 [2009] SGCA 46.
50 [2013] 4 SLR 1.
51 AIR 1973 SC 1461 (Supreme Court of India (India SC)).

52 There appeared to be some confusion between these two doctrines in *Yong Vui Kong v Public Prosecutor* [2015] 2 SLR 1129.
53 Bruce Ackerman, *We the People: Foundations* (Belknap Harvard 1991) 60–61.
54 Ackerman has a sophisticated theory distinguishing the former as higher politics and the latter as normal politics. Higher politics occurs when the People (with a capital 'P') are roused, and participate in the decision-making process, and a constitutional position emerges based on the clear choices of the majority. Normal politics, in comparison, involves decisions made by the government on a daily basis. This means that politicians wishing to change the earlier decisions made by the People will need to overcome higher obstacles in order to be able to claim the authority to speak for the People and change the constitution: ibid 6–7.
55 See further discussion of Ackerman's theory in Michael W McConnell, 'The Forgotten Constitutional Moment' (1994) 11 Constitutional Commentary 115.
56 Notably, however, there are events in the course of Singapore's constitutional history that could arguably attain the status of constitutional moments, such as the 1964 racial riots, separation from the Federation of Malaysia, as well as the Marxist Conspiracy in the late 1980s, that do impact the constitutional environment and constitutional interpretation. For instance, the racial riots continue to form the constitutional narrative that justifies elevating racial and religious harmony, and the related principle of freedom from offence in sedition cases, to quasi-constitutional status. This is not directly discussed in the chapters, but has been addressed in other scholarly articles. See eg Jaclyn Ling-Chien Neo, 'Seditious in Singapore! Free Speech and the Offence of Promoting Ill-will and Hostility between Different Racial Groups' (2011) Singapore Journal of Legal Studies 351.
57 The imprecision of language was noted by Chief Justice Sundaresh Menon in his discussion as to why there are often disputes on interpretation of legal texts. Although his focus was on statutes and contracts, some clear parallels can be drawn. Menon (n 1) 7.
58 [2008] 2 SLR(R) 239 (Sing HC).
59 [2012] 4 SLR 947 (Sing HC).
60 [2013] 4 SLR 1 (Sing CA).
61 Robert Post, 'Theories of Constitutional Interpretation' (1990) 30 Representations 13.
62 ibid.

Bibliography

Ackerman, Bruce, *We the People: Foundations* (Belknap Harvard 1991).

Ackerman, Bruce, 'The Holmes Lectures: The Living Constitution' (2007) 120(7) Harvard Law Review 1737.

Bickel, Alexander M, *The Least Dangerous Branch* (2nd edn, Yale University Press 1986).

Bosland, Jason and Jonathan Gill, 'The Principle of Open Justice and the Judicial Duty to Give Public Reasons' (2014) 38(2) Melbourne University Law Review 1.

Chan, Sek Keong, 'The Courts and the 'Rule of Law' in Singapore' (2012) Singapore Journal of Legal Studies 209.

da Cunha, Derek, *Singapore in the New Millennium: Challenges Facing the City-State* (Institute of Southeast Asian Studies 2002).

de Smith, SA, *Constitutional and Administrative Law* (Harry Street and Rodney Brazier eds, 5th edn, Penguin Books 1986).

Goldsworthy, Jeffrey, 'Introduction' in Jeffrey Goldsworthy (ed), *Interpreting Constitutions: A Comparative Study* (Oxford University Press 2007).

Goldsworthy, Jeffrey, 'Constitutional Interpretation' in Michel Rosenfeld and András

Sajó (eds), *The Oxford Handbook of Comparative Constitutional Law* (Oxford University Press 2012).

Lee, Jack Tsen-Ta, 'Foreign Precedents in Constitutional Adjudication by the Supreme Court of Singapore, 1963–2013' (2015) 24(2) Washington International Law Journal 253.

McConnell, Michael W, *The Forgotten Constitutional Moment* (1994) 11 Constitutional Commentary 115.

Menon, Sundaresh, 'The Interpretation of Documents: Saying What They Mean or Meaning What They Say' (2014) 32 Singapore Law Review 3.

Neo, Jaclyn Ling-Chien, 'Seditious in Singapore! Free Speech and the Offence of Promoting Ill-will and Hostility between Different Racial Groups' (2011) Singapore Journal of Legal Studies 351.

Patmore, Glenn, 'Making Sense of Representative Democracy and the Implied Freedom of Political Communication in the High Court of Australia' (1998) 7(1) Griffith Law Review 97.

Post, Robert, 'Theories of Constitutional Interpretation' (1990) 30 Representations 13.

Rajah, Jothie, *Authoritarian Rule of Law: Legislation, Discourse and Legitimacy in Singapore* (Cambridge University Press 2012).

Rajah, Jothie and Arun Thiruvengadam, 'Of Absences, Masks and Exceptions: Cause Lawyering in Singapore' (2014) 31(3) Wisconsin International Law Journal 646.

Rehnquist, William H, 'The Notion of a Living Constitution' (2006) 29 Harvard Journal of Law & Public Policy 401.

Scalia, Antonin and Bryan A Garner, *Reading Law: The Interpretation of Legal Texts* (Thomson/West 2012).

Tan, Kevin YL, *The Constitution of Singapore: A Contextual Analysis* (Bloomsbury 2015).

Thio, Li-ann, 'The Right to Political Participation in Singapore: Tailor-making a Westminster-modelled Constitution to Fit the Imperatives of 'Asian' Democracy' (2002) 6 Singapore Journal of International & Comparative Law 181.

Thio, Li-ann, 'Singapore: Regulating Political Speech and the Commitment "to Build a Democratic Society"' (2003) 1(3) International Journal of Constitutional Law 516.

Thio, Li-ann, 'In Search of the Singapore Constitution: Retrospect and Prospect' in Kevin YL Tan and Li-ann Thio (eds), *Evolution of a Revolution: Forty Years of the Singapore Constitution* (Routledge-Cavendish 2009).

Tushnet, Mark, 'Authoritarian Constitutionalism' (2015) 100 Cornell Law Review 391.

Part I

Theoretical frameworks

1 Intepreting the Singapore Constitution

VK Rajah, SC[1]

I Introduction

Our Constitution did not have a storied birth. There were no grand speeches by founding fathers at constitutional conventions. We came into nationhood suddenly, and needed a working constitution in short order. This was supplied by the Republic of Singapore Independence Act,[2] which was passed shortly after independence and backdated to 9 August 1965. The Act provided for the 1963 State Constitution[3] and certain provisions of the Federal Constitution of Malaysia to continue in force, and made some additional provisions.[4] Amendments were made as we found our feet as a nation.[5] The result was a patchwork constitution. In 1970, then Prime Minister Lee Kuan Yew felt that this mess had to be polished up and asked the British Foreign and Commonwealth Office for a complete redraft.[6] Mr Lee thought that the draft provided by the British was a first-rate job, but rejected it after further reflection. He preferred to retain the constitutional arrangements that had worked for Singapore than to pursue some unworkable perfection.[7] In the end, the different pieces of our constitution were consolidated and published as a single document, the Constitution of the Republic of Singapore.

The origins of our Constitution have led some to assert that Singapore operates under a system of parliamentary supremacy.[8] Whatever the theoretical niceties, we have today a constitution that is indisputably supreme in law and in fact. It shares many features with other constitutions: parliamentary democracy and cabinet government in the Westminster mould, the rule of law and the separation of powers, an independent judiciary, a bill of rights. Its interpretation is the province of the judiciary. The body of constitutional case law is still small but surely increasing. Apart from litigated cases, legal advisers and legislative drafters in my Chambers handle on a daily basis many matters that engage the Constitution and its attendant principles. Their advice on constitutional matters is taken seriously by government officials and proposals have been significantly changed as a result. To my officers, interpreting the Constitution is not a rarefied exercise.

II Fidelity to the text

How should the Constitution be interpreted? I want to start by going back to basics and stating the obvious: the interpretation of the Constitution must be faithful to the constitutional text. In a way this is a truism: how can one claim to interpret a text without being faithful to it? But, there are also higher principles involved. Underlying the notion of written law is a belief in the power of the written word: that words have meaning; that words are important; that words can bind. This is all the more so for a written constitution that is the supreme law of the land – its words are meant to bind the state and secure the rights of the people. Fidelity to the idea of a written constitution must mean fidelity to its text.

A What fidelity requires

What does fidelity to the constitutional text require? In the first place, it requires that where constitutional provisions are clear, they must be given effect to. And many of our constitutional provisions are clear enough that little is required by way of interpretation. Article 9(4) is a good example. It provides that a person cannot be detained beyond forty-eight hours without being produced before a Magistrate, and cannot be detained further without the authority of the Magistrate. This is the essence of the writ of habeas corpus. There is little that is doubtful in this provision; it does not make for long judgments or academic musings.[9] But, it is this absolute clarity that makes the provision a bulwark of personal liberty. It is the same clarity that secures regular general elections,[10] the independence of the judiciary[11] and the very sanctity of the Constitution,[12] among other things.

But, fidelity to the constitutional text does not stop at giving effect to the literal meaning of the text. Sometimes, value judgments have to be made in interpreting and applying the Constitution.

This is because the Constitution is not drawn like tax or criminal statutes, which are intended to have meanings that cleave to the text. Some constitutional provisions, most significantly the fundamental liberties, are broadly framed, and intentionally so. Concepts such as equal protection and free speech may have a clear general meaning, but their application to specific facts requires exposition and value judgments.

There are also implied concepts and principles in the Constitution. Some degree of implication is unavoidable in any written document, and especially so in a document with a scope as wide as the Constitution. In fact, many important concepts in the Constitution are implied. For instance, the principle of separation of powers is nowhere stated in the Constitution, but is everywhere implied in the system of government that it prescribes.[13] Value judgments are needed to identify this and other propositions that are reflected in or assumed by the express provisions of the Constitution and without which the express provisions would be meaningless or unworkable.

I would make a short detour here and briefly mention constitutional conventions. These are not rules of law and are not enforceable by the courts.[14] But they are essential to a complete understanding of how the Constitution works in practice, which may be very different from how the legal rules are framed. One would, for instance, have a very mistaken view of the British Constitution if one did not appreciate the convention that the Sovereign acts on the advice of the government of the day. Singapore has imported some conventions from the UK, such as the practice of the House of Commons, which is relevant where the Standing Orders of our Parliament are silent.[15] We have also evolved our own conventions – for instance, it is the Government's practice to consult the President before introducing constitutional amendments that affect the President's discretionary powers, and to state the President's views when the amendments are debated in Parliament.[16] The written Principles[17] agreed between the President and the Government on the protection of our past reserves is another example of a constitutional convention.[18] As we mature as a polity, the development of constitutional conventions is likely to become a rich area for study.

As is evident from my earlier observations, a literal approach is not always sufficient in interpreting the Constitution and understanding how it works in practice. In the context of constitutional interpretation, there will be cases where judges are called upon to look beyond the plain words and exercise a degree of value judgment. I think we can be frank and acknowledge that the process involves a degree of judicial law-making occurring in the interstices of the written law. The power of the court in such cases is significant; short of a constitutional amendment, the interpretations they lay down are final, and what they hold to be within the domain of the Constitution is thereby removed from the ordinary processes of democracy.

Conspicuous fidelity to the constitutional text is, therefore, even more important in such cases, where the judge is, by necessity, required to go beyond the plain words. A failure to justify each decision by reference to the constitutional text taints the courts with the suspicion of preferring their personal views under the guise of interpreting the Constitution, of asserting judicial supremacy under the guise of upholding constitutional supremacy.

In practical terms, fidelity to the text in such cases means that judges must reach their decisions guided only by considerations that flow from the text and the structure of the Constitution, and the principles that undergird the text and the Constitution. Some of the more general considerations are well known. The Privy Council has said that the fundamental liberties must be given a generous interpretation that avoids the austerity of tabulated legalism.[19] There is also the consideration that the Constitution is founded on the separation of powers and its provisions are to be interpreted accordingly.[20]

Sometimes the constitutional text leads inexorably to one interpretation, even though it is not explicit. For example, if you read Article 4 and Article 93 together, there can be no doubt that the courts have the power to strike down unconstitutional laws. Another example is the right to vote. The Constitution does not, in terms, create such a right. But, if there were no such right, the system of parliamentary democracy established under Part VI and the requirement for general elections in Articles 65 and 66 would be no better than a mockery. My predecessors as Attorney-General have therefore advised, and the Government has accepted in Parliament, that there is, in principle, an implied constitutional right to vote.[21]

In other cases, the process of interpretation may be more involved and judges may have to decide between reasonable alternatives. But, this is an exercise that a judge is well-equipped to handle, using the usual tools of judicial reasoning. There will, of course, be debates on whether the judge in a given case reached the best possible interpretation of the text, and that is fine and healthy. But so long as the judge is guided by proper textual considerations, properly articulated, the interpretation that he or she reaches will be a legitimate one, even though another judge might legitimately reach a different conclusion.

In reaching their conclusions, it is critical that judges articulate their reasoning.[22] The legitimacy and strength of unelected judges lies in a consistent and visible adherence to the law and to legal method. Every decision must be capable of justification with reference to legal rules, principles and precedents. A failure to give proper reasons undermines the legitimacy of the judicial process.

The guarantee of equal protection in Article 12(1) illustrates some of the points I have just made. The broad language of the clause has lent itself to much litigation. In *Taw Cheng Kong*'s case, the Court of Appeal[23] disagreed with the High Court[24] on the strength of the nexus between the purpose of a law and the classification adopted by the law that is required under the reasonable classification test. In *Lim Meng Suang*'s case,[25] the Court of Appeal was presented with wide-ranging arguments for reinterpreting Article 12(1).

After extensive analysis, the court confirmed that the established reasonable classification test was applicable, albeit with some interesting glosses, the practical implications of which remain to be seen. The judges in each of these decisions took slightly different views on what Article 12(1) required. Constitutional scholars may prefer one of these decisions over the other, or argue for yet other interpretations. But each of these decisions can be said to be legitimate interpretations because they were guided by considerations that flowed from the text of Article 12 and the Constitution. As discussed in *Lim Meng Suang*,[26] some of these considerations include: the principle that fundamental liberties ought to be generously construed; the countervailing principle that judges should avoid open-ended tests that, in effect, place them in the position of policy-makers, thereby breaching the separation of powers; and the specific consideration that Article 12(2) lays down a closed list of grounds on which discrimination is prohibited.

This very brief discussion of Article 12 case law also illustrates how there is room for judicial interpretation of the Constitution to change and evolve in response to changing social and national circumstances, and yet remain legitimate and faithful to the text. But, such evolution is ultimately constrained by the constitutional text. If the constitutional text does not change, there is necessarily an outer limit to its scope. A fixed constitutional text cannot have an ever-expanding meaning.

I should also say that while the Constitution must be ultimately interpreted within its four walls, the process does not require us to bury our heads in the sand. The Constitution shares many basic ideas with other written constitutions, even though its architecture and the precise wording of specific provisions may differ. It is therefore helpful to look at how the courts in other countries have interpreted their constitutions. For instance, the *Kable* principle[27] in Australia holds that you cannot confer a function on the courts that is incompatible with their constitutional character as independent repositories of judicial power. The principle obviously has resonance in the context of our Article 93.

Of course, we have not always followed foreign case law. But even in such cases a proper consideration of comparative jurisprudence imposes a salutary discipline on the quality of our judicial reasoning. On this point I am of course preaching to the converted – the judgments of our courts on constitutional law regularly discuss foreign case law and woe betide the counsel who is not prepared to address the court on relevant foreign case law. State counsel, for their part, regularly consider relevant comparative law in giving advice on constitutional issues. I have also asked for regular digests of international developments to be shared within my Chambers, not least because these are sometimes bellwethers for constitutional issues that could arise in Singapore.

B Non-textual approaches

I now wish to deprecate what might politely be called non-textual approaches to interpreting the Constitution. Their premise is this: there are some laws or policies that are so deplorable that there must be some constitutional remedy, even if the most anxious consideration of the constitutional text, in the light of all that I have said earlier, points to none.

It is clear to me that such approaches are neither lawful nor legitimate. I have mentioned that fidelity to the text does not preclude arguments about the best interpretation of the text, and sometimes these arguments can be very involved. But there is an important distinction to be made between an interpretive exercise where there is a bona fide commitment to be guided only by textual considerations, and one that is overtly or covertly motivated by outcomes that a judge wants to achieve.

If judges go beyond textual considerations in interpreting the Constitution, they are really repudiating the Constitution and constitutional supremacy and substituting their personal views. In doing so, they would be undermining the legitimacy of the courts as impartial tribunals guided only by the law. They would also be usurping the law-making province of the democratically elected branches and, ultimately, diluting every citizen's democratic choice. Some argue that it is comforting that judges stand ready to provide a remedy in extreme cases.

To me, there is nothing comforting about judges who are willing to bend or ignore the law. And in matters outside of the law, why should judges purport to know better than the rest of us?

It is helpful to compare the due process clause of the United States Constitution, Article 21 of the Indian Constitution and Article 9(1) of our own Constitution. At first blush, these are similarly worded provisions. But, there are significant differences in drafting and in how each provision has been interpreted, and these differences illustrate some of the points I have just made.

In the United States, the due process clause prohibits the deprivation of liberty … without due process of law. The US courts have created various substantive rights under the doctrine of substantive due process. This included the economic liberties created in the *Lochner* era,[28] which have since been repudiated. Today, the liberties recognised under the due process clause include personal decisions relating to marriage, procreation, contraception, family relationships, child rearing, and education.[29] There is no clear basis in the US Constitution for these rights and the US courts have not articulated any clear framework for how these unenumerated rights are identified and defined. It is difficult to resist the conclusion that these rights are entirely a judicial creation.

The difficulties with the due process clause and its jurisprudence were known even in the late 1940s when the Indian Constitution was drafted. The drafters deliberately drafted Article 21 of the Indian Constitution to avoid importing substantive due process jurisprudence. The ambit of Article 21 was confined to personal liberty as opposed to liberty generally. And personal liberty could be removed by procedure established by law.[30] Yet, the Indian courts have gone ahead and created numerous substantive rights under Article 21.[31] In my opinion, this is a clear instance of judicial creativity.

Our Article 9(1) is derived from the Indian Article 21. In the context of Article 9 as a whole, it is obvious that the clause is concerned only with unlawful executions and unlawful detentions. Our courts have firmly and quite rightly refused invitations to read the clause to include the freedom of contract and notions of personal dignity or sexual autonomy.[32] In *Yong Vui Kong*'s case, the Court of Appeal specifically declined to follow the activist approach of the Indian courts and tests that 'hinge[d] on the court's view of the reasonableness of the law in question, and requires the court to intrude into the legislative sphere of Parliament as well as engage in policy making'.[33]

To be sure, there are matters that some of us hope can be placed under constitutional protection, with all its attendant implications. But this is an argument for constitutional change and is not relevant to constitutional interpretation. In interpreting the constitution, we must be guided by what the text is, not what we hope for it to be. To venture beyond the text of the Constitution and enunciate a meaning that reflects what the law should be, is to disrespect the principle of separation of powers – this is an exercise that violates rather than upholds the Constitution.

By way of illustration, I want to briefly touch on a fairly recent discussion on whether there is a basic structure to the Constitution that cannot be amended. To me the issue is fairly straightforward. The Constitution has made very plain and specific provisions on how its various provisions may be amended. Every provision can be amended by the prescribed process, and even the most fundamental provisions can be amended (by national referendum[34]). There is therefore no question of any provision of the Constitution, however fundamental, being immune from amendment. There may be valid arguments for amending the

Constitution to make this the case, but those arguments have no bearing on what the law is today.

III Conclusion

In concluding, I want to place constitutional interpretation in context, using an example from the United States. Constitutional lawyers rightly celebrate *Brown v Board of Education*,[35] where the Supreme Court led by Chief Justice Earl Warren in 1954 emphatically struck down segregation in schools. But, it is sobering to also remember that racial integration was viscerally opposed in many parts of the United States and was not fully achieved until many years later. In 1957, President Eisenhower had to send in the army to escort black children to school in Little Rock, Arkansas.

The United States experience with desegregation is salutary. The role of judges in faithfully interpreting and applying the Constitution is important and indispensable. But judges alone cannot secure the health and vitality of the Constitution. The judiciary must be supported in its role by the other branches of government who must see it as their duty to abide by the Constitution and to give effect to judicial interpretations of the Constitution. The Constitution itself recognises this in a small but significant way: in addition to the judges of the Supreme Court, the President and the Members of Parliament all swear an oath to preserve, protect and defend the Constitution.[36]

Beyond the organs of state, the strength of the Constitution ultimately depends on its acceptance by the people: by you and me and our fellow citizens. Here I want to quote from a parliamentary speech made by Prime Minister Lee Kuan Yew in 1984:[37]

> From my experience, constitutions have to be custom-made, tailored to suit the peculiarities of the person wearing the suit. Perhaps, like shoes, the older they are, the better they fit. Stretch them, soften them, resole them, repair them. They are always better than a brand new pair of shoes.
>
> Our people have got used to and understand the present system. It takes a long time … Any fundamental change takes a long time. But most important of all, the Constitution works. Many countries have tried and gone through several constitutions since independence … They have not brought stability or legitimacy. I believe it is better to stretch and ease an old shoe when we know that the different shape and fit of a younger generation requires a change.

There is wisdom in those words. Despite its humble and patchwork beginnings, the Constitution devised by then Prime Minister Lee and his colleagues have served us well for the past fifty years. As we look ahead, each succeeding generation must decide for itself if the Constitution continues to reflect its aspirations and our national conditions, and have the strength of conviction and the boldness of spirit to make any necessary change. It is through this continuous process of refinement, stretching and easing that we work out our constitutional salvation.

Notes

1 Attorney-General and Public Prosecutor, Singapore. This article is slightly edited from the keynote address I gave on 28 May 2015 at the conference, 'Judging the Constitution; the Theory and Practice of Constitutional Interpretation in Singapore', organised by the Centre for Asian Legal Studies, Faculty of Law, National University of Singapore. The address was also published in *The Straits Times* on 30 May 2015. I am indebted to Mr Seow Zhixiang, from the Legislation Division in my Chambers, for his work on this article.

2 (1985 Rev Ed), No 9 of 1965.

3 The 1963 State Constitution is found in the Sabah, Sarawak and Singapore (State Constitutions) Order in Council 1963 (SI 1493/1963).

4 Because of this approach, some of the long titles of our early constitutional amendments read 'An Act to amend the Constitution of Singapore', referring to the 1963 State Constitution, while others read 'An Act to amend the Constitution of Malaysia in its application to Singapore'.

5 One of the more significant amendments was the creation of the Presidential Council for Minority Rights as a result of the recommendations of the Wee Chong Jin Commission.

6 Singapore Parliamentary Debates, Official Report (25 July 1984) vol 44, cols 1818–19.

7 ibid.

8 AJ Harding, 'Parliament and the Grundnorm in Singapore' (1983) 25 Malayan Law Review 351.

9 Earlier this year, there was a misguided attempt to read the provision as conferring on a detained person an absolute right to be brought before a Magistrate (as opposed to a right to be brought before a Magistrate only if the detention exceeds forty-eight hours). The Court of Appeal did not hesitate to dismiss the challenge: see *Yan Jun v AG* [2015] 1 SLR 752 [89]–[96].

10 See the provisions on the dissolution of Parliament and the holding of general elections in Articles 65 and 66.

11 See the protections afforded to judicial office-holders in Articles 98 and 99.

12 See the provisions for the amendment of the Constitution in Articles 5(1) and (2), 5A and 8.

13 See eg *Mohammad Faizal bin Sabtu v Public Prosecutor* [2012] 4 SLR 947 [11]–[12].

14 *Patriation Reference* [1981] 1 SCR 753.

15 Standing Order 110 of the Standing Orders of the Parliament of Singapore.

16 Singapore Parliamentary Debates, Official Report (21 October 2008) vol 85, cols 532ff (Mr Lee Hsien Loong, the Prime Minister).

17 These Principles have been set out in a White Paper entitled *The Principles for Determining and Safeguarding the Accumulated Reserves of the Government and the Fifth Schedule Statutory Boards and Government Companies* (Cmd 5, 1999), presented to Parliament on 2 July 1999.

18 Thio Li-ann refers to the Principles as 'the clearest example of soft constitutional law as it relates to institutionalised interaction': see Thio Li-Ann, *A Treatise on Singapore Constitutional Law* (Academy Publishing 2012) para 01.206.

19 *Ong Ah Chuan v Public Prosecutor* [1979–1980] SLR (R) 710.

20 See eg *Mohammad Faizal* (n 13) [11]–[12].

21 Singapore Parliamentary Debates (16 May 2001) vol 73, cols 1725–28 (Mr Wong Kan Seng, Deputy Prime Minister and Leader of the House); Singapore Parliamentary Debates (13 February 2009) vol 85, cols 3157–61 and 3174–79 (Mr K Shanmugam, Minister for Law).

22 I have written on behalf of the Court of Appeal on the general judicial duty to give reasons in *Thong Ah Fat v PP* [2012] 1 SLR 676.

23 *PP v Taw Cheng Kong* [1998] 2 SLR(R) 489.
24 *Taw Cheng Kong v PP* [1998] 1 SLR(R) 78.
25 *Lim Meng Suang v AG* [2015] 1 SLR 26.
26 ibid.
27 *Kable v DPP (New South Wales)* (1996) 189 CLR 51.
28 *Lochner v New York* 198 US 45 (1905).
29 *Planned Parenthood v Casey* 505 US 833 (1992) 851.
30 See B Shiva Rao (ed), *The Framing of India's Constitution: A Study* (The Indian Institute of Public Administration 1968) 235–38.
31 See the examples quoted in *Yong Vui Kong v Public Prosecutor* [2010] SGCA 20, [2010] 3 SLR 489 [83].
32 *Lo Pui Sang v Mamata Kapildev Dave* [2008] SGHC 116, [2008] 4 SLR(R) 754; *Lim Meng Suang* (n 25).
33 *Yong Vui Kong* (n 31) [80].
34 See Articles 5(2A), 5A and 8. Articles 5(2A) and 5A are not in operation but are, nonetheless, part of the law of the land: see the reasoning in *Constitutional Reference No 1 of 1995* [1995] SGCT 1, [1995] 1 SLR(R) 803.
35 347 US 483 (1954).
36 *Constitution of the Republic of Singapore* (1999 Rev Ed), Art 20(2) and 61, and First Schedule.
37 Singapore Parliamentary Debates (24 July 1984) vol 73, cols 1735–36.

Bibliography

Harding, AJ, 'Parliament and the Grundnorm in Singapore' (1983) 25 Malaya Law Review 351.

Shiva, Rao B, *The Framing of India's Constitution: A Study* (The Indian Institute of Public Administration 1968).

Thio, Li-ann, *A Treatise on Singapore Constitutional Law* (Academy Publishing 2012).

2 Does the 'basic structure doctrine' apply in Singapore's Constitution?

An inquiry into some fundamental constitutional premises

Andrew J Harding

I Introduction

Any form of constitutional interpretation engages, or should engage, with fundamental constitutional principles. Purely pragmatic or knee-jerk solutions could prove very awkward if the deep structural implications of a particular interpretation are not carefully considered as a matter of legal reasoning within a particular frame of reasoning. In a rule-of-law society, consistency in the way the law deals with difficult issues such as constitutional interpretation is of the utmost importance, and therefore lawyers are always concerned with 'basic structure' in one way or another: the chapters in this book are a paean to this idea. In this sense, basic structure is always with us when we reason legally. When judging the constitutionality of legislation, for example, we do not do so in the abstract, as it were, but by reference to the totality of the constitution's provisions and the intentions and assumptions that gave rise to them.[1] Basic structure or basic features[2] can hardly be avoided when performing this task. A good example of this is those decisions that preserve the independence of the judiciary; it is unexceptional to interpret constitutional provisions in line with the separation of powers as an aspect of 'basic structure', as was done by Chan Sek Keong CJ in *Mohammad Faizal bin Sabtu*.[3] This case raised the question of whether statutory provision for a mandatory penalty in a criminal case constituted an unconstitutional interference with the judicial power. In deciding that it did not do so, Chan CJ accepted that the separation of powers between the legislature, the executive and the judiciary was part of the basic structure of Singapore's Constitution,[4] being based on Westminster model principles.[5]

The words 'basic structure doctrine' in the title of this chapter, however – and let us be quite clear – go much further than the above paragraph. They refer to the constitutional doctrine set out by India's Supreme Court in the epoch-making case of *Kesavananda Bharati* in 1973.[6] Under this doctrine, a law seeking *to amend the Constitution* is not constitutionally valid if it is judged to be inconsistent with what the court called the 'basic structure' of the Constitution. Thus, constitutional amendments are subject to an implied limitation under the Constitution of India:

the limitation that no amendment has power to destroy the Constitution's basic structure, *even if* the procedure prescribed by the Constitution for effecting an amendment is complied with. This limitation is implied because the Constitution of India (unlike some others[7]) at no point places *express* limits on the substance of the power the legislature has to amend the Constitution. The limits on this power are, on the face of the Constitution, limits only in the procedural sense, namely, that a majority of two-thirds of the membership of each House in favour of a bill seeking to amend the Constitution is required before the amendment can take effect.[8]

A similar procedural limit is, as it happens, expressly imposed by the Constitution of Singapore, which provides that a bill for amending the Constitution must be supported by at least two-thirds of the total number of the Members of Parliament at second and third readings (except, of course, that the Singapore legislature is unicameral, not bicameral).[9] However, Article 6 protects Singapore's sovereignty with a further requirement of a referendum in which two-thirds of the votes cast must be in favour of surrendering sovereignty for the amendment to be valid. A similar requirement also applies (Article 8) to amendments to this very Article 6, as well as to amendments falling under Articles 5(2A) and 5A, which concern fundamental rights and the tenure, powers and privileges of the President, and of course to Articles 5(2A) and 5A themselves (although these provisions are not yet operational). The amendment provisions themselves have been subject to amendment on several occasions. The two-thirds-majority requirement itself, we might note, was removed in 1965 and then reinstated in 1979.[10] We can also note that the supremacy clause[11] itself was introduced only in 1979 by virtue of the process of 'reprinting' the Constitution.[12] The amendment process itself seems therefore not to have been regarded as part of the Constitution of Singapore's basic structure; indeed the special majority requirement was removed and then reinstated for purely strategic or contingent reasons.[13] Singapore's Constitution therefore contains no express limits with regard to the substance or subject matter of an amendment, so that on the face of the Constitution it allows an amendment of any of its provisions to be effective if it complies with the relevant procedural requirements, even if it has the effect of destroying the Constitution's basic structure. The question addressed here is whether in Singapore there is an implied substantive limitation on the power of constitutional amendment, as there is in India.

In this chapter, I am therefore concerned only with implied, substantive limits, not with procedural ones. In the latter case, we can readily grant that the courts would have power to strike down a purported constitutional amendment that failed to comply with the procedure set out in the Constitution. This might occur if, for example, Parliament purported to pass a bill for amending the Constitution by acclamation rather than a proper parliamentary vote; or if a referendum requirement were abused by posing the question in a prejudicial manner or miscounting the votes.

The notion of judicial review of the *substance* of a constitutional amendment as opposed to reviewing compliance with procedure is startling, if such a great power is being *implied* into the provisions of a constitution. In such a case, we are assuming that the required procedure has been impeccably complied with. We might indeed be inclined to say that a special majority (even more so, a referendum) should be determinative if the express words of the Constitution require nothing else. Imagine what chaos there might be in a football match if the rules, as interpreted by the referee, required, for the scoring of a goal, that the ball must not just cross the goal line but must cross it after being kicked by the goalkeeper's opponent within (not just the stated rules of the governing body but) the basic structure or spirit of the game. Players, managers, officials and spectators would be confused as to when a goal had been scored or even how to legitimately score a goal. They would no doubt suspect the referee of bias or arbitrary decision. Confusion would reign.

That a notion is startling should not in itself, however, prejudice our minds against it. There is no doubt that in the USA of the early nineteenth century, lawyers and others were shocked when the Supreme Court proclaimed without any textual support that the courts could review the constitutionality of legislation.[14] Two hundred years later, it is still not entirely accepted by everyone as a matter of principle, but it is hardly contestable as a constitutional fact: the recent gay marriage case illustrates both the fact that the Supreme Court decides fundamental questions relating to rights and that its doing so (in this instance by the slenderest majority of one) is almost always controversial.[15] Just as the US Constitution does not indicate any express power of judicial review of legislation and the Supreme Court in *Marbury v Madison*[16] felt compelled to find this to be a power implied in the Constitution's provisions (one might add that it did so as a matter of the Constitution's basic structure), so the Indian Supreme Court felt compelled in *Kesavananda* to go a stage further and decide it had the power to strike down a constitutional amendment on substantive grounds despite the lack of any textual support for the existence of such a power.[17]

Naturally, there are those who will argue that the constitution-makers (in, for example, India) apparently made a conscious choice *not* to place any express limits on the power of constitutional amendment. They could clearly have done so, and there are indeed, as we have seen, constitutions in which some provisions have been *expressly* placed completely beyond the amending power.[18] The counter-argument is that the constitution-makers could not have considered, or must have assumed it impossible, that a constitutional amendment that destroys the basic structure of the edifice they erected could be regarded as valid; why, otherwise, would they have drafted a constitution that contained the seed of its own destruction?

I do not wish here to go into the merits of these arguments, which are as interesting as they are extensive; my argument is simply that the correct position is to be ascertained only by looking at the context (historical and textual) of the Constitution or constitutional provisions in question.

The decision in *Kesavananda*, controversial as it was, set off a process of consideration of the applicability of the basic structure doctrine (in the sense in which I am using the term here) in the constitutions of the region – in Pakistan,[19]

Sri Lanka[20] and Malaysia[21] – and also in Singapore.[22] This chapter accordingly discusses the arguments for and against interpreting the Constitution in line with the basic structure doctrine, and argues that this doctrine (strictly, that is, in the narrow sense indicated above) has no application to Singapore's Constitution. This, it is argued here, is due to the manner in which Singapore's Constitution was laid down in the months and years following Singapore's separation from Malaysia in 1965, that critical moment when a new republic was born in the crucible of international political events.[23]

What we see in Singapore's constitutional history, it is argued here, is not an act of a constituent body such as occurred in India, but rather a constitutional evolution via a gradual legislative process of combining different sources,[24] and subsequent piecemeal attempts to redesign the constitutional apparatus, a process which appears to be still continuing as Singapore celebrates fifty years of independence under its patchwork Constitution. In advancing this thesis, I argue that the basic structure doctrine is *contextually based*. What I mean by this is that a constitutional principle of this kind cannot be regarded as *generally applicable* in any given constitutional order. Its applicability will depend on a number of factors that include the actual wording of a given constitution, the circumstances of its drafting, the presumed intention of the constitution-makers, and the perceived role of the judiciary. Accordingly, it makes no sense to ask whether someone 'believes in' the basic structure doctrine, as it would if you were to ask if they 'believe in' the rule of law or judicial independence. The saliency and even the content (ie what features are basic?) of the basic structure doctrine will vary according to the constitutional context in question. It may well be that the doctrine applies in Malaysia, for example, due to the different context of its constitution-making.

Since this idea is fundamental to my argument, let me briefly explain it further.

When we confront the basic structure doctrine, should we adopt a contextual or a normative approach? Do we say that legal principle is so inherent in the nature of constitutional ordering (or conceivably, in the eyes of some, Westminster model-type constitutional ordering) that what is true in one constitutional order is potentially true in another, especially if the two are genetically connected in some sense? Or is every response on this issue in a given society dependent on its own relevant factors, some of which are listed above?

There may well be many relevant factors and indeed many ways of posing this question, but my point here is that the salience of the basic structure doctrine is *contextual*, and these relevant contextual factors will therefore vary considerably between constitutional orders. Indeed the basic structure doctrine in India depends very much on contingent factors of this kind, being based on what Krishnaswamy calls 'a coherent reading of the constitutional text', as well as historical facts and statements in the Constituent Assembly.[25] It is not, in my view, necessary or appropriate to argue for a general position on this issue because no such general position is logically possible. Constitutions do not emerge from some wellspring of theory so that their principles are abstracted from any particular time and place. On the contrary, they are contingent expressions of what is desired in a particular society at a given point in time, and which are to be judged according to their fitness for the desired purposes. These purposes may of course change over time: hence the need for constitutional change (even Singapore's relatively stable Constitution has actually been amended twenty-one times since the 1992 revised edition). I doubt if any constitution-maker could properly assume a kind of Olympian omniscience and omnipotence in laying down a constitution for a particular society for ever, let alone a general constitutional theory that is universally or eternally applicable.[26] Even 'constitutionalism' as an inherent quality of constitutions is not universal or certain in its content: it has a core of meaning, no doubt, but needs to be calibrated according to the nature and development of constitutional law and constitutional ideas current in the jurisdiction in question. In Singapore's case, we can note, *fundamental* changes have been made within the last generation to both the process of constitutional amendment itself and to the presidency. These are basic issues in constitutional ordering and have defined (not perhaps finally) the nature of constitutional law in Singapore.

In this chapter, arguing as I do that the basic structure doctrine has no application in Singapore, I maintain that any conditions for application of the doctrine were simply not present at the critical moment of separation in 1965 and beyond.[27] In the last part of the chapter I take the argument a stage further by asking a hypothetical question: if I am right, what would the consequences be in terms of any future attempt to entrench the Constitution, or a constitution, in Singapore? Just as the basic structure doctrine does not apply, as I argue, because of the events at Singapore's founding, could it *become* part of the constitutional law of Singapore under different future circumstances that might attract its application? If the doctrine is contingent rather than necessary, could the relevant contingencies change?

II Basic structure and basic sources in Singapore's Constitution

When Singapore unexpectedly became an independent republic after ceasing to be part of the Malaysian Federation on 9 August 1965, that was potentially what Ackerman calls a 'constitutional moment'.[28] Of course, it was determinative in the sense that Singapore sovereignty was thereby established. But constitutionally it proved not in fact to be simply a 'moment', but rather the beginning of a process of adjustment which may be regarded as ongoing even after fifty years.[29] While one would have expected – and indeed it was indicated at the time – that this event would lead to a consideration of Singapore's constitutional future, what actually happened was rather different. A Constitutional Commission was indeed established but the Commission, rather than looking anew at Singapore's constitutional issues in this unexpected situation, simply looked at a few issues, and some, but not all, of its recommendations were adopted.[30] It was not a review of the entire Constitution. This was all in sharp distinction from India (and indeed many other jurisdictions), where the process of independence led to a Constituent Assembly which drafted India's constitution. In Singapore a piecemeal approach was taken that knitted together, largely from existing sources, a renovated rather than a wholly new constitution.

First, the Singapore Parliament passed the Republic of Singapore Independence Act 1965 (RSIA),[31] which made provision for Singapore's newly established independence. This was in essence a constitutional statute.[32]

Second, the RSIA also continued in force the Constitution of Singapore of 1963, which applied to Singapore as a State of the Malaysian Federation under the Federal Constitution; this State Constitution had been derived from its colonial predecessors and agreed under the Malaysia Agreement of 1963.[33]

Third, certain applicable provisions of the Malaysian Constitution were also continued in force by the RSIA, notably the fundamental rights provisions now in Part IV of the Constitution of Singapore and the citizenship provisions now in Part X.[34] Essentially, this meant that the constitutional status quo continued (*mutatis mutandis*, of course – a new republic was, after all, being formed, but at that point who knew for how long?) as opposed to a new constitution being drafted.

Fourth, in 1979, Parliament empowered the Attorney-General to consolidate these various provisions, together with subsequent amendments, into one document, which was not itself passed by Parliament, but became the Revised Edition of the Constitution of the Republic of Singapore 1980. The actual text of the Constitution, including the numbering of its provisions, was thus, remarkably, settled by an executive rather than legislative or constituent act, under the general authority of Parliament. This revised edition was succeeded by further revised editions in 1992 and 1999.

While *Mohammad Faizal bin Sabtu*[35] discusses the idea of a basic structure in the context of interpretation, *Teo Soh Lung*'s case[36] and *Vincent Cheng v Minister of Home Affairs*[37] deal directly with the issue of the validity of constitutional amendments. In the former case, the High Court rejected the applicability of the basic structure doctrine in relation to the Constitution (Amendment) Act 1989,[38] which had the effect of depriving the applicant of the benefit of judicial review by means of amendment to the Internal Security Act and Article 149 of the Constitution, under which the Act was passed. These amendments followed a decision of the Court of Appeal in *Chng Suan Tze v Minister of Home Affairs*,[39] following which the applicant had been released on a writ of habeas corpus, only to be re-arrested under fresh documentation. Chua J held that the *Kesavananda* doctrine was 'not applicable to our Constitution' because of 'the differences in the making of the Indian and our Constitution'. He further held that '[i]n any case none of the amendments complained of has destroyed the basic structure of the Constitution'. In *Vincent Cheng*, Lai J decided along the same lines, approving Chua J's judgment in *Teo Soh Lung*.

III Basic structure and governance innovation

We have seen that the moment for drafting an entirely new constitution passed in 1965/1966 and another, more pragmatic, inductive approach was taken. Most notably, an amendment of 1991 introduced an elected presidency having some executive powers.[40] The merits of this major change are not a subject for this chapter, but it can be noted nonetheless that it might be argued, if the basic structure doctrine applies in Singapore, that by altering the nature of the presidency in this way Parliament had indeed altered the basic structure of the Constitution away from the Westminster model, a model that one sees indelibly engraved in its original, if evolutionary, form in 1963–1965. It has even been argued that the elected presidency *has actually become* part of the basic structure of Singapore's Constitution.[41]

This latter proposition is puzzling if examined from the perspective of the basic structure doctrine. If a constitutional amendment is passed that fundamentally alters the structure of government, how could that amendment at the same time (a) be valid in spite of destroying by alteration the existing basic structure of the Constitution, and (b) become part of that basic structure, and hence immune from amendment? If it is retorted that the basic structure can change over time, then surely the correct response is that that is indeed correct, which in turn establishes the point that the power of constitutional amendment is there precisely to provide a process for such change, whether that change is incremental or fundamental. While one can see arguments for entrenching fundamental rights so as to render them beyond not just legislative but even constitutional amendment,[42] still, as a matter of political morality, it is hard to see how such entrenchment can be appropriate for a particular structure of government. Structures of government are not necessarily moral or immoral: they are simply designed to fulfil the need for stable, effective and accountable government, and this need may produce different results in different societies at different times. If we consider all those countries, even within the ambit of the 'Westminster model', that have changed their government structure from parliamentary to presidential (actually around half of the countries in the present Commonwealth[43]), is it really the case that these constitutional changes are all invalid as destroying the basic (Westminster) structure of their respective constitutions? If so, these countries might argue, we are saddled with British constitutionalism *forever*. The constitution-makers, one imagines, could not have desired or intended such an absurd result. It is of course significant in this regard that *Kesavananda* itself was concerned with fundamental rights and *not* specifically with the structure of government.[44]

In Singapore's case, the original Constitution embraced parliamentary democracy with its distinctive Westminster-type conventions, including those deriving from a distinction between the (non-executive) head of state and the (executive) head of government, and an independent judiciary.[45] One could of course argue, in the alternative to the argument addressed above, that such basic structure was altered, but not in any way *destroyed*, by the change in this form of government that took place when the elected presidency was introduced. One could point here to the purely negative, veto-like powers of the President, which are more like reserve powers than executive powers in the plenary and ordinary sense of the term. On this argument, the elected presidency would be merely an incidental modification of the Constitution, which preserves the possibility of the basic structure doctrine being applied to Singapore's Constitution. A more convincing argument (and one that is consistent with the view taken in this chapter) might be that Singapore's Parliament is, and should be, entitled to change the structure of government away from the Westminster model in whatever manner it chooses. The actual constitutional power to do this (as opposed to the expediency of such a change) does not appear to have been an issue anywhere else in the Commonwealth, despite many such structural changes.[46]

In Singapore there have, in addition, been several changes to the system of elected parliamentary representation; for example, the introduction of the GRC (Group Representation Constituency), NMP (Nominated Member of Parliament) and NCMP (Non-Constituency Member of Parliament). Parliament could, for instance, on the view advanced here, abolish the elected presidency, thereby restoring the status quo ante; or create a hybrid presidency in which the head of government is head of state and enjoys the confidence of the parliament in which he or she sits; or change the entire electoral system to one of proportional representation; or abolish constituencies as the geographical basis of representation. Singapore would not, in any of such events, be the first country to commence with a Westminster model constitution upon independence and then proceed to modify it several times over.[47] Singapore is not a federation but the argument might equally apply to changes in federal and unitary structures. If, shall we say, Malaysia decided to establish peninsular Malaysia as a unitary state in federation with Sabah and Sarawak; or if it admitted Brunei or readmitted Singapore to the existing Federation on favourable terms, reducing the powers of existing states – would these changes really be *juridically impossible* due to the applicability of the basic structure doctrine? Such a stance in opposition to a majority or consensus would invite constitutional revolution and the avoidance or even the overthrow of judicial power.[48]

The contextual point I wish to emphasise, however, remains that in Singapore there was no constitutional moment in which Singapore's Constitution was created, and therefore no process whereby constitution-makers expressly or impliedly laid down a basic structure for Singapore's Constitution which could not be destroyed by constitutional amendment. Rather, Singapore's Constitution fell into place by a process of piecemeal legislative actions directed towards specific issues. If Singapore had any 'constitution-makers' as such, they might have been the parliamentarians of 1965–1979, the period in which constitutional flexibility was espoused, but, even these members owed much to those who drafted the Constitution of the Federation of Malaya in 1957 and the State Constitution of Singapore of 1963. Furthermore, 1979 should not be seen as the *culmination* of a process of experimentation leading to consolidation but on the contrary as marking the *beginning* of such a process, which has yet to find its endpoint.

It is, of course, arguable that a constitution-drafting process should have been iterated in 1965, and indeed it is surprising that this did not happen, given the novel circumstances in which this new, unintended republic found its way into the world. Arguable as this might be, it does not, however, represent historical fact. The Constitutional Commission, despite its name, was not mandated to draft a new constitution. The view was held that current arrangements were quite satisfactory, but merely needed some adjustment to the new circumstances. This theory of constitutional change seems still to apply. One can of course readily imagine that a drafting process would have been highly charged politically, given the controversial circumstances of 1965 and the fact that a substantial number of sitting MPs belonging to the Barisan Sosialis Party regarded the whole process of enacting the RSIA as unconstitutional, and boycotted Parliament.[49] A process to draft a new constitution in these circumstances would have proved very difficult, although not perhaps impossible. In the event, what we can discern is a gradual, pragmatic attempt to adjust, experiment with, and entrench the new constitutional arrangements over a lengthy period – fifty years to be precise, and counting.

If the basic structure doctrine does, contrary to my argument, apply in Singapore, we are faced with some intractable questions. We might argue about the fundamental or merely incidental nature of the changes to the presidency, but we could hardly argue that the process of constitutional amendment itself is not fundamental, as it determines who has the power to amend the legal system's most fundamental law, and therefore stands in a sense superior in legal hierarchy over those laws. Nor (to pursue this logic) could we argue that Singapore's sovereignty is not fundamental to the constitutional order. It is so basic that a referendum is required in order to surrender it.

In short, if there is a basic structure to Singapore's Constitution, then these aspects, at the very least, must be part of it.[50] But, consider again the changes to the amendment process: on the basis of the basic structure doctrine these changes, introduced via procedurally correct process, must have been (virtually by definition) invalid. By the same token, if Singapore's sovereignty were surrendered in terms envisaged by Article 6, and such surrender were to be supported by a two-thirds vote at a referendum, we would nonetheless be forced to conclude that any necessary amendments were invalid because they destroyed the Constitution's basic structure. The same argument would of course apply to the entrenchment of fundamental rights and the elected presidency, yet to be completed under the changes to Articles 5 and 5A.[51]

Seen in this light, the inapplicability of the basic structure doctrine in Singapore seems highly compelling. Singaporeans would be astonished to learn that all these changes that have actually occurred, or whose occurrence is envisaged by the express terms of the Constitution itself, were unconstitutional. If they were, the Constitution would be confined within a straitjacket of its own making that effectively allowed for virtually no development.

Does this take the position too far? Is there merit in at least leaving the door open for future application of the basic structure doctrine in the event of an extreme event – let us suppose an attempt to amend the Constitution in such a way as to abolish the separation of judicial power completely[52] and vest it in the legislature or the executive? I suggest that in this event, the niceties of constitutional interpretation become irrelevant, because here we enter the realm of revolutionary politics. If the basic structure doctrine were to be used in a judicial decision striking down an amendment of this kind, it seems to me that the legitimacy or otherwise of such a devastating change would be a political rather than a legal question. What role the judiciary might play in such a scenario is impossible to predict. I see no convincing argument here for deliberately leaving open the possibility of applying the basic structure doctrine.

IV Grundnorms and evolving norms

In an article published more than thirty years ago,[53] I argued for a position similar to that set out in this chapter, based on the uniqueness of Singapore's constitutional transition from being a post-colony State of Malaysia to an independent republic. The burden of my argument in that article was that in August 1965, one could discern a shift in Singapore's *grundnorm*. Instead of the orchestration of a constitution-drafting process, Singapore's Parliament (actually the Legislative Assembly of the Malaysian State of Singapore in continued de facto operation) stepped in and legislated Singapore's Constitution in the manner set out a few pages above. By doing so, I argued, this Parliament established a form of parliamentary sovereignty as opposed to constitutional supremacy. In other words, Parliament had exercised constituent power in enacting Singapore's Constitution, and therefore analytically the situation was similar in a sense to that in England in 1688, where Parliament stepped in to legislate for the royal succession having deemed King James II to have abdicated. Of course, we can see from the history of the UK that parliamentary sovereignty is also capable of evolving, and few these days would maintain it still exists in unadulterated form.[54] Could it be that this 'grundnorm' has shifted over time in Singapore? Or if not, could it be changed? Can parliamentary sovereignty be consistent with the Constitution's apparent adoption of constitutional supremacy (a feature distinguishing Singapore's Constitution from that of the UK, as Chan CJ argued in *Mohammad Faizal*[55])?

In identifying the grundnorm in parliamentary sovereignty, my point was that Singapore's Parliament assumed the right to lay down Singapore's Constitution. When it did so, Parliament was exercising constituent power, as was recognised in *Taw Cheng Kong*.[56] It does not necessarily exercise that power all the time. Indeed, by laying down a procedure for amending the Constitution, it has in effect bound itself procedurally in such a case. However, on this argument, there is no inherent reason why the constituent power could not be revived if Parliament chose to revoke the Constitution and substitute a new one. It seems consistent with the argument in this chapter that such a constituent act could not be impugned by arguing that the Constitution's basic structure has been (a fortiori, of course, if the entire Constitution is revoked) destroyed, rendering this constituent act unconstitutional. In explaining this, I do not mean to argue that this would be the best or even an appropriate way of bringing about constitutional change. That, as I have said, is a political question to be decided if and when the time comes to decide it. My point is simply that Parliament has the power to do this given the precedent of 1965 and the propositions that that precedent has established.

Of course, a citizen could plausibly argue that the real issue is that the people of Singapore have never been asked what kind of constitution they would like. Given that they have, in the last 25 years or so, expressed strong views on such issues as the elected presidency, GRCs, nominated and non-constituency MPs, the constitutional position of the People's Action Party as a 'national movement', and on freedom of expression, there seems little doubt that a debate about Singapore's future constitution would be intense. This is an issue for the political process to decide. Currently, there is no demand for the drafting of a new constitution; hence the concern in this book with the issue of interpreting the constitution. The question, nonetheless, might arise whether and how one might see the adoption of the basic structure doctrine, were it thought to be an appropriate innovation. It is my view that, while there is much to be said for the basic structure doctrine, the entire tenor of the argument in this chapter is that its applicability needs to be calibrated against constitutional facts, and these will vary according to the jurisdiction and its constitutional history. These facts in relation to Singapore appear, we have seen, to lead to the conclusion that the doctrine has no application in Singapore, and the courts, as we have also seen, endorse this position. But, as a matter of speculation as to constitutional fundamentals, and as promised in the title of this chapter, the argument seems to require an answer to the question whether Singapore could have the benefit of the doctrine. And if so, how?

The argument of this chapter rests on the issue of how the Constitution came into effect. If it were decided at some future juncture that Singapore needed an entirely new constitution in which the citizens and/ or their representatives got to debate and adopt such a new constitution, would such a process allow for the basic structure doctrine as a plausible basis of interpretation, imposing implied substantive limitations on the power of constitutional amendment? How indeed would we *know* if this occurs?

A new constitution could, of course, be achieved in different ways.

First, it would be possible for the present constitution to be simply amended in line with whatever might be agreed, via some political process, as newly desirable principles or provisions. I leave aside whether a referendum or other approval process would or should be required. Here we would, on the argument presented here, encounter little difficulty: such amendments, even if destroying the basic structure of the constitution, would be valid because the basic structure doctrine has no application. The intention might well, depending on the extent of the amendments, be precisely to destroy the constitution's basic structure. In this event, I see no good reason why the expressed, concerted political will of the community should be struck down by the courts.

Of course, it is also possible in this case that newly introduced provisions might make some provisions expressly unamendable; in this case, the Constitution would have defined its own basic structure and the doctrine as such would be redundant, and would indeed be made redundant by such provisions, which would protect certain provisions by express, as opposed to implied, limitations on the amending power. Such provisions are not unknown in constitutional law generally, as we have seen. One could go further and argue that if a constitution provides different *levels* of entrenchment according to their 'basic-structure-ness' (as the current constitution actually does if one considers Article 6), then the doctrine is impliedly excluded because the Constitution has actually provided a process for amending the basic structure, that structure being in effect defined by the expressly enacted scope of the deepest level of entrenchment.[57]

Second, however, it might be thought appropriate to amend the present constitution in such a way as to contemplate its own eclipse and the bringing into effect of a new constitution – as it were from the womb of the old. One can imagine various ways in which this might be done, but the central point would be that there would be a form of legal continuity. In this case, whether the basic structure doctrine had application in these new circumstances would, I suggest, be moot, and would depend on the wording of what we might call the 'midwife provisions', ie those facilitating the birth of the new constitution. As against the current situation and consistently with the manner in which I present it, it might be arguable that the basic structure doctrine applied to the new constitution. Much would depend, I suggest, on the nature of the exercise, the intention of the constitution-makers, and what the courts might feel able make of those intentions. The point is that the basic structure doctrine could become relevant in this scenario. Again, it would be possible (and, I would suggest, highly desirable) for the constitution-makers to address the issue directly if they chose to do so, either by providing for (or indeed excluding, if they preferred) judicial review of the new constitution's basic structure. It is suggested that the basic structure doctrine is too important an issue to simply leave for judicial interpretation. Given the deeply contested applicability of this doctrine, if it were thought desirable to give the courts this power it should be provided *expressly* as an act of constitution-drafting: indeed, given what is now known about this issue it would, I suggest, be nothing short of a dereliction of duty not to make provision clarifying whether the doctrine applies or not.

Third, one could imagine a scenario in which Singapore decided to organise a complete legal break with the current constitution by simply ignoring it or revoking it and basing a new constitution on some kind of an act of popular sovereignty. This was effected quite deliberately in Sri Lanka in 1972,[58] and is actually embraced as a possibility in the German Basic Law's Preamble, despite its totally entrenched provisions as indicated in Article 79(3). In this scenario I suggest that the arguments adduced in *Kesavananda* would become of relevance; for the contextual reasons stated above I cannot say if they would be ultimately persuasive. It does not mean that the basic structure doctrine would have to be adopted. After all, the courts might find the arguments against the doctrine attractive in spite of the new legal situation; or they might not. Courts in the region, apart from the Indian courts, that have considered the doctrine, as we saw earlier, have generally not looked on it with favour. As with the second scenario above, it would be preferable in this case to make express provision for judicial review of the basic structure. Given that the constitution-makers and those debating the issues, as above, would be presumptively aware of *Kesavananda* and its aftermath, it would be hardly forgivable if they offered no solution, or no hint as to the answer, leaving it to the judiciary to decide with (on this hypothesis) no evidence on which to draw.

Here, let me explain further a point, mentioned above, that could be relevant to the evolution of Singapore's Constitution over time. To the extent that a constitution provides differing levels of entrenchment, it could in effect elaborate its own basic structure. Let us suppose, for example, that the most important provisions in the Constitution are entrenched more deeply than other more detailed provisions (contrast, let us say, the role and position of the President being amendable by an ordinary law, with detailed provisions concerning his/her appointment/election/qualification which could only be altered after a referendum). Let us suppose, to follow the trend in Singapore, that the 'basic' provisions are protected by a referendum requirement. In this event, the Constitution will have defined its own basic structure, but, crucially, in the process it will also have defined *the manner of amendment applicable to this basic structure*. In India, there is no such protection for basic provisions, which could help to explain the role of the Supreme Court using the basic structure doctrine to strike down amendments, these being within the power of the legislature alone to effect. If the Constitution thereby defines its own basic structure and the manner of amendment, it is very hard to see any role for the judiciary in contradicting the clear decision of both the legislature and one or more other elements of the state such as the electorate. If Singapore's judiciary is squeamish about overturning the will of Parliament in ordinary legislation, as is set out in several chapters of this book,[59] it is hard to imagine that they could adopt an aggressive stance towards constitutional amendments, especially if Parliament and the consensus of citizens have expressed their preference.

V Conclusion

Let me finally attempt to summarise with clarity the argument in this chapter.

Under Singapore's current constitution, it is not convincingly arguable that the basic structure doctrine applies in Singapore. The conclusions of the courts on this point are correct.

For the future, I argue, in the event of constitutional change of a fundamental nature, it may become arguable that the doctrine applies. However, a better solution would be to decide this issue as a matter of constitution-making rather than leaving it to the courts to decide. The constitution-makers should decide (in this event) whether any, and if so which, provisions of Singapore's constitution should be beyond the power of constitutional amendment. There is, of course, much more to be said on the subject of what a good process for amending the Constitution would be. There are, in my view, dangers in giving such a power of hyper-judicial-review, as we might put it, to the courts, which gives them power to strike down not just legislation passed by a parliamentary majority, but also the considered view of the community operating the stated process for constitutional amendment. Of course, arguments will continue as to the desirability of the basic structure doctrine (I have separated out here the issue of applicability). It is an unruly doctrine – when does it apply? What is the basic structure? When has it been 'destroyed'? While arguments will continue as to the merits of the basic structure doctrine, this chapter argues that, as things are, the doctrine has no application in Singapore.

Notes

1 For an example of this, see Kevin YL Tan, 'Into the matrix: interpreting the Westminster model constitution', Chapter 3 of this book, and *Mohammad Faizal bin Sabtu v Public Prosecutor* [2012] 4 SLR 947 (SGHC) [11]–[12] (Chan CJ). For further discussion, see Calvin Liang and Sarah Shi, 'The Constitution of Our Constitution, A Vindication of the Basic Structure Doctrine' (2014) Singapore Law Gazette (August 2014); Benjamin Joshua Ong, 'The Basic Structure Doctrine in Singapore: A Reply' (2014) Singapore Law Gazette (November 2014).

2 In Chapter 3 of this book Kevin YL Tan uses 'basic structure' in the general sense indicated here, and 'basic features' to indicate limitations on the power of constitutional amendment. In this chapter I use the term 'basic structure' for both of these, but as I explain here the chapter deals with the second meaning. I accept Kevin Tan's distinction but prefer the terminology I have used here.

3 *Mohammad Faizal bin Sabtu* (n 1); see also *Liyanage v The Queen* [1967] 1 AC 259 (JCPC); *Hinds v The Queen* [1977] AC 195 (JCPC); *Australian Capital Television Pty Ltd v Commonwealth of Australia* (1992) 177 CLR 106, 135. Liang and Shi (n 1) use 'basic structure doctrine' to embrace both meanings indicated here. In this chapter, I am concerned only with basic structure doctrine as affecting the *scope of valid constitutional amendments*, not the scope of constitutional provisions per se. The authors state, consistently with what is argued here, that 'Singapore courts tend to use the basic structure doctrine as an interpretive tool, as opposed to the role it has traditionally occupied in other jurisdictions as a trump to strike down errant constitutional amendments': ibid [27]; Kevin YL Tan and Thio Li-ann, *Constitutional Law in Malaysia and Singapore* (3rd edn, LexisNexis 2010) 174–79; Thio Li-ann, *A Treatise on Singapore Constitutional Law* (Academy Publishing 2012) 4.055–4.061; and the discussion of the Singapore cases below.

4 Constitution of the Republic of Singapore (1985 Rev Ed, 1999 Reprint) (the constitution).

5 See further Kevin YL Tan, 'Into the matrix: interpreting the Westminster model constitution', Chapter 3 of this book.

6 *Kesavandanda Bharati v State of Kerala* AIR 1973 SC 1461. For a very thorough study of the doctrine in India, see S Krishnaswamy, *Democracy and Constitutionalism in India: A Study of the Basic Structure Doctrine* (Oxford University Press 2011); SP Sathe, 'Limitation on Constitutional Amendment: "Basic Structure" Principle Re-examined' in Rajeev Dhavan and Alice Jacob (eds), *Indian Constitution: Trends and Issues* (Tripathi 1978); *Minerva Mills Ltd v Union of India* (1980) 2 SCC 591.

7 Some constitutions contain 'eternity' clauses, which expressly preclude constitutional amendment of some clauses. For a well-known example, see the Basic Law for the Federal Republic of Germany, Article 79(3).

8 Article 368, the Constitution of India. There are other modes of amendment that are not relevant to the argument here.

9 Article 5(1) of the constitution. There is also a referendum requirement in the event of a proposal to surrender the sovereignty of Singapore, under Article 6. This would

apply, for example, to a bill to amend the Constitutionto enable Singapore to rejoin the Malaysian federation.

10 Acts 8/1965 and 10/1979.

11 Article 4 of the constitution.

12 A Harding, 'Parliament and the Grundnorm in Singapore', 25 Malaya Law Review 351, 357; for discussion of issues surrounding this Reprint, see Kevin YL Tan, 'The Evolution of Singapore's Modern Constitution: Developments from 1946 to the Present Day' (1989) 1 Singapore Academy of Law Journal 1, 17–23; *Public Prosecutor v Taw Cheng Kong* [1998] 2 SLR 410, 417–22 (Court of Appeal).

13 Essentially, the objective was to create a temporary period of constitutional flexibility as a result of Singapore's sudden, unplanned independence. According to Prime Minister Mr Lee Hsien Loong, the presidency, too, is in the process of being refined, as well as the 'ironing out of issues that can arise in the light of experience': Singapore Parliamentary Debates, Official Report (21 October 2008) vol 85, col 532.

14 M Tushnet, *The Constitution of the United States of America: A Contextual Analysis* (2nd edn, Hart Publishing 2015) 132–34.

15 See eg 'Justice Scalia's Gay Marriage Ruling Slapdown' *New York Post* (New York, 26 June 2015) http://nypost.com/2015/06/26/justice-scalias-gay-marriage-ruling-slapdown accessed 17 August 2015.

16 5 US 137 (1803) (USCS).

17 For a well-edited version of this epic case, see Tan and Thio (n 3) 157ff.

18 See n 6.

19 *Zafar Ali Shah v Pervez Musharraf* PLD 2000 SC 869 (Supreme Court of Pakistan), and a recent case on the 18th and 21st Amendments, reported in Nasir Iqbal, 'Military Courts Get Supreme Court Nod' (*Dawn*, 5 August 2015) www.dawn.com/news/1198533 accessed 17 August 2015. The Pakistan Supreme Court rejected the applicability of the basic structure doctrine to constitutional amendments.

20 See *Re the Thirteenth Amendment to the Constitution and the Provincial Councils Bill* [1990] LRC (Const) 1 (Supreme Court of Sri Lanka).

21 See *Phang Chin Hock v Public Prosecutor* [1980] 1 MLJ 70 (Federal Court); *Mark Koding v Public Prosecutor* [1982] 2 MLJ 120 (Federal Court); AJ Harding, 'The Death of a Doctrine? *Phang Chin Hock v Public Prosecutor*', [1979] 21 MLR 365. In *Sivarasa Rasiah v Badan Peguam Malaysia* [2010] 3 CLJ 507 (Federal Court) [8], Gopal Sri Ram FCJ stated (obiter) and without reference to *Phang Chin Hock*, that 'any statute (including one amending the Constitution) that offends the basic structure may be struck down as unconstitutional'. The doctrine has also been the subject of two recent decisions in Belize, for which see Derek O'Brien, 'The Basic Structure Doctrine and the Courts of the Commonwealth Caribbean' (*UK Constitutional Law Association*, 28 May 2013) http://ukconstitutionallaw.org/2013/05/28/derek-obrien-the-basic-structure-doctrine-and-the-courts-of-the-commonwealth-caribbean accessed 17 August 2015.

22 *Teo Soh Lung v Minister for Home Affairs* [1989] 2 MLJ 449 (SGHC). See below for discussion.

23 See further Tan (n 12).

24 For citations, see n 12.

25 Krishnaswamy (n 6) 2, 25–42.

26 The Constitution of Japan contains some provisions, eg the controversial pacifist provision in Article 9, that envisage eternally applicable principles – the renunciation of war 'forever' and that armed forces will 'never' be maintained. See also, for the Singapore context, Jaclyn Neo, 'Should Constitutional Principles be Eternal?' *The Straits Times* (Singapore, 6 October 2014) www.straitstimes.com/opinion/should-constitutional-principles-be-eternal accessed 17 August 2015.

27 Harding (n 12); LR Penna, 'Diceyan Perspective of Supremacy of the Constitution of Singapore' (1990) 32 Malaya Law Review 207, 231; cf *Teo Soh Lung v Minister for Home Affairs* [1989] 1 SLR(R) 461 (SGHC) [47] per Chua J.

28 Bruce Ackerman, *We the People: Foundations* (Belknap Publishing 1993).
29 Arguably, all constitutions are always in a process of adaptation. In Singapore's case, as we will see, independence was not, as it turned out, a reason to inaugurate a constitutional moment, even though some might have said it should have been.
30 Report of the Constitutional Commission 1966 (Government Publications Bureau 1966); for discussion, see Kevin YL Tan, 'A Short Legal and Constitutional History of Singapore', in Kevin YL Tan (ed), *Essays in Singapore Legal History* (Singapore Academy of Law and Marshall Cavendish 2005).
31 Act 9/1965.
32 See, regarding the constitutional primacy of the RSIA, Harding (n 12) 354ff.
33 Agreement relating to Malaysia between United Kingdom of Great Britain and Northern Ireland, Federation of Malaya, North Borneo, Sarawak and Singapore (adopted 9 July 1963, entered into force 16 September 1963) 750 UNTS 4.
34 Interestingly enough for our purposes, these Malaysian provisions were never subjected to the 'two-thirds' requirement for constitutional amendment until they purported to be so subjected by the Attorney-General's Reprint of 1979. The point can be made that the Attorney-General was not entrusted by Parliament with the power to make such a sweeping constitutional change: Tan (n 12).
35 *Mohammad Faizal* (n 1).
36 *Teo Soh Lung* (n 22).
37 [1990] 1 MLJ 449 (SGHC).
38 Act 1/1989.
39 [1989] 1 SLR (R) 461 (SGHC), [35]. The decision was appealed but the Court of Appeal ([1990] 2 MLJ 129) found it unnecessary to consider the basic structure doctrine.
40 For this issue, see Tan and Thio (n 3) 420ff. For discussion in relation to the basic structure doctrine, see Ravneet Kaur, 'The Basic Features Doctrine and the Elected President Act' (1994) 15 Singapore Law Review 244.
41 Liang and Shi (n 1).
42 Krishnaswamy goes into this question in the particular context of India's Constitution: (n 6) Chapter 1.
43 Andrew Harding, 'The "Westminster Model" Constitution Overseas: Transplantation, Adaptation and Development in Commonwealth States' (2004) 4(2) Oxford University Commonwealth Law Journal 143.
44 See further Penna (n 27).
45 See *Mohamad Faizal* (n 1) (Chan CJ).
46 Harding (n 43).
47 ibid. A study of this issue across the countries of the modern Commonwealth shows that about half of its member states have done precisely that.
48 We can bear in mind here that when Malaysia was created from the existing Federation of Malaya, Singapore, Sabah and Sarawak in 1963, there was indeed a 'basic structure' challenge to the fundamental change involved, on the eve of the Federation, in *Government of the State of Kelantan v Government of the Federation of Malaya and Tunku Abdul Rahman Putra Al-Haj* [1963] MLJ 355 (High Court, Federation of Malaya). The challenge failed, although the applicability of the basic structure doctrine was left open. Yet, Kelantan's case is maintainable in the sense that such a fundamental alteration to the federal structure plausibly required that Kelantan be consulted over this change. One does not need to resort to the basic structure doctrine to argue this; it can be seen as a requirement of convention, and therefore an implied *procedural* rather than substantive requirement.
49 'Barisan MPs Won't Be There' *The Straits Times* (Singapore, 8 December 1965).
50 Thio Li-ann (n 3) 4.059 and *Chan Hiang Leng Colin v Public Prosecutor* [1994] 3 SLR (R) 209 (SGHC) [64].
51 For the complexity and continuing story of changes to the process of constitutional amendment, see Tan and Thio (n 3) 116ff.

52 This is, in fact, virtually what was argued by Lord Lester QC in *Teo Soh Lung*'s case (n 22).
53 Harding (n 12).
54 P Leyland, *The Constitution of the United Kingdom: A Contextual Analysis* (2nd edn, Hart Publishing 2012) Chapter 3.
55 *Mohammad Faizal* (n 1).
56 *Taw Cheng Kong* (n 12).
57 An interesting case is Myanmar, whose 2008 Constitution entrenches basic provisions with a special majority plus a referendum requirement, while leaving detailed provisions to special majority protection only. It is submitted that by doing so, the constitution-makers effectively defined the basic structure and provided a means to change it. Accordingly, in my view, basic structure has no relevance in this context: Andrew Harding, 'Constitutional Change in Myanmar: Process v Substance' (2014) Myanmar Law Working Paper No 2, Centre for Asian Legal Studies, National University of Singapore http://law.nus.edu.sg/pdfs/cals/working_papers/Myanmar/MWPS002.pdf accessed 17 August 2015.
58 N Jayawickrama, 'Reflections on the Making and Content of the 1972 Constitution: An Insider's Perspective' in A Welikala (ed), *The Sri Lankan Republic at 40: Reflections on Constitutional History, Theory and Practice* (Centre for Policy Alternatives 2012).
59 See eg Yap Po Jen, 'Uncovering originalism and textualism in Singapore', Chapter 5; Jaclyn L Neo, 'Balancing act: the balancing metaphor as deference and dialogue in constitutional adjudication', Chapter 7; Swati Jhaveri, 'The broader case for developing the content of fundamental rules of natural justice under Article 9 of the Constitution: a place for proportionality-type adjudication?', Chapter 8; David Tan, 'Whither the autochthonous narrative of freedom of speech? A guide to defaming politicians and scandalising judges in Singapore', Chapter 9; Arun K Thiruvengadam, 'The continuing resistance to foreign law in constitutional adjudication in Singapore', Chapter 12, all of this book.

Bibliography

Ackerman, Bruce, *We the People: Foundations* (Belknap Publishing 1993).

Harding, AJ, 'The Death of a Doctrine? Phang Chin Hock v Public Prosecutor' (1979) 21 Malaya Law Review 365.

Harding, A, 'Parliament and the Grundnorm in Singapore' (1983) 25 Malaya Law Review 351.

Harding, Andrew, 'The "Westminster Model" Constitution Overseas: Transplantation, Adaptation and Development in Commonwealth States' (2004) 4 Oxford University Commonwealth Law Journal 143.

Harding, Andrew, 'Constitutional Change in Myanmar: Process v Substance', Myanmar Law Working Paper No 2 (2014) Centre for Asian Legal Studies, National University of Singapore http://law.nus.edu.sg/pdfs/cals/working_papers/Myanmar/MWPS002.pdf.

Iqbal, Nasir, *Military Courts Get Supreme Court Nod*, 5 August 2015 www.dawn.com/news/1198533.

Jayawickrama, N, 'Reflections on the Making and Content of the 1972 Constitution: An Insider's Perspective' in A Welikala (ed), *The Sri Lankan Republic at 40: Reflections on Constitutional History, Theory and Practice* (Colombo, Centre for Policy Alternatives 2012).

Kaur, Ravneet, *The Basic Features Doctrine and the Elected President Act* (1994) 15 Singapore Law Review 244.

Krishnaswamy, S, *Democracy and Constitutionalism in India: A Study of the Basic Structure Doctrine* (Oxford University Press 2011).

Leyland, P, *The Constitution of the United Kingdom: A Contextual Analysis* (2nd edn, Hart Publishing 2012).

Neo, Jaclyn, 'Should Constitutional Principles Be Eternal?' *The Straits Times* (Singapore, 6 October 2014).

O'Brien, Derek, 'The Basic Structure Doctrine and the Courts of the Commonwealth Caribbean', 28 May 2013, http://ukconstitutionallaw.org/2013/05/28/derek-obrien-the-basic-structure-doctrine-and-the-courts-of-the-commonwealth-caribbean.

Ong, Benjamin Joshua, 'The Basic Structure Doctrine in Singapore: A Reply' (2014) Singapore Law Gazette (November).

Penna, LR, 'Diceyan Perspective of Supremacy of the Constitution of Singapore' (1990) 32 Malaya Law Review 207.

Sathe, SP, 'Limitation on Constitutional Amendment: "Basic Structure" Principle Re-examined' in Rajeev Dhavan and Alice Jacob (eds), *Indian Constitution: Trends and Issues* (Tripathi 1978).

Scalia, Antonin, 'Justice Scalia's Gay Marriage Ruling Slapdown', *New York Post* (26 June 2015) http://nypost.com/2015/06/26/justice-scalias-gay-marriage-ruling-slapdown.

Shi, Sarah and Calvin Liang, 'The Constitution of our Constitution: A Vindication of the Basic Structure Doctrine' (2014) Singapore Law Gazette (August 2014) 12.

Tan, Kevin YL, 'A Short Legal and Constitutional History of Singapore' in Kevin YL Tan (ed), *Essays in Singapore Legal History* (Singapore Academy of Law and Marshall Cavendish 2005).

Tan, Kevin YL, 'The Evolution of Singapore's Modern Constitution: Developments from 1946 to the Present Day' (1989) 1 Singapore Academy of Law Journal 1.

Tan, Kevin YL and Li-ann Thio, *Constitutional Law in Malaysia and Singapore* (3rd edn, LexisNexis 2010).

Thio, Li-ann, *A Treatise on Singapore Constitutional Law* (Academy Publishing 2012).

Tushnet, Mark, *The Constitution of the United States of America: A Contextual Analysis* (2nd edn, Hart Publishing).

Unknown, 'Barisan MPs Won't Be There' *The Straits Times* (Singapore, 8 December 1965).

3 Into the matrix

Interpreting the Westminster model constitution

Kevin YL Tan

I Words and their meanings

It is a truism that words carry meanings and that these meanings are necessarily limited (or extended) by what those words traditionally or habitually mean, as well as the context in which they are used.

The meaning of words can stretch or contract, depending on circumstances, but the elasticity of meanings is necessarily limited by the words themselves. For example, take the word 'ball'. I think you will agree that a two-dimensional representation of a circle or circular object might be called a 'ball', just as might any three-dimensional, spherical object. By analogy, the word 'ball' may be extended to anything that looks round or spherical, so you can have 'balls' of pearls in bubble tea, for example. However, there is a limit to how far you can stretch that meaning. Thus, a cube cannot in any way be said to be a 'ball' any more than an ice-cream cone can.

When we use the words 'constitution' or 'constitutional' or 'constitutionalism' to describe something, we all have an idea of what it means or is intended to mean. So, a newspaper report cannot be a constitution any more than a textbook on constitutional law can. We all understand the word 'constitution' to refer to (in most cases) a written document embodying the highest laws of the land, or a set of *legal* rules demarcating the relationship between a state and its polity, and between the branches of government *inter se*.

Adjectives further enhance or limit the meaning of words. So, when we talk about a 'Westminster constitution' we do not mean any kind of constitution, but a particular type of constitution derived from the institutions, arrangements and rules of government in Great Britain. Indeed, the words contain elements that provide us with a background and framework in which to understand the words themselves. I call this the *matrix*.

The word 'matrix' derives from the French word *matrice* meaning 'womb', and from the Latin *matrix* meaning 'pregnant animal', which, in turn, derives its meaning from the word *mater*, meaning 'mother'.[1] It is, pardon the pun, a word that is pregnant with meaning. Today, the *Oxford English Dictionary* defines it as 'the cultural, social or political environment in which something develops'. A matrix, therefore, includes a holistic background against which a word is used, elucidated and understood. Words must thus be understood in context. For that reason, lawyers develop guiding principles and maxims of construction such as the *ejesdem generis* and *noscitur a sociis* rules of interpretation when faced with ambiguous words, while our courts adopt a *purposive approach* to interpretation.

So, what are the matrices we need to consider when interpreting a constitution? More specifically, what matrix should we employ when interpreting a Westminster-style or -model constitution like Singapore's? This is an important question as the matrix necessarily circumscribes what the Constitution is all about, and constrains its meaning. A constitutional matrix contains specific meanings that are not only ordinarily understood, but a whole host of assumptions about those meanings. For instance, when a politician implores his parliamentary colleagues to 'uphold the constitution', we assume several things: (a) everyone understands what the Constitution is; (b) everyone understands what constitutionalism requires; and (c) those who are being exhorted believe in the legitimacy of the constitutional rules, whatever they might be. We can add several other assumptions to this equation, but I think the point is evident.

This chapter traces the roots of the Westminster model matrix from its origins in the Privy Council decisions of the 1960s and 1970s. It will then examine its application to Singapore through the 1980 appeal of *Ong Ah Chuan v Public Prosecutor*, which formally established the matrix which the courts now use for interpreting the Singapore Constitution. I will argue that despite having been independent for half a century, Singapore courts still assiduously adopt the Westminster model and its attendant matrix, and that this directly impacts the way in which judges interpret the constitution.

II Westminster constitutions and the Privy Council

While Britain has no written constitution of its own, it drafted no less than fifty constitutions for its former colonies as part of its decolonisation process.

As Andrew Harding observed:

> At the present time about 30 per cent of the world's population (1.7 billion people) who live in the 54 states comprising the Commonwealth live under constitutional arrangements which correspond, albeit roughly, to the 'Westminster-model' constitution, or else have been heavily influenced by it. These states, with the exception of Mozambique, have a constitution that conforms to most, even if not all, of the essential principles of the Westminster model; or at least one can say that this model forms a very important part of the state's constitutional history and is important in understanding its present constitution, even if that constitution has evolved considerably, and that evolution involved some degree of deliberate divergence from the Westminster model.[2]

The content and meaning of this Westminster model were articulated and sustained by the Judicial Committee of the Privy Council. While it is unclear exactly when the King-in-Council (the predecessor of the Privy Council) began hearing appeals from the colonies,[3] the passage of the Privy Council Appeals Act in 1832[4] and the Judicial Committee Act in 1833[5] officially transformed the Privy Council into the highest appellate court for the colonies.[6] As the final court of the Empire, the Privy Council quite naturally interpreted colonial laws with the English constitutional structure and arrangements and the common law as its matrices, while making exceptions in matters of personal law where required.[7] One of the earliest cases was the 1932 decision in *Abyeskera v Jayatilake*[8] where the Privy Council had occasion to consider whether the King had reserve powers to amend an Order in Council made by the Ceylonese Legislative Council. Lord Darling, on behalf of the Judicial Committee, held that the King had such legislative powers as Ceylon was a conquered territory rather than one that was 'constituted as a colony' with its own constitution that limited the sovereign's power.

Even after becoming independent from Great Britain, many of these territories not only continued to preserve the common law system of administration of justice, but also retained the Privy Council as their final court of appeal. Some territories such as India and Pakistan ended appeals to the Privy Council upon independence, while others such as Nigeria, Sri Lanka (formerly Ceylon), Malaya and Singapore only 'withdrew from the system some considerable time after independence'.[9] And for as long as these new states continued to send appeals to the Privy Council, the Judicial Committee continued to develop a jurisprudence that interpreted the post-colonial constitutions as codifications of British practice and in a manner that was consonant with the Westminster matrix. For example, in the Ceylonese case of *Attorney-General of Ceylon v de Livera*,[10] in considering the role of the member of the House of Representatives in Ceylon, Lord Radcliffe said:

> A member of the House of Representatives in Ceylon derives his constitutional status from the Ceylon (Constitution) Order in Council, 1946, which prescribed the existing Constitution of the Island. The system thereby established is that of a bi-cameral legislature in the form of a Parliament, which itself consists of the Sovereign, represented by the Governor, the Senate and the House of Representatives; an independent Judiciary; and an Executive, the powers of which are vested in the Governor. The general direction and control of government are, however, entrusted to a Cabinet of Ministers under a Prime Minister, and the Cabinet is by section 46 of the Order declared to be 'collectively responsible to Parliament'. Moreover, section 49 (2) provides that a Minister must cease to hold his office at the expiration of any period of four consecutive months during which he has not been a member of either Chamber. Thus, the Constitution is explicitly designed to secure the subordination of the Executive to the Legislature through their common meeting ground in the procedures of Parliament and, although there are many variations in matters of detail, its general conceptions are seen at once to be those of a parliamentary democracy founded on the pattern of the constitutional system of the United Kingdom.[11]

III Embedding constitutional supremacy

Despite operating within assumptions of transplanted continuity, British judges in the Privy Council were also patently conscious of the fact that all these post-independence constitutions were written constitutions and thus had to be interpreted differently from one in which Parliament was sovereign. Whether it declared itself to be supreme or not, the written constitution was to be treated as the supreme law, and any law that went against the Constitution was void. This happened in in the Ceylonese case of *The Bribery Commissioner v Pedrick Ranasinghe*.[12] In that case, the respondent, who had been prosecuted and convicted under the Bribery Amendment Act, challenged the validity of the Act and the appointment of the appellant Bribery Commissioner. Among other things, the 1958 Act provided for the creation of Bribery Tribunal, the appointment of members to that Tribunal, and the appointment of a Bribery Commissioner. The appellant argued that the appointment of the Bribery Commissioner and members of the Tribunal was unconstitutional as the Bribery Amendment Act violated Section 55 of the Ceylon Constitution, which provides that appointment of all 'judicial officers' can only be made through the Judicial Service Commission. The respondent argued that when the Ceylonese Parliament passed the Bribery Amendment Act in 1958, it had the force of a constitutional amendment under Section 29 of the Constitution and made an exception to the requirements of Section 55:

> Under Section 29 of the Constitution, no law to amend the Constitution shall be presented for Royal Assent unless it has endorsed on it a certificate under the hand of the Speaker that the number of votes cast in favour thereof in the House of Representatives amounted to not less than two-thirds of the whole number of Members of the House (including those not present).

It was not disputed that the Bribery Amendment Bill did not have such a certificate and was not passed by the requisite two-thirds majority. Counsel for the respondent then argued that the Amendment Bill was not invalid only by reason of its procedural defect 'since the Ceylon Parliament is sovereign and had the power to pass it' and the courts are not entitled 'to look behind the Act to see if it was validly passed'.[13] The Privy Council held:

> Once it is shown that an Act conflicts with a provision in the Constitution, the certificate is an essential part of the legislative process. The court has a duty to see that the Constitution is not infringed and to preserve it inviolate. Unless, therefore, there is some very cogent reason for doing so, the court must not decline to open its eyes for doing so.[14]

Approving what was said by the Privy Council in *McCawley v The Queen*,[15] the Judicial Committee added:

> ...a legislature has no power to ignore the conditions of law-making that are imposed by the instrument which itself regulates its power to make law. This restriction exists independently of the question whether the legislature is sovereign, as is the legislature of Ceylon, or whether the Constitution is 'uncontrolled', as the Board held the Constitution of Queensland to be. Such a Constitution can, indeed, be altered or amended by the legislature, if the regulating instrument so provides and if the terms of those provisions are complied with; and the alteration or amendment may include the change or abolition of those very provisions. But, the proposition which is not acceptable is that a legislature, once established, has some inherent power derived from the mere fact of its establishment to make a valid law by the resolution of a bare majority which its own constituent instrument has said shall not be a valid law unless made by a different type of majority or by a different legislative process.[16]

This judgment made it clear that even if a constitution was 'uncontrolled' or easily amended, it is the constitutional instrument that determined the method and process of amendment and that where a written constitution exists, no extra-constitutional plenary power exists. Thus, in the interpretation of all written constitutions founded on the Westminster model, the starting point would always be the Constitution itself.

IV Explicating the Westminster constitutional model: Lord Diplock at the Privy Council

From the 1960s to the 1980s, in decisions on appeals from various former British colonies, the Judicial Committee of the Privy Council formulated and explicated on the matrix of what has come to be known as the Westminster model constitution. The term itself was first used by Lord Diplock in the case of *Moses Hinds v The Queen*,[17] but discussions on the nature and the structure of this kind of constitution had already occupied the minds of the law lords in the Privy Council more than a decade and a half earlier, starting with the case of *Don John Francis Douglas Liyanage v The Queen.*[18] In this section, we examine the series of Privy Council decisions in which the Westminster model came to be 'created'.

A Don John Francis Douglas Liyanage v The Queen

In *Liyanage*, the Ceylon Parliament passed two statutes ('the 1962 Acts') to deal specifically with the perpetrators of a failed coup that took place on 27 January 1962. Among other things, these new laws regularised the appellants' otherwise illegal detention, altered the mode of trial for their offences, and inserted a minimum punishment of not less than ten years and a forfeiture of all property in the event of conviction. The nature of the offence of 'waging war against the Queen' was amended to the extent that a new offence was created *ex post facto*. The appellants challenged the validity of their conviction on three grounds. First, that the Ceylon Parliament was limited in its competence in that it could not 'pass legislation which is contrary to fundamental principles of justice'[19] and the 1962 Acts were not only 'directed against individuals but also *ex post facto* create crimes and punishments, and destroy fair safeguards by which those individuals would otherwise be protected'.[20] Second, it was argued that the 1962 Acts offended the Constitution in that 'they amounted to a direction to convict the appellants or to a legislative plan to secure the conviction and severe punishment of the appellants' and this:

> constituted an unjustifiable assumption of judicial power by the legislature, or an interference with judicial power, which is outside the legislature's competence and is inconsistent with the severance of power between the legislature, executive, and judiciary which the Constitution ordains.[21]

Finally, it was argued that the wording of the 1962 Acts was insufficient to 'deprive the appellants of the right to a jury' trial.[22]

The Privy Council rejected the first argument on grounds that various legislative enactments, including the Ceylon Independence Act, had 'the result of giving to the Ceylon Parliament the full legislative powers of a sovereign independent State'.[23] As such, there was no fetter on Parliament's power to make law, and the Privy Council was not prepared to 'accept the view that the legislature … left in existence a fetter of repugnancy to some vague unspecified law of natural justice'.[24]

In respect of the second argument, the respondents argued that since there was no 'express vesting of judicial power in the courts' as in the United States of America or Australia, the judicial power could not be breached. The Privy Council disagreed. Lord Pearce held that the nature of Ceylon's judiciary was different from that of the USA or Australia because, in those countries, 'there were no federal courts apart from the Constitution' and unless 'such courts were created and invested with power by the Constitution they had no existence or power'.[25] In the case of Ceylon, the change in sovereignty – from colony to independent state in 1947 – 'did not in itself produce any apparent change in the constituents or the functioning of the Judicature' and the work of the courts 'continued unaffected by the new Constitution, and the Ordinances under which they functioned remained in force'.[26]

The Privy Council noted that the Constitution was divided into parts:

> Part 2 The Governor-General, Part 3 The Legislature, Part 4 Delimitation of Electoral Districts, Part 5 The Executive, Part 6 The Judicature, Part 7 The Public Service, Part 8 Finance.
>
> And although no express mention is made of vesting in the judicature the judicial power which it already had and was wielding in its daily process under the Courts Ordinance, there is provision under Part 6 for the appointment of judges by a Judicial Service Commission, which shall not contain a member of either House but shall be composed of the Chief Justice and a

> judge and another person who is or shall have been a judge. Any attempt to influence any decision of the Commission is made a criminal offence. There is also provision that judges shall not be removable except by the Governor-General on an address of both Houses.
>
> These provisions manifest an intention to secure in the judiciary a freedom from political, legislative and executive control. They are wholly appropriate in a Constitution which intends that judicial power shall be vested only in the judicature. They would be inappropriate in a Constitution by which it was intended that judicial power should be shared by the executive or the legislature. The Constitution's silence as to the vesting of judicial power is consistent with its remaining, where it had lain for more than a century, in the hands of the judicature. It is not consistent with any intention that henceforth it should pass to or be shared by, the executive or the legislature.[27]

It should be noted that in *Liyanage*, the Privy Council actually offered two connected reasons for the vesting of judicial power in the Constitution. The first was on the basis of legal continuity while the second was based on structure. The legal continuity argument is based on the fact that Ceylon's judiciary had been established by the Charter of Justice of 1833 which provided, among other things, the exclusive vesting of judicial power in the judiciary.[28] While the 1947 Constitution established a Supreme Court and provided for its constitution, it did not provide for an explicit vesting of 'judicial power' in the courts. This was unnecessary since the 1947 Constitution left undisturbed the terms of the 1833 Charter of Justice. The second connected argument is that as the new Constitution is divided into parts, it must be assumed that the judicial power should vest in the judicial branch and nowhere else.

B Hinds v The Queen

In *Moses Hinds & Ors v The Queen*,[29] the appellants, who had been charged and convicted for firearms offences under the Gun Court Act, challenged the constitutionality of the Act. The Jamaican Parliament passed the Gun Court Act 1974 as an ordinary statute. The object of the Act was to establish a new court called the Gun Court with three different divisions: a Resident Magistrate's Division; a Full Court Division; and a Circuit Court Division. The appellants argued that the Gun Court, which exercised similar jurisdiction to that of the criminal courts of Jamaica, was unconstitutional because its judges, especially those of its Full Court Division, did not enjoy the same safeguards of judicial independence as other members of the higher judiciary and, as such, this violated the judicial power of Jamaica.

Lord Diplock, on behalf of the majority of the Privy Council (with Lord Simon of Glaisdale and Lord Edmund-Davies), began by pointing out two common types of arguments made in relation to the interpretation of written constitutions: first 'judicial reasoning which depended on the express words used in the particular constitution under consideration' and second, 'reasoning which depended on what, though not expressed, is nonetheless a necessary implication from the subject matter and structure of the Constitution and the circumstances in which it had been made'.[30] This may conveniently be called the 'argument from text' and the 'argument from structure', respectively.

All constitutions 'have two things in common that have an important bearing on their interpretation'. First, constitutional rules are supreme law, quite unlike ordinary acts of the legislature; and second, post-colonial constitutions are an embodiment of

> an agreement reached between representatives of the various shades of political opinion in the state as to the structure of the organs of government through which the plenitude of the sovereign power of the state is to be exercised in future.[31]

All such constitutions were negotiated and drafted by

> persons nurtured in the tradition of that branch of the common law of England that is concerned with public law and familiar in particular with the basic concept of separation of legislative, executive and judicial power as it had been developed in the unwritten constitution of the United Kingdom.[32]

All post-colonial peoples were thus already living under a system of public law in 'which government was carried on' through the legislature, the executive and the courts. The evolutionary, rather than revolutionary, character of these post-colonial constitutions

> provided for continuity of government through successor institutions, legislative, executive and judicial, of which the members were to be selected in a different way, but each institution was to exercise powers which, although enlarged, remained of a similar character to those that had been exercised by the corresponding institution that it had replaced.[33]

Having established the nature of the post-colonial constitution and its evolution, Lord Diplock then proceeded to advance a structural argument about the separation of powers based on the nature of the 'Westminster model' constitution. His Lordship argued that because of the way constitutional bargains are struck and post-colonial constitutions framed,

> ... [a] great deal can be, and in drafting practice often is, left to necessary implication from the adoption in the new constitution of a governmental structure which makes provision for a legislature, an executive and judicature. It is taken for granted that the basic principle of separation of powers will apply to the exercise of their respective functions by these three organs of government. Thus, the constitution does not normally contain any express

> prohibition upon the exercise of legislative powers by the executive or of judicial powers by either the executive or the legislature. As respects the judicature, particularly if it is intended that the previously existing courts shall continue to function, the constitution itself may even omit any express provision conferring judicial power upon the judicature. Nevertheless, it is well established as a rule of construction applicable to constitutional instruments under which this governmental structure is adopted that the absence of express words to that effect does not prevent the legislative, the executive and the judicial powers of the new state being exercisable exclusively by the legislature, by the executive and by the judicature respectively.[34]

Lord Diplock then explained the nature of the 'Westminster model' constitution. It 'can be discerned', his Lordship continued, 'in all those constitutions which have their origin in an Act of the Imperial Parliament at Westminster or in an Order in Council, a common pattern and style of draftsmanship which may conveniently be described as "the Westminster model" '.[35]

According to Lord Diplock (emphasis added):

> All Constitutions on the Westminster model deal under separate Chapter headings with the legislature, the executive and the judicature. The Chapter dealing with the judicature invariably contains provisions dealing with the method of appointment and security of tenure of the members of the judiciary, which are designed to assure to them a degree of independence from the other two branches of government. It may, as in the case of the Constitution of Ceylon, contain nothing more. To the extent to which the Constitution itself is silent as to the distribution of the plenitude of judicial power between various courts it is implicit that it shall continue to be distributed between and exercised by the courts that were already in existence when the new Constitution came into force; but the legislature, in the exercise of its power to make laws for the 'peace, order and good government' of the state, may provide for the establishment of new courts and for the transfer to them of the whole or part of the jurisdiction previously exercisable by an existing court. What, however, is *implicit in the very structure of a Constitution on the Westminster model* is that judicial power, however it be distributed from time to time between various courts, is to continue to be vested in persons appointed to hold judicial office in the manner and on the terms laid down in the Chapter dealing with the judicature, even though this is not expressly stated in the Constitution: *Liyanage v. The Queen* [1967] 1 AC 259, 287–288c.[36]

The structure of the Westminster model constitution not only provides the matrix by which it is to be interpreted but also acts to limit the extent to which such a constitution may be changed. Applying his logic to the facts at hand, Lord Diplock held that by enacting the Gun Court Act, the Jamaican Parliament had effected a transfer of judicial power from the judiciary to the executive branch of government.

Viscount Dilhorne and Lord Fraser of Tullybelton disagreed with the majority, holding that the creation of the Gun Court through the Gun Court Act was a perfectly valid exercise of legislative power by the Jamaican Parliament. With regard to what Lord Diplock 'felicitiously called "the Westminster model"',[37] the dissenting judges observed that while such constitutions 'were evolutionary and not revolutionary' it did 'not follow from that that the Parliament of a territory cannot by ordinary enactment alter the jurisdiction and powers of any court named in the Constitution'.[38] Their Lordships further noted:

> A written constitution must be construed like any other written document. It must be construed to give effect to the intentions of those who made and agreed to it and those intentions are expressed in or to be deduced from the terms of the constitution itself and not from any preconceived ideas as to what such a constitution should or should not contain. It must not be construed as if it was partly written and partly not. We agree that such constitutions differ from ordinary legislation and this fact should lead to even greater reluctance to imply something not expressed. While we recognise that an inference may be drawn from the express provisions of a constitution ... we do not agree that on the adoption of a constitution a great deal is left to necessary implication. If this were so, a written constitution would largely fail to achieve its object. If it does not define clearly what Parliament can do and cannot do by ordinary enactment, then the Government and Parliament of a territory may find that as a result of judicial decision after a considerable lapse of time all the time spent in legislating has been wasted and that laws urgently required have not been validly enacted. No doubt the Constitution of Jamaica was drafted by persons nurtured in the common law. That is apparent from the Constitution itself. The principle that there should be a separation of powers between the three organs of government is not just taken for granted. Effect is given to that principle by the written terms of the Constitution and consequently there is no room for the assumption.[39]

Quite clearly, Viscount Dilhorne and Lord Fraser were uncomfortable with the idea that a constitution should include elements and content to be implied through its origins and structure. Instead, their Lordships favoured a theory of constitutionalism that gave the greatest potency to parliamentary intent, with no structural limitations to how the Constitution can be amended.

V 'Law' at the commencement of the Westminster constitution

Besides establishing the structural framework of constitutions under the Westminster model, the Privy Council took for granted the fact that whilst colonies may have transited to independence, the legal system established in colonial times would continue in operation. In most cases, where power transited peacefully, this would have been effected by transitional constitutional provisions. For example, when Singapore became independent from the United Kingdom in 1963 and became a constituent state of the Federation of Malaysia, Article 105(1) of the Sabah, Sarawak and Singapore (State Constitutions) Order in Council 1963[40] provided that 'all existing laws shall continue in force on and after the coming into operation of this Constitution'. Such transitional provisions were worked into many independence constitutions drafted by the British. At the same time, these post-colonial constitutions typically contained interpretation clauses in which the word 'law' would be spelt out. In the case of Singapore's 1963 State Constitution, Article 91(1) provides that the word

> includes written law and any legislation of the United Kingdom or other enactment or instrument whatsoever which is in operation in the State and the common law in so far as it is in operation in the State and any custom or usage having the force of law in the State.

The legal continuity that was assured by such transitional provisions provides the constitutional matrix with its other internal logic – that the common law remains part of the corpus of laws of the new state, and that all rights that citizens had accrued up to that time, remain intact. Let us consider two of the earliest cases that touch on this point.

The first is the Privy Council case of *Director of Public Prosecutions v Nasralla.*[41] In this 1967 appeal from Jamaica, a key question before the Judicial Committee was whether the respondent could rely on the common law plea of *autrefois acquit*. In issue was the interpretation of Section 20(8) of the Constitution of Jamaica, which provided:

> No person who shows that he has been tried by any competent court for a criminal offence and either convicted or acquitted shall again be tried for that offence or for any other criminal offence of which he could have been convicted at the trial for that offence.

In holding for the respondent, Lord Devlin noted that Chapter III of the Jamaican Constitution – dealing with fundamental rights and liberties – 'proceeds upon the presumption that the fundamental rights which it covers are already secured to the people of Jamaica by existing law'.[42] The object of the provisions under Chapter III 'is to ensure that no future enactment shall in any matter which the chapter covers derogate from the rights which at the coming into force of the Constitution the individual enjoyed'.[43]

The second case is the 1976 appeal from Trinidad and Tobago, *F Michael de Freitas v George Ramoutar Benny & Ors.*[44] In this case, the appellant, who was convicted of murder and sentenced to death, argued that the death penalty was unconstitutional as it was 'cruel and unusual punishment'; and alternatively, that even if it was not 'cruel and unusual', the average lapse of time between the pronouncement of the death sentence and the carrying out of the sentence 'has become substantially greater since the commencement of the Constitution and this has the effect of making it unconstitutional to carry out the death penalty'.[45] Reliance was placed on Section 105(1) of the Constitution, which defined 'law' as including 'any instrument having the force of law and any unwritten rule of law'. In relation to Section 105(1), Lord Diplock observed:

> The 'unwritten law' in force in Trinidad and Tobago at the commencement of the Constitution was the common law and doctrines of equity that were in force in England on March 1, 1848, in the case of Trinidad, and on January 1, 1889, in the case of Tobago, so far as these had not been abrogated by enacted law. This unwritten law has been preserved after the commencement of the Constitution by section 12 of the Supreme Court of Judicature Act 1962.[46]

The appellant's alternative argument that a delay between the pronouncement and execution of the death penalty breached 'unwritten law' was rejected by the Privy Council who dismissed the appeal because this not only attributed to the expression 'unwritten rule of law' in Section 105 'a meaning which it is incapable of bearing, but it conflicts with the very concept of the nature of a law'.[47]

By the time the case of *Maharaj v AG of Trinidad and Tobago (No 2)*[48] came before the Privy Council in 1979, the matrix advanced by Lord Diplock in *Hinds* had become widely adopted and used by the Judicial Committee. Lord Diplock himself was on the bench in *Majaraj*'s case and he once again repeated his structural argument, pronouncing, as a preliminary, that:

> The structure and the presumptions that underlie Chapter I of the Constitution of Trinidad and Tobago and the corresponding chapters in other constitutions on the Westminster model that provide for the recognition and protection of fundamental human rights and freedoms, have been referred to in a number of previous cases that have come before the Judicial Committee...[49]

Even in the dissenting judgment, Lord Hailsham of St Marylebone made reference to 'Westminster model legislation'.[50]

VI The Westminster model in Singapore: fundamental rules of natural justice

The first time the Westminster constitutional model was invoked as an 'interpretive aid' in Singapore was in the case of *Ong Ah Chuan v Public Prosecutor*,[51] a drug-trafficking case in which the meaning of the word 'law' in the fundamental liberties provisions came up for consideration. The word 'law' was held to embody 'fundamental rules of natural justice', which formed part of the common law at the time the Constitution came into being. Westminster-style constitutions were thus presumed to implicitly include rules of the common law as well. This was followed soon after by the case of *Haw Tua Tau v Public Prosecutor*[52] in which the court was asked to consider if a change in criminal procedure amounted to a breach of the 'fundamental rules of natural justice' embodied within the meaning of the word 'law' under the Constitution. Both cases were appealed all the way to the Privy Council.

A Ong Ah Chuan v Public Prosecutor

In June 1977, a 29-year-old unemployed man, Ong Ah Chuan, was arrested in Singapore for the possession and trafficking of 210 grams of heroin. Section 15 of the Misuse of Drugs Act provided that any person who

> is proved or presumed to have had in his possession more than 2 grams of diamorphine (heroin) contained in any controlled drug, shall, until the contrary is proved, be presumed to have had such controlled drug in his possession for the purpose of trafficking therein.

Also under the Misuse of Drugs Act, any person convicted of trafficking in more than 15 grams of heroin attracted the mandatory death penalty and Ong was accordingly sentenced to death. Ong's appeal to the Court of Criminal Appeal was dismissed and his appeal to the Privy Council was heard alongside that of another drug trafficker, Koh Chai Cheng, in *Ong Ah Chuan & Anor v Public Prosecutor*.[53] On appeal, Ong launched what Lord Diplock called an 'eleventh-hour attack … on the constitutional validity of the presumption'[54] under section 15 of the Misuse of Drugs Act. The appellants argued that the statutory presumption went against the 'presumption of innocence', which was 'a fundamental human right protected by the Constitution' and which could not 'be limited or diminished by any Act of Parliament' save for a constitutional amendment. This 'presumption of innocence' was said to have been 'imported' into the Singapore Constitution by Articles 9(1) and 12(1), which provide respectively:

> 9. —(1) No person shall be deprived of his life or personal liberty save in accordance with law.
> 12. —(1) All persons are equal before the law and entitled to the equal protection of the law.

Lord Diplock began by rephrasing the words of Lord Wilberforce in *Minister of Home Affairs & Anor v Collins MacDonald Fisher & Anor*:[55]

> That the way to interpret a Constitution on the Westminster model is to treat it not as if it were an Act of Parliament but 'as *sui generis*, calling for principles of interpretation of its own, suitable to its character … without necessary acceptance of all the presumptions that are relevant to legislation of private law'. As in that case, which concerned fundamental rights and freedom of the individual guaranteed by the Bermuda Constitution, their Lordships would give to Pt IV of the Singapore Constitution 'a generous

interpretation, avoiding what has been called "the austerity of tabulated legalism", suitable to give to individuals the full measure of the [fundamental liberties] referred to'.[56]

Lord Diplock then proceeded to explain how the word 'law', found in both Articles 9(1) and 12(1) of the Singapore Constitution, ought to be interpreted by the Judicial Committee (emphasis added):

> 26 In a Constitution founded on the Westminster model and particularly in that part of it that purports to assure to all individual citizens the continued enjoyment of fundamental liberties or rights, references to 'law' in such contexts as 'in accordance with law', 'equality before the law', 'protection of the law' and the like, in their Lordships' view, *refer to a system of law which incorporates those fundamental rules of natural justice that had formed part and parcel of the common law of England that was in operation in Singapore at the commencement of the Constitution.* It would have been taken for granted by the makers of the Constitution that the 'law' to which citizens could have recourse for the protection of fundamental liberties assured to them by the Constitution would be a system of law that did not flout those fundamental rules. If it were otherwise, it would be misuse of language to speak of law as something which affords 'protection' for the individual in the enjoyment of his fundamental liberties, and the purported entrenchment (by Art 5) of Arts 9(1) and 12(1) would be little better than a mockery.

This oft-cited passage reiterates the matrix and jurisprudence that the Privy Council had been developing since the 1960s. The reasoning is consistent with that of the Judicial Committee in past cases and may be summarised as follows: (a) Great Britain drafted many constitutions for its former colonies as part of the decolonisation process, almost all of which are based on the Westminster model; (b) Constitutions based on the Westminster model share a common structure, history and past upon which we base a number of assumptions about how the constitutions work; and (c) the assumptions imported by the constitutional matrix also inform our understanding about the nature of substantive provisions within the constitution. It has, of course, become a matter of great controversy[57] what the Privy Council meant by the 'fundamental rules of natural justice' since the Judicial Committee had, up to this case, only used this phrase once – in *Ramesh Lawrence Maharaj v Attorney-General of Trinidad and Tobago (No 2)*[58] – in reference to the right to be heard.

Coming back to the appeal in *Ong Ah Chuan*, the Privy Council went on to consider if the presumption complained of violated the constitution, and reasoned:

> 27 One of the fundamental rules of natural justice in the field of criminal law is that a person should not be punished for an offence unless it has been established to the satisfaction of an independent and unbiased tribunal that

> he committed it. This involves the tribunal's being satisfied that all the physical and mental elements of the offence with which he is charged, conduct and state of mind as well where that is relevant, were present on the part of the accused. To describe this fundamental rule as the 'presumption of innocence' may, however, be misleading to those familiar only with English criminal procedure. Observance of the rule does not call for the perpetuation in Singapore of technical rules of evidence and permitted modes of proof of facts precisely as they stood at the date of the commencement of the Constitution. These are largely a legacy of the role played by juries in the administration of criminal justice in England as it developed over the centuries. Some of them may be inappropriate to the conduct of criminal trials in Singapore. What fundamental rules of natural justice do require is that there should be material before the court that is logically probative of facts sufficient to constitute the offence with which the accused is charged.[59]

This finding is totally consistent with the Privy Council's approach and the interpretive matrix it had systematically adopted. The 'fundamental rule of natural justice' insofar as this case was concerned, was satisfied as long as an 'independent and unbiased tribunal' had determined that the accused had committed the offence. There was no need to perpetuate technical rules of evidence and proof in post-independent Singapore as long as the evidence adduced was 'logically probative' of the facts upon which the charge was based.

B Haw Tua Tau v Public Prosecutor

Singapore's legal fraternity lost no time in digesting the Judicial Committee's decision in *Ong Ah Chuan* and, shortly after, used the 'fundamental rules of natural justice' argument once again in the case of *Haw Tua Tau v Public Prosecutor and other Appeals*.[60] Haw, a hawker, was charged and convicted for the murder of another hawker, Phoon Ah Leong, and Phoon's mother. On appeal, Haw argued that the amendment to the Criminal Procedure Code (through Act 10 of 1976) – which abolished the right of an accused to make an unsworn statement from the dock and gave the court the right to draw adverse inferences from the accused choosing to remain silent – was in breach of the fundamental rules of natural justice. The Privy Council did not consider it necessary to decide whether, 'under the common law system of criminal procedure', it is a fundamental rule of natural justice that

> a person who is standing trial before a court of justice charged with an offence which he does not admit, must not be ordered by the court, under threat of legal sanctions in the event of disobedience, to disclose what he knows about the matter which is the subject of the charge.[61]

The Judicial Committee found no such prohibition in either the Universal Declaration of Human Rights nor in the European Convention on Human Rights 1950 and held that it did not conflict with 'the undoubted fundamental rule of natural justice' that '[e]veryone charged with a criminal offence shall be presumed innocent until proved guilty according to law'.[62] The Privy Council added that when 'considering whether a particular practice adopted by a court of law offends against a fundamental rule of natural justice, that practice must not be looked at in isolation, but in the light of the part which it plays in the complete judicial process'.[63] Lord Diplock added, as a final observation:

> 26 Their Lordships recognise, too, that what may properly be regarded by lawyers as rules of natural justice change with the times. The procedure for the trial of criminal offences in England at various periods between the abolition of the Court of Star Chamber and High Commission in the 17th century and the passing of the Criminal Evidence Act in 1898 involved practices, particularly in relation to the trial of felonies, that nowadays would unhesitatingly be regarded as flouting fundamental rules of natural justice. Deprivation until 1836 of the right of the accused to legal representation at his trial and, until 1898, of the right to give evidence on his own behalf are obvious examples. Nevertheless, throughout all that period the rule that an accused person could not be *compelled* to submit to hostile interrogation even in trials for misdemeanours, at which he was a competent witness on his own behalf, remained intact; and if their Lordships had been of the opinion that there was any substance in the argument that the effect of the amendments made to the Criminal Procedure Code by Act 10 of 1976 was to create a genuine *compulsion* on the accused to submit himself at his trial to cross-examination by the Prosecution, as distinguished from creating a strong *inducement* to him to do so, at any rate if he were innocent, their Lordships, before making up their own minds, would have felt it incumbent on them to seek the views of the Court of Criminal Appeal as to whether the practice of treating the accused as not compellable to give evidence on his own behalf had become so firmly based in the criminal procedure of Singapore that it would be regarded there by lawyers as having evolved into a fundamental rule of natural justice by 1963 when the Constitution came into force.[64]

Since these two cases were decided, the phrase 'fundamental rules of natural justice' has been relied on in argument in several subsequent cases, although in none of them has any law been struck down as being in breach of the 'fundamental rules of natural justice'. In deciding these cases, the courts have typically restricted themselves to considering whether the impugned rule violates these 'fundamental rules' without explaining what these rules entail. The only instance when an effort was made to probe the meaning of what was said in *Ong Ah Chuan* was in the 2010 decision of *Yong Vui Kong v Public Prosecutor & Anor Matter*[65] when Chan Sek Keong CJ, on behalf of the Court of Appeal, said:

> … beyond what was actually decided in *Ong Ah Chuan* itself, it is not clear what the Privy Council had in mind *vis-à-vis* the kind of legislation that

> would not qualify as 'law' for the purposes of Art 9(1). Perhaps, the Privy Council had in mind colourable legislation which purported to enact a 'law' as generally understood (*i.e.* a legislative rule of general application), but which in effect was a legislative judgment, that is to say, legislation directed at securing the conviction of particular known individuals (see *Don John Francis Douglas Liyanage v The Queen* [1967] 1 AC 259 at 291), or legislation of so absurd or arbitrary a nature that it could not possibly have been contemplated by our constitutional framers as being 'law' when they crafted the constitutional provisions protecting fundamental liberties (*i.e.* the provisions now set out in Pt IV of the Singapore Constitution).[66]

However, in the latest ruling in *Yong Vui Kong v Public Prosecutor*,[67] the Court of Appeal appears to have restricted the meaning of the phrase 'fundamental rules of natural justice' strictly to 'procedural rights aimed at securing a fair trial'.[68] In this case, the issue was whether caning was unconstitutional in that it violated a 'fundamental rule of natural justice'. The court held that it did not.

VII Westminster's basic structure

From the foregoing, it is clear that Westminster-style constitutions are necessarily imbued with a particular structural form and suffused with the substantive rules of the common law, including the so-called 'fundamental rules of natural justice'. Let us now consider two cases that involved an interpretation of the Westminster constitution's structural form – what the Singapore courts have called the 'basic structure' of the constitution.

The first case is *Law Society of Singapore v Phyllis Tan*,[69] a disciplinary show-cause action against the respondent, who had attempted to procure conveyancing work by offering monetary reward to individuals who referred such work to her. In the course of its judgment, the High Court (sitting as a panel of three) had occasion to consider the nature of prosecutorial discretion in Singapore. Chan Sek Keong CJ, delivering the judgment of the court, began by looking at the structure of Singapore's Constitution and the manner in which the various powers are separated under the Constitution:

> 143 In Singapore, the Constitution establishes a form of parliamentary government (based on the Westminster model) based on the separation of the legislative, executive and judicial powers. Each arm of the government operates independently of the other and each should not interfere with the functions of the other. As each of them is limited in its authority and power by the Constitution itself, it is necessary that there should exist a means whereby each arm may be prevented from acting beyond its constitutional powers. Under the Constitution, the means adopted and recognised by all three arms of government is the judicial power of the court to review the legality of legislative and executive acts and declare them unconstitutional and of no legal effect if they contravene the provisions of the Constitution.

> The modifications to the Constitution that established the office and powers of the elected President do not affect this feature of the Constitution. However, the Constitution also expressly provides for the separation of the judicial power from the prosecutorial power.[70]

The court held that Article 93 and Article 35(8) of the Constitution provided separately for the judicial and prosecutorial functions respectively, and that 'both organs have an equal status under the Constitution, and neither may interfere with each other's functions'.[71] However, the court is constitutionally empowered to ensure that the prosecutorial power is not exercised unconstitutionally. In that sense, the 'judicial power may circumscribe the prosecutorial power in two ways'; first, to declare the wrongful exercise of prosecutorial power as unconstitutional; and second, in the control of all judicial proceedings once the prosecution commences in the courts.

Chan Sek Keong CJ was even more explicit in his use of a structural argument in the case of *Mohammad Faizal bin Sabtu v Public Prosecutor*,[72] a case concerning the constitutionality of an amended section of the Misuse of Drugs Act. In this case, the petitioner was charged with one count of consuming morphine under section 8(b)(ii) of the Misuse of Drugs Act. As he had two previous admissions to a drug rehabilitation centre, he was considered a repeat offender under section 33A(1)(a) of the Act, which provided for mandatory minimum punishment of five years' imprisonment and three strokes of the cane. He argued that section 33A(1)(a) was unconstitutional in that it was an infringement of the separation of powers because it amounted to a legislative direction to the judiciary to mete out the mandatory minimum punishment on him.

After reciting the facts and framing the issues, Chan CJ started by setting out Singapore's constitutional framework before locating the judicial power within this framework:

> The Singapore Constitution is based on the Westminster model of constitutional government ('the Westminster model'), under which the sovereign power of the State is distributed among three organs of state, *viz*, the Legislature, the Executive and the Judiciary. In the UK (where the Westminster model originated), the Legislature is the UK parliament (comprising the House of Commons and the House of Lords), the Executive is the UK government and the Judiciary consists of the UK judges. Likewise, under the Singapore Constitution, the sovereign power of Singapore is shared among the same trinity of constitutional organs, *viz*, the Legislature (comprising the President of Singapore and the Singapore parliament), the Executive (the Singapore government) and the Judiciary (the judges of the Supreme Court and the Subordinate Courts). *The principle of separation of powers, whether conceived as a sharing or a division of sovereign power between these three organs of state, is therefore part of the basic structure of the Singapore Constitution.* Article 38 of the Singapore Constitution vests the legislative power of Singapore in the Legislature consisting of the President and Parliament. Article 23(1) of the

> Singapore Constitution vests the executive power (or authority) of Singapore in the President, which power is 'exercisable subject to the provisions of this Constitution by him or by the Cabinet or any Minister authorised by the Cabinet'. Article 93 of the Singapore Constitution vests the judicial power of Singapore in 'a Supreme Court and in such subordinate courts as may be provided by any written law for the time being in force'[73].

In support of his holding, Chan CJ quoted with approval Lord Diplock's statement in *Hinds* that Westminster model constitutions take for granted that 'the basic principle of separation of powers will apply to the exercise of their respective functions' by the three organs of government – the legislature, the executive and the judiciary. This passage in the judgment is remarkable, not only in its wholesale adoption of the Westminster model logic (and matrix), but also in holding categorically that the separation of powers between the three branches of government forms part of the 'basic structure' of the Singapore constitution. It begs the question as to what else might be part of this 'basic structure'.

Chan CJ went further to discuss two 'fundamental differences' between the UK and Singapore versions of the Westminster model. The first is the supremacy of the constitutional document in the case of Singapore. The UK does not have a written constitution and as such, Parliament is supreme, which means that a UK court has no power to declare an Act of the UK Parliament unconstitutional and, subsequently, null and void. The second difference is the manner in which the courts are vested with 'judicial power'. In the case of the UK, judicial power vests in the UK courts either at common law or by statute. The situation is quite different in Singapore:

> In contrast, under Singapore's Westminster model, the judicial power of Singapore is vested (by Art 93 of the Singapore Constitution) in the Supreme Court and 'in such subordinate courts as may be provided by any written law for the time being in force'. The Singapore Constitution thus provides for two different sources of judicial power. The first and much more significant source is the Singapore Constitution itself. The judicial power of the Supreme Court is a constitutional power derived directly from Art 93 and, hence, may be said to be co-equal in constitutional status with the legislative power and the executive power, subject only to the limitations expressed in the Singapore Constitution. The second source of judicial power, which applies to courts subordinate to the Supreme Court, is, in contrast, statutory in nature (see the words 'any written law for the time being in force' in Art 93).[74]

The petition was dismissed as Chan CJ found that the mandatory punishment provided for under the Misuse of Drugs Act did not usurp the judicial power and was, therefore, constitutional.

More recently, the Court of Appeal had occasion to consider the nature of the 'basic structure' doctrine in the case of *Yong Vui Kong v Public Prosecutor*,[75] where it was argued that 'a prohibition against torture and inhuman punishment should be read into the Constitution because such practices violate "first principles of natural law"'.[76] In support of this argument, counsel for the appellant referred to the passage in *Mohammad Faizal bin Sabtu v Public Prosecutor*[77] referring to the 'basic structure of the Singapore Constitution' as set out above. The Court of Appeal then launched into a confused and confusing explanation as to the nature of the 'basic structure' doctrine.

Sundaresh Menon, who succeeded Chan Sek Keong as Chief Justice in November 2012, delivered the judgment of the court and held:

> The basic structure doctrine postulates that there are certain fundamental features of a constitution that cannot be amended by Parliament. It derives from the decision of the Supreme Court of India in *Kesavananda Bharati v State of Kerala* AIR 1973 SC 1461 ('*Kesavananda*'), where the court held that 'every provision of the Constitution can be amended provided in the result the basic foundation and structure of the Constitution remains the same' (at [316]). An example of a feature that is part of the basic structure of the Constitution is the separation of powers (as was held in *Mohammad Faizal*). Another example is possibly the right to vote. This right cannot be found in the Constitution; indeed, like the prohibition against inhuman punishment it was one of the rights which the constitutional commission chaired by Wee Chong Jin CJ recommended to be included in the Constitution (*Report of the Constitutional Commission 1966* (27 August 1966) at para 43), but which ultimately was not adopted by the Government. Nonetheless, in relation to the right to vote, the Government acknowledged in 2001 that this is part of the basic structure of the Constitution…

These examples show that in order for a feature to be considered part of the basic structure of the constitution, it must be something fundamental and essential to the political system that is established thereunder.[78]

With due respect, the Court of Appeal might have misunderstood what Chan CJ meant when he spoke of 'basic structure' in *Mohammad Faizal*, mistaking it for the controversial 'basic features doctrine' propounded by the Indian Supreme Court in *Kesavananda*'s case in 1973. Under this doctrine, certain 'basic features' of the Indian Constitution may not be amended even by a validly passed constitutional amendment. However, the Indian judges found themselves unable to agree on exactly what these extra-constitutional 'basic features' were. Chan CJ's 'basic structure' argument is quite different and rather more limited in scope. The 'basic structure' of the Constitution derives from the Westminster model which separates or distributes state power between the three functional branches of government, and which 'adopted and codified most, if not all, of the laws, customs, conventions and practices of the British constitutional and parliamentary system'.[79] Chan CJ's 'basic structure' derives from the matrix of the Westminster model and is grounded in history, legal precedent, and the logic of legal continuity. Put another way, so long as Singapore purports to have a constitution founded on the Westminster model, such a basic structure must exist. It would be an abuse and travesty to otherwise call it a Westminster-style constitution.

By adopting the 'basic structure' argument, the court puts minimal constraints on Parliament's powers to amend the Constitution. Provided the requisite procedures are followed and the necessary majorities obtained, the Constitution may be amended. The only constraints are those imposed by the structural matrix and by the common law. This necessarily limits what the courts can do to thwart Parliament's power, unlike the much more expansive 'basic features' doctrine under which a constellation of judicially determined extra-constitutional 'features' serve to limit the amendment power of the Constitution itself. The latter is not a structural argument but was formulated by the Indian judges reading the Preamble and the whole scheme of the Constitution. Such an interpretive approach gives judges much greater latitude in determining what constraints it can place on parliamentary power.

This begs the question: Who determines whether Singapore's Constitution is based on the Westminster model? The short answer would be – the courts. In many ways, it is a claim to identity, a self-proclamation of sorts. So long as the courts continue to hold Singapore's Constitution to be based on the Westminster model, the matrix holds true and limits Parliament's amendment powers only insofar as it destroys the structure of the Constitution. Thus, if Parliament decides to abolish the judiciary completely, the court can strike it down as destroying the Constitution's 'basic structure'. Likewise, it can be argued that Parliament has not the power to obliterate the fundamental liberties provisions under Part IV of the Constitution as all constitutions based on the Westminster model have a bill of rights.

We end with the case of *Vellama d/o Marie Muthu v Attorney-General*,[80] where the Court of Appeal was invited to probe beyond the structural matrix of Singapore's Constitution and consider if there was a constitutional right to vote. The case arose shortly after the parliamentary seat for Hougang constituency was declared vacant following the sacking of its erstwhile Member of Parliament by his own political party. In the aftermath of this dramatic turn of events, Prime Minister Lee Hsien Loong intimated that he had the discretion to decide whether or not to call a by-election. Madam Vellama, a resident of Hougang constituency then applied for a declaration that the Prime Minister had no such discretion and that he was duty-bound to call for a by-election within a reasonable time. The Court of Appeal held:

> Having regard to the role of an MP in the Westminster form of government and on a plain reading of Art 49, it seems clear to us that the Constitution places a duty upon the Prime Minister to call a by-election (unless he intends to dissolve Parliament in the near future) to fill casual vacancies of elected MPs which may arise from time to time.[81]

In this last case, the Court of Appeal read into the Constitution a duty on the part of the Prime Minister to call a by-election within a reasonable time even though such an obligation is neither found in the Constitution nor in written law. The court was prepared to extrapolate such a duty using the matrix of the Westminster system of government and the form of parliamentary representation it embodies.

VIII Conclusion

The American constitutional law scholar, Charles Black, made this point in his Edward Douglas White Lectures in 1969 when he argued that in interpreting constitutional provisions, courts may build 'inferences from the existence of constitutional structures and the relationships which the Constitution ordains among' them.[82] But, it is not enough just to look at structural connections; we need to do more to probe the matrix of the constitution we are interpreting. As Lord Wilberforce, speaking for the Privy Council, urged in *Minister of Home Affairs & Anor v Collins MacDonald Fisher & Anor*:[83]

> A Constitution is a legal instrument giving rise, amongst other things, to individual rights capable of enforcement in a court of law. Respect must be paid to the language which has been used and to the traditions and usages which have given meaning to that language. It is quite consistent with this, and with the recognition that rules of interpretation may apply, to take as a point of departure for the process of interpretation a recognition of the character and origin of the instrument, and to be guided by the principle of giving full recognition and effect to those fundamental rights and freedoms with a statement of which the Constitution commences.[84]

All these ingredients – structural relationships, traditions and usages –form part of the matrix that provides the key as to how judges need to interpret the Constitution. The matrix is not an invitation for judicial adventurism and neither is it a straitjacket that would cripple judicial imagination. Instead, it provides a grid of values that breathes life into the Constitution.

Notes

1 Robert K Barnhart (ed), *Chambers Dictionary of Etymology* (Chambers 1999) 641–42.
2 Andrew Harding, 'The "Westminster Model" Constitution Overseas: Transplantation, Adaptation and Development in Commonwealth States' (2004) 4 Oxford University Commonwealth Law Journal 143, 143.
3 PA Howell, *The Judicial Committee of the Privy Council 1833–1876: Its Origins, Structure and Development* (Cambridge University Press 1979).
4 2 & 3 Will 4 c 92.
5 3 & 4 Will 4 c 41. Section 3 of the Act provides:

> All appeals or complaints in the nature of appeals whatever, which either by virtue of this Act, or of any law, statute, or custom, may be brought before His Majesty or His Majesty in Council from or in respect of the determination, sentence, rule, or order of any court, judge, or judicial officer, and all such appeals as are now

> pending and unheard, shall from and after the passing of this Act be referred by His Majesty to the said Judicial Committee of his Privy Council, and such appeals, causes, and matters shall be heard by the said Judicial Committee, and a report or recommendation thereon shall be made to His Majesty in Council for his decision thereon as heretofore, in the same manner and form as has been heretofore the custom with respect to matters referred by His Majesty to the whole of his Privy Council or a committee thereof (the nature of such report or recommendation being always stated in open court).

6 Howell (n 3) Chapters 3 and 4.

7 For such an instance in the Straits Settlements, see *Choa Choon Neoh v Spottiswoode* (1869) 1 Kyshe 216, 221, where Sir Peter Benson Maxwell held:

> In this Colony, so much of the law of England as was in existence when it was imported here and is of general (and not merely local) policy, and adapted to the conditions and wants of the inhabitants, is the law of the land; and further, that law is subject, in its application to the various alien races established here, to such modifications as are necessary to prevent it from operating unjustly and oppressively on them.

8 [1932] AC 260 (PC).

9 David B Swinfen, *Imperial Appeal: The Debate on the Appeal to the Privy Council, 1833–1986* (Manchester University Press 1987) Chapter 6.

10 [1963] AC 103 (PC).

11 ibid 118.

12 [1965] AC 152 (PC).

13 ibid 193.

14 ibid 194.

15 [1920] AC 691 (PC).

16 ibid 197–98.

17 *Moses Hinds v The Queen* [1977] 1 AC 195 (PC).

18 [1967] AC 259 (PC).

19 ibid 283.

20 ibid.

21 ibid.

22 ibid.

23 ibid 286.

24 ibid 284.

25 ibid 286.

26 ibid.

27 ibid 287–88.

28 Clause 4 of the 1833 Charter provides:

> And to provide for the administration of justice hereafter in Our said Island Our will and pleasure is, and We do hereby direct that the entire administration of justice, civil and criminal therein, shall be vested exclusively in the courts erected and constituted by this Our Charter…

29 *Hinds* (n 17).

30 ibid 211.

31 ibid.

32 ibid 212.

33 ibid.

34 ibid.

35 ibid.

36 Emphasis added, ibid 213.

37 ibid 233.
38 ibid 235.
39 ibid 238–39.
40 SI 1963/1493.
41 [1967] 2 AC 238 (PC).
42 ibid 247.
43 ibid 248.
44 [1976] AC 239 (PC).
45 ibid 245.
46 ibid 244.
47 ibid 247.
48 [1979] AC 385 (PC).
49 ibid 395.
50 ibid 407.
51 *Ong Ah Chuan v Public Prosecutor* [1980] SGPC 6, [1979–1980] SLR(R) 710.
52 *Haw Tua Tau v Public Prosecutor* [1981] SGPC 1, [1981–1982] SLR(R) 133.
53 *Ong Ah Chuan* (n 51).
54 ibid 720.
55 *Minister of Home Affairs & Anor v Collins MacDonald Fisher & Anor* [1980] AC 319 (PC).
56 *Ong Ah Chuan* (n 51) 721.
57 In the context of Singapore, see, TKK Iyer, 'Article 9(1) and Natural Justice' (1981) 23 Malaya Law Review 213 and AJ Harding, 'Natural Justice and the Constitution' (1981) 23 Malaya Law Review 226.
58 [1979] 1 AC 385 (PC).
59 *Ong Ah Chuan* (n 51) 722–23.
60 *Haw Tua Tau* (n 52).
61 ibid 143–44.
62 ibid 144.
63 ibid.
64 ibid 144–45.
65 [2010] SGCA 20, [2010] 3 SLR 489.
66 ibid 500.
67 *Yong Vui Kong v Public Prosecutor* [2015] SGCA 11, [2015] 2 SLR 1129.
68 ibid 1156.
69 [2007] SGHC 207, [2008] 2 SLR(R) 239.
70 ibid 310.
71 ibid 311.
72 Emphasis added. *Mohammad Faizal bin Sabtu v Public Prosecutor* [2012] SGHC 163, [2012] 4 SLR 947.
73 ibid 956–57.
74 ibid 958.
75 *Yong Vui Kong* (n 67).
76 ibid 1158.
77 *Mohammad Faizal* (n 72).
78 *Yong Vui Kong* (n 67) 1158–59.
79 *Jeyaretnam Joshua Benjamin v Attorney-General* [1987] SGHC 36, [1987] SLR(R) 472, 475 (Chua J); cited with approval in *Mohammad Faizal* (n 72) 957 (Chan CJ).
80 [2013] SGCA 39, [2013] 4 SLR 1.
81 ibid 35.
82 Charles L Black Jr, *Structure and Relationship in Constitutional Law* (Ox Bow Press 1969) 7.
83 *Fisher* (n 55).
84 ibid 329.

Bibliography

Barnhart, Robert K (ed), *Chambers Dictionary of Etymology* (Chambers 1999).

Black, Charles L Jr, *Structure and Relationship in Constitutional Law* (Ox Bow Press 1969).

Harding, AJ, 'Natural Justice and the Constitution' (1981) 23 Malaya Law Review 226.

Harding, Andrew, 'The "Westminster Model" Constitution Overseas: Transplantation, Adaptation and Development in Commonwealth States' (2004) 4 Oxford University Commonwealth Law Journal 143.

Howell, PA, *The Judicial Committee of the Privy Council 1833–1876: Its Origins, Structure and Development* (Cambridge University Press 1979).

Iyer, TKK, 'Article 9(1) and Natural Justice' (1981) 23 Malaya Law Review 213.

Swinfen, David B, *Imperial Appeal: The Debate on the Appeal to the Privy Council, 1833–1986* (Manchester University Press 1987).

4 Principled pragmatism and the 'third wave' of communitarian judicial review in Singapore

Thio Li-ann

I Introduction: principle and pragmatism at tension?

In the fifty years since the Republic's inception on 9 August 1965, three waves of approaches towards constitutional interpretation may be discerned. The third and current wave is captured by what may be described as Singapore's brand of 'principled pragmatism', broadly traceable to judgments delivered during the era of former Chief Justice Chan Sek Keong (11 April 2006–6 November 2012) and present Chief Justice Sundaresh Menon (from 7 November 2012). The phrase 'principled pragmatism' may sound oxymoronic, and certainly suggests values in tension. 'Principle' speaks of 'first things', of fixity in terms of a priori objective norms of what is just, true or good and of consistency in norm application, which is a rule of law virtue. 'Pragmatism' speaks of 'last things', of what works; it operates in the vernacular of experience, expediency, practicality, rather than abstract formalism.

Can these values co-exist? We live in a sceptical age, where realist propensities translate into a trashing of the model of Objective Law; 'law is politics', not autonomous of politics; law is indeterminate and judicial interpretation is not necessarily value-free. What might 'principled pragmatism' applied to constitutional adjudication look like, where 'principle' suggests structured legal reasoning and some degree of objectivity, and 'pragmatism' suggests a relaxing of these features?

As a starting point, this chapter affirms the view that a distinction, however imperfect, can be drawn between law and politics, between 'legal' and 'extra-legal' factors. Judicial power is functionally separate from executive and legislative powers and entails the courts 'making a finding on the facts as they stand, applying the relevant law to those facts and determining the rights and obligations of the parties concerned for the purposes of governing their relationship for the future'.[1] Article 93 of the Singapore Constitution exclusively vests judicial power in the courts, which at common law is 'an entity with certain characteristics'.[2] As the Court of Appeal recently averred in relation to a politically divisive issue, 'in the midst of a cacophony of voices', only one was relevant, 'it is the voice of the law, which represents the voice of objectivity'. All other voices are irrelevant; indeed, they generate unnecessary heat (and distraction) rather than needful (and illuminating) light'.[3] Singapore courts have repeatedly asserted that judicial usurpation of the legislative function would violate the separation of powers thereby undermining the constitutional order where courts are co-equal with, not superior to, the legislature and executive.[4]

Whether characterised as 'activist', 'restrained', or 'deferential', the scope of judicial review implicates questions relating to normative constitutionalism, including the well-worn question of the democratic legitimacy of judicial review as a counter-majoritarian check. The rule of law is weakened where a legal decision turns on the political preferences of unelected judges. In some jurisdictions, judges may justify the striking down of legislation in the name of a 'living tree'[5] brand of constitutional interpretation. This empowers judges to alter the meaning of the Constitution, in accordance with their 'progressive' vision of the realities of modern life; this frequently involves declaring new rights for individuals or groups which otherwise find no basis in the constitutional text. This approach is said to ensure that the Constitution remains flexible and does not become obsolete. It is often contrasted with other interpretive approaches that emphasise fidelity to the constitutional text, structure or framers' intentions. However, '[a] counter-majoritarian Court can appear either as hero or villain, depending on one's political preferences and the flow of history'. It is not self-evident that courts would do 'a better job than majoritarian politics of selecting the right minority groups for protection'.[6]

Interpretation is not a mechanical, value-free exercise. However, there can be a third way between formalism and judicial legislation. Indeed, Attorney-General VK Rajah articulated the mainstream view that 'a degree of judicial lawmaking [occurs] in the interstices of the written law'.[7] In upholding the centrality of the constitutional text in interpretation, the courts have consistently maintained that calls to introduce new rights or to abolish statutory provisions should be addressed before Parliament, and should not be effected 'by the courts under the guise of constitutional interpretation'.[8] A sharp distinction is drawn between constitutional *interpretation* and constitutional *change* by the amendment process, which fall within the judicial province and legislative forum respectively. Judicial circumspection might be especially apposite because amending the Constitution in Singapore is a political and practical possibility. As the supreme law of the land,[9] the Constitution is controlled[10] but remains flexible, as the government in a dominant party state can easily muster the two-thirds parliamentary majority to activate the amendment process under Article 5(2). The Court of Appeal affirmed: '[T]he possibility of constitutional amendment … furnishes our Parliament with *the necessary flexibility to ensure that the Singapore Constitution reflects the prevailing social mores as well as aspirations of Singapore society*.'[11] Constitutional fossilisation is thus unlikely and judicial activism is not an imperative.

This chapter does not present a theory *of* constitutional adjudication; rather it is a theory *about* constitutional adjudication in Singapore, in terms of 'principled' judicial impulses to intervene and 'pragmatic' impulses to refrain or practice restrained review. Descriptively, it examines whether the idea of 'principled pragmatism' accurately captures contemporary constitutional interpretive approaches or what I describe as the 'third wave', as distinct from the preceding two waves of interpretive approaches. In evaluative terms, it assesses the desirability of this approach in terms of whether constitutional principles or values are adequately vindicated. This relates to the continuing debate over whether courts should primarily demonstrate fidelity to legal reasoning and the text, or whether their role is to connect the law with evolving social values. It considers the extent to which institutional constraints operate on courts, such as the principle of separation of powers or the need to protect public confidence in the administration of justice as a public good. This is tied to expectations of judicial impartiality and fair hearings. This should illumine attitudes towards the issue of the democratic legitimacy of judicial review.[12]

Part I establishes the conceptual framework and studies the concepts of principles and pragmatism as ideas which shape interpretation, and unpacks two ways in which principled pragmatism may be understood as capturing Singapore's approach to constitutional adjudication. As a protean term, 'pragmatism' has a 'spongy' or substantively empty quality,[13] and can be used to service any ideological agenda, being 'neutral between alternative prophecies and thus neutral between democrats and fascists'.[14] The strain of outcome-oriented American legal pragmatism,[15] which has been used to justify activist forms of judicial review, 'living tree' to some, 'make it up as you go along' to others, will be examined with the purpose of identifying and distinguishing the Singapore strain of pragmatism in relation to judicial review. Part II contextualises the discussion by examining the three waves of constitutional interpretive approaches since independence. Part III interrogates in greater detail how principled pragmatism is evident in Singapore case law, both as a judicial method that identifies legitimate legal sources, and in terms of judicial attitude towards intervening in disputes or demonstrating restraint. Part IV evaluates principled pragmatism in terms of understanding the judicial role and offers concluding observations.

II Principled pragmatism: unpacking the components

While 'principle' as fundamental truths or foundational norms are oriented to the general and abstract as the 'one right answer', 'pragmatism' leans towards the experiential and particular, distrusting grand theory and foregrounding the consequences of a proposition. A pragmatic orientation evaluates a project by whether it serves social or human needs, although this itself requires a theory of the good as not every claim based on human need is self-evident. Pragmatism is critical of formalistic, over-rigid, structured ways of answering legal questions that only consider *some* criteria. Borrowing from Oliver Wendell Holmes, law is about prediction rather than right reason, tradition, custom or the command of a sovereign.[16] Integral to pragmatism is a move to relax the weight accorded to precedent, to reduce the force of general principle from being coercive to persuasive. Legal pragmatism focuses on context and the real-world consequences of decisions, values practical judgment, and prioritises the particular. It is antifoundationalist and rejects deduction from grand theories. Law is thus not a brooding omnipresence in the sky, which judges identify and declare, but 'our creation, an activity we engage in to advance our social purposes'.[17] It is a practical instrument of social policy. On this view, law is inherently uncertain, 'predictive rather than subsisting'.[18] Judicial autonomy and creativity tends to be lauded as these facilitate the touting of 'progressive' visions of the Good. Legal pragmatists are particularly partial to 'living tree' approaches to constitutional interpretation, where the focus is on moral theory or the political preferences of judges, which are usually autonomy-oriented and rights-expansive in liberal jurisdictions. While judges would not entirely disregard history, precedents, traditions, customs in determining what serves the community interests, they might, however, discount their weight. Legal pragmatists of this ilk decry critiques that unelected judges should not engage in judicial law-making, condemning as 'legal fundamentalists' those who have a 'misplaced faith in majoritarian government' to resolve disagreements between the powerful and powerless.[19] However, if representative democracy is a form of government by elites, to validate expansive judicial law-making powers is merely to substitute one form of government by elites for another – rule by aristocratic judges.[20]

Principled pragmatism suggests a tension between two competing impulses: a desire for continuity and certainty, which allies itself to fidelity to text and framers' intent. The focus on text, history and precedent reins in judicial discretion in the interpretive process and favours a vision of law as objective, impersonal, even transcendent, with its own logic and coherence. It is important to note that because the need to maintain a distinction between law and politics is a dominant motif in Singapore public law cases, judgments gravitate towards textualism, historicism, precedent, and more recently, principle or constitutional theory. The next section examines the case law more closely and identifies the three waves of interpretive approaches.

III Three waves of constitutional interpretative approaches in Singapore

This section examines the three waves of interpretive approaches – to ascertain whether these evince pragmatic components, to give content to this protean[21] term, and to assess the extent to which principle weighted past decisions. It is argued that there has been a distinctive, if evolutionary and modest, shift in methods of interpreting the Constitution over the past fifty years. The waves are not strictly chronological and should be thought of in terms of models or typologies of interpretation that dominated constitutional interpretation during the tenure of Singapore's first four Chief Justices. The descriptor 'principled pragmatism' is largely reserved for decisions given during the twenty-first century, associated with the Chan and Menon bench. It is well to remember that the self-perception by judges of their role and functions is influenced by public perception and expectations as to the institutional role of the courts, which is a product of constitutional principle, history and political culture. In Singapore, courts have the power to review both the constitutionality of legislation and the legality of administrative action.[22]

A The first wave: stability, continuity, survivability, thinking administratively

The first wave is broadly associated with the early decades of Singapore's independence, where Wee Chong Jin was Chief Justice and the bench was staffed by judges well-schooled in the English common law traditions, and where decisions were made against the backdrop of a system of parliamentary supremacy. As Kevin Tan has noted, constitutional law for these judges 'was little more than an extension of English administrative law, transposed to suit local conditions'.[23] Further, this was a relatively immature version of English administrative law, where robust principles of objective review had yet to develop. Indeed, prior to the seminal 1984 House of Lords decision of *Council of Civil Service Unions v Minister for the Civil Service*,[24] English judges accorded the broadest latitude to Parliament. Singapore judges similarly did so, influenced by the development imperative as well as concerns about national security. At this point in time, the judicial role was to ensure the optimal operation of the inherited legal system, in accordance with known and accepted legal precepts. Stability was primary and the court was focused on resolving immediate disputes in a workmanlike fashion, rather than making long-term and more wide-reaching pronunciations or engaging in constitutional jurisprudence.

Such deference to the executive was reflected in the subjective test of review which effectively rendered ministerial discretion beyond judicial scrutiny, as was evident in the 1971 case of *Lee Mau Seng v Minister for Home Affairs*[25] where the court declined to enquire whether there were sufficient grounds to justify the issuance of a detention order under the Internal Security Act (ISA).[26] According to the court, this would be

> wholly inconsistent with the scheme of the Act under which the power to issue a detention order has been made to depend upon the existence of a state of mind in the President acting in accordance with the advice of the Cabinet which is a purely subjective condition.[27]

This may be described as a form of submissive deference insofar as the courts refused to scrutinise the weight of executive reasons for this decision. Instead, accountability for such broad powers was parked at the feet of weak political checks, bearing in mind that the incumbent government held all parliamentary seats in 1971. It is noteworthy that towards the end of his tenure as Chief Justice, Wee Chong Jin was party to the seminal decision of *Chng Suan Tze v Minister of Home Affairs*[28], which remains a high watermark for constitutional law in Singapore. After a studied consideration of Commonwealth case law and principle, the Court of Appeal reversed the subjective test in *Lee Mau Seng* and applied an objective test that permitted judicial review of detention orders. This rested on the principle that exercises of executive discretion not subject to judicial review would effectively be arbitrary, and that it was 'no answer to refer to accountability to Parliament as an alternative safeguard'.[29] In a ringing endorsement of the rule of law, the Court of Appeal declared that 'all power has legal limits and the rule of law demands that the courts should be able to examine the exercise of discretionary power'.[30]

Parliament by constitutional amendment swiftly overruled this decision, insofar as it pertained to preventive detention under the ISA, on the basis that the court had intruded upon executive prerogatives. These amendments severely truncated judicial review, cabining it to scrutiny of non-compliance with procedure.[31] Presumably chastened by the Government's view that the courts had overstepped their role, the courts subsequently retreated to deciding issues on the facts,[32] becoming more solicitous in ensuring that its decisions did not fall beyond the pale of what important political actors could tolerate.

The *Chng* decision, which expanded judicial review, was itself moderated by the application of the principle of non-justiciability on grounds of national security, as such matters were considered better suited to executive judgment; as such, it is a better fit with the third wave, an early precursor which became one of the pillars of principled pragmatism. Of the first wave, one may conclude that it was a season from which one could glean little in terms of constitutional principles and normative thinking. Instead, it was a time of minimal judicial control where a 'strong state,' with its emphasis on survivability, was able to effectively enforce its political programmes and priorities.

B The second wave: statist pragmatism – thinking bureaucratically

The second wave approach towards constitutional interpretation is most closely associated with decisions emanating from the bench under Chief Justice Yung Pung How, who assumed office from 1990 to 2006. Efficiency was a prime value at a time when the judiciary was being built up to service the needs of a flourishing commercial centre and Yong CJ was lauded for clearing the judicial backlog. The approach towards constitutional interpretation at this time was driven by the values of statist pragmatism. Statism (which affirms power and supports the strong, efficient state) must not be confused with communitarian values.[33] Pragmatism was evident in both the methods and the values prioritised in constitutional cases, often at the cost of individual liberty. Foremost considerations were pragmatic matters relating to common sense,[34] administrative convenience,[35] efficiency and practical experience[36] rather than theory. This manifested a bureaucratic ethos and was status-quo oriented; this bench evinced a clear distrust of scholarly writings and foreign precedents[37] that advocated giving more weight to rights in the adjudicatory process.

While eclectic in methodology, which itself manifests a pragmatic bent in deploying whatever is useful, cases from the Yong bench were consistent in terms of the statist ideology they espoused, preferring claims that were supportive of state power rather than individual rights. This is illustrated by *Public Prosecutor v Mazlan bin* Maidun,[38] which concerned Article 9(1). This provides that a person shall not be deprived of life or personal liberty save 'in accordance with law'. It was contended that the meaning of 'law', which incorporated what the

Privy Council had described as 'fundamental rules of natural justice',[39] included an implied right or privilege against self-incrimination, which protects the criminal process rights of an accused person. The Court of Appeal refused to read this in, noting, 'To say that the right of silence is a constitutional right would be to elevate an evidential rule to constitutional status despite its having been given no explicit expression in the Constitution.' Further, it involved 'a degree of adventurous extrapolation which we do not consider justified' as such implication was 'not a mere matter of balancing'.[40] The court thus declined to declare what would in its view be a new right, refusing to conceptualise the matter as one involving a recalibration of the balance between a competing interest and an existing right (which could have been developed by building on precedent and elaborating on what fundamental rules of natural justice entailed). The lynchpin of this strict textualist approach was Yong CJ's view that if the right to silence was a constitutional right rather than an evidentiary one, it would have been 'given specific parliamentary expression if the Legislature had intended to guarantee full protection for it'.[41] Similarly, in *Rajeevan Edakalavan v Public Prosecutor*,[42] the High Court refused to read in a right to be told of the existing Article 9(3) right to counsel. In a burst of populist rhetoric, Yong CJ declared that 'any proposition to broaden the scope of the rights accorded to the accused should be addressed in the political and legislative arena'; matters relating to fundamental liberties were 'sensitive issues' and the judiciary was not positioned to decide whether legislation was 'fair or reasonable' as this was 'very subjective'. Instead, it fell to 'the people of Singapore' to decide if any law contravened 'the principles of justice' through their freely elected parliamentary representatives.

However, an alternative way of characterising such an implied right, which is facilitative of an express right (not involving the declaration of a controversial substantive right) is that this is what constitutes a generous interpretation of liberties in Part IV of the Constitution, long accepted as the appropriate way to read fundamental liberties to ensure individuals enjoy the 'full measure' of said liberties.[43]

However, the decision of Yong CJ in *Colin Chan v Public Prosecutor*[44] reflected an enthusiastic embrace of extra-textual adventurous extrapolation in declaring, in the absence of a textual basis, that the unwritten 'paramount mandate' of the Singapore Constitution was the 'sovereignty, integrity and unity of Singapore.' Effectively, Yong CJ fashioned an extra-textual statist trump that effectively negated a religious liberty claim under Article 15. The means (a non-textual approach) justified the end (statism) in *Chan*, as it did in *Mazlan*.

Statism, which valorises the centralisation of public power as a determinative value, permeated the entire judgment in various respects. This is evident in how the importance of individual rights in Part IV, which embody a principle of justice, was minimised. The use of the term 'balancing' to frame judicial decisions where there were clashes between fundamental liberties and community interests was rhetorical. The High Court in *Chan*, while affirming that religious freedom must be 'reconciled' with the state's right to exercise sovereign power to ensure peace and security, nonetheless applied the statist trump to declare that anything 'including religious beliefs and practices which tend to run counter to these objectives must be restrained'. This was a categorical rather than balancing approach; once a statist public order trump was invoked, the matter was determined in favour of the state. No consideration was made about the value of fundamental liberties or the reasonableness of restrictive state action. Indeed, the judicial reasoning painted something of a caricature in pointing out the 'danger of allowing absolute freedom of religion which might create a complete denial of a government's authority and ability to govern individuals or groups asserting a religious affiliation'.[45] Attention to 'tendencies' and over-wrought speculation of how 'absolute' freedoms might bring about a state of anarchy prevented a balancing exercise that seeks to optimise competing interests, which does not require swinging to the extreme of declaring rights as determinative trumps. The conflation of 'national security', which the Jehovah Witnesses supposedly endangered by being conscientious objectors to compulsory military service, with 'public order', a constitutionally recognised ground for restraining religious liberty, also demonstrates statism.

This 'no-balancing' balancing approach was evident in *Chee Soon Juan v Public Prosecutor*,[46] which also deployed the rhetoric of engagement with 'a balancing exercise' between free speech guaranteed under Article 14 and 'broader societal concerns such as public peace and order'. The appellant was charged with a statutory offence for holding a May Day rally at the Istana without a permit. The reasoning was curt. Yong CJ did not find the statutory provisions 'in any way contrary to our Constitution'; to him it 'seemed eminently clear'[47] that the legislature had the power to enact the Public Entertainments and Meeting Act under Article 14(2)(a), which allows for eight grounds of derogation, including public order. Lip service was paid to balancing, in an under-reasoned judgment that accepted that any statutory regime based on an express ground of derogation was constitutional, without more.[48]

This brand of statist pragmatism gives short shrift to norms that seek to constrain public power, including fundamental liberties. It was an unhealthy form of pragmatism insofar as it devalued legal reasoning through cursory treatment of the disputed issues or in the invocation of public order trumps which eviscerated rights clauses of meaningful content in parsimonious fashion. This also provided little insight into whether, and how, balancing of competing interests took place and the invocation of this rhetorical trump was unhappily repeated as precedent in subsequent cases.[49] While efficiency and stability are not irrelevant considerations, they cannot be the primary concern within a constitutional order that seeks to regulate public power. To accord these values determinative weight to uphold government reasons for restricting rights, whether because courts are *ad idem* with government priorities and/or wish to adopt a posture of submissive deference to the government, is a matter of alarm to those who appreciate that courts have a role as a bulwark against a tyrannical government. To critics, this stream of pragmatism was thus cast in a pejorative light as an apology for power or misplaced paean to efficiency.

C *The third wave: principled pragmatism – thinking constitutionally*

1 *General developments*

One might argue that a 'sea change' was initiated when the third Chief Justice, Chan Sek Keong, took office and public law jurisprudence began to focus more on the intrinsic value of norms. I have previously observed that the bench 'now regularly engages with foreign case law and international legal arguments, produces expository judgments,[50] references academic opinion and has demonstrated a culture of elaborate reason-giving, as opposed to the statist, cursory judgments of a former age'. If these judgments reflect a concern with communitarian values rather than autonomist Western liberal values, driven by local conditions and a desire for autochthony, this is a welcome trend towards a form of 'particularism without parochialism'.[51]

In stylistic terms, the judgments have increased in length. In substantive terms, the quality has improved in terms of judicial reasoning. The allergy to theory and scholarly writings seems to have been cured, and one might discern a new affinity for theory and ideas, with increasingly regular references in judgments to local academics and eminent jurists such as Dworkin, Hart, Bentham and Devlin, for example.[52] Increasingly the courts have considered cases on 'first principles' in the absence of precedent[53] or where precedent was criticised, demonstrating a freedom to contemplate changes in doctrine. In altering the test for the contempt of scandalising the court from the laxer 'inherent tendency' test to the stricter 'real risk' test, it was clear that the High Court was keen not to present the change as a radical rupture from past practice. The criticism of the inherent tendency test was that, taken literally, it would not adequately protect free speech because the risk to public confidence in the administration of justice could be remote or speculative. Loh J noted that the formula was 'susceptible of controversy and misunderstanding' such that 'if it were a pure question of semantics', he would not have departed from the original test. He asserted that properly understood, the inherent tendency test required a contextual analysis but preferred the real risk test for its clarity. He noted that cases decided under the inherent tendency test would have satisfied his formulation of the real risk test.[54] This gentle correction of apparent misunderstandings of what a legal test entailed was also evident in a discreet aside where the Court of Appeal unobtrusively sought to correct how critics have misread another case, which was not directly on point.[55]

This section examines the nature of this sea change in general, and highlights those aspects of judicial review that provide grist to support the mill of principled pragmatism.

2 *Beyond statism to communitarianism?*

Statism focuses on considerations of the strong, effective and efficient state, valorising public order considerations at the expense of individual liberties A strong state operates through issuing top-down *diktats*, rather than seeking community-evolved consensus. In the last decade of Singapore's constitutional history, however, there has been a turn from statism towards a more communitarian philosophy in judicial reasoning. This manifests in a move beyond the liberal dichotomy of 'individual versus state', to a more sophisticated recognition of various actors, such as the interest of the individual, ethnic groups, the larger community and the state.[56].This envisages a set of shared values. In Singapore, the Government has put out a white paper on shared values that espouses communitarianism,[57] while the courts have ventured to articulate these common values in public law cases. Communitarian values like 'the preservation of morality, the protection of the person, the preservation of public peace and order, respect for institutions and the preservation of the state's wider interest' have been identified.[58] In the 2009 case of *Kalpanath Singh s/o Ram Raj Singh v Law Society of Singapore*, the High Court declared that although Singaporeans within a secular society did not subscribe to a common religion, 'this does not mean that there cannot be shared values that our society, as a collective whole, may adopt. We believe that one such common value is forgiving those who have trespassed against us.'[59] This may be seen as the judicial contribution towards a national identity, some variant of constitutional patriotism which undergirds the polity, and an articulation of a thicker conception of public good. The weight given to community values and appreciation of the social value of law[60] is also evident in cases where the importance of legislative objectives such as countering drug trafficking, even where entrapment is involved, is judicially affirmed.[61]

3 Taking constitutional theory more seriously: articulating principles

There are a noticeable number of third wave cases that identify and address the unwritten principles underlying Singapore's practice of constitutional democracy. While the rule of law was most strongly articulated in the 1988 case of *Chng Suan Tze*, it has become the vindicated cornerstone of Singapore public law. The Court of Appeal in *Yong Vui Kong* (2011)[62] noted that the 'full amplitude' of the *Chng* principle of objective review of discretionary powers was 'left untouched' by Parliament outside of the Internal Security Act regime, which constituted an implicit endorsement.[63] Since then, the *Chng* principle has been regularly cited and has taken pride of place in many third wave judgments.[64]

Other judicially affirmed constitutional principles include the separation of powers and the principle of judicial independence as well as the presumption of constitutionality or regularity (*omnia praesumuntur rite esse acta*).[65] The Court of Appeal also noted that the basis for judicial review was 'very much tied up with democratic theory'[66] and underscored the importance of parliamentary representation as a facet of democracy, where parliamentarians were 'not just the mouthpiece but the voice of the people of the constituency.'[67] These principles interact with and influence the scope of review, as will be discussed further below.

4 Taking rights a little more seriously?

It is clear that Singapore courts have never treated rights as Dworkinian trumps; indeed, constitutional rights have been little more than defeasible interests to be sacrificed at the altar of stability and efficiency, particularly during the first and second waves. Constitutional rights as limits on state power are, by nature, inefficient. Unsurprisingly, considerations of efficiency have dominated under the old statist paradigm in the second wave of constitutional interpretation. However, there are signs this is being moderated insofar as more weight is given to the importance of a right. Today, case law indicates that rights are, in principle, to be balanced[68] against a wide range of competing rights, interests and duties.[69] They are not to be rendered the exception to the rule nor unduly subordinated to a public good trump as in *Colin Chan*. As Loh J noted, when balancing a freedom against a recognised limit, minimally, 'neither can be defined in such a way that renders the other otiose'.[70] In discussing political defamation, the Court of Appeal in *Review Publishing v Lee Hsien Loong*[71] proffered a fourfold typology of rights beyond the concept of a right as trump, which it describes as a fundamental right. Others in the typology include preferential rights, co-equal rights and subsidiary rights. Preferential and co-equal rights may be useful in developing a rights jurisprudence within a communitarian context in assigning weights to rights as against converse and correlative duties[72] and public goods.[73]

The greater prominence given to rights-based concerns is evident in relation to case law on Article 9(3), which provides that '[w]here a person is arrested, he shall be informed as soon as may be of the grounds of his arrest and shall be allowed to consult and be defended by a legal practitioner of his choice'. The provision itself does not stipulate the point in time when this entitlement applies and in past cases like *Jasbir Singh v Public Prosecutor*,[74] a 'second wave' era case, the position was that this right did not accrue immediately upon arrest and that a 'reasonable time' was to afford the police 'a degree of latitude in carrying out their investigations';[75] whether the right was available depended 'entirely on investigative needs' as opposed to arising upon request. Choo J in *James Raj s/o Ariokiasamy v Public Prosecutor*[76] questioned whether the correct reading should be that the right to consult counsel was immediate upon arrest, but a 'reasonable time' should be allowed for 'any necessary or unavoidable delay occasioned by practical or administrative concerns'. This could include transferring the arrested person to the place of remand or the time taken to contact counsel.[77] Nonetheless, Choo J was bound to follow the Court of Appeal precedent of *Jasbir*.[78] However, Choo J clarified that efficiency could not trump other competing concerns particularly when the constitutional rights of accused persons were at stake. While what constituted a 'reasonable time' was fact-based, Choo J stated that the onus fell on the police to prove to the court's satisfaction that granting the right to counsel would impede police investigations, and that it was 'necessary and not merely desirable or convenient to derogate from it'.[79] This was an attempt to ensure greater protection for the accused. Fears that consultations with lawyers might deprive the police of questioning time could be addressed 'by delineating the content of the right to counsel',[80] such as time limits for consultation, rather than depriving the applicant of the enjoyment of the right.

Thus, efficiency arguments simpliciter now curry less judicial favour in an age where more attention is paid to rights, while not treating rights as trumps. The greater solicitude for individual liberties is also evident in cases where there have been efforts to recalibrate the balance between liberty and order concerns. For example, in relation to contempt of court law, there has been a shift away from speech with a 'tendency' to impair public confidence in the administration of justice, that is, the inherent tendency test which was celebrated by Tay J in *Attorney-General v Hertzberg Daniel*,[81] for two reasons, based on expediency. First, there was no need to prove that public confidence was impaired and second, the court could pre-emptively step in before any damage was done.[82] Further, the High Court judge gave the hypothetical example that if someone ranted at a dinner party that the judiciary was completely biased, and no one cared or was affected, the real risk test, which would require an evidential basis to show there was more than a remote possibility of harm, would mean the speaker would not be cited for contempt. The judge considered it 'more logical' to first hold that contempt was committed, and then investigate whether public confidence had been impaired in deciding the question of punishment. This approach may be criticised as insufficiently protective of free speech and was rejected by another High Court judge, Loh J, who adopted the real risk test in *Shadrake No. 1*. He considered that only an 'overzealous judiciary' would consider a dinner party rant – which no one took serious notice of – a threat to public confidence in the administration of justice. He asserted the need for a test based on the 'potential adverse effect of impugned conduct'.[83] This affords greater protection to free speech.

Another clear indication of a move towards actual rather than rhetorical balancing is the elaboration of the defence of fair criticism in relation to the contempt of scandalising the court, first articulated by Prakash J in *Attorney-General v Tan Liang Joo John*,[84] later broadly affirmed by the High Court and Court of Appeal in the *Shadrake* litigation.[85] This enhanced the weight to be attributed to free speech. Prakash J not only identified all items to be placed on the balancing scale, but also investigated their weight and rationale in a non-cursory fashion, paying special attention to the importance of free speech. Speech made in good faith, in a respectful and temperate fashion, would be protected speech. Fair criticism also needed to be supported by 'reasonable argument or expostulation',[86] as opposed to a bare assertion. The intent to vilify the court could be inferred from abusive language; in contrast, 'temperate balanced criticism' actually protected the rationale behind free speech to promote democratic debate as it 'allows for rational debate' of the issues raised, which could improve the administration of justice. In contrast, 'scurrilous and preposterous attacks' would likely have the opposite effect.[87] This contributes towards an understanding of what speech is valued and protected and what is not, underscoring that speech is not the end, but the means to an end – rational debate.

5 The turn to autochthony beyond the four walls: particularism without parochialism

The Singapore courts have long cut an autochthonous trajectory in public law cases, which was formally recognised in the 1994 Practice Statement on Judicial Precedent[88] issued after the Privy Council ceased to be the apex court.[89] Divergence, rather than convergence with transnational standards (international law and foreign cases), characterised public law cases which were meant to reflect 'fundamental values of Singapore society'. Second and third wave approaches towards transnational sources are distinct.

Prior to the third wave, Singapore courts demonstrated a nationalist orientation and a 'parochial' attitude towards international law arguments, discounting these without consideration as in *Colin Chan*.[90] In other cases, 'local conditions' were invoked without sustained reasoning. For example, Sinnathuray J in the contempt of court decision of *Attorney-General v Wain Barry J*[91] was content to observe that Singapore had 'many and varied' local conditions but, he was 'not going to touch on the socio-political and economic conditions' which made 'our island nation ... markedly different' from other countries. He only stressed the indifferent factor that because Singapore had abolished jury trials, judges were triers of both law and fact, which must 'weigh heavily' such that charges of partiality had to be 'firmly dealt with'. As judges exercised more responsibility, the argument was that they required more protection from accusations of partiality that were 'harmful to public interest'. The more compelling counter-argument is that with greater power comes a need for greater accountability, given that free speech critical of the judiciary had value within a democratic society. Evidently unimpressed, the Court of Appeal in the 2011 decision of *Shadrake Alan v AG*[92] blandly described this argument from *Wain* as 'neutral at best'.

As far as foreign precedents were concerned, these were considered and selectively referenced to support statist values or existing laws. For example, the courts rejected free speech decisions in the USA,[93] while approving decisions upholding the death penalty.[94]

In the 2000s, a series of challenges against the mandatory death penalty based on Article 5 of the Universal Declaration of Human Rights (UDHR) (which prohibits torture, and cruel, inhuman and degrading treatment) brought international law arguments to the fore, accompanied by copious citations of foreign decisions, particularly from Commonwealth countries. During this third wave, the Singapore courts demonstrated a proficient, sophisticated understanding of international law, its sources and how it was received within the domestic legal order.[95] While accepting that Article 5 of the UDHR embodied customary international law (CIL), it disagreed with arguments that administering the death penalty by hanging[96] or the mandatory death penalty[97] itself fell within its ambit as 'inhuman punishment', pointing to the lack of 'extensive and virtually uniform state practice'[98] needed to support this claim. A similar context and fact-sensitive approach was evident in obiter remarks about how the implementation of caning in Singapore fell short of international law prohibitions against torture,[99] showing a deft awareness of international and regional jurisprudence.

Case law has now made it clear that Singapore practises a dualist system,[100] such that international law (whether treaty, which must be legislatively incorporated,[101] or CIL, which must be judicially recognised[102]) did not automatically apply within the domestic legal order. On reception, CIL norms were ranked at the bottom rung of the hierarchy of legal sources as common law norms. As such, clear domestic legislation prevailed over international law norms, even if it was a *jus cogens* norm, although international responsibility would be attracted.[103] It is clear that national law is primary, even if the general position is that Singapore law should be interpreted in a manner consistent with its international law obligations. The Court of Appeal noted there were 'inherent limits' on the extent to which international human rights law may factor into constitutional interpretation; this would not be appropriate 'where the express wording of the Singapore Constitution is not amenable to the incorporation of the international norms in question, or where Singapore's constitutional history is such as to militate against the incorporation of those international norms'.[104] It stated that 'neither CIL nor treaty law' could trump a clear and unambiguous domestic law, and 'pretending that the court is engaged in an interpretative exercise does not change this'.[105]

The courts now regularly engage with foreign cases as models, anti-models[106] or inspiration in crafting local solutions,[107] with the understanding that Singapore common law has to be 'developed by our Judiciary for the common good'[108] to build 'an autochthonous or indigenous legal system sensitive to the needs and mores of the society of which it is a part'.[109] In this respect, the courts have expressed reticence towards giving weight to decisions from other common law countries whose public law or constitutional bills of rights were influenced by the European Convention on Human Rights (ECHR), eg the UK under its Human Rights Act (1998), or various Caribbean countries.[110] Cases influenced by ECHR jurisprudence accord greater weight to individual rights by adopting the more intrusive standard of proportionality review. This was rejected by the High Court in *Chee Siok Chin v Minister for Home Affairs*[111] because this was 'a continental European jurisprudential concept' which the UK imported to satisfy its ECHR obligations, a regional treaty Singapore is not party to.

This does not mean, however, that the court is adopting a moral relativist stance; it does recognise universal principles.[112] Just as there are core human rights and contested human rights claims,[113] Singapore courts do recognise that we live in a plural world and that tensions between liberties and competing interests involve a 'delicate balancing exercise' that includes particularities such as 'societal values, pluralism, prevailing social and economic considerations as well as the common good of the community'. Further, the 'margins of appreciation for public conduct vary from country to country as do their respective cultural, historical and political evolutions as well as circumstances'.[114] Context is key, as pragmatic jurists would agree.

Thus, there is no slavish following of Western precedents from liberal jurisdictions and indeed the Court of Appeal has with confidence argued that US case law is exceptional rather than normative or universal.[115] Foreign cases may also be used as foils against which to distinguish Singapore particularities. Differences do exist between states in a plural world and the people of any country may '*lay down the rules by which they wish their state to be governed* and they are not bound to give effect in their Constitution to norms and standards accepted elsewhere, perhaps in very different societies'.[116] Furthermore, where an applicant cites a foreign case, this is often done selectively, and thus is of 'no weight' for two main reasons. First, Singapore as 'an independent nation with its own unique history, geography, society and economy' is entitled to forge its own path as a matter of the prerogative of a sovereign state, particularly where a contentious norm is argued for. Second, to assert 'the world is changing' in arguing for a contentious norm, and to cite cases in support, is unhelpful as this can be countered by examples that show 'shifts in the opposite direction'.[117]

In an age where human rights have become politicised, it is important to remember that imposing a contested norm on a society in the name of a false universalism constitutes a form of moral imperialism. Singapore courts have shown a concern about this in their appeal to democracy and the principle of self-determination; even with respect to a peremptory norm, this did not automatically acquire the status of a constitutional norm. The primacy of national and popular sovereignty is evident in the observation that, otherwise:

> It would mean the content of our Constitution could be dictated by the views of other states, regardless of what the people of Singapore, expressing their will through their elected representatives, think.[118]

An approach which favours national democracy and the supremacy of domestic law, but which actively engages in-depth with transnational sources, warrants the descriptor, 'particularism without parochialism', a shift from the parochialism of past waves. Furthermore, judicial reasoning takes place within the matrix of the constitutional framework and both shapes, and is shaped by, constitutional principles and specific prudential concerns.

IV Principled pragmatism and Singapore case law

The judicial imperative of maintaining a distinction between the arenas of law and politics and of confining the court's role to the realm of the former (to legal rather than non-legal factors) is examined in this section.

A Principled pragmatism as judicial method: the importance of text and history and the identification of legitimate unwritten sources

The idea of balancing in constitutional adjudication suggests the adoption of a reasonable consideration of all relevant factors and coming to some kind of accommodation of these factors. Here, the Constitution is not treated as providing a set of peremptory norms. All factors are relevant, not determinative, and balancing involves a fact-sensitive exercise. This is a pragmatic methodology and bears some similarity to common law administrative law reasoning.

However, the Singapore variant of legal pragmatism is not results-driven or consequentialist – insofar as it is reined in by principle – in the sense of judicial prioritisation of certain legal sources or factors in an interpretive method which is understood as distinctively legal, involving structured decision-making. This must be understood against the backdrop of the judicial role and attitude towards judicial intervention, where the courts disavow the role of engaging in social engineering and acting as a second legislative chamber. This is discussed further below.

In terms of judicial method, factors such as text, intent and precedent certainly were core aspects of first and second wave cases, and continue to be central in third wave interpretation cases where there is fidelity to the formulation of specific textual provisions and the context of that provision drawn from the structure of the text. Historical intent is also given determinative weight and, where this is ambiguous, preference is given to upholding the status quo and judicial adventurism is eschewed. These few examples illustrate this.

First, the actual textual formulation of the right to freedom of speech under Article 14 was given close scrutiny in *Chee Siok Chin v MHA*,[119] just as it had been in the earlier second wave case of *Jeyaretnam Joshua Benjamin v Lee Kuan Yew*.[120] Rajah JC, in particular, noted that Parliament could enact legislative restrictions to Article 14 'in the interests of public order' which allows for more expansive readings of legislative discretion than the term 'the maintenance of public order', which justified a 'prophylactic approach' to statutory regulation of a fundamental liberty.[121] Minimalist review was thus derived from taking the specific words of the text seriously. American legal pragmatists would reject giving such weight to specific words in the text.

Second, the record of constitutional history shaped judicial interpretation in *Yong Vui Kong v PP* (2010).[122] Although the Government had expressed before Parliament an in-principle acceptance of a recommendation by the 1966 Constitutional Commission to include a proposed Article 13 prohibiting torture and cruel and inhuman punishment, it was ultimately excluded from the final constitutional text. The reasons for this were ambiguous. The Court of Appeal determined that it was not at liberty, 'via an interpretative exercise',[123] to read Article 13 into the meaning of 'law' in Article 9(1) to expand its scope.

During all three waves, judicial attention was directed at non-textual bases for interpretation, although there are developments in the third wave that build on the existing jurisprudence. During the first wave, the Privy Council in *Ong Ah Chuan v Public Prosecutor*[124] had identified unwritten constitutional norms embodied in Westminster constitutions such that the word 'law' in the fundamental liberties chapter incorporated 'fundamental rules of natural justice' which could constrain the exercise of public power. However, this came to a standstill during the second wave, when a literalist approach towards reading 'law'[125] was adopted and extra-textualism was deployed to serve statist, *power-confirming* ends.[126] The issue of the meaning of 'law' in Article 9 and the content of unwritten principles it might embody came to the fore during the third wave in various constitutional challenges. However, the development of the meaning of 'fundamental rules of natural justice', whether these were procedural or substantive in nature,[127] was slow until clear guidance was provided by the Court of Appeal in *Yong Vui Kong v PP* (2015).[128] This highlights the greater willingness in third wave cases to articulate constitutional theory as a clear basis for guiding interpretation, as was done in *Vellama*[129] where appeal was made to democratic principles.

In *Yong* (2015), unwritten norms or rights were to be derived not from abstract appeals to natural law (which could easily masquerade as subjective politics),[130] but from historical understandings of rights clauses. In *Yong* it was argued that caning was a deprivation of life and personal liberty not in accordance with law, violating Article 9. To derive a 'correct interpretation'[131] of Article 9(1), the Court of Appeal traced its historical lineage, wading through its Malaysian and Indian constitutional precursors, the rejection of the US due-process formulation by Indian constitutional framers, and ultimately back to Clause 39 of the Magna Carta,[132] which was influenced by Blackstone's *Commentaries*.[133] Clause 39 went beyond the right not to be unlawfully incarcerated to include unlawful uses of force against a person and unlawful seizure of his property, protecting the three rights of personal security, personal liberty and private property. Aside from property rights, which were deliberately excised from the Indian and Singapore Constitutions, the Court of Appeal clarified that 'life' could be deprived not only by arbitrary execution or incarceration, but also the 'unlawful use of force against a person, including by way of amputations, mutilations, assaults, beatings and woundings'.[134]

Thus, freestanding unenumerated rights or norms would not be judicially read into the constitutional text. Only those rights that were facilitative or integral to the system of parliamentary government would be adopted. This could include the unwritten implied right to vote, integral to how parliamentary systems operate, but not an implied prohibition against torture.[135] This provides a principled basis for identifying and limiting the range of unenumerated norms, distinct from American legal pragmatism's focus on results (which begs a normative debate in politically rifted societies) and which refuses to preclude any factor from the balancing process.

Thus, principled pragmatism is evident in third wave judicial methodology. Pragmatically, an implied right to vote is needed for parliamentary systems to function; in terms of principle, the courts have found a basis on which to admit or reject an argument for an implied *power-constraining* right or norm which ultimately stands on constitutional theory and the nature of the Singapore constitutional order.

B Principled pragmatism as judicial attitude towards intervention

1 Expansive standing?

Standing is a requirement an applicant for judicial review needs, to have access to a judicial remedy. Common law judges make the rules that govern 'standing', which reflect an underlying political theory implicating the role of the court and of the citizen within the public life of a polity; namely, is the chief task of a judicial forum to prevent public wrong by serving as a venue for advancing social justice claims, or is it to protect the private rights of individuals where these have been violated?

The latter reflects the model of a traditional adversarial litigation process where the court relies on the aggrieved individual to apply for judicial review and seeks to resolve a legal dispute between the immediate parties. This fits in easily with the green light theory discussed by Chan Sek Keong in an extra-judicial lecture,[136] which the Court of Appeal referenced,[137] to the effect that other regulatory institutions such as the political process and public avenues could promote good governance, rather than seeking redress for bad government through the courts. As such, standing rules are stricter.

In the former instance, standing rules are more lax and the courts in jurisdictions such as India are concerned with public policy and treated as fora to advance social justice agendas. The individual acts *qua citizen* rather than *qua aggrieved individual* in this brand of public interest litigation, which is complemented by enlarged judicial powers to conduct *suo moto* investigations, to appoint committees to make enquiries and to supervise compliance with rulings.

The Singapore courts have demonstrated vigilance against becoming a politicised forum; rules on standing reflect a vision of the traditional adversarial litigation process which relies on a legally wronged person to bring a cause of action and to frame the issues to be adjudicated. The court in *Jeyaretnam*[138] expressed concern that suits relating to 'public interest' ran the risk of having citizens running amok after their own whims and fancies in relation to 'taxpayers' actions questioning all nature of administrative acts'; these were commonplace in other jurisdictions and there was 'an established body of case law and jurisprudence on the topic'. The courts were lukewarm towards the idea of public interest litigation and the spectre of the frivolous and vexatious litigant it may conjure.

In a typical case where a private right is involved, the aggrieved person applies for judicial review. Where a public right is concerned, which affects society at large or a sector thereof, an applicant has to show 'special damage' over and above what other members of the public suffered through the violation of a public right, and this serves to filter litigants. The Court of Appeal in *Vellama* stated that this 'special damage' requirement also 'safeguards against essentially political issues' which are 'camouflaged as legal questions' and which are 'more appropriately ventilated elsewhere'.[139] In demonstrating a desire not to descend into the political thicket, the Court of Appeal stated:

> Taken collectively, these rules on standing espouse an ethos of judicial review focused on vindicating personal rights and interests through adjudication rather than determining public policy through exposition. Matters of public policy are the proper remit of the Executive, and decoupling judicial review from the fundamental precepts of adversarial litigation would leave the courts vulnerable to being misused as a platform for political point-scoring.[140]

The Court of Appeal in *Kenneth Jeyaretnam* identified Singapore more closely with what it termed the classical Dicey-an constitution where the emphasis in regulating public wrong was on a responsible government subject to parliamentary scrutiny. This was contrasted against a communitarian civic republican tradition where courts were in the frontline of regulating public wrongs and promoting social justice, consonant with the 'red light theory', facilitated by standing rules allowing decisions to be brought on behalf of groups or broader communities.

The issue framed by the appellant in *Jeyaretnam* related to whether Singapore had acted constitutionally in making a loan to the International Monetary Fund in 2012 and whether Article 144 of the Constitution had been violated. Article 144 requires that parliamentary and presidential approval be obtained when loans are raised, not given, so it was not breached. In effect, the appellant was trying to question the wisdom of the loan and the court noted that neither the President nor Parliament 'had thought fit to question the propriety of the promised loan'; in addition, the President could have requested an advisory opinion from an ad hoc tribunal of three judges under Article 100. The court noted that 'The nature of the issue is entirely political'[141] and 'should be resolved as such'. Political modes of accountability were available to check the wisdom of the loan. The legality, not merits, of the decision could be reviewed and the courts were concerned 'only with the individual's rights and interests, and not matters of public policy, which rightfully remains in the remit of proper political process'.[142] This view is shaped by the imperatives of pragmatism:

> The recognition that members of the public do not have the right per se to call upon the courts to review every decision made by public bodies is not only undergirded by the obvious pragmatism of minimizing disruptiveness caused by vexatious claims to the functioning of those bodies, but also exists as a reflection of the very ethos of our adversarial system.[143]

2 Separation of powers – institutional autonomy and accountability

The scope of judicial review is shaped by the interaction of constitutional principles, particularly that of the rule of law, which urges principled intervention where legal questions are concerned, and the separation of powers. This latter principle may locate a matter within the province of the legislature or executive, in part for pragmatic considerations, because it is a matter of policy, polycentric in nature or, for democratic reasons, to leave the matter to a politically accountable branch. A clear example or model of 'principled pragmatism' is evident in the elaboration of the Singapore political questions doctrine, which identifies what is non-reviewable. This involves questions of 'high policy', as described by Menon JC in *Lee Hsien Loong v Review Publishing*,[144] such as the conduct of foreign relations, making treaties, deploying armed forces or dissolving Parliament. These fell squarely within 'provinces of executive decision-making that are, and should be, immune from judicial review', which was a reflection of 'the constitutional doctrine of the separation of powers'.[145]

However, what is manifestly clear is that the courts do not advocate a blanket 'hands off, no review' approach. Rather, a case which is prima facie non-justiciable might be justiciable on closer scrutiny, such as where it raises an international law question which 'in fact bears on the application of domestic law' or where 'the courts are able to isolate a pure question of law' from what appears to be a non-justiciable area. The separation of powers doctrine was to be 'interpreted and applied sensibly'. Rather than adopt a 'rigid and categorical approach' in deciding what was not justiciable, Menon JC recommended that the intensity would depend upon 'the context in which the issue arises and upon common sense', which considers that an unelected judiciary has no role with respect to certain questions.[146]

Pragmatism is imbued in the four guidelines provided. First, the views of the executive should be regarded as 'highly persuasive, if not decisive' where it has 'access to the best materials available to resolve the issue'. Second, the courts should shy away from reviewing the merits of government policy matters which requires 'the intricate balancing of various competing policy considerations' that judges are ill-equipped to adjudicate because 'of their limited training, experience and access to materials'. Third, the court should abstain from making pronouncements that might embarrass or impede the work of another branch of government regarding affairs traditionally falling within executive purview. Fourth, courts should exercise restraint in taking note of the fact that all branches of government are co-equal and that there are some areas of prerogative power democratically elected bodies are entrusted with, and that it is to the electorate rather than courts that the political branches are ultimately accountable.

V From 'no review' to 'calibrated review' of executive powers

Beyond the political questions doctrine, the shift from 'no review', which would be an abdication of the rule of law virtue of judicial control of government powers, to 'calibrated review' is evident in the exercise of other forms of executive power and in rights adjudication.[147] Judicial review's empire appears to have expanded to reject arguments that absolute discretion lay with respect to clemency powers, prosecutorial discretion, or the Prime Minister's powers to call by-elections. However, this principled availability of judicial review is moderated by judicial modesty in realising that certain decisions are best left to the elected branches of government as a matter of expertise or propriety, and deployed through calibrated intensities of review, presumptions of constitutionality, and assignment of the onus of proof, all of which inform the contours of the Singapore conception of the separation of powers.[148] Pragmatism as a method in this conception speaks of a trade-off or compromise, familiar to the 'balancing' method of interpretation. However, it still is necessary in the balancing process to have recourse to principle, to identify the background political philosophy in order to understand how balancing items are prioritised against each other, given that pragmatism is itself not value-neutral.

A Clemency and prosecutorial powers: Articles 22P and 35(8)

The Court of Appeal in *Ramalingam Ravinthran v AG*[149] moved away from a previously expressed view that the Public Prosecutor enjoyed 'wide discretion'[150] in determining what charges to prefer against a particular offender under Article 35(8). The case itself concerned the differential charging of two persons involved in the same drug-trafficking act: Ramalingam was charged with a capital offence and his accomplice, Sundar, with a non-capital offence under the Misuse of Drugs Act (Cap 185).

Consonant with the high constitutional office of the Public Prosecutor, the Court of Appeal stated that courts should apply a presumption of constitutionality or lawfulness with respect to an exercise of prosecutorial discretion, unless otherwise shown.[151] Such a presumption should not be regarded as judicial deference as it merely applies 'the established principle that the acts of high officials of state should be accorded a presumption of legality or regularity, especially where such acts are carried out in the exercise of constitutional powers'.[152]

However, this discretion was not absolute but subject to legal limits; the *Chng* rule of law principle was invoked to this effect.[153] Prosecutorial discretion could not be exercised arbitrarily or pursuant to an extraneous purpose; nor could it contravene constitutional rights such as the equal protection clause under Article 12. Within the Article 12(1) context, the court was required 'to give unbiased consideration to every offender and to avoid taking into account any irrelevant consideration'.[154] This embodies a limited model of review of Article 35(8), that constitutional powers were not immune from judicial correction.

Although Sundar had been, for the same criminal act, charged with an offence carrying a less onerous sentence, the court differentiated between Sundar and Ramalingam and found that Article 12 was not contravened. The Court of Appeal stressed there were 'many legitimate reasons' for a prosecution to differentiate between bringing charges against different offenders involved in same the same criminal enterprise.[155] Such differentiation per se does not raise an inference that Article 12(1) had been breached – as an absence of contrary prima facie evidence might;[156] the inference would be that the differentiation was based on 'relevant considerations'.

Aside from considerations of legal guilt, the Public Prosecutor must consider 'a wide range of factors'[157] in exercising power under Article 35(8), including the 'legitimate factor'[158] that Sundar had acted as prosecution witness, as well as these following extra-legal factors:

> [the] moral blameworthiness, the gravity of the harm caused to the public welfare by his criminal activity, and a myriad of other factors, including whether there is sufficient evidence against a particular offender, whether the offender is willing to co-operate with the law enforcement authorities in providing intelligence, whether one offender is willing to testify against his co-offenders, and so on – up to and including the possibility of showing some degree of compassion in certain cases.[159]

These policy-oriented factors which the Public Prosecutor can take into account when exercising prosecutorial discretion are matters not readily subject to judicial review; prosecutorial discretion might include factors such as the enforcement priorities of the Government which are 'not readily susceptible to the kind of analysis the courts are competent to undertake'.[160] Principled pragmatism cautions restraint in such cases.

With respect to the clemency power under Article 22P, the court in *Yong Vui Kong v AG*[161] noted that granting a pardon was an executive power conferred as a matter of grace, rather than of legal right. Decisions to pardon were based on policy considerations of public welfare, and the merits of the decision lay exclusively with the executive as a facet of the separation of powers.[162] However, as Article 22P was a constitutional power and not an extra-legal power beyond legal restraint,[163] it was subject to limited review on grounds including compliance with stipulated procedural safeguards and the rule against bias and bad faith, bearing in mind that presumptive legality applied and that individuals holding 'high constitutional offices' were engaged in the Article 22P decision-making process.[164]

B Calling by-elections under Article 49 – polycentricity, policy and exceptional review

While insisting on judicial review, courts hearing cases during this 'third wave' show sensitivity towards the boundaries of their power.[165] This manifestation of principled pragmatism is evident in *Vellama d/o Marie Muthu v* AG,[166] which involved an interpretation of Article 49, more specifically, that when a parliamentarian vacated his parliamentary seat, 'the vacancy shall be filled by election in the manner' provided by the Parliamentary Elections Act (Cap 218).

The High Court and Court of Appeal differed in their interpretive approach. The High Court focused on text, structure and history and read Article 49 as referring to the process or method of filling parliamentary seats. The Court of Appeal, on the other hand, gave determinative weight to constitutional theory, specifically, democratic and rule of law values. It read Article 49 as requiring an event to take place. It considered that history shed little light on how to construe Article 49, in relation to the fact that the time limit, which qualified Article 49 (or its precursors), was removed at independence in 1965. The lack of a specific time limit did not mean that the Prime Minister had absolute discretion as to when to call a by-election.[167] The Court of Appeal resorted to democratic theory to anchor its decision, noting that parliamentarians represented their voters and were 'the voice of the people of the constituency'.[168] Given the role of the Member of Parliament in a Westminster-based government, the Court of Appeal concluded that the Prime Minister was under a constitutional duty to call a by-election.[169] While this was a discretionary power, it was not unfettered; a limit was read into the interpretation and derived from Section 52 of the Interpretation Act (Cap 1), which prescribes the standard of 'with all convenient speed', thereby enshrining the common law concept of 'reasonable time'.[170] This transcended considerations of logistics and the court recognised that the question of when to hold by-elections was a 'polycentric matter' involving considerations 'beyond mere practicality'. In assessing reasonableness of conduct, it noted that no pre-determination of what constituted relevant considerations in the face of a 'dynamic situation' was warranted. Justified considerations could include the physical well-being of the country, such as delaying by-elections in the event of a public health crisis like SARs or the haze. Nonetheless, this discretion, which was subject to legal limits after the *Chng* principle, did not extend to indefinite delay, as an unrepresented constituency raised the 'serious risk of disenfranchising the residents of that constituency'.[171]

The Court of Appeal deployed the terminology of 'balance' in expressing the need to strike a *via media* between the Prime Minister's 'substantial measure of discretion'[172] and voter rights in a parliamentary system and noted the fact-sensitive' nature of valid exercises of discretion. It concluded by emphasising that judicial review would only be exceptionally warranted; review was available, but would be rare. This reflects a form of deference as respect for the executive, according weight to its reasons but nonetheless evaluating these reasons and indicating that these could be rejected if found to stray beyond the range of defensible reasonable options with respect to the law and facts. As a matter of principle, the court would not abdicate its responsibility to prevent abuses of public power and refused a posture of submissive deference. As a matter of pragmatism, it appreciated that restraint was prudent and deferential respect warranted, where faced with extra-legal considerations.

VI Separation of powers, democracy and public morals legislation

Singapore courts have demonstrated restraint in constitutional cases where the 'morals question' doctrine arises. This arises most frequently in cases involving the equality guarantee under Article 12. Equality is an empty concept in the sense that it is parasitic on an independent substantive theory that is needed if we are to know when differences drawn between two objects are permissible or legitimate.[173] This is necessary as legislation of necessity draws distinctions. It is thus susceptible to political capture, in service of any agenda and notably, there is wide and wild disagreement on what should be equal to what.

The Singapore courts in reading Article 12 have been informed by a sense of perspective and proportion and have avoided what may be described as a 'dogmatic and finical approach'.[174] The constitutional test adopted and consistently affirmed has been that of 'reasonable classification', which comes with a strong presumption of constitutionality[175] predicated on the view that Parliament best understands the needs of the people. In declining to adopt more intrusive tests of review, such as that of proportionality, the courts have been strongly influenced by separation of powers considerations, as where social policy issues are characterised as matters of legislative concern.[176] This has included issues pertaining to the constitutionality of the mandatory death penalty under the Misuse of Drugs Act (Cap 185),[177] of the caning regime under the 2012 amended Misuse of Drugs Act[178] and of provisions criminalising acts of gross indecency between two males in public or private under section 377A of the Penal Code (Cap 224).[179]

The reasonable classification test as the standard to be applied in judicial intervention is a pragmatic formula. The first limb requires that the legislative classification be based on 'intelligible differentia'. The second limb requires that this differentia bear a 'rational relation' to the statutory objective. Intelligibility is a 'relatively low threshold' designed to avoid a consideration of 'substantive moral, political and/or ethical issues', which could be controversial, because reasonable people can have reasonable disagreement on many issues. The courts were not to engage in resolving such issues except where a legal point is involved.[180] They were confined to 'requiring logic and coherence' in the relevant statute, serving a 'minimal threshold function', as the first limb is oriented towards 'value neutrality'.[181]

Over- or under-classifications are not fatal, as they might be under proportionality review, which is indicative of the wide latitude given to legislative choices. For example, in testing the reasonableness of the differentia where traffickers dealing with at least 15 g of heroin were subject to the mandatory death penalty, the Court of Appeal in *Yong Vui Kong v PP*[182] required that the quantity of trafficked drugs be 'broadly proportionate' to such factors as the drug dealers' scale of operations and degree of harm posed to society, that is, the legislative purpose of the relevant Act. The differentia utilised did not have to be 'the most effective means' to achieve the statutory objective as long as it was 'not one so far removed' from the objective which would result in 'an unreasonable and unjust relation between the two'.[183] All that is needed is a plausible relation between classification and objective, as opposed to a more stringent requirement that a classification be 'least restrictive' in relation to rights. Where 'plausible justifications' exist for legislation 'within the context of Singapore's societal mores and norms' and where Parliament has adopted a clear position over a contested issue, the courts 'should not readily dismiss the views of one portion of society in favour of those of another portion of society'.[184] If the differentia was 'broadly effective' to achieve the objective, the court was not to displace Parliament's decision in prescribing the legislative classification. This is because as reasonable people could disagree upon what constituted the most effective differentia to secure the legislative object, 'this matter lay within the legislative and not judicial province, being a matter of social policy'. The courts must respect 'the constitutional role of the legislature', which required that they did not second-guess whether Parliament could have 'devised a more efficacious differentia'.[185]

Nonetheless, although the reasonable classification test is a low threshold test, it does not mean that legislation cannot be impugned as unconstitutional. The onus is on the party impugning the legislation 'to place relevant materials and evidence before the court'.[186] The pragmatic judge harbours great enthusiasm for using empirical materials and social sciences data to resolve constitutional issues. Singapore courts are cautious but not entirely closed to statistical data as an avenue for questioning legislative wisdom, opening the door to the issue of how might weight be ascribed to the views of Parliament embodied in legislation.[187] In *Nguyen Tuong Van v PP*,[188] the Court of Appeal noted an Indian case where the lack of sociological data showing that life convicts had a greater propensity to commit murder meant there was 'no rational justification' to treat life convicts differently from other prisoners and to subject them to a mandatory death sentence under section 303 of the Indian Penal Code. In *Nguyen* itself, no 'comparable material'[189] was submitted to assess whether the 15 g classification under the Misuse of Drugs Act was supportable. This seems to indicate a willingness to consider such materials. This reflects some pragmatic sensibility in not being blind to social realities when developing the law. However, there is considerable caution in considering these non-traditional factors. For instance, in discussing the deterrent effect of the mandatory death penalty (MDP) in *Yong Vui Kong v PP*[190], Chan CJ acknowledged that it was arguable whether there was insufficient evidence that the MDP did indeed deter serious crimes such as murder, but 'it can equally be said that there is insufficient evidence that the MDP does not have such a deterrent effect'. He noted that statistical studies and surveys from one country could 'never be conclusive' where another country was concerned. The issue was a policy question best left to legislative purview.[191]

As a matter of principle and pragmatism, the Court of Appeal rejected the High Court's view in *Lim Meng Suang* that a test of legitimacy of legislative objective may apply 'over and above its power of scrutinising legislation pursuant to the reasonable classification test'.[192] This is because such a test would confer a judicial licence to usurp the legislative function in declaring a legislative object illegitimate. It would involve the court 'adjudicating on controversial issues of policy, ethics or social values' falling within the legislative sphere.[193] This reflects a commitment to a principled understanding of separation of powers in avoiding questions of moral controversy and affirming the legislative management of such questions. One might also detect the pragmatic desire not to embroil the court in issues where there is no clear legal standard to apply. However, the Court of Appeal noted that a statute could be struck down for violating Article 12(1) where there were 'serious flaws' regarding the intelligibility of its legislative differentia, or where a clear disconnect existed between the differentia and legislative purpose. This incorporated a 'limited element of illegitimacy' as *an aspect* of the reasonable classification test, not independent of it.[194] Where legislative classifications manifested 'extreme illogicality and/or incoherence', a statute would fail the reasonable classification test and violate Article 12.[195] The Court of Appeal in *Yong Vui Kong* (2015) further elaborated upon the reasonable classification test by stating that statutes with a 'manifestly discriminatory object' would fail its first limb; it imported a moral rather than logical element into 'unintelligible' by understanding it in the sense that 'no *reasonable* person would consider such a differentiating factor to be functional as an intelligible differentia' even if such differentia clearly identifies what is and is not covered by law.[196] Such cases would 'necessarily be rare',[197] which speaks to judicial restraint as well as the desire to reserve to the court the inherent power to do justice in extreme cases where non-intervention would outrage the moral conscience, primordial considerations of humanity, or any other descriptor that thinly veils a natural law justice-based impulse.

Nonetheless, the courts have sought to give a wide berth to ideologically driven arguments which diverge from deliberative legislative choices. The judicially endorsed 'reasonable classification' test, which speaks of restrained judicial review in not dogmatically insisting upon perfect classifications, allows them space to manoeuvre in this regard. For example, the Court of Appeal in *Yong Vui Kong v PP* (2015) rejected an argument that it was patronising and outdated to regard females as the more delicate sex requiring protection, as a justification for exempting them from caning as a punishment.[198] It made the common sense observation that there were 'obvious physiological differences' between male and female, which Parliament could legitimately consider in prescribing punishments; exempting women from caning reflected the 'moral sense of the community', which was legislatively captured. As such, it was inappropriate for the court to 'pass judgment on the soundness or rationality of such gendered social attitudes'.[199] It was uninfluenced by the rhetorical labelling of the caning regime as a 'colonial relic', again referring to legislative choice as a proxy for extant mainstream social attitudes. The fact that the caning regime was re-enacted in a 2010 amendment to the Criminal Procedure Code indicated that social attitudes towards the acceptability of inflicting corporal punishment on women had 'yet to change'; the social values underlying this regime which might have originated from a colonial era law was, in fact, ratified and represented contemporary opinion.[200]

The age of a law is itself indifferent to its merits or otherwise, unless one is a chronological snob or easily swayed by emotional assertions. Review is available but restrained, and the courts have refused to be drawn into making value judgments on social policies, which they consider resides within the province of the legislature. The 'reasonable classification' test adopted reflects this principled sensibility in delineating the boundaries of the various government branches and in pragmatically not upsetting legislative will.

A last point worth making relates to matters pertaining to the constitutional concept of public morality,[201] which conceptually differs from the morality of the majority, which may be located in legislative enactments. Where public morals legislation is concerned, one of the issues raised is whether law should

enforce public morality.[202] The courts are unconcerned with purely rhetorical arguments, such as the argument that section 377A of the Penal Code represented the 'tyranny of the majority'. Indeed, this could be turned on its head with the majority insisting they not be subjected to the 'tyranny of the minority' as the Court of Appeal observed in *Lim Meng Suang*.[203] Jurisprudential arguments relating to the Millian Harm principle and competing conceptions of intangible harm, as well as Lord Devlin's argument that law could regulate societal morality, were considered matters appropriate to the legislative sphere.[204] Thus, in relation to matters muddied by politicised science, such as whether homosexuality was immutable, the courts have observed that medical and scientific evidence remained 'divided and inconclusive at best' and that 'plausible evidence' existed for both sides of the argument. In adopting a posture of ambivalence over charged controversies, the courts have sought to defuse emotion rather than pour oil onto fire by 'affirming' one side, recognising that both sides have deep moral claims and recognising that the responsibility for this political decision lay with the legislature.[205] It demonstrated a concern not to engage in heavy-handed judicial intervention 'ahead of democratic change',[206] as exemplified in the anti-model of the still contentious US decision of *Roe v Wade*.[207]

Thus, while Quentin Loh J recognised in *Lim Meng Suang* that even where society has shifted towards one side in relation to a controversial issue, the appropriate judicial role was that of an interlocutor rather than final adjudicator, where courts could 'call on Parliament to consider changing the law'.[208] This recognises the primacy of judicial decision-making over social policy or moral questions which are primarily questions about value choice rather than interpretation. Change should be channelled through political actors,[209] in the view of those who support the legislative rather than judicial model of moral reasoning.[210] Legislative reasoning with many individuals participating in the debate is a method of 'reasoning in the name of a whole society' when it is appropriate that the issue be debated on the merits unconstrained by existing texts, doctrines or precedents, such as in relation to watershed rights issues or 'major issues of political philosophy'.[211] The Singapore court in its insistence that it cannot be a mini-legislature[212] subscribes to this view. It distances itself from alternative views that see the court as a 'forum of principle'[213] which promotes a political conception of justice celebrating 'the priority of the right over the good'.[214] In principle, the courts do not entirely disavow the power, albeit in rare cases, to say that 'a certain principle of law is outmoded and should no longer be enforced'.[215] However, this is tempered by the pragmatic bent when speaking to social change, to recognise the primary responsibilities shouldered by the legislature and to adopt the tone of persuasion and recommendation, rather than to impose dogma through judicial *diktats*.

VII Concluding observations: principled pragmatism – between the nightmare and the noble dream?

This chapter has set forth the proposition that 'principled pragmatism' is a descriptively accurate term for describing the interpretive approach and jurisprudence of the 'third wave' Singapore bench. It also argues that this brand of normative realism has virtues against both an activist form of review which privileges the substantive values of judges and an inert form of review which has no predictive or protective value, bearing in mind the constitutional role of the courts in restraining abuses of constitutional powers. Principled pragmatism may be seen to tread a line between judicial hubris and judicial obsequiousness, between 'law as politics' and rigid legal formalism, to stake a claim between the Hartian Nightmare and the Noble Dream,[216] in aid of preserving the distinctive identity of courts as impartial dispute arbiters.

In principle, Singapore courts today are not disposed towards refusing judicial review, although review itself might be restrained, limited or exceptional, owing to pragmatic considerations. In terms of methodology, the courts hold firm to maintaining a distinction between law and politics, legal and extra-legal considerations. However, this is not done in an unconscious or dogmatic fashion as 'we do not believe in fairy tales any more', as associated with the idea that judges only declare rather than make law.[217] Courts are aware and accept that courts 'make' law but being 'separate and distinct from the Legislature' as a facet of the separation of powers, this is 'only permissible in the context of the interpretation of statutes and the development of the principles of common law and equity'. Courts cannot 'arrogate to themselves legislative powers'. While having a duty to 'interpret' statutes, courts cannot 'amend or modify statutes' based on their 'own personal preference or fiat'.[218] In other words, they will not accede to invitations to adopt a 'more activist'[219] approach as 'bold spirits' when this entails acting beyond their jurisdictional sphere, invoking extra-legal considerations to declare statutes illegitimate which would permit appellants '*to obtain by the (judicial) backdoor what they ought to have sought to obtain by the (legislative) front door*'.[220] Arguments that a focus on relevant 'legal arguments' was tantamount to the court acting 'like an ostrich whose head is buried in the sand' insofar as it was ignoring the need 'to achieve a substantively fair result' were rightly rejected on two scores. First, that there was no reason why a 'substantively fair result' could not be achieved by consideration of legal arguments. Second, if the court were to transgress its 'legitimate jurisdiction' in considering extra-legal arguments within the purview of Parliament, this would be contrary to both substantive and procedural fairness.[221]

Clearly, courts are concerned about maintaining institutional legitimacy, which is derived from the discipline of argument and public reason-giving, and preserving public confidence in the administration of justice. If the court is seen as a forerunner in social reform, so as to become decision-makers indistinguishable from the legislative chamber, this could thwart expectations and elicit a political backlash and demise in public support. Nonetheless, the Singapore courts, while evincing a distaste for the spectre of juristocracy and judicialised politics, accept a dialogical function when it comes to questions of moral controversy where it speaks in the language of recommendation rather than adjudication in respect of legislative will and democratic legitimacy.

To maintain judicial prestige, impartiality – actual and perceived – must be preserved; there must be some limits on the decisional freedom of judges who must and do demonstrate fealty to a principled form of decision-making. Unlike other jurisdictions where the political branches are dysfunctional, law is not seen as a corrective for failed politics. Trust in political constitutionalism is more apparent in the restraint the courts adopt where matters of non-judicial expertise or of democratic legitimacy arise. Deference to the political branches is less a matter of subservience and more one of respect for the institutional relationships, the superior qualities of other decision-makers or for prudential reasons.[222] Courts will not override the decisions of political branches, even if they are critical of them, just because they can think of a better alternative.[223]

There is thus an appreciation that constitutionalism is evident where public power is constrained to ensure it does not subvert the values it seeks to promote, and that the judicial role is central to this project and must not capitulate in anaemic fashion to political will. The accent is on the separation of powers in the delineation of the scope of judicial review within a communitarian polity, which avoids confrontation with the political branches and escapes charges of a legitimacy deficit which undue judicial legislation attracts. Its context-sensitive standard of review prioritises the particular and practical, moderated by constitutional principle; continuity is prized, yet principled change is possible.

Singapore courts have consistently held to the faith/fiction that 'Law' is objective; in the third wave, the courts maintain fidelity to legal craft and embrace the discipline of judicial reasoning by reference to text, history, structure, precedent shared values, sound analysis and logic. They strenuously reject the result-oriented reasoning evident in the brand of legal pragmatism which sees no duty to abide by legal texts and promotes rights-based liberal constitutionalism. The Singapore brand of principled pragmatism is not given to excessive abstraction, does not see historic intent as trivial or harmful, takes text seriously and embraces the judicial discipline of structured, reason-giving culture, sensitive to the question of what reasons are relevant to a judge. It operates in the tone of moderation, akin to a 'common law' 'incremental change' method of adjudication where the wisdom of past authorities is distilled, without loss of the critical capacity to reject or modify past approaches. It is committed to the distinctive quality of legal reasoning.[224]

Judicial reasoning evinces a commitment to maintain a law/politics distinction in an age where this is decried by realists and sceptics. This may be for various reasons. First, as a principle of judicial restraint and aspiration, where the debate hovers over the acceptable degree of judicial law-making. A second reason may relate to the public image of the court, as embedded in the declaratory theory's vision of the judicial role. This theory, which the courts have observed is 'no longer part of the current orthodoxy',[225] posits that judges find and apply pre-existing law to the immediate case, rather than make it. Mishkin argued that 'the image of the declaratory judge has strong public appeal' in relation to the American context, although this observation might equally apply to how the Singapore public understands the judicial decision-making process:

> The declaratory theory expresses a symbolic concept of the judicial process on which much of the court's prestige and power depend. This is the

> strongly held and deeply felt belief that judges are bound by a body of fixed overriding law, that they apply that law impersonally as well as impartially, that they exercise no individual choice and have no program of their own to advance.[226]

This is reflected in this judicial statement:

> Drawing such *a line in the legal sand* is imperative. If this is not done, the court will necessarily be sucked into and thereby descend into the *political* arena, which would in turn undermine (or even destroy) the very role which constitutes the *raison d'être* for the court's existence in the first place – namely, to furnish an *independent, neutral and objective* forum for deciding, on the basis of objective legal rules and principles (*inter alia*), what rights parties have in a given situation.[227]

Efforts to maintain a distinction between 'law' and 'politics' may well involve a latter day telling of what Plato called a 'noble lie'; noble because of its 'civic purpose' to inspire ruler or, at least, citizen to care for the city[228] or in contemporary parlance, to be devoted or committed to a constitutional order, to nurture some form of constitutional patriotism, within liberal or non-liberal polities.[229] Through fostering national loyalty, social stability is promoted. The maintenance of a law–politics distinction (rather than law/politics dichotomy) might also be dependent on what has been called the 'Tinkerbell Effect'[230] (something exists as long as you believe that it does), whereby the urge to distinguish between the 'lawfulness' or 'political' quality of something remains forever aspirational, never to be perfectly realised, but it nonetheless serves as a useful aspiration and orientation which feeds into judicial postures, self-image and reasoning processes.

This objectivity of law as a key cornerstone of 'principled pragmatism' may be criticised for being mythical or impossible, but like originalism, it might constitute the 'lesser evil'.[231] It positions judges not to have to don the garb of an indefatigable idealist desiring an unrealisable utopia, or to capitulate to serving as apologists for the status quo. Law must serve the virtues of consistency and legality, without neglecting its normative dimensions or disregarding local traits such as a predilection towards communitarianism. In this sense, 'principled pragmatism' is an imperfect interpretive approach for an imperfect world, and that is not necessarily a bad thing.

Notes

1 *Mohammad Faizal bin Sabtu v Public Prosecutor* [2012] SGHC 163, [2012] 4 SLR 947 [27].
2 ibid [17].
3 *Lim Meng Suang v Attorney-General* [2014] SGCA 53, [2015] 1 SLR 26 [5] ['*Lim Meng Suang (CA)*'].
4 *Mohd Faizal* (n 1) [16] (Chan CJ).

5 *Edwards v Canada (Attorney-General)* [1930] AC 124 (PC) 124; *Reference Re Same Sex Marriage* [2004] 3 SCR 698 (Supreme Court of Canada) [22].
6 Michael J Klarman, 'What's So Great About Constitutionalism?' (1998) 93 Northwestern University Law Review 145, 162.
7 VK Rajah, 'Interpreting the Singapore Constitution', Chapter 1 of this book.
8 *Yong Vui Kong v Public Prosecutor* [2010] SGCA 20, [2010] 3 SLR 489 [122] ['*Yong Vui Kong (2010)*'].
9 Article 4, Republic of Singapore Constitution: The High Court in *Mohd Faizal* (n 1) [14] noted that 'Singapore's Westminster model is based on the supremacy of the Singapore Constitution'.
10 A controlled constitution (unlike an uncontrolled one) is one that must be amended by a super-majority, rather than a simple parliamentary majority: *McCawley v The King* [1920] 28 CLR 106 (PC) 114–15. Where parliament is supreme, the non-documentary constitution is amended by a simple majority.
11 *Lim Meng Suang (CA)* (n 3) [92].
12 What Bickel called the 'counter-majoritarian difficulty', given the super-majoritarian commitment to the supremacy of the constitution as a check on contemporary politics; competing theories include what has been known as the 'dead-hand' problem, the question of why the current generation of contemporary majorities should be bound by the dictate of past (dead) generations (rule from the grave). See Alexander Bickel, *The Least Dangerous Branch: The Supreme Court at the Bar of Politics* (Yale University Press 1962). Arguments that assert that courts have a democratic function in providing multiple routes to power bring to the fore the real question at issue: what sort of democracy do we want?
13 Richard A Posner, *The Problematics of Moral and Legal Theory* (Belknap Press of Harvard University Press 1999) 240.
14 Richard Rorty, 'The Professor and the Prophet' (1992) 52 Transition 70, 75.
15 Thomas C Grey, 'Judicial Review and Legal Pragmatism' (2003) 38 Wake Forest Law Review 473; Andrew J Morris, 'Some Challenges for Legal Pragmatism: A Closer look at Pragmatic Legal Reasoning' (2007) 28 Northern Illinois University Law Review 1; Christopher H Schroeder, 'Some Notes on a Principled Pragmatism' (2007) 95 California Law Review 1703.
16 Oliver Wendell Holmes Jr, 'The Path of the Law' (1897) 10 Harvard Law Review 457, 460–61: 'The prophecies of what the courts will do in fact, and nothing more pretentious, are what I mean by the law.'
17 Brian Tamanaha, 'Pragmatism in US Legal Theory: Its Application to Normative Jurisprudence, Sociolegal Studies and the Fact-Value Distinction' (1996) 41 American Journal of Jurisprudence 315, 354.
18 EW Thomas, *The Judicial Process: Realism, Pragmatism, Practical Reasoning and Principles* (Cambridge University Press 2008) 18.
19 Thomas (n 18) 77, 80.
20 James Grant, 'The Rise of Juristocracy' (2010) 34(2) Wilson Quarterly 16.
21 Mark S Kende, 'Constitutional Pragmatism, The Supreme Court and Democratic Revolution' (2012) 89(3) Denver University Law Review 635.
22 *Chng Suan Tze v Minister for Home Affairs* [1988] SGCA 16, [1988] 2 SLR (R) 525 [86]; *Public Prosecutor v Taw Cheng Kong* [1988] SGCA 37, [1998] 2 SLR (R) 489 [89].
23 Kevin YL Tan and Thio Li-ann, *50 Constitutional Moments that Defined a Nation* (Marshall Cavendish 2015) (forthcoming).
24 [1985] 1 AC 374 (HL).
25 *Lee Mau Seng v Minister for Home Affairs* [1971] SGHC 10, [1971–1973] SLR(R) 135.
26 (Cap 143).
27 *Lee Mau Seng* (n 25) [54].

28 *Chng Suan Tze* (n 22).
29 ibid [56].
30 ibid [86].
31 As set out in the Internal Security Act.
32 For example, in *Teo Soh Lung v Minister of Home Affairs* [1990] SGCA 5, [1990] 1 SLR(R) 347 [44], the Court of Appeal declined to consider whether judicial review under the new Internal Security Act amendments were subject to 'red hair' review, whether the amendments were beyond the extraordinary law-making power conferred by Article 149 or whether the amendments violated the basic structure of the Constitution. See also Michael Hor, 'Constitutionalism and Subversion: An Exploration' in Li-ann Thio and Kevin YL Tan (eds), *Evolution of a Revolution: Forty Years of the Singapore Constitution* (Routledge-Cavendish 2009).
33 As Yash Ghai points out,

> The community and state are different institutions ... The community ... depends on popular norms developed through forms of consensus and which are enforced through mediation and persuasion. The state is an imposition on society and unless humanized and democratized ... it relies on edicts, the military, coercion and sanctions. It is the tension between them which has underpinned human rights.
> Yash Ghai, 'Asian Perspectives on Human Rights' (1993) 23(3) Hong Kong Law Journal 342, 352

34 In rejecting an American 'clear and immediate danger' test as a test for legitimate restrictions on religious freedom, Yong CJ in *Colin Chan v Public Prosecutor* [1994] SGHC 207, [1994] 3 SLR(R) 209 [59] said that if such a test applied, it would be 'too late' as the danger sought to be prevented 'would have transpired'. Further, 'any administration which perceives the possibility of trouble over religious beliefs and yet prefers to wait until trouble is just about to break out before taking action must be not only pathetically naïve but also grossly incompetent'.
35 ibid [72]: Yong CJ, in upholding a blanket ban on Jehovah Witnesses' publications issued under the Undesirable Publications Act, declared (without investigating how many publications were produced within a specific time frame) that 'any order other than a total blanket order would have been impossible to monitor administratively'.
36 In response to an argument that not to read in an implied right to be told of an existing right to counsel would 'effectively amount to a negation of the right to counsel itself', Yong CJ said that this was 'pushing the case too far'. Without further reasoning or citing authority, he barely stated: 'The practical experiences in our judicial system bear testimony to the fact that such a conclusion is wholly speculative and unwarranted': *Rajeevan Edakalavan v Public Prosecutor* [1998] SGHC 2, [1998] 1 SLR (R) 10 [21].
37 Although the High Court in *Colin Chan* (n 44) [51] advocated interpreting a constitution primarily within its own 'four walls', it was receptive to foreign precedents which advocated the primacy of statist values, such as the wartime Australian case of *Adelaide Co of Jehovah's Witnesses Inc v The Commonwealth* (1943) 67 CLR 116 (HCA), approvingly discussed at [60]–[61].
38 *Public Prosecutor v Mazlan bin Maidun* [1992] 3 SLR (R) 968 [13].
39 *Ong Ah Chuan v Public Prosecutor* [1980] SGPC 6, [1979–1980] SLR(R) 710 [26]–[27].
40 *Mazlan* (n 38) [14].
41 ibid [17].
42 [1998] SGHC 2, [1998] 1 SLR (R) 10.
43 *Ong Ah Chuan* (n 39) [23].
44 *Colin Chan v Public Prosecutor* [1994] SGHC 207, [1994] 3 SLR(R) 209.
45 ibid [78].
46 [2003] SGHC 122, [2003] 2 SLR 445.

47 ibid [20].

48 There are earlier decisions that suggest that a test of 'reasonableness' in terms of evaluating statutory restrictions on free speech may apply, insofar as a statutory scheme predicated on absolute discretion could not be constitutional: *Jeyaretnam Joshua Benjamin v Public Prosecutor* [1989] SGHC 90, 2 SLR (R) 419.

49 Eg *Peter Williams Nappalli v Institute of Technical Education* [1998] SGHC 351 [46].

50 For example, there was an extended discussion of whether or not the *Reynolds* qualified privilege defence to defamation would be imported into Singapore in *Review Publishing v Lee Hsien Loong* [2009] SGCA 46, [2010] 1 SLR 52, a defence which may apply to citizens, even though the case itself only involved non-citizens. In more recent times, the court has reined in the tendency to exposit, as where it did not decide whether the basic features doctrine was part of Singapore law because it was not at issue in *Yong Vui Kong v Public Prosecutor* [2015] SGCA 11, [2015] 2 SLR 1129 [72].

51 Thio Li-ann, *A Treatise on Singapore Constitutional Law* (Academy Publishing 2012) xiii.

52 *Yong Vui Kong (2010)* (n 8) [58]; *Lim Meng Suang (CA)* (n 3) [6], [162]. There was a reference to Rousseau in the 1998 High Court decision of *Taw Cheng Kong v Public Prosecutor* [1998] SGHC 10, [1998] 1 SLR(R) 78 [54], but this was unusual for its time.

53 *Ramalingam Ravinthran v Attorney-General* [2012] SGCA 2, [2012] 2 SLR 49 [42]. In the administrative law context, whether to import in substantive legitimate expectations was also examined from 'first principles': *Chiu Teng @ Kallang Pte Ltd v Singapore Land Authority* [2013] SGHC 262, [2014] 1 SLR 1047 [111].

54 *Attorney-General v Shadrake Alan* [2011] 2 SLR 445 [43], [50]–[51] ('*Shadrake No. 1*').

55 This was the case of *Jabar bin Kadermastan v Public Prosecutor* [1995] 1 SLR(R) 326, as discussed by the Court of Appeal in *Yong Vui Kong (2010)* (n 8) [17]–[19].

56 *Public Prosecutor v Koh Song Huat Benjamin* [2005] SGDC 272 [8].

57 *Shared Values*:

> While stressing communitarianism, we must remember that in Singapore society the individual also has rights which should be respected and not lightly encroached upon. The shared values should make it clear that we are seeking a balance between the community and the individual, not promoting one to the exclusion of the other.
>
> Parliament of Singapore, *Shared Values White Paper* (Cmd 1, 1991) para 30

58 *Public Prosecutor v Kwong Kok Hing* [2008] SGCA 10, [2008] 2 SLR 684 [17].

59 [2009] 4 SLR(R) 1018 [23].

60 The law is taken seriously as a potential source of correct or preferable norms of human conduct: see Peter Cane, 'Taking Law Seriously: Starting Points of the Hart/Devlin Debate' (2006) 10 Journal of Ethics 21, 26.

61 The prosecution of the drug trafficker but not an undercover police officer involved in the entrapment was held not to violate the equal protection clause, because without entrapment, which had a deterrent effect, many instances of drug trading, which posed a 'grave menace' to society (even if it may be considered a 'victimless crime' involving two consenting adults in a private transaction), would be hard to detect: *Mohamed Emran bin Mohamed Ali v Public Prosecutor* [2008] SGHC 103, [2008] 4 SLR 411.

62 *Yong Vui Kong v Attorney-General* [2011] SGCA 9, [2011] 2 SLR 1189 [*Yong Vui Kong (2011)*].

63 ibid [79].

64 *Law Society of Singapore v Tan Guat Neo Phyllis* [2007] SGHC 207, [2008] 2

SLR(R) 239; *Ramalingam* (n 53) [51]; *Vellama d/o Marie Muthu v Attorney-General* [2013] SGCA 391, [2013] 4 SLR 1 [85].

65 *Yong Vui Kong (2011)* (n 62) [139], affirmed in *Ramalingam* (n 53) [45]–[47].

66 *Jeyaretnam Kenneth Andrew v Attorney-General* [2013] SGCA 56, [2014] 1 SLR 345 [35], [48]–[50].

67 *Vellama* (n 64) [79], [85].

68 'Balancing' as opposed to categoric reasoning is pragmatically oriented, as it consists not of applying the priority of peremptory rights but balancing all relevant interests. T Alexander Aleinikoff in 'Constitutional Law in the Age of Balancing' (1987) 96 Yale Law Journal 943 notes that 'balancing' is anti-theory as it shifts the focus from categoric rights to the question of whether a decision which restricts rights was reasonable in all circumstances. This was the approach adopted in *Chee Siok Chin v Minister for Home Affairs* [2005] SGHC 216, [2006] 1 SLR (R) 582 [126].

69 *Koh Song Huat Benjamin* (n 56). The courts have also greatly expanded upon the value of non-constitutional interests such as reputation in the context of political defamation: see *Lee Hsien Loong v Singapore Democracy Party* [2008] SGHC 173, [2009] 1 SLR 642; *Lim Eng Hock Peter v Lin Jian Wei* [2010] SGCA 26, [2010] 4 SLR 357.

70 *Shadrake No. 1* (n 54) [57].

71 *Review Publishing v Lee Hsien Loong* [2009] SGCA 46, [2010] 1 SLR 52 [286]–[289].

72 *Chee Siok Chin v Minister for Home Affairs* [2005] SGHC 216, [2006] 1 SLR(R) 582 [135], [202].

73 See generally, Thio (n 51) 610–27.

74 [1994] SGCA 46, [1994] 1 SLR(R) 782.

75 As discussed in *James Raj s/o Ariokiasamy v Public Prosecutor* [2014] SGHC 10, [2014] 2 SLR 307 [3]–[5].

76 ibid.

77 ibid [6].

78 The Court of Appeal affirmed that *Jasbir* represented settled and good law in *James Raj s/o Arokiasamy v Public Prosecutor* [2014] SGCA 33 at [36].

79 ibid [12].

80 ibid [14].

81 [2008] SGHC 218, [2009] 1 SLR(R) 1103.

82 ibid [33].

83 *Shadrake No. 1* (n 54) [47]–[48].

84 *Attorney-General v Tan Liang Joo John* [2009] SGHC 41, [2009] 2 SLR(R) 1132.

85 *Shadrake No. 1* (n 54) [70]–[76]; *Shadrake Alan v Attorney-General* [2011] SGCA 26, [2011] 3 SLR 778 [81]–[82] (the Court of Appeal thought fair criticism went towards liability for contempt of court rather than acting as a defence).

86 *Tan Liang Joo John* (n 84) [16].

87 ibid [19].

88 [1994] SGCA 148, [1994] 2 SLR 689. While Privy Council decisions did not bind the Court of Appeal, they would be departed from sparingly. However, in taking note of the enormous changes in the 'political, social and economic circumstances of Singapore' since independence, it asserted that 'the development of our law should reflect these changes and the fundamental values of Singapore society'.

89 Notably during the 'first wave' in *Haw Tua Tau v Public Prosecutor* [1981] 2 MLJ 49 (PC), the Privy Council stated that in construing the meaning of law in Article 9(1) which incorporated fundamental rules of natural justice, reference could be made to comparative cases as well as international human rights documents like the 1948 Universal Declaration of Human Rights and the 1950 European Convention on Human Rights. See generally, Thio Li-ann, 'Trends in Constitutional Interpretation: Oppugning Ong, Awakening Arumugam?' (1997) Singapore Journal of Legal

Studies 240 on 'first wave' cases; for 'second wave' cases, see Li-ann Thio, 'Beyond the "Four Walls" in an Age of Transnational Judicial Conversations: Civil Liberties, Rights Theories and Constitutional Adjudication in Malaysia and Singapore' (2006) 19(2) Columbia Journal of Asian Law 428.

90 The court said:

> The ban was therefore described by the appellants as being, in the circumstances, irrational, oppressive, unreasonable, overboard, a violation of the freedom of religion as enshrined in the constitution and also a violation of international declarations of human rights. All things being said, I think that the issues here are best resolved by a consideration of the provisions of the Constitution, the Societies Act and the UPA alone.
>
> *Colin Chan* (n 44) [54]

91 [1991] SGHC 8, [1991] 1 SLR(R) 85 [38].

92 *Shadrake Alan v Attorney-General* [2011] SGCA 26, [2011] 3 SLR 778 [31] [*Shadrake (CA)*].

93 *Jeyaretnam Joshua Benjamin v Lee Kuan Yew* [1992] SGCA 27, [1992] 1 SLR(R) 791, rejecting *New York Times v Sullivan* (1964) 376 US 254 (Supreme Court of the USA).

94 *Jabar bin Kadermastan v Public Prosecutor* [1995] SGCA 18, [1995] 1 SLR(R) 326, citing the case of *Richmond v Lewis* 948 F 2d 1373 (US Court of Appeals, Ninth Circuit) in relation to the 'death row phenomenon'.

95 Eg *Yong Vui Kong (2010)* (n 8).

96 *Nguyen Tuong Van v Public Prosecutor* [2004] SGCA 47, [2005] 1 SLR(R) 103 [91]–[92].

97 *Yong Vui Kong (2010)* (n 8).

98 ibid [98].

99 *Yong Vui Kong v Public Prosecutor* [2015] SGCA 11, [2015] 2 SLR 1129 [76]–[99] [*Yong Vui Kong (2015)*].

100 *Public Prosecutor v Tan Cheng Yew* [2012] SGHC 241, [2013] 1 SLR 1095 [56].

101 *The 'Sahand'* [2011] SGHC 27, [2011] 2 SLR 1093.

102 *Yong Vui Kong (2010)* (n 8) [91].

103 *Yong Vui Kong (2015)* (n 99) [26]–[38].

104 *Yong Vui Kong (2010)* (n 8) [59], [61]–[72], [122]. Where the framers of the Constitution deliberately considered an 'anti-torture' clause for inclusion into the constitutional text, which eventually was not included, this prevented the courts from importing the contents of such a clause in through another more general provision, as this would be tantamount to legislation 'under the guise of constitutional interpretation'.

105 *Yong Vui Kong (2015)* (n 99) [50].

106 The USA free speech model is rejected in *Shadrake (CA)* (n 92) [41], which described the 'clear and present danger' test as rooted in the 'unique culture' of the First Amendment, pointing out that making free speech paramount

> is *not*, with respect, *necessarily* an approach that *ought* to be emulated as it could actually result in possible *abuse* and *consequent negation* of the right itself. This is no mere parochial rhetoric but is, rather, premised on logic and commonsense. Hence, it is no surprise, therefore, that jurisdictions across the Commonwealth (including Singapore) adopt, instead, the approach from *balance*…

107 In relation to political defamation, the Court of Appeal in *Review Publishing* (n 71) [297] contemplated borrowing the UK *Reynolds* test of 'responsible journalism' as a defence or qualified privilege to libel, but rather than applying it to questions of liability, it could be modified to be a relevant factor 'in adjusting the quantum of damages payable' as this would deter irresponsible journalism.

108 *Nguyen Tuong Van* (n 96) [88].
109 *Tang Kin Hwa v Traditional Chinese Medicine Practitioners Board* [2005] SGHC 153, [2005] 4 SLR(R) 604 [27] (in discussing the appropriateness of importing English law).
110 *Yong Vui Kong (2010)* (n 8) [61] (pointing out that the ECHR formerly applied to Singapore when it was a British colony as it did for other British colonies, but that Singapore did not model its constitution after the ECHR, unlike other former colonies such as Belize or Jamaica).
111 *Chee Siok Chin* (n 72) [87].
112 *See Toh Siew Kee v Ho Ah Lam Ferrocement (Pte) Ltd* [2013] SGCA 29, [2013] 3 SLR 284 [22] (recognising that Lord Atkin's 'neighbour' principle, although Biblically inspired, was a global standard and also 'reflects the mores of Asian societies' as a 'universal communitarian value').
113 This distinction was drawn by Foreign Minister Wong Kan Seng in his speech entitled, 'The Real World of Human Rights' (World Conference on Human Rights, Vienna, 16 June 1993), reproduced in [1993] Singapore Journal of Legal Studies 602.
114 *Chee Siok Chin* (n 72) [52], [132].
115 *Shadrake (CA)* (n 92) [41].
116 Lord Bingham in *Reyes v R* [2002] 2 AC 235 (PC), cited in *Yong Vui Kong (2010)* (n 8) [73].
117 In relation to an argument that there was a worldwide movement to decriminalise homosexual activity, Loh J pointed out that other former British colonies such as Botswana, Malaysia, Sri Lanka, Sudan, Tanzania, Yemen and the Solomon Islands had criminalised *female* homosexual conduct while retaining their respective equivalents of s 377A of the Penal Code which criminalises homosexual sodomy: *Lim Meng Suang v AG* [2013] SGHC 73, [2013] 3 SLR 118 [133].
118 *Yong Vui Kong (2015)* (n 99) [38].
119 *Chee Siok Chin* (n 72) [45]–[49].
120 *JB Jeyaretnam* (n 93). The Court of Appeal noted at [56] that while the First Amendment denoted a strong free speech policy, and while Article 10 of the European Convention of Human Rights permitted only those restrictions 'necessary in a democratic society', Article 14 of the Singapore Constitution authorised Parliament to make restrictions it considered 'necessary or expedient' on eight grounds of permissible derogation.
121 *Chee Siok Chin* (n 72) [50].
122 *Yong Vui Kong (2010)* (n 8).
123 ibid [74].
124 *Ong Ah Chuan* (n 39).
125 *Jabar* (n 94). However, the High Court in *Public Prosecutor v Nguyen Tuong Van* [2004] SGHC 54, [2004] 2 SLR(R) 328 [77] opined that law could encompass 'the processes for passing an act or its constitutional validity'.
126 As discussed above in relation to *Colin Chan* (n 44) [78].
127 The Court of Appeal in *Yong Vui Kong (2010)* (n 8) speculated that 'law' under Article 9 would exclude colourable legislation which constituted a legislative judgment or legislation 'so absurd or arbitrary' in nature that the constitutional framers could not have contemplated it as being 'law when crafting the fundamental liberties chapter'.
128 *Yong Vui Kong (2015)* (n 99). For further discussion on the fundamental rules of natural justice, see Swati Jhaveri, 'The broader case for developing the content of fundamental rules of natural justice under Article 9 of the Constitution: a placeholder for proportionality-type adjudication?', Chapter 8 of this book.
129 *Vellama* (n 64) [85]. The Court of Appeal made reference to *Vellama* in *Yong Vui Kong (2015)* (n 99) [70].

130 The Court of Appeal in *Yong Vui Kong (2015)* (n 99) [73] noted that

> where a right cannot be found in the constitution (whether expressly or by necessary implication), *the courts do not have the power to create such a right out of whole cloth simply because they consider it to be desirable* or perhaps to put in terms that might *appear* more principled, to be part of natural law.

131 *Yong Vui Kong (2015)* (n 99) [16].
132 ibid [16]–[23].
133 ibid at [18], referencing William Blackstone, *Commentaries on the Laws of England* (Book I, Clarendon Press 1765) 125–34. Blackstone defined personal security as relating to 'a person's legal and uninterrupted enjoyment of his life, his limbs, his body, his health and his reputation'. A person's body was also entitled to security from 'insults of menaces, assaults, beatings, and wounding' not rising to destruction of life or limb.
134 *Yong Vui Kong (2015)* (n 99) [22].
135 ibid [69]–[72]. The Court of Appeal noted that there is 'nothing inherent' in the government system which required a finding that a prohibition against torture formed a part of the constitutional basic structure.
136 Chan Sek Keong, 'Judicial Review – From Angst to Empathy' (2010) 22 Singapore Academy of Law Journal 469 [48]–[49].
137 *Kenneth Jeyaretnam* (n 66) [48].
138 ibid [62].
139 *Vellama* (n 64) [33].
140 ibid [34].
141 *Kenneth Jeyaretnam* (n 66) [61].
142 ibid [56].
143 ibid [62].
144 [2007] SGHC 24, [2007] 2 SLR(R) 453.
145 ibid [95]–[96].
146 ibid [98].
147 See generally, Thio Li-ann and David Chong, 'The Chan Court and Constitutional Adjudication: "A Sea Change into Something Rich and Strange?" ' in Chao, Phang, Rajah and Yeo (eds), *The Law in His Hands: A Tribute to Chief Justice Chan Sek Keong* (Academy Press 2012).
148 For more on the presumption of constitutionality and balancing, see Jack Tsen-Ta Lee, 'Rethinking the presumption of constitutionality', Chapter 6 of this book, and Jaclyn L Neo, 'Balancing act: the balancing metaphor as deference and dialogue in constitutional adjudication', Chapter 7 of this book.
149 *Ramalingam* (n 53).
150 *Thiruselvam s/o Nagaratnam v Public Prosecutor* [2001] SGCA 13, [2001] 1 SLR(R) 362 [32] (Thean JA), with reference to the holding in *Sim Min Teck v Public Prosecutor* [1987] SGCA 3, [1987] SLR(R) 65.
151 *Ramalingam* (n 53) [44]–[45].
152 ibid [46].
153 ibid [51].
154 ibid.
155 ibid [71].
156 ibid.
157 ibid [63].
158 ibid [72].
159 ibid [52].
160 ibid [50], citing the decision of *United States v Christopher Lee Armstrong* 517 US 456 (1996) (Supreme Court of the United States) in relation to deferring to the Attorney-General on matters of prosecution.

161 *Yong Vui Kong (2011)* (n 62).
162 ibid [74].
163 ibid [76].
164 ibid [84].
165 This could be contrasted with 'second wave' cases where certain decisions might be criticised for intruding on religious freedom by engaging in theology in defining what a religion did, and did not, require. See *Nappalli Peter Williams v Institute of Technical Education* [1999] SGCA 41, [1999] 2 SLR(R) 529 [28]; a contrasting approach was adopted by the court in *Ebralinag v Division of Superintendent of Schools of Cebu* [1993] 219 SCRA 256 (Supreme Court of the Philippines):

> The State cannot interpret the Bible for them; only they can read it as they see fit. Right or wrong, the meaning they derive from it cannot be revised or reversed except perhaps by their own acknowledged superiors. But certainly not the State. It has no competence in this matter. Religion is forbidden territory that the State, for all its power and authority, cannot invade.

See Thio Li-ann, 'Courting Religion: The Judge between Caesar and God in Asian Courts' (2009) Singapore Journal of Legal Studies 52.
166 *Vellama* (n 64).
167 ibid [78].
168 ibid [79].
169 ibid [82].
170 ibid [84].
171 ibid [84]–[85].
172 ibid [87]. The Prime Minister had a continuing duty to assess the circumstances and to call for by-elections if and when the circumstances changed.
173 Peter Westen, 'The Empty Idea of Equality' (1995) 95 Harvard Law Review 537; Thio (n 51) 706–16. The Court of Appeal noted this point in referencing Westen's article in *Lim Meng Suang (CA)* (n 3) [61].
174 *Datuk Haji bin Harun Idris v Public Prosecutor* [1977] 2 MLJ 155 (Federal Court, Malaysia) (Suffian LP), quoting with approval the decision of *M Chhagganlal v Greater Bombay Municipality*, AIR 1974 SC 2009 (Supreme Court of India).
175 *Taw Cheng Kong v Public Prosecutor* [1998] SGHC 10, [1998] 1 SLR(R) 78 [16].
176 *Ong Ah* Chuan (n 39) [37]

> ...whether this dissimilarity in circumstances justifies any differentiation in the punishments imposed upon individuals who fall within one class and those who fall within the other, and, if so, what are the appropriate punishments for each class, are questions of social policy. Under the Constitution, which is based on the separation of powers, these are questions which it is the function of the legislature to decide, not that of the Judiciary.

177 *Yong Vui Kong (2010)* (n 8); *Nguyen Tuong Van* (n 96).
178 *Yong Vui Kong (2015)* (n 99).
179 *Lim Meng Suang (CA)* (n 3).
180 ibid [65].
181 ibid [66].
182 *Yong Vui Kong (2010)* (n 8).
183 ibid [94].
184 *Lim Meng Suang v Attorney-General* [2013] SGHC 73, [2013] 3 SLR 118 [127] (Loh J) [*Lim Meng Suang (HC)*]. Thus, in relation to why homosexual rather than lesbian sex was criminalised, a plausible reason was a traditional preoccupation with procreation and family lineage 'which is focused on males rather than females'.
185 *Yong Vui Kong (2010)* (n 8) [95].
186 *Lim Meng Suang (HC)* (n 184) [104].

187 *Nguyen Tuong Van* (n 96) [73], rejecting the view that the judicial role was simply the 'blind acceptance of legislative fiat'.
188 *Nguyen Tuong Van* (n 96).
189 ibid [77]. The Indian case discussed was *Mithu v State of Punjab* AIR 1983 SC 473 (Supreme Court of India) [72].
190 *Yong Vui Kong (2010)* (n 8).
191 ibid [118].
192 *Lim Meng Suang (CA)* (n 3) [82].
193 *Yong Vui Kong (2015)* (n 99) [106].
194 *Lim Meng Suang (CA)* (n 3) [84].
195 ibid [86].
196 *Yong Vui Kong (2015)* (n 99) [106].
197 ibid [111].
198 ibid [109].
199 ibid [111].
200 ibid [111]; see also [119] in noting that Singapore's Parliament had adopted a colonial era law.
201 Eg Robert George, 'The Concept of Public Morality' (2000) 45 American Journal of Jurisprudence 17 argues that public morality is a common good which generates obligations in justice for all.
202 One may argue that the more accurate question is *whose* morality law should enforce since all laws have a moral basis.
203 *Lim Meng Suang (CA)* (n 3) [169].
204 Notably, the court rejected the attempt to ground a 'limited right to privacy and personal autonomy allowing a person to enjoy and express affection and love towards another human being' which would encompass homosexual sodomy as residing in the meaning of 'personal liberty' under Article 9(1) in *Lim Meng Suang (CA)* (n 3). The court had noted that historically, the word 'personal' was included to limit potentially unhinged readings of 'liberty'. This novel reading of Article 9(1) lacks a textual root and can only proceed from a freestanding theory of radical autonomy so beloved of activist judges. The court also noted at [49] that the right claimed contained 'the seeds of an unlimited right' and could be read 'to encompass and to legalise all manner of subjective expressions of love and affection' which could 'embody content that may be wholly unacceptable from the perspective of broader societal policy', such as consensual adult incest, bestiality or paedophilia. This resort to 'rights language' was an attempt to transform what the criminal law identified as grossly indecent acts into an expression of (sexual) love, which would constitute a radical assault on existing conceptions of public sexual morality. This is best left for legislative debate.
205 *Lim Meng Suang (HC)* (n 184) [59]–[63].
206 ibid [143].
207 410 US 113 (1973) (Supreme Court of the USA), discussed in *Lim Meng Suang (HC)* (n 184) [142].
208 *Lim Meng Suang (HC)* (n 184) [139].
209 Eg the Court of Appeal in *Yong Vui Kong (2015)* (n 99) [121] noted that 'any campaign to abolish caning is a matter that must be taken up in the legislative sphere'. See also *Yong Vui Kong (2010)* (n 8) [122] on the mandatory death penalty and *Lim Meng Suang (CA)* (n 3) at [190] on the constitutionality of laws criminalising sodomy.
210 Jeremy Waldron, 'Do Judges Reason Morally?' in Grant Huscroft (ed), *Expounding the Constitution: Essays in Constitutional Theory* (Cambridge University Press 2008) 64. He argues that debate should be conducted 'in a morally responsible manner, and fairness demands that they be debated in a way that reflects the fact that a decision is being made, not just for an individual, but for the whole society'.

Distrust is directed towards unelected and unaccountable judges where judicial review in relation to rights questions over which deep disagreement exists 'disenfranchises ordinary citizens and brushes aside cherished principles of representation and political equality in the final resolution about rights': Jeremy Waldron, *Law and Disagreement* (Oxford University Press 1999) 8.

211 ibid 63.

212 This was a recurrent refrain in *Lim Meng Suang (CA)* (n 3) [70], [77], [82], [84], [93], [101], [173], [189].

213 Ronald Dworkin, *A Matter of Principle* (Harvard University Press 1985) 71.

214 John Rawls, *Political Liberalism* (Columbia University Press 2005) 176.

215 Loh J, *Lim Meng Suang v AG* [2013] 3 SLR 118 at [139].

216 Professor Hart described American constitutional jurisprudence as oscillating between the 'Nightmare' and the 'Noble Dream': The Nightmare is that judges make up law as they go along while the Noble Dream is that judges never make law but simply apply existing principles already embedded in the law: HLA Hart, 'American Jurisprudence through English Eyes: The Nightmare and the Noble Dream' (1977) 11 Georgia Law Review 5.

217 Quoting Lord Reid's extra-judicial lecture, 'The Judge as Law Maker' (1972–1973) 12 JSPTL (NS) 22, in *Lim Meng Suang (CA)* (n 3) [78].

218 *Lim Meng Suang (CA)* (n 3) [76].

219 ibid [81].

220 ibid [83].

221 ibid [12].

222 See generally Aileen Kavanagh, 'Deference or Defiance? The Limits of the Judicial Role in Constitutional Adjudication' in Grant Huscroft (ed), *Expounding the Constitution: Essays in Constitutional Theory* (Cambridge University Press 2008) 38; J Jowell, 'Judicial Deference: Servility, Civility or Institutional Capacity' (2003) Public Law 592.

223 Ruth Gavison, 'The Role of Courts in Rifted Democracies' (1993) 33 Israel Law Review 216, 242 (arguing that even if courts disagree with political decisions, they should not 'delegitimize' the elected branches).

224 This is distinct from the legal pragmatist view that there is no such thing as legal reasoning: Richard A Posner, *The Problems of Jurisprudence* (Harvard University Press 1990) at 459.

225 *Review Publishing Co Ltd v Lee Hsien Loong* [2010] 1 SLR 52 at [239].

226 Paul J Mishkin, 'The Supreme Court, 1964 Term Foreword: The High Court, the Great Writ and the Due Process of Time and Law' (1965) 79 Harvard Law Review 56, 61. See generally Schroeder (n 15) 1703.

227 *Lim Meng Suang (CA)* (n 3) [7].

228 Malcolm Schofield, 'The Noble Lie' in GRF Ferrari (ed), *The Cambridge Companion to Plato's Republic* (Cambridge University Press 2007).

229 See generally Jan-Werner Müller, *Constitutional Patriotism* (Princeton University Press 2007).

230 See Cameron Stewart, 'The Rule of Law and the Tinkerbell Effect: Theoretical Considerations, Criticisms and Justifications for the Rule of Law' (2004) 4 Macquarie Law Journal 135.

231 Judge Antonin Scalia argues that problems notwithstanding, originalism does establish a 'historical criterion' conceptually separate from judicial preference: Antonin Scalia, 'Originalism: The Lesser Evil' (1989) 57 University of Cincinnati Law Review 849.

Bibliography

Aleinikoff, T Alexander, 'Constitutional Law in the Age of Balancing' (1987) 96 Yale Law Journal 943.

Bickel, Alexander, *The Least Dangerous Branch: The Supreme Court at the Bar of Politics* (Yale University Press 1962).

Blackstone, William, *Commentaries on the Law of England* (Book I, Clarendon Press 1765).

Calo, Zachary R, 'Religion, Human Rights and Post Secular Legal Theory' (2014) 85(2) St John's Law Review 495.

Chan, Sek Keong, 'Judicial Review – From Angst to Empathy' (2010) 22 Singapore Academy of Law Journal 469.

Dworkin, Ronald, *A Matter of Principle* (Harvard University Press 1985).

Gavison, Ruth, 'The Role of Courts in Rifted Democracies' (1993) 33 Israel Law Review 216.

George, Robert, 'The Concept of Public Morality' (2000) 45 American Journal of Jurisprudence 17.

Ghai, Yash, 'Asian Perspectives on Human Rights' (1993) 23(3) Hong Kong Law Journal 342.

Goldsworthy, Jeffery, 'Constitutional Cultures, Democracy and Unwritten Principles' (2012) University of Illinois Law Review 683.

Grant, James, 'The Rise of Juristocracy' (2010) 34(2) Wilson Quarterly 16.

Grey, Thomas C, 'Judicial Review and Legal Pragmatism' (2003) 38 Wake Forest Law Review 473.

Hart, HLA, 'American Jurisprudence through English Eyes: The Nightmare and the Noble Dream' (1977) 11 Georgia Law Review 5.

Holmes, Oliver Wendell Jr, 'The Path of the Law' (1897) 10 Harvard Law Review 457.

Hor, Michael, 'Constitutionalism and Subversion: An Exploration' in Li-ann Thio and Kevin YL Tan (eds), *Evolution of a Revolution: Forty Years of the Singapore Constitution* (Routledge-Cavendish 2009).

Jowell, J, 'Judicial Deference: Servility, Civility or Institutional Capacity' (2003) Public Law 592.

Kavanagh, Aileen, 'Deference or Defiance? The Limits of the Judicial Role in Constitutional Adjudication' in Grant Huscroft (ed), *Expounding the Constitution: Essays in Constitutional Theory* (Cambridge University Press 2008).

Kende, Mark S, 'Constitutional Pragmatism, The Supreme Court and Democratic Revolution' (2012) 89(3) Denver University Law Review 635.

Klarman, Michael J, 'What's So Great About Constitutionalism?' (1998) 93 Northwestern University Law Review 145.

Mishkin, Paul J, 'The Supreme Court, 1964 Term Foreword: The High Court, the Great Writ and the Due Process of Time and Law' (1965) 79 Harvard Law Review 56.

Morris, Andrew J, 'Some Challenges for Legal Pragmatism: A Closer Look at Pragmatic Legal Reasoning' (2007) 28 Northern Illinois University Law Review 1.

Müller, Jan-Werner, *Constitutional Patriotism* (Princeton University Press 2007).

Posner, Richard A, *The Problems of Jurisprudence* (Harvard University Press 1990).

Posner, Richard A, *The Problematics of Moral and Legal Theory* (Belknap Press of Harvard University Press 1999).

Rawls, John, *Political Liberalism* (Columbia University Press 2005).

Reid, Lord, 'The Judge as Law Maker' (1972–1973) 12 JSPTL (NS) 22.

Rorty, Richard, 'The Professor and the Prophet' (1992) 52 Transition 70.
Scalia, Antonin, 'Originalism: The Lesser Evil' (1989) 57 University of Cincinnati Law Review 849.
Schofield, Malcolm, 'The Noble Lie' in GRF Ferrari (ed), *The Cambridge Companion to Plato's Republic* (Cambridge University Press 2007).
Schroeder, Christopher H, 'Some Notes on a Principled Pragmatism' (2007) 95 California Law Review 1703.
Shapiro, Martin, *Courts: A Comparative and Political Analysis* (University of Chicago Press 1986).
Stewart, Cameron, 'The Rule of Law and the Tinkerbell Effect: Theoretical Considerations, Criticisms and Justifications for the Rule of Law' (2004) 4 Macquarie Law Journal 135.
Tamanaha, Brian, 'Pragmatism in US Legal Theory: Its Application to Normative Jurisprudence, Sociolegal Studies and the Fact-Value Distinction' (1996) 41 American Journal of Jurisprudence 315.
Thio, Li-ann, 'Trends in Constitutional Interpretation: Oppugning Ong, Awakening Arumugam?' (1997) Singapore Journal of Legal Studies 240.
Thio, Li-ann, 'Beyond the "Four Walls" in an Age of Transnational Judicial Conversations: Civil Liberties, Rights Theories and Constitutional Adjudication in Malaysia and Singapore' (2006) 19(2) Columbia Journal of Asian Law 428.
Thio, Li-ann, 'Courting Religion: The Judge between Caesar and God in Asian Courts' (2009) Singapore Journal of Legal Studies 52.
Thio, Li-ann, *A Treatise on Singapore Constitutional Law* (Academy Publishing 2012) xiii.
Thio, Li-ann and David Chong, 'The Chan Court and Constitutional Adjudication: A Sea Change into Something Rich And Strange?' in Chao, Phang, Rajah and Yeo (eds), *The Law in His Hands: A Tribute to Chief Justice Chan Sek Keong* (Academy Press 2012).
Thio, Li-ann and Kevin YL Tan, *50 Constitutional Moments that Defined a Nation* (Marshall Cavendish 2015).
Thomas, EW, *The Judicial Process: Realism, Pragmatism, Practical Reasoning and Principles* (Cambridge University Press 2008).
Waldron, Jeremy, *Law and Disagreement* (Oxford University Press 1999).
Waldron, Jeremy, 'Do Judges Reason Morally?' in Grant Huscroft (ed), *Expounding the Constitution: Essays in Constitutional Theory* (Cambridge University Press 2008).
Westen, Peter, 'The Empty Idea of Equality' (1995) 95 Harvard Law Review 537.
Wong, Kan Seng, 'The Real World of Human Rights' (World Conference on Human Rights, Vienna, 16 June 1993) [1993] Singapore Journal of Legal Studies 602.

5 Uncovering originalism and textualism in Singapore

Yap Po Jen

I Introduction

Our judges in Singapore, like many of their counterparts in the West, tend to present adjudication merely as a mechanical exercise of applying the law to the facts of a specific case. In so doing, it would appear that the law can truly be separated from politics and judges merely follow pre-determined rules and exercise little discretion when making decisions.[1]

However, if we were to closely examine the prevailing theories of interpretation that our judges purport to rely upon when they resolve constitutional disputes, we may discover that these principles are often mere constitutional 'fig leaves' that cover their normative choices. In particular, two such interpretive modalities are flourishing in Singapore: originalism and textualism.

But, I must emphasise that that these fig leaves seek not to mislead anyone about what the courts are doing. As astutely observed by Professor Christopher Forsyth in his seminal article:

> The point about the fig-leaf metaphor (and why it is so apt) is that fig leaves do not deceive anyone as to what lies beneath them. The fig leaf, like the swimming costume on a crowded beach, is to preserve the decencies. It enables individuals to interact in an appropriate manner without threatening the social order.[2]

Similarly, the use of fig leaves in Singapore demonstrates that our judges implicitly accept the constitutional role that they are expected to play within our political system;[3] and the truth is, our judges, on their own, can do very little.

The political reality is that, in Singapore, the state has been governed by the same ruling party, the People's Action Party (PAP), since the nation's independence, and will be so governed for the foreseeable future. When legislative and executive powers are consolidated by a *semi-permanent* party, the dominant political entity in question can display its disagreement by overriding a constitutional decision easily with a constitutional amendment.[4] Our judges, operating in such a political system, would not be oblivious to this fact. More significantly, Singapore has experienced a judicial crisis, which arguably has cast a pall over the state of constitutional review. When the Court of Appeal ruled against them in 1989, for the first and last time on constitutional grounds, the Government swiftly overturned this decision via a series of constitutional and statutory amendments within a month of the judgment. In that seminal decision of *Chng Suan Tze v Minister of Home Affairs*,[5] the Court of Appeal, after surveying a litany of Commonwealth precedents, quashed the preventive detention orders issued under the Internal Security Act (ISA) against alleged Marxist conspirators and also concluded in obiter that the ministerial discretion to detain personnel under the ISA would be subject to an 'objective' test of review by the courts as constitutionally required under Articles 9[6] and 12[7] of the Singapore Constitution.[8] This decision proved to be disquieting to the Government, so much so that in the subsequent amendments, it restricted judicial review in ISA cases to only narrow procedural grounds.

Part II of this chapter begins by identifying and uncovering the judicial use of 'originalism' as an interpretive modality. Part III continues with a close examination of the judicial reliance on 'textualism' as another preferred mode of constitutional interpretation. In essence, I shall seek to illustrate that the judicial decisions reached by our courts are neither mandated by the text nor the history of our Constitution, but are the consequence of normative choices made by our judges.

II Originalism

Originalism, as a constitutional theory, presents itself as a resolution to the tension between constitutionalism and democracy. So far as courts only implement the original understanding of a constitution, judges would be adjudicating in a democratically legitimate way as they are merely enforcing the original meaning of the constitutional text that was duly enacted by the people via their representatives.[9] It is thus believed that originalism, as a mode of constitutional interpretation, can best promote predictability and also prevent illegitimate constitutional change under the guise of judicial interpretation.[10]

This brand of originalism has been termed 'hard originalism'.[11] It is largely defended by judges and scholars who seek to transform constitutional law into a system of rules. According to these originalists, legal predictability is enhanced by this judicial turn to history.[12] Judicial discretion is fettered and is perceived to be more democratic by virtue of its connection to past judgments of the constitutional framers. Originalists often caution that if judges are allowed to stray from the original understanding of a constitution, they will be given free rein to amend it. In the process, judges, who are non-elected officials, would be imposing norms that the people have not accepted through their democratically elected representatives.[13]

An originalist understanding of the Singapore Constitution was explicitly endorsed by the Court of Appeal in the 2010 case of *Yong Vui Kong v Public Prosecutor* ('*Yong (2010)*').[14] On the facts, the accused was sentenced to death by the trial judge, under the Misuse of Drugs Act, for trafficking 47.27 g of diamorphine, a controlled drug. On appeal, the accused argued that the mandatory death penalty (MDP) as imposed by the impugned statute was not 'in accordance with law' as required under Article 9(1)[15] of the Singapore Constitution – the expression 'law' enshrined under Article 9(1) excluded inhuman forms of punishment; accordingly, he could not be statutorily deprived of his life in this manner.

Specifically, counsel for the accused had sought to ask the court to follow a series of Privy Council decisions from the Caribbean States[16] where the Law Lords in the United Kingdom had overturned the MDP imposed by the respective state legislations. Nevertheless, the Court of Appeal flatly rejected their applicability. According to the Court of Appeal, Singapore's due process clause was based on its equivalent in the 1963 Malaysian Federal Constitution,[17] which was likewise based on the 1957 Malayan Constitution drafted pursuant to the advice of the Federation of Malayan Constitutional Commission chaired by Lord Reid (the Reid Commission). Unlike those foreign decisions that involved constitutions that expressly prohibited inhuman punishments, the Court of Appeal held that the Singapore Constitution did not expressly include such a prohibition. According to the court, the fact that the Reid Commission did not recommend in favour of an express prohibition against inhuman punishment, even though such a provision existed in the European Convention on Human Rights – an instrument that applied in all the British colonies (including Singapore and Malaysia) prior to their independence – clearly illustrated that the omission was deliberate and was not due to ignorance or oversight.[18]

Furthermore, the Court of Appeal also noted that the Singapore Government, in 1969, had unambiguously rejected a proposal by the Constitutional Commission[19] to include a provision expressly prohibiting the state imposition of inhuman punishment. Therefore, according to the Court of Appeal, it was 'not legitimate for this court to read into Art 9(1) a constitutional right which was decisively rejected by the Government in 1969, especially given the historical context in which that right was rejected'.[20] The Court of Appeal's originalist understanding of the Singapore Constitution meant that our judiciary would only invalidate 'legislation of so absurd or arbitrary a nature that it could not possibly have been contemplated by our constitutional framers as being 'law when they crafted the constitutional provisions protecting fundamental liberties'.[21]

However, the espousal of 'hard originalism' as the preferred theory of constitutional adjudication in Singapore by the Court of Appeal in *Yong (2010)* is not unproblematic, and it is to this aspect that we now turn.

First, the constitutional text of Singapore's Fundamental Liberties Clauses, of which the due process clause is one of them, was not deliberated upon by a Constituent Assembly of the independent state in question. Instead, upon gaining independence from Malaysia in 1965, the Singapore legislature simply made most fundamental liberties provisions found in the Malaysia Federal Constitution applicable to Singapore via the Republic of Singapore Independence Act.[22] Certainly, the fact that the legislature of a newly sovereign republic had consciously adopted those provisions thereby conferred upon these Singaporean liberties a legal life of their own. But the mere enactment of the law does not provide us with a clue as to the original meaning that the framers attached to very provisions they adopted. Furthermore, since Singapore's constitutional framers did not deliberate upon the phraseology of the Fundamental Liberties Clauses, but merely imported them as a matter of expedience from Malaysia, one does wonder whether it is even possible to discern at all what original meaning they attached to those provisions adopted from Malaysia. At best, one can try to discern the original intent of the framers (and, indeed, the members of the Reid Commission) when the Malaysian Constitution was drafted and adopted, but it would be a very curious state of affairs for Singapore judges in modern independent Singapore to give effect to and be fettered by the original intent of another nation-state's constitutional framers.[23]

Second, in relation to the Court of Appeal's application of this originalist mode of interpretation in *Yong (2010)*, the court was unwilling to accept that Article 9(1) could be interpreted to include an implied general prohibition against inhuman punishment because the Singapore Government had, in 1969, unambiguously rejected a proposal by a Constitutional Commission to amend the Constitution and provide for such an express right. However, one must remember that the Fundamental Liberties Clauses of the Singapore Constitution came into effect in 1965, soon after Singapore's independence that same year. Hence, it is unclear, even on an originalist understanding of the Singapore Constitution, whether it was legitimate for the court to discern the original intent of the constitutional framers in 1965, when they imported the applicable Fundamental Liberties Clauses from Malaysia, from a parliamentary decision taken four years later to reject a proposal that would have provided for an express prohibition against inhuman punishment.

Even if we assume that the intent of the constitutional framers in 1969 to reject a constitutional prohibition against torture and inhuman punishment mirrored that of the framers in 1965, to be consistent, this would mean that whatever recommendations the Constitutional Commission made in 1966, but were not taken up subsequently by the Government in 1969, should also not be judicially deemed a constitutional right. In an earlier commentary, I have observed that if this argument is taken to its logical conclusion, the right to vote would also not be a constitutionally protected fundamental liberty because it is not expressly enshrined in the Singapore Constitution. Moreover, the Constitutional Commission in the 1960s had failed to convince the Government to entrench this right.[24] After all, if one takes the view that there can be no implied right against inhuman punishment under Article 9(1) because the Singapore Government expressly refused to entrench this right in 1969, then to be consistent, the courts cannot also read in an implied right to vote because the Singapore Government equally refused to entrench an express right to vote then. In that referenced article, I had argued that such a position would be very worrying because this would mean that the Singapore Parliament can pass legislation to allow only elite segments of society to vote in general elections or abolish confidential voting at general elections.

(Fortunately, the Court of Appeal, in a more recent constitutional challenge against judicial caning, took pains to suggest in obiter that the right to vote could 'possibly'[25] form part of the basic structure of the Singapore Constitution and that this right may not even be removed by a validly passed constitutional amendment.)

Despite dismissing the argument that Article 9(1) included an implied general prohibition against inhuman punishment, the court in *Yong (2010)* observed, 'This conclusion does not mean that, because the proposed [constitutional amendment by the Constitutional Commission 1966] included a prohibition against torture, an Act of Parliament that permits torture can form part of 'law' for the purposes of Art 9(1).'[26] It appears that the court was suggesting that there existed an implied prohibition against torture under Article 9(1). Whilst one should certainly applaud this judicial concession, this pronouncement is very puzzling. As a matter of logic, if the Court of Appeal were reluctant to expand, via an interpretive exercise, the scope of Article 9(1) so as to include a constitutional prohibition against inhuman punishment because Parliament had deliberately refused to enact such a provision, surely this reasoning must also bar any elevation of a prohibition against torture to a constitutional right since this proposal, too, was deliberately rejected by the Government in 1969. The Court of Appeal interestingly justified this distinction on the basis that in 1987, Singapore's Minister of Home Affairs had explicitly recognised that torture was wrong and that torture, insofar as it caused harm to another's body with criminal intent, was already criminalised under the Singapore Penal Code.

With respect, the logic of this argument eludes the author. One does wonder how a mere statement from the Home Minister during Parliamentary Debates in 1987 would license the court, on an originalist understanding of the Singapore Constitution, to elevate a prohibition against torture into a constitutional right, and the fact that bodily assault is a crime in Singapore would surely not have any bearing on this matter. Unfortunately, the Court of Appeal, whilst recognising that Article 9(1) prohibited torture, went on to state unequivocally that 'currently, no domestic legislation permits torture',[27] thereby insulating all current official state practices from a challenge on this ground, and in particular judicial caning, a commonplace punishment for vandalism and rape in Singapore.[28] [More importantly, in 2015, the Court of Appeal in *Yong Vui Kong v Public Prosecutor*[29] ('*Yong (2015)*') has addressed the inconsistency in *Yong (2010)* by stating unequivocally that Article 9(1) does not implicitly prohibit torture.]

In the same vein, the Court of Appeal in *Yong (2010)* dismissed the alternate Article 9(1) argument that the MDP was unconstitutional because Customary International Law (CIL) formed part of the laws of Singapore under Article 9(1) and that CIL prohibited the imposition of the MDP. As observed by the Court: Given that the Government [in 1969] deliberated on but consciously rejected this suggestion of incorporating into the Singapore Constitution an express prohibition against inhuman punishment generally, a CIL rule prohibiting such punishment – let alone a CIL rule prohibiting the MDP specifically as an inhuman punishment – cannot now be treated as 'law' for the purposes of Art 9(1).[30]

In other words, the court was suggesting that since the Singapore Government in 1969 had rejected an express prohibition against inhuman punishment *in general*, any CIL norm that evolved after 1969 that might prohibit inhuman punishment *in general* or any CIL norm prohibiting a specific form of inhuman punishment, would *never* be judicially treated as part of Singapore law for the purposes of Article 9(1).

This judicial pronouncement is startling as it is certainly contrary to the approach taken by the Court of Appeal in the earlier decision of *Nguyen Tuong Van v Public* Prosecutor.[31] In that decision, the Court of Appeal, inter alia, had to decide whether the accused's specific mode of execution, ie judicial hanging, was contrary to the prohibition under CIL against inhuman punishment and therefore unconstitutional because CIL norms were implicitly recognised as part of Singapore law under Article 9(1). The court in *Nguyen Tuong Van* stated, 'It is quite widely accepted that the prohibition against cruel and inhuman treatment or punishment does amount to a rule in customary international law'.[32] However, on the facts, the court concluded that there was insufficient state practice to show that a specific CIL norm prohibited hanging as a mode of execution and, in any event, such a CIL norm could be overridden in Singapore by domestic statute. Hence, whilst the Court of Appeal in *Nguyen Tuong Van*, with regard to Article 9(1), would be amenable to incorporating any specific CIL norm against inhuman punishment in the absence of a conflicting domestic statute, the Court of Appeal after *Yong* would now reject the applicability of all such CIL norms because the constitutional framers (arguably) had deliberately rejected the inclusion of a constitutional clause prohibiting inhuman punishment *in general*. While the Court of Appeal in *Yong (2010)* was probably right on the facts to conclude that a specific CIL norm had yet to develop against the use of the MDP for drug-trafficking offences, it is another thing altogether to reject outright the notion that a *general* CIL norm prohibiting inhuman punishments could ever form part of the law of Singapore under Article 9(1). More startlingly, the Court of Appeal in *Yong (2015*), upholding the constitutionality of judicial corporal punishment, stated, 'even where a CIL rule has acquired the status of *jus cogens*, it cannot override a domestic statute whose meaning and effect is clear'.[33]

The appeal of originalism persisted in the Singapore Court of Appeal's encounter with the same appellant, Yong Vui Kong, in the 2011 case of *Yong Vui Kong v Attorney-General* [*Yong (2011)*]. On the facts, the applicant argued, inter alia, that the clemency powers conferred on the President under Article 22P[34] of Singapore Constitution was exercisable by him acting in his own discretion, and he was not bound by any advice given by the Cabinet. The Court of Appeal surveyed the legislative history of Article 22P and concluded that the 'legislative history of the clemency power in this jurisdiction indicates plainly that Art 22P excludes any role for the President's personal discretion in the exercise of the clemency power'.[35] In particular, the court seized upon the speech given by then Prime Minister Lee Kuan Yew during the Second Reading of the Republic of Singapore Independence Bill, which included clause 8, which is textually identical to the current Article 22P:

> Clause 8 … invests the power of pardon in the President who will exercise it in accordance with the advice of the Cabinet.[36]

In view of the Prime Minister's parliamentary speech in 1965, the Court of Appeal opined as follows:

> Nothing can be clearer than the above words in showing that the clemency power, although exercised by and in the name of the President, is to be exercised in accordance with the advice of the Cabinet.[37]

In ascertaining the meaning of Article 22P, the court is certainly not wrong to have recourse to its constitutional history, since history is always an important resource for constitutional construction. However, one must note that the court's historical understanding of Article 22P *arguably* flies in the face of a textual reading of the said provision. Article 22P provides that the President 'may, on the advice of the Cabinet' grant a pardon. It is thus certainly possible that the usage of the permissive word 'may' indicates that the President is conferred with a personal discretion to reject the advice given by the Cabinet. The statutory language of Article 22P can be contrasted with Article 21(1), which expressly provides that 'except as provided by this Constitution, the President *shall*, in the exercise of his functions under this Constitution or any other written law, *act in accordance with* the advice of the Cabinet'. Ostensibly, the use of the permissive word 'may' suggests that the President has the subjective discretion to reach a different conclusion from the Cabinet's, while the phrase 'shall … act in accordance with' suggests that he has an obligation and duty to conform to the Cabinet's decision. So, it would not be misplaced for one to argue that, on an ordinary reading of the terms 'may' and 'shall', distinct and separate meanings must be accorded to the scope of discretion that the President possessed when he exercised the said constitutional powers. Yet, for the Court of Appeal, this linguistic distinction appeared to be immaterial; the President is obliged to obey the Cabinet's decision in either scenario. In response to the phraseological differences between the two terms, the Court of Appeal had this pithy reply:

> The word 'may' in that context does not connote a personal discretion which allows the President to reject the advice of the Cabinet as to how the clemency power is to be exercised in a particular case – otherwise, the advice of the Cabinet would be pointless. The word 'may' in Art 22P(1) simply vests the President with the constitutional power to make a clemency order … on the advice of the Cabinet – ie, that word has an authorising or enabling effect, absent which the President would have no legal power to make any decision under Art 22P.[38]

With respect, this argument is problematic for two reasons. First, it is not evident why the conferring of a personal discretion on the President would render the advice of the Cabinet 'pointless'. After all, it is equally possible and logical for

Article 22P to have conferred a duty on the Cabinet to consider the matter in the first instance, and have the President reconsider the issue in light of the former's advice.[39] By the logic of the Court of Appeal's own argument, any decision handed down by the High Court of Singapore would be 'pointless' merely because the Court of Appeal would always have the discretion to overturn it. Second, the fact that the word 'may' has an authorising or enabling effect in no way answers the question of whether the Cabinet's decision is binding on the President. After all, the word 'shall' also has an authorising or enabling effect, in the absence of which the President would have no legal power to make any decision under Article 21(1) either. The words 'shall' and 'may' are two modal auxiliary verbs that are used to express a future action; in other words, both words have an enabling effect on an actor to engage in a future activity although the word 'shall' suggests that the enabling effect on the actor is mandatory – the actor is not only enabled to act, he or she is compelled to so. On the other hand, the use of the word 'may' suggests that while the actor is also enabled to perform an act, this grant of power is permissive in nature; ie he or she may choose not to act.

In a separate concurring opinion, then Chief Justice Chan Sek Keong, on originalist grounds, also held that an offender sentenced to death had no right to be heard during the clemency process. One must note that there is nothing in Article 22P that expressly forbids the right to a hearing. But, as observed by the learned Chief Justice:

> [T]he clemency power is derived from the prerogative of mercy, which is a common law power. Historically, at common law, an offender seeking mercy had no right to be heard during the clemency process ... This was the position in Singapore when the clemency power was a prerogative power. After the clemency power in Singapore became a constitutional power ... the common law position that an offender had no right of hearing during the clemency process continued to apply.... In short, the hearing rule has never applied to the clemency process in Singapore, both during the time when the clemency power was a prerogative power and, subsequently, after this power became a constitutional power.[40]

In short, historical practice alone militated against the recognition of the right to a hearing prior to the exercise of the clemency power.[41]

Such judicial appeal to history is particularly puzzling as the Court of Appeal in this case had already chosen to depart from historical understandings when deciding that the exercise of the clemency power was justiciable.[42] The Court of Appeal had noted that, up until 1971, the clemency power was not reviewable in the English courts, and even today, the clemency power is not reviewable in the Malaysian courts.[43] If the historical understanding of a particular constitutional provision at the time of its enactment is determinative, then surely the clemency power in Singapore, in view of the English and Malaysian positions, must also be non-justiciable. If the Singapore judiciary is able to depart from historical practices on the reviewability of the clemency power, it should also be able to depart from past practices and recognise an offender's right to a hearing prior to the President's exercise of his clemency power.

In *Yong (2015)*, another interesting state of affairs presents itself.[44] The applicant argued inter alia that his sentence of caning violated Article 9(1) of the Singapore Constitution and the Court of Appeal once again (ostensibly) reaffirmed its originalist stance:

> In order to determine the correct interpretation of Art 9(1), it is necessary to go back in history and consider how its predecessor provisions were understood.[45]

Although the text of Article 9(1) only expressly protects an individual against deprivations of his/her life or liberty, the court held that acts of amputation and mutilations would also fall within the ambit of Article 9(1), as this was the historical understanding of 'life and personal liberty' that dated back to Blackstone and even the Magna Carta.[46] More interestingly, even though the Reid Commission had made no mention of other forms of deprivation of life and liberty when the Malayan constitution was drafted, the court held that this was immaterial:

> In the absence of clear words signifying an intention to depart from the traditional understanding of 'life and personal liberty', little weight can be placed on this omission.[47]

Furthermore, this expansive reading of 'life and personal liberty' was equally applicable in Singapore as there is 'no evidence in the historical record to indicate that this understanding of 'life' had been altered by the time Art 9(1) was adopted into the Constitution of Singapore'.[48] While we should congratulate the Court of Appeal for not giving 'life and personal liberty' a parsimonious reading, it is noteworthy that this generous reading was inferred by the court from mere historical *silence*.

Even more oddly, despite choosing to read the phrase 'life and personal liberty' more broadly and generously, the court went on to narrow the protective ambit of Article 9(1) by stating that the said provision had no application *after* the accused had been convicted in a criminal trial. As observed by the court:

> In our judgment, therefore, even assuming the common law prohibition of torture extends to caning in the context of a punishment to be imposed on a convicted person after trial, it would not have constitutional force because this would not come within the ambit of fundamental rules of natural justice in the sense in which it was referred to in *Ong Ah Chuan*.[49]

Yet, if the Court of Appeal had indeed found Blackstone's definition of life and personal liberty to be determinative of the interpretive scope of Article 9(1), one would note that Blackstone himself had not limited these same rights to pre-conviction detainees![50] The court's selective use of history is indeed very surprising.

Finally, even if a state practice, eg the use of mandatory capital punishment or judicial caning, was generally accepted at the time the constitutional provisions were adopted, this does not prove that the framers had intended to constitutionalise that convention for all subsequent generations to obey. It is equally possible that the framers had given little thought to that issue, or were divided on it and preferred to let future generations decide the matter for themselves. This 'evolving' interpretation of the Constitution is also more consistent with a textual reading of the constitutional provisions. The Singapore framers, like framers of other national constitutions, have used both specific and broad provisions within the constitutional text, thus indicating that separate clauses should be interpreted with different levels of generality. Where the framers wanted the constitutional clauses to be read strictly, they used highly specific and particular words. For example, a member of the Singapore Parliament must be 'of the age of 21 years or above'.[51] The Singapore Constitution does not say that a Member of Parliament must be of sufficient maturity in age. The Singapore Parliament, unless sooner dissolved, shall continue for five years from the date of its first sitting and shall then stand dissolved.[52] Our constitution does not say that the Singapore Parliament, unless sooner dissolved, shall continue for a *reasonable* period of years and shall then stand dissolved.

Given that the Singapore framers had intentionally left the constitutional provisions enshrining terms such as 'in accordance with law' or 'equal protection' ambiguously worded, fully comprehending that the language was not specific and could be interpreted in various ways, the choice to adopt a broader principle must therefore be respected. After all, if a prohibition's reach is restricted to the practices that were thought to fall foul of the Constitution at the time the provisions were adopted, it would leave no room for a reasoned adjudication of practices that scientific and technological advancements or changed socio-economic circumstances bring.[53] Thus, such broadly phrased constitutional clauses have to embody abstract principles rather than merely encapsulate and enshrine historical practices.

As Jack Balkin has observed:

> [Constitutional adopters] choose vague standards or abstract principles because they want to channel political judgment but delegate the task of construction and application to future generations.[54]

Fidelity to the Constitutionrequires judges to pay credence to the framers' choice of rules and/or standards in the bill of rights. However, what is problematic is that the Singapore judiciary has placed dispositive weight on the expectations of the constitutional framers in deciding whether some impugned legislation is constitutional. Pursuant to this hard-line originalist approach, if the framing or pioneer generation was of the view that a statutory practice was constitutional in their time, then it follows that it must continue to be constitutional today. But there is no historical evidence available to indicate that our constitutional framers had intended the Constitutionto merely enumerate a static understanding of constitutional rights. Such attempts to shackle the Constitution to the framers' original specific application of the text at the time of enactment – as the 'hard originalism' approach would require – when the framers had deliberately chosen vague, open-textured language, may be inconsistent with the original intent as manifested in the constitutional language of enacting an enduring instrument with constitutional standards and spaces that allow future generations of law-makers and judges to design and build over time, through the processes of constitutional construction.[55]

Therefore, it is evident that the judicial recourse to 'hard originalism' in Singapore is not mandated by the text or history of the country's supreme law; rather it is the consequence of the court's deliberate choice to defer to the contemporary policy choices of the dominant PAP government, which has ruled Singapore without interruption since the nation's independence and has not taken well to robust judicial review. While it is not uncommon for judges in all countries to act prudentially when they seek to avoid legislative or electoral outrage, this concern about political reprisals is particularly accentuated or pronounced in countries with a semi-permanent form of government in power. Where a dominant disciplined political party/coalition is in control, the less space their courts have in which to operate. As Professor Tom Ginsburg has observed, the extent of political diffusion within the legislative/executive structures determines how successfully courts can assert their judicial power.[56] Where divided government exists, the 'policy space'[57] of the courts is greater because the opposing parties in the legislature have to co-operate to effectuate any disagreement with the judiciary. Bipartisan legislative agreement to overrule judges would be less likely and frequent in liberal democracies. In contrast, where legislative and executive power is consolidated by a single party or coalition, as is the case in Singapore, these dominant political parties/coalitions can display their displeasure more easily by ousting judicial review altogether.[58] Therefore, as observed by Professor Michael Hor, '[I]t might well have been a certain 'political' conception of the proper reach of the judiciary into the governmental sphere [that] foreclosed any possibility'[59] of judicial intervention, and constitutional history has been merely relied upon as a convenient proxy for judicial inaction.

III Textualism

Textualism is an interpretive method that allows judges to derive the meaning of the constitution from its language, as situated within the linguistic practice of the community, alongside the accepted canons of interpretation. Proponents of textualism, like advocates of 'hard originalism', argue that the role of a judge is to merely interpret the law as enacted by the legislature. In their view, the word 'interpret' is a transitive verb, ie judges must interpret text.[60] If judges were to depart from the text of the constitution, they would be imposing on society prescriptions that have not been endorsed by the political process.

An excellent illustration of textualism in practice would be the High Court of Singapore's decision in *Chee Siok Chin v Minister for Home Affairs.*[61] On the facts, three applicants commenced proceedings seeking declarations that the Police Commissioner had acted unlawfully in ordering them to disperse when they had engaged in a peaceful protest outside a government building. A central issue that arose was whether the Miscellaneous Offences (Public Order and Nuisance) Act could curtail their right to assembly. The High Court acknowledged that every Singapore citizen has the right to assemble peaceably, but the learned judge noted that Article 14(2) of the Singapore Constitution also qualifies this right by allowing the government to impose 'such restrictions as it considers necessary *or expedient* in the interest of … public order'. Notably, the High Court observed as follows:

> It bears emphasis that the phrase 'necessary or expedient' confers on Parliament an extremely wide discretionary power and remit that permits a multifarious and multifaceted approach towards achieving any of the purposes specified in Art 14(2) of the Constitution … there can be no questioning of whether the legislation is 'reasonable'. All that needs to be established is a nexus between the object of the impugned law and one of the permissible subjects stipulated in Art 14(2) of the Constitution.[62]

Simply put, the High Court was arguing that the literal text of the Singapore Constitution did not authorise the judiciary to examine the reasonableness of the impugned legislative measure. According to the judge, the constitutional right to free speech and assembly in Singapore is expressly qualified such that the government may impose 'such restrictions as it considers necessary *or expedient*'. Given that the terms 'reasonable' and 'expedient' are used disjunctively, the court concluded that there was no need for the courts to examine whether the impugned legislation is reasonable at all. Mere legislative expedience would suffice to justify the passage of any rights-infringing law on free assembly. Furthermore, given that the legislative power to circumscribe the right to free assembly is 'delineated by what is "in the interest of public order" and not confined to "the maintenance of public order"'[63], the court reasoned that Parliament is constitutionally conferred a wider legislative remit and is thereby textually authorised to take a prophylactic approach in the maintenance of public order. More significantly, the court argued that a 'generous and not a pedantic interpretation'[64] should be given to the legislative purposes underpinning these statutory restrictions.

In *Ong Ah Chuan v Public Prosecutor*[65] and *Chng Suan Tze v Minister of Home Affairs*,[66] our highest courts have exhorted that constitutional rights be given 'a generous interpretation, avoiding what has been called "the austerity of tabulated legalism", suitable to give to individuals the full measure of the [fundamental liberties] referred to'.[67] Now, not only were both appellate decisions not cited by the High Court, the learned judge had turned the iconic interpretive maxim on its head by deciding to give a generous interpretation to a statutory restriction instead of a constitutional right.

Textualism equally prevailed insofar as the High Court in *Chee Siok Chin* distinguished the applicability of Indian case law in Singapore. Unlike in Singapore, the limitations clause in India only allows for 'reasonable restrictions' to be imposed on the citizenry's right to free speech and assembly.[68] A fortiori, the Singapore High Court judge reasoned that the Indian courts have the power to declare a law restricting the constitutional right to assembly invalid on the basis that 'it does not create and/or form a reasonable restriction'.[69] In contrast, and with regard to Singapore, 'there can be no questioning of whether the legislation is "reasonable"'[70] and the 'court's sole task, when a constitutional challenge is advanced, is to ascertain whether an impugned law is within the purview of any of the permissible restrictions'.[71]

Nevertheless, our courts might want to reconsider its stance in the light of recent developments in Malaysia. In *Dr Mohd Nasir Hashim v Menteri Dalam Negeri Malaysia*,[72] the Court of Appeal upheld the constitutionality of an administrative policy which required a political party seeking registration at a national level to include in the party's committee at least one member from the seven states in the Federation of Malaysia. What is fascinating about this decision was the court's take on Article 10(2) of the Federal Constitution, which, similar to Singapore's Article 14(2), allows the government to limit a citizen's right to free expression, assembly and association if the restrictions are 'necessary or expedient' in the interests of, inter alia, security or public order. Nevertheless, the Malaysian Court of Appeal held that 'we can read the word "reasonable" before the word "restrictions"'[73] in Article 10(2). Furthermore, the 'court is therefore entitled to strike down state action on the ground that it is disproportionate to the object sought to be achieved'.[74] This judicial approach stands in stark contrast to that taken by the Singapore High Court in *Chee Siok Chin*, as discussed above. It is perhaps even more significant that the Malaysian Court of Appeal in *Nik Nazmi bin Nik Ahmad v Public Prosecutor*[75] invalidated section 9(5) of the Peaceful Assembly Act, which imposes criminal sanctions on organisers who fail to notify the police at least ten days before a proposed public assembly. While the court accepted that it was constitutional to impose a notification requirement on organisers, the judges took the view that it was *unreasonable* to automatically impose criminal sanctions for non-compliance with the notice requirement when the police retained a host of criminal law powers to address disorderly and unlawful assemblies should they occur. Therefore, insofar as the Malaysian judges have chosen to depart from such a literal reading of their limitations clause, which is practically identical to ours, it might be timely for our courts to re-examine the High Court's decision in *Chee Siok Chin*.

Furthermore, even if our courts are committed to textualism as an interpretive theory, the judicial application of textualism in *Chee Siok Chin* is not unproblematic. In Singapore, where parliamentary supremacy was expressly jettisoned in favour of a constitutional arrangement post-independence – an arrangement that places fundamental rights beyond the reach of majoritarian politics – it is logically inconceivable that the constitutional right to free assembly can be circumvented merely when it is *expedient* for the government of the day to override it. Even if one is an ardent textualist, one would note that the absurdity doctrine is a well-accepted canon of textual interpretation. As Lord Wensleydale observed in the 1857 decision of *Grey v Pearson*:

> [I]n construing … all written instruments, the grammatical and ordinary sense of the words is to be adhered to, unless that would lead to some absurdity, or some repugnance or inconsistency with the rest of the instrument, in which case, the grammatical and ordinary sense of the words may be avoided, so as to avoid that absurdity and inconsistency, but no farther.[76]

This, in essence, echoes Blackstone's observation that 'where words bear … a very absurd signification, if literally understood, we must a little deviate from the received sense of them'.[77] Therefore, in *Chee Siok Chin*, it would have been perfectly plausible, even as a textualist, for the learned judge to apply the absurdity doctrine and state that the Singapore Constitution only authorises Parliament to pass such legislative restrictions that are necessary *and* expedient in the interest of public order. Otherwise, *any* ordinary legislation that Parliament passes pursuant to the ends of public order could automatically trump the constitutionally enshrined right to free assembly. By reading the words 'necessary' and 'expedient' conjunctively, rather than disjunctively, the court would have corrected an obviously absurd and unintended disposition that would allow a constitutional exception to swallow up the constitutional rule that seeks to safeguard the citizenry's fundamental freedoms.

The key feature of textualism, as applied in the Singapore decision of *Chin Siok Chin*, is that it allows judges to focus on the literal language of a constitutional text, narrow the range of decisional opportunities open to them, and direct any changes to the impugned legislation to the legislature instead.

Lest one thinks that textualism is necessarily only a tool to justify judicial passivity, it must be pointed out that textualism has also been harnessed by Singapore judges to justify a more liberal and democratic reading of the Singapore Constitution. In *Vellama d/o Marie Muthu v Attorney-General*[78], the Court of Appeal had to decide whether the Prime Minister had a constitutional duty under Article 49 of the Constitution[79] to call for a by-election when a casual vacancy arose. Very laudably, the court rejected the government's argument that the Prime Minister had an unfettered discretion whether to call for a by-election, and instead imposed a constitutional duty on the Prime Minister to fill a casual vacancy within a 'reasonable time'.[80]

In view of the fact that Article 49 of the Singapore Constitution states that a 'vacancy *shall* be filled by election', the Court of Appeal advanced the following textual argument:

> The implication of a less definitive and directory rather than mandatory verb where the word 'shall' is used, and where its ordinary sense is not open to question, is simply unwarranted.[81]

The appeal of textualism is that it allows judges to defend the legal result they want by disguising their normative choices 'in the language of definitional inexorability'.[82] The 'our Constitution made us do it' argument allows judges to deny that they have an option in the matter, and obscures questions on how the judicial decision was made and whether it could have been made differently.[83]

IV Conclusion

This chapter has shown that originalism and textualism, as practised in Singapore, have been inconsistently observed and applied. Furthermore, the constitutional text and its history would rarely mandate the specific outcomes reached by the courts. In a constitutional system where a dominant party is in control, it is not inconceivable that a robust judicial reading of the Constitution could precipitate another constitutional crisis when the government responds to an adverse judicial ruling. After all, when the legislature is exempt from the usual pressures and constraints imposed by electoral competition, it can more likely rein in the courts when it is displeased with a judicial decision. In Singapore, where the ruling People's Action Party guards its prerogative to determine the constitutionality of the legislation it enacts, it is very plausible that any judicial attempt to invalidate duly enacted legislation would prove to be a Pyrrhic victory for the courts, as Parliament can respond with a constitutional amendment that reverses any confrontational judicial decision. Therefore, prudent judges in Singapore might decide to avoid heading for the constitutional precipice by choosing to preserve the legislative status quo instead.

Therefore, the deployment of originalism and textualism in Singapore as interpretive tools helps to obscure the strategic political choices judges make in support of preserving this status quo. As observed by Michael Hor, it is not easy for common law judges to be open about 'larger non-strictly legal motivations in judicial decision-making'.[84] Judges in the USA and UK, too, have admitted that judicial sensitivity to the consequences of decisions is 'not an exceptional or aberrant aspect of judicial decision making'.[85] Even jurists as eminent as Lord Bingham have pointed out that courts make their decisions 'in light of legal principle and such authority as there is, and having regard to the *apprehended practical consequences* of one decision as opposed to another ...' (emphasis added).[86]

So, perhaps, we should not chafe against these constitutional fig leaves for they do serve an important social function, which is to preserve judicial legitimacy and maintain political stability. As rightly argued by Christopher Forsyth:

> Those who consider that the fig leaf should be stripped away to reveal the awful truth to all the world do not, with respect, appreciate the subtlety of the constitutional order in which myth but not deceit plays so important a role and where form and function are often different.[87]

But, since textualism and originalism are mere fig leaves in Singapore and precisely because neither the text nor the history of our constitution inexorably mandates the results reached by our courts, the judicial outcomes should not be viewed as immutable, and they should and can be reviewed by a future appellate bench in the not-too-distant future when political circumstances evolve.

Notes

1 See also Jeff King, 'Institutional Approaches to Judicial Restraint' (2008) 28 Oxford Journal of Legal Studies 409; Erwin Chemerinsky, 'Getting Beyond Formalism in Constitutional Law: Constitutional Theory Matters' (2001) 54 Oklahoma Law Review 1.

2 Christopher Forsyth, 'Of Fig Leaves and Fairy Tales: The Ultra Vires Doctrine, The Sovereignty of Parliament and Judicial Review' (1996) 55 Cambridge Law Journal 122, 136.

3 ibid.

4 The People's Action Party has been the ruling party in Singapore since its independence and the party has controlled over 90 per cent of the elected seats in Parliament since 1968. See also Tom Ginsburg, *Judicial Review in New Democracies: Constitutional Courts in Asian Cases* (Cambridge University Press 2003) 82–83.

5 *Chng Suan Tze v Minister of Home Affairs* [1988] 2 SLR(R) 525. (Singapore Court of Appeal [Sing CA]).

6 Constitution of the Republic of Singapore (1985 Rev Ed, 1999 Reprint) ('Singapore Constitution') Article 9(1) states: 'No person shall be deprived of his life or personal liberty save in accordance with law.'

7 ibid Art 12(1): 'All persons are equal before the law and entitled to the equal protection of the law.'

8 One must, however, note that the Court of Appeal had merely quashed the detention order on a technicality and did not actually objectively review the Minister's exercise of his statutory powers of detention. The appeal primarily turned on the court's interpretation of section 8(1) of the ISA, which authorised the Minister of Home Affairs to issue a detention order if the President of Singapore was satisfied that this was necessary to prevent a person from acting in any manner prejudicial to the security of Singapore. On the facts, the detention orders were signed only by the Permanent Secretary of Home Affairs and his affidavit merely testified to the fact that the government was satisfied that the detention orders were necessary. The court held unanimously that this recital was insufficient. Instead, the court opined that, in the absence of direct evidence from the President, the Cabinet or the authorised Minister must provide evidence that the Cabinet (or the authorised Minister) was satisfied and that the President, after receiving the government's advice, was satisfied that these measures were necessary.

9 Aileen Kavanagh, 'Original Intention, Enacted Text, and Constitutional Interpretation' (2002) 47 American Journal of Jurisprudence 255, 261.

10 See Robert Bork, *The Tempting of America: The Political Seduction of the Law* (Free Press 1990) 143–60; Antonin Scalia, 'Common Law Courts in a Civil Law System: The Role of the United States Federal Courts in Interpreting the Constitution and Laws' in Amy Gutmann (ed), *A Matter of Interpretation* (Princeton University Press 1998) 17.

11 Cass Sunstein, *Legal Reasoning and Political Conflict* (Oxford University Press 1996) 173. There are many strands of 'originalist' thought. Hard originalists would focus on the original intent of the Constitution's framers or the public meaning of the constitutional text when it was originally adopted. Liberal originalists disagree that contemporary judges are bound by the original expected application of the constitutional text; instead, fidelity to the constitutional text would require judges to construe the broad and vague contours of the constitutional text in light of changing circumstances.

See Yvonne Tew, 'Originalism at Home and Abroad' (2014) 52 Columbia Journal of Transnational Law 780.

12 Bork (n 10); Scalia (n 10).

13 Antonin Scalia, 'Commentary' (1996) 40 St Louis University Law Journal 1119.

14 *Yong Vui Kong v Public Prosecutor* [2010] SGCA 20 (Sing CA).

15 Singapore Constitution (n 6) Art 9(1).

16 See *Reyes v The Queen* [2002] 2 AC 235; *Fox v The Queen* [2002] 2 AC 284; *R v Hughes* [2002] 1 AC 259.

17 Singapore became a constituent state of Malaysia in 1963 and gained full independence as a sovereign republic in 1965.

18 *Yong (2010)* (n 14) [62].

19 The Singapore Constitutional Commission was tasked by the Singapore government in 1966 to make recommendations on constitutional changes that might be necessary to protect the rights of minorities in Singapore.

20 *Yong (2010)* (n 14) [72].

21 ibid [16].

22 For example, the Singapore Parliament deliberately omitted to include Article 13 of the Federal Constitution that guarantees the right to property and provides for adequate compensation for depreciation of this right. See Kevin Tan and Min-Yeo Thio, *Constitutional Law in Malaysia and Singapore* (LexisNexis 2010) 74; Kevin YL Tan, 'State and Institution Building through the Singapore Constitution 1965–2005' in Li-ann Thio and Kevin Tan (eds), *Evolution of a Revolution: Forty Years of the Singapore Constitution* (Routledge-Cavendish 2009) 54.

23 For a fuller discussion of this case, see Yap Po Jen, 'Constitutionalising Capital Crimes: Judicial Virtue or Originalism Sin?' (2011) Singapore Journal of Legal Studies 281.

24 ibid.

25 *Yong Vui Kong v Public Prosecutor* [2015] SGCA 11 (Sing CA) [69].

26 *Yong (2010)* (n 14) [75].

27 ibid.

28 In *Yong Vui Kong v Public Prosecutor* [2015] SGCA 11 (Sing CA), the Court of Appeal affirmed that the statutory authorisation of caning does not breach Art 9(1) of the Constitution.

29 *Yong Vui Kong v Public Prosecutor* [2015] SGCA 11 (Sing CA).

30 *Yong (2010)* (n 14) [92].

31 [2005] 1 SLR 103 (Sing CA).

32 ibid [91].

33 *Yong (2015)* (n 29) [38].

34 Singapore Constitution (n 6) Art 22P(1):

> The President, as occasion shall arise, may, on the advice of the Cabinet —
>
> *(a)* grant a pardon to any accomplice in any offence who gives information which leads to the conviction of the principal offender or any one of the principal offenders, if more than one;
>
> *(b)* grant to any offender convicted of any offence in any court in Singapore, a pardon, free or subject to lawful conditions, or any reprieve or respite, either indefinite or for such period as the President may think fit, of the execution of any sentence pronounced on such offender; or
>
> *(c)* remit the whole or any part of such sentence or of any penalty or forfeiture imposed by law.

35 *Yong Vui Kong v Attorney-General* [2011] 2 SLR 1189 (Sing CA) [174].

36 ibid [172].

37 ibid [173].

38 *Yong Vui Kong* (n 35) [157].
39 Shubhankar Dam, 'Presidential Pardon in Singapore: A Comment on *Yong Vui Kong v Attorney-General*' (2013) 42 Common Law World Review 48, 51.
40 *Yong Vui Kong* (n 35) [114].
41 ibid [113]–[114].
42 ibid [83].
43 ibid [37], [72].
44 *Yong (2015)* (n 29).
45 ibid [16].
46 ibid [16]–[18].
47 ibid [20].
48 ibid [23].
49 ibid [64].
50 ibid [18].
51 Singapore Constitution (n 6) Art 44(2)(b).
52 ibid Art 65(4).
53 Mark D Greenberg and Harry Litman, 'The Meaning of Original Meaning' (1998) 86 Georgetown Law Journal 569, 580.
54 Jack M Balkin, 'Nine Perspectives on Living Originalism' (2012) University of Illinois Law Review 815, 817.
55 ibid 815–16.
56 Ginsburg (n 4) 19.
57 ibid 81.
58 See Po Jen Yap, *Constitutional Dialogue in Common Law Asia* (Oxford University Press 2015) 77–78.
59 Michael Hor, 'Singapore's Death Penalty: The Beginning of the End?' in Roger Hood and Surya Deva (eds), *Confronting Capital Punishment in Asia: Human Rights, Politics, and the Public Opinion* (Oxford University Press 2013) 149.
60 Antonin Scalia and Bryan A Garner, *Reading Law: The Interpretation of Legal Texts* (Thomson/West 2012) Preface xxx.
61 *Chee Siok Chin v Minister for Home Affairs* [2006] 1 SLR 582 (Singapore High Court [Sing HC]).
62 ibid [49].
63 ibid [50].
64 ibid [49].
65 *Ong Ah Chuan v Public Prosecutor* [1980–1981] SLR 48 (Privy Council [PC]).
66 *Chng Suan Tze* (n 5).
67 *Ong Ah Chuan* (n 65) [23]; see also *Chng Suan Tze* (n 5) [80]–[82].
68 Article 19(3) of the Constitution of India, 1950:

> Nothing in sub-clause (b) of the said clause … shall affect the operation of any existing law in so far as it imposes or prevents the State from making any law imposing, in the interest of the sovereignty and integrity of India or public order, reasonable restrictions on the exercise of the right conferred by the said sub-clause.

69 *Chee Siok Chin* (n 61) [46].
70 ibid [49].
71 ibid [49].
72 [2006] 6 MLJ 213 (Malaysia Court of Appeal [Malaysia CA]).
73 ibid [9].
74 ibid [8]. The Court of Appeal justified this reading on the basis that the 'court must not permit restrictions upon the rights conferred … that render those rights *illusory*' (emphasis added). See [11].
75 [2014] 4 MLJ 157 (Malaysia CA).
76 (1857) 6 HL Cas 61,106.

77 2 Bl Comm 60.
78 *Vellama d/o Marie Muthu v Attorney-General* [2013] 4 SLR 1 (Sing CA).
79 Singapore Constitution (n 6) Art 49(1): 'Whenever the seat of a Member, not being a non-constituency Member, has become vacant for any reason other than a dissolution of Parliament, the vacancy shall be filled by election.'
80 *Vellama* (n 78) [84].
81 ibid [77].
82 Frederick Schauer, 'Formalism' (1988) 97 Yale Law Journal 509, 513–14.
83 ibid.
84 Hor (n 59) 149.
85 Aileen Kavanagh, 'Judicial Restraint in the Pursuit of Justice' (2010) 60 University of Toronto Law Journal 23, 33.
86 Lord Bingham, 'The Courts and the Constitution' (1996/1997) 7 King's College Law Journal 12, 16.
87 Christopher Forsyth, 'Of Fig Leaves and Fairy Tales: The Ultra Vires Doctrine, The Sovereignty of Parliament and Judicial Review' (1996) 55 Cambridge Law Journal 122, 136.

Bibliography

Balkin, Jack M, 'Nine Perspectives on Living Originalism' (2012) University of Illinois Law Review 815.

Bingham, Lord T, 'The Courts and the Constitution' (1996/1997) 7 King's College Law Journal 12.

Bork, Robert, *The Tempting of America: The Political Seduction of the Law* (Free Press 1990).

Chemerinsky, Erwin, 'Getting Beyond Formalism in Constitutional Law: Constitutional Theory Matters' (2001) 54 Oklahoma Law Review 1.

Dam, Shubhankar, 'Presidential Pardon in Singapore: A Comment on *Yong Vui Kong v Attorney-General*' (2013) 42 Common Law World Review 48.

Forsyth, Christopher, 'Of Fig Leaves and Fairy Tales: The Ultra Vires Doctrine, The Sovereignty of Parliament and Judicial Review' (1996) 55 CLJ 122.

Garner, Bryan A and Antonin Scalia, *Reading Law: The Interpretation of Legal Texts* (Thomson/West 2012) Preface xxx.

Ginsburg, Tom, *Judicial Review in New Democracies: Constitutional Courts in Asian Cases* (Cambridge University Press 2003).

Greenberg, Mark D and Harry Litman, 'The Meaning of Original Meaning' (1998) 86 Georgetown Law Journal 569.

Hor, Michael, 'Singapore's Death Penalty: The Beginning of the End?' in Roger Hood and Surya Deva (eds), *Confronting Capital Punishment in Asia: Human Rights, Politics, and the Public Opinion* (Oxford University Press 2013).

Kavanagh, Aileen, 'Original Intention, Enacted Text, and Constitutional Interpretation' (2002) 47 American Journal of Jurisprudence 255.

Kavanagh, Aileen, 'Judicial Restraint in the Pursuit of Justice' (2010) 60 University of Toronto Law Journal 23.

King, Jeff, 'Institutional Approaches to Judicial Restraint' (2008) 28 Oxford Journal of Legal Studies 409.

Scalia, Antonin, 'Common Law Courts in a Civil Law System: The Role of the United States Federal Courts in Interpreting the Constitution and Laws' in Amy Gutmann (ed), *A Matter of Interpretation* (Princeton University Press 1998).

Schauer, Frederick, ‘Formalism’ (1988) 97 Yale Law Journal 509.
Sunstein, Cass, *Legal Reasoning and Political Conflict* (Oxford University Press 1996).
Tan, Kevin YL, ‘State and Institution Building through the Singapore Constitution 1965–2005’ in Li-ann Thio and Kevin YL Tan (eds), *Evolution of a Revolution: Forty Years of the Singapore Constitution* (Routledge-Cavendish 2009).
Tew, Yvonne, ‘Originalism at Home and Abroad’ (2014) 52 Columbia Journal of Transnational Law 780.
Thio, Li-ann and Kevin YL Tan, *Constitutional Law in Malaysia and Singapore* (LexisNexis 2010).
Yap, Po Jen, ‘Constitutionalising Capital Crimes: Judicial Virtue or Originalism Sin?’ (2011) Singapore Journal of Legal Studies 281.
Yap, Po Jen, *Constitutional Dialogue in Common Law Asia* (Oxford University Press 2015).

Part II

Interrogating assumptions

6 Rethinking the presumption of constitutionality

Jack Tsen-Ta Lee[1]

Legal cases are often won or lost on the burden of proof, and constitutional claims are no exception. In Singapore, what makes such claims particularly difficult to succeed in is a doctrine called the presumption of constitutionality. The doctrine surfaced in a 1977 case, *Lee Keng Guan v Public Prosecutor*,[2] involving Article 12(1) of the Constitution,[3] which guarantees to all persons the rights to equality before the law and the equal protection of the law. Since then it has been consistently adverted to by the courts, and while it remains closely associated with equality jurisprudence, the courts have made it clear that it applies to all constitutional claims. In addition, another rule expressed in the Latin maxim *omnia praesumuntur rite esse acta* – all things are presumed to have been done rightly – has been regarded as justifying the application of the presumption to acts and decisions of government officials.

In judicial review proceedings, the overall legal burden of establishing the case undoubtedly lies on the claimant. In the United Kingdom and certain other jurisdictions, he or she must raise a prima facie case that the Government has acted unlawfully, whereupon it is for the Government to discharge its evidential burden by proving the contrary. However, in Singapore, the presumption of constitutionality, as it has been explained by the courts, has the effect of imposing an additional and substantial onus on the claimant to produce material or factual evidence to justify the claim before the court will require the Government to respond substantively to it. At the same time, the court assumes the existence of any plausible facts pointing towards the constitutionality of the executive or legislative act being challenged, without requiring the Government to adduce any supporting evidence. In this chapter, I consider whether imposing this onus on claimants is justified.

I The presumption of constitutionality in Singapore

The presumption of constitutionality was first applied in Singapore in cases involving Article 12(1) of the Constitution,[4] which guarantees rights to equality before the law and the equal protection of the law. It was adopted from *Shri Ram Krishna Dalmia v Shri Justice S R Tendolkar*,[5] a decision of the Supreme Court of India interpreting Article 14 of the Indian Constitution,[6] which is similar in all material respects to Article 12. The following statement from *Shri Ram Krishna Dalmia*[7] was approved by two cases of the Singapore Court of Appeal, *Lee Keng Guan*[8] (referred to earlier) and *Public Prosecutor v Taw Cheng Kong*:[9]

> [T]here is always a presumption in favour of the constitutionality of an enactment and this burden is upon him who attacks it to show that there has been a clear transgression…

In *Taw Cheng Kong*, the Court of Appeal characterised the presumption as a 'strong presumption of constitutional validity',[10] even though the adjective *strong* does not appear in the Indian judgment. It neither explained what it regarded as the difference between a strong and an ordinary presumption, nor why a strong presumption applied in that case instead of an ordinary one. The subsequent case of *Lim Meng Suang v Attorney-General*[11] may shed some light on the matter, although the Court of Appeal did not say it was explaining its statement in *Taw Cheng Kong*. The court noted that the strength of the presumption is not monolithic, but may vary according to the circumstances of each case.[12] The presumption does not, for instance, apply as strongly to laws predating the commencement of the independent Republic of Singapore's Constitution on 9 August 1965 because many of such laws were formulated in the absence of a constitutional bill of rights.[13] On the other hand, the presumption is said to apply with full force to post-independence laws as these were 'promulgated in the context of, inter alia, an elected legislature which, it can be assumed, would have fully considered all views before enacting the (post-Independence) laws concerned'.[14] This would include section 37(1) of the Prevention of Corruption Act,[15] the constitutionality of which was questioned in *Taw Cheng Kong*, because it was introduced in 1966.[16] In any event, it is clear that the presumption extends to all constitutional challenges and not only to those in which Article 12(1) is invoked,[17] although it is in such cases that the rule has been most fully described.

Closely allied to the presumption of constitutionality is the principle expressed in the maxim *omnia praesumuntur rite esse acta*, which was translated in *Yong Vui Kong v Attorney-General*[18] as 'all things are presumed to have been done rightly and regularly, *ie*, in conformity with the law'.[19] In *Ramalingam Ravinthran v Public Prosecutor*,[20] the Court of Appeal applied the principle to prosecutorial decisions, by virtue of the constitutional standing of the office of the Attorney-General who is the Public Prosecutor.[21] In the light of this, it concluded that a presumption of constitutionality applies to prosecutorial decisions.[22] The court noted that the presumption also applies to the decisions of administrative officials without constitutional standing because the *omnia praesumuntur* principle is applicable to them as well. However, the presumption does not operate as strongly.[23]

The presumption has the following effects. The court '*prima facie* leans in favour of constitutionality and supports the impugned legislation if it is reasonable to do so', and 'it is for the party who attacks the validity of a piece of legislation to place relevant materials and evidence before the court'.[24] In *Taw Cheng Kong*, the Court of Appeal elaborated on the issue in these terms:[25]

> [U]nless the law is *plainly arbitrary* on its face, postulating examples of arbitrariness would ordinarily not be helpful in rebutting the presumption of constitutionality. This is because another court or person can well postulate an equal number if not more examples to show that the law did not operate arbitrarily. If postulating examples of arbitrariness can always by themselves be sufficient for purposes of rebuttal, then it will hardly be giving effect to the presumption that Parliament knows best for its people, that its laws are directed at problems made manifest by experience, and hence its differentiation is based on adequate grounds. Therefore, *to discharge the burden of rebutting the presumption, it will usually be necessary for the person challenging the law to adduce some material or factual evidence to show that it was enacted arbitrarily or had operated arbitrarily.* Otherwise, there will be no practical difference between the presumption and the ordinary burden of proof on the person asserting unconstitutionality.

The presumption of constitutionality tips the scales very much in the Government's favour. If an applicant claims, for example, that a legislative provision infringes one of the fundamental liberties in the Constitution and 'if any state of facts reasonably can be conceived that would sustain it, the existence of that state of facts at the time the law was enacted must be assumed' by the court.[26] In other words, the Government may simply submit to the court at least one plausible reason for the impugned law or executive action, and the court will assume it is true. The Government is relieved of the need to produce evidence to justify the constitutionality of the law or action. Only where there are no credible justifications will the court decline to make any inferences. In the context of the constitutional protection of equality, it has been said that

> if there is nothing on the face of the law or the surrounding circumstances brought to the notice of the court on which the [legislative] classification may reasonably be regarded as based, the presumption of constitutionality cannot be carried to the extent of always holding that there must be some undisclosed and unknown reasons for subjecting certain individuals or corporations to hostile or discriminating legislation.[27]

In contrast to the foregoing, to overcome the presumption and to require the Government to discharge its evidential burden of proving the constitutionality of the provision in question, it is not enough that the applicant is able to posit examples of how the provision operates unjustly. Instead, he or she must adduce material or factual evidence that is compelling or cogent which demonstrates that the provision was enacted arbitrarily or operated arbitrarily.[28] The standard is pitched at arbitrariness,[29] with the consequence that laws and executive actions are subjected to a mere rationality test. A legislative provision is not unconstitutional unless it is arbitrary or irrational.[30]

It is difficult to see what evidence applicants can find to show arbitrary enactment of a provision. Given how unlikely it is that legislators will admit openly in Parliament that they intend to discriminate against a certain class of people, applicants will have to rely on statements having only circumstantial effect. The court would probably deem such inferences too speculative to rebut the presumption.

As for arbitrary operation, in *Lim Meng Suang and another v Attorney-General*[31] the High Court held out the United States Supreme Court decision *Yick Wo v Hopkins*[32] as a 'good example'[33] of an appellant having brought cogent material and factual evidence before the court to establish that certain municipal authorities in San Francisco had discriminated against him in the implementation of a fire-safety regulation in violation of the Fourteenth Amendment.[34] The regulation stipulated that the authorities' consent was required to operate a laundry in a building not constructed of brick or stone. The appellant's petition to the court had alleged that he and 200 other Chinese persons who were not United States citizens had been denied consent to continue operating their laundries in wooden buildings, which they had done for over twenty years. Yet, all the requests (save one) made by persons who were not Chinese had been granted. Moreover, while the appellant and more than 150 of his countrymen had been arrested for continuing to operate their businesses without the requisite consent, none of the laundrymen in the same position who were not Chinese citizens had been detained. These asserted facts were admitted to by the respondent, the sheriff of the city and county of San Francisco, under whose custody the appellant had been placed.[35]

If the Singapore Government declines to stipulate to facts as the respondent in *Yick Wo* did, it appears that an applicant may have to incur the potentially substantial expense of arranging for statistically significant surveys to be conducted in order to have cogent evidence to adduce. What is more, it could prove somewhat easier to obtain evidence of unconstitutional *implementation* of a law (as was the case in *Yick Wo*) than evidence that a law is intrinsically unconstitutional. This is because the latter is more readily proved through reasoned arguments. If the adduction of 'material or factual evidence' is a prerequisite to applicants displacing a presumption of constitutionality in a situation of this sort, it is not immediately clear what sort of evidence they should compile to demonstrate this.

II Justifications and criticisms

A Deference to the legislature

Since the presumption of constitutionality was adopted by the Singapore courts from Indian case law, an examination of the origin of the presumption in that jurisdiction is apposite. A 1950 Indian case, *Chiranjit Lal v Union of India*,[36] justified the presumption's existence by relying upon the following sentence from the decision of the United States Supreme Court in *Middleton v Texas Power and Light Company*:

> It must be presumed that a Legislature understands and correctly appreciates the needs of its own people, that its laws are directed to problems made manifest by experience and that its discriminations are based upon adequate grounds.[37]

It is submitted that the courts' reliance on *Middleton* to justify the presumption is misplaced. This judgment was delivered in 1919, before a major shift in US constitutional law was wrought in 1938 by Justice Harlan Stone's Footnote Four of the *Carolene Products* case.[38] In this famous footnote, Justice Stone suggested that the courts should apply a stricter standard of scrutiny where the Government has classified persons in a way that offends fundamental rights in the Constitution (such as those set out in the first ten amendments) or where such a classification results from 'prejudice against discrete and insular minorities'.[39] Singapore cases have not examined decisions subsequent to *Carolene Products*, such as *Heller v Doe*,[40] in which the US Supreme Court made clear that in equal protection analyses, a statutory classification is only accorded a strong presumption of validity if it neither involves fundamental rights nor proceeds 'along suspect lines'.[41]

This rosy view of the legislature is not the only justification the Singapore courts have relied on. In *Lim Meng Suang*, the High Court regarded the presumption as 'intimately tied to the idea of separation of powers'.[42] The doctrine of justiciability is likewise based on the separation of powers, and in this context it was said in *Lee Hsien Loong v Review Publishing*[43] that the intensity of judicial review must take into account 'the simple fact that there are certain questions in respect of which there can be no expectation that an unelected judiciary will play any role'.[44] Therefore, the court held that 'where issues of social morality are concerned', it should adopt an approach 'tilted in favour of persons who are elected and entrusted with the task of representing the people's interests and will'.[45]

In the Singapore context, therefore, the presumption of constitutionality seems to be justified by the fact that Parliament has considered the matter and regards the legislation in question as constitutional. The same rationalisation would appear to apply to the *omnia praesumuntur* principle – that government officials have made an assessment of the constitutionality of their actions and decisions. Where legislation is concerned, particularly where 'issues of social morality' are dealt with, this opinion is accorded significant weight due to the legislature's democratic credentials. The implication is that the legislature is accountable to the people for its decisions. The Supreme Court of Ireland has justified the application of a presumption of constitutionality in a similar way. In *Pigs Marketing Board v Donnelly*,[46] for example, it was said:[47]

> When the Court has to consider the constitutionality of a law it must, in the first place, be accepted as an axiom that a law passed by the Oireachtas [the legislature of Ireland], the elected representatives of the people, is presumed to be constitutional unless and until the contrary is established.

We should, therefore, examine whether courts are right in making the above assumptions. In the first instance, where the legislation in question was enacted before any legally enforceable bill of rights applied to Singapore, it is hard to see how the legislature can be regarded as having considered the 'constitutionality' of the legislation. For instance, when section 377A was introduced into the Penal Code in 1938,[48] the Attorney-General of the Straits Settlements said only that the provision was necessary to align the local law with English criminal law in order to enable stronger action to be taken against acts of 'gross indecency' between men, which were regarded as undesirable.[49] Unless a counterfactual and speculative analysis of these facts surrounding the legislation's enactment is embarked upon, it cannot honestly be said that the Legislative Assembly took any account of whether section 377A intruded excessively into the private lives of men to whom the provision might apply, or discriminated against them. Although in *Lim Meng Suang* the Court of Appeal took the view that a presumption of constitutionality would still apply, albeit less strongly,[50] it is submitted the better view is that no presumption ought to apply at all.

As for legislation enacted after a bill of rights applied to Singapore, it should be asked whether it is in fact sufficiently scrutinised for constitutionality as it makes its way through Parliament. There are few formal requirements, unlike in the United Kingdom where section 19 of the Human Rights Act 1998[51] obliges a Minister of the Crown in charge of a bill in either House of Parliament, before the Second Reading of the bill, to either make a 'statement of compatibility', that is, one to the effect that in his view the provisions of the bill are compatible with the rights protected by the Act, or to declare that the Government wishes the House to proceed with the bill even though he is unable to make such a statement. This procedure requires the Government to direct its mind towards considering if the bill is compliant with human rights. In addition, a permanent Joint Committee on Human Rights comprising members of both Houses exists, and one of its main functions is to scrutinise parliamentary bills for conformity with the Act.[52]

Although this parliamentary safeguard does not exist in Singapore, Part VII of the Constitution requires all bills that are given a final reading and passed by Parliament (apart from some exceptions) to be sent to the Presidential Council for Minority Rights before being presented to the President for assent.[53] The Council examines the legislation and must draw attention to any 'differentiating measure',[54] namely,

> any measure which is, or is likely in its practical application to be, disadvantageous to persons of any racial or religious community and not equally disadvantageous to persons of other such communities, either directly by

prejudicing persons of that community or indirectly by giving advantage to persons of another community.[55]

If the Council renders an adverse report in respect of a bill, Parliament may either amend the bill and resubmit it to the Council for further consideration, or proceed to present the bill to the President for assent after a motion for that purpose has been passed by the affirmative vote of not less than two-thirds of the total membership of Parliament.[56] It is clear that the Council's remit is narrow. It ensures that legislation does not disadvantage racial or religious communities, arguably in line with the rights to equality and freedom of religion, and to non-discrimination in respect of education, respectively guaranteed by Articles 12, 15 and 16 of the Constitution. The Council has no role to ensure that laws comply with other fundamental liberties in Part IV of the Constitution, such as the prohibition against deprivation of life or personal liberty save in accordance with law, and the rights to free speech and assembly.[57] To date, no adverse report has been rendered by the Council.[58]

Another means that might be employed to test the constitutionality of a bill is the advisory opinion procedure established by Article 100 of the Constitution. The President may refer to a tribunal, consisting of no less than three judges of the Supreme Court, for its opinion any question on the effect of any provision of the Constitution that has arisen or that appears likely to arise.[59] This includes asking the tribunal to rule on the constitutionality of a bill, and if the bill is found to be constitutional, no court has the jurisdiction to question the validity of the law resulting from the passing of the bill.[60] However, the procedure is fairly limited. The President can only refer a question to the Constitution of the Republic of Singapore Tribunal if he is advised by the Cabinet to do so; he lacks personal discretion in this regard.[61] Thus, if the Government takes the view that legislation it has initiated is constitutional, it seems unlikely it will advise the President to trigger the advisory opinion procedure. Furthermore, former Chief Justice Chan Sek Keong has taken the extra-judicial view that Article 100 was enacted as a means to resolve disputes between constitutional organs rather than to enable individuals to obtain court rulings on constitutional issues,[62] although it has to be said that a plain reading of the provision does not contain any such limitation. On 29 January 1999, the President's principal private secretary, responding to the opposition politician and lawyer JB Jeyaretnam's request that the question of the constitutionality of an Act his client had been charged under be referred to the Constitutional Tribunal, said that the advisory opinion procedure should be invoked only 'when there is no other forum available to a person who claims that his constitutional rights have been infringed to have such claim tested'.[63] This must no doubt be taken as the Government's view. As at the time of writing the procedure had only been used once, in 1995.[64] In the circumstances, the Constitutional Tribunal cannot really be regarded as a routine and dependable means of ensuring the constitutionality of legislation.

Apart from these concerns about the legal framework, it may be asked whether there is in fact a practice of examining the constitutionality of bills in

Parliament. On a number of occasions, the Government has consulted the Attorney-General on constitutional matters and disclosed in Parliament the opinion expressed. For example, this was done on 14 January 1998 to explain why Article 144 of the Constitution[65] did not require the President's concurrence to a loan made by the Singapore Government to the Government of Indonesia.[66] Subsequently, the Attorney-General's opinion that the right to vote is to be implied into the Constitution was endorsed in Parliament by the Government on 16 May 2001 and again on 13 February 2009.[67] However, none of these incidents related to the constitutionality of a bill, and it is unclear whether the Attorney-General is consistently asked for his views on this type of issue. Even if he is, Hansard appears to indicate that the Government does not regularly inform MPs of the Attorney-General's opinions so that they can be discussed in Parliament.

There have been instances when fundamental liberties were mentioned in the House during the Second Readings of bills. The rights to freedom of expression, assembly and movement[68] were raised in Parliament during the legislative lead-up to the Public Order Act[69] which, among other things, refined the regulation of cause-related assemblies and processions through the issuance of permits, and granted new powers to the police to order people to 'move on' from a particular place, and to seize films or pictures taken of law enforcement activities. Non-Constituency Member of Parliament (NCMP) Sylvia Lim and Nominated Members of Parliament (NMPs) Siew Kum Hong and Thio Li-ann argued that provisions in the bill did not necessarily strike an appropriate balance between public order and the fundamental liberties in question,[70] whereas Second Minister for Home Affairs K Shanmugam and other Members of Parliament (MPs) of the ruling People's Action Party (PAP) took the opposing view.[71] In contrast, while the right to freedom of religion was mentioned by a number of parliamentarians during debates on the bill that led to the Maintenance of Religious Harmony Act,[72] the constitutionality of the bills in question was not debated in detail. The Government asserted the necessity of imposing restrictions on rights, and this was largely unquestioned by a number of PAP MPs.[73]

Arguably, therefore, the extent to which the constitutionality of bills is legislatively examined is inconsistent. Assuming that the Government does in fact assert in Parliament that a particular bill is constitutional, given the large majority of parliamentary seats held by the PAP[74] and its strong enforcement of the party whip system, it seems unlikely that most MPs (being PAP backbenchers) would disagree with the Government's view. Conversely, it is doubtful that opposition MPs, NCMPs and NMPs would be able to convince the Government that a bill needs to be altered since their votes are not needed for the enactment of bills.[75]

Parliament's nature as a democratic institution does not by itself justify a presumption of constitutionality. It is jarring for critics to argue that Singapore's system of strong constitutional review, under which the courts are empowered to strike down laws incompatible with the Constitution, is somehow undemocratic, when it was established through a democratic process. Moreover, a richer conception of representative democracy goes beyond majority rule to comprehend due respect for the fundamental rights of minorities,[76] which the courts must protect through judicial review. The court process can also be regarded as democratic in its own right, since it involves a hearing (usually public) before an impartial judge at which all parties are able to present their respective cases.[77] Eventually, if the court decides to declare the law in question unconstitutional, this stimulates a constitutional dialogue between the judiciary and the political branches of government, in the course of which the latter will have to decide whether to accept the court's judgment or seek to overturn it through a constitutional amendment. Members of the public are free to participate in the dialogue. With the benefit of a reasoned court judgment and statements from politicians both in and outside Parliament, they can 'examine and criticise the human rights compatibility of legislation, as well as the desirability of a continuing restraint over legislation in order to protect human rights'.[78] Through public discussion, engagement with MPs and, ultimately, their electoral votes, they are in a position to help to shape the political branches' decision on the matter.

Brian Foley argues in the Irish context that it is appropriate for the courts to demonstrate deference to Parliament's views in some circumstances. However, Alison Young analyses Foley's view of deference as involving respect for the legislature rather than submission to it. The difference is that a court should not meekly accept that the legislature has correctly decided that a law is constitutional. Instead, it must come to its own decision on the matter, but may give weight to the legislature's views.[79] This factor therefore militates against the application of a presumption of constitutionality.

Second, Foley says that deference should be applied 'non-spatially' and not 'spatially'. A spatial approach means that the court defers to Parliament when a matter falls within a specified category, such as national security. This takes a rigid view of the separation of powers and may, for example, assume there is a clear divide between policy and law, only matters involving the latter being suitable for judicial determination. The presumption of constitutionality is problematic because it takes a spatial approach towards deference.[80] When a court does so it overlooks the fact that the separation of powers doctrine is best understood not as requiring a strict distribution of functions between the three branches of government, but rather as 'a network of rules and principles which ensure that power is not concentrated in the hands of one branch'.[81] Thus, checks and balances between the branches *inter se*, and in particular the subjection of acts of the political branches to judicial review by the judicial branch, must be regarded as integral to the doctrine. In contrast, if deference is applied non-spatially, the court does not presuppose a rigid divide between law and policy, and 'defer[s] only when required according to the specific interests of national security raised in the precise question before the court'.[82]

Thus, irrespective of whether Parliament has indeed given serious thought to a bill's constitutionality, it is submitted that the courts have a responsibility to independently ascertain whether the legislators have determined the issue correctly. If a court concludes too readily that the political branches have acted lawfully or that a matter is simply not justiciable, there is a danger that judicial review will become a blunted tool and fundamental liberties will be insufficiently protected.

The Canadian experience is instructive. A presumption of proportionality applies in constitutional cases where the issue is whether a law must be invalidated because the power to enact it lay with the federal legislature rather than the provincial legislature or vice versa.[83] The effect of the presumption in such cases is moderated by the fact that, according to the Constitution, if one level of government has no power to act, the other level does.[84] Conversely, the presumption has been held to be inapt in cases involving the Canadian Charter. In *Manitoba (AG) v Metropolitan Stores Ltd*,[85] the Supreme Court of Canada stated that 'the innovative and evolutive nature of the *Canadian Charter of Rights and Freedoms* conflicts with the idea that a legislative provision can be presumed to be consistent with the *Charter*'.[86] Similarly, the application of legally enforceable fundamental liberties to Singapore when it became a state of Malaysia in 1963, and their inclusion in the Singapore Constitution upon the nation's full independence in 1965, indicate a deliberate departure from the assumption that individual rights are adequately protected by the legislature. Instead, the courts were given the weighty responsibility of scrutinising executive and legislative acts for compliance with constitutional principles.

In *Operation Dismantle v The Queen*,[87] the Supreme Court of Canada drew a distinction between a court pronouncing on the wisdom of the executive's exercise of its defence powers, which it considers inappropriate, and determining if an executive act violated the rights of citizens. In the latter case, 'it is not only appropriate that we answer the question; it is our obligation under the *Charter* to do so'.[88] This, it is submitted, is the correct approach, since the Singapore High Court itself in *Lim Meng Suang* affirmed that

> [i]t is both the duty and the constitutional role of our courts to ensure that Parliament does not contravene the rights enshrined in the constitution for it is the Constitution, and not Parliament, that is supreme in our legal system. Our courts are the guardians who ensure that the rule of law and all that it entails is observed and prevails.[89]

B The presumption of constitutionality as a canon of construction

The Supreme Court of Canada pointed out in the *Metropolitan Stores* case that the term *presumption of constitutionality* can also signify a 'rule of construction under which an impugned statute ought to be construed, whenever possible, in such a way as to make it conform to the Constitution'.[90] Indeed, this appears to be the common law understanding of the presumption. In *Attorney-General of the Gambia v Jobe*,[91] the Privy Council said the presumption of constitutionality[92]

> ...is but a particular application of the canon of construction embodied in the Latin maxim magis est ut res valeat quam pereat which is an aid to the

> resolution of any ambiguities or obscurities in the actual words used in any document that is manifestly intended by its makers to create legal rights or obligations.... Where, as in the instant case, omissions by the draftsman of the law to state in express words what, from the subject matter of the law and the legal nature of the processes or institutions with which it deals, can be inferred to have been Parliament's intention, a court charged with the judicial duty of giving effect to Parliament's intention, as that intention has been stated in the law that Parliament has passed, ought to construe the law as incorporating, by necessary implication, words which would give effect to such inferred intention, wherever to do so does not contradict the words actually set out in the law itself and to fail to do so would defeat Parliament's intention by depriving the law of all legal effect.

In other words, the presumption does not impose on the challenger of a law any particularly burdensome evidential onus, but is in line with 'the elementary rule of legal procedure according to which "the one who asserts must prove", with the consequence that "the onus of establishing that legislation violates the Constitution undeniably lies with those who oppose the legislation"', which the Supreme Court in *Metropolitan Stores* regarded as another way in which the presumption of constitutionality may be understood.[93]

Cases applying the *omnia praesumuntur* rule are to like effect. The Court of Appeal of England and Wales commented in *Knight v Harris*:[94]

> The maxim expresses an inference which may reasonably be drawn when an intention to do some formal act is established; when the evidence is consistent with that intention having been carried into effect in a proper way; but when the actual observance of all due formalities can only be inferred as a matter of probability. The maxim is not wanted where such observance is proved, nor has it any place where such observance is disproved. The maxim only comes into operation where there is no proof one way or the other; but where it is more probable that what was intended to be done was done as it ought to have been done to render it valid; rather than that it was done in some other manner which would defeat the intention proved to exist, and would render what is proved to have been done of no effect.

The rule applies to legislation as much as to acts and decisions,[95] but the courts of the United Kingdom have treated it as having no greater effect than affirming the general duty of the applicant to establish a prima facie case of unlawfulness,[96] whereupon the Government must discharge its own evidential burden of establishing that the impugned legislation or action was in fact lawful.[97] Indeed, in *Buxton v Jayne*[98] the Court of Appeal declined to apply the rule at all '[i]n a matter which touches the liberty of the subject',[99] and this position was also taken by the House of Lords in *R v Secretary of State for the Home Department, ex p Khawaja*,[100] Lord Scarman noting that

> in cases where the exercise of executive discretion interferes with liberty or property rights … the burden of justifying the legality of the decision [is] upon the executive. Once the applicant has shown a prima facie case, this is the law.[101]

Since constitutional claims in Singapore are manifestly akin to cases where a claimant alleges that such rights have been infringed, I would submit that the presumption of constitutionality should be reinterpreted in line with the cases described above.

The decision of the Hong Kong Court of Final Appeal in *Secretary for Justice v Yau Yuk Lung*,[102] also an equality case, takes what I believe to be the correct approach. The court did not apply a Singapore-style presumption of constitutionality; instead, in conjunction with adopting a proportionality analysis,[103] it held:

> The *burden is on the Government* to satisfy the court that the justification test is satisfied. Where one is concerned with differential treatment based on grounds such as race, sex or sexual orientation, the court will *scrutinize with intensity* whether the difference in treatment is justified [my emphasis].[104]

It was for this reason that the Hong Kong Court of Appeal had, in an earlier case, rejected the argument that the courts should apply a concept akin to the presumption of constitutionality – the margin of appreciation – in favour of the legislature whenever the constitutionality of legislation was challenged.[105]

III Concluding thoughts

The presumption of constitutionality, and the concomitant *omnia praesumuntur rite esse acta* rule, are tools that have been used by the courts in constitutional cases to maintain a fairly deferential stance towards the political branches of the government. Such deference stems from the courts' modest conception of their role in judicial review, which can also be discerned from cases narrowing the scope of standing and declining to subject administrative and legislative action to rigorous scrutiny, among others. As regards the former, in *Jeyaretnam Kenneth Andrew v Attorney-General*[106] the Court of Appeal expressed a preference for a 'green-light' rather than a 'red-light' view of judicial review – that is, 'seek good government through the political process and public avenues rather than redress bad government through the courts'.[107] The court said that judicial review should be concerned with individual rights rather than public policy, and appeared to import into constitutional adjudication the administrative law concept that

> judicial review finds its place as an avenue for parties to bring claims of *legality* to the courts, and not for the purposes of challenging the very *merits* of a policy decision. Extensive judicial intervention in the administrative process is by no means the only avenue by which good governance can be

> ensured. Some regulatory functions can be better performed by other institutions or organs of state.[108]

Ultimately, it held that the appellant's status as a citizen and taxpayer did not clothe him with sufficient standing to challenge the Government's alleged failure to comply with the Constitution by seeking the concurrence of the President before offering a contingent loan of US$4 billion to the International Monetary Fund – no personal right of his, nor any public rights, had been infringed.[109]

In *Lim Meng Suang v Attorney-General*,[110] the Court of Appeal dismissed claims that section 377A of the Penal Code,[111] which criminalises acts of 'gross indecency' between male persons whether occurring in public or private, violated the guarantee of equality before the law and equal protection of the law in Article 12(1) of the Constitution. It reached this result by affirming that it would only subject the correlation between statutory classifications and objectives to a mere rationality test,[112] and commented that 'the requisite rational relation will – more often than not – be found' because 'there is *no* need for *a perfect* relation or "*complete* coincidence" [emphasis added] between the differentia in question and the purpose and object of the statute concerned'.[113] The court declined to assess whether the object of the statutory provision itself was illegitimate, as doing so would, in its view,

> *be to confer on the court a licence to usurp the legislative function in the course of becoming (or at least acting like) a 'mini-legislature'*.... The *courts* ... have *no* such power – *nor ought they to have such power*.[114]

Thus, submissions such as whether it is appropriate for a majority in society to impose its moral views on a minority to the detriment of their individual rights[115] were regarded as 'extra-legal arguments ... *which this court is not equipped to assess*' [emphasis in original].[116]

This hesitance to engage in robust judicial review goes a long way towards explaining why the courts, following the Indian example, adopted a form of the presumption of constitutionality qualitatively different from its original common law incarnation as a canon of construction which does not impose a significant evidential burden on claimants. I have attempted to show that the presumption makes unwarranted assumptions about the extent to which issues of constitutionality are examined by Parliament, and the undemocratic nature of judicial review. At any rate, even if legislators have given considered thought to whether a bill is consistent with fundamental liberties in the Constitution, the judiciary has a legal duty to ensure they have done so correctly. I argue that the presumption is better treated as a technique for reading down potentially unconstitutional statutes, and as a reminder that claimants must discharge their ordinary evidential burden of raising a prima facie claim against the Government. Unfortunately, it does not seem likely that the courts will do so until there is a fundamental mindset change concerning their role in the constitutional order.

Notes

1 This chapter is dedicated to Dr jur Thorsten Winkler (1969–2015).
2 *Lee Keng Guan v Public Prosecutor* [1977–1978] SLR(R) 78 (Singapore Court of Appeal [Sing CA]) [19].
3 Constitution of the Republic of Singapore (1985 Rev Ed, 1999 Reprint) ('Singapore Constitution').
4 ibid Art 12(1), which states, 'All persons are equal before the law and entitled to the equal protection of the law.'
5 *Shri Ram Krishna Dalmia v Shri Justice S R Tendolkar* AIR 1958 SC 538, [1959] SCR 279 (India Supreme Court [India SC]).
6 Constitution of India, 1950 Art 14 states, 'The State shall not deny to any person equality before the law or the equal protection of the laws within the territory of India.'
7 *Shri Ram Krishna Dalmia* (n 5) 297.
8 *Lee Keng Guan* (n 2).
9 [1998] 2 SLR(R) 489 (Sing CA) [79] ('*Taw Cheng Kong* (CA)'), citing ibid *Taw Cheng Kong* (CA) has been cited in *Ng Chye Huay v Public Prosecutor* [2006] 1 SLR(R) 157 (Singapore High Court [Sing HC]) [37]; *Johari bin Kanadi v Public Prosecutor* [2008] 3 SLR(R) 422 (Sing HC) [10]; *Ramalingam Ravinthran v Public Prosecutor* [2012] 2 SLR 49 (Sing CA) [43]–[44]; *Chan Kin Foo v City Developments Ltd* [2013] 2 SLR 895 (Sing HC) [23]; *Lim Meng Suang and another v Attorney-General* [2013] 3 SLR 118 (Sing HC) [103] ('*Lim Meng Suang* (HC)'); *Lim Meng Suang and another v Attorney-General* [2015] 1 SLR 26 (Sing CA) [4] ('*Lim Meng Suang* (CA)').
10 *Taw Cheng Kong* (CA) (n 9) [60].
11 *Lim Meng Suang* (CA) (n 9).
12 ibid [107]–[108].
13 In *Lim Meng Suang* (CA) (n 9), the Court of Appeal indicated it felt that a weaker presumption should apply to all pre-independence laws (that is, those enacted before 9 August 1965). However, it would be more accurate to regard the relevant date as 16 September 1963 when Singapore became a state of the Federation of Malaysia because it was with effect from that date that the fundamental liberties contained in the Federal Constitution were extended to Singapore.
14 ibid [107].
15 Cap 241, 1993 Rev Ed.
16 As the Prevention of Corruption (Amendment) Act 1966 (No 10 of 1966) s 31A.
17 See eg *Chan Hiang Leng Colin v Public Prosecutor* [1994] 3 SLR(R) 209 (Sing HC) [56] (Art 15 – right to freedom of religion); *Kok Hoong Tan Dennis v Public Prosecutor* [1996] 3 SLR(R) 570 (Sing HC) [34] (freedom of religion); *Chee Siok Chin v Minister for Home Affairs* [2006] 1 SLR(R) 582 (Sing HC) [49] (Art 14 – rights to freedom of speech and assembly).
18 *Yong Vui Kong v Attorney-General* [2011] 2 SLR 1189 (Sing CA).
19 ibid [139].
20 *Ramalingam* (n 9). The case was applied in *Yong Vui Kong v Public Prosecutor* [2012] 2 SLR 872 (Sing CA) [28].
21 Singapore Constitution (n 3) Art 35(8): 'The Attorney-General shall have power, exercisable at his discretion, to institute, conduct or discontinue any proceedings for any offence.'
22 *Ramalingam* (n 9) [44]–[46], citing *Yong Vui Kong* (n 18) [139]. See also *Akar v Attorney-General of Sierra Leone* [1970] AC 853 (Privy Council (PC)) 868 (constitutional amendment bill assumed to have been properly passed by the legislature in the absence of contrary evidence); *Re Section 22 of the Mutual Assistance in Criminal Matters Act* [2009] 1 SLR(R) 283 (Sing CA) [19] (principle applies to an exercise of

discretion by the Attorney-General to apply for a court order that a bank should produce material concerning one of its clients at the request of a foreign country, pursuant to the Mutual Assistance in Criminal Matters Act (Cap 190A, 2001 Rev Ed)).

23 *Ramalingam* (n 9) [47], citing *Howe Yoon Chong v Chief Assessor* (n 30) [13], which in turn cited *Sunday Lake Iron Co v Township of Wakefield* 247 US 350, 352 (1918) ('The good faith of such officers and the validity of their actions are presumed; when assailed, the burden of proof is upon the complaining party.') See also *R v Inland Revenue Commissioners, ex p TC Coombs & Co* [1989] STC 520 (CA) 534, cited on appeal in [1991] 2 AC 283 (HL) 299–300, which was distinguished in *Gibbs v Rea* [1998] AC 786 (PC) 798; *Dow Jones Publishing Co (Asia) Inc v Attorney-General* [1989] 1 SLR(R) 637 (Sing CA) [19] (principle applies to Minister for Communications and Information declaring a foreign newspaper to have engaged in the domestic politics of Singapore pursuant to the Newspaper and Printing Presses Act (Cap 206, 1985 Rev Ed) s 16, now the Newspaper and Printing Presses Act (Cap 206, 2002 Rev Ed) s 24); *Aspinden Holdings Ltd v Chief Assessor* [2006] 3 SLR(R) 99 (Sing HC) [52], [57] (Chief Assessor exercising powers under the Property Tax Act (Cap 254, 2005 Rev Ed)).

24 *Lim Meng Suang* (HC) (n 9) [104], citing *Public Prosecutor v Su Liang Yu* [1976] 2 MLJ 128 (Malaysia High Court (Malaysia HC)) 131, which was also cited in *Taw Cheng Kong* (CA) (n 9) [60].

25 Emphasis added. *Taw Cheng Kong* (CA) (n 9) [80], cited in *Lim Meng Suang* (HC) (n 9) [105].

26 *Lindsley v Natural Carbonic Gas Co* 220 US 61, 78 (1911), cited in *Malaysian Bar v Government of Malaysia* [1987] 2 MLJ 165 (Malaysia Supreme Court (Malaysia SC)) 166–67, and in *Taw Cheng Kong* (CA) (n 9) [57].

27 *Shri Ram Krishna Dalmia* (n 5) 297–98, cited in *Lee Keng Guan* (n 2) [19], and in *Lim Meng Suang* (HC) (n 9) [107].

28 *Lim Meng Suang* (HC) (n 9) [101], [105].

29 The point was emphasised in *Lim Meng Suang* (HC) (n 9) [113] by the citation of a series of cases including *Ong Ah Chuan v Public Prosecutor* [1979–1980] SLR(R) 710 (PC) [37] (Art 12 is not infringed '[p]rovided that the factor which the Legislature adopts as constituting the dissimilarity in circumstances *is not purely arbitrary* but bears a reasonable relation to the social object of the law'); *Kedar Nath Bajoria Hari Ram Vaid v State of West Bengal* AIR 1953 SC 404, [1954] SCR 30 (India SC) 38 ('the legislative classification *must not be arbitrary*'); *Chiranjit Lal v Union of India* AIR 1951 SC 41, [1950] SCR 869 (India SC) 911–12 ('the classification [prescribed] *should never be arbitrary*') (all emphasis added).

30 In *Eng Foong Ho v Attorney-General* [2009] 2 SLR(R) 542 (Sing CA) [30], the Court of Appeal said, 'An executive act may be unconstitutional if it amounts to intentional and arbitrary discrimination' (citing *Public Prosecutor v Ang Soon Huat* [1990] 2 SLR(R) 246 (Sing HC) [23], which in turn cited *Howe Yoon Chong v Chief Assessor* [1990] 1 SLR(R) 78 (PC) [17]), and noted that '[a]rbitrariness implies the lack of any rationality' (citing *Ang Soon Huat*).

31 *Lim Meng Suang* (HC) (n 9).

32 *Yick Wo v Hopkins* 118 US 356 (1886).

33 *Lim Meng Suang* (HC) (n 9) [106].

34 US Const Amend XIV § 1. Section 1 of the 14th Amendment to the United States Constitution states, in part: '… nor shall any State deprive any person of life, liberty, or property, without due process of law; nor deny to any person within its jurisdiction the equal protection of the laws'.

35 *Yick Wo* (n 32) 359.

36 *Chiranjit Lal* (n 29).

37 249 US 152, 157 (1919), cited in *Chiranjit Lal* (n 29) 913. The same sentence was cited in *Lim Meng Suang* (HC) (n 9) [103].

38 304 US 144, 152, n 4 (1938).
39 ibid.
40 509 US 312 (1993).
41 ibid 319, citing *City of New Orleans v Dukes* 427 US 297, 303 (1976) (rational basis review does not authorise the judiciary to 'sit as a superlegislature to judge the wisdom or desirability of legislative policy determinations made in areas *that neither affect fundamental rights nor proceed along suspect lines*' [emphasis added]).
42 *Lim Meng Suang* (HC) (n 9) [110].
43 [2007] 2 SLR(R) 453 (Sing HC).
44 ibid [98], citing *R (on the application of Marchiori) v Environment Agency* [2002] EWCA Civ 3 (CA) [39].
45 *Lim Meng Suang* (HC) (n 9) [110].
46 [1939] IR 413 (Ireland Supreme Court (Ireland SC)).
47 ibid 424.
48 Through the Penal Code (Amendment) Ordinance 1938 (No 12 of 1938) (Straits Settlements).
49 Proceedings of the Legislative Council of the Straits Settlements (13 June 1938) B49 (CG Howell (Attorney-General), speech during the Second Reading of the Penal Code (Amendment) Bill), cited in *Lim Meng Suang* (CA) (n 9) [119].
50 See nn 12–14 and the accompanying text. Curiously, in *Lim Meng Suang* (CA) (n 9) the Court of Appeal did not explicitly say how the presumption applied to the facts of the case.
51 1998 c 42 (UK).
52 See, for example, Alison L Young, 'Deference, Dialogue and the Search for Legitimacy' (2010) 30(4) Oxford Journal of Legal Studies 815, 824.
53 Singapore Constitution (n 3) Art 76(1). Subsidiary legislation must also be sent to the Council by the minister promulgating it within 14 days of publication: ibid Art 80(1).
54 ibid Art 77.
55 ibid Art 68.
56 ibid Art 78(6)(c). A similar procedure applies to subsidiary legislation, save that if Parliament wishes to confirm such legislation in the face of an adverse report, a resolution passed with a simple majority suffices: ibid Art 80(4)(b).
57 ibid Arts 9, 14.
58 For further commentary and criticism on the Presidential Council for Minority Rights, see Thio Su Mien, '[The Presidential Council:] Paper I' (1969) 1 Singapore Law Review 1; David S Marshall, '[The Presidential Council:] Paper II' (1969) 1 Singapore Law Review 9; Francis Khoo Kah Siang, '[The Presidential Council:] Paper III' (1969) 1 Singapore Law Review 14.
59 Singapore Constitution (n 3) Art 100(1).
60 ibid Art 100(4).
61 *Tan Eng Hong v Attorney-General* [2012] 4 SLR 476 (Sing CA) [103].
62 Chan Sek Keong, 'Judicial Review – From Angst to Empathy: A Lecture to Singapore Management University Second Year Law Students' (2010) 22 Singapore Academy of Law Journal 469, [4], cited in *Tan Eng Hong*, ibid. See also Singapore Parliamentary Debates, Official Report (25 August 1994) vol 63, cols 428–32 (Lee Hsien Loong (Deputy Prime Minister), speech during the Second Reading of the Constitution of the Republic of Singapore (Amendment No 2) Bill).
63 'Constitutional Tribunal Plea Rejected' *The Straits Times* (Singapore, 30 January 1999) 54.
64 *Constitutional Reference No 1 of 1995* [1995] 1 SLR(R) 803 (Constitutional Tribunal).
65 Singapore Constitution (n 3) Art 144(1) states:

> No guarantee or loan shall be given or raised by the Government — (a) except under the authority of any resolution of Parliament with which the President concurs; (b) under the authority of any law to which this paragraph applies unless the President concurs with the giving or raising of such guarantee or loan; or (c) except under the authority of any other written law.

66 Singapore Parliamentary Debates, Official Report (14 January 1998) vol 68, cols 82–86 (Ho Peng Kee (Minister of State for Law and Home Affairs), 'Respect for the Judiciary'). The Attorney-General's opinion of 12 January 1998 addressed to S Jayakumar, the Minister for Law, is reproduced at cols 133–36; parts of it were quoted by the High Court in *Jeyaretnam Kenneth Andrew v Attorney-General* [2013] 1 SLR 619 (Sing HC) [19].

67 Singapore Parliamentary Debates, Official Report (16 May 2001) vol 73, col 1726 (Wong Kan Seng (Minister for Home Affairs and Leader of the House), 'Is Voting a Privilege or a Right?'); Singapore Parliamentary Debates, Official Report (13 February 2009) vol 85, col 3158 (K Shanmugam (Minister for Law), 'Head R – Ministry of Law').

68 Singapore Constitution (n 3) Art 13(2):

> Subject to any law relating to the security of Singapore or any part thereof, public order, public health or the punishment of offenders, every citizen of Singapore has the right to move freely throughout Singapore and to reside in any part thereof.

69 No 15 of 2009, now Cap 257A, 2012 Rev Ed.

70 See, for instance, Singapore Parliamentary Debates, Official Report (13 April 2009) vol 85, cols 3684–85 (Sylvia Lim (Non-Constituency Member of Parliament), speech during the Second Reading of the Public Order Bill); ibid cols 3696–99, 3768 (Siew Kum Hong (Nominated Member of Parliament)); ibid cols 3711–25 (Thio Li-ann (NMP)).

71 ibid cols 3658–62, 3747–58, 3662, 3766, 3768–69 (K Shanmugam (Second Minister for Home Affairs)); ibid cols 3682–83 (Alvin Yeo (Hong Kah); ibid cols 3738–3739 (Sin Boon Ann (Tampines).

72 No 26 of 1990, now Cap 167A, 2001 Rev Ed.

73 Singapore Parliamentary Debates, Official Report (22 February 1990) vol 54, cols 1048, 1050 (S Jayakumar (Minister for Home Affairs), speech during the Second Reading of the Maintenance of Religious Harmony Bill); and see the remarks by Tay Eng Soon (Senior Minister of State for Education): ibid col 1061, Wong Kan Seng (Minister for Foreign Affairs and Community Development): ibid col 1089, Tan Cheng Bock (Ayer Rajah): ibid col 1124, and S Dhanabalan (Minister for National Development) speaking on 23 February 1990: ibid col 1168.

74 As of 23 May 2015 when Lee Kuan Yew, the founding Prime Minister of independent Singapore, died, the PAP held 79 of the 87 elected seats in Parliament.

75 Compare Brian Foley, 'Democracy, Deference and the Presumption of Constitutionality' in *Deference and the Presumption of Constitutionality* (Institute of Public Administration, Dublin 2008) 242 (citing Michael Gallagher, 'Parliament' in John Coakley and Michael Gallagher (eds), *Politics in the Republic of Ireland* (4th edn, Routledge in association with PSAI Press 2005) 211, 219: 'Ultimately the government sees its plans approved by parliament pretty much as a matter of course. There is no feeling that the opposition's views need to be taken into account or that its agreement is required for the passage of legislation.'), 245.

76 Paul C Weiler, 'Rights and Judges in a Democracy: A New Canadian Version' (1984) 18 University of Michigan Journal of Law Reform 51, 67–68.

77 ibid 66.

78 Young (n 52) 830. Further on constitutional dialogue, see Jaclyn L Neo, 'Balancing

act: the balancing metaphor as deference and dialogue in constitutional adjudication', Chapter 7 of this book.

79 ibid 817–18, citing Foley, 'The Constitutional Context and Nature of Deference' in *Deference and the Presumption of Constitutionality* (Institute of Public Administration, Dublin 2008) 6–10.

80 Foley, 'Deference, Rights, Policy and Spatial Distinctions' in *Deference and the Presumption of Constitutionality*, (Institute of Public Administration, Dublin 2008) 173–209; see also Young (n 52) 818–19.

81 Eric Barendt, 'Separation of Powers and Constitutional Government' (1995) Public Law 599, 608–609.

82 Young (n 52) 819.

83 See eg *Re Anti-Inflation Act* [1976] 2 SCR 373 (Supreme Court of Canada [Canada SC]) 423 (party seeking to uphold the law need only provide 'a rational basis for the legislation which it is attributing to the head of power invoked in this case in support of its validity'). According to Peter W Hogg, *Constitutional Law of Canada* (5th edn, Thomson Carswell, Ontario 2007) 813–14, § 60.2(f), this creates a presumption of constitutionality that is exceedingly difficult to overcome.

84 Hogg (n 83) 120, § 38.5.

85 *Manitoba (AG) v Metropolitan Stores Ltd* [1987] 1 SCR 110 (Canada SC).

86 ibid 122. See also Hogg (n 83) 120, § 38.5; Hogg (n 83) 813–14, § 60.2(f).

87 [1985] 1 SCR 441 (Canada SC).

88 That is, the Canadian Charter of Rights and Freedoms: ibid 472.

89 See *Lim Meng Suang* (HC) (n 9) [112], and the cases cited therein.

90 *Metropolitan Stores* (n 85) 125.

91 [1984] AC 689 (PC).

92 ibid 702, cited in *Hector v Attorney-General of Antigua and Barbuda* [1990] 2 AC 312 (PC) 319; *De Freitas v Permanent Secretary of Ministry of Agriculture, Fisheries, Lands and Housing* [1999] 1 AC 69 (PC) 77–78.

93 *Metropolitan Stores* (n 85) 124–25, citing Dale Gibson, *The Law of the Charter: General Principles* (Carswell, Toronto 1986), 56, 58.

94 (1890) LR 15 PD 170 (CA) 179–80, cited in *Re Estate of Bercovitz* [1962] 1 WLR 321 (CA) 327 (rule not applied to execution of a will as there was insufficient evidence of compliance with formalities).

95 For instance, *Pillai v Mudanayake* [1953] AC 514 (PC) 528–29 (Acts of Parliament); *McEldowney v Forde* [1971] AC 632 (HL) 655 (subsidiary legislation); *F Hoffmann-la Roche & Co AG v Secretary of State for Trade and Industry* [1975] AC 295 (HL) 357–58 (subsidiary legislation).

96 *Inland Revenue Commissioners v Rossminster Ltd* [1980] AC 952 (HL) 1006–1007:

> When taking so many documents as were taken in this case [from the respondents by the Inland Revenue], mistakes may occur and some documents be taken that should not have been. But the fact that they should not have been does not, in my opinion, justify the conclusion that the other documents taken were not taken after adequate examination and in the belief that they might be required in evidence. *Omnia praesumuntur rite esse acta.* If the respondents … assert that following a lawful entry, documents and things were seized and removed when there was no right to take them, the onus, in my opinion, lies on them to establish a prima facie case of that…

See also *McEldowney* (n 95) 661; *Standard Commercial Property Securities Ltd* v *Glasgow City Council* 2007 SC (HL) 33 [74].

97 Compare Clive Lewis, *Judicial Remedies in Public Law* (4th edn, Sweet & Maxwell 2009) 394 [9-115]:

> The burden is on the claimant to establish that a ground for review exists [*R v Reigate Justices, ex p Curl* [1991] COD 66 (Div Ct)].… [O]nce the claimant has

established a ground for review, the burden is on the defendant to show some adequate reason why the court should exercise its discretion and refuse a remedy.

98 [1960] 1 WLR 783 (CA).
99 ibid 794 (person admitted to mental hospital against her will).
100 *R v Secretary of State for the Home Department, ex p Khawaja* [1984] AC 74 (HL). See also Lewis (n 97) [12–014]–[12–015]; William Wade and Christopher Forsyth, *Administrative Law* (10th edn, Oxford University Press 2009) 248–49.
101 *Khawaja* (n 100) 112. See also *Eleko v Government of Nigeria* [1931] AC 662 (PC) 670, cited in *Khawaja* (n 100) 110–11:

> In accordance with British jurisprudence no member of the executive can interfere with the liberty or property of a British subject except on the condition that he can support the legality of his action before a court of justice. And it is the tradition of British justice that judges should not shrink from deciding such issues in the face of the executive.

102 (2007) 10 HKCFAR 335 (Hong Kong Court of Final Appeal [Hong Kong CA]).
103 On proportionality analysis in constitutional interpretation, see Jack Tsen-Ta Lee, 'According to the Spirit and not to the Letter: Proportionality and the Singapore Constitution' (2014) 8(3) Vienna Journal on International Constitutional Law 276; and Swati Jhaveri, 'The broader case for developing the content of fundamental rules of natural justice under Article 9 of the Constitution: a placeholder for proportionality-type adjudication?', Chapter 8 of this book.
104 *Yau Yuk Lung* (n 102) [21], citing *Ghaidan v Godin-Mendoza* [2004] 2 AC 557 (HL) 568.
105 *Leung v Secretary of Justice* [2006] 4 HKLRD 211 (Hong Kong CA) [52]–[53].
106 [2014] 1 SLR 345 (Sing CA).
107 ibid [48], citing Chan Sek Keong, 'Judicial Review – From Angst to Empathy: A Lecture to Singapore Management University Second Year Law Students' (2010) 22 Singapore Academy of Law Journal 469, [29].
108 ibid [56].
109 ibid [65]. The court also held that there was no case on the merits, as the appellant's interpretation of the relevant provision of the Constitution (n 3) Art 144, was wrong: ibid [10]–[28].
110 *Lim Meng Suang* (CA) (n 9).
111 Cap 224, 2008 Rev Ed.
112 *Lim Meng Suang* (CA) (n 9) [61]–[71].
113 ibid [68], citing *Lim Meng Suang* (HC) (n 9) [98].
114 ibid [82].
115 ibid [162]–[174].
116 ibid [173]. For commentary on this case, see Jack Tsen-Ta Lee, "Equality and Singapore's First Constitutional Challenges to the Criminalization of Male Homosexual Coduct" (2015) 16(1–2) Asia-Pacific Journal on Human Rights and the Law 150; Jaclyn L Neo, "Equal Protection and the Reasonable Classification Test in Singapore: After Lim Meng Suang v Attorney-General" [2016] Singapore Journall of Legal Studies 95; and Benjamin Joshua Ong, "New Approaches to the Constitutional Guarantee of Equality before the Law: Lim Meng Suang v Attorney-General; Tan Eng Hong v Attorney-General" (2016) 28 Singapore Acandemy of Law Journal 320.

Bibliography

Chan, Sek Keong, 'Judicial Review – From Angst to Empathy: A Lecture to Singapore Management University Second Year Law Students' (2010) 22 Singapore Academy of Law Journal 469.

Foley, Brian, 'Democracy, Deference and the Presumption of Constitutionality', 'The Constitutional Context and Nature of Deference' and 'Deference, Rights, Policy and Spatial Distinctions' in *Deference and the Presumption of Constitutionality* (Institute of Public Administration, Dublin 2008).

Forsyth, Christopher and William Wade, *Administrative Law* (10th edn, Oxford University Press 2009).

Gallagher, Michael, 'Parliament' in John Coakley and Michael Gallagher (eds), *Politics in the Republic of Ireland* (4th edn, Routledge in association with PSAI Press 2005).

Gibson, Dale, *The Law of the Charter: General Principles* (Carswell 1986).

Hogg, Peter W, *Constitutional Law of Canada* (5th edn, Thomson Carswell 2007).

Khoo, Francis Kah Siang, '[The Presidential Council:] Paper III' (1969) 1 Singapore Law Review 14.

Lee, Jack Tsen-Ta, 'According to the Spirit and Not to the Letter: Proportionality and the Singapore Constitution' (2014) 8(3) Vienna Journal on International Constitutional Law 276.

Lewis, Clive, *Judicial Remedies in Public Law* (4th edn, Sweet & Maxwell 2009).

Marshall, David S, '[The Presidential Council:] Paper II' (1969) 1 Singapore Law Review 9.

Thio, Su Mien, '[The Presidential Council:] Paper I' (1969) 1 Singapore Law Review 1.

Weiler, Paul C, 'Rights and Judges in a Democracy: A New Canadian Version' (1984) 18 University of Michigan Journal of Law Reform 51.

Young, Alison L, 'Deference, Dialogue and the Search for Legitimacy' (2010) 30(4) Oxford Journal of Legal Studies 815.

7 Balancing act

The balancing metaphor as deference and dialogue in constitutional adjudication

*Jaclyn L Neo**

I Introduction

In Singapore, the assertion that rights are not absolute is often accompanied by a corresponding claim that rights need to be balanced against other important interests. Balancing is invoked to explain and justify the outweighing of a right/interest over another, or alternatively, to explain a rule as having struck the appropriate balance between or among different rights/interests.[1] Judges engaging in balancing analyse a constitutional question by first identifying interests implicated by the case; second, explicitly or implicitly assigning values to the identified interest; and, finally, reaching a decision. In the process of reaching that decision, the court may construct a rule of constitutional law as encompassing the outcome of the identified and balanced rights/interests.[2] In this regard, a distinction is sometimes made between ad hoc balancing and what is called definitional balancing, which involves the construction of a generalisable rule that can be applied in later cases.[3] This contrasts with ad hoc balancing, which merely applies the balancing method to reach an outcome in a particular case, based on the particular facts of that case. As Melville B Nimmer explains, the 'profound difference between ad hoc and definitional balancing lies in the fact that a rule emerges from definitional balancing which can be employed in future cases without the occasion for further weighing of interests'.[4] Ad hoc balancing however appears to take each case on its own terms. Furthermore, while ad hoc balancing is usually explicit on the identification, valuation, and comparison of competing interests, definitional balancing tends to (although not necessarily) engage in these steps implicitly.[5] This raises one criticism of definitional balancing. Where judges do not explicitly refer to a balancing process in constructing a rule, the projection of a balancing approach may be criticised as reconstructive and not necessarily reflective of the reasoning process. Indeed, one advantage of the balancing metaphor is that it makes explicit the court's reasoning process.[6]

Explicit reference to balancing started appearing in constitutional law cases in the1990s. It has since gained traction in constitutional thinking and is now firmly part of the constitutional law lexicon.[7] This articulation of constitutional reasoning in balancing terms was initially and had for some time served to justify the prioritisation of state/public interests over constitutional rights. In several of the earlier constitutional law cases, while the balancing metaphor was used, it often justified a particular outcome without a clear enunciation of the identified rights/interests, the value to be assigned, or the comparison that was made. Therefore, it could be argued that while the term balancing was used, the method of balancing was not actually carried out. In recent years, however, there has been a shift in how balancing has been used in constitutional law cases. While earlier cases saw balancing refer to state/public interests trumping constitutional rights, later cases appear to embrace balancing as a way to articulate a reasoning process whereby identified rights/interests are weighed against each other to arrive at a reasonable outcome or to construct a particular rule in constitutional law. This, I argue, could suggest a greater openness to the idea of constitutional law as a 'battleground of competing interests'[8] where state/public interests do not always trump constitutional rights. In other words, later cases suggest that constitutional rights stand at least on an equal footing with state/public interests.

This chapter examines this development in the use of the balancing metaphor in Singapore. I argue that the earlier use of the balancing metaphor shows that it was used as an interpretive tool for strong judicial deference. Its enhanced use in later cases, however, shows that there has been a departure from this strong judicial deference towards a weaker form of judicial deference. In this regard, balancing has become a useful interpretive tool in an emerging judicial dialogue with the legislature and the executive on constitutional meaning. It should here be clarified that the enquiry is directed primarily at the reasoning process, and not at the conclusion of the cases. Indeed, the record remains that no legislation has been struck down as being unconstitutional by the Singapore courts. Nonetheless, this shift in judicial reasoning is important as it signifies a more robust notion of judicial review.

Part II of this chapter introduces balancing as being particularly conducive to constitutional rights adjudication because rights tend to be conceptualised as principles. Part III examines the early cases employing the balancing metaphor and argues that balancing was invoked as a mode of judicial deference to legislative choices. This strong deference suggests a judicial predilection towards de facto parliamentary supremacy. Part IV examines later cases and suggests that they show a gradual shift towards a greater role for judicial balancing as a legitimate modality of constitutional adjudication. This represents a departure from strong judicial deference towards a weaker form of deference. Part V contextualises this shift within broader social, political and legal contexts, and argues that the balancing metaphor is a particularly appropriate interpretive tool for an emerging constitutional dialogue because of its capacity to allow judges to assert a greater judicial role in the shaping of constitutional meaning while giving due recognition to state interests where necessary. Part VI provides some concluding reflections.

II Balancing and rights

A Constitutional rights as principles

It has been said that the balancing approach appears particularly apposite for constitutional adjudication because of the broad language used. Indeed, it has been argued that 'balancing as a type of legal decision-making is more typical of constitutional law' than in the interpretation of statutes because constitutions contain more abstract provisions than statutes.[9] This is premised on the idea that there is greater scope and, indeed, a need for balancing where the provisions are more abstract.[10] Alexy explains this further by distinguishing between rules and principles. He argues that, essentially, constitutional rights have the character of principles, which renders them particularly conducive to balancing. This is because principles are what he calls 'optimization requirements', ie 'norms requiring that something be realized to the greatest extent possible, given the legal and factual possibilities'.[11] He contrasts principles with rules, which he defines as norms that require something definitive. Rules are definitive commands and they are applied in the form of a subsumption. What this means is this:

> If a rule is valid and applicable, it is definitively required that exactly what it demands be done. If this is done, the rule is complied with; if this is not done, the rule is not complied with.[12]

In contrast, as principles, constitutional rights can be 'satisfied to varying degrees'.[13]

Notably, constitutional rights and other constitutional provisions may be expressed as rules, not necessarily as principles. One constitutional right that is arguably expressed as a rule is Article 10 of the Singapore Constitution, which states, 'No person shall be held in slavery.' That said, constitutional rights do tend to be expressed in a manner that is more like principle rather than definitive command. This is reflected in most of the provisions within Part IV of the Singapore Constitution. For instance, on freedom of speech, Article 14 states:

> (1) Subject to clauses (2) and (3) – (a) every citizen of Singapore has the right to freedom of speech and expression; …
> (2) Parliament may by law impose – (a) on the rights conferred by clause (1)(a), such restrictions as it considers necessary or expedient in the interest of the security of Singapore or any part thereof, friendly relations with other countries, public order or morality and restrictions designed to protect the privileges of Parliament or to provide against contempt of court, defamation or incitement to any offence.

This provision is expressed in a way that requires judges to look at rights and interests in competing terms and might therefore be considered to particularly invite a balancing approach.

Even where the constitutional provision is not explicitly expressed in this manner, a balancing approach may still appear more conducive where judges find themselves needing to legitimately take into account the government's interests in decision-making. One example is the equal protection guarantee under Article 12(1). Unlike Article 14, Article 12(1) is not expressed in a clearly qualified manner. It states:

> All persons are equal before the law and entitled to the equal protection of the law.

However, the courts have not treated this as a clear rule, but as a principle and have relied on the reasonable classification test to measure constitutionality under Article 12(1). This test, which looks at whether the impugned legislation contains an intelligible differentia, and whether there is a rational nexus between the differentia and the purpose, is justified on the basis that differentiation is a necessary part of legislation. In the recent case of *Tan Eng Hong v Attorney-General*, the High Court of Singapore explained it as such:

> Inherent in this [reasonable classification] test is a *balance* between, on the one hand, the protection of the fundamental right to equality and, on the other, the political autonomy afforded to Parliament to legislate within the bounds of the Constitution.[14]

The Court of Appeal reiterated this view in the 2014 case of *Lim Meng Suang v Attorney-General*, where it clearly stated that:

> the threshold nature of the 'reasonable classification' test helps to *balance* the need to accord as much legislative leeway as possible to the Legislature against the need to ensure that laws which are patently illogical and/or incoherent do not pass legal muster.[15]

By adopting a balancing approach, judges are able to conceptualise constitutional rights as principles, conducive to varying degrees of satisfaction.[16] Balancing also conforms with the notion of rational decision-making as being necessarily contextual.[17] In the case of Singapore, the manner in which the balancing metaphor has been used and how it has evolved reflects a shift from strong judicial deference to a weaker form of judicial deference. Before I go on to discuss the cases, I will discuss these two forms of judicial deference.

B Balancing and levels of deference

Judicial deference is not, by itself, controversial. Judges, as one of the three branches of government, operate within a constitutional framework where they do have to give due regard to the functions and expertise of the other branches of government. It should be clear that there is no one fixed understanding of deference. Indeed, there are different levels of deference.[18] In the strongest sense of the word, deference could mean that judges suspend their own judgment in favour of the judgment of another constitutional actor, typically another branch of government.[19] Similarly, it has been emphasised that '[j]udicial deference acknowledges that, based on the interpretation of another branch of government, a court *might* arrive at a conclusion different from one it would otherwise reach'.[20] This strong sense of deference overlaps with what has been called the model of 'deference as submission', which occurs when courts submit to the authority of the legislature. In this model, the courts accept the legislature's assessment that its legislation does not contravene rights as correct.[21] In this regard, I am taking strong deference as including the scenario where the court *suspends judgment* in favour of another branch of government as well as where it *adopts the judgment* of another branch as to the relative weight of state or public goals vis-à-vis the implicated constitutional right(s).

Strong deference thus suggests that the court is refraining from re-evaluating a particular legislative or executive act. In comparison, weak deference could suggest a tendency to give due weight to the constitutionality or legality of a legislative or executive act. Thus, for instance, Foley defines deference as a situation where a decision-making body decides a case 'not on the basis of its own independent assessment, but by treating the decision of some other decision-making body … as, in some degree, authoritative for its own … decision'.[22] This presents deference as a form of 'respect' whereby 'courts give weight to the opinion of the legislature but do not automatically accept that the decision of the legislature is correct'.[23] On the contrary, the courts reach their own conclusion as to the constitutionality of legislation while giving due weight to legislative choices.[24]

It might, on the face of it, appear contradictory to suggest that the balancing metaphor could be used as an interpretive tool for judicial deference. This is because balancing suggests judicial engagement in determining whether an appropriate balance has been struck between competing rights and interests, or whether a right/interest has outweighed another right/interest. Balancing evokes the idea of active judging, whereas deference, especially in the strong sense that was defined above, suggests some judicial passivity. In identifying, valuing and weighing the implicated rights/interests, judges are not, strictly speaking, deferring to the impugned branch of government in the sense that they suspend their own judgment in its favour. However, on closer examination, the judicial act of balancing itself encompasses an attitude of deference, not least because it acknowledges the legitimate role and judgment of the legislature or executive in placing limits on constitutional rights.[25] Furthermore, the weight judges assign to constitutional rights or interests could reflect the degree of deference that it adopts towards the other branches of government.

III Balancing as an interpretive tool for strong judicial deference

A Strong deference to the executive

In Singapore, early constitutional law cases reflect a strong degree of deference to the government. Judges tended to accept the government's evaluation of the importance of a state or public interest (where there is a tendency to conflate state and public interests) and thereby defer to this evaluation in balancing constitutional rights. An example of balancing in this strongly deferential manner is the 1994 case of *Jasbir Singh and another v Public Prosecutor*.[26] There, balancing was used to justify restricting the constitutionally guaranteed right to counsel under Article 9 of the Constitution. In rejecting the argument that the right to counsel could be exercised immediately, the Court of Appeal opined that postponing the exercise of the right to counsel was necessary in order to balance the arrested person's right to legal advice and the duty of the police to protect the public by carrying out effective investigations.[27] The court held that the right to counsel need only be granted 'within a reasonable time' after a person's arrest and 'the element of allowance for police investigations and procedure' is built into such 'reasonable time'.[28] It went on to hold that an interval of two weeks between arrest and access to counsel was reasonable. The judgment was fairly brief and did not elaborate on why two weeks was reasonable. Instead, the court employed the balancing metaphor to give determinative weight to the police's judgment on the amount of time needed to carry out effective investigations. In doing so, the court was strongly deferring to the judgment of the police as to what is necessary to ensure efficacious investigations, rather than independently determining how much time is reasonable.

B Strong deference to legislative balancing

The use of the balancing metaphor in these early cases also demonstrates a strong deferential disposition towards the legislature, or more specifically towards legislative balancing. This is especially evident in cases addressing the constitutional right to free speech. For instance, in the 2003 case of *Chee Soon Juan v Public Prosecutor*,[29] the High Court was asked to consider the constitutionality of the Public Entertainments and Meetings Act[30] (PEMA), which requires persons intending to hold public talks, rallies, and exhibitions, inter alia, to apply for a licence. Having been charged for attempting to hold a public rally without a licence, opposition politician Chee Soon Juan challenged the constitutionality of PEMA on the basis of Article 14 of the Constitution, which guarantees every citizen the right to freedom of speech and expression. The High Court rejected the constitutional challenge. The court stated that '[b]roader societal concerns such as public peace and order must be engaged in a balancing exercise with the enjoyment of this personal liberty'.[31] As in the cases discussed above, the court's use of the balancing metaphor provides a two-stage reasoning process of first asserting the non-absolute nature of free speech rights,[32] and second the assignment of determinative weight to competing interests.

Indeed, the High Court took the view that this idea of balancing was 'embodied in Article 14(2)(a)',[33] which is the limitation clause to Article 14(1)'s guarantee of free speech. In this case, while the court did not identify specifically which competing interest found in Article 14(2)(a) PEMA supposedly serves, it may be surmised that PEMA is arguably justified as a law restricting speech on the basis of public order. Indeed, the court concluded that the provisions of PEMA were not 'in any way contrary to our Constitution'.[34]

Further, what is interesting here is that despite the High Court's invocation of the balancing methodology, it did not appear to engage in actual balancing of the constitutional right against the interest advanced by PEMA. This is not only because the court did not actually identify public order as the competing interest. In merely concluding that it 'seemed eminently clear that the enactment of PEMA was fully within the power of the legislature pursuant to the power granted to it by Article 14(2)(a)',[35] the court appeared to take a strongly deferential stance towards the legislature. Indeed, in referring to balancing, the court did not appear to be addressing its own process of decision-making. Instead, it was used to assert the legislature's power to restrict the right to freedom of speech. In other words, balancing here appears to refer to legislative balancing rather than judicial balancing.

Therefore, it would seem that in Article 14 cases, the balancing metaphor was used to refer to, if not to signify strong deference to, legislative balancing, which could be understood as suspending judgment in favour of the legislative branch whether by reason of relative expertise or due to a certain constitutional interpretation. This reading of Article 14 was evident in the High Court in a free speech and assembly case, *Chee Siok Chin v Minister of Home Affairs*.[36] In this case, the High Court expressly and comprehensively addressed balancing as legislative balancing. At issue was whether the Miscellaneous Offences (Public Order and Nuisance) Act[37] and police action empowered under the Act were unconstitutional for being inconsistent with the freedom of speech and expression, and freedom of peaceful assembly guaranteed under Article 14 of the Constitution. The applicants had held a 'peaceful protest' outside a government building and were told by the police to disperse. The applicants then commenced proceedings seeking declarations that the Minister for Home Affairs and the Commissioner of Police had acted in an unlawful and/or 'unconstitutional manner' in ordering the applicants to disperse during their protest and in seizing their protest items.

This case provides two important clarifications about Article 14. First, the High Court held that the threshold for legitimacy is whether the curtailment is 'necessary or expedient' in the interest of one of the stated bases.[38] Second, while at one part the court refers to what the Constitution considers necessary or expedient,[39] in the ultimate analysis, the court takes the view that it is Parliament's estimation of what is necessary or expedient that determines whether a law is valid under Article 14.[40] Consequently, the High Court concluded that a court's 'sole task' is to ascertain whether the impugned law is within the purview of any of the permissible restrictions.[41] In order to ascertain this, all that is required is a 'nexus between the object of the impugned law and one of the permissible subjects stipulated in Article 14(2) of the Constitution'.[42] This nexus does not entail any consideration of reasonableness, much less a balancing exercise. Instead, all that is required is for the government to 'satisfy the court that there is a factual basis' for Parliament to consider it necessary or expedient to pass a law in the interest of one of the expressly stated bases.[43]

The High Court alluded to balancing in the following way:

> The tension between the individual's right to speak and/or to assemble freely and the competing interests of security and/or public order calls into play a *delicate balancing exercise* involving several imponderables and factors such as societal values, pluralism, prevailing social and economic considerations as well as the common good of the community. Consideration of such public policy is exceedingly complex and multifaceted. While the clarion call for unfettered individual rights is almost irresistibly seductive, it cannot, however, be gainsaid that individual rights do not exist in a vacuum. Permitting unfettered individual rights in a process that is value-neutral is not the rule of law. Indeed, that form of governance could be described as the antithesis of the rule of law – a society premised on individualism and self-interest.[44]

The court was right to point out that qualified rights are not unusual.[45] Notably, however, this case conceptualised a theory of constitutional law, specifically for freedom of speech, assembly and association cases, where the balancing exercise takes place within the legislative arena, with the court's role limited to determining whether such an exercise has taken place. In other words, the legislature balances, while the court merely ensures (if it does so at all) that such a balancing has taken place, without any evaluation of whether the balancing was proper. This arguably takes a common objection that judicial balancing improperly duplicates legislative function even further as it contemplates a very limited role for the court in ensuring constitutionality.[46] Later cases, including on Article 14, however, show a slightly different use of the balancing metaphor, and this is discussed below.

Nonetheless, the strong level of judicial deference underlying the use of balancing in these early cases is consistent with how judges conceptualised their role within the constitutional order during this time. While the Singapore Constitution is *de jure* supreme, there is evidence that the prevailing constitutional culture remained deeply influenced by the theory and practice of parliamentary supremacy.[47] For instance, Yong Pung How CJ then affirmed that the duty of the judge is merely to 'adjudicate and interpret the laws passed by Parliament with the aim of ensuring that justice is upheld'.[48] This means that the judiciary is 'to ensure that the intention of Parliament as reflected in the Constitution and other legislation is adhered to'[49] and that the judge 'is in no position to expand the scope of or imply into the Constitution and other legislation his own interpretation of the provisions which is clearly contrary to Parliament's intention'.[50] In particular, such strong deference to Parliament presumably proceeds from a constitutional theory that gives greater weight to majoritarian institutions and perhaps overly compensates for the counter-majoritarian difficulty. According to this view, 'Members of Parliament are freely elected by the people of Singapore' and, therefore, 'represent the interests of the constituency who entrust them to act fairly, justly and reasonably'.[51] The people have the right to determine if any law passed by Parliament goes against the principles of justice or otherwise and, if so, they should exercise this right through the ballot box.[52]

C Strong deference and prioritisation of state interests

Consequently, this view of the judicial role within the constitutional order had inevitably led to a tendency for the courts to accept the prioritisation of collective welfare over individual rights.[53] The balancing metaphor has also been associated with the almost lexical prioritisation of state or public interests over constitutional rights, such that it would appear that no amount of constitutional rights could override the competing governmental interests in these cases. There is however a stronger use of balancing in a few religious freedom cases where the courts invoking balancing have done so in such a way as to affirm the prioritisation of state or public interests over constitutional rights explicitly. Thus, while the intensity of review is strongly deferential, there are aspects of the judgment where balancing appears to be used to positively support (rather than defer) to executive power. It may be said that the qualified nature of Article 15 guaranteeing the right to freedom of religion makes it especially conducive to a balancing exercise. Article 15(1) provides that '[e]very person has the right to profess and practise his religion and to propagate it', but it is subject to a limitation clause under Article 15(4), which states that '[t]his Article does not authorize any act contrary to any general law relating to public order, public health or morality'. In *Colin Chan v Public Prosecutor*,[54] a case concerning the religious freedom of Jehovah's Witnesses in Singapore, the court opined that the right to freedom of religion 'must be reconciled with the right of the state to employ the sovereign power to ensure *peace*, *security* and *orderly living* without which constitutional guarantee of civil liberty would be a mockery'.[55] While the judgment did not expressly use the word 'balancing', it clearly adopted the balancing methodology in its judicial reasoning. Like in *Jasbir Singh*, this balancing methodology allowed the High Court (presided over by then Chief Justice Yong Pung How) to first assert the non-absolute nature of the right to religious freedom and next to assign determinative weight to competing state interests. However, the court went further than strongly deferring to the government in this regard when it famously stated that:

> The sovereignty, integrity and unity of Singapore are undoubtedly the paramount mandate of the Constitution and *anything*, including religious beliefs and practices, which *tend to run counter* to these objectives must be *restrained*.[56]

Arguably, this goes further than strong deference or 'deference as submission', which merely entails the courts accepting the legislature or executive's assessment as correct. The court, in proclaiming that the 'sovereignty, integrity and unity of Singapore' are the 'paramount mandate of the Constitution', is opining actively as to the priority of these interests over constitutional rights. Balancing is also used in this way to affirm the priority of state interests over religious freedom in another case involving Jehovah's Witnesses, *Peter Williams Nappalli v Institute of Technical Education*.[57] Here, while the High Court stated that 'there must be a careful *balance* between the interest of the State in the education system and the religious beliefs of the plaintiff', it nonetheless concluded that this was 'one case where the interest of the State in the education system *must prevail* over those of the individual'.[58] While the judgments demonstrate strong deference in some parts, one might argue that here balancing was used in a more active manner to positively affirm the prioritisation of state interests over constitutional rights. This goes beyond deference, even in the strong sense.

IV The advancement of judicial balancing: towards a weaker form of judicial deference?

Starting from the late 2000s, the cases show a judicial willingness to depart from the previous view of the seemingly lexical priority of competing interests over rights. Instead, there appears to be an increasing openness to the idea that judicial balancing is a legitimate mode of constitutional adjudication and within the proper scope of the judicial role. Taking balancing seriously means that the judiciary is not merely determining the narrow question of whether the legislature or the executive had acted in good faith (ie in taking into consideration the competing rights and interests, whatever the outcome), but, at least in some cases, the courts appear willing to consider whether the other branches of government had acted 'reasonably'. The language of balancing facilitates this shift into a reasonableness enquiry.

A Balancing and the limits on discretionary power

A case where the balancing metaphor was used to introduce a reasonableness enquiry was the case of *Vellama d/o Marie Muthu v Attorney-General.*[59] The case concerned whether the Prime Minister had a constitutional obligation to call for by-elections when a parliamentary seat in a single-member constituency fell vacant. Article 49 of the Constitution states that:

> [w]henever the seat of a Member ... has become vacant for any reason other than a dissolution of Parliament, the vacancy *shall be filled* by election in the manner provided by or under any law relating to Parliamentary elections for the time being in force.[60]

However, no by-election was called immediately following the confirmation that the seat had become vacant. Almost three weeks after, on 9 March 2012, the

Prime Minister was asked in Parliament if he would be calling a by-election for Hougang, to which he replied that he had the intention to do so, but had not decided when. He stated that he would 'take into account all relevant factors including the well-being of Hougang residents, issues on the national agenda, as well as the international backdrop which affects our prosperity and security'. However, the Prime Minister nonetheless asserted that he had absolute discretion in calling the by-elections.[61] He stated:

> The timing of the by-election is at the discretion of the Prime Minister. The Prime Minister is not obliged to call a by-election within any fixed time frame. This absence of any stipulated time frame is the result of a deliberate decision by Parliament to confer on the Prime Minister the discretion to decide when to fill a Parliament vacancy.[62]

So, does the Prime Minister have absolute discretion when and even whether to call a by-election when a parliamentary seat falls vacant?[63] Put another way, are there any limits to the exercise of this discretion to call for a by-election or can it be exercised in any way such that a by-election may never be called and the vacancy becomes subsumed under the next general elections, to be held possibly years later? The by-election not having been called, Ms Vellama, a resident in the Hougang constituency, filed a suit seeking a declaration that the Prime Minister does not have unfettered discretion whether and when to announce by-elections in the Hougang constituency, and she sought a mandatory order to require the Prime Minister to call for a by-election within three months or within a reasonable time.[64]

Clearly, the case hinged on the interpretation of the phrase 'shall be filled by election' in Article 49(1) of the Constitution. In a well-elucidated judgment, the Court of Appeal opined that the Prime Minister's discretion was 'not unconditional', and that he was constitutionally obliged to call for an election 'within a reasonable time'.[65] Nonetheless, the court stated that the Prime Minister 'retains a substantial measure of discretion as to the timing of an election to fill a casual vacancy' and 'is entitled to take into account all relevant circumstances'.[66] It is interesting that the Court of Appeal turned to balancing to frame its conclusion and to justify it as striking the appropriate balance between the right of the voters and the discretionary powers of the Prime Minister. In rejecting the argument that the Prime Minister had absolute discretion, the court clearly stated that:

> There is … a need to *balance* the rights of the voters in a Parliamentary system of government and the discretion vested in the Prime Minister to decide when to call for by-elections to fill a vacancy.[67]

Furthermore, balancing in the case of *Vellama* seems to be a departure from strict interpretation. In *Vellama*, the Court of Appeal's approach and conclusion differed greatly from those of the High Court. To fully appreciate the Court of Appeal's invocation of the balancing metaphor, one has to look to the High

Court's judgment, which it rejected. Relying on a textual, contextual and historical reading of the provision, the High Court concluded that there was no requirement in the Constitution for the Prime Minister to call elections to fill vacancies.[68] It opined that Article 49 merely prescribes that parliamentary vacancies can only be filled by elections (ie the process of elections) and no other means (eg nominations or appointments), but it did not mean that elections must be called (ie the event of elections). Following from this, the High Court determined that there was 'no prescribed time within which such elections must be called'.[69] The High Court approached the constitutional question by examining the meaning and intent of those who wrote the constitutional language. The Court of Appeal, however, took a divergent view, holding that the text, context and history of the clause did not necessarily lead to the High Court's interpretation of Article 49.[70] It is interesting that the court drew from first principles (based on certain normative foundations underlying a Westminster constitution[71]) to support its derivation of an implied right of voters to vote.

B Balancing and ad-hoc adjudication

Another way in which the use of balancing has shifted is in the provision of explicit content to constitutional tests and in stressing the need to decide cases based on the specific legal and factual considerations involved. This was manifested in recent cases where balancing was used to determine 'reasonable time' for the purposes of the right to counsel under Article 9(3) of the Constitution. Recall that in *Jasbir Singh v Public Prosecutor*[72] it was affirmed that the constitutional right to counsel was not exercisable immediately but rather only within a reasonable time.[73] The Court of Appeal reaffirmed this in the 2014 case of *James Raj s/o Arokiasamy v Public Prosecutor*.[74] The *James Raj* decision has been criticised for failing to properly re-examine the imposition of reasonable time as a limit on the constitutional right to counsel.[75] That criticism is valid. However, what this chapter is concerned with is the invocation of the balancing metaphor and what it means. I suggest that there are significant albeit subtle differences between *James Raj* and the earlier cases. This is because, unlike in *Jasbir Singh*, the Court of Appeal articulated clearly that the determination of reasonable time involves a balancing exercise. Chief Justice Sundaresh Menon, delivering the opinion of the court, explained:

> The exercise of the right of access to counsel was framed in this way to strike a balance that was considered appropriate to our circumstances between, on the one hand, the arrested person's undoubted right to legal representation and, on the other hand, the public interest in enabling the police to discharge their duty and carry out investigations effectively and expeditiously.[76]

As to what constitutes 'reasonable time', the Court of Appeal further explained that this was 'inherently a question of fact', which would involve 'a factual inquiry of all the relevant considerations'. Since the question was raised in the context of a motion to refer a question of law to the Court of Appeal, the court declined to give a definite answer as to what would constitute 'reasonable time'. The court explained that it was not a question of law that could be answered in the abstract.[77] What is significant is that the court did not merely say that 'reasonable time' is determined solely by what is required for effective police investigation, which appears to be the approach in the earlier cases. Instead of the prioritisation of state/public interests, as appears to be the situation in earlier cases, the judgment suggests a willingness to examine each case to determine whether there are good reasons to delay access to counsel.[78]

The balancing metaphor has also been used to rationalise the courts' approach to locus standi. In *Tan Eng Hong v Attorney-General*, the Court of Appeal had to consider whether to liberalise the locus standi rules and opted for a rule based on balancing. In addressing the question of whether the very existence of an allegedly unconstitutional law in the statute books suffices to show a violation of constitutional rights, the Court of Appeal opined that the position that it takes has to properly balance the various considerations in ensuring access to justice. It thus argued that while relaxing the requirements for locus standi would ensure some applicants greater access to justice, the requirements must also be such that it would not amount in an increase in unmeritorious cases which may have the effect of delaying access to justice for other claimants. Thus, the court stated:

> Keeping in mind the need for a balance, we will not lay down a general rule that the very existence of an allegedly unconstitutional law in the statute books suffices to demonstrate a violation of an applicant's constitutional rights. Each case must turn on its own facts, and the courts must remain mindful that lax standing rules could 'seriously curtail the efficiency of the Executive in practising good governance'.[79]

Balancing thus effectively presents courts with the discretion to determine cases according to the legal and factual conditions of each case.

C Balancing and co-equal rights

In taking balancing seriously, later cases also suggest a shift from the asserted prioritisation of state interests towards giving rights, at the least, co-equal status. A significant case in this regard is *Review Publishing Co Ltd and Another v Lee Hsien Loong and another appeal*,[80] which is more notable for its dicta rather than its result. The case concerned a defamation claim against Far Eastern Economic Review (FEER) for an article that the plaintiffs argued had claimed that they were unfit for office because they were corrupt and had, therefore, set out to sue and suppress those who would question them for fear that such questioning would expose their corruption. The Court of Appeal had to consider whether FEER could raise the defence of qualified privilege based on responsible journalism. This specific defence had not been incorporated into Singapore law. It was developed by the English courts only after Singapore's independence, specifically in the case of *Reynolds v Times Newspapers Ltd.*[81] Unlike in earlier cases, Singapore's Court of Appeal did not find it conclusive that the test of responsible journalism had been developed in response to the United Kingdom's obligations under the European Convention of Human Rights. Instead, the court accepted that it could exercise independent judgment as to whether the test could be adopted in Singapore. What deserves emphasis here is that the court affirmed that freedom of speech had the status of a constitutional right and, therefore, was of a higher-order status than common law rights.

The court asserted that it had to decide how the balance between constitutional free speech and protection of reputation should be struck in Singapore.[82] Unlike in the earlier generation of cases, the court now did more than merely assert that the balance had already been struck by the legislature. The Court of Appeal contemplated whether courts should 'shift the existing balance between constitutional free speech and protection of reputation in favour of the former where the publication of matters of public interest is concerned'.[83] According to the court, applying the *Reynolds* rationale would mean that 'constitutional free speech would become the rule and restrictions on this right become the exception'.[84]

This assertion of judicial function in determining the appropriate balance between free speech rights and reputational rights is interesting especially since the Court of Appeal also acknowledged that Article 14(2)(a) 'expressly provides that it is Parliament which has the *final say* on how the balance between constitutional free speech and protection of reputation should be struck'.[85] While this appears to contradict the earlier contemplation as to whether the judiciary should reconsider the balance between free speech and reputational rights, this should be understood as the court placing itself in dialogue with the legislature and acknowledging that the Constitution envisages legislative responses.[86] This departs from one conventional understanding of judicial review according to which the courts are the final arbiter on constitutional matters.[87] However, the court's reasoning is significant when contrasted with earlier judicial pronouncements that the court has no role in determining whether an appropriate balance has been struck. Even in the case of *Chee Siok Chin*, the court's role was limited to asking whether there was a nexus between the law and Parliament's stated objectives in restricting free speech and assembly rights.

To be sure, the court's preliminary statements as to the considerations involved in determining whether to shift the balance may be regarded as fairly circumspect. It stated that considerations such as political climate, the role of the media in Singapore and the local emphasis on honesty and integrity in public discourse would be relevant but not exhaustive factors in answering the key question.[88] The judgment, nonetheless, suggests openness towards reconsideration while also cautioning that any reconsideration would require a preponderance of evidence that change is appropriate. As the Court of Appeal noted:

> Proponents of change must produce evidence of a change in our political, social and cultural values in order to satisfy the court that change is necessary

> so as to provide greater protection against the existing law of defamation for defendants where the publication of matters of public interest is concerned.[89]

The fundamental question as to whether a new balance should be struck between free speech rights and reputational rights remains unresolved because the court held that the Constitution extended free speech rights only to citizens. The defendants in this case were not citizens of Singapore.[90]

Nonetheless, the judgment in *Review Publishing Co Ltd v Lee Hsien Loong*[91] demonstrates willingness by the court to conceptualise rights as no longer 'subsidiary' to state interests. It however did not go so far as to accept that constitutional rights are 'preferential' or 'fundamental'.[92] In this case, the Court of Appeal differentiated subsidiary, co-equal, preferential and fundamental rights. It states that when a right is treated as preferential, the balances are tilted in its favour but could be outweighed under certain conditions.[93] A fundamental right, however, serves largely as a trump.[94] In comparison, when rights are regarded as co-equal, there is no presumption in favour of either. The outcome has to be determined through an 'ultimate balancing test'.[95] The Court of Appeal acknowledged that the idea of a subsidiary right reflects the dominant interpretation of Article 14 as subjecting free speech rights to the expressly permitted restrictions under Article 14(2)(a) of the Constitution.[96] A recalibration of the balance between the right to freedom of speech and the right to reputation however would give stronger recognition to the status of free speech as a constitutional right.

To be clear, the Court of Appeal in *Review Publishing* did suggest that constitutional rights are usually conceptualised as preferential or fundamental. It introduced the idea of co-equal rights seemingly as an afterthought. However, this idea of co-equality is useful as it suggests another evolutionary point on the continuum between lexical prioritisation of state interest, on the one hand, and constitutional rights as trumps, on the other. Arguably, the balancing metaphor is currently used to co-equalise constitutional rights to competing state interests. It does not currently go so far as to give constitutional rights preferential or even fundamental status, but should be seen as an improvement from the prior treatment of rights as subsidiary to state interests. At the very least, balancing is now used to describe and justify treating constitutional rights as co-equal, and not to describe and justify the subordination of constitutional rights to competing state interests. That said, the expansive use of the presumption of constitutionality could continue to limit the impact of this recognition of the co-equal status of rights within the balancing test since it effectively gives preference to competing state interests.[97] Consequently, there is a need, going forward, to reconsider the use of this presumption, as well as to further grapple with how courts value and weigh constitutional rights/interests against other constitutional rights/interests in a balancing test.

V Balancing act: theorising the judicial turn to balancing in Singapore

A Balancing and a contextual approach to the law

As a whole, the use of the balancing metaphor in more recent cases suggests a less deferential judicial attitude towards the executive and legislature. It is consistent with the model of deference as respect rather than submission. The judiciary respects the opinion of the executive or legislature, but still examines whether legislation or administrative/executive action is constitutional.[98] This use of balancing arguably allows judges to take a more evolutionary and dialogic approach to constitutional review. This could be particularly apposite in Singapore's constitutional context where no legislation has thus far been struck down for being inconsistent with the Constitution.[99] Balancing allows judges to give greater weight to constitutional rights while still explicitly affirming legitimate governmental interests. Thus, for instance, a court could legitimately consider good relations between religious groups as part of the corpus of public order considerations which in the context of Singapore have been incorporated into the Constitution. At the same time, balancing puts forward a view of the law as being contextual and responsive.[100] It is seen as desirable because it suggests a particularistic, case-by-case, common law approach that accommodates gradual change and rejects absolutes.[101] The outcome of a case would turn on a careful analysis of the particular interests at stake.[102] In addition, balancing provides courts with flexibility since it does not commit the court to any one ideological position. It keeps everyone in the game, thereby enhancing its legitimacy.[103]

Those advocating stronger judicial protection of rights may, however, eschew balancing because it supposedly deprives constitutional rights of their normative power. Balancing, it is said, downgrades rights to the level of goals, policies and values. Rights therefore lose their 'strict priority'.[104] Dworkin goes further in arguing that treating 'rights' as interests that can be overcome by other non-constitutional interests does not conform to the essential nature of a 'right'.[105] This conceptualises rights as trumps, which presumably can never be outweighed by public interests, although it is questionable whether they can be outweighed by other rights. Some have even argued that the nature of rights is such that they cannot be included in the cost-benefit analysis which is characteristic of balancing, or even in proportionality tests, since such an exercise would place them on an equal footing with non-constitutional interests.[106] This criticism goes to the status of rights within the constitutional order. If rights exist on a higher-order plane than interests, then no amount of governmental or other competing interests could ever outweigh rights. In other words, rights are always lexically prior to interests.

This criticism of balancing is particularly apposite in the Singapore context. Indeed, some have argued that balancing gives governments too much leeway because it allows laws that arguably exceed constitutional limits to be enacted, as long as the government can cite sufficient justification.[107] As mentioned, this problem is exacerbated when a presumption is applied in favour of legislative or executive constitutionality.[108] This could be understandable since the court has to balance the right against 'the compelling force of a particular legislative judgment as molded in the law which has been violated'.[109] Such an approach, if not taken to the extreme, may also be said to give due consideration to the separation of powers and acts as a guard against charges of counter-majoritarianism.

Singapore's political context, where there appears to be a preference for a dominant party and an efficient state, suggests that a rights-as-trumps approach is unlikely to be accepted as legal doctrine or have much traction in society.[110] A more realistic view is that there is greater likelihood for Singapore courts to treat rights as co-equal or even preferential, rather than fundamental, at least in the foreseeable future. Balancing is the manifestation of judicial philosophy on rights, not a cause of that philosophy. Nonetheless, one way to give adequate protection to rights is for judges to ensure that only public interests that have the status of higher norms are weighed against rights.[111] Interestingly, any fears that balancing gives judges too much power to take into account non-enumerated *interests* in constitutional adjudication often underestimate the capacity of the balancing approach to also allow judges to recognise and justify the introduction of non-enumerated *rights*. The case of *Vellama*, for instance, referred to the rights of the voters (presumably to vote), which is not a right expressly provided for in the Constitution.

B Balancing and the principle of legality

One might see balancing as facilitating the courts' engagement in a slightly more robust form of judicial review while at the same time cautiously guarding against charges of judicial activism.[112] Externalising the balancing process allows judges to avoid the criticism of supplanting legislative acts with their personal preferences.[113] Judges merely search for relevant interests in society at large and give them the *weight* that *history*, *tradition* and *current society attribute* to them. This way, balancing could be seen as primarily descriptive[114] and thereby less intrusive of legislative and executive powers.[115] There remains a tone of deference, albeit in a weaker form, which pre-empts criticisms that judicial review is counter-majoritarian.[116] In *Vellama*, for instance, the Court of Appeal justified the imposition of limits on the Prime Minister's discretionary powers on the basis of the rule of law, ie that it is 'a basic proposition of the rule of law that all discretionary power is subject to legal limits'.[117] Nonetheless, the court was careful to emphasise that:

> [w]hilst the Prime Minister's discretion as to the timing of an election to fill a casual vacancy is subject to judicial review, it is in the nature of such a fact-sensitive discretion that judicial intervention would only be warranted in exceptional cases.[118]

How does one take into account the sensitive facts? Through balancing.

The reference to legal limits of discretionary power is important. This 'principle of legality', as former Chief Justice Chan Sek Keong characterised it, underlies and has been expressly invoked to justify assertions of judicial review. The principle has its jurisprudential genesis locally in *Chng Suan Tze v Minister for Home Affairs*, a case widely considered as a high watermark for constitutional law in Singapore. There, the Court of Appeal famously stated, '[T]he notion of a subjective or unfettered discretion is contrary to the rule of law.'[119] It followed with these now widely recited words: 'All power has legal limits and the rule of law demands that the courts should be able to examine the exercise of discretionary power.'[120] According to this, judicial review is necessitated by the rule of law. In an extra-judicial lecture in 2010, Chan CJ posited that '[t]he basic principle in constitutional and administrative judicial review is the principle of legality'.[121] This principle requires the Government to act in accordance with the law. This means that legislative and executive acts must conform to the Constitution. In addition, an executive action must also conform to the written law and the common law principles of natural justice.[122]

This principle of legality, as an aspect of the rule of law, provides the judiciary with a strong and persuasive basis for a more robust approach towards judicial review. Its invocation to justify judicial balancing is interesting because it suggests that balancing rights/interests is an *aspect* of ensuring legality of legislative and executive action according to the Constitution. The emphasis on legality rather than on the fundamentality of rights presumably pre-empts any objection that balancing constitutes a form of judicial intrusion into the legislative domain and unnecessarily duplicates legislative function. This objection states that relevant constitutional interests were balanced when the Constitution was drafted and courts should not recalibrate those interests.[123] Indeed, judicial balancing replicates the legislative function in a democracy and, worse, supplants the decision that the legislature had arrived at through the process of balancing.[124] It is clearly linked to the counter-majoritarian difficulty. Since the legislature is popularly elected and has a link to the electorate, the court's exercise of its constitutional review powers to strike down a law that the legislature had enacted may seem to be undemocratic.[125]

By hinging judicial balancing on the rule of law, judges may argue that the exercise only focuses on legality according to the Constitution rather than on purposes with which legislators are concerned such as maximising social welfare or voters' interests.[126] The principle of legality not only legitimates judicial balancing but also distinguishes the judicial exercise from the legislative one. This pre-empts the criticism that judicial balancing is unnecessary. Furthermore, one might respond to the counter-majoritarian objection by arguing that the court reinforces representation because it ensures that the interests of unpopular or under-represented groups are taken into account.[127] In this regard, the court improves the balancing process by giving weight to interests that the legislature ignores or undervalues.[128] Another response lies in the conceptual differences between judicial and legislative balancing. While both institutions employ the balancing method, their process of reasoning is conceptually dissimilar. This is because the primary focus of judicial balancing is the Constitution. The court is 'searching for a reasonable understanding of the Constitution – one that harmonizes constitutional provisions and values with important governmental interests'.[129] This contrasts with legislative balancing, which is essentially concerned with making judgments of good social policy.[130]

C Co-equal branch and constitutional dialogue

In the Singapore context, the use of judicial balancing has an added function of allowing judges to legitimately take into account the interests and concerns of the legislators. The court that balances can arrive at a reasonable understanding of the Constitution, which harmonises constitutional provisions and values with important governmental interests.[131] In this regard, the legislative act and the attendant interests could be taken as a measure of social importance but they do not act as a trump over rights. Indeed, one might say, as Alexy does, that all the constitutional court is concerned with is ensuring that legislative outcomes are within a broad range of legal acceptability (by constitutional standards). Alexy highlights the differences between legislative and judicial function as such:

> The majority in parliament cannot issue a law that says no more than it is possible to decide both for and against a certain regulation. A constitutional court can make such a decision, and it in effect has to do so in all cases of discretion. This implies that constitutional review is confined to controlling the limits of the competence of the legislature.[132]

Seen from this perspective, judicial balancing strikes the right balance (pun intended) between robust judicial review and counter-majoritarian concerns.

In addition, the shift towards judicial balancing could be viewed as the judiciary coming into its role as a co-equal but not superordinate branch in the government. In this regard, it must be seen as an attempt to engage in constitutional dialogue with the other branches of government.[133] Judges may be increasingly seeing themselves as primary actors in the constitutional dialogue and are legitimate participants in the institutional process through which decisions about constitutional meaning are made. Judges, as well as legislators and the executive, are equally involved in enunciating a shared meaning of the Constitution.[134] This idea of dialogue is most notably present in the *Review Publishing* case discussed earlier. The dicta on the relevant considerations for reforming the law of defamation signals a need for the legislature to reconsider the status quo. One might see this as a form of judicial advice-giving where judges use a range of pro-active interpretive and decision-making techniques in order to recommend particular courses of action to the political branches and to advise them of ways to avoid constitutional problems.[135] The use of non-binding dicta allows judges to convey their views on constitutional meaning but without necessarily striking down the law or administrative action at that instance. This presumably gives the political branches the opportunity to reconsider their position by amending the law or enacting a new one or to rectify ambiguities and/or vagueness from the law in order to survive future constitutional challenges.[136] Such judicial advice-giving 'creates the conditions for productive dialogue between the courts and the political branches about constitutional meaning and responsibility'.[137]

Constitutional dialogue is more than judicial advice-giving, and broadly speaking, this idea of a constructive dialogue has many virtues. For one, it has the potential to resolve counter-majoritarian concerns because of its recognition that non-judicial actors play a key role in constitutional interpretation. This is due to the thinking that 'the concerns that judicial review necessarily sets judges against the electorally accountable branches of government are greatly attenuated if the political branches are able to respond to judicial decisions with which they disagree'.[138] This co-operative view of judicial review is particularly appropriate in the context of a democratising non-liberal state. Courts can play an important role in this process of democratisation, but how they negotiate this process in the context of existing autocratic predilections could determine their status and effectiveness in the long term. Couching their approach in a dialogic sense pre-empts criticisms of judicial activism and retaliation from the political branches.[139] As Kent Roach puts it, '[U]nder a dialogic approach, the dilemma of judicial activism in a democracy diminishes perhaps to the point of evaporation.'[140] This is because the court does not present itself as the final arbiter of constitutional meaning but recognises its place as a co-equal and co-operative player in constitutional law and politics.

Consequently, judicial balancing serves the court's dialogic assertions because it characterises legal solutions as being subject to contextual determinations and thereby to differing outcomes. To an extent, it is a way to hedge one's bets as it invites counter-meanings to be articulated for future cases. In this way, the legislature and the executive could respond to a court's articulation of constitutional meaning in a non-antagonistic fashion. This enhances the judiciary's status and legitimacy as a constitutional actor. Balancing provides judges with a way to develop the law further in a way that would not appear overly activist, while also giving voice to rights discourse.

VI Conclusion

In one of the early cases on constitutional law, the Privy Council cautioned that judges should give fundamental liberties 'a generous interpretation, avoiding what has been called "the austerity of tabulated legalism", suitable to give to individuals the full measure of the [fundamental liberties] referred to'.[141] The adoption of judicial balancing could be criticised for falling short of giving individual rights the full measure of what would be expected under a liberal democracy. The current embrace of judicial balancing is a modest development for Singapore constitutional law. Indeed, the act of balancing treats rights as defeasible by other rights and/or public interests.[142]

However, considering the tendency in earlier cases to regard constitutional rights as subsidiary to governmental interests, the promise of judicial balancing

lies in its capacity to raise the status of constitutional rights to co-equal or perhaps even preferential status in the future. At the very least, it signifies increasing judicial engagement with the Constitution, particularly with constitutional rights. It is notable that this engagement is taking place amidst increased citizen engagement in Singapore's dominant party democracy.[143] Courts should further enunciate how they value and attach weight to constitutional rights as opposed to state interests in the balancing process. It is here that courts will, arguably, have to articulate their conception of constitutional rights. In this context, judicial balancing is a progressive, but ongoing, shift in favour of greater rights-recognition, and with the potential for greater rights-protection.

Notes

* I am grateful to David Tan, Swati Jhaveri and Ho Hock Lai for their comments on previous drafts.

1 T Alexander Aleinikoff, 'Constitutional Law in the Age of Balancing' (1987) 96(5) Yale Law Journal 943, 946.
2 ibid 945.
3 See generally Norman Deutsch, 'Professor Nimmer Meets Professor Schauer (and Others): An Analysis of "Definitional Balancing" as a Methodology for Determining the "Visible Boundaries of the First Amendment"' (2006) 39 Akron Law Review 483.
4 Melville B Nimmer, 'The Right to Speak from Times to Time: First Amendment Theory Applied to Libel and Misapplied to Privacy' (1968) 56(4) California Law Review 935, 944–45.
5 ibid 943.
6 Note, however, Aleinikoff's critique, which is that definitional balancing is not that different from ad hoc balancing because it does not foreclose arguments that new considerations or factors should be taken into account where applicable. If that is the case, meaning if new interests and different weights are allowed to re-open the balancing process, then every case would still entail an 'ad-hoc' balance whereby the rule it establishes really only applies to that specific case: Aleinikoff (n 1) 980.
7 The balancing metaphor is also used in other areas of law, such as in company law (see eg *The Oriental Insurance Co Ltd v Reliance National Asia Re Pte Ltd* [2008] 3 SLR(R) 121), conflict of laws (see eg *Evergreen International SA v Volkswagen Group Singapore Pte Ltd and others* [2004] 2 SLR(R) 457), ad-hoc admission under the Legal Professions Act (see eg *Re Beloff Michael Jacob QC* [2013] 4 SLR 849) and admissibility of entrapment or illegally obtained evidence (see eg *Law Society of Singapore v Tan Guat Neo Phyllis* [2008] 2 SLR(R) 239 [113]).
8 ibid.
9 Marko Novak, 'Three Models of Balancing (in Constitutional Review)' (2010) 23(2) Ratio Juris 101, 101.
10 ibid.
11 Robert Alexy, 'Constitutional Rights, Balancing, and Rationality' (2003) 16(2) Ratio Juris 131, 135.
12 Robert Alexy, 'The Construction of Constitutional Rights' (2010) 4(1) Law & Ethics of Human Rights 21.
13 ibid.
14 Emphasis added. *Tan Eng Hong v Attorney-General* [2013] 4 SLR 1059 [89].
15 Emphasis added. *Lim Meng Suang v Attorney-General* [2015] 1 SLR 26 [70].
16 Alexy (n 12) 21.

17 Aleinikoff points out that in the context of the USA, balancing is seen as uncontroversial because it resonates with prevailing conceptions of law and notions of rational decision-making: Aleinikoff (n 1) 944.

18 There could also be different types of deference. For instance, Alexy differentiates between structural and epistemic deference: Robert Alexy, *A Theory of Constitutional Rights* (J Rivers tr, first published 1985, Oxford University Press 2002).

19 See generally Paul Horwitz, 'Three Faces of Deference' (2008) 83(3) Notre Dame Law Review 1061. To be sure, Horwitz does not differentiate between strong and weak senses of deference.

20 Emphasis added. Robert A Schapiro, 'Judicial Deference and Interpretive Coordinacy in State and Federal Constitutional Law' (2000) 85 Cornell Law Review 656, 665.

21 Alison L Young, 'Deference, Dialogue, and the Search for Legitimacy' (2010) 30(4) Oxford Journal of Legal Studies 815, 817.

22 Brian Foley, *Deference and the Presumption of Constitutionality* (Institute of Public Administration, Dublin 2008) 4.

23 Young (n 21) 817–18. This distinction between deference as submission and deference as respect is drawn from Dyzenhaus' work: see David Dyzenhaus, 'The Politics of Deference: Judicial Review and Democracy' in M Taggard (ed), *The Province of Administrative Law* (Hart Publishing 1997) 186, 279.

24 In the United Kingdom, this idea of deference as respect underlies the doctrine of due deference. See Alison L Young, 'In Defence of Due Deference' (2009) 72 MLR 554, 559.

25 Interestingly, Brady has provided a book-length account of the inter-relationship between proportionality and deference. Alan DP Brady, *Proportionality and Deference under the UK Human Rights Act 1998: An Institutionally Sensitive Approach* (Cambridge University Press 2012).

26 [1994] 1 SLR(R) 782.

27 The court discussed this in the context of addressing a relevant Malaysian case, which had held that the right to counsel begins immediately but that its exercise could be delayed because the right of the accused must be balanced against the interests of effective police investigations: ibid [46].

28 *Jasbir Singh* (n 26) [48].

29 *Chee Soon Juan v Public Prosecutor* [2003] SGHC 122, [2003] 2 SLR(R) 445.

30 (Cap 257, 2001 Rev Ed Sing).

31 *Chee Soon Juan* (n 29) [20].

32 ibid.

33 ibid.

34 ibid.

35 ibid.

36 *Chee Siok Chin v Minister of Home Affairs* [2006] 1 SLR(R) 582.

37 (Cap 184, 1997 Rev Ed Sing).

38 *Chee Siok Chin* (n 36) [44].

39 ibid [2].

40 ibid [42].

41 ibid [49].

42 ibid.

43 ibid.

44 ibid [52], emphasis added. At another point, the High Court used the balancing language to refer to the Constitution:

> In the ultimate analysis, the overarching issue is what the Constitution of the Republic of Singapore (1999 Rev Ed) ("the constitution") considers "necessary or

> expedient" so as to strike a balance between the exercise of certain individual rights on the one hand and the perceived wider public interest on the other hand.
>
> ibid [2]

45 *Chee Siok Chin* (n 36) [51]–[52].

46 For a more complete discussion on Article 14 jurisprudence, see David Tan, 'Whither the autochthonous narrative of freedom of speech? A guide to defaming politicians and scandalising judges in Singapore', Chapter 9 of this book.

47 See further discussion of this point in Jaclyn Ling-Chien Neo and Yvonne CL Lee, 'Constitutional Supremacy: Still a Little Dicey' in Li-ann Thio and Kevin YL Tan (eds), *Evolution of a Revolution: Forty Years of the Singapore Constitution* (Routledge-Cavendish 2009) 153.

48 Although this case did not invoke balancing, it nonetheless is consistent with the courts' view of judicial review during this period: *Rajeevan Edakalavan v PP* [1998] SGHC 2, [1998] 1 SLR(R) 10 [19].

49 *Rajeevan Edakalavan* (n 48) [21].

50 ibid [19]. Similar sentiments were expressed in *Jabar bin Kadermastan v* Public Prosecutor [1995] SGCA 18, [1995] 1 SLR(R) 326 where Yong CJ opined:

> Any law which provides for the deprivation of a person's life or personal liberty ... is valid and binding so long as it is validly passed by Parliament. The court is not concerned with whether it is also fair, just and reasonable as well.

Note, however, the Court of Appeal's reading of *Jabar* as being restricted to the facts in *Yong Vui Kong v Public Prosecutor* [2010] SGCA 20, [2010] 3 SLR 489 [18]–[19].

51 *Rajeevan Edakalavan* (n 48) [21].

52 ibid.

53 Thio Li-ann, 'Protecting Rights' in Thio Li-ann and Kevin YL Tan (eds), *Evolution of a Revolution: Forty Years of the Singapore Constitution* (Routledge-Cavendish 2009) 193, 195.

54 [1994] 3 SLR(R) 209.

55 ibid [64].

56 ibid.

57 [1998] SGHC 351.

58 ibid [53]. The plaintiff in this case was a teacher at a public institution who refused to take the National Pledge or sing the National Anthem because he considered these acts to contravene his beliefs as a Jehovah's Witness. Jehovah's Witnesses believe that worship is reserved exclusively for God and that the act of taking the National Pledge or singing the National Anthem is effectively an expression of religious devotion. ibid [2]–[3]. The Court of Appeal affirmed the High Court's decision, albeit by denying the plaintiff's view that the Pledge and the Anthem constitute religious ceremonies, and thereby fall within the protection of Article 15. See *Nappalli Peter Williams v Institute of Technical Education* [1999] 2 SLR(R) 529.

59 [2013] 4 SLR 1 ('*Vellama (CA)*').

60 (Emphasis added).

61 Singapore Parliamentary Debates, Official Report (9 March 2012) vol 88.

62 ibid.

63 Notably, the issue was focused on single-member constituencies since section 24(2A) of the Parliamentary Elections Act (Cap 218, Rev Ed Sing) provides that no writ of election shall be issued to fill a Group Representation Constituency (GRC) vacancy 'unless all the Members for that constituency have vacated their seats'. One could, nonetheless, question whether s 24(2A) of the Parliamentary Elections Act could be challenged on constitutional grounds. See discussion on the GRC and by-elections here: Thio Li-ann, 'By-election Case: A Legal or Political Question?' *The*

Straits Times: Singapolitics (Singapore, 24 September 2013) www.singapolitics.sg/views/election-case-legal-or-political-question accessed: 12 May 2015.

64 It should be noted that while the matter was pending, the Prime Minister called for a by-election, rendering the case largely moot.

65 *Vellama (CA)* (n 59) [87] and [92].

66 ibid [87] and [92].

67 ibid [85], emphasis added.

68 *Vellama d/o Marie Muthu v Attorney-General* [2012] 4 SLR 698 [115] ('*Vellama (HC)*'). The High Court's judgment could be criticised for being too formalistic in that it justified its conclusion on linguistic inexorability, which it supported through textual, contextual and historical sources. As Schauer explains, the critique of formalism is directed at legal reasoning that denies the presence of choice for the decision-maker. This denial often relies on an assertion that there is an inexorable meaning to the language in which the rules are written. See Frederick Schauer, 'Formalism' (1998) 97 Yale Law Journal 509.

69 *Vellama (HC)* (n 68) [115].

70 As the Court of Appeal stated:

> Even reading the word "election" in the context as prescribing only a process, we *fail to see how that necessarily leads* to the conclusion that the Prime Minister has thereby an unfettered discretion as to whether he will tender advice to the President to issue a writ of election.
>
> *Vellama (CA)* (n 59) [75]

71 See Kevin YL Tan, 'Into the matrix: interpreting the Westminster model constitution', Chapter 3 of this book.

72 *Jasbir Singh* (n 26).

73 This was reiterated by the High Court in *Public Prosecutor v Leong Siew Chor* [2006] 3 SLR(R) 290 [87], where the court stated that giving effect to the right of access to counsel entailed balancing the rights of the arrested person against the public interest that crime be effectively investigated. Like in *Jasbir Singh* (n 26), the case however did not involve a balancing exercise. The identification of the public interest in effective investigation of crime was merely identified and asserted as a competing interest that justified the limiting of the constitutional right to counsel.

74 *James Raj s/o Arokiasamy v Public Prosecutor* [2014] 3 SLR 750 [31].

75 Ho calls the case a non-development of the right to counsel. See Ho Hock Lai, 'Recent (Non-) Developments in an Arrested Person's Right to Counsel' (2014) Singapore Journal of Legal Studies 267.

76 *James Raj* (n 74) [31] referring to *Jasbir Singh* (n 26) [46].

77 *James Raj* (n 74) [39].

78 Ho, however, criticises this approach, preferring instead the approach by the High Court (*James Raj s/o Arokiasamy v Public Prosecutor* [2014] 2 SLR 307) in the same case. He argues that the question of whether it is reasonable to deprive a person of access to counsel should not be approached as a question of fact, but as a matter of legal principle, or more specifically as a question of fairness. Ho Hock Lai, 'Criminal Justice and Constitutional Rights' (Criminal Justice Conference 2015: Criminal Justice and the Singapore Constitution, Singapore, 15 August 2015) (on file with author).

79 *Tan Eng Hong v Attorney-General* [2012] 4 SLR 476 [109] (citing Chan Sek Keong, 'Judicial Review – From Angst to Empathy' (2010) 22 Singapore Academy of Law Journal 469, 481).

80 *Review Publishing Co Ltd and Another v Lee Hsien Loong and another appeal* [2009] SGCA 46, [2010] 1 SLR 52.

81 [2001] 2 AC 127 (HL).

82 *Review Publishing* (n 80) [268]–[271].

83 ibid [267].
84 ibid [266].
85 ibid [270].
86 Notably, the court opined that 'striking the balance between freedom of expression and protection of reputation would call for a *value judgment which depended upon local political and social conditions*'. ibid [271].
87 See eg *Marbury v Madison* 5 US 137 (1803).
88 *Review Publishing* (n 80) [273]–[285].
89 ibid [273].
90 ibid [266]–[267].
91 ibid.
92 In this case, the court considered four possible ways to conceptualise rights: as 'preferential', as 'fundamental', as 'co-equal' or as 'subsidiary'; ibid [286]–[289].
93 *Review Publishing* (n 80) [287].
94 ibid [288].
95 ibid [289].
96 ibid [260].
97 See Jack Tsen-Ta Lee, 'Rethinking the presumption of constitutionality', Chapter 6 of this book.
98 Note, however, Young's point that the distinction is open to misinterpretation and that it could be difficult to distinguish between the two. Young proposes instead three possible models of the way in which the court could give weight to the opinions of the legislature or the executive, which are deference as submission, as submission plus correction, and as respect. See Young (n 21) 559–64.
99 Former Chief Justice Chan Sek Keong briefly discussed a common perception about the futility of judicial review in Keong (n 79).
100 See Aleinikoff's discussion of the American experience. Aleinikoff (n 1) 958.
101 Aleinikoff (n 1) 961.
102 ibid. Specifically, in the American context there was a shift towards an instrumental view of the law as:

> an attempt to satisfy, to reconcile, to harmonize, to adjust … overlapping and often conflicting claims and demands, either through securing them directly and immediately, or through securing certain individual interests, or through delimitations or compromises of individual interests, so as to give effect to the greatest total of interests or to the interests that weigh most in our civilization, with the least sacrifice of the scheme of interests as a whole.
>
> Roscoe Pound, 'A Survey of Social Interests' (1943) 57 Harvard Law Review 1, 39

103 ibid.
104 Jürgen Habermas, *Between Facts and Norms: Contributions to a Discourse Theory of Law and Democracy* (W Rehg tr, Oxford, Polity Press 1996) 256.
105 Ronald Dworkin, *Taking Rights Seriously* (Duckworth 1977) 193–94, 269 (arguing inter alia that '[t]he prospect of utilitarian gains cannot justify preventing a man from doing what he has a right to do').
106 See Habermas (n 104).
107 For a discussion of this in the United States context, see Thomas A Balmer and Katherine Thomas, 'In the Balance: Thoughts on Balancing and Alternative Approaches in State Constitutional Interpretation' (2012/2013) 76(4) Albany Law Review 2027, 2043.
108 See Jack Tsen-Ta Lee, 'Rethinking the presumption of constitutionality', Chapter 6 of this book.
109 Melville B Nimmer, 'The Right to Speak from Times to Time: First Amendment Theory Applied to Libel and Misapplied to Privacy' (1968) 56(4) California Law

Review 935, 940 (discussing the balancing approach as applied to free speech cases).

110 The ruling party's recent electoral success suggests that the electorate is comfortable with a dominant party government. Sumiko Tan, 'GE2015: PAP vote share increases to 69.9%, party wins 83 of 89 seats including WP-held Punggol East' *The Straits Times* (Singapore, 12 September 2015) www.straitstimes.com/politics/ge2015-pap-vote-share-increases-to-699-wins-83-of-89-seats-including-wp-held-punggol-east accessed 7 October 2015. For a more extensive analysis of the 2015 General Elections, see Tommy Koh, 'Ten Reflections on GE 2015' *The Straits Times* (Singapore, 17 September 2015) www.straitstimes.com/opinion/ten-reflections-on-ge-2015 accessed 7 October 2015.

111 Matthias Kumm, 'Political Liberalism and the Structure of Rights: On the Place and Limits of the Proportionality Requirement' in G Pavlakos (ed), *Law, Rights, and Discourse: The Legal Philosophy of Robert Alexy* (Hart Publishing 2007).

112 For criticisms, see eg Ran Hirschl, *Towards Juristocracy* (Harvard University Press 2007).

113 Aleinikoff (n 1) 962–63.

114 ibid 963.

115 This restrained approach may also explain why judges have not embraced proportionality to the same extent as they have balancing, even though balancing could be said to be an integral part of a broader principle of proportionality. Alexy points out that:

> [i]n German constitutional law balancing is one aspect of what is required by a more comprehensive principle, namely, the principle of proportionality (Verhältnismäßigkeitsgrundsatz). The principle of proportionality consists of three subprinciples: the principles of suitability, of necessity and of proportionality in its narrow sense. All these principles give expression to the idea of optimization.
> Robert Alexy, 'Balancing, Constitutional Review and Representation' (2005) 3(4) International Journal of Constitutional Law 572, 572

116 For an exposition on the counter-majoritarian difficulty, see Alexander Bickel, *The Least Dangerous Branch: The Supreme Court at the Bar of Politics* (Yale University Press 1986).

117 *Chng Suan Tze v Minister for Home Affairs* [1988] SGCA 16, [1988] 2 SLR(R) 525 [86].

118 ibid [85].

119 ibid [86].

120 ibid.

121 Keong (n 79) [8].

122 ibid [9].

123 Balmer and Thomas (n 107) 2041.

124 Aleinikoff (n 1) 984.

125 The counter-majoritarian difficulty was famously raised by Bickel in *The Least Dangerous Branch* (n 116).

126 Aleinikoff (n 1) 985–86.

127 For instance, John Hart Ely addresses the counter-majoritarian difficulty by emphasising the court's representation reinforcing role. See John Hart Ely, *Democracy and Distrust* (Harvard University Press 1980).

128 Aleinikoff (n 1) 984.

129 ibid 985.

130 ibid 985–86.

131 ibid.

132 Robert Alexy, 'Constitutional Rights and Constitutional Review' (2014), http://ius.bg.ac.rs/konferencije/2014.10.24.%20Fundamental%20Rights/Alexy.pdf. Alexy has

characterised the representative claim of a constitutional court as 'purely argumentative': Robert Alexy, 'Balancing, Constitutional Review, and Representation' (2005) 3 International Journal of Constitutional Law 579.

133 For more, see generally Yap Po Jen, *Constitutional Dialogue in Common Law Asia* (Oxford University Press 2015).

134 For an overview of theories on constitutional dialogue, see Christine Bateup, 'The Dialogic Promise – Assessing the Normative Potential of Theories of Constitutional Dialogue' (2005–2006) 71 Brooklyn Law Review 1109.

135 ibid 1124.

136 ibid 1123–24. See also Neal Kumar Katyal, 'Judges as Advicegivers' (1998) 50 Stanford Law Review 1709.

137 Bateup (n 134) 1124–25. Bateup however points out that there are strong criticisms against characterising the conversation as a form of active judicial advice-giving, not least because it adopts a position of superiority and seemingly shows an underlying distrust of the political branches; ibid, 1125–28.

138 ibid 1118.

139 One might argue that the Court of Appeal in *Chng Suan Tze* was right in law to strike down the detention orders and in enunciating an objective test of review of detention powers, but that it was too progressive for its time. This coincides with Ginsburg's observation that '[i]n autocratic settings, courts may on occasion seek to trigger a democratic tipping, but this is a dangerous course that rarely succeeds'. Tom Ginsburg, 'The Politics of Courts in Democratization' in Diana Kapiszewski and others (eds), *Consequential Courts: Judicial Roles in Global Perspective* (Cambridge University Press 2013) 64.

140 Kent Roach, 'Constitutional and Common Law Dialogues Between Supreme Court and Canadian Legislatures' (2001) 80 Canadian Bar Review 481, 532.

141 *Ong Ah Chuan v PP* [1981] 1 AC 649.

142 Thio Li-ann, *A Treatise on Singapore Constitutional Law* (Academy Publishing 2012).

143 This takes place within the context of increasing litigation by citizens seeking to vindicate their constitutional rights. VK Rajah, 'The Rule of Law', Speech at the Opening of the Legal Year 2015, edited excerpt *The Straits Times* (Singapore, 7 January 2015) www.agc.gov.sg/DATA/0/Docs/NewsFiles/OPENING%20OF%20LEGAL%20YEAR%202015_ATTORNEY-GENERAL%20V%20K%20RAJAH'S%20SPEECH_5%20JAN_checked%20against%20delivery.pdf accessed 7 January 2015.

Bibliography

Aleinikoff, T Alexander, 'Constitutional Law in the Age of Balancing' (1987) 96(5) Yale Law Journal 943.

Alexy, Robert, *A Theory of Constitutional Rights* (J Rivers tr, first published 1985, Oxford University Press 2002).

Alexy, Robert, 'Constitutional Rights, Balancing, and Rationality' (2003) 16(2) Ratio Juris 131.

Alexy, Robert, 'Balancing, Constitutional Review and Representation' (2005) 3(4) International Journal of Constitutional Law 572.

Alexy, Robert, 'The Construction of Constitutional Rights' (2010) 4(1) Law & Ethics of Human Rights 21.

Bateup, Christine, 'The Dialogic Promise – Assessing the Normative Potential of Theories of Constitutional Dialogue' (2005–2006) 71 Brooklyn Law Review 1109.

Bickel, Alexander, *The Least Dangerous Branch: The Supreme Court at the Bar of Politics* (Yale University Press 1986).

Brady, Alan DP, *Proportionality and Deference under the UK Human Rights Act 1998: An Institutionally Sensitive Approach* (Cambridge University Press 2012).
Chan, Sek Keong, 'Judicial Review – From Angst to Empathy' (2010) 22 Singapore Academy of Law Journal 469.
Deutsch, Norman, 'Professor Nimmer Meets Professor Schauer (and Others): An Analysis of "Definitional Balancing" as a Methodology for Determining the "Visible Boundaries of the First Amendment"' (2006) 39 Akron Law Review 483.
Dworkin, Ronald, *Taking Rights Seriously* (Duckworth 1977).
Dyzenhaus, David, 'The Politics of Deference: Judicial Review and Democracy' in M Taggard (ed), *The Province of Administrative Law* (Hart Publishing 1997).
Ely, John Hart, *Democracy and Distrust* (Harvard University Press 1980).
Foley, Brian, *Deference and the Presumption of Constitutionality* (Institute of Public Administration, Dublin 2008).
Ginsburg, Tom, 'The Politics of Courts in Democratization' in Diana Kapiszewski, Gordon Silverstein and RA Kagan (eds), *Consequential Courts: Judicial Roles in Global Perspective* (Cambridge University Press 2013).
Habermas, Jürgen, *Between Facts and Norms: Contributions to a Discourse Theory of Law and Democracy* (W Rehg tr, Polity Press 1996).
Hirschl, Ran, *Towards Juristocracy* (Harvard University Press 2007).
Ho, Hock Lai, 'Recent (Non-) Developments in an Arrested Person's Right to Counsel' (2014) Singapore Journal of Legal Studies 267.
Ho, Hock Lai, 'Criminal Justice and Constitutional Rights' (Criminal Justice Conference 2015: Criminal Justice and the Singapore Constitution, Singapore, 15 August 2015).
Horwitz, Paul, 'Three Faces of Deference' (2008) 83(3) Notre Dame Law Review 1061.
Koh, Tommy, 'Ten Reflections on GE 2015' *The Straits Times* (Singapore, 17 September 2015) www.straitstimes.com/opinion/ten-reflections-on-ge-2015.
Kumm, Matthias, 'Political Liberalism and the Structure of Rights: On the Place and Limits of the Proportionality Requirement' in G Pavlakos (ed), *Law, Rights, and Discourse: The Legal Philosophy of Robert Alexy* (Hart Publishing 2007).
Neo, Jaclyn Ling-Chien and Yvonne CL Lee, 'Constitutional Supremacy: Still a Little Dicey' in Li-ann Thio and Kevin YL Tan (eds), *Evolution of a Revolution: Forty Years of the Singapore Constitution* (Routledge-Cavendish 2009).
Nimmer, Melville B, 'The Right to Speak from Times to Time: First Amendment Theory Applied to Libel and Misapplied to Privacy' (1968) 56(4) California Law Review 935.
Novak, Marko, 'Three Models of Balancing (in Constitutional Review)' (2010) 23(2) Ratio Juris 101.
Pound, Roscoe, 'A Survey of Social Interests' (1943) 57 Harvard Law Review 1.
Rajah, VK, 'The Rule of Law', Speech at the Opening of the Legal Year 2015, edited excerpt *The Straits Times* (Singapore, 7 January 2015) www.agc.gov.sg/DATA/0/Docs/NewsFiles/OPENING%20OF%20LEGAL%20YEAR%202015_ATTORNEY-GENERAL%20V%20K%20RAJAH'S%20SPEECH_5%20JAN_checked%20against%20delivery.pdf.
Roach, Kent, 'Constitutional and Common Law Dialogues between Supreme Court and Canadian Legislatures' (2001) 80 Canadian Bar Review 481.
Schapiro, Robert A, 'Judicial Deference and Interpretive Coordinacy in State and Federal Constitutional Law' (2000) 85 Cornell Law Review 656.
Schauer, Frederick, 'Formalism' (1998) 97 Yale Law Journal 509.
Tan, Sumiko, 'GE2015: PAP Vote Share Increases to 69.9%, Party Wins 83 of 89 Seats Including WP-held Punggol East' *The Straits Times* (Singapore, 12 September 2015)

www.straitstimes.com/politics/ge2015-pap-vote-share-increases-to-699-wins-83-of-89-seats-including-wp-held-punggol-east.

Thio, Li-ann, 'Protecting Rights' in Li-ann Thio and Kevin YL Tan (eds), *Evolution of a Revolution: Forty Years of the Singapore Constitution* (Routledge-Cavendish 2009).

Thio, Li-ann, *A Treatise on Singapore Constitutional Law* (Academy Publishing 2012).

Thio, Li-ann, 'By-election Case: A Legal or Political Question?' *The Straits Times: Singapolitics* (Singapore, 24 September 2013) www.singapolitics.sg/views/election-case-legal-or-political-question.

Yap, Po Jen, *Constitutional Dialogue in Common Law Asia* (Oxford University Press 2015).

Young, Alison L, 'In Defence of Due Deference' (2009) 72 MLR 554.

Young, Alison L, 'Deference, Dialogue, and the Search for Legitimacy' (2010) 30(4) Oxford Journal of Legal Studies 815.

8 The broader case for developing the content of fundamental rules of natural justice under Article 9 of the Constitution

A placeholder for proportionality-type adjudication?

*Swati Jhaveri**

I Introduction

Article 9 of the Constitution of the Republic of Singapore states that '[n]o person shall be deprived of his life or personal liberty, *save in accordance with law*' (emphasis added). The precise scope of the latter part of this provision has been the subject of extensive judicial discussion. Applicants have sought to introduce content to the meaning of the phrase 'in accordance with law' through various means.[1] For example, they have sought to argue that 'law' includes norms of customary international law, the prohibition against cruel and inhuman punishment, and procedural and substantive rights that must be respected in depriving one of life or liberty. This chapter focuses on one example of this extra-textual content to the proviso to Article 9(1),[2] namely, the concept of the 'fundamental rules of natural justice' (FRNJ). This chapter will look at how 'law' has been interpreted to include the concept of FRNJ and how this concept has evolved over time. The discussion surrounding the meaning of FRNJ is noteworthy for two reasons. First, it is the only extra-textual inclusion to the meaning of the word 'law' that has been successfully introduced and retained in cases[3] and, second, it was an innovative introduction into local constitutional jurisprudence at a time when constitutional interpretation was relatively more textual and literal in its approach.[4] It thus provides an interesting vantage point for understanding the different interpretive techniques of the court and for evaluating possible trajectories of the interpretation of Part IV of the Constitution. As will be discussed further in Section III below, a particularly interesting trajectory would be the possible development of proportionality as a mode of adjudicating on limitations on rights as set out in Part IV of the Constitution. This trajectory is discussed in light of the more recent judgments on the concept of FRNJ and, in particular, the use of (albeit embryonically) similar analytical considerations as traditionally found within proportionality (which has thus far been rejected).

The start of the discussion on FRNJ can be traced back to the case of *Ong Ah Chuan v Public Prosecutor* ('*Ong Ah Chuan*').[5] In that case, in adopting a generous approach to constitutional interpretation, the Privy Council held that the meaning of the phrase 'in accordance with law' in the context of Article 9(1) refers to 'law' that incorporates 'fundamental rules of natural justice'. In *Ong Ah Chuan*, the Privy Council left open the precise scope and meaning of the phrase. This task was left to subsequent case law. Subsequent cases have noted the open-ended nature of the concept of FRNJ. In *Haw Tua Tau & Ors v Public Prosecutor* ('*Haw Tua Tau*'),[6] the Privy Council considered it would be premature to attempt to make a comprehensive list of what constitutes FRNJ: it is a concept that should evolve over time.[7] These thoughts were echoed in *Tan Eng Hong v Attorney-General* ('*Tan Eng Hong*')[8] where Loh J remarked that:

> [T]he authorities are not definitive on a number of difficult aspects, in particular: (a) what is the concept of the fundamental rules of natural justice in a constitutional setting; and (b) what is the scope of the fundamental rules of natural justice? The dearth of binding authority on these issues appears to indicate some reluctance to venture forth into this unchartered territory, lest it proves even worse than the metaphorical unruly horse.... Lord Diplock in [*Haw Tua Tau*] suggested it was a concept whose meaning would evolve over time. In this context, it is therefore not entirely surprising, considering the lack of clarity with regard to the somewhat amorphous and nebulous concept of the fundamental rules of natural justice, that there has been extremely limited development of the scope of these rules in a constitutional setting.[9]

This chapter will analyse the way the courts have interpreted FRNJ in subsequent case law. The aim of this analysis is not just to identify the interpretive direction that the proviso to Article 9(1) may take but also to highlight the possibility of utilising some of the more recent interpretations of FRNJ to recognise the possibility of introducing some form of proportionality-type reasoning into local constitutional jurisprudence as an adjudicative tool for evaluating limitations on the rights set out in Part IV of the Constitution.

The chapter identifies four different tracks that the discussion on FRNJ has taken in the case law. Here it is important to clarify the terminology that will be used to discuss the various tracks. This article uses four labels: procedural rights; procedural standards; substantive rights; and substantive standards. The distinction is between the 'procedural' and the 'substantive' and between 'rights' and 'standards'. 'Procedural rights' refer to interests (typically borrowed from the criminal context) that the applicant argues must be respected during the process of depriving them of life or liberty in order for such a deprivation to be compliant with the FRNJ and 'in accordance with law'. This includes, for example, protecting the presumption of innocence or the privilege against self-incrimination.[10] 'Procedural standards' on the other hand include criteria guiding the decision-making process on the part of the executive or the legislature. They refer to the procedural benchmarks that the applicant argues are part of the FRNJ that the decision-maker must respect in order to successfully assert that they have constitutionally deprived an individual of life or liberty 'in accordance with law'. This includes providing the applicant with all aspects of a fair hearing and ensuring the absence of bias in the decision-maker.[11] 'Substantive rights' refer to interests that cannot be violated in depriving of life or liberty irrespective of the process followed by the decision-maker. These include depriving a person of life or liberty in a way that would violate the prohibition[12] against torture or in a way that would constitute a form of cruel and inhuman punishment.[13] 'Substantive standards' refer to content-based benchmarks that the content of any restriction on life or liberty must meet: for example, the law or executive action that seeks to restrict life or liberty cannot be 'absurd' or 'arbitrary'.[14] These are terms that the courts have developed, as will be further discussed below.[15]

This study will track these developments of the judicial interpretation of the proviso to Article 9. In particular, it will analyse the reluctance to interpret the proviso as having any strong substantive content (either rights or standards). It will highlight how the courts have instead preferred a more procedural approach to interpretation: one that focuses on procedural standards of decision-making relying on administrative law standards of fair hearing and the rule against bias. This is in preference to incorporating procedural rights relating to the presumption of innocence or the privilege against self-incrimination into the concept of FRNJ.

The analysis will, however, show that there is scope for a modified substantive content to this proviso which incorporates some elements of the proportionality-type adjudication typically seen in rights adjudication. This conclusion draws on the recent approach to evaluating deprivations of life and liberty in cases such as *Tan Eng Hong* and *Lim Meng Suang*. These cases borrow aspects of the reasonable classification test under Article 12 to assess the 'arbitrariness' of a law purporting to restrict life and liberty under Article 9 by reference to its purpose and means, which are inquiries that can be located within proportionality-type of reasoning in constitutional adjudication. Such an approach can be generalised in its usage when assessing whether a particular deprivation of life or liberty is 'in accordance with law'. This analysis into the law's purpose in restricting a particular constitutional right or interest is making an appearance elsewhere and is not an unfamiliar judicial exercise.[16] It may be possible to expand its usage to other rights in Part IV of the Constitution. These issues will be discussed further in Section III below.

II Developing FRNJ: key defining moments

A Procedural rights: FRNJ and aspects of criminal procedure

The two key cases discussing procedural rights within the concept of FRNJ are *Ong Ah Chuan* and *Haw Tua Tau.* The applicants in *Ong Ah Chuan* had been convicted of trafficking drugs contrary to section 3 of the Misuse of Drugs Act

1973 (MDA). They both received the mandatory death penalty (MDP) under the legislation. In *Ong Ah Chuan* they sought to challenge the constitutionality of the presumption of trafficking arising from the possession of a certain weight of drugs under section 15 of the MDA, as well as the constitutionality of the MDP.[17] The applicants contended that the presumption as well as the MDP were not restrictions 'in accordance with law' within the meaning of Article 9.

In interpreting Article 9, the Privy Council recognised that constitutional interpretation is *sui generis* and when it comes to fundamental rights and freedoms the courts will give 'a generous interpretation, avoiding what has been called "the austerity of tabulated legalism", suitable to give to individuals the full measure of the [fundamental liberties] referred to'.[18] The Privy Council accordingly rejected the respondent's position that the legislation in question was legal as long as it was duly passed by the legislature and was general in its application. The Privy Council instead held that in a constitution which protects rights of citizens, references to 'law' in Part IV refer to a system of law which incorporates those FRNJ that had formed part of the common law of England that was in force in Singapore at the commencement of the Constitution. Although this was worded in historical terms with reference to the rules of the common law in force in England at the time of the enactment of the Constitution, the Privy Council did have a more normative concern to ensure that narrow interpretations of 'law' did not make a mockery of the entrenchment of rights. Academic commentators have argued elsewhere that the reason for recognising a richer notion of 'law' was not to assure Singaporeans of the continuance of the notion once the Constitution came into force but to reinforce the idea that it is normatively appealing to prevent Parliament from enacting laws which take away a person's liberty without observing rules of natural justice in reaching a decision on the guilt of that person to justify the removal of liberty.[19]

In applying the concept of the FRNJ to the case, the Privy Council was not willing to go as far as recognise that the presumption of innocence is a FRNJ (largely because they regarded this as an outdated and misunderstood rule).[20] However, it did recognise that one of the rules is that a person should not be punished for an offence unless it has been established to the satisfaction of an independent and impartial tribunal that he committed it. This involves the tribunal being satisfied that all the physical and mental elements of the offence were made out sufficient to constitute the offence with which the accused is charged. The Privy Council held that there had been no breach of this rule. Although the court did not use the language of balancing, it focused on issues relating to the 'reasonableness' of the presumption. In reaching their decision, they focused on the fact that it would not be unfair to have a presumption of trafficking that was based on the weight of drugs in the defendant's possession. Such a presumption is based on facts consistent with trafficking and is based on an unlawful fact (possession of a controlled substance for which there is no innocent explanation possible). It is also not unreasonable to have a presumption because the facts and evidence relating to the purpose of possession are within the knowledge of the defendant who is, therefore, in the best position to rebut the presumption.[21]

The first major case dealing with the interpretation of FRNJ following *Ong Ah Chuan* was *Haw Tua Tau*. The case concerned amendments to the Criminal Procedure Code. Under the Criminal Procedure Code, as it stood when the Constitution came into force in 1963, the accused had the option of either making an unsworn statement from the dock on which he could not be cross-examined, or of giving evidence on oath or affirmation and thereby submitting himself to cross-examination. This was subsequently amended with the effect that the option to make an unsworn statement without being subjected to cross-examination was abolished. Instead, an accused person would be warned at the end of the prosecution's case that he had the option of either giving evidence on the stand and subjecting himself to cross-examination, or to remain silent. However, the court could draw such inferences as would appear proper from his refusal to give evidence. The appellants in *Haw Tua Tau* were charged and convicted of capital offences (murder and drug trafficking) and were sentenced to death. At their trial, each of them had been called upon to give evidence at the end of the prosecution's case, which they did. In their appeal to the Privy Council the applicants contended that the amendments to the Criminal Procedure Code essentially compelled an accused person to give evidence in his defence (because if they did not the court could draw inferences from their silence), and to subject himself to cross-examination. The applicants argued that this infringed the accused person's privilege against self-incrimination, which they argued was a FRNJ, and was thus unlawful as it was inconsistent with Article 9(1) of the Constitution of Singapore.

The Privy Council held that it would be open to considering whether compulsion to give evidence breached a possible FRNJ embodied in the privilege against self-incrimination, but this was not necessary because there was no such compulsion in the case: there was only a strong inducement. They drew support from the fact that section 195(3) of the Criminal Procedure Code makes it clear that the accused has a legal right to refuse to give evidence at his trial and no legal sanctions can be imposed upon him if he chooses to remain silent. It is only if he elects to give evidence that he exposes himself to the risk of being compelled to answer questions put in cross-examination.

The applicants also argued that notwithstanding this, the very act of calling on the accused at the conclusion of the prosecution's case to give evidence and informing him of the consequences of a refusal to do so has the practical effect of putting the accused under a compulsion to give evidence. The applicants tried to argue that the FRNJ are concerned as much with the practical effect of a rule as with the legal aspects of the rule itself. The Privy Council did not respond to this aspect of the argument on the practical effects of FRNJ. Instead, the Privy Council concluded, on narrower grounds,[22] that even before the amendments to the Criminal Procedure Code withdrew the option of making an unsworn statement, the accused would be aware that adverse inferences might be drawn if he failed to go into the witness box, based on the nature of the evidence that had been adduced against him. This could constitute an inducement to give evidence. The Criminal Procedure Code did not alter or increase the possible inferences that could be drawn in any particular case.

Accordingly, while the applicant was successful in convincing the Privy Council that it may be possible that the FRNJ included the privilege against self-incrimination, the Privy Council did not conclusively decide the issue because in this case, there was no compulsion to give evidence which breached a possible FRNJ embodied in the privilege against self-incrimination. For a procedure to violate Art 9(1) it would have to be seriously unfair, in the words of Lord Diplock. Thus, following *Ong Ah Chuan*, the courts have continued to give a fairly narrow reading of process-based rights within the framework of FRNJ and, where possible, have been reluctant to enlarge the scope of process-based rights.[23]

B Procedural standards: FRNJ and the fair hearing rule and rule against bias

The discussion thus far shows mixed success with interpreting FRNJ to include procedural rights. However, the courts have been willing to incorporate procedural decision-making standards from the administrative law context into the concept of FRNJ.[24] This was the case in *Yong Vui Kong Clemency*.[25] The applicant had been convicted of trafficking drugs and had received the MDP under the MDA. He filed a petition for clemency to the President, which was rejected. He sought to challenge the President's decision on the grounds that, inter alia, it breached the FRNJ, namely, the requirement for a fair hearing (which required full disclosure of all relevant materials) and the rule against bias in relation to the decision-maker. The applicant relied on, inter alia, Article 9(1) to make the argument. The applicant argued that the clemency process is an integral part of the process of depriving a person of his life 'in accordance with law' for the purposes of Article 9(1) of the Singapore Constitution. The term 'law' in Article 9(1) incorporates the FRNJ, which, in this case, consisted of the administrative law rules of natural justice.

The Court of Appeal observed that while the administrative rules of natural justice and FRNJ are different – the latter being constitutional in source and effect[26] – the scope and content of the rules are the same, namely, the rule against bias and the fair hearing rule. The court also commented that, as recognised in *Ong Ah Chuan*, in the specific context of criminal procedures that deprive a person of liberty, the fair hearing rule and rule against bias require that (a) the accused be convicted only if the ingredients of the offence have been proven according to the applicable criminal standard of proof; (b) the tribunal trying the accused must be independent and unbiased; and (c) the accused must be heard on his defence. Legislation or procedure that infringes on any of these FRNJ can be challenged for being inconsistent with Article 9(1). This was recently reinforced in *Yong Vui Kong Caning*, where the court went even further to say that these procedural standards make up the complete content of FRNJ. This runs counter to comments made elsewhere in cases like *Haw Tua Tau* on the need to develop the concept over time (as discussed above). Specifically, the court noted that the FRNJ do not have any substantive content. It is to this discussion that we now turn.

C Substantive rights: FRNJ and prohibitions against cruel and inhuman punishment and torture and rules of customary international law

The majority of the cases where the applicants have sought to introduce substantive rights into the concept of FRNJ involve challenges to the MDP. Applicants have sought to argue that the MDP constitutes cruel and inhuman punishment. The applicants argued that such punishment is not in 'accordance with law' under Article 9(1), which contains an implied prohibition against such punishment or, in the alternative, incorporates a rule of customary international law prohibiting such punishment. The latter argument asserts that customary international law is part and parcel of the definition of 'law' under Article 9(1). Until recently these conversations revolved around the meaning of the words 'law' and 'in accordance with law' under Article 9(1). However, as will be further discussed below, the conversation has recently relocated itself to the concept of FRNJ, as evidenced by the most recent case of *Yong Vui Kong Caning*.

These arguments were first made in *Nguyen Tuong Van v Public Prosecutor*.[27] The applicant tried to argue that the MDP was 'arbitrary' in its application and this arbitrariness constituted 'cruel and inhuman punishment'. They sought to argue that 'law' in Article 9(1) went beyond Parliament-sanctioned legislation to include FRNJ, including prohibitions against cruel punishment, an integral part of which was the need for proportionate and individualised sentencing. On this, the court held that the issue of the weight of trafficked drugs sufficiently discriminated between individuals, thereby obviating any inhumanity in the law's operation, which was therefore constitutional. The applicant also argued that the mode of execution by hanging constituted cruel and inhuman punishment which was contrary to customary international law's prohibition against such punishment. The court was willing to accept the possibility of customary international law being a FRNJ within the meaning of 'law' under Article 9(1). The court even held that the applicant had successfully argued that a prohibition on cruel and inhuman punishment was a norm of customary international law. However, the applicant had not shown that there is a specific prohibition against hanging as a mode of execution. For this to happen, any customary international law rule must be clearly and firmly established before its adoption by the courts. In enforcing customary international law under Article 9, the court recognised their responsibility and duty to consider and give effect to any rule concomitant with the civil and civilised society which must be preserved and protected.

This was the position, especially on the issue of customary international law potentially being part of the definition of FRNJ and 'law' under Article 9(1) until *Yong Vui Kong MDP*.[28] The applicant in this case again challenged the MDP on the basis that it, inter alia, violated Article 9(1): the expression 'law' included customary international law and such law prohibited the MDP as inhuman. The applicant argued that the MDP was inhuman because it precluded the courts from considering the circumstances of the case, and thus the moral blameworthiness of the offender, in sentencing. The court decided that Article 9(1) contained no express prohibition against cruel and inhuman punishment and could not be interpreted to contain such an implied prohibition. Domestic law, including Singapore's Constitution, should as far as possible be interpreted so as to be consistent with Singapore's international legal obligations. However, there had to be limits to this interpretive exercise; it would not be appropriate for the courts to legislate new rights into the Constitution through 'interpretation'. This point is especially pertinent because an express constitutional provision prohibiting cruel and inhuman punishment was proposed by the Wee Commission[29] and rejected.[30]

The Court of Appeal was also of the opinion that customary international law cannot be incorporated into the meaning of the word 'law' in Article 9(1) of the Constitution. The court held that customary international law rules do not have any status in domestic law until they are first accepted and adopted as part of domestic law. This happens when a rule is incorporated into a statute (in which case, it becomes domestic law) or when it is judicially declared to be part of the common law of Singapore. At common law the incorporation of customary international law can only be done when it is not inconsistent with existing domestic laws. Given the existence of the MDP in several Singapore statutes, the customary international law rule prohibiting inhuman punishment could not be regarded as part of Singapore common law. And, in any event, it could be overridden by subsequent statutory provisions. The final blow to the customary international law argument was the court's recognition that in view of the decisive rejection of a constitutional prohibition against inhuman punishment in the Singapore Constitution, any changes in customary international law would have no effect on the scope of Article 9(1). Any changes would have to be made by the legislature as a matter of social policy and not by the courts via constitutional 'interpretation'.[31]

Thus far the discussion on substantive rights above had focused on the word 'law'. However, recently applicants have sought to relocate the debate to the concept of FRNJ. This is apparent in *Yong Vui Kong Caning*, where the applicant sought to argue that caning amounted to torture and that a prohibition against torture was a FRNJ under Art 9. This argument had some success.[32] The court reiterated its view from *Yong Vui Kong MDP* on customary international law: namely, that although the prohibition against torture was a peremptory norm of customary international law, its implementation into domestic law was a task for the legislature. The court was however willing to recognise that there was a prohibition on torture at common law that had been incorporated into the law of Singapore, albeit only with a narrow remit. The prohibition related only to the torture of suspects or witnesses for the purpose of extracting confessions, but not in the context of the punishment of criminals after they had been found guilty of their crimes following a fair trial. This limited prohibition did form a FRNJ that could not be abrogated by legislation. The background for this recognition of a limited prohibition on torture relating to the extraction of pre-trial evidence is based on, inter alia, the fact that the court held that the content of the FRNJ was procedural and focused on securing a fair trial. The court was conclusive that FRNJ do not contain substantive rights, especially not rights relating to the punishment meted out after a trial. This is an unusual restriction on a prohibition against 'torture'; generally elsewhere the prohibition applies even in the context of punishment for crimes committed.[33] The phrase does not lend itself to a restriction to the narrow procedural context drawn out by the Court of Appeal in *Yong Vui Kong Caning*. The restriction appears to be motivated more by how to interpret FRNJ than what it means to interpret the prohibition against torture independently of the concept of FRNJ. Thus, the former served as a limiting force on the latter.[34] In any event, following *Yong Vui Kong Caning*, it could be difficult for an applicant to introduce substantive *rights* into the concept of FRNJ. However, as the following section will demonstrate, there is still scope for substantive standards of law to be incorporated into the meaning of FRNJ: substantive standards that hold that a law must not be 'arbitrary, absurd or vague' in its deprivation of life or liberty under Article 9. As the discussion below demonstrates, the courts have introduced aspects of a proportionality-type of reasoning to assess 'arbitrariness' under Article 9.

D Substantive standards: FRNJ and prohibitions against arbitrary, absurd and vague laws[35]

Aside from the context of the death penalty, applicants in other situations have sought to import more substantive limits on legislation within the proviso of Article 9 of the Constitution. The cases relating to section 377A of the Singapore Penal Code are examples of this. The key case dealing with this argument is *Tan Eng Hong*[36] where the applicant argued that section 377A was void for being inconsistent with Article 12(1) of the constitution, and that his arrest, investigation and detention under section 377A infringed his rights under Article 9(1). On the latter point, the applicant argued that section 377A was contrary to the FRNJ because it was absurd and arbitrary, undermined access to justice, and was vague and uncertain. The applicant was unsuccessful.

In ascertaining the precise scope of FRNJ, the court recognised that the authorities are not definitive. The court further observed that the most recent exposition of FRNJ was in *Yong Vui Kong MDP* (the case pre-dates *Yong Vui Kong Caning*), where the Court of Appeal was only willing to go beyond the procedural interpretation of it as far as to say that the Privy Council in *Ong Ah Chuan* may have had two possible types of legislation in mind: (a) legislation which aimed at securing the conviction of particular individuals (being legislation which was effectively legislative judgment); or (b) laws that were absurd or arbitrary. The court in *Tan Eng Hong* focused on the second category of legislation. In doing so, the court observed that when speaking of law as arbitrary, it would only make sense if one is speaking of the law *in the context* of its purpose. Thus, in *Yong Vui Kong MDP*,[37] the court looked at the arbitrary argument in the context of the reasonable classification test used to consider Article 12 arguments:

> [the Article 9 argument] raises an issue which is, in essence, no different from the question of whether mandatory death penalty legislation is consistent with the right under Article 12(1) of the Singapore Constitution, ie the right to equal protection of the law.

Accordingly, in *Yong Vui Kong MDP*, the Court of Appeal considered the arbitrariness of the 15 gram-threshold within the legal matrix of the 'reasonable classification' test.

In the context of *Tan Eng Hong*, the High Court remarked that section 377A is not arbitrary for the purposes of Article 12(1) because the legislature has articulated a clear social purpose (the prevalence of grossly indecent acts between males – whether in public or in private – as not desirable[38]) for which section 377A is its chosen means for implementation. The Court of Appeal in *Yong Vui Kong MDP* did not think that it was appropriate to inquire into the legislature's prerogative for determining that 15 g was the right threshold for the implementation of the mandatory death penalty. Likewise, in *Tan Eng Hong*, the court stopped short of looking into whether the mode of implementing its purpose via section 377A was arbitrary for the purpose of Article 9(1).[39]

A further aspect of the applicant's argument relating to the absurdity of section 377A was not one of 'equality' under Article 12 but the fact that section 377A was based on an immutable and natural trait or attribute of the applicant; deprivation of liberty on this basis was unconstitutional. An immutable attribute for the purposes of showing an alleged breach of the Constitution was one that was (a) innate or inborn; and (b) unchanging or unable to be changed. The court concluded that whether homosexuality, as a form of sexual orientation, is a natural and immutable attribute of a person is a factual question, which can only be resolved by adducing evidence. The court was not satisfied it was able to reach a conclusion on this issue on the basis of the comparative case law or medical and other scientific literature available. There was clear evidence of a division of opinion on the issue of homosexuality and immutability in such material. Accordingly, the court felt that it was not necessary to make any conclusions as to whether legislation that criminalises conduct which is tied to a natural and immutable human attribute is absurd and against FRNJ.

Finally, the applicant also submitted that section 377A was contrary to the FRNJ because it undermined access to justice by criminalising victims of homosexual assaults and homosexual domestic abuse. The court did not agree. With regard to the latter situation, the victims could prosecute the complaint of domestic abuse if they so wished, and the fear that the victims themselves would be prosecuted for the commission of some other offence could not per se undermine access to justice. With regard to the former situation, section

377A arguably did not make criminals out of male victims of sexual assaults by other males. On a purposive interpretation of section 377A, it is not the intention to capture male victims (even if consent is not an aspect of the definition of the offence) and the wording of section 377A actually captures those who actively seek out such sexual conduct.

E Summary of developments

The above survey of cases highlights that: (a) the courts have been prepared to recognise some procedural content to FRNJ (limited criminal process rights and rules of natural justice analogous to those found in administrative law); (b) the courts have not been willing to import substantive rights in the form of prohibitions against cruel and inhuman punishment into the scope of FRNJ or 'law' in Article 9(1); (c) the courts have been unwilling to import other systems of law, namely customary international law, into the concept of FRNJ; and (d) there is some substantive content in the form of tests of absurdity, which borrows from discussions taking place within the confines of Article 12(1) ('equal before the law') and, in particular, the reasonable classification test in that context. In relation to the optimal approach to take when interpreting the proviso in Article 9(1), this next section will focus on the last of these developments[40] as it contains the largest scope for developing a consistent and coherent approach to cases under the proviso. The discussion starts by highlighting that it is a welcome development if we recognise the substantive constraints to what constitutes proper 'law' restricting life or liberty. However, as it stands, the substantive analysis of the final approach in *Tan Eng Hong* would benefit from further structure and depth. The following discussion will propose how these issues can be resolved.

III Adjudicating restrictions on life and liberty under Article 9(1): *quo vadis*?

This section discusses the possibility of further developing the interpretation of the proviso to Article 9(1) (and its equivalent in other jurisdictions) to allow judges to consider whether the executive or legislature can constitutionally restrict personal liberty for a particular purpose and in a particular manner. Such a development would involve evaluating the potential of the approach already adopted by the courts in cases like *Tan Eng Hong* (as discussed in Section II(D) above). The said approach would not be forestalled by the text of Article 9(1) which only states that any restriction must be 'in accordance with law'.[41] Expanding such an approach would involve going further than restricting the legislature from enacting what would be deemed to be procedurally unsound laws; it would amount to restricting laws that fall short of certain substantive standards, for example, laws that are 'irrational' or 'disproportionate' in nature.

A preliminary concern about developing the justificatory assessment, stemming from cases such as *Tan Eng Hong* on Article 9(1) rights, is the use of 'FRNJ' as a label – as was done in *Ong Ah Chuan* – to define the content of 'law' in Article 9(1). Academics argue that the only natural meaning to be attached to FRNJ is the idea of fair procedure.[42] However, there is no reason why the justificatory assessment in cases such as *Tan Eng Hong* should continue to be housed within concepts such as FRNJ; they can be relocated more generally to an assessment of whether any deprivation of life or liberty was 'in accordance with law'. Accordingly, while it may be true that, as a matter of wording, the concept of FRNJ lends itself to be interpreted in a more procedural manner, 'law' has a much broader scope and, more importantly, stronger aspirations. It may be appropriate, therefore, to incorporate this more substantive inquiry into the general proviso to Article 9(1).[43]

Beyond this, there are the usual concerns with advancing the law in this direction. For instance, recognising and allowing a more substantive inquiry into the restrictions under Article 9(1) would allow judges to engage in an analysis of the merits or political wisdom of legislative decisions. Indeed, loyalty to the principles of the separation of powers has meant that the Singapore courts have traditionally been reluctant to review the content of a legislative (or administrative) decision. For this reason, the courts have eschewed adjudicative tools such as proportionality as a ground for judicial review.[44] A proportionality-type of inquiry typically involves an assessment of the legitimacy of the purpose of a particular law or executive decision; the suitability of the means used by the government to achieve that purpose; the necessity of said means and the proportionality of said means.[45] As has already been seen in the context of *Tan Eng Hong* (discussed in Section II(D) above), the courts have started a very early entrance into reviewing aspects of this form of an inquiry under the cover of analysing whether particular legislation is 'absurd'. From this embryonic analysis in *Tan Eng Hong*, it is clear that concerns about judicial activism and overreaching are more apparent than real. There is clear evidence to suggest that notwithstanding this foray into the substantive, the courts have also exercised restraint where they felt it appropriate. This is evident in cases such as *Tan Eng Hong* itself where the court unequivocally concluded that they would not evaluate the wisdom of pursuing a particular purpose in enacting legislation; they would, instead, restrict their inquiry to checking if the means used to achieve the purpose bore a reasonable connection to said purpose. This is a more reduced form of proportionality analysis than is apparent in other jurisdictional contexts.[46]

This, in fact, leads to an opposing concern: that the scope of substantive control introduced in *Tan Eng Hong* in the form of an analysis of the arbitrariness or absurdity of the law is too vague and deferential to be considered a robust constitutional tool for adjudication. This is a real concern and one that presents itself in more current case law that rely on notions such as 'absurdity' to frame the substantive discussion at hand. Does the legislation in question constitute 'law' under Article 9(1)? The courts' struggle with a lack of structure is evident in the fact that they rely on the more structured framework of the reasonable classification test under Article 12 within which to frame their discussion.

At this juncture, one must revisit the proportionality debate. The concern with existing 'balancing' tests, such as that of reasonable classification, is that they lack rigour, structure and examination of legislative action.[47] This has been discussed extensively elsewhere, especially in the context of concerns relating to separation of powers and the role of the judiciary.[48] However, although the law is currently some distance away from engaging in a full proportionality adjudication of constitutional restrictions, it may be necessary to acknowledge that the aspects of it which are currently in place need to be organised and structured. The reasonable classification test under Article 12 comes the closest to this structuring of the inquiry. The question is how to take the law forward from its current position. Here, there are three things to note.

First, it is important to note that proportionality-type adjudication is not a universally accepted solution for constitutional adjudication of restrictions on rights;[49] neither is it being argued that it should be recognised as such. Rather, the point being made is that constitutional adjudication inevitably touches on aspects of the analytical framework of proportionality. The constitutional conversation eventually touches on issues relating to why there is a restriction on a right and the scope of that restriction. This is apparent from the jurisprudence thus far under Articles 9 and 12. It is proposed that this constitutional conversation be formalised.

Second, it must be pointed out that the proposal is not to immediately introduce proportionality. The balancing tests, including the reasonable classification test and the absurdity test under Article 9, are tests that will need to evolve incrementally over time in line with changes in the general landscape of public law and judicial review in Singapore. In the current climate and its emphasis on the separation of powers and the limits on the scope of judicial discretion, the introduction of full-blown proportionality review as found elsewhere would clearly be impossible. A gradual and incremental introduction of aspects of it into the justificatory conversation relating to permissible restrictions on rights is however possible. The possibility of such an incremental development is already evident from cases like *Lim Meng Suang*. There the court suggested that the justificatory conversation could evolve to include some judicial consideration of the legitimacy of the legislative purpose and involve not just the one-sided identification of the purpose set out by the respondent, and judicial deference to this purpose.[50] This could be a precursor to further expanding the conversation to assessing two matters. The first is aspects of the suitability and necessity of any law or executive act that seeks to restrict a constitutional right – analytical questions apparent elsewhere in a typical proportionality discussion. Even here other jurisdictions have developed review of variable intensity: for example, in assessing the 'necessity' of a measure, the courts have alternated between looking at whether it was manifestly unreasonable[51] and whether it pursued 'a pressing social need' (or a 'compelling social interest'), subjecting the challenged measure to 'close scrutiny' and requiring 'very weighty reasons' to rationalise the restriction on the right in question.[52] This alternation between the different formulations of the suitability and necessity inquiry is predicated on the subject matter in dispute (eg a matter of high policy or related to the allocation of economic resources) and also on the importance or centrality of the counter-interest or right on the part of the applicant. This sliding scale of review is apparent in a nascent form from the discussion in cases like *Lee Hsien Loong v Review Publishing*[53] where the court indicated that judicial involvement may vary depending on the subject matter in question in any particular case at hand. The second matter to be assessed is the importance of the applicant's right (or interests), whether there has been an infringement or harm to that right (or interest) and the extent of the infringement.

Related to the second issue is a further concern about the 'spirit' of any evolution of proportionality or balancing-type adjudication. The concern is that should the courts further develop the balancing approach, it could actually evolve into a savings and justificatory exercise driven by the respondent rather than a tool for genuine dialogue and constitutional negotiation in which the applicants are equal participants. This concern could be borne out by the cautious attitude taken towards the scope of the judicial role and the maintenance of the separation of powers, a theme that is apparent from the discussion in Section II above. The proposed incremental development of proportionality review under Part IV more generally is therefore premised on a similar evolution, development and re-balancing of the roles of the respective institutions of government within the constitutional landscape.

IV Conclusion

The ultimate aim of the proposed use of proportionality-type adjudication is the eventual internalisation of the intellectual focus of proportionality: identifying the important interests on both sides and seeking to adopt a more optimal constitutional balance between the individual and broader communitarian interests inherent in any constitutional problem. The function of judicial review in setting standards is clear in this context. Recent case law indicates movements in the approach to constitutional interpretation that could signal the evolution of constitutional law to embrace more substantive standards in assessing constitutionality issues. The courts have, for example, indicated a willingness to imply norms and concepts from the Constitution's normative foundations into its text. For example, the courts recently recognised an entitlement to have a political representative in one's constituency in Parliament in the absence of any specific text specifying such a right but on the basis that this is what is expected in a Westminster model of government in Singapore as embodied in the Constitution.[54] Other examples include a broader more normative consideration of the scope of 'liberty' within Article 9.[55] A final example includes the courts recognition that there are certain features of the Constitution (including non-enumerated features) that are part of the basic structure of the Constitution and that cannot, therefore, be (easily) amended.[56] Developing the proviso to Article 9(1) will require paying close attention to the trajectory of the law under Article 12(1) and, in particular, the reasonable classification test. Similarly, refining the mode of assessing restrictions on other rights in Part IV of the Constitution would involve paying close attention to how the post-*Tan Eng Hong* interpretation of the Article 9(1) proviso develops. In *Ong Ah Chuan*, the Privy Council suggested that the concept of FRNJ applies equally to the definition of 'law' under Article 12(1).[57] Ultimately, in developing principles in the context of judicial review, we need to do so in a way that optimises the constitutional realisation of the protections set out in Part IV of the constitution.

Notes

* I would like to thank Jaclyn Neo and Ho Hock Lai for valuable comments on this chapter. All errors remain my own.

1 The precise scope of the permissible restrictions on liberty rights is an issue that not only the Singapore courts face. This has been the subject of prolific judicial and academic discussion in most common law jurisdictions, including India, the USA, Canada and South Africa. The different judicial responses to the question could come down to different formulations of the liberty rights in the Constitution. For example, the limitation in Article 9 of the Singapore Constitution is that any restriction must be 'in accordance with the law'. This is much broader, in its wording, than other constitutions which refer specifically to procedural restrictions on liberty rights (for example, the US Constitution: '[N]or shall any person … be deprived of life, liberty, or property, without due process of law' and the Indian Constitution: 'No person shall be deprived of his life or personal liberty except according to procedure established by law'). *Prima facie*, the differences in text could reveal the possible interpretive choices open to the courts in each jurisdiction on the scope of the restrictions (for example, a plain reading of the text in the US and Indian constitutions points towards a more procedural approach to defining the scope of restrictions). This can be compared with Article 9, which is, on the text, less prescriptive. However, as has been highlighted elsewhere, none of the jurisdictions mentioned have taken an exclusively textual approach to interpretation, but have also relied on the underlying purpose or spirit of the Constitution (in the case of India and the USA, they have adopted a more substantive reading of their liberty provisos whereas Singapore has taken a more procedural approach. See also V Ramraj, 'Four Models of Due Process' (2004) 2(3) International Journal of Constitutional Law 492, 495). The use of 'procedural' and 'substantive' as labels to characterise the various approaches will be further elaborated on in Section II.

2 This chapter, therefore, will not focus on interpretations of 'life' and 'liberty' in the first part of Article 9. For example, one of the applicant's in *Lim Meng Suang v Attorney-General* [2015] 1 SLR 26 (Singapore Court of Appeal (Sing CA)) ('*Lim Meng Suang*') unsuccessfully argued that section 377A of the Penal Code, which criminalises sexual conduct between consenting male adults was impermissible as a restriction on a right to privacy, which they argued is part and parcel of 'liberty' under Article 9. Although, as will be discussed in Section IV below, the courts have recently adopted a more normative approach to interpretation based on features of the 'Westminster' constitutional system (versus a purely textual and literal approach), they were not willing to adopt such a broader interpretation of 'liberty' under Article 9.

3 There is some discussion that there were attempts to expunge FRNJ from the meaning of 'law' under Article 9: see, for example, *Jabar v Public Prosecutor* [1995] 1 SLR 615 (Sing CA) where Yong Pung How CJ stated that (at 631B): '*Any law which provides for the deprivation of a person's life or personal liberty, is valid and binding so long as it is validly passed by Parliament. The court is not concerned with whether it is also fair, just and reasonable as well*' (emphasis added). See also *Public Prosecutor v Ahmad Bin Kidam* [2007] SGDC 113 (Singapore District Courts (Sing DC)). Although, as will be discussed below, there is an alternative and less restrictive reading of this dicta from *Jabar*: see text accompanying (n 31).

4 See for example *Chan Hiang Leng Colin v Public Prosecutor* [1994] 3 SLR(R) 209 (Singapore High Court (Sing HC)).
5 [1979–1980] SLR(R) 710 (Privy Council (PC)).
6 [1981–1982] SLR(R) 133 (PC).
7 ibid [9] (Lord Diplock).
8 [2013] SGHC 199 (Sing HC).
9 ibid [31]–[33]. See also Thio Li-ann, *A Treatise on Singapore Constitutional Law* (Academy Publishing 2012) paras 12.021–12.045: 'As far as the constitutional concept [of FRNJ] has developed, this relates largely to the conduct of a fair trial … [and is the subject of] gradual or incremental development through case by case exposition.'
10 See, for example, *Ong Ah Chuan* (n 5) on the presumption of innocence; *Haw Tua Tau* (n 6) on the privilege against self-incrimination – both cases are discussed further in Section II.
11 *Yong Vui Kong v Attorney-General* [2011] 2 SLR 1189 (Sing CA) ('*Yong Vui Kong Clemency*'), which was followed in *Yong Vui Kong v Public Prosecutor* [2015] 2 SLR 1129 (Sing CA) ('*Yong Vui Kong Caning*').
12 Although the examples in the text above are worded in terms of a 'prohibition' (eg prohibition against torture and cruel and inhuman punishment), the applicant argued that he had a 'right' or 'interest' in being protected from such torture and punishment. Accordingly, this chapter tracks the phraseology used in the cases.
13 *Nguyen Tuong Van v Public Prosecutor* [2005] 1 SLR 103 (Sing CA) ('*Nguyen*'), *Yong Vui Kong v Public Prosecutor* [2010] 3 SLR 489 (Sing CA) ('*Yong Vui Kong MDP*') and *Yong Vui Kong Caning* (n 11).
14 See, for example, *Tan Eng Hong* (n 8) and *Lim Meng Suang* (n 2).
15 I acknowledge further the possibility of overlap in usage of the labels: for example, it is possible that the rule against bias could constitute both a procedural standard and a procedural right (ie someone can equally argue they have a 'right' to an unbiased trial). Similarly, the presumption of innocence could constitute a procedural rule, but it contains a standard (the right to be proved guilty according to the standard of proof beyond reasonable doubt). And the substantive standards ('absurd', 'arbitrary') apply or can apply equally to procedural rules (eg, as judges have remarked, rebuttable presumptions of law that are arbitrary cannot pass constitutional muster). I am grateful to Professor Ho Hock Lai for highlighting this. However, this chapter seeks to use these labels to organise the way in which FRNJ as a tool has been developed under Article 9: it is clear that the categories will not be watertight or exclusive and independent of each other. This chapter is not the place to address the major epistemological issues relating to concepts such as 'rights' versus 'standards' and 'process' versus 'substance' (on which see, for example, L Alexander, 'Are Procedural Rights Derivative Substantive Rights?' (1998) Law and Philosophy 17, 19–42; D Dyzenhaus, 'Process and Substances as Aspects of the Public Law Form' (2015) 74(2) Cambridge Law Journal 284–306)). However, where relevant, it will address the particular conceptual issues relating, in particular, to the distinction drawn between process and substance by the courts (and in particular, in relation to the courts' interpretation of the prohibition against torture in Section II(C)).
16 See, for example, *Chiu Teng @ Kallang Pte Ltd v Singapore Land Authority* [2014] 1 SLR 1047 (Sing HC) where the court held that in the context of the doctrine of substantive legitimate expectations, a government body needs to point to some overriding public interest that justifies departing from the legitimate expectation.
17 The latter was challenged under both Article 9 and Article 12 (relating to equality before the law). In the context of their Article 12 argument, the applicants asserted that the broadly drawn nature of the MDP based on the weight of the drugs (15 grams or above) contravened the principle of equality in not allowing the court to consider the relative blameworthiness of different offenders. The applicants pointed to the fact

that, for example, an addict who supplies to a friend 15 grams of heroin would get the death penalty whereas a drug dealer who is in the business of supplying drugs would receive a lesser penalty if they supplied 14.99 grams. The Privy Council explained that the equality provision does not forbid discrimination in prescribing different punishments for different classes of individuals where the differentiation is based on the circumstances of the offence, and such differentiation would be constitutional as long as the differentiation criteria that the legislature adopts as the differentiating factor is not arbitrary but bears a 'reasonable relation to the social object of the law'. In the present case this was satisfied. The purpose of the legislation is to combat the illegal drugs trade and this objective is 'broadly proportional to the quantity of addictive drugs' brought into the market. In any event the legislature is entitled to decide on the appropriate boundary to be drawn between varying classes of persons: this is a question best left to the legislature. It is worth nothing that the remarks in *Ong Ah Chuan* (n 5) on the FRNJ applied to both Article 9 and Article 12. In the case of the latter, the reasonable classification test for assessing whether legislation is discriminatory was part of the analysis of whether such legislation complied with the FRNJ. The latter interpretation of FRNJ in the context of Article 12 is not restricted to questions of 'procedure' but went further in its analysis to questions of substance under the framework of the 'reasonable classification' test, including whether the legislation embodied differential treatment and whether this differential treatment could be rationalised. This latter part of the *Ong Ah Chuan* (n 5) analysis has been picked up in the context of Article 9 in the cases of *Tan Eng Hong* (n 8) and *Lim Meng Suang* (n 2) as will be further discussed in Section II(D).

18 *Ong Ah Chuan* (n 5) [23].

19 See Andrew Harding, 'Natural Justice and the Constitution' (1981) 23 Malaya Law Review 226, 230–31.

20 See also Hock Lai Ho, 'The Presumption of Innocence as a Human Right' in Paul Roberts and Jill Hunter (eds), *Criminal Evidence and Human Rights: Reimagining Common Law Procedural Traditions* (Hart Publishing 2012) 259 for a discussion on the nature of the presumption of innocence.

21 The applicant's arguments under Article 9 on the MDP focused on the fact that the mandatory nature of the sentence rendered it arbitrary since it debarred the court from discriminating between offenders according to their individual blameworthiness. The Privy Council clarified that it was not going to comment on the wisdom of capital punishment. This was for the legislature in Singapore to decide (including deciding which offences attract the death penalty). This is especially because Article 9(1) specifically allows for the deprivation of life in accordance with the law. The Privy Council further commented that there was nothing unusual in a capital sentence being mandatory as its efficacy as a deterrent could be diminished otherwise. This discussion happened more in the context of the meaning of 'law' rather than within the parameters of the concept of FRNJ.

22 Harding has also remarked on the unjustifiably narrow grounds for this decision (Harding (n 19) 232):

> [I]nstead of deciding whether this principle (*nemo debet se ipsum prodere*) is a fundamental principle of natural justice, the court preferred to decide the case on a narrower ground. Having drawn a distinction between 'a genuine compulsion on the accused to submit himself at his trial to cross-examination by the prosecution' and 'a strong inducement to him to do so,' it was concluded that the 1976 amendments constituted the latter rather than the former, so that the right had not been removed. However, the amendments in question had the double effect of removing the accused's right to make an unsworn statement and allowing the court to draw adverse inferences from his failure to give sworn evidence and submit himself to cross-examination. In view of this the distinction between a compulsion

and an inducement seems almost grotesque when used in relation to a person accused of an offence carrying a mandatory death sentence; certainly the amendments do not legally compel an accused person to give evidence, but to conclude from this that the right of silence has not been removed is surely to be guilty of the very legalist fallacy which natural justice was designed to rectify.

23 An applicant in the subsequent case of *Public Prosecutor v Mazlan bin Maidun and Another* [1992] SGCA 90 (Sing CA) was similarly unsuccessful in importing further procedural rights into the notion of FRNJ: in this case, the right to silence. A failure to inform the accused of his right to remain silent was not a breach of his constitutional rights. The court reasoned that the right of silence was historically an evidential rule and to elevate it to a constitutional right would stretch beyond interpretation to enumeration of rights under Article 9(1). The right to silence would have been given specific parliamentary expression if the legislature had intended to guarantee full protection for it.

24 Other administrative law arguments have been unsuccessful. In *Ahmad Bin Kidam* (n 3) the applicant attempted to argue that the doctrine of substantive legitimate expectations was part of the definition of 'law' and that the removal of liberty without compliance with such substantive legitimate expectations was not 'in accordance with law'.

25 *Yong Vui Kong Clemency* (n 11).

26 ibid [88]–[105], where the Court of Appeal observed that:

> [T]he Ong Ah Chuan rules of natural justice were articulated and applied in the context of a constitutional challenge to the validity of legislation, and not in the judicial review context, where what is challenged is an administrative decision made pursuant to valid legislation. For this reason, it is my view that a distinction must be made... This distinction stems from the difference in the juridical status of these two categories of rules of natural justice ... the Ong Ah Chuan rules of natural justice operate at the constitutional level in relation to the validity of legislation, whereas the administrative law rules of natural justice operate at an executive level in relation to the validity of administrative decisions... It follows that these fundamental rules have the status of constitutional rules and, thus, can only be abrogated or amended by a constitutional amendment under Art 5 of the Singapore Constitution. In contrast, the administrative law rules of natural justice, which apply to judicial review of administrative decisions made under valid legislation, can be abrogated or disapplied by ordinary legislation either directly or indirectly.

27 *Nguyen* (n 13).

28 *Yong Vui Kong MDP* (n 13).

29 Singapore Government Printer, Report of the Constitutional Commission, 1966 (Chairman: Wee Chong Jin) (OCLC 51640681, 1966).

30 The Court of Appeal refused to be persuaded by decisions of the Privy Council which decided otherwise (ie held that the death penalty does constitute cruel and inhuman punishment) in the context of other jurisdictions because such other jurisdictions had explicit restrictions on such punishment (in some form) in their constitutional documents.

31 Another strategy utilised by applicants in relation to the death penalty has been to argue that the *delay in execution* constitutes cruel and inhuman punishment and that this specific norm is embodied within the understanding of 'law' under Article 9(1): *Jabar* (n 3). The court rejected this argument. It did so, however, on narrow grounds relating to the separation of powers. The court held that judges in Singapore do not have discretion to consider whether events after the judicial process have ended constitute a constitutional infringement. Once the Court of Appeal had disposed of the

appeal against conviction and had confirmed the sentence of death, it was *functus officio*. *Jabar* (n 3) is sometimes used as authority for the proposition that Singapore has adopted a 'formal' approach to interpreting 'law' for the purposes of Article 9. In other words, such law has to be validly passed for it to comply with Article 9 (see, for example, the discussion in Ramraj (n 1) 496). However, *Yong Vui Kong MDP* (n 13) highlighted that when Yong Pung How CJ observed in *Jabar* that 'any law is valid and binding so long as it is validly passed by Parliament and the court is not concerned with whether it is fair, just and reasonable' (*Jabar* (n 3) 631B), the judge was referring to the issue of the constitutionality of *carrying out the MDP* versus the constitutionality of the MDP per se. The court was simply asserting the fact that the question of whether the MDP was fair, just and reasonable was not in issue and Yong CJ's statement should be read in this context and not as a definitive interpretation of what 'law' means for Article 9(1) – to conclude otherwise would contradict *Nguyen*'s affirmation of *Ong Ah Chuan* (where Yong CJ was also presiding).

32 The case is also an advancement in some respects in terms of the constitutional interpretation of the earlier part of Article 9 in its recognition that 'liberty' under Article 9 is not just a reference to the process leading up to incarceration but also the punishment meted out after trial (*Yong Vui Kong Caning* (n 11) [22]–[23]):

> Art 9 does not protect only against arbitrary execution or incarceration. It also prohibits the unlawful use of force against a person, including by way of amputations, mutilations, assaults, beatings, woundings, etc. Such acts would result in a deprivation of 'life' ... Art 9(1) is engaged by the execution (or proposed execution) of a sentence of caning on the Appellant, and in order to pass constitutional muster it has to be 'in accordance with law'.

This can be contrasted with *Lim Meng Suang* (n 2).

33 See, for example, the Convention against Torture and Other Cruel, Inhuman or Degrading Treatment or Punishment (adopted 10 December 1984, entered into force 26 June 1987) 1465 UNTS 85 Art 1.1, which defines the scope of the prohibition as: '"torture" means any act by which severe pain or suffering, whether physical or mental, is intentionally inflicted on a person for such purposes as ... punishing him for an act he or a third person has committed ...'

34 *Yong Vui Kong Caning* (n 11) [62]–[64]:

> As one commentator puts it (Frederick F Schauer, 'English Natural Justice and American Due Process: An Analytical Comparison' (1976) 18 William & Mary Law Review 47 at 48): 'The basis of procedural protection in the English system is the concept of natural justice. Natural justice is not, despite its name, a general natural law concept; the name is a term of art that denotes specific procedural rights in the English system. The first, audi alteram partem, relates to the right to be heard; the second, nemo debet esse judex in propria sua causa or nemo judex in re sua, establishes the right to an unbiased tribunal' ... To similar effect, the Privy Council in [*Haw Tua Tau* (n 6)] noted: 'It would be imprudent of their Lordships to attempt to make a comprehensive list of what constitutes fundamental rules of natural justice applicable to procedure for determining the guilt of a person charged with a criminal offence.... The fundamental rules of natural justice in the common law are therefore procedural rights aimed at securing a fair trial. Torture in its narrow sense (where it is used to extract evidence to be used as proof in judicial proceedings) would violate the fundamental rules of natural justice; to convict a person based on evidence procured by torture strikes at the very heart of a fair trial. But the fundamental rules of natural justice have nothing to say about the punishment of criminals after they have been convicted pursuant to a fair trial. In our judgment, therefore, even assuming the common law prohibition of torture extends to caning in the context of a punishment to be imposed on a convicted

person after trial, it would not have constitutional force because this would not come within the ambit of fundamental rules of natural justice in the sense in which it was referred to in Ong Ah Chuan.'

35 This argument was made in the context of *Nguyen* (n 13) to argue that arbitrary laws do not constitute 'laws' – it did not succeed in that context, but the courts in the cases discussed in this section did accept the notion of 'arbitrariness' as part of FRNJ.

36 *Tan Eng Hong* (n 8). *Lim Meng Suang* (n 2) echoes the more detailed ratio of *Tan Eng Hong* (n 8) on the question of FRNJ under Article 9 and so the discussion here focuses on the ratio and dicta from *Tan Eng Hong* (n 8).

37 *Yong Vui Kong MDP* (n 13) [86].

38 See also *Lim Meng Suang* (n 2) [67]–[68]. The court also found that the differentia adopted in section 377A – ie that of males who perform acts of gross indecency on other males – is intelligible. The acts which are captured and the acts which are not captured (eg male–female sexual acts and female–female sexual acts) are clearly identifiable: ibid [48].

39 For a criticism of this aspect of the decision see PJ Yap, 'Section 377A and Equal Protection in Singapore: Back to 1938?' (2013) 25 Singapore Academy of Law Journal 630.

40 In this respect, this chapter moves beyond the debate on whether we should adopt a procedural or substantive due process model, which is the main debate surrounding the Fifth and Fourteenth Amendments of the US Constitution (as discussed by Ramraj (n 1)). This debate appears to have been foreclosed in the Singapore context (*Yong Vui Kong Caning* (n 11)). This chapter does not revisit this conclusion but focuses on those avenues that have been left open by the courts thus far.

41 *Tan Eng Hong v Attorney-General* (n 8).

42 Harding (n 19) 235.

43 See also Ramraj (n 1) 523, who remarks that a broader substantive interpretation is more in line with the 'robust' constitutionalism promised in constitutions, including Part IV of the Singapore Constitution. See also Thio Li-ann, 'Pragmatism and Realism Do Not Mean Abdication: A Critical and Empirical Inquiry into Singapore's Engagement with International Human Rights Law' (2004) 8 Singapore Year Book of International Law 41, on the need to focus more on the issue of whether an appropriate balance has been struck between the rights in question and the wider communitarian goals that the legislature is striving for.

44 See, for example, *Chan Hiang Leng Colin v Minister for Information and the Arts* [1996] 1 SLR(R) 294 (Sing CA) [38]–[47]; *Chng Suan Tze v Minister of Home Affairs* [1988] 2 SLR 525 (Sing CA) [108]–[121].

45 There are, of course, significant variances in the proportionality tests used in the various local and regional jurisdictions. However, they broadly share these analytical emphases (see, for example, discussion in M Klatt and M Meister, *The Constitutional Structure of Proportionality* (Oxford University Press 2012) 7–13).

46 For example, the European or Canadian contexts that allow the courts to investigate the legitimacy or wisdom of pursuing a particular purpose (see M Cohen-Eliya and I Porat, *Proportionality and Constitutional Culture* (Cambridge University Press 2013) 2, 17).

47 See Jaclyn L Neo, 'Balancing act: the balancing metaphor as deference and dialogue in constitutional adjudication', Chapter 7 of this book.

48 See, for example, Yap (n 39). See also former Chief Justice Chan Sek Keong, 'Judicial Review – From Angst to Empathy' (2010) 22 Singapore Academy of Law Journal 469; and Daniel Tan, 'Substantive Review in Administrative Law' (2013) Singapore Academy of Law Journal 319.

49 See, for example, A Bahrak, *Proportionality: Constitutional Rights and their Limitations* (Cambridge University Press 2012) Chapter 19 for a discussion of common

alternatives. This includes, for example, a 'categorical' approach (which focuses on the interpretation of the scope of rights and then protects the core of the right absolutely).

50 *Lim Meng Suang* (n 2) [101].

51 See, for example, Case T-13/99 *Pfizer Animal Health v Council* [2002] ECR II-3305 (European Court of Justice) and Case C-12/03 P *Commission v Tetra Laval* [2005] ECR I-987.

52 See, for example, *Handyside v United Kingdom* (1979) 1 EHRR 737 (European Court of Human Rights).

53 *Lee Hsien Loong v Review Publishing Co Ltd* [2007] SGHC 24 per Sundaresh Menon JC (as he then was) at paras 998(b).

54 *Vellama d/o Marie Muthu v Attorney-General* [2013] SGCA 39 (Sing CA) [79]:

> At this juncture, it is vital to remind ourselves that the form of government of the Republic of Singapore as reflected in the Constitution is the Westminster model of government, with the party commanding the majority support in Parliament having the mandate to form the government. The authority of the government emanates from the people. Each Member represents the people of the constituency who voted him into Parliament. The voters of a constituency are entitled to have a Member representing and speaking for them in Parliament. The Member is not just the mouthpiece but the voice of the people of the constituency.

See also Kevin Tan, 'Into the matrix: interpreting the Westminster model constitution', Chapter 3 of this book.

55 See n 32.

56 *Yong Vui Kong Caning* (n 11) [71]: 'In order for a feature to be considered part of the basic structure of the Constitution, it must be something fundamental and essential to the political system that is established thereunder.' See also, *Mohammad Faizal bin Sabtu v PP* [2012] 4 SLR 947 [11]:

> The Singapore Constitution is based on the Westminster model of constitutional government ('the Westminster model'), under which the sovereign power of the State is distributed among three organs of state, viz, the Legislature, the Executive and the Judiciary. In the UK (where the Westminster model originated), the Legislature is the UK parliament (comprising the House of Commons and the House of Lords), the Executive is the UK government and the Judiciary consists of the UK judges. Likewise, under the Singapore Constitution, the sovereign power of Singapore is shared among the same trinity of constitutional organs, viz, the Legislature (comprising the President of Singapore and the Singapore parliament), the Executive (the Singapore government) and the Judiciary (the judges of the Supreme Court and the Subordinate Courts). The principle of separation of powers, whether conceived as a sharing or a division of sovereign power between these three organs of state, is, therefore, part of the basic structure of the Singapore Constitution.

57 Although, the court expressed caution against doing this in the case of *Tan Eng Hong* (n 8), this was specifically in the context of Article 12 rather than Part IV more generally: ibid [24]–[29]. Commentators have suggested that this is a welcome clarification on the usage of FRNJ. See, for example, Harding (n 19) 235:

> A law, if considered under Article 12(1), must either offend or not offend that provision. If it offends, it is void under Article 4 so that any incidental inconsistency with natural justice is immaterial. If it does not offend, in the sense that it provides a reasonable classification having a nexus with the purpose of the statute, can it be argued that it is still void because it offends natural justice? Such an argument in my submission is wrong, because it means that any law which does not offend

Article 12(1) because it does not involve unconstitutional discrimination can nonetheless be void for inconsistency with natural justice; in other words, any Act of Parliament whatsoever is open to being struck down on the ground that it offends natural justice.

Bibliography

Alexander, L, 'Are Procedural Rights Derivative Substantive Rights?' (1998) Law and Philosophy 17.

Bahrak, A, *Proportionality: Constitutional Rights and Their Limitations* (Cambridge University Press 2012).

Chan, Sek Keong, 'Judicial Review – From Angst to Empathy' (2010) 22 Singapore Academy of Law Journal 469.

Cohen-Eliya, M and I Porat, *Proportionality and Constitutional Culture* (Cambridge University Press 2013).

Dyzenhaus, David, 'Process and Substance as Aspects of the Public Law Form' (2015) 74(2) Cambridge Law Journal.

Harding, Andrew, 'Natural Justice and the Constitution' (1981) 23 Malaya Law Review 226.

Klatt, M and M Meister, *The Constitutional Structure of Proportionality* (Oxford University Press 2012).

Ramraj, Victor, 'Four Models of Due Process' (2004) 2(3) International Journal of Constitutional Law 492–524.

Schauer, Frederick F, 'English Natural Justice and American Due Process: An Analytical Comparison' (1976) 18 William & Mary Law Review 47.

Tan, D, 'Substantive Review in Administrative Law' (2013) Singapore Academy of Law Journal 319.

Thio, Li-ann, 'Pragmatism and Realism Do Not Mean Abdication: A Critical and Empirical Inquiry into Singapore's Engagement with International Human Rights Law' (2004) SGYrBkIntLaw 41.

Thio, Li-ann, *A Treatise on Singapore Constitutional Law* (Academy Publishing 2012).

Yap, PJ, 'Section 377A and Equal Protection in Singapore: Back to 1938?' (2013) 25 Singapore Academy of Law Journal 630.

9 Whither the autochthonous narrative of freedom of speech?

A guide to defaming politicians and scandalising judges in Singapore

David Tan

I Introduction

The infamous 'four walls' approach to constitutional interpretation in Singapore was succinctly stated by former Chief Justice Yong Pung How who unequivocally expressed his preference for interpreting the Singapore Constitution 'within its four walls and not in the light of analogies drawn from other countries, such as Great Britain, the United States of America or Australia'.[1] The 'four walls' doctrine as a theory of constitutional interpretation does not demand an exclusive reliance on domestic legal sources, but it severely restricts the engagement with foreign and international sources of law that may inform or influence local constitutional interpretation.[2] Furthermore, it suggests an insularity discordant with the vigorous interest in 'transnational judicial conversations' within a growing 'world community of courts'.[3]

However, there is criticism that the 'four walls' appears to be a euphemism for

> [S]trategic moves to orientate future public law developments along an 'autochthonous', localized, or indigenous track, particularly in relation to civil liberties jurisprudence … [and] to insulate domestic cases from external influences especially when they were rights-expanding.[4]

Indeed, the 'four walls' doctrine appears to fit in very well with the Court of Appeal's main interpretive modalities of originalism and textualism, which have been used to construe constitutional rights restrictively – albeit with a few notable exceptions[5] – when considering both vertical applications and horizontal effects.

Much of the jurisprudence concerning vertical applications of constitutional rights in Singapore, both in terms of constitutional validity of legislation and in the area of administrative law, are covered by other authors in this book. I will focus instead on two issues relating to how Article 14 of the Singapore Constitution[6] can affect the development of the common law. The first concerns the horizontal effects[7] of a fundamental constitutional right of freedom of speech; I will interrogate how courts have interpreted Article 14 to operate as between two private parties in defamation actions. The second relates to how the courts have attempted to establish a balancing test that gives weight to Article 14 in scandalising contempt proceedings – a common law offence – and the recent laudable efforts of the courts going beyond the 'four walls' to articulate a formulation that draws Singapore closer to its Commonwealth counterparts. This nascent willingness to refer with approval to appropriate foreign decisions in forging an autochthonous free speech jurisprudence augurs well for the future development of a broader qualified privilege for Singapore citizens in defamation law.

Defamation actions by politicians in Singapore have always attracted much international attention. The author agrees with numerous observations made by Andrew Kenyon and Ang Hean Leng in their analysis of the developments in qualified privilege in Malaysian law,[8] and their suggestion that '*Reynolds* is clearly within the Malaysian common law of defamation, given its origins in English common law and its suitability for a "modern pluralistic democracy" '.[9] This chapter continues where Kenyon and Ang have left off, discussing how the Court of Appeal has left tantalising hints in *Review Publishing Co Ltd v Lee Hsien Loong*[10] that it was willing to consider arguments for the adoption of a broader qualified privilege for Singapore citizens, in accordance with Article 14 of the Singapore Constitution, in a future case. The chapter will also advance a theoretical autochthonous framework for the articulation of this defence.

The judicial interpretation of Article 14 in defamation cases must be viewed in the context of the scandalising contempt decisions in order to understand the permissible limits of freedom of speech in Singapore when an individual criticises a branch of government or an office-holder in a branch of government (eg Prime Minister or Chief Justice). It is often a fine line between what qualifies as fair or justified criticism of the conduct of the courts or the individual judges in their administration of justice and what constitutes an undue interference with the administration of justice that would amount to 'scandalising the judiciary'.

Although the Singapore Court of Appeal has interpreted Article 14 with deference to the 'government's assessment of the needs of public order without requiring that the restrictions be informed by substantive standards of reasonableness, proportionality, or necessity within a democratic society',[11] there is perhaps greater leeway for the courts to make an evaluation of how an appropriate balance may be struck between freedom of speech and the social interests in preserving public confidence in the integrity of the judiciary and the administration of justice. Recent decisions such as *Shadrake Alan v Attorney-General*[12] and *Attorney-General v Au Wai Pang*[13] indicate that courts in Singapore are indeed attuned to the need to strike such a balance.

Part II of this chapter provides a brief overview of the dominant rationales that are said to underlie freedom of speech, and it evaluates how the autochthonous narrative in Singapore combines a neo-Confucianist ethos with a principled pragmatic orientation.

Part III examines one of the horizontal effects of Article 14 as it applies to the law of defamation, and argues that the justifications behind the *Lange* and *Reynolds* privileges are relevant to the Singapore experience, and that courts in

Singapore ought to consider a broader qualified privilege applicable to citizens that takes into account the *Reynolds* factors in defamation suits involving political public figures.

Part IV questions whether the 'four walls' approach to constitutional interpretation is really tenable in the twenty-first century, and suggests that recent decisions of the Court of Appeal and High Court in scandalising contempt scenarios indicate a judicial willingness to align certain aspects of free speech jurisprudence in Singapore with developments in other Commonwealth common law jurisdictions.

Part V concludes that exciting times lie ahead for freedom of speech jurisprudence in Singapore as the country enters a new phase of experimenting with a more consultative style of government and encouraging a more active citizenry.

II Free speech – theories, practice and Singaporean pragmatism

A Rationales for free speech

There is a preponderance of academic literature that discusses various rationales that are said to underlie freedom of speech. Three rationales are most often considered: 'furthering a search for knowledge; supporting practices of politics, particularly forms of democratic self-government; and establishing self-development or autonomy'.[14] Such analyses have also been described as displaying variations within and between three purposes: cognitive, political and ethical.[15]

Similarly, mutually supportive theories for the First Amendment have been said to rest on the tripartite goals that comprise sponsoring enlightenment or the discovery of truth, self-fulfilment and citizen participation in a deliberative democracy.[16] There are numerous writings by political philosophers and jurists that advocate for the protection of free speech principles, but this chapter will not be revisiting the arguments by theorists such as John Stuart Mill, Alexander Meiklejohn, Thomas Emerson and Ronald Dworkin.[17] In interpreting Article 10 of the European Convention on Human Rights, the House of Lords also affirmed the three universal rationales.[18]

In its earlier conceptions, the goal of enlightenment or the discovery of truth is represented most prominently by Oliver Wendell Holmes' theory of a 'marketplace of ideas' in which 'the ultimate good desired is … reached by free trade in ideas',[19] and that 'the best test of truth is the power of the thought to get itself accepted in the competition of the market'.[20] The marketplace theory is perhaps 'the most famous and rhetorically resonant of all free speech theories'[21] but it also exhibits a strong underlying democratic theory, evident in the oft-quoted phrase that there is a 'profound national commitment' to the principle that 'debate on public issues should be uninhibited, robust, and wide-open'.[22] However, the concept of a marketplace of ideas 'has long been subject to devastating objections based on its various imperfections, inefficiencies, and internal contradictions'[23] and it is rarely embraced in doctrinal formulations outside of the USA.

In contrast, the self-development or autonomy function shifts the attention from the ideas marketplace to individual dignity.[24] While the US Supreme Court has acknowledged that 'the human spirit ... demands self-expression',[25] there have been relatively few decisions that discuss this as a central goal of the First Amendment.[26] Moreover, no significant decision from the European Court of Human Rights or the English courts has used this rationale to bolster the formulation of judicial tests. While it has been mentioned in decisions outside of the USA as one of the objectives of a constitutional free speech guarantee,[27] its narrow focus on the autonomous individual simply does not comport with the complex reality of living in a community. Nevertheless, it has been argued that although this theory might regard the right to express personal beliefs and political attitudes as a reflection of what it means to be human, the exercise of free speech might be also seen to be of value to the concept of democracy in 'leading to the development of more reflective and mature individuals and so benefitting society as a whole'.[28]

However, the US Supreme Court appears to have been more engaged in recent years with a 'participatory theory of democracy'[29] – one that commands greater acceptance across the European and Commonwealth common law jurisdictions and that is concerned with the enlightenment of public decision-making in a democracy through enabling public access to information and promoting public discourse.[30] Often known in the USA as the Madisonian ideal of deliberative democracy, different but related versions of this theory have been prominently championed by constitutional scholars such as Robert Post,[31] Cass Sunstein[32] and Jack Balkin.[33] The participatory theory is also supported by the more philosophical writings of Meiklejohn,[34] Dworkin[35] and Owen Fiss.[36] Justice Stephen Breyer, speaking in an extra-judicial capacity, has advocated an approach to constitutional adjudication centred on 'active liberty' similar to Post's participatory theory.[37]

An acceptance of the participatory theory has important implications for the continuing development of judicial approaches in resolving the tension between free speech values and other societal interests protected in defamation and scandalising contempt proceedings because it focuses not on an abstract notion of the quest for truth, but on how the nature and content of communication can 'ensure that the individual can effectively participate in and contribute to our republican system of self-government'.[38] In a contemporary formulation, Post advances the concept of 'public discourse' – defined as 'the forms of communication constitutionally deemed necessary for formation of public opinion'[39] – to convey the idea that the 'necessary condition for democratic legitimacy' is seen in people 'being free to participate in the formation of public opinion' and government being responsive to that opinion.[40] Post postulates that:

> Speakers participating in public discourse are constitutionally presumed to be engaged in the formation of public opinion, to the end of making government responsive to their views. All citizens within public discourse, and their audiences within public discourse, have equal autonomy in this regard,

which reflects the political equality that all citizens enjoy within a democracy.[41]

His thesis that the 'purpose of [the First Amendment] is to protect the free formation of public opinion that is the *sine qua non* of democracy'[42] resonates with numerous decisions in the Commonwealth common law world[43] as well as the European Court of Human Rights.[44] Such decisions often emphasise the primacy of free communication of information, opinions and argument about the laws a state should enact and the policies that a government should pursue as an essential condition of a truly democratic process.

B Singapore – the autochthonous narrative

In Singapore, the constitutional guarantee of freedom of speech is found in Article 14 of the Constitution and it applies *only* to citizens of Singapore.[45] The Article states, inter alia, that:

> 14 (1) Subject to clauses (2) and (3) —
> (a) every citizen of Singapore has the right to freedom of speech and expression;
> ...
> (2) Parliament may by law impose —
> (a) on the rights conferred by clause (1)(a), such restrictions as it considers necessary or expedient in the interest of the security of Singapore or any part thereof, friendly relations with other countries, public order or morality and restrictions designed to protect the privileges of Parliament or to provide against contempt of court, defamation or incitement to any offence.

The eight grounds upon which freedom of speech may be restricted have been 'construed expansively, both in ministerial pronouncements and judicial interpretation'.[46] Despite the presence of the supremacy clause,[47] in a consistent line of cases since the 1990s, the Singapore Court of Appeal, the highest appellate court, has interpreted Article 14 with deference to the 'government's assessment of the needs of public order without requiring that the restrictions be informed by substantive standards of reasonableness, proportionality, or necessity within a democratic society'.[48]

This judicial deference stands in stark contrast to the First Amendment jurisprudence in the USA,[49] but it resonates with the purported communitarian ideology or neo-Confucian ethos of the Singapore system, which emphasises the community's interest in social cohesion and stability above individual rights and liberties.[50]

Professor Thio Li-ann recently coined the term 'paternal democracy' as a useful framing device for understanding the distinctive brand of constitutional democracy practised in Singapore; one that is characterised by a governmental prescription of

> political stability, combined with a legal environment that protected property rights and ensured commercial certainty … [and where economic prosperity] was to be achieved by discipline, rather than rambunctious democracy, and through curtailing an over-robust exercise of civil and political rights.[51]

Thio cautions that '[i]n developing an autochthonous rights jurisprudence, both the Scylla of hyper-individualism and the Charybdis of collectivism must be avoided',[52] and that:

> Even as an autochthonous legal system may be celebrated as an expression of self-determination, autochthony per se is not an unalloyed good; the values and the virtues which it espouses matter greatly, including its vision of the 'rule of law', as do the vices it fosters.[53]

This pragmatic political ideology[54] centred on economic progress, effective governance and a harmonious multiracial and multicultural society has been articulated in an official document released by the Singapore government.[55] Much of this climate of speech regulation stems from the concerns that the fragile ethnic and religious harmony in Singapore must be preserved to prevent the recurrence of the race riots that the country experienced in the 1960s.[56] For example, political commentator Melanie Chew explains this 'ideology of survival' as the 'siege mentality' where the political leadership of Singapore 'perceives Singapore as being small, vulnerable, and fragile' resulting in all human rights considerations being 'subordinate to the task of ensuring the economic and physical survival of the nation and the community'.[57]

Fidelity to a written constitution is of fundamental importance.[58] It requires that 'we do our best to respect the text's allocation of freedom and constraint for future constitutional construction, and thus its particular allocation of trust and distrust with respect to later generations'.[59]

However, it is highly unlikely that the drafters intended the meaning of the Constitution text to be frozen at the time of its adoption. As the Attorney-General VK Rajah concurred, '[c]oncepts like equal protection and free speech may have a clear general meaning, but their application to specific facts require exposition and value judgments'.[60]

The idea of a living constitution that adapts to changing times and conditions is not a new one.[61] In advocating a theory of 'living constitutionalism' and a 'framework originalism' approach to constitutional construction, Jack Balkin makes a persuasive argument of how fidelity to a plan for self-government built on a written legal framework that continues over time can be compatible with both history and democratic legitimacy:

> When we engage in this inquiry, we *are* interested in … the expectations and intentions that adopters had about their choice of linguistic technologies of freedom and constraint; we are interested in the economy of trust and distrust they created through their choice of publicly available language.[62]

The reason that one should be interested in these expectations and intentions is that they help us to understand the nature of the social compact that the citizens of a particular democratic state, in the present, have accepted as their own. This approach not only has 'the advantage of describing the actual history of our nation',[63] but it also explains 'how constitutional construction occurs in response to constitutional politics' taking into account the 'work of the political branches, courts, political parties, social movements, interest groups, and individual citizens'.[64]

The author takes a more charitable view of the Court of Appeal's interpretive methodologies in Article 14 jurisprudence than that expressed by Yap Po Jen in this book.[65] It appears that the court under the leadership of Chief Justice Chan Sek Keong has gone beyond the mere constitutional 'fig leaves' of originalism and textualism, as was evident in the court's comprehensive discussion in *Review Publishing* on how the broader qualified privilege in the law of defamation may be argued for a Singapore citizen in the future, and the emphasis on the importance of adducing evidence to show that the contemporary political, social and cultural values in Singapore would support such a development.[66] The judicial dicta was expressed in a manner not incompatible with Balkin's living constitutionalism/framework originalism approach. The above strongly suggests that constitutional interpretation in Singapore must be situated within the evolving context of a paternalistic democracy and a neo-Confucianist statist framework.

The Singapore government's espousal of 'Asian values' – a form of cultural relativism and economic particularism – repudiates the liberal Western notion of distrust of government that informs much of First Amendment jurisprudence[67] and instead embraces respect for honourable, trustworthy gentleman-governors (*junzi*) derived from the Confucian tradition.[68] Although drawn from Confucian ideals, it was explained that these values are 'secular'[69] in nature, 'common to all the major groups in Singapore'[70] and are 'shared by all communities'.[71] The 'gist of Confucianism' is the notion that 'human society expresses itself through a finite number of hierarchical relationships'.[72]

The late former Prime Minister and founding father of Singapore, Lee Kuan Yew, had reiterated the 'Confucianist belief that society works best where every man aims to be a gentleman' and that this *junzi* adheres to the Five Relationships or *Wu-Lun*.[73] Since the elected politician is a gentleman-governor and is, therefore, a *junzi* deserving of respect in a Confucian social order of hierarchical relations, substantial public harm can result if criticism deterred such candidates from taking public office.

The justifications for freedom of speech are relatively well accepted within liberal democratic theory. What is interesting is that freedom of speech can also be justified from this neo-Confucianist philosophy that the Singapore government espouses. The traditional Confucian preference of rites over laws, the glaring weakness in its approach to government insofar as it relies on the inherent goodness of the *junzi* and on the moral restraints of ritual and benevolence to curb the excesses of autocratic power, has resulted in a neo-Confucianist movement that attempts to adapt Confucianism to the realities of political life. From a neo-Confucianist perspective, one accepts that the five Confucian paradigms of human relationships are premised on respect being shown according to specific norms of behaviour called 'rites' (*li*) which exist as a social constitution that is preferable to governmental enforcement of laws (*fa*). In the Confucian view, especially as expounded by his follower Mencius, the cultivation of personal virtue (*ren*), expressed through voluntary adherence to *li*, should be sufficient to order social activity without the interference of *fa*.[74]

Contrary to popular belief, Confucianism does not support a highly interventionist state. Instead, communitarian goals are to be promoted through the cultivation of personal virtue and the practice of rites within what Mencius describes as a 'co-operative community'.[75] Admittedly, neither Confucius nor Mencius explicitly advocated freedom of expression, but it has been pointed out that 'a Confucian perspective would have a reason, albeit an *instrumental* one, to endorse freedom of expression'.[76] They both saw the value of public criticism of the ruler and those holding public office as conducive to preventing those in power from indulging in wrongdoing, and to the pursuit of *ren*.[77] In the late nineteenth century, Liang Qichao's journal *Renewing the People* (*Xinmin Congbao*) interpreted Confucian political doctrine as emphasising that the people as a 'new citizenry' possessed rights (*quanli*) both individually and collectively, had a consciousness of its own identity, and actively participated in the determination of its own destiny in a world of many contending peoples. This contemporary form of Confucian constitutionalism underscores accountability and the value of public discussion of governmental matters (*gongyi*) and the discussion of learning (*jiangxue*).[78]

It is the author's contention that the model of good government and good governance in Singapore[79] – reinforced in part by a commitment to build a democratic society, and in part by notions of Confucian communitarian ideology – necessitates, *minimally*, a recognition and protection of the freedom of speech that relates to communications pertaining to the conduct of the elected *junzi* and *gongyi*. The days of pursuing a rhetorical political Confucianism in pursuit of authoritarian statist ends belong to the 1990s. If one wants to make a coherent and intellectual connection between Confucianism and communitarian Asian values today, then one will have to accept a statist conception of society *but with an emphasis on participatory community*. It would be a misunderstanding of Confucianism to insist on the right of the state to act on behalf of the people as a whole (*gong*), often at the expense of the individual (*si*), purporting to find its mandate in the enforcement of rites (*li*). The development of the community compact in a later neo-Confucian tradition tended to misappropriate *li* and calcified them in *fa*, characteristic of a more authoritarian and bureaucratic state.

There is some concern that the government has misunderstood the requirements of Confucian philosophy. This stems from pronouncements about the need for a strong state. For instance, the late Lee Kuan Yew once stated that if Singapore as a small nation 'embarked on any of these romantic ideas, to revive a mythical past of greatness and culture' rather than to avoid 'racial conflict, linguistic strife, religious conflict', Singapore would be a failed state.[80] Referring to a 'pragmatist' approach to government where Singapore is constantly 'fighting for survival' in contrast to a 'classical, Western, liberal approach',[81] he revealed that Singapore's extraordinary success is dependent on economic and political alliances based on the nation's 'security, stability and predictability'.[82] However, although Lee maintained that his ideology-free pragmatic approach to running a country is the key to success, he had on several occasions affirmed the virtues of a representative democracy.[83]

At its most basic level, a democracy entails a choice of rulers by the people, where each citizen is entitled to a say in the choice of rulers, and the rulers are in turn accountable to the people.[84] The Singapore National Pledge, recited at numerous public events and school assemblies, is an oath of allegiance to Singapore and the ideals that it embodies. It was written by one of Singapore's founding fathers, the late S Rajaratnam, in 1966 after Singapore's independence and was revised by the then Prime Minister Lee Kuan Yew and subsequently approved by the Cabinet:[85]

> We, the citizens of Singapore,
> pledge ourselves as one united people,
> regardless of race, language or religion,
> *to build a democratic society*
> based on justice and equality
> *so as to achieve happiness, prosperity and*
> *progress for our nation.*[86]

The national commitment to 'build a democratic society' as a means to achieving the articulated ends as enshrined in the Pledge is a significant indication that the establishment of a 'democratic society' in Singapore is quintessential to the achievement of 'happiness, prosperity and progress' for the nation. One of the five stars on the Singapore flag represents democracy.[87] Although such declarations are non-legal in nature, the widespread public recital of the Pledge at a plethora of national events, and its unequivocal endorsement by the Singapore government, demonstrates the unique consensual nature of the Pledge that has, arguably, attained the status of a social compact: that the citizens of Singapore, including the government, are committed to *building a democratic society.*

Furthermore, the need to maintain 'good government' and 'good governance' has been consistently emphasised by political leaders of Singapore and senior public officials.[88] The late Lee Kuan Yew himself thought that this represented a government that was 'honest, effective and efficient in protecting its people, and allowing opportunities for all to advance themselves in a stable and orderly society'.[89] Ambassador-at-Large Tommy Koh argued that indicators of good government included 'wise and honest political leaders; a competent and clean bureaucracy; ... social policies in such fields as housing, education and health care that make every citizen feel like a stakeholder'.[90]

This democratic society envisaged is by no means identical to a Western liberal democratic model, but is shaped by a communitarian ethos and the priority to ensure a system of 'good government'.[91] However, at the bare minimum, one should accept that,

> [A]t a pragmatic level, freedom to disseminate and receive information on political matters is essential to the proper functioning of the system of parliamentary democracy ... This freedom enables those who elect representatives to Parliament to make an informed choice, regarding individuals as well as policies, and those elected to make informed decisions.[92]

Consequently, the aims of good government and good governance as understood from a neo-Confucianist, communitarian perspective and the commitment to building a democratic society necessitates, *minimally*, a recognition and protection of some freedom of political speech.

III Beyond the four walls – representative democracy and responsible government

A Overview of the 'broader' qualified privilege in defamation

In a landmark decision, the House of Lords held that a 'broader' qualified privilege – subsequently known as the *Reynolds* privilege – should be available to media defendants with respect to publications of defamatory statements which are of public interest provided they can establish 'responsible journalism'. Generally, a media article will be protected by the *Reynolds* privilege where the information is 'of sufficient value to the public that, in the public interest, it should be protected'.[93]

Qualified privilege, therefore, was interpreted more broadly in *Reynolds* than in the traditional qualified privilege defence that requires a reciprocal duty and interest between the publisher and the recipient of the statement in question.[94] In recognising this broader qualified privilege, the House of Lords noted that 'freedom to disseminate and receive information on political matters is essential to the proper functioning of the system of parliamentary democracy'.[95] According to the Privy Council, this defence was capable of applying to 'publications made by *any person* who published material of public interest in any medium, so long as the conditions framed by Lord Nicholls [in *Reynolds*] as being applicable to "responsible journalism" are satisfied'.[96] This point was affirmed by the Supreme Court of the United Kingdom (UKSC) in *Flood v Times Newspaper Ltd.*[97]

In *Jameel (Mohammed) v Wall Street Journal Europe Sprl*, Lord Bingham explained:

> The rationale of [the responsible journalism] test is ... that there is no duty to publish and the public have no interest to read material which the publisher *has not taken reasonable steps to verify* ... [T]he publisher is protected if he has taken such steps as a responsible journalist would take to try and ensure that what is published is accurate and fit for publication.[98]

As Kenyon and Ang have also pointed out, the *Reynolds* privilege is different from the traditional duty–interest privilege

> in that an occasion on which public interest material is published *and* responsible journalism is practised is now an occasion of qualified privilege. The defence focuses [more closely] on the material at issue and the underlying circumstances, in determining whether an occasion of privilege exists, more than earlier forms of the defence.[99]

One should also be cognisant that the *Reynolds* privilege does *not* necessarily result in greater freedom for the media or any individual to publish baseless allegations or scandalous falsehoods. All the circumstances surrounding the verification of sources, gathering of information, manner and tone of its reporting and opportunity to reply for the person against whom an allegation has been made are material to the privilege being successfully argued.[100] Despite the House of Lords' emphasis in *Jameel* that the *Reynolds* factors do not represent individual hurdles to be cleared by the media defendant,[101] a point that was reiterated by the UKSC in *Flood*,[102] the lower courts, nonetheless, appear to insist that the media demonstrates high standards in terms of ethics and responsibility before the *Reynolds* privilege would be permitted to stand. The decision in *Flood* suggests that a sharp divide will continue to exist in the manner between how the *Reynolds* privilege is more expansively applied by the highest English appellate court[103] and the overwhelming insistence on a more rigorous standard of responsible journalism by the lower courts.[104] In a comprehensive analysis of English cases and interviews with practitioners, it has been observed that 'media defendants have failed on *Reynolds* privilege in almost all the cases', but 'the reasoning in the decisions does not suggest that *Reynolds* privilege is narrow in its scope nor necessarily weak in its strength'.[105] In *Flood*, Lord Mance restated the *Reynolds* privilege both as a 'public interest defence' and a 'defence of public interest privilege'.[106] This description of the *Reynolds* privilege is similar to the public interest defence of 'responsible communication' on matters of public interest recognised by the Supreme Court of Canada.[107]

1 The nature of political communication in a representative democracy

In Australia, the landmark judicial recognition in 1992 of an implied constitutional freedom of political communication,[108] based on its indispensability to the efficacious working of the system of representative democracy and responsible government provided by the Australian Constitution, suggests that political communication may have a broad ambit that can embrace the discussion of all matters of public affairs[109] and the 'free flow of information and ideas bearing on Commonwealth, State and Territory government, government arrangements and institutions'.[110] However, a subsequent unanimous decision of the High Court of Australia in *Lange v Australian Broadcasting Corporation* anchored the doctrine to the necessary implications from the text and structure of the Constitution,[111] and framed the freedom more narrowly as 'freedom of communication between the people concerning political and government matters which enables the people to exercise a free and informed choice as electors'.[112]

Furthermore, the High Court has been 'reticent about using the language of rights to describe [this] freedom'.[113] The court has emphasised that this Australian implication is negative in character, being a restriction on the exercise of legislative and executive power rather than a source of positive rights.[114]

In addition, the High Court noted that the 'protection of the reputations of those who take part in the government and political life of this country from false and defamatory statements is conducive to the public good';[115] this is a view also echoed by the Singapore judiciary.[116] While eschewing any notion of a positive right to freedom of speech being granted by this implied freedom of political communication, the unanimous decision in *Lange* nevertheless adopts an 'extended defence of qualified privilege'[117] where the defendant has to meet the standard of 'reasonableness' which is defined by a number of factors akin to the *Reynolds* list. It has also been observed that the High Court has borrowed much from Strasbourg jurisprudence on the European Convention on Human Rights.[118] As a general rule, a defendant's conduct in publishing material giving rise to a defamatory imputation will not be reasonable 'unless the defendant had reasonable grounds for believing that the imputation was true, took proper steps, so far as they were reasonably open, to verify the accuracy of the material and did not believe the imputation to be untrue'.

Furthermore, the defendant is expected to have 'sought a response from the person defamed and published the response made (if any) except in cases where the seeking or publication of a response was not practicable or it was unnecessary to give the plaintiff an opportunity to respond'.[119] The *Lange* privilege in fact 'imposes fairly onerous conditions upon the defendant and should ensure that the extended defence of qualified privilege is not easily invoked'.[120] Like in *Reynolds*, the *Lange* privilege has established a high standard of responsible journalism for the media while protecting the freedom of political communication.

2 Freedom of political communication and a public interest defence of responsible communication

The relevance of these developments for Singapore law lies in the strong emphasis of the UK and Australian courts on the relationship between political or public interest communications and representative government. As discussed, the High Court of Australia has viewed the ambit of political communication as necessary in a system of representative government. In *Lange*, the court held unanimously that the ambit encompasses relevant information concerning the functioning of government and about the policies of political parties and candidates; communications between electors and elected representatives, between electors and candidates for election, between the electors themselves; communications concerning the conduct of executive branch officials, including ministers, the public service, statutory authorities and utilities.[121]

Similarly, Lord Nicholls, who wrote the leading judgment in *Reynolds*, took as the starting point the need for the common law to assist electors in making informed choices about who should govern their country, and whether the elected were governing well.[122] But his Lordship cautioned about placing too much emphasis on freedom of the press, and explained the need for a balanced approach to giving effect to Article 10:

> [I]n the absence of any additional safeguard for reputation, a newspaper, anxious to be first with a 'scoop', would in practice be free to publish seriously defamatory misstatements of fact based on the slenderest of materials. Unless the paper chose later to withdraw the allegations, the politician thus defamed would have no means of clearing his name, and the public would have no means of knowing where the truth lay. Some further protection for reputation is needed if this can be achieved without a disproportionate incursion into freedom of expression.[123]

Generally, the unifying thread in a number of decisions that recognise the broader qualified privilege from the various Commonwealth common law jurisdictions – whether the *Reynolds* privilege or its variant such as the public interest defence of responsible communication – is the argument that stems from the necessity of enabling robust political communications, which is essential to allowing voters to participate in the democratic process. While this conception of freedom of political communication is much narrower than Post's theory of participatory democracy and the Meiklejohnian notion of self-government, it nonetheless draws implicitly from aspects of these writings. Even in the absence of Article 10 of the ECHR,[124] it is possible to derive a broader qualified privilege defence from the notion of accountability of elected politicians and public officials within a system of representative democracy. In the Privy Council's judgment in *Hector v Attorney-General of Antigua and Barbuda*, the court suggested that:

> In a free democratic society, it is almost too obvious to need stating that those who hold office in government and who are responsible for public administration must always be open to criticism. Any attempt to stifle or fetter such criticism amounts to political censorship of the most insidious and objectionable kind.[125]

Lord Bridge also thought that the stifling of public criticisms of government officials hindered the citizenry's capacity to make informed electoral choices[126] – a view that is reflected in the *Lange* decision of the Australian High Court.

Thus, while one can distinguish the constitutional framework of Singapore from Australia and the United Kingdom, it is important to note that it is the 'national democratic elections [that] provide the basis for the implication',[127] and as such, Singapore does share significant similarities with these jurisdictions in this regard. Moreover, the Singapore Constitution provides an express grant of a positive right to freedom of speech for the citizens of Singapore, which presents a stronger case for a more robust protection of such communications relevant to a system of representative government under Article 14. It is also important to note that in *Vellama d/o Marie Muthu v Attorney-General*, the Singapore Court of Appeal acknowledged that the Singapore Constitution establishes a representative democracy and emphasised that:

> [I]t is vital to remind ourselves that the form of government of the Republic of Singapore as reflected in the Constitution is the Westminster model of government, with the party commanding the majority support in Parliament having the mandate to form the government. *The authority of the government emanates from the people. Each Member represents the people of the constituency who voted him into Parliament. The voters of a constituency are entitled to have a Member representing and speaking for them in Parliament.* The Member is not just the mouthpiece but the voice of the people of the constituency.[128]

Consequently, when interpreting Article 14 in the future, it is inevitable that the courts will have to revisit the implications for freedom of speech for voters in Singapore who are critical of how Members of Parliament discharge their official functions.

B Climbing over the walls – relevance to interpretation of Article 14 of the Singapore Constitution

The Court of Appeal left many questions unanswered in *Review Publishing* regarding the possible application of *Reynolds* in defamation cases involving a Singapore citizen–defendant. If the development in the United Kingdom of common law qualified privilege can be shaped by Article 10 of the ECHR, then it is not tenuous to argue that qualified privilege as it applies to Singapore citizens could also be bolstered by Article 14(1)(a) of the Singapore Constitution[129] and guided by English decisions in this area. Although the *Reynolds* privilege is not currently part of Singapore's common law,[130] the author postulates that 'a *contemporary* consideration of what the common convenience and welfare of [Singapore] society require[s]'[131] makes a persuasive case for its adoption as a qualified privilege available to Singapore citizens.

If a good government 'accepts the obligation to face the electorate',[132] then this accountability, which is quintessential to good governance, leads inevitably to the electorate being able to communicate matters relating to good government and governance amongst themselves and with the political leaders. In Singapore, the citizens' desire for a shift to a more participatory democracy is palpable. In October 2010, former Prime Minister Goh Chok Tong explained:

> In politics, the government encourages feedback and participation. We want to engage you. Singaporeans have become better educated and have higher expectations. This is natural, as is the growing desire of Singaporeans to want more say over matters which affect their lives and future. This is a healthy development.[133]

The last Singapore parliamentary elections in 2011, in which the People's Action Party (PAP) lost a historic six seats, clearly illustrated the demand by the electorate for greater accountability and more active involvement in government.[134] Academic commentator Alan Chong noted that 'the people are sending a strong message to the PAP: Listen to us.'[135] In his post-election press conference, Prime Minister Lee Hsien Loong conceded that this election 'marks a distinctive shift in our political landscape' and that 'many [Singaporeans] wish for the Government to adopt a different style and approach to government, in keeping with a new generation and a new era which we're living in'.[136] PM Lee later promised that the ruling party would evolve to accommodate more views and citizen participation, and said, '[N]ever forget we're the servants of the people, not their masters.... Never lord it over the people we're looking after and serving.'[137]

It would seem that the year 2011 marks a perceptible shift from the authoritarian-style politics that had characterised the PAP government to one of 'public servant-hood'.[138] The promised transformation of the PAP is an unequivocal signal that 'the balance struck on 16 September 1963 between constitutional free speech and protection of reputation'[139] is unlikely to be the same today in the light of events after the May 2011 elections. Perhaps this is the 'evidence of a change in our political, social and cultural values' that would satisfy the Court of Appeal 'that change [to the defence of qualified privilege] is necessary so as to provide greater protection against the existing law of defamation for defendants where the publication of matters of public interest is concerned'.[140]

The Australian free speech jurisprudence, premised on facilitating political communication in order to ensure that citizens are well informed when it comes to exercising their right to vote, is instructive to Singapore. Even in the absence of an express free speech provision like Article 10 of the ECHR, the High Court of Australia held that it was necessary to find an implied constitutional freedom of communication in respect of government and political matters, which accords an analogous but much narrower right to the press to report matters of public interest.[141] In fact, the High Court has stated that unlike the US Constitution, the Australian Constitution does *not* create rights of communication; the freedom protected is not freedom to communicate, but 'a freedom *from* laws that effectively prevent the members of the Australian community from communicating with each other about political and government matters relevant to the system of representative and responsible government'.[142] The High Court in a unanimous and joint opinion framed the implied freedom narrowly:

> [t]hat each member of the Australian community has an *interest* in disseminating and receiving information, opinions and arguments concerning government and political matters that affect the people of Australia.[143]

Framed in this manner, with the basis of freedom of speech fundamentally originating from its necessity in a system of representative democracy and responsible government, free speech may be properly circumscribed by other competing community interests and *yet* be given adequate breathing space to manifest in robust political debate. Moreover, the communication of information about political and government matters remains consistent with democratic values.

In Singapore, the 'dominant community interest is invariably identified with assuring respect for the reputations of politicians and public institutions',[144] but this does not mean that one has to abandon the community interest in robust political debate and political communication that are implicit in the words '*to build a democratic society*', which are enshrined in the Pledge. In fact, the Pledge strengthens the argument that Article 14(2) of the Constitution ought to be interpreted in the context of this national commitment to democracy. Koh concedes that despite a Singaporean 'culture favouring consensus-building', the nation, nonetheless, subscribes to 'a form of participatory democracy'.[145] Moreover, as McHugh J points out in *Stephens v West Australian Newspapers Ltd*:

> In the last decade of the twentieth century, the quality of life and the freedom of the ordinary individual in Australia are highly dependent on the exercise of functions and powers vested in public representatives and officials by a vast legal and bureaucratic apparatus funded by public moneys. How, when, why and where those functions and powers are or are not exercised are matters that are of real and legitimate interest to every member of the community ... It follows, in my opinion, that the general public has a legitimate interest in receiving information concerning matters relevant to the exercise of public functions and powers vested in public representatives and officials.[146]

These observations are equally pertinent to Singapore, especially where voting is compulsory for citizens under the Parliamentary Elections Act.[147] Furthermore, as Anne-Marie Slaughter persuasively argues, there is an underlying 'simple desire [amongst the highest appellate courts of any jurisdiction] to look around the world for good ideas' and this reflects 'a spirit of genuine transjudicial deliberation within a newly self-conscious transnational community'.[148] Slaughter posits that when a 'core judicial function ... to protect individuals against abuses of state power' is engaged, courts may well 'feel a particular common bond with one another' as they have to determine 'the appropriate level of protection in light of a complex matrix of historical, cultural, and political needs and expectations'. However, '[a]ctual decisions must be highly individualized'.[149] Hence, 'constitutional cross-fertilization'[150] is a perfectly legitimate process in an era of globalisation that allows courts to import ideas from other jurisdictions and benefit from 'comparative deliberation'[151] when adapting them to the particular circumstances of their jurisdictions.

C Implications for defamation laws in Singapore

The author does not suggest that Singapore embrace either the *Reynolds* privilege or the *Lange* privilege in its entirety. Indeed, the historical, geographical, political, social and cultural circumstances of Singapore are markedly different from England or Australia. However, they do share a common commitment to a system of representative democracy and responsible government, insofar as citizens require information relating to matters of public interest and government matters to enable them to competently exercise their votes. The *Lange* privilege contains elements present in the *Reynolds* list of ten non-exhaustive factors, and will not be examined separately here.[152]

The author proposes that the Singapore Court of Appeal consider adopting or adapting the *Reynolds* privilege to give effect to Article 14(1)(a) of the Singapore Constitution by extending it to any Singaporean – whether an ordinary citizen or journalist – when articulating his or her views on matters of public interest relating to government and governance. As legal commentator William Buss observes, at some point, the common law might fall short of what the Constitution requires.[153] The court should then develop the common law to fit the requirements of the Constitution.[154] Presently, section 12 of the Defamation Act (Singapore) sets out particular circumstances where qualified privilege shall not apply; it does not, however, define the defence of qualified privilege, thus leaving it to the courts to interpret qualified privilege in the common law.[155]

Section 12, states, inter alia, that:

> 12 (4) Nothing in this section shall be construed as limiting or abridging any privilege subsisting (otherwise than by virtue of the repealed Defamation Ordinance 1960 [Ordinance 7 of 1960]) immediately before 6th May 1965.

Since the defence of qualified privilege was already in existence before the commencement of the Defamation Act, it is part of the common law in Singapore.[156] But, one should not ask the question whether the *Reynolds* qualified privilege is a natural development of the common law, or a different jurisprudential creature that grew out of Article 10 of the ECHR.[157] This is an incorrect inquiry. Rather, one should reason from first principles whether the common law of qualified privilege adequately gives effect to Article 14(1) of the Constitution, and whether, in the light of developments over the last fifty years since Singapore declared its independence *and* Singapore's commitment to building a democratic society based on a system of representative government, a multi-factorial approach to giving effect to a broader common law defence of qualified privilege is applicable today. Undoubtedly, *more* weight can be given to the reputation of honourable men and women whose vocation of serving the public is their 'whole life',[158] but the current judicial approach to criticisms of elected public figures in defamation claims does not give sufficient weight to a constitutional norm that guarantees freedom of speech.

Former Chief Justice Chan Sek Keong had indicated in an extra-judicial address that the judiciary is the 'lynchpin of a democratic society and the rule of law'.[159] Hence, even under the narrowest literal construction of Article 14, in the absence of the Singapore Parliament passing a law that circumscribes the defence of qualified privilege, it is open to the Court of Appeal to develop the defence of qualified privilege under the common law in the direction of the *Reynolds* privilege *and* still accord greater weight to reputation in recognition of Singapore's purportedly neo-Confucianist and paternalistic democratic culture. While the court in *Review Publishing* conceded that 'the *rationale* behind the *Reynolds* privilege ... is equally relevant to our citizens because of Art 14(1)(a) of the Singapore Constitution',[160] it stopped short of declaring that the adoption of the *Reynolds* factors – or a combination thereof – would be appropriate to ensure that the citizens of Singapore are able to exercise their constitutional right to express views on matters of public interest relating to government and governance.

Furthermore, the Court of Appeal has also conceded that:

> We should, however, clarify that this does not mean that public leaders may not be criticised at all. They certainly should be strongly – and perhaps even mercilessly – criticised for incompetence, insensitivity, ignorance, and any number of other human frailties where the critique does not go to the extent of besmirching their integrity, honesty, honour, and such other qualities that make up the reputation of a person.[161]

The *Reynolds* privilege contains a number of factors to which the Singapore courts can accord different weight or emphasis.[162] The *Reynolds* responsible journalism standard is not as broad as the Court of Appeal in *Review Publishing* made it out to be; it is focused on ensuring that journalists take reasonable steps to check on the accuracy of any allegations that they report.[163] Perhaps the Canadian Supreme Court's more nuanced formulation of the privilege as a 'defence of responsible communication on matters of public interest' more accurately captures the essence of this privilege, and might be more palatable in the Singaporean context. In *Grant*, the court observed that 'the proper functioning of democratic governance, has profound resonance in this context',[164] but at the same time, '[i]t is vital that the media act responsibly in reporting facts on matters of public concern, holding themselves to the highest journalistic standards'.[165] One should also be cognisant that the *Reynolds* privilege does *not* necessarily result in greater freedom for the media or any individual to publish baseless allegations or scandalous falsehoods. All the circumstances surrounding the verification of sources, gathering of information, manner and tone of its reporting and opportunity to reply for the person against whom an allegation has been made are material to the privilege being successfully argued.[166] In fact, the *Reynolds* privilege skews the emphasis towards the protection of reputation, places an onerous burden on the publisher to prove that he or she has behaved responsibly and discourages publication of information that is likely to be false. In short, the *Reynolds* privilege does not merely protect responsible journalism; it also *ensures* responsible journalism and comment.

In the recent case of *Lee Hsien Loong v Roy Ngerng Yi Ling*, it was disappointing that the defence for the blogger – a Singapore citizen – failed to even raise the issue of the *Reynolds* privilege when the facts presented a fertile opportunity to capitalise on the opportunities that *Review Publishing* had presented.[167] It was held that the Singaporean blogger had defamed the plaintiff, the Prime Minister of Singapore and the Chairman of GIC, in that the natural and ordinary meaning of the published words and images conveyed that the Prime Minister was guilty of criminal misappropriation of the monies paid by Singaporeans to the Central Provident Fund. Unfortunately, and perplexingly, the sole defence was that the law of defamation contravenes Article 14 of the Constitution of the Republic of Singapore.[168] A defence that the law of defamation was unconstitutional would obviously fail; such an argument would not succeed even in the most liberal speech-protective jurisdiction, such as the USA. Based on the facts of *Ngerng*, where a Singapore citizen was commenting on a matter of public interest and on good governance that is of great importance to the electorate,[169] it would have been the paradigmatic test case to revisit judicial recognition of a broader qualified privilege akin to the *Reynolds* privilege.

IV Scaling the four walls – scandalising the judiciary

A Global appreciation of scandalising contempt

Scandalising the court or judiciary has been described as an 'archaic title'[170] but it generally embodies '[a]ny act done or writing published calculated to bring a court or a judge of the court into contempt, or to lower his authority'.[171] However, there can be a fine line between what qualifies as fair or justified criticism of the conduct of the courts or the individual judges in their administration of justice and what constitutes an 'undue interference with the administration of justice'[172] that amounts to contempt. Indeed it has been observed that 'the law of contempt has been considered, not just in Singapore, but in other jurisdictions as well, to be a justifiable restriction on the right to freedom of speech'.[173]

The law of contempt of court in English common law was examined by the Interdepartmental Committee on the Law of Contempt chaired by Lord Justice Phillimore over forty years ago.[174] The Phillimore Report divided contempt of court into a number of categories,[175] but the eventual passage of the Contempt of Court Act 1981 (UK) focused only on the last-mentioned category, ie conduct may be treated as a contempt of court 'tending to interfere with the course of justice in particular legal proceedings regardless of intent to do so', and the 'strict liability rule' applies only to 'a publication which creates a substantial risk that the course of justice in the [active] proceedings in question will be seriously impeded or prejudiced'.[176] The regulation of conduct that scandalises the court has been left largely to the interpretation of judges in the development of the common law governing contempt of court, but it was abolished by statute in the UK after a lengthy consultative process.[177]

As Lord Diplock declared in *Attorney-General v Times Newspaper Ltd*, '[t]he provision of such a system for the administration of justice by courts of law and *the maintenance of public confidence in it, are essential if citizens are to live together in peaceful association with one another*'.[178]

The due administration of justice requires, inter alia, that citizens

> [S]hould be able to rely upon obtaining in the courts the arbitrament of a tribunal which is free from bias against any party and whose decision will be based upon those facts only that have been proved in evidence adduced before it in accordance with the procedure adopted in courts of law; and … that, once the dispute has been submitted to a court of law, they should be able to rely upon there being no usurpation by any other person of the function of that court to decide it according to law.[179]

Indeed, public confidence in the judiciary is a fundamental tenet of any democratic society. In Australia, it was noted that 'scandalising is thriving' and 'this head of contempt [is] becoming increasingly potent in Australia'.[180]

Even in a highly pro-speech jurisdiction such as the USA, cogent exhortations have been advanced that 'public confidence in the court demands at least that it acts according to professional standards and adheres to principled reasoning in its decisions'.[181] US Supreme Court Chief Justice John Roberts has also referred to concerns of institutional legitimacy in explaining why the court should avoid 5–4 decisions in cases 'involving the most controversial questions in American politics'.[182] It is also interesting to note that even the judiciary in the USA 'does not always appreciate having its own integrity questioned'.[183]

Academic commentator Margaret Tarkington observed that

> [t]hroughout the United States, state and federal courts discipline and sanction attorneys who make disparaging remarks about the judiciary and thereby impugn judicial integrity. In so doing, courts have almost universally rejected the constitutional standard established by the U.S. Supreme Court in the seminal 1964 case *New York Times Co. v Sullivan* for punishing speech regarding government officials.[184]

B A real risk of transnational judicial conversations?

In *Attorney-General v Shadrake Alan*,[185] the Singapore High Court rejected the 'inherent tendency' test for deciding whether acts and words complained of should be held in contempt of court, and held that the Attorney-General had to prove that the publications posed real risks of undermining public confidence in the administration of justice.[186] Quentin Loh J explained that such an approach 'strikes an adequate balance between the freedom of speech and the countervailing constitutional interest in ensuring that public confidence in the administration of justice does not falter as a result of scandalous publications'.[187] This can be said to be an effective departure from previous decisions of the High Court that seemed to endorse the inherent tendency test.[188]

Hitherto, the Singapore Court of Appeal has not decided on the applicable test for liability for contempt of court on the ground of scandalising the judiciary ('scandalising contempt'); neither is there any legislative provision that articulates the appropriate standard to be applied for contempt cases.[189] However, in considering Alan Shadrake's appeal, the Court of Appeal made an important pronouncement:

> We, therefore, unequivocally state that the 'real risk' test is the applicable test vis-à-vis liability for scandalising contempt in Singapore.[190]

In *Shadrake I*, Loh J found Alan Shadrake in contempt of court for eleven of the fourteen impugned statements, but the Court of Appeal held that only nine of the statements were contemptuous.[191] Nonetheless, the Court of Appeal unanimously affirmed the sentence, and was of the view that 'this is still the worst case of scandalising contempt that has hitherto come before the Singapore courts … [and] the Appellant's conduct merits a substantial custodial sentence'.[192]

The 'real risk' standard, as correctly pointed out by Loh J in *Shadrake I*, has been adopted in the United Kingdom,[193] Australia,[194] New Zealand[195] and Hong Kong.[196]

Loh J emphasised that the law of scandalising contempt is concerned with 'the potential effect on public confidence in the administration of justice'.[197] However, there is always a danger that scandalising contempt will have a significant chilling effect on a citizen's right to freedom of speech, especially when the impugned criticism of the judiciary implicates public interest in the administration of justice by the courts.[198] The Court of Appeal in *Shadrake III* acknowledged this tension, when it commented that:

> [I]t should be noted that the law relating to contempt of court operates against the broader legal canvas of the right to freedom of speech that is embodied both within Article 14 of the Constitution of the Republic of Singapore … as well as the common law. The issue, in the final analysis, is one of *balance*: just as the law relating to contempt of court ought not to unduly infringe the right to freedom of speech, by the same token, that right is not an absolute one, for its untrammelled abuse would be a negation of the right itself.[199]

Many of the reasons proffered by the Singapore courts in defamation cases – for example, the fragile ethnic and religious harmony in Singapore that must be preserved to prevent the recurrence of the race riots that the country experienced in the 1960s[200] – when reading down the ambit of available defences, do not apply to contempt of court scenarios. While earlier High Court cases in Singapore appeared to have rejected the defences of fair comment, justification and fair criticism,[201] Loh J in *Shadrake I* considered a number of Australian and English cases and concluded that there is a defence of fair criticism, subject to three conditions. Perhaps emboldened by VK Rajah JA's recent comment,[202] Loh J was of the view that 'it is very much in the public interest that judicial impropriety should be brought to light'[203] and that 'the public should be able to debate judicial conduct'.[204]

Acknowledging that 'while it would be inappropriate to import wholesale the defence of fair comment [from defamation] into the law of contempt … it may well be that there is in the final analysis some functional similarity between fair comment and fair criticism', Loh J relied on the analysis of Prakash J in *Attorney-General v Tan Liang Joo John* ('*Tan*') that fair criticism does not amount to contempt of court.[205]

Adopting a more liberal approach than any of the earlier Singapore decisions on contempt of court proceedings, Loh J eschewed a categorical approach to defences available for contempt, and intimated that 'there should be no limit to the kind of criticisms which can be made against the court subject to the above three criteria being met'.[206] This formulation departs from previous formulations of the High Court by Goh J in *Attorney-General v Lingle and Others*,[207] by Ang J in *Lee Hsien Loong v Singapore Democratic Party and Others*[208] and by Tay J in *Attorney-General v Hertzberg Daniel and Others*.[209] The problem with these pre-*Shadrake* formulations of fair criticism is the requirement that the publication or conduct does not impugn the integrity or impartiality of the judge or the court. This requirement renders the 'fair criticism' defence impotent as the published criticism is, in fact, calling into question the very integrity or impartiality of the judiciary, thus resulting in prima facie contempt. It is only because, as Loh J points out in *Shadrake I*, that this criticism has an objective basis, is made in good faith and is temperate in tone, that it qualifies as 'fair criticism'.

However, Loh J's endorsement of an independent legal defence of fair criticism was rejected by the Court of Appeal. Andrew Phang JA examined a number of English and Australian decisions,[210] as well as treatises[211] and law commission reports,[212] and concluded that 'the *nature, tenor and thrust* of these statements of principle are, in our view, more consistent with the concept of fair criticism as going towards *liability* instead'.[213] According to the Court of Appeal, fair criticism therefore will be evaluated within the ambit of *liability* for scandalising contempt, through an analysis of a number of factors articulated by Prakash J in *Tan* (which were also cited by Loh J in *Shadrake I*).[214]

These factors include (i) the extent to which the allegedly fair criticism is rationally supported by argument and evidence; (ii) the manner in which the alleged criticism is made; (iii) the party's attitude in court; and (iv) the number of instances of contemning conduct. The practical result of this is

> the *evidential* burden would be on the party relying on it [and the] *legal* burden, on the other hand, would be on the [Attorney-General] to prove beyond a reasonable doubt that the impugned statement does not constitute fair criticism, and that it presents a real risk of undermining public confidence in the administration of justice.[215]

As Prakash J astutely observed in *Tan*, such bona fide, temperate and balanced criticism 'allows for rational debate about issues raised and thus may even contribute to the improvement and strengthening of the administration of justice'.[216] Although the judicial appointment process in Singapore is nowhere as politically contentious as the appointments to the US Supreme Court, the judges on the highest appellate court of any nation still need to earn their credibility through their reasoning process. Louis Fisher was of the view that the court's decisions 'must build from acceptable premises to reach plausible conclusions'.[217] Decisions 'that are mere edicts or assertions anchored in vague suppositions are not credible'[218] and the court may be seen by the public 'as acting in an arbitrary and capricious manner'.[219]

Hence, judicial decisions, especially those of the highest appellate court, should be more exposed to public scrutiny and rational debates. The Confucian ethos of placing 'demanding standards of moral behavior on rulers and gentlemen' and 'moral edification by example'[220] would apply equally to judges and politicians. The cultivation of virtue by the *junzi*-judge would not be immune from public scrutiny. As the case law develops, an evaluation of fair criticism in scandalising contempt cases can perhaps draw on some of the elements of the *Reynolds* test for responsible journalism.[221] For instance, an allegation of bias against a High Court judge, which is a very serious matter that could affect public confidence in the administration of justice in Singapore, must be supported by rigorous efforts to verify the information suggesting the existence of bias, and the publication should display a clear demarcation of facts from comments and be expressed in a temperate tone.

The much-welcomed clarification by the Court of Appeal in *Shadrake III* brings the law of scandalising contempt in Singapore more in line with other Commonwealth counterparts. Thio agrees that the decisions in *Tan* and *Shadrake III*

> demonstrate not only careful reasoning and a ready engagement with foreign decisions, but also a confidence in treading the path of developing an autochthonous public law jurisprudence, one 'sensitive to the needs and mores of the society of which it is a part'.[222]

In applying the 'real risk' test, the court

> must avoid either extreme on the legal spectrum, *viz*, of *either* finding that contempt has been established where there is only a remote or fanciful possibility that public confidence in the administration of justice is (or might be) undermined *or* finding that contempt has been established *only* in the *most* serious situations.[223]

It is also clear that an objective analysis should be undertaken of 'the precise facts and context in which the impugned statement is made' and 'the court must not substitute its own subjective view for the view of the average reasonable person'.[224] Furthermore, it must be beyond a reasonable doubt that there is a real risk that the impugned statement would undermine public confidence in the administration of justice in Singapore.[225]

In *Attorney-General v Au Wai Pang*, handed down by the High Court in 2015, Belinda Ang J agreed with the present author that the decision in *Shadrake III* 'strikes an appropriate balance between safeguarding, on the one hand, freedom of speech and, on the other hand, the public interest in protecting public confidence in the administration of justice in Singapore'.[226] In *Au Wai Pang*, the Attorney-General brought committal proceedings against the respondent Au in connection with two articles he published on the internet on his blog, the Yawning Bread, which the AG said amounted to contempt of court in the form of scandalising the Supreme Court of Singapore. Although Ang J did not explicitly refer to how the respondent as a Singapore citizen was specifically entitled to freedom of speech under Article 14, a point that was crucial in *Review Publishing*, her Honour was concerned that 'the law relating to contempt of court ought not to unduly infringe the right to freedom of speech'.[227] Ang J concluded that the 'combination of the "real risk" test and the placing of the legal burden on the Prosecution "calibrates" appropriately the tension between freedom of speech and the public interest in protecting public confidence in the administration of justice'.[228]

It would appear that the dominion of the illiberal 'four walls' approach has been diminished in constitutional free speech jurisprudence as Ang J sought to reason that the real risk test 'is also in line with the test applied in other common law jurisdictions such as Australia, New Zealand and Hong Kong'.[229] However, this does not mean that Singapore should be open to an alacrity to align itself with every aspect of doctrinal developments in this area. It would appear that an autochthonous approach does not entail an erection of 'four walls' that are impervious to all foreign influences, but the walls do act as a filter for courts to evaluate which developments are instructive in the context of Singapore's history, constitutionalism and form of representative democracy. For example, in *Au*, Ang J considered the recent Privy Council decision on scandalising contempt in *Dhooharika v Director of Public Prosecutions*[230] and held, inter alia, that '*Dhooharika* is distinguishable from our Court of Appeal's decision in *Shadrake* ... given the respective local circumstances and constitutional contexts in which these two cases were decided'.[231] The appeal in *Dhooharika*, from a decision rendered by the Supreme Court of Mauritius, concerns a publication in a weekly newspaper making allegations of serious wrongdoing against the Chief Justice. Lord Clarke, delivering the judgment for the Privy Council, concluded that the 'specific ingredients of the offence may vary across jurisdictions'[232] and that 'local conditions are relevant to the continued existence of the offence'.[233]

The decisions in *Au* and *Shadrake III* resonate with the extra-judicial comments of former Chief Justice Chan Sek Keong, who pointed out:

> [M]echanisms such as the doctrine of contempt should not be used to stifle fair and reasonable criticism of the work of the Judiciary and also judicial decisions. The right to criticise is only part of the freedom of speech and expression the citizen enjoys in a democracy and its exercise will encourage or ensure that judges are independent in their decision-making ... Fair and objective criticism of judicial decisions will instil accountability and greater discipline in decision-making. If no one is allowed to judge judges, there

could be lawless courts and irresponsible judging. But, criticism of judgments should not lead to the denigration of judges.[234]

V Conclusion

Asian constitutionalism generally 'occupies a distinctive space on the spectrum between universalism and particularism in the world of the 21st century'[235] and 'both local constitutional difference and national constitutional identity are significant phenomena with which judicial engagement [with foreign sources] ... must deal'.[236] With Singapore's commitment 'to build a democratic society',[237] albeit a neo-Confucianist, communitarian or paternal democracy, and bolstered by the free speech guarantee in Article 14(1), the 'four walls' cannot shut out relevant considerations of how Singapore and her citizens might benefit from recognising what good government and good governance entail in a number of Commonwealth common law jurisdictions. Thus, the common law of defamation should be more expansively interpreted to include a multi-factorial approach to the qualified privilege defence that draws on the *Reynolds* factors. The *Reynolds* privilege – or in more nuanced *Grant* parlance, the defence of responsible communication on matters of public interest – offers a better balance between the protection of the reputation of honourable men in politics and freedom of speech in relation to scrutiny by the electorate of the conduct of these honourable men when holding office.[238]

The consideration of the *Reynolds* factors in a broader qualified privilege defence raised by the citizens of Singapore is compatible with both the Constitution and Singapore's democratic system, which emphasises good government and good governance. Indeed, there is an 'Asian version of a social contract between the people and the state'.[239] This social contract, even if argued to be paternalistic and communitarian in nature, nonetheless requires the leaders of the state to be accountable to the people. Similarly, this neo-Confucianist philosophy of good government grounds an argument for expanding the scope of fair criticism in the law on contempt of court. As the Singapore judiciary has observed, even judges should be subject to 'fair and reasonable criticism of [their] work' and 'the right to criticise is only part of the freedom of speech and expression the citizen enjoys in a democracy'.[240]

Joseph Chan has compellingly argued that Confucianism would justify civil liberties such as freedom of expression on instrumental grounds as a means for society to ensure that rulers would not indulge in wrongdoing.[241] Good government depends on 'good institutions virtuously administered'.[242] Even in the *Shared Values* White Paper released by the Singapore Parliament to explain its governing ideology, it was stated that '[t]he electorate must uphold the democratic process ... Elected politicians and career civil servants who are entrusted with authority over their fellow citizens must exercise power responsibly, as trustees of the people'.[243]

In the Singapore context of an Asian system of government of 'good men',[244] the behaviour of these men should still be subject to appropriate scrutiny by the citizens of Singapore to ensure that they remain 'good'. Robust debate and rigorous scrutiny should not be confined only to the hallowed chambers of Parliament House. In any democracy, the government must be accountable to the electorate. A well-informed and well-educated citizenry that can more freely discuss and debate matters of public interest relating to government and governance will more intelligently and effectively supervise the organs of the state. In developing this autochthonous narrative of responsible freedom, one should take heed of the words of James Madison: 'A popular Government, without popular information, or the means of acquiring it, is but a Prologue to a Farce or a Tragedy.'[245]

Notes

1 *Chan Hiang Leng Colin & Ors v Public Prosecutor* [1994] 3 SLR(R) 209 (Singapore High Court (Sing HC)) [51] ('*Colin Chan*') (quoting *Government of the State of Kelantan v Government of the Federation of Malaya* [1963] MLJ 355 (Federation of Malaya High Court (Malaya HC)) 359 (Thomson CJ)).

2 *Colin Chan* (n 1) [53]:

> The social conditions in Singapore are, of course, markedly different from those in the United States. On this basis alone, I am not influenced by the various views as enunciated in the American cases cited to me but instead must restrict my analysis of the issues here with reference to the local context.

3 Thio Li-ann, 'Beyond the "Four Walls" in an Age of Transnational Judicial Conversations: Civil Liberties, Rights Theories, and Constitutional Adjudication in Malaysia and Singapore' (2006) 19 Columbia Journal of Asian Law 428, 430 (citing Anne-Marie Slaughter, 'A Global Community of Courts' (2003) 44 Harvard International Law Journal 191).

4 Thio (n 3) 431. As Cheryl Saunders points out in her study, '[a]ll the Asian courts with constitutional adjudication for which data is readily available use foreign law experience as an aid although not, of course, as a binding source of law, in resolving constitutional questions brought before them.' (Cheryl Saunders, 'Judicial Engagement' in Rosalind Dixon and Tom Ginsburg (eds), *Comparative Constitutional Law in Asia* (Edward Elgar 2014) 80, 85). Saunders was of the view that the 'four walls' doctrine as propounded in Singapore was not a denial of the legitimacy of any use of foreign law but rather 'a comparative methodology that favours particularism': ibid 89. See also *Yong Vui Kong v Public Prosecutor* [2015] SGCA 11 (Singapore Court of Appeal (Sing CA)) [33]–[38]. In particular, Sundaresh Menon CJ held (at [38]):

> [T]he content of our Constitution could [not] be dictated by the views of other states, regardless of what the people of Singapore, expressing their will through their elected representatives, think … [E]ven where a CIL rule has acquired the status of *jus cogens*, it cannot override a domestic statute whose meaning and effect is clear.

5 Eg *Vellama d/o Marie Muthu v Attorney-General* [2013] 4 SLR 1 (Sing CA) [83]–[85]; *Ong Ah Chuan v Public Prosecutor* [1980–1981] SLR 48 (Privy Council (PC)) [23]; *Chng Suan Tze v Minister for Home Affairs* [1988] 2 SLR(R) 525 (Sing CA) [80]–[86].

6 Constitution of the Republic of Singapore (1985 Rev Ed, 1999 Reprint) ('Singapore Constitution') Art 14.

7 The 'horizontal effects' doctrine relates to the effects of a constitutional provision on private law actions where courts are obliged to interpret and apply existing law in a manner that is compatible with the constitutional guarantee. See generally, Murray

Hunt, 'The Horizontal Effect of the Human Rights Act' (1998) Public Law 423; Gavin Phillipson, 'Transforming Breach of Confidence? Towards a Common Law Right of Privacy under the Human Rights Act' (2003) 66 Modern Law Review 726; Gavin Phillipson, 'Clarity Postponed: Horizontal Effect After *Campbell*' in Helen Fenwick, Gavin Phillipson and Roger Masterman (eds), *Judicial Reasoning under the UK Human Rights Act* (Cambridge University Press 2007) 143.

8 Andrew T Kenyon and Ang Hean Leng, '*Reynolds* Privilege, Common Law Defamation and Malaysia' (2010) Singapore Journal of Legal Studies 256.

9 ibid 272. In 2007, Justice Tee Ah Sing in the High Court applied the *Reynolds* privilege and examined the ten factors as laid out by Lord Nicholls. See *Irene Fernandez v Utusan Melayu (M) Sdn Bhd* (2008) 2 Current Law Journal 814 (Malaysia High Court (Malaysia HC)). See also Kenyon and Ang (n 8) 266–70. However, it should also be noted that 'Malaysian law has reached the awkward position of the Federal Court having endorsed both the English *Reynolds* defence and the Australian *Lange* defence': ibid 263.

10 [2010] 1 SLR 52 (Sing CA) ('*Review Publishing*').

11 Thio Li-ann, 'Singapore: Regulating Political Speech and the Commitment "to Build a Democratic Society"' (2003) 1 International Journal of Constitutional Law 516, 516. See, eg *Jeyaretnam Joshua Benjamin v Lee Kuan Yew* [1992] 1 SLR(R) 791 (Sing CA) ('*Jeyaretnam*'); *Tang Liang Hong v Lee Kuan Yew* [1997] 3 SLR(R) 576 (Sing CA) ('*Tang*'); *Goh Chok Tong v Jeyaretnam Joshua Benjamin* [1998] 2 SLR(R) 971 (Sing CA) ('*Goh*'); *Review Publishing* (n 10).

12 [2011] 3 SLR 778 (Sing CA).

13 [2015] 2 SLR 352 (Sing HC).

14 Andrew T Kenyon, 'Assuming Free Speech' (2014) 77 Modern Law Review 379, 379.

15 Robert C Post, *Democracy, Expertise, Academic Freedom: A First Amendment Jurisprudence for the Modern State* (Yale University Press 2012) 6.

16 Rodney Smolla argues that all three theories should be understood 'not as *mutually exclusive* defences of freedom of speech, but rather as *mutually supportive* rationales': Rodney A Smolla and Melville B Nimmer, *Smolla and Nimmer on Freedom of Speech: A Treatise on the First Amendment* (3rd edn, M Bender 2008) § 2:7. See also Rodney A Smolla, *Free Speech in an Open Society* (Knopf 1992) 14–17; Eric Barendt, *Freedom of Speech* (2nd edn, Oxford University Press 2005) 7–21. There have been different variations of the goals advanced by the First Amendment, but they cover essentially the same themes. Eg *Whitney v California* 274 US 357, 375 (1927) (Brandeis J) ('*Whitney*'); Thomas I Emerson, *The System of Freedom of Expression* (Random House 1970) 6; C Edwin Baker, *Human Liberty and Freedom of Speech* (Oxford University Press 1989) 47; Martin H Redish, 'The Value of Free Speech' (1982) 130 University of Pennsylvania Law Review 591, 593.

17 For an excellent review of such works, see eg Barendt (n 16) 1–36; Frederick Schauer, *Free Speech: A Philosophical Enquiry* (Cambridge University Press 1982) 35–46. See also John Stuart Mill, *On Liberty and Other Essays* (John Gray ed, Oxford University Press 1998); Alexander Meiklejohn, *Free Speech and Its Relation to Self-Government* (Harper Brothers Publishers 1948); Thomas I Emerson, *Toward A General Theory of the First Amendment* (Random House 1966); Ronald M Dworkin, *Freedom's Law* (Harvard University Press 1996).

18 *R v Secretary of State for the Home Department, ex p Simms* [2000] 2 AC 115 (HL) 126 (Lord Steyn). The European Court of Human Rights also remarked that communications of especial importance in a representative democracy include publications 'capable of contributing to a debate in a democratic society relating to politicians in the exercise of their functions': *Von Hannover v Germany* (2005) 40 EHRR 1 [63] ('*Von Hannover*').

19 *Abrams v United States* 250 US 616, 630 (1919) ('*Abrams*'). See also *Whitney* (n 16).

20 ibid.
21 Smolla and Nimmer (n 16) § 2:4.
22 *New York Times Co v Sullivan* 376 US 254, 270 (1964) ('*NYT*') as quoted in *NAACP v Claiborne Hardware Co* 458 US 886, 913 (1982) ('*NAACP*'); *Boos v Barry* 485 US 312, 318 (1988) ('*Boos*'). The democratic variant of the marketplace of ideas theory was first discussed in *Thornhill v Alabama* 310 US 88, 96, 101–02 (1940).
23 Post (n 15) xi.
24 Eg C Edwin Baker, 'Scope of the First Amendment Freedom of Speech' (1978) 5 UCLA Law Review 964, 990–91; Genevieve Blake, 'Expressive Merchandise and the First Amendment in Public Fora' (2007) 34 Fordham Urban Law Journal 1049, 1081–83.
25 *Procunier v Martinez* 416 US 396, 427 (1974).
26 Eg *Stanley v Georgia* 394 US 557, 565 (1969); *Cohen v California* 403 US 15, 26 (1971). For a useful discussion of this theory of the First Amendment, see Brian C Murchison, 'Speech and the Self-Realization Value' (1998) 33 Harvard Civil Rights-Civil Liberties Law Review 443. There has also been much criticism that individual self-actualisation or autonomy cannot provide a sound basis for the First Amendment. Eg Patrick M Garry, 'The First Amendment and Non-Political Speech: Exploring a Constitutional Model that Focuses on the Existence of Alternative Channels of Communication' (2007) 72 Missouri Law Review 477, 514; Stanley Ingber, 'Rediscovering the Communal Worth of Individual Rights: The First Amendment Institutional Contexts' (1990) 69 Texas Law Review 1, 19.
27 Eg n 18.
28 Tom Campbell, 'Rationales for Freedom of Communication' in Tom Campbell and Wojciech Sadurski (eds), *Freedom of Communication* (Dartmouth 1994) 33–34; Barendt (n 16) 13.
29 Eg Robert C Post, 'Reconciling Theory and Doctrine in First Amendment Jurisprudence' (2000) 88 California Law Review 2353, 2371. See also Barendt (n 16) 18–21; Dworkin (n 17) 15–26. Smolla refers to this as the 'democratic self-governance' rationale: Smolla and Nimmer (n 16) § 2:28.
30 Eg *Virginia v Black* 538 US 343, 365 (2003) ('*Black*'); *Reno v American Civil Liberties Union* 521 US 844, 885 (1997) ('*Reno*'); *Hustler Magazine Inc v Falwell* 485 US 46, 53 (1988) ('*Falwell*'); *Virginia State Board of Pharmacy v Virginia Citizens Consumer Council* 425 US 748, 765 (1976) ('*Virginia Pharmacy*'). At the Circuit level, see also *King v Federal Bureau of Prisons* 415 F 3d 634, 637 (7th Cir, 2005); *Prometheus Radio Project v FCC* 373 F 3d 372, 435 (3rd Cir, 2004); *United States v Rowlee* 899 F 2d 1275, 1278 (2nd Cir, 1990).
31 Eg Post (n 15); Robert C Post, 'Meiklejohn's Mistake: Individual Autonomy and the Reform of Public Discourse' (1993) 64 University of Colorado Law Review 1109; Robert C Post, 'The Constitutional Concept of Public Discourse: Outrageous Opinion, Democratic Deliberation, and *Hustler Magazine v Falwell* (1990) 103 Harvard Law Review 601 ('Constitutional Concept').
32 Eg Cass R Sunstein, *Democracy and the Problem of Free Speech* (The Free Press 1993) 17–23, 241–52; Cass R Sunstein, *Designing Democracy: What Constitutions Do* (Oxford University Press 2001) 6–9, 96–101, 239–423.
33 Balkin argues that the purpose of free speech is to promote a

> 'democratic culture' that is even broader than deliberation about public issues such that each individual has 'a fair chance to participate in the production of culture, and in the development of the ideas and meanings that constitute them and the communities and subcommunities to which they belong.
>
> Jack M Balkin, 'Digital Speech and Democratic Culture: A Theory of Freedom of Expression for the Information Society' (2004) 79 New York University Law Review 1, 4

See also Jack M Balkin, 'Populism and Progressivism as Constitutional Categories' (1995) 104 Yale Law Journal 1935, 1948–1949.

34 Eg Alexander Meiklejohn, *Political Freedom: The Constitutional Powers of the People* (Oxford University Press 1965) 19–28.

35 Eg Dworkin (n 17) 15–26.

36 Eg Owen M Fiss, 'Free Speech and Social Structure' (1986) 71 Iowa Law Review 1405, 1409–10.

37 Stephen Breyer, 'Lecture: Our Democratic Constitution' (2002) 77 New York University Law Review 245, 246. The participatory theory also appears to have the support of Brian Murchison who, through an analysis of judgments of the Supreme Court, contends that the 'self-governance value' underpins the First Amendment: Brian C Murchison, 'Speech and the Self-Governance Value' (2006) 14 William & Mary Bill of Rights Journal 1251, 1291.

38 *Globe Newspaper Co v Superior Court* 457 US 596, 604 (1982). See also Post (n 29) 2369. See also Barendt (n 16) 48–49.

39 Post (n 15) 15.

40 Robert C Post, 'Understanding the First Amendment' (2012) 87 Washington Law Review 549, 553.

41 Robert C Post, 'Participatory Democracy and Free Speech' (2011) 97 Virginia Law Review 477, 562.

42 Post (n 15) 15.

43 Eg *R (Animal Defenders International) v Secretary of State for Culture, Media and Sport* [2008] UKHL 15; [2008] 1 AC 1312 (HL) [27]–[28], [48]; *Grant v Torstar Corp* [2009] 3 SCR 640 (Supreme Court of Canada (Canada SC)) [1]; *Lange v Australian Broadcasting Corporation* (1997) 189 CLR 520 (High Court of Australia (Australia HC)) 557–62.

44 Freedom of political debate is accepted to be at the 'very core of the concept of democratic society which prevails throughout the Convention': *Lingens v Austria* (1986) 8 EHRR 103 [42]. See also *Özgür Gündem v Turkey* (2001) 31 EHRR 1082 [43]; *Von Hannover* (n 18) [58]–[59].

45 Singapore Constitution (n 6) Art 14.

46 Thio (n 11).

47 Singapore Constitution (n 6) Art 4, 'This Constitution is the supreme law of the Republic of Singapore and any law enacted by the Legislature after the commencement of this Constitution which is inconsistent with this Constitution shall, to the extent of the inconsistency, be void.'

48 Thio (n 11). See eg *Jeyaretnam* (n 11); *Tang* (n 11); *Goh* (n 11); *Review Publishing* (n 10). This may be contrasted with the more liberal approach of the Federal Court of Malaysia in recent years. Eg *Sivarasa Rasiah v Badan Peguam Malaysia* [2010] 3 CLJ 507 (Federal Court of Malaysia (Malaysia FC)) [3] ('the provisions of the Constitution, in particular the fundamental liberties guaranteed under Part II, must be generously interpreted and that a prismatic approach to interpretation must be adopted').

49 The vertical application of the First Amendment – including content/viewpoint discrimination, time-place-manner restrictions and public forum doctrine – is beyond the scope of this chapter. However, in terms of its horizontal effect in common law defamation, the Supreme Court has imposed the actual malice standard with respect to public figure plaintiffs. See *NYT* (n 22); *Gertz v Robert Welch Inc* 418 US 323, 344–45 (1974). Under the *NYT/Gertz* rules, the public official who is defamed in the USA today has little ability to correct a falsehood published about him or her in the media. In *Dun & Bradstreet Inc v Greenmoss Inc*, Justice White issued a trenchant warning about the diabolical effects of the actual malice standard: 472 US 749, 769 (1985). Nevertheless, the Supreme Court has steadfastly refused to establish judicial standards of conduct relating to responsible journalism. Eg *Curtis Publishing v Butts*

388 US 130, 164–65 (1966); *Miami Herald Publishing Co v Tornillo* 418 US 241, 247–58 (1974). For criticisms of the actual malice standard, see, eg Benjamin Barron, 'A Proposal to Rescue *New York Times v Sullivan* by Promoting a Responsible Press' (2007) 57 American University Law Review 73.

50 This has been well chronicled in a number of publications. Eg Thio Li-ann, 'An "i" for an "I": Singapore's Communitarian Model of Constitutional Adjudication' (1997) 27 Hong Kong Law Journal 152; Kishore Mahbubani, 'The Dangers of Decadence: What the Rest Can Teach the West' (1993) 72(4) Foreign Affairs 10; Bilahari Kausikan, 'Asia's Different Standard' (1993) 92 Foreign Policy 24; Melanie Chew, 'Human Rights in Singapore: Perceptions and Problems' (1994) 34(11) Asian Survey 933. cf eg Aryeh Neier, 'Asia's Unacceptable Standard' (1993) 92 Foreign Policy 42; Tommy Koh, *The Quest for World Order: Perspectives of a Pragmatic Idealist* (Institute of Policy Studies 1998) 352–66.

51 Thio Li-ann, 'Between Apology and Apogee, Autochthony: The "Rule of Law" Beyond the Rules of Law in Singapore' (2012) Singapore Journal of Legal Studies 269, 283. Thio also suggests that (at 283):

> [P]aternal democracy captures the changing nature of the relationship between the Singapore government and the governed as reflected in the government's self-perception, institutional developments, the rules of engagement with respect to the conduct of public debate which are in flux.

52 ibid 279.

53 ibid 297.

54 See the discussion in Thio Li-ann, 'Principled pragmatism and the "third wave" of communitarian judicial review in Singapore', Chapter 4.

55 Singapore, *Shared Values* (White Paper, Cm 1, 1991) ('*Shared Values*'). The shared values identified are: nation before community and society above self; upholding the family as the basic building block of society; resolving major issues through consensus rather than contention; and stressing racial and religious harmony.

56 Thio (n 11) 519.

57 Chew (n 50) 945. See also Lee Kuan Yew, *From Third World to First: The Singapore Story: 1965–2000* (HarperCollins Publishers 2000) 760–63.

58 See VK Rajah, 'Interpreting the Singapore Constitution', Chapter 1. The Attorney-General also noted (at p 24), 'But fidelity to the constitutional text does not stop at giving effect to the literal meaning of the text. Sometimes value judgments have to be made in interpreting and applying the Constitution.'

59 Jack M Balkin, *Living Originalism* (Belknap Press 2011) 46.

60 Rajah (n 58) 4.

61 For an excellent analysis, see Vicki C Jackson, 'Constitutions as "Living Trees"? Comparative Constitutional Law and Interpretive Metaphors' (2006) 75 Fordham Law Review 921.

62 Balkin (n 59) 46.

63 ibid 278.

64 ibid 279.

65 See discussion in Yap Po Jen, 'Uncovering originalism and textualism in Singapore', Chapter 5.

66 *Review Publishing* (n 10) [265]–[297].

67 Eg Eric Barendt, *Freedom of Speech* (2nd edn, Oxford University Press 2005) 21–23; Frederick Schauer, *Free Speech: A Philosophical Enquiry* (Cambridge University Press 1982) 85–86.

68 Eg *Shared Values* (n 55) [41]. This has been observed to be 'an unusually well-defined, explicit state ideology': Adrienne Stone, Rishad Chowdhury and Martin Clark, 'The Comparative Constitutional Law of Freedom of Expression in Asia' in Dixon and Ginsburg (eds), *Comparative Constitutional Law in Asia* (n 4) 227, 236.

69 *Shared Values* (n 55) [46].
70 ibid [9].
71 ibid [40].
72 M Ulric Killion, 'Post-WTO China and Independent Judicial Review' (2004) 26 Houston Journal of International Law 507, 516–17.
73 Tom Plate, *Conversations with Lee Kuan Yew – Citizen Singapore: How to Build a Nation* (Marshall Cavendish Editions 2010) 177.
74 Eg William Theodore De Bary, *Asian Values and Human Rights: A Confucian Communitarian Perspective* (Harvard University Press 1998) 17–40.
75 ibid 33. See also Jeremy T Paltiel, 'Cultural and Political Determinants of the Chinese Approach to Human Rights' in Errol P Mendes and Anne-Marie Traeholt (eds), *Human Rights: Chinese and Canadian Perspectives* (Human Rights Research and Education Centre, University of Ottawa 1997) 25.
76 Joseph Chan, 'A Confucian Perspective on Human Rights for Contemporary China' in Joanne R Bauer and Daniel A Bell (eds), *The East Asian Challenge for Human Rights* (Cambridge University Press 1999) 212, 228 (emphasis added).
77 ibid 229.
78 De Bary (n 74) 109–16.
79 According to former Chief Justice Chan Sek Keong, 'good government' refers to 'pursuing good policies in building a modern successful society, and not in turning it into an economically or socially failed state', while 'good governance' refers to 'the institutional rules of procedure and decision-making processes of administrative bodies in implementing government policies in accordance with the law': Chan Sek Keong, 'Judical Review – From Angst to Empathy' (2010) 22 Singapore Academy of Law Journal 469, 471–72.
80 Leonard Apcar, Wayne Arnold and Seth Mydans, 'Excerpts from an Interview with Lee Kuan Yew' *The New York Times* (New York, 29 August 2007) www.nytimes.com/2007/08/29/world/asia/29iht-lee-excerpts.html?ref=asia accessed 15 August 2015 ('Lee Interview'). Lee Kuan Yew stepped down as Prime Minister in 1990 and was appointed Senior Minister and then reappointed Minister Mentor from 2004–2011. Lee stepped down from Cabinet after the 2011 General Elections and passed away on 23 March 2015.
81 ibid See also Koh (n 50) 356–66.
82 Lee Interview (n 80).
83 Lee believed in a government of elected parliamentarians who would be accountable to the electorate, and that a Western-style Westminster system of parliamentary democracy would be adjusted to fit the needs and requirements of Asian societies with an emphasis on good government. Eg Alex Josey, *Lee Kuan Yew: The Crucial Years* (Times Books International 1968) 65–71; Lee, *From Third World to First* (n 57) 547–49; Lee Kuan Yew, 'What People Want is Good Government' (Keynote Address at Create 21 Asahi Forum, Tokyo, 20 November 1992) as quoted in Han Fook Kwang, Warren Fernandez and Sumiko Tan, *Lee Kuan Yew: The Man and His Ideas* (Singapore Press Holdings 1998) 381. However, a pragmatic ideology nonetheless pervades government decision-making. See Beng-Huat Chua, *Communitarian Ideology and Democracy in Singapore* (Routledge 1995) 57–78.
84 Eg Christine Sypnowich, 'Ruling or Overruled? The People, Rights and Democracy' (2007) 27 Oxford Journal of Legal Studies 757, 765. Other more sophisticated and developed democracies – or idealised democracies – may require principles of liberty, egalitarianism and reciprocity to be adhered to. Eg Ronald Dworkin, *A Bill of Rights for Britain* (Chatto & Windus 1990) 35; Wil Waluchow, *A Common Law Theory of Judicial Review: The Living Tree* (Cambridge University Press 2007) 106–09; Amy Guttman and Dennis Thompson, *Democracy and Disagreement* (Harvard University Press 1996) 93. For a description of different forms of democracy, including the meaning of a 'pragmatic democracy', see Peter N Amponsah,

Libel Law, Political Criticism, and Defamation of Public Figures: The United States, Europe and Australia (LFB Scholarly Publishing LLC 2004) 9–17.

85 The National Pledge, http://app.singapore.sg/about-singapore/national-symbols/national-pledge.

86 ibid, emphasis added.

87 *Shared Values* (n 55) [51]. The other four stars represent equality, peace, progress and justice.

88 Eg Singapore Parliamentary Debates, Official Report (16 May 2001) vol 73, col 1726 (Wong Kan Seng (Minister for Home Affairs)). See also *Shared Values* (n 55) [29], [47], [48], [51]. It was also proposed by academic commentator Jon Quah that national values of 'honest government' as well as 'compassion for the less fortunate' be included to supplement the four shared values. See Jon ST Quah, 'Searching for Singapore's National Values' in Jon ST Quah (ed), *In Search of Singapore's National Values* (Times Academic Press for the Institute of Policy Studies 1990) 91, 98–101.

89 Lee Keynote Address (n 83) 380.

90 Eg Koh (n 50) 365. See also ibid 208 (explaining the elements of 'good governance').

91 Eg Han, Fernandez and Tan (n 83) 380–83. It has also been emphasised on numerous occasions by Lee Kuan Yew that Singapore is built on a system of good government by *good* men. Eg ibid 87–101.

92 *Reynolds v Times Newspapers Ltd* [2001] 2 AC 127 (HL) 200.

93 ibid 195. While the UK Parliament had abolished the Reynolds privilege in 2013, its statutory replacement in section 4 of the Defamation Act 2013 – a defence on matter of public interest – is substantially similar to the common law privilege.

94 The traditional qualified privilege defence is also known as the duty-interest privilege. See *Adam v Ward* [1917] AC 309 (HL) 334. In *Jameel*, Lord Hoffmann and Lady Hale viewed the qualified privilege as being of a 'different jurisprudential creature', which evolved from the traditional qualified privilege: *Jameel (Mohammed) v Wall Street Journal Europe Sprl (No. 3)* [2007] 1 AC 359 (HL) [50], [146]. Nevertheless, under the broader *Reynolds* privilege, 'where a publication related to a matter of public interest, it was accepted that the reciprocal duty and interest could be found even where publication was by a newspaper to a section of the public or the public at large': *Jameel* ibid [29].

95 *Reynolds* (n 92) 200.

96 *Seaga v Harper* [2009] 1 AC 1 (PC) 9 ('*Seaga*'). It was also clarified by the House of Lords that the *Reynolds* privilege was not confined only to media defendants but was also available to any individual who published material of public interest in any medium. See *Jameel* (n 94) [54].

97 [2012] UKSC 11 [44] ('*Flood III*').

98 *Jameel* (n 94) 377.

99 Andrew T Kenyon and Ang Hean Leng, '*Reynolds* Privilege, Common Law Defamation and Malaysia' (2010) Singapore Journal of Legal Studies 256, 278.

100 David Tan, 'The *Reynolds* Privilege in a Neo-Confucianist Communitarian Democracy: Reinvigorating Freedom of Political Communication in Singapore' (2011) Singapore Journal of Legal Studies 456, 478.

101 *Jameel* (n 94) 377 (Lord Bingham), 384 (Lord Hoffmann).

102 Eg *Flood III* (n 97) [75] (Lord Phillips), [124] (Lord Mance).

103 Eg *Jameel* (n 94); *Seaga* (n 96).

104 Eg *James Gilbert Ltd v MGN* [2000] EMLR 680 (QB); *Grobbelaar v News Group Newspapers* [2001] 2 All ER 437 (CA); *Loutchansky v Times Newspaper (No 2)* [2002] QB 783; *Galloway v Telegraph Group* [2006] EWCA Civ 17, [2006] EMLR 221; *Malik v Newspost Ltd* [2008] QB 502; *Radu v Houston* [2008] EWCA Civ 921 ('*Radu*').

105 Andrew T Kenyon, *Defamation: Comparative Law and Practice* (UCL Press 2006) 209. See also Eric Barendt, 'Balancing Freedom of Expression and the Right to Reputation: Reflections on *Reynolds* and Reportage' (2012) 63 Northern Ireland Legal Quarterly 59, 61.
106 ibid [122], [138].
107 *Grant v Torstar Corp* [2009] 3 SCR 640 (Canada SC) ('*Grant*'); *Cusson v Quan* [2009] 3 SCR 712 (Canada SC) ('*Cusson*').
108 *Nationwide News Pty Ltd v Wills* (1992) 177 CLR 1 (Australia HC) ('*Nationwide News*'); *Australian Capital Television Pty Ltd v Commonwealth* (1992) 177 CLR 106 (Australia HC) ('*ACTV*'). See also Dan Meagher, 'What is Political Communication: The Rationale of the Implied Freedom of Political Communication' (2004) 28 Melbourne University Law Review 438; Adrienne Stone, 'Freedom of Political Communication, the Constitution and the Common Law' (1998) 26 Federal Law Review 219.
109 Eg *ACTV* (n 108) 142; *Theophanous v Herald & Weekly Times Ltd* (1994) 182 CLR 104 (Australia HC) 121–23 ('*Theophanous*').
110 *ACTV* (n 108) 217.
111 (1997) 189 CLR 520 (Australia HC) 559–60, 566 ('*Lange*').
112 ibid 520, 560. It is however not confined to election periods. ibid 561–62. See also *Levy v Victoria* (1997) 189 CLR 579 (Australia HC) 606 ('*Levy*').
113 Adrienne Stone, 'Australia's Constitutional Rights and the Problem of Interpretive Disagreement' (2005) 27 Sydney Law Review 29, 33. See also *Lange* (n 111) 560 ('These sections do not confer personal rights on individuals.'); *Cunliffe v Commonwealth* (1994) 182 CLR 272 (Australia HC) 327.
114 Eg *Theophanous* (n 109) 125–26; *Lange* (n 111) 560, 567, 575; *Levy* (n 112) 622.
115 *Lange* (n 111) 568.
116 Eg *Jeyaretnam* (n 11) 818 (citing *Campbell v Spottiswoode* (1863) 32 LJ QB 185, 200 (Cockburn CJ)).
117 *Lange* (n 111) 571.
118 Amponsah (n 84) 77–78.
119 *Lange* (n 111) 575. See also *Stephens v West Australian Newspapers Ltd* (1994) 182 CLR 211 (Australia HC) 252–53.
120 Andrew Lynch, 'Unanimity in a Time of Uncertainty: The High Court settles its differences in *Lange v Australian Broadcasting Corporation*' (1997) 6 Griffith Law Review 211, 217.
121 *Lange* (n 111) 560–61. This concept of political communication was also referred to in *Reynolds*. See *Reynolds* (n 92) 200. In *Hinch*, French CJ was of the view that

> [t]he range of matters that may be characterised as 'governmental and political matters' for the purpose of the implied freedom is broad. They are not limited to matters concerning the current functioning of government. They arguably include social and economic features of Australian society.
>
> *Hogan v Hinch* [2011] HCA 4 [49]

In Canada, the Supreme Court would consider public interest to cover even a broader range of topics than in Australia, holding that the public 'has a genuine stake in knowing about many matters, ranging from science and the arts to the environment, religion, and morality': *Grant* (n 107) [106].
122 *Reynolds* (n 92) 200.
123 ibid 201.
124 Article 10 of the European Convention on Human Rights and Fundamental Freedoms (ECHR) states, inter alia, that, 'Everyone has the right to freedom of expression. This right shall include freedom to hold opinions and to receive and impart information and ideas without interference by public authority and regardless of frontiers': Convention for the Protection of Human Rights and Fundamental Freedoms (ECHR, as amended) Art 10.

125 [1990] 2 All ER 103 (PC) 106.
126 ibid.
127 William G Buss, 'Alexander Meiklejohn, American Constitutional Law, and Australia's Implied Freedom of Political Communication' (2006) 34 Federal Law Review 421, 427.
128 *Vellama d/o Marie Muthu v Attorney-General* [2013] 4 SLR 1 (Sing CA) [79] (emphasis added).
129 Chan Sek Keong, 'Opening Address: Singapore Academy of Law Conference 2011 – Developments in Singapore Law 2006–2010' (Singapore, 24 February 2011) [14] ('[f]reedom of speech in Singapore is also a higher legal order right because it is a constitutional right under Art 14 of the Constitution').
130 ibid 171.
131 ibid 166.
132 Koh (n 50).
133 Senior Minister Goh Chok Tong, *Speech at the NTU Students' Union Ministerial Forum* (Singapore, 29 October 2010) www.news.gov.sg/public/sgpc/en/media_releases/agencies/micacsd/speech/S-20101029–1 [26] accessed 15 August 2015.
134 See eg Zuraidah Ibrahim, '81–6: Workers' Party wins Aljunied GRC; PAP vote share dips to 60.1%' *The Sunday Times* (Singapore, 8 May 2011) 1, 4.
135 'PAP's share of vote declines again' *The Sunday Times* (Singapore, 8 May 2011), 13.
136 'Pledge to serve responsibly and humbly' *The Sunday Times* (Singapore, 8 May 2011) 3.
137 '3Ps behind PAP's image problem' *The Straits Times* (Singapore, 27 May 2011) A28.
138 Thio (n 51) 285 (referring to Letter from the Prime Minister's Office to all PAP MPs reported in 'PM Lee's letter to MPs' *Asiaone News* (Singapore, 28 May 2011), http://news.asiaone.com/News/AsiaOne+News/Singapore/Story/A1Story20110528–281111.html accessed 15 August 2015). In that communique, PM Lee stated:

> Singapore is in a new phase of its political development. The PAP government has to operate and govern in a different way than before. But, two things should not change. First, we must always hold fast to the spirit of service to the people, and work hard on their behalf. Second, we must never compromise the high standards of honesty and integrity, which have enabled the PAP to keep trust with the people all these decades.

139 *Review Publishing* (n 10) 178.
140 ibid.
141 In *Lenah Game Meats*, Kirby J also pointed out that the US First Amendment 'has no counterpart in the Australian Constitution' and that analogous First Amendment principles have been rejected by both the High Court and the House of Lords; the public interest in free speech will not always trump individual interests: *Australian Broadcasting Corporation v Lenah Game Meats Pty Ltd* (2001) 208 CLR 199 (Australia HC) 283, 285.
142 *Levy* (n 112) 622 (McHugh J). See also ibid 594 (Brennan CJ), 641 (Kirby J).
143 *Lange* (n 111) 571.
144 Thio (n 46) 523.
145 Koh (n 50) 208. It is worth noting that just before taking office in 2004, PM Lee had delivered a speech urging citizens not to be 'passive bystanders' but to 'debate issues with reason, passion and conviction'. See Thio (n 51) 286 (citing Lee Hsien Loong, 'Building a Civic Society' (Speech delivered at the Harvard Club of Singapore's 35th Anniversary Dinner, Singapore, 6 January 2004) unpan1.un.org/intradoc/groups/public/documents/APCITY/UNPAN015426.pdf accessed 15 August 2015).
146 (1994) 182 CLR 211 (Australia HC) 264.

147 Parliamentary Elections Act (Cap 218, 2011 Rev Ed) s 43. See also Singapore Constitution (n 6) Art 39(1)(a) ('Parliament shall consist of – such number of elected Members as is required to be returned at a *general election by the constituencies* prescribed by or under any law made by the Legislature.') (emphasis added).
148 Anne-Marie Slaughter, *A New World Order* (Princeton University Press 2004) 78.
149 ibid 79–80.
150 ibid 69–79. See also Christopher McCrudden, 'A Common Law of Human Rights?: Transnational Judicial Conversations on Constitutional Rights' (2000) 20 Oxford Journal of Legal Studies 499; Sujit Choudhry, 'Globalization in Search of Justification: Toward a Theory of Comparative Constitutional Interpretation' (1999) 74 Indiana Law Journal 819.
151 ibid 75. See also Frederick Schauer, 'The Politics and Incentives of Legal Transplantation' in Joseph S Nye and John D Donahue (eds), *Governance in a Globalizing World* (Brookings Institution Press 2000) 253, 256–58.
152 *Lange* (n 111) 571–75.
153 Buss (n 127) 435.
154 Eg Buss (n 127) 434–35; Stone (n 108) 227–45; Adrienne Stone, 'The Australian Free Speech Experiment and Scepticism about UK Human Rights Act' in Tom Campbell, KD Ewing and Adam Tomkins (eds), *Sceptical Essays on Human Rights* (Oxford University Press 2001) 391, 395–99.
155 Defamation Act (Cap 75, 2014 Rev Ed). One should also note other legislative limitations on the application of qualified privilege pertaining to publication in respect of any such report or matter as stipulated in Part II of the Schedule (s 12(2)) and to statements in elections (s 14).
156 Eg Application of English Law Act (Cap 7A, 1994 Rev Ed) s 3. See also *Pang Koi Fa v Lim Djoe Phing* [1993] 2 SLR(R) 366 (Sing HC) [22]:

> The courts in Singapore are not strictly bound by decisions of the English courts in the sense that the courts in England are not part of the hierarchy of courts in Singapore, this being especially true since legislative amendments have limited appeals to the Judicial Committee of the Privy Council; nonetheless, in respect of decisions in common law, particularly in the area of tort in general and negligence in particular, decisions of the highest court in England should be highly persuasive if not practically binding.

157 *Review Publishing* (n 10) 173–76.
158 ibid (citing *Crampton v Nugawela* (1996) 41 NSWLR 176 (Supreme Court of New South Wales (New South Wales SC)) 193).
159 Chan Sek Keong, 'Securing and Maintaining the Independence of the Court in Judicial Proceedings' (2010) 22 Singapore Academy of Law Journal 229, 230 (citing Lydia Brashear Tiede, 'Judicial Independence: Often Cited, Rarely Understood' (2006) 15 Journal of Contemporary Legal Issues 129, 129).
160 *Review Publishing* (n 10) 175.
161 *Lim Eng Hock Peter v Lin Jian Wei and another and another appeal* [2010] SGCA 26 (Sing CA) [13].
162 *Reynolds* (n 92) 205.
163 Eg *Flood v Times Newspapers Ltd* [2010] EWCA Civ 804; [2010] EMLR 26.
164 *Grant* (n 107) [52].
165 ibid [53].
166 The issues involving trial by jury as highlighted by the English courts and academic commentators will be of limited relevance in a Singapore context of trial by judge. Eg *Loutchansky v Times Newspapers* [2001] EMLR 38 (QB); *Gregson v Channel Four Television* [2002] EWCA Civ 941; Andrew T Kenyon, *Defamation: Comparative Law and Practice* (UCL Press 2006) 209–11; Paul Mitchell, *The Making of the Modern English Law of Defamation* (Hart Publishing 2000) 117.

167 [2014] SGHC 230 (Sing HC) ('*Ngerng*').

168 ibid [13]–[14].

169 The Central Provident Fund (CPF) is a comprehensive social security system that enables working Singapore citizens and Permanent Residents to set aside funds for retirement. It also covers healthcare, home ownership, family protection and asset enhancement. As at March 2014, it had 3.53 million members and S$260 billion under management. See Central Provident Fund Board, 'CPF Overview' https://mycpf.cpf.gov.sg/members/aboutus/about-us-info/cpf-overview accessed 15 August 2015; Central Provident Fund Board, 'CPF: How It Works' https://mycpf.cpf.gov.sg/Assets/common/PublishingImages/CPFHowItWorks.jpg accessed 15 August 2015.

170 *Attorney-General v Wong Hong Toy* [1982–1983] SLR 398 (Sing HC) 403.

171 *Attorney-General v Pang Cheng Lian and Others* [1972–1974] SLR 658 (Sing HC) 662 (following *R v Gray* [1900] 2 QB 36, 40 (Lord Russell CJ)).

172 *R v Davies* [1906] 1 KB 32, 40.

173 *Attorney-General v Hertzberg Daniel* [2009] 1 SLR(R) 1103 (Sing HC) [21] ('*Hertzberg*'). It has also received much recent academic attention. See eg, Kim Gould, 'Scandalising Contempt in Australia: Dead? Dying? In much Danger? … (not!) …' (2010) 15 Media & Arts Law Review 23; Eli Fisher, 'The Courts' Scandal: Scandalising the Courts in Australia' (2011) 16 Media & Arts Law Review 73; Tsun Hang Tey, 'Scandalising the Singapore Judiciary' (2010) 12 Australian Journal of Asian Law 59.

174 *Sunday Times v United Kingdom* (1979–80) 2 EHRR 245 [36] ('*Sunday Times*'). See also *Attorney-General v Times Newspaper Ltd* [1974] AC 273 (HL). It should be noted that *Sunday Times* did not concern conduct scandalising the judiciary but was an appeal to the European Court of Human Rights regarding an injunction restraining publication of an article with the aim of assisting parents of 'thalidomide children' to obtain a more generous settlement in legal proceedings against the drug manufacturers. The court by 11 votes to 9 found that the restriction was not justified by a 'pressing social need' and could not be regarded as 'necessary' within the meaning of Art 10(2) of the European Convention on Human Rights. The dissenters disagreed with the majority's holding on the necessity of interference with regard to the due administration of justice and the margin of appreciation that is to be allowed to the national authorities.

175 *Sunday Times* (n 174) [18].

176 Contempt of Court Act 1981 (UK) ss 1–4. There is also a saving provision that gives effect to the discussion of matters of public interest where

> [a] publication made as or as part of a discussion in good faith of public affairs or other matters of general public interest is not to be treated as a contempt of court under the strict liability rule if the risk of impediment or prejudice to particular legal proceedings is merely incidental to the discussion

ibid s 5.

177 Crime and Courts Act 2013 (UK) s 33. See also The Law Commission, 'Contempt of Court: Scandalising the Court' (2012) www.lawcom.gov.uk/wp-content/uploads/2015/06/lc335_scandalising_the_court.pdf accessed 15 August 2015.

178 [1974] 1 AC 273 (HL) 307 ('*Times Newspaper*') (as cited in *Attorney-General v Shadrake Alan* [2010] 2 SLR 445 (Sing HC) [7] ('*Shadrake I*')).

179 ibid 309 (as cited in *Shadrake I* (n 178) [7]).

180 Fisher (n 173) 82.

181 Amnon Reichman, 'The Dimensions of Law: Judicial Craft, Its Public Perception, and the Role of the Scholar' (2007) 95 California Law Review 1619, 1623. See also Paul Mishkin, 'The Uses of Ambivalence: Reflections on the Supreme Court and the Constitutionality of Affirmative Action' (1983) 131 University of Pennsylvania Law Review 907, 929, 930 (arguing that 'the Court … must rest its decision

on an analytically sound principle', that is, a notion 'which transcends the particular case, [that] is rationally defensible on those general terms, and [that] is analytically adequate to support the result').

182 Lawrence Baum and Neal Devins, 'Why the Supreme Court Cares About Elites, Not the American People' (2010) 98 Georgetown Law Journal 1515, 1520 (citing Jeffrey Rosen (Op-Ed), 'The Trial of John Roberts' *The New York Times* (New York, 13 September 2009) WK18).

183 Margaret Tarkington, 'A Free Speech Right to Impugn the Judiciary in Court Proceedings' (2010) 51 Boston College Law Review 363, 363–64.

184 ibid 364. See also Margaret Tarkington, 'The Truth Be Damned: The First Amendment, Attorney Speech, and Judicial Reputation' (2009) 97 Georgetown Law Journal 1567, 1569, 1571–72, 1587–91.

185 *Shadrake I* (n 178) (Quentin Loh J). See also *Attorney-General v Shadrake Alan* [2010] 2 SLR 506 (Sing HC) [3] (Quentin Loh J) ('*Shadrake II*') (where the Appellant was sentenced to six weeks' imprisonment and a fine of $20,000).

186 ibid [77].

187 ibid.

188 Eg *Attorney-General v Wain Barry* [1991] 1 SLR(R) 85 (Sing HC) ('*Wain*'); *Attorney-General v Lingle* [1995] 1 SLR(R) 199 (Sing HC) ('*Lingle*'); *Attorney-General v Chee Soon Juan* [2006] 2 SLR(R) 650 (Sing HC)('*Chee*'); *Hertzberg* (n 173); *Attorney-General v Tan Liang Joo John* [2009] 2 SLR(R) 1132 (Sing HC) ('*Tan*').

189 Article 14 of the Singapore Constitution states, inter alia, that:

> 14 (1) Subject to clauses (2) and (3) —
> (a) every citizen of Singapore has the right to freedom of speech and expression;
>
> ...
>
> (2) Parliament may by law impose —
> (a) on the rights conferred by clause (1)(a), such restrictions as it considers necessary or expedient in the interest of the security of Singapore or any part thereof, friendly relations with other countries, public order or morality and restrictions designed to protect the privileges of Parliament or *to provide against contempt of court*, defamation or incitement to any offence.

Singapore Constitution (n 6) Art 14 (emphasis added). But, the Singapore Parliament has not enacted relevant legislation governing the appropriate test to be applied to determine contempt of court. There are, however, laws in place for criminal contempt and for both the subordinate courts and the Supreme Court to punish acts of contempt. Eg Criminal Procedure Code (Cap 68, 1985 Rev Ed); Subordinate Courts Act (Cap 321, 2007 Rev Ed); Supreme Court of Judicature Act (Cap 322, 2007 Rev Ed).

190 [2011] 3 SLR 778 (Sing CA) [57] ('*Shadrake III*').

191 ibid [149].

192 ibid [153]. The court also held that '[t]here are also no mitigating factors, whatsoever, in this case that could possibly be considered in the Appellant's favour' and 'that there has not been an iota of remorse demonstrated by the Appellant who continues to stand by the statements made': ibid [151].

193 Eg *R v Duffy, ex p Nash* [1960] 2 QB 188, 200; *Times Newspaper* (n 178) 298–99, 312.

194 Eg *R v Hoser and Kotabi Pty Ltd* [2001] VSC 443 (Supreme Court of Victoria (Victoria SC)) [55], [226]; *McGuirk v University of NSW* [2009] NSWSC 1058 (New South Wales SC) [239]–[272].

195 Eg *Solicitor-General v Radio Avon Ltd* [1978] 1 NZLR 225 (Wellington Court of Appeal (Wellington CA)) 234.

196 Eg *Wong Yeung Ng v Secretary of Justice* [1999] 3 HKC 143 (Hong Kong Court of Final Appeal (Hong Kong CFA) [13] (affirming *Wong Yeung Ng v Secretary for Justice* [1999] 2 HKC 24 (Hong Kong CFA); *Secretary for Justice v Oriental Press Group Ltd and others* [1998] 2 HKC 627 (Hong Kong Court of First Instance (Hong Kong CFI) [55]).

197 *Shadrake I* (n 178) [53].

198 The Court of Appeal observed that 'justice is not a cloistered virtue but a public one' [citing *Ambard v Attorney-General for Trinidad and Tobago* [1936] AC 322 (PC) 335 (Lord Atkin)]. The court also cited its own decision in *Pertamina Energy Trading Ltd v Karaha Bodas Co LLC* [2007] 2 SLR(R) 518 (Sing CA) [22] ('It is imperative to note … that the doctrine of contempt of court is not intended, in any manner or fashion whatsoever, to protect the dignity of the judges as such; its purpose is more objective and is [more importantly] rooted in the public interest.').

199 *Shadrake III* (n 190) [17].

200 Thio (n 11) 519.

201 Eg *Chee* (n 188) and *Hertzberg* (n 173).

202 VK Rajah JA is a judge on the Court of Appeal. He has pronounced that '[a] culture of openness has long since taken firm root in our courts, with mistakes being acknowledged openly rather than being papered over'. See *Shadrake I* (n 178) [76], citing *Tan Lai Kiat v Public Prosecutor* [2010] 3 SLR 1042 (Sing HC) [63] (Rajah JA).

203 *Shadrake I* (n 178) [67].

204 ibid [68].

205 ibid [70] (referring to *Tan* (n 188) [15]–[23]). See also *Lingle* (n 188) 700 (referring to *Ambard* (n 198) 335). See also *Shadrake I* (n 178) [72]–[75] (where Loh J sets out the elements of the defence of fair criticism).

206 ibid [76].

207 *Lingle* (n 188) 701 ('This right to criticise is, however, exceeded and contempt of court is committed if the publication impugns the integrity and impartiality of the court, even if it is not so intended.').

208 [2009] 1 SLR 642 (Sing HC) [173]:

> The criticism of a judge's conduct or the conduct of the court does not constitute contempt of court so long as fair criticism is not exceeded, ie, so long as the criticism is fair, temperate, made in good faith and not directed at the personal character of a judge or at the impartiality of a judge or a court.

209 *Hertzberg* (n 173) [54] ('[s]o long as the criticism is within the boundaries of "reasonable argument or expostulation", is made in good faith and is not directed at the impartiality of the courts or seeks to impute improper motives to the judges, it will not constitute contempt of court').

210 *Shadrake III* (n 190) [60]–[67].

211 ibid [70].

212 ibid [71]–[73].

213 ibid [68].

214 ibid [81]–[85]. See also ibid [86]:

> In approaching this concept, the court should bear in mind the various factors set out (albeit non-exhaustively) in *Tan Liang Joo John* … The court ought always to apply this concept not only in relation to *the precise facts and context but also bearing in mind the following key question throughout*: does the impugned statement constitute fair criticism, or does it go on to cross the legal line by posing a real risk of undermining public confidence in the administration of justice – in which case it would constitute contempt instead? (emphasis in original).

215 ibid [78].

216 *Tan* (n 188) [19].
217 Louis Fisher, 'Judicial Credibility' in Bruce Peabody (ed), *The Politics of Judicial Independence: Courts, Politics, and the Public* (Johns Hopkins University Press 2011) 225, 225.
218 Fisher, ibid.
219 ibid 226.
220 Joseph Chan, 'A Confucian Perspective on Human Rights for Contemporary China' in Bauer and Bell (eds), *The East Asian Challenge for Human Rights* (n 76) 212, 233.
221 See generally, *Review Publishing* (n 10) 175–88; *Reynolds* (n 92) 200–04.
222 Thio (n 51) 296 (citing *Tang Kin Hwa v Traditional Chinese Medicine Practitioners Board* [2005] 4 SLR(R) 604 (Sing HC) [27]).
223 *Shadrake III* (n 190) [36].
224 ibid.
225 For example, one of the statements was found in *Shadrake III* (n 190) not to pose 'a real risk of undermining public confidence in the administration of justice in so far as the Respondent has failed to prove beyond a reasonable doubt the logically prior step that the second statement refers to the courts': ibid [105]. See also ibid [142].
226 [2015] 2 SLR 352 (Sing HC) [10] ('*Au*'). See also David Tan, 'A "real risk" of undermining public confidence in the administration of justice' (2011) 16 Media & Arts Law Review 191, 202. I suggested that this balance is appropriately achieved by the application of the 'real risk' test for liability, coupled with the placing of the onus on the party bringing the committal proceedings (typically, the prosecuting authorities of the jurisdiction concerned) ('the Prosecution') to prove the elements of the offence based on the criminal standard of beyond reasonable doubt.
227 *Au* (n 226) [9] (citing *Shadrake III* (n 190) [17]).
228 ibid [11].
229 ibid [11].
230 [2014] 3 WLR 1081 (PC) ('*Dhooharika*').
231 ibid [19].
232 ibid [38]. The Privy Council referred to 'modern examples' of scandalising contempt offences in Australia, Canada, Hong Kong, India, Malaysia, New Zealand, Singapore, Fiji, Swaziland and Zimbabwe: ibid Annex A.
233 ibid [41]. The Privy Council also noted that the European Court of Human Rights has not declared the existence of scandalising contempt to be incompatible with Art 10 of the ECHR: ibid [39] (citing *De Haes and Gijsels v Belgium* (1998) 25 EHRR 1 and *Zugic v Croatia* App no 3699/08 (European Court of Human Rights (ECHR), 31 May 2011).
234 Chan Sek Keong, 'Securing and Maintaining the Independence of the Court in Judicial Proceedings' (2010) 22 Singapore Academy of Law Journal 229, 239–40 (internal citations omitted).
235 Saunders (n 4) 83.
236 ibid 98.
237 See nn 85–86 and accompanying text.
238 In *Grant* (n 107), the Supreme Court noted (at [62]):

> If the publisher fails to take appropriate steps having regard to all the circumstances, it will be liable. The press and others engaged in public communication on matters of public interest, like bloggers, must act carefully, having regard to the injury to reputation that a false statement can cause. A defence based on responsible conduct reflects the social concern that the media should be held accountable through the law of defamation.

Since the relative weight placed on reputation of political public figures in Singapore vis-à-vis freedom of speech is clearly different from that in the UK,

Singapore courts can therefore accord different emphases to each of the *Reynolds* factors – eg an allegation of corruption against a senior public official, which is a very serious charge, must be counterbalanced by, inter alia, thorough steps taken to verify the information, a clear distinction of facts from comments and a publication of the plaintiff's side of the story. See Tan (n 100) 484.

239 Koh (n 50) 350.

240 Chan (n 234).

241 Chan (n 220) 237.

242 Peter Berkowitz, *Virtue and the Making of Modern Liberalism* (Princeton University Press 1999) 163. It is important to note that liberalism is not a monolithic ideology that places the rights of the individual over the cultivation of virtue. Berkowitz, for example, argues that 'stability in democracies depends on citizens who can discipline the democratic inclination to do as one pleases so as to defer immediate gratification in the interest of long-term benefits' and that in 'a liberal polity ... it will be necessary for its citizens, both those who do and those who do not occupy political office, to exercise virtue': ibid 177, 191.

243 *Shared Values* (n 55) [48]. See also Gerald E Caiden, 'The Problem of Ensuring the Public Accountability of Public Officials' in Joseph G Jabbra and OP Dwivedi (eds), *Public Service Accountability: A Comparative Perspective* (Kumarian Press 1988) 17.

244 Eg Lee Kuan Yew, 'Speech in Parliament on White Paper on Ministerial Salaries' (1 November 1994) as quoted in Han, Fernandez and Tan (n 83) 89.

245 Letter from James Madison to WT Barry (4 August 1822), reprinted in Gaillard Hunt (ed), *9 The Writings of James Madison* (GP Putnam's Sons 1910) (as cited in Post (n 15) 35).

Bibliography

Amponsah, Peter, N, *Libel Law, Political Criticism, and Defamation of Public Figures: The United States, Europe and Australia* (LFB Scholarly Publishing LLC 2004).

Baker, C Edwin, 'Scope of the First Amendment Freedom of Speech' (1978) 5 UCLA Law Review 964.

Baker, C Edwin, *Human Liberty and Freedom of Speech* (Oxford University Press 1989).

Balkin, Jack M, 'Populism and Progressivism as Constitutional Categories' (1995) 104 Yale Law Journal 1935.

Balkin, Jack M, 'Digital Speech and Democratic Culture: A Theory of Freedom of Expression for the Information Society' (2004) 79 New York University Law Review 1.

Balkin, Jack M, *Living Originalism* (Belknap Press 2011).

Barendt, Eric, *Freedom of Speech* (2nd edn, Oxford University Press 2005).

Barendt, Eric, 'Balancing Freedom of Expression and the Right to Reputation: Reflections on Reynolds and Reportage' (2012) 63 Northern Ireland Legal Quarterly 59.

Barron, Benjamin, 'A Proposal to Rescue New York Times v Sullivan by Promoting a Responsible Press' (2007) 57 American University Law Review 73.

Baum, Lawrence and Neal Devins, 'Why the Supreme Court Cares about Elites, Not the American People' (2010) 98 Georgetown Law Journal 1515.

Berkowitz, Peter, *Virtue and the Making of Modern Liberalism* (Princeton University Press 1999).

Breyer, Stephen, 'Lecture: Our Democratic Constitution' (2002) 77 New York University Law Review 245.

Buss, William G, 'Alexander Meiklejohn, American Constitutional Law, and Australia's Implied Freedom of Political Communication' (2006) 34 Federal Law Review 421.
Caiden, Gerald E, 'The Problem of Ensuring the Public Accountability of Public Officials' in Joseph G Jabbra and OP Dwivedi (eds), *Public Service Accountability: A Comparative Perspective* (Kumarian Press 1988).
Campbell, Tom, 'Rationales for Freedom of Communication' in Tom Campbell and Wojciech Sadurski (eds), *Freedom of Communication* (Dartmouth 1994).
Chan, Joseph, 'A Confucian Perspective on Human Rights for Contemporary China' in Joanne R Bauer and Daniel A Bell (eds), *The East Asian Challenge for Human Rights* (Cambridge University Press 1999).
Chan, Sek Keong, 'Judicial Review – From Angst to Empathy' (2010) 22 Singapore Academy of Law Journal 469.
Chan, Sek Keong, 'Securing and Maintaining the Independence of the Court in Judicial Proceedings' (2010) 22 Singapore Academy of Law Journal 229.
Chew, Melanie, 'Human Rights in Singapore: Perceptions and Problems' (1994) 34(11) Asian Survey 933.
Choudhry, Sujit, 'Globalization in Search of Justification: Toward a Theory of Comparative Constitutional Interpretation' (1999) 74 Indiana Law Journal 819.
Chua, Beng-Huat, *Communitarian Ideology and Democracy in Singapore* (Routledge 1995).
De Bary, William Theodore, *Asian Values and Human Rights: A Confucian Communitarian Perspective* (Harvard University Press 1998).
Dworkin, Ronald M, *A Bill of Rights for Britain* (Chatto & Windus 1990).
Dworkin, Ronald M, *Freedom's Law* (Harvard University Press 1996).
Emerson, Thomas I, *Toward a General Theory of the First Amendment* (Random House 1966).
Emerson, Thomas I, *The System of Freedom of Expression* (Random House 1970).
Fisher, Eli, 'The Courts' Scandal: Scandalising the Courts in Australia' (2011) 16 Media & Arts Law Review 73.
Fisher, Louis, 'Judicial Credibility' in Bruce Peabody (ed), *The Politics of Judicial Independence: Courts, Politics, and the Public* (Johns Hopkins University Press 2011).
Fiss, Owen M, 'Free Speech and Social Structure' (1986) 71 Iowa Law Review 1405.
Garry, Patrick M, 'The First Amendment and Non-Political Speech: Exploring a Constitutional Model that Focuses on the Existence of Alternative Channels of Communication' (2007) 72 Missouri Law Review 477.
Gould, Kim, 'Scandalising Contempt in Australia: Dead? Dying? In much Danger? … (not!) …' (2010) 15 Media & Arts Law Review 23.
Guttman, Amy and Dennis Thompson, *Democracy and Disagreement* (Harvard University Press 1996).
Han, Fook Kwang, Warren Fernandez and Sumiko Tan, *Lee Kuan Yew: The Man and His Ideas* (Singapore Press Holdings 1998).
Hunt, Murray, 'The Horizontal Effect of the Human Rights Act' (1998) Public Law 423.
Ingber, Stanley, 'Rediscovering the Communal Worth of Individual Rights: The First Amendment Institutional Contexts' (1990) 69 Texas Law Review 1.
Jackson, Vicki C, 'Constitutions as 'Living Trees?' Comparative Constitutional Law and Interpretive Metaphors' (2006) 75 Fordham Law Review 921.
Josey, Alex, *Lee Kuan Yew: The Crucial Years* (Times Books International 1968).
Kausikan, Bilahari, 'Asia's Different Standard' (1993) 92 Foreign Policy 24.
Kenyon, Andrew T, 'Assuming Free Speech' (2014) 77 Modern Law Review 379.

Kenyon, Andrew T, *Defamation: Comparative Law and Practice* (UCL Press 2006).

Kenyon, Andrew T and Ang Hean Leng, 'Reynolds Privilege, Common Law Defamation and Malaysia' (2010) Singapore Journal of Legal Studies 256.

Killion, M Ulric, 'Post-WTO China and Independent Judicial Review' (2004) 26 Houston Journal of International Law 507.

Koh, Tommy, *The Quest for World Order: Perspectives of a Pragmatic Idealist* (Institute of Policy Studies 1998).

Lee, Kuan Yew, *From Third World to First: The Singapore Story: 1965–2000* (Harper-Collins Publishers 2000).

Lynch, Andrew, 'Unanimity in a Time of Uncertainty: The High Court Settles Its Differences in Lange v Australian Broadcasting Corporation' (1997) 6 Griffith Law Review 211.

McCrudden, Christopher, 'A Common Law of Human Rights?: Transnational Judicial Conversations on Constitutional Rights' (2000) 20 Oxford Journal of Legal Studies 499.

Madison, James, 'Letter from James Madison to WT Barry' (4 August 1822), reprinted in Gaillard Hunt (ed), *The Writings of James Madison* (vol 9, GP Putman's Sons 1910).

Mahbubani, Kishore, 'The Dangers of Decadence: What the Rest Can Teach the West' (1993) 72(4) Foreign Affairs 10.

Meagher, Dan, 'What is Political Communication: The Rationale of the Implied Freedom of Political Communication' (2004) 28 Melbourne University Law Review 438.

Meiklejohn, Alexander, *Free Speech and Its Relation to Self-Government* (Harper Brothers Publishers 1948).

Meiklejohn, Alexander, *Political Freedom: The Constitutional Powers of the People* (Oxford University Press 1965).

Mill, John Stuart, *On Liberty and Other Essays* (John Gray ed, Oxford University Press 1998).

Mishkin, Paul, 'The Uses of Ambivalence: Reflections on the Supreme Court and the Constitutionality of Affirmative Action' (1983) 131 University of Pennsylvania Law Review 907.

Mitchell, Paul, *The Making of the Modern English Law of Defamation* (Hart Publishing 2000).

Murchison, Brian C, 'Speech and the Self-Realization Value' (1998) 33 Harvard Civil Rights-Civil Liberties Law Review 443.

Murchison, Brian C, 'Speech and the Self-Governance Value' (2006) 14 William and Mary Bill of Rights Journal 1251.

Neier, Aryeh, 'Asia's Unacceptable Standard' (1993) 92 Foreign Policy 42.

Paltiel, Jeremy T, 'Cultural and Political Determinants of the Chinese Approach to Human Rights' in Errol P Mendes and Anne-Marie Traeholt (eds), *Human Rights: Chinese and Canadian Perspectives* (Ottawa: Human Rights Research and Education Centre 1997).

Phillipson, Gavin, 'Transforming Breach of Confidence? Towards a Common Law Right of Privacy under the Human Rights Act' (2003) 66 Modern Law Review 726.

Phillipson, Gavin, 'Clarity Postponed: Horizontal Effect after Campbell' in Helen Fenwick, Gavin Phillipson and Roger Masterman (eds), *Judicial Reasoning under the UK Human Rights Act* (Cambridge University Press 2007).

Plate, Tom, *Conversations with Lee Kuan Yew – Citizen Singapore: How to Build a Nation* (Marshall-Cavendish Editions 2010).

Post, Robert C, 'The Constitutional Concept of Public Discourse: Outrageous Opinion, Democratic Deliberation, and Hustler Magazine v Falwell' (1990) 103 Harvard Law Review 601.

Post, Robert C, 'Meiklejohn's Mistake: Individual Autonomy and the Reform of Public Discourse' (1993) 64 University of Colorado Law Review 1109.

Post, Robert C, 'Reconciling Theory and Doctrine in First Amendment Jurisprudence' (2000) 88 California Law Review 2353.

Post, Robert C, 'Participatory Democracy and Free Speech' (2011) 97 Virginia Law Review 477.

Post, Robert C, *Democracy, Expertise, Academic Freedom: A First Amendment Jurisprudence for the Modern State* (Yale University Press 2012).

Post, Robert C, 'Understanding the First Amendment' (2012) 87 Washington Law Review 549.

Quah, Jon ST, 'Searching for Singapore's National Values' in Jon ST Quah (ed), *In Search of Singapore's National Values* (Times Academic Press for the Institute of Policy Studies 1990).

Redish, Martin H, 'The Value of Free Speech' (1982) 130 University of Pennsylvania Law Review 591.

Reichman, Amnon, 'The Dimensions of Law: Judicial Craft, Its Public Perception, and the Role of the Scholar' (2007) 95 California Law Review 1619.

Saunders, Cheryl, 'Judicial Engagement' in Rosalind Dixon and Tom Ginsburg (eds), *Comparative Constitutional Law in Asia* (Edward Elgar 2014).

Schauer, Frederick, *Free Speech: A Philosophical Enquiry* (Cambridge University Press 1982).

Schauer, Frederick, 'The Politics and Incentives of Legal Transplantation' in Joseph S Nye and John D Donahue (eds), *Governance in a Globalizing World* (Brookings Institution Press 2000).

Slaughter, Anne-Marie, *A New World Order* (Princeton University Press 2004).

Smolla, Rodney A, *Free Speech in an Open Society* (Knopf 1992).

Smolla, Rodney A and Melville B Nimmer, *Smolla and Nimmer on Freedom of Speech: A Treatise on the First Amendment* (3rd edn, M Bender 2008).

Stone, Adrienne, 'Freedom of Political Communication, the Constitution and the Common Law' (1998) 26 Federal Law Review 219.

Stone, Adrienne, 'The Australian Free Speech Experiment and Scepticism about UK Human Rights Act' in Tom Campbell, KD Ewing and Adam Tomkins (eds), *Sceptical Essays on Human Rights* (Oxford University Press 2001).

Stone, Adrienne, 'Australia's Constitutional Rights and the Problem of Interpretive Disagreement' (2005) 27 Sydney Law Review 29.

Stone, Adrienne, Rishad Chowdhury and Martin Clark, 'The Comparative Constitutional Law of Freedom of Expression in Asia' in Rosalind Dixon and Tom Ginsburg (eds), *Comparative Constitutional Law in Asia* (Edward Elgar 2014).

Sunstein, Cass R, *Democracy and the Problem of Free Speech* (The Free Press 1993).

Sunstein, Cass R, *Designing Democracy: What Constitutions Do* (Oxford University Press 2001).

Sypnowich, Christine, 'Ruling or Overruled? The People, Rights and Democracy' (2007) 27 Oxford Journal of Legal Studies 757.

Tan, David, 'The Reynolds Privilege in a Neo-Confucianist Communitarian Democracy: Reinvigorating Freedom of Political Communication in Singapore' (2011) Singapore Journal of Legal Studies 456.

Tan, David, 'A "Real Risk" of Undermining Public Confidence in the Administration of Justice' (2011) 16 Media & Arts Law Review 191.

Tarkington, Margaret, 'The Truth Be Damned: The First Amendment, Attorney Speech, and Judicial Reputation' (2009) 97 Georgetown Law Journal 1567.

Tey, Tsun Hang, 'Scandalising the Singapore Judiciary' (2010) 12 Australian Journal of Asian Law 59.

Thio, Li-ann, 'An "i" for an "I": Singapore's Communitarian Model of Constitutional Adjudication' (1997) 27 Hong Kong Law Journal 152.

Thio, Li-ann, 'Singapore: Regulating Political Speech and the Commitment "to Build a Democratic Society"' (2003) 1 International Journal of Constitutional Law 516.

Thio, Li-ann, 'Beyond the 'Four Walls' in an Age of Transnational Judicial Conversations: Civil Liberties, Rights Theories, and Constitutional Adjudication in Malaysia and Singapore' (2006) 19 Columbia Journal of Asian Law 428.

Thio, Li-ann, 'Between Apology and Apogee, Autochthony: The 'Rule of Law' Beyond the Rules of Law in Singapore' (2012) Singapore Journal of Legal Studies 269.

Waluchow, Wil, *A Common Law Theory of Judicial Review: The Living Tree* (Cambridge University Press 2007).

Part III

Rethinking boundaries

10 The interpretation of the Singapore Constitution

Towards a unified approach to interpreting legal documents

Goh Yihan

I Introduction

The interpretation of the Constitution of the Republic of Singapore (1985 Rev Ed, 1999 Reprint) ('the Constitution') takes place alongside the interpretation of other legal documents, such as statutes and contracts. However, the relationship between the interpretation of one type of legal document and another is seldom, if ever, discussed.[1] It is usually assumed that the interpretation of each type of legal document takes place within the confines of its own rules, with little or no relationship to the interpretation of other legal documents. Indeed, Lord Wilberforce has said in *Minister of Home Affairs v Fisher*[2] that constitutions should be treated as *sui generis* and be interpreted on their own terms.

In contrast, another view holds that the interpretation of all legal documents should follow broadly the same approach. For example, VK Rajah JA in *Zurich Insurance (Singapore) Pte Ltd v B-Gold Interior Design & Construction Pte Ltd* suggested that 'the adoption of the contextual approach to contractual interpretation is conceptually broadly similar to the purposive approach which our courts now adopt vis-à-vis statutory interpretation'.[3] Similarly, Lord Neuberger in the UK Supreme Court decision of *Marley v Rawlings*[4] said that the way by which all legal documents, such as contracts or wills, are interpreted should not be too dissimilar. While Lord Neuberger may not have had constitutional interpretation in mind, it is likely that any grand theory of interpretation would have to include constitutions (and statutes) as well. Academics have likewise sought to draw parallels between the interpretations of different legal documents.[5]

It is important to consider how the Constitution should be interpreted in the light of other legal documents. This is because the answer to this question sheds light on a broader question: what is the judicial function in the interpretation of legal documents? Is it to give effect to the drafter's intention, or does the court have a broader responsibility than that? This chapter is concerned with whether the interpretation of the Constitution in Singapore should be different from the interpretation of other legal documents, such as statutes and contracts. In order to answer this question, this chapter proceeds along several parts. First, it will distil the areas of similarities and differences across the interpretation of the Constitution, statutes and contracts in Singapore. Second, it attempts to justify, where possible, such similarities and differences, before concluding in a third part as to whether a unified approach ought to be taken with regard to the interpretation of the Constitution, statutes and contracts in Singapore. Ultimately, this chapter will suggest that the Constitution should be interpreted from the same starting point as any other legal document, with any differences restricted to the application of that starting point.

II The interpretation of the Constitution in Singapore

The interpretation of the Constitution has had many evolutions over the years. It has also been covered extensively by other chapters in this book.[6] This chapter will, therefore, focus on the more recent cases since those will show the courts' most current approach. One of the latest cases in this regard of the Constitution is the Court of Appeal case of *Yong Vui Kong v Public Prosecutor*.[7] In that case, the appellant argued that the sentence of caning imposed on him violated Articles 9(1) and 12(1) of the Constitution. In dealing with the correct interpretation of Art 9(1), the court held that 'it is necessary to go back in history and consider how its predecessor provisions were understood'.[8] The court traced the history of Article 9(1) to Clause 39 of the Magna Carta.[9] Using that as the starting point, it next considered whether the ambit of protection embodied in Clause 39 of the Magna Carta changed when it was adapted into the constitutions of other countries, and finally in Singapore. After an extensive examination of the constitutional lineage of Article 9(1), it considered that its ambit was narrowed along its evolution. In the end, it laid down three propositions relating to Article 9(1), namely:[10]

(a) to the extent specific rights are dealt with elsewhere, for instance the prohibition of forced slavery and labour in Art 10, or of banishment and curtailment of freedom of movement in Art 13, these would not be included within the ambit of the protection conferred by Art 9;
(b) to the extent potential rights were considered and excluded, for instance the right to property, those also would not be included in Art 9;
(c) beyond this, Art 9 does not protect only against arbitrary execution or incarceration. It also prohibits the unlawful use of force against a person, including by way of amputations, mutilations, assaults, woundings, etc. Such acts would result in a deprivation of 'life', according to Blackstone.

The court placed particular attention on the fact that this understanding of 'life' had not been altered by the time Article 9(1) was adopted in Singapore.

From this passage, a few points about the courts' approach to the interpretation of the Constitution emerge. First, the Singapore courts' starting point is the intention of the drafter. Indeed, this is mandated by section 9A(1) of the Interpretation Act, which mandates a purposive approach for the interpretation of all written law, including the Constitution. Such an approach is evinced by the court's attention to the lineage of Art 9(1) and whether the drafters of the Constitution had narrowed its ambit. Indeed, when they have, as exemplified by Parliament's express exclusion of protection over property rights, the courts will respect it.[11] More than that, the courts do not regard themselves as having the power to read into the Constitution what its drafter never intended. Thus, slightly later on in *Yong Vui Kong*, the Court of Appeal considered that it had no right to read unenumerated rights, such as on the basis of natural law, into the Constitution as that would result in judges sitting as a 'super-legislature' and 'enacting their personal views of what is just and desirable into law'.[12] This, the court noted, is 'not only undemocratic but also antithetical to the rule of law'.[13] This sentiment was also evident in the Court of Appeal case of *Lim Meng Suang v Attorney-General*.[14] The court in that case acknowledged that the courts were distinct and separate from Parliament, and that the courts' function was to furnish an independent, neutral and objective forum for deciding, on the basis of objective legal rules and principles, the parties' rights.[15] Such an approach must be contrasted with the wider approach taken by the Privy Council in *Ong Ah Chuan v Public Prosecutor*,[16] where Lord Diplock held that the word 'law' in Arts 9(1) and 12(1) of the Constitution must include 'fundamental rules of natural justice that formed part and parcel of the common law of England that was in operation in Singapore at the commencement of the constitution'.[17] However, the court in *Yong Vui Kong* explained Lord Diplock's statement on the basis that the fundamental rules of natural justice in the common law are procedural as opposed to substantive rights.[18] This further emphasises the role that the drafter's intention plays in the courts' interpretation of the Constitution: in this case, even assuming that values of natural justice feature in Arts 9(1) and 12(1), the exact content of such values must be derived from the drafter's intention. The upshot of these developments appears to be that, in so far as the interpretation of the Constitution is concerned, the Singapore courts aim to give effect primarily to the drafter's intention.

Moreover, as Professor Thio Li-ann notes, the Singapore courts in more recent times have evinced adherence more to the specific intent of the constitutional framers.[19] She raises the example of *Yong Vui Kong v Public Prosecutor*,[20] where the argument was raised that Article 9's reference to 'law' included a prohibition against inhuman punishment which, in that case, meant that the mandatory death penalty should be avoided. The Court of Appeal had no difficulty rejecting this argument, holding that the constitutional history showed that the 1966 Constitutional Commission's recommendation of an Article that prohibited inhumane punishment was conscientiously rejected by the Government of the day. Thus, this original, specific intent was used by the Court of Appeal to conclude that Art 9(1) did not encompass an implied prohibition against inhuman punishment.

However, adherence to the drafter's intention is only the starting point. How is the court supposed to know what the drafter intended? The second point therefore from the approach taken in *Yong Vui Kong* is that the Singapore courts are willing to consider historical materials in discerning the drafter's intention.

Therein is the implicit assumption, as Professor Kevin Tan notes in his chapter,[21] that the Constitution was not drafted in a vacuum. Rather, it is presumed that the drafter had in mind the historical genesis of various constitutional protections embedded within the Constitution. Thus, in *Yong Vui Kong*, the court was prepared to consider the historical lineage of Art 9(1) all the way back to the Magna Carta, and to carefully chart how that original genesis of the protection accorded by Art 9(1) has been changed over the course of history. Another similar example is *Lim Meng Suang*, where the Court of Appeal cautioned that foreign cases that have conferred an expansive constitutional right to life and liberty should be approached 'with circumspection because they were decided in the context of their unique social, political and legal circumstances'.[22] The presumption therefore is that the drafter intended to incorporate into the constitutional wording the social, legal and political contexts at the time of writing. These presumptions may or may not be factually true in so far as the drafter's actual intentions are concerned, but they are an important characteristic of how the Constitution is interpreted in Singapore.

This also shows that the courts are open to looking at extrinsic materials in the interpretation endeavour but, it seems, only recourse to materials that are historically tied to the Constitution. On the whole, as David Tan notes in his chapter,[23] the Singapore courts have enacted a 'four walls' doctrine, starting with *Colin Chan v Public Prosecutor*,[24] which states that the Constitution is primarily to be interpreted within its own four walls and not in the light of analogies drawn from other countries such as Great Britain, the United States of America or Australia. This appears to cement the view that foreign cases and international law-based arguments are generally not relevant extrinsic materials to refer to in the interpretation of the Constitution. Indeed, this stance seems to preclude the reference to foreign cases in formulating judgment on the constitution.

A third point is that the drafter may also be presumed to have intended certain non-express rights in the Constitution. Thus, while the Singapore courts attach some importance to the text of the Constitution, as Professor Kevin Tan notes in his chapter,[25] its structure can lead to certain non-express rights being read into it. However, these non-express rights must be in line with the broader purpose and structure of the Constitution. For example, in *Yong Vui Kong*, the Court of Appeal alluded to the views expressed by Chan Sek Keong CJ in the High Court case of *Mohammad Faizal bin Sabtu v Public Prosecutor*.[26] In that case, Chan CJ had held that the principle of separation of powers is part of the 'basic structure' of the Constitution. Thus, the very nature of a constitution necessitates the recognition of several implied rights built into it, all necessary to give effect to that underlying nature.[27] An example of such a right is the right to vote, as Minister Wong Kan Seng acknowledged in Parliament.[28] Thus, while the Court of Appeal in *Yong Vui Kong* did not decide whether the 'basic structure' doctrine, which postulates that there are certain fundamental features of a constitution that *cannot* be taken away by Parliament, applies in Singapore, it is clear that the court did acknowledge the presence of non-express rights within the Constitution, as long as they did not contradict but, in fact, gave effect to the express provisions in the Constitution. This appears clear from the court's judgment, which clearly distinguished its understanding of when there is such an non-express right found in the Constitution, and the more controversial idea introduced by the Indian Supreme Court in *Kesavananda Bharati v State of Kerala*[29] that these non-express rights, once established, can never be taken away.[30]

The Singapore courts' approach to the interpretation of the Constitution can be summarised in three broad points. First, they seek to give effect to the drafter's intention. Second, in discerning the drafter's intention, they recognise that the Constitution was not drafted in a vacuum and that the drafter intended to incorporate into the Constitution the prevailing norms at the time of drafting. These norms are not limited to the social, legal and political landscape, but also the way that predecessor constitutions had interpreted similar constitutional provisions. In order to discern what these norms are, the courts are willing to consider *relevant* extrinsic materials. Third, the courts also accept that the Constitution is not confined to only its express words but may include implied rights that are in line with the overall purpose of the document. Ultimately, the Singapore courts' approach in interpreting the Constitution may be summed up by the case of *Constitutional Reference No 1 of 1995*,[31] when the Constitutional Tribunal described the proper interpretative approach as interpreting the Constitution to give effect to the intent and will of Parliament, in accordance with section 9A(1) of the Interpretation Act. As has been said, although the purposive approach has been adopted, what remains to be seen is whether the 'purpose' will be read to enhance or regulate state power.[32]

This chapter will now compare these three points with the courts' corresponding approaches in the interpretation of statutes and contracts in Singapore.

III The interpretation of the Constitution compared with the interpretation of statutes and contracts in Singapore: the proper interpretative approach

A ***Broad similarities***

Just like the interpretation of the Constitution, the search for the drafter's intent also forms the Singapore courts' starting point in interpreting statutes and contracts.

1 Statutes

In so far as the interpretation of statutes is concerned, the Singapore High Court in *Public Prosecutor v Low Kok Heng* ('*Low Kok Heng*')[33] has affirmed that section 9A(1) of the Interpretation Act (Cap 1, 1993 Rev Ed) mandates the purposive approach as the dominant interpretative approach.[34] Accordingly, any other common law interpretative approach, such as the plain meaning rule and the strict construction rule, must yield to the purposive approach.[35] Indeed, more recently, the Court of Appeal in *Chief Assessor v First DCS Pte Ltd*[36] has explained the effect of section 9A(1) as follows:[37]

> When construing statutory provisions, it is important to consider the purpose for which Parliament enacted the provision in question. It would be incorrect to read the provision as if it existed in a vacuum. Indeed, by virtue of s 9A of the Interpretation Act (Cap 1, 2002 Rev Ed), the courts must prefer an interpretation which supports the intended purpose of a provision over an interpretation that does not. The effect of that section is to make the purposive approach the paramount rule of construction in our jurisprudence: *PP v Low Kok Heng* [2007] 4 SLR(R) 183.

The similarities between this approach and the approach taken by the Court of Appeal in *Yong Vui Kong* in interpreting the Constitution are obvious. The courts regard their role as giving effect to the drafter's intention. In this case, the drafter of both Constitution and statutes is Parliament. The courts do not regard themselves as having the power to overrule what Parliament has enacted. Indeed, in *AXA Insurance Singapore Pte Ltd v Chandran s/o Natesan*,[38] the High Court held that where Parliament has considered an area of law statutorily, the courts do not have the power to intervene even where such consideration was broad and not specific.[39]

2 Contracts

Similarly, the broad starting position for the interpretation of contracts is the same. In this regard, the Singapore cases are united in the view that contractual interpretation is an effort to understand the meaning of the contractual text as intended by the parties. Thus, as was held in *Zurich Insurance*, interpretation 'usually denotes the process of uncovering meaning in and seeking to understand a text where there is some doubt or room for a difference of opinion'.[40] The same sentiment was conveyed in *Sembcorp Marine Ltd v PPL Holdings Pte Ltd*, where it was said that interpretation refers to the 'process of ascertaining the meaning of expressions in a contract'.[41] The Singapore courts, following the English common law, have thus said that contractual interpretation is done objectively, that is, recourse is had to the parties' expressed intention in the contractual language rather than their actual intention.[42] This, according to *Zurich Insurance*, is the 'cornerstone of the theory of contract and permeates our entire approach to contractual interpretation'.[43] An objective approach usually means that evidence of the parties' subjective declarations of intention is not admissible.[44]

In addition, contractual interpretation is also to be done 'contextually'. Much emphasis has been made of the fact that contracts are not made in a vacuum, and that words are at times 'penumbral'.[45] The context is all-important; hence, the extrinsic evidence admissible under the Evidence Act can assist the court in coming to the objectively correct meaning of the contractual language, especially where the contractual language is 'ambiguous or capable of having more than one meaning'.[46] As a preliminary matter, it was held in *Lee Chee Wei v Tan Hor Peow Victor* that the presence of an entire agreement clause does not generally prevent the adoption of the contextual approach.[47] Also, a contextual understanding would be especially important where the contract was not drafted properly.[48] In *International Research Corp PLC v Lufthansa Systems Asia Pacific Pte Ltd*, the High Court noted that the contextual approach does not usurp the plain meaning rule; rather, the plain meaning rule operates within the contextual method.[49] To be more precise, what the court probably meant is that at times the plain meaning of the words, in light of the context, sufficiently gives effect to the parties' intentions. There is, therefore, no need to depart from that plain meaning.[50] Even this purported use of the objective and contextual approach admits of several questions, which we deal with below.

Pursuant to the contextual approach, context is derived both externally and internally. External context largely refers to the surrounding circumstances including 'facts and circumstances which were (or ought to have been) in the mind of the [drafter] when he used those words'.[51] This can also include the attributes of the document in question,[52] the 'legal, regulatory and factual matrix constituting the background in which the contract was drafted or the utterance made',[53] the commercial purpose of the transaction or provision,[54] and such facts can also be provided for by the recitals to the contract. In *Tiger Airways Pte Ltd v Swissport Singapore Pte Ltd*, the High Court explained that recitals are often the ready source of the 'background' or 'factual matrix', even if they do not bind the parties contractually.[55] However, context that is not relevant would not be used in the interpretative exercise. In *LW Infrastructure*, the High Court found that the parties did not have regard to standard forms when they concluded the contract in question and hence, such evidence was not part of the context.[56]

Again, the similarities with the approach taken in *Yong Vui Kong* are obvious. First, the courts are concerned with discerning the drafter's intent. Second, the search is for the drafter's objective as opposed to actual intent. Thus, just like in the interpretation of the Constitution, the drafter is presumed to know or intend certain things. For example, the drafter is intended to desire the internal coherence of the contract such as that an interpretation favouring such coherence is preferred to one that does not. Similarly, the drafter is taken to have intended non-express terms to be implied into the contract, but only if necessary for the overall working of the contract. And, of course, in discerning the drafter's intent, the approaches taken in the interpretation of the Constitution and contracts are again similar in that they acknowledge that the respective documents are not drafted in a vacuum but that the context can, and should, be taken into account.

While the broad starting point is similar, if not identical, differences appear when one considers the courts' approaches more specifically in so far as their application of the purposive approach is concerned.

B Specific differences

1 The meaning of 'purpose' under the purposive approach

One specific difference between the Singapore courts' interpretation of the three classes of legal documents is whether the courts are concerned with the broad or specific intent of the drafter. In so far as the interpretation of the Constitution is concerned, as Professor Thio Li-ann notes, courts in more recent times have evinced adherence more to the specific intent of the constitutional framers.[57] However, the same cannot be said about the interpretation of statutes, where there is some uncertainty as to whether the courts look at the broad or specific intent of the drafter.

A STATUTES

An example of a court taking a 'general' view of the purpose of a statute is *Raffles City Pte Ltd v Attorney-General* ('*Raffles City*').[58] That case concerned the interpretation of the phrase 'a storey of an approved development project' in the Property Tax Order 1967.[59] The question was whether the phrase covered three modern multiplexes comprising of a total of 138 stories. LP Thean J thought that the Minister's comments made it clear that 'he certainly did not contemplate – not surprisingly as the speech was made more than 25 years ago – a construction of an immense multi-building complex with which we are familiar today'.[60] Instead, Thean J placed greater emphasis on the fact that the Minister's comments disclosed that the *general* purpose underlying the Order was to encourage private participation in urban redevelopment and it was pursuant to that general purpose that the court found for the defendants.[61] Thus, the court did not think that Parliament was capable of thinking through each and every exact consequence of its statutory provisions and viewed the relevant statutory intent as being a general purpose underlying the statute. Yet another example can be found in *The 'Seaway'*,[62] where the High Court thought that the Minister's 'reference to damage to facilities at PSA' was merely 'illustrative in nature' and 'not intended to be exhaustive in nature and scope'.[63]

On balance, it appears that the Singapore courts focus not only on the specific purpose but more on the general purpose of statutes, which, depending on the circumstances, can supersede the more specific consequential purpose. Indeed, in *ADP v ADQ*,[64] the Court of Appeal held that the court should discern the statutory intent from the provisions as a whole and their context instead of other parts of the same provisions.[65] Similarly, in *W Y Steel Construction Pte Ltd v Osko Pte Ltd*,[66] the Court of Appeal referred to using the 'guiding philosophy' behind a statute to interpret it.[67] The utility of a court looking at the 'general' purpose of a statute can be seen in *PP v Mohammad Ashik bin Aris*,[68] where the High Court rightly pointed out that purposive interpretation is needed to 'facilitate the effective operation of the written law at the application level',[69] especially if the legislator could not have anticipated all the consequences of a statute. If a court were focused on specific purposes, it might miss out the general purposes that better suit the statutory purpose. Similarly, as we have seen from *Raffles City*, a strict adherence to the Minister's speech, which clearly illustrates a specific consequential purpose but did not foresee the multiplexes of the present time, would actually have frustrated the general purpose behind the statute. That would have fallen foul of the statutorily mandated approach under s 9A(1) of the Interpretation Act.

Thus, compared with the Court of Appeal's approach towards the interpretation of the Constitution in *Yong Vui Kong*, the Singapore courts' approach towards the interpretation of statutes appears broader in the sense that it is less tied to what the drafter originally thought. Instead, the courts appear more willing to consider the more general purpose behind the statute concerned and to acknowledge that the legislator may not have thought of all the consequences of the statute. In slight contrast, the Singapore courts appear to take a more restrictive view in interpreting the Constitution, preferring to focus on exactly what the drafter had in mind. To be fair though, given that the Constitution is drafted at a higher degree of generality compared to statutes, it may be that, practically speaking, it is not possible to discern what the general purpose of the Constitution is. Thus, rather than risk imposing their own views of what that general purpose is, the courts have rightly interpreted the Constitution with regard to its specific purposes, as evinced from the historical materials.

B CONTRACTS

A similar difference also exists when one compares the interpretation of the Constitution with the interpretation of contracts. In contractual interpretation, related to the importance of context is the specific proposition that a commercially sensible interpretation would generally be preferred for commercial contracts. In *Ang Tin Yong*, a deed was construed in a way that accorded with 'business common sense and its commercial purposes'.[70] In doing so, the Court of Appeal endorsed Lord Steyn's explanation for such an approach in *Mannai Investment Co Ltd v Eagle Star Life Assurance Co Ltd* – a commercial interpretation would more likely give effect to the parties' intention in a commercial situation.[71] Thus, where the context is commercial in nature, it is more likely that a commercially sensible interpretation would be preferred. In doing so, the courts appear to read into contracts a broad intention that the contract is meant to be commercially sensible.

Again, there is, in contrast, no such broad purpose behind the interpretation of the Constitution. The courts have rightly to pay great attention to the specific purpose behind each provision, and to recognise the importance of the historical lineage.

2 The purposive approach and literal words

A second specific difference relates to methodology: what does the purposive approach actually allow? Specifically, how does the purposive approach relate to a literal reading of a provision? The position for the interpretation of the Constitution appears to be clear: the courts attach importance to the literal words of the Constitution as the starting point in their interpretation. Thus, in *Yong Vui Kong*, the Court of Appeal first considered the meaning of Article 9(1) based on a 'plain reading' of it.[72] It appears that the plain meaning of the provisions is taken as the presumptive intent of the drafter. In that sense, the courts would adopt a stricter reading of the Constitution.

A STATUTES

However, the position in relation to the interpretation of statutes is not as clear. Indeed, there appear to be three views among the Singapore courts. The first view is that the purposive approach may permit a literal reading of a statutory provision if such reading gives effect to the statutory purpose. However, the text controls the extent to which a 'non-literal' meaning may be reached. An example of this view may be found in *Low Kok Heng*, where Rajah JA thought that a purposive approach should not be construed as being at odds with a literal reading of the statutory provision.[73] In essence, the court is bound by the text as enacted,[74] but the statutory purpose may be discerned through a non-literal reading of the text within reasonable confines. This view was also expressed in the Court of Appeal case of *ADP v ADQ*,[75] where the court emphasised that it ought not to superimpose what it feels *ought* to be the meaning of the statutory provision concerned, notwithstanding the plain meaning of the statutory language.[76] This is the view most similar to the Court of Appeal's approach towards the interpretation of the Constitution in *Yong Vui Kong*.

A second view taken by the Singapore courts, which is quite opposite from the first view, is that the statutory purpose is completely independent of the statutory text. An expression of such a view may be found in *Public Prosecutor v Knight Glenn Jeyasingam*[77] (*'Knight Glenn Jeyasingam*'). In that case, the 'without prejudice' rule contained in Section 23 of the Evidence Act (Cap 97, 1997 Rev Ed) (which applies to civil proceedings) was applied to criminal proceedings on the basis that the Evidence Act was a 'facilitative statute' which permitted the introduction of 'common law rules not expressly provided for under the ... Act' in accordance with 'the will and intent of Parliament'.[78]

A third view taken by the Singapore courts straddles the first and second views: while the statutory purpose must be given effect to, such statutory purpose will *always* be found in precise and unambiguous statutory text. Thus, where the statutory provision is indeed so clear, it will be literally interpreted because that will give effect to the statutory purpose. Thus, it was held in the Court of Appeal case of *Public Prosecutor v Manogaran s/o R Ramu*[79] ('*Manogaran s/o R Ramu*') that the 'cardinal rule' in statutory interpretation was to give effect to the intention 'expressed in the provision itself', such that if the statutory wording is precise and unambiguous, then *all that the court had to do* was to expound the words in their ordinary and natural sense.[80]

B CONTRACTS

In so far as the interpretation of contracts is concerned, the courts have stressed the anchoring effect of the contractual language in the interpretative process. As the cases have repeatedly stressed, the meaning derived through the process of interpretation cannot stray too far from the contractual language used. Indeed, there cannot be, as *Sembcorp Marine* put it, 'interpretation of a non-expression, ie a non-existent expression'.[81] The fidelity to the contractual language also derives a more practically relevant point: the distinction between 'interpreting' and 'contradicting, varying, adding to or subtracting from' contractual terms lies in the continued authority of the underlying language. This distinction is important because, as mandated by the Evidence Act, extrinsic evidence that has the latter effect is inadmissible, whereas evidence is almost always admissible to *interpret* a contract. As was held in *Zurich Insurance*, extrinsic evidence that interprets a contract 'does not usurp the authority of the written document or contradict, vary, add to or subtract from its terms'; rather, '[i]t is the writing which operates'.[82] In other words, 'extrinsic evidence [which interprets] does no more than assist in [the operation of the writing] by assigning a definite meaning to terms capable of such explanation or by pointing out and connecting them with the proper subject-matter'.[83] In *Pender Development Pte Ltd v Chesney Real Estate Group LLP*,[84] evidence, if admitted, would have led the court to ignore an express clause of the contract. The High Court held that such an outcome was not an interpretative exercise and that if the parties wanted to argue that the wrong words were used (and hence should be rejected), the correct cause of action was rectification.[85]

Fidelity to the contractual language also implies that ambiguity or absurdity is necessary before the court will assign a different (albeit equally possible) meaning to that language. This is because such fidelity implies that the language has a default meaning that must be adhered to (hence its anchoring effect) unless ambiguity or absurdity necessitates a departure from such meaning. This, as noted in *Zurich Insurance*, is somewhat antithetical to the modern contextual approach, which posits that words have no default meanings and that everything is dependent on context.[86] Indeed, the statutory framework in Singapore (via the Evidence Act) necessitates a continued adherence to the default meanings of words such that, consistent with the courts' pronouncements, some degree of ambiguity or absurdity is indeed required before an alternative meaning can be given to the contractual language in its plain meaning sense.

Out of the three legal documents, this is probably the strictest adherence to the plain meaning of the text. While the interpretation of the Constitution requires some adherence to the text, there is nothing to say that the court cannot depart from it if the context shows otherwise. The case is the same, if not stronger, for statutes. However, contractual interpretation in Singapore suffers from a very close adherence to the textual meaning, which can only be departed from in limited circumstances.

3 The purposive approach and 'outdated' documents

A final (and related) question is how the Singapore courts should interpret a document that is 'outdated'. This is a particularly relevant issue in Singapore because of the number of antiquated statutes present from the British colonial times, such as the Evidence Act and the Penal Code. Indeed, the Constitution itself will be more and more detached from the original time it was drafted, much like how the US Constitution is today regarded in that country. It is clear, as the Court of Appeal emphasised in *Lim Meng Suang*, that the interpretation of the Constitution must not be unduly influenced by modern developments. The courts are, therefore, concerned with giving effect to the drafter's intention as discerned from the time the Constitution was drafted, thereby rejecting the living constitutionalism approach.

A STATUTES

In so far as the interpretation of statutes is concerned, the position is not quite the same. There appear to be two relevant principles. First, the High Court in *BFC v Comptroller of Income Tax*[87] stated that the statutory purpose is to be determined at or around the time the law is passed. As such, subsequent statutory provisions are *generally* irrelevant to the interpretation of the earlier statutory provisions.

However – and this marks a distinction from the interpretation of the Constitution – although subsequent statutory provisions cannot be used to affect the interpretation of an older statutory provision, the Court of Appeal in *AAG v Estate of AAH, deceased*[88] ('*AAG*') stated that '[i]t is a settled principle that a statutory provision should be construed in a manner which will take into account new situations which may arise and which were not within contemplation at the time of its enactment'.[89] Thus, in contrast to subsequent statutory provisions, subsequent *circumstances* may be used to affect the interpretation of an older statutory provision. This is a marked departure from the interpretation of the Constitution.

What is not as clear is the extent to which changed circumstances could affect the interpretation of statutes. Indeed, in *AAG* itself, the Court of Appeal had to interpret sections 2 and 3(1) of the Inheritance (Family Provision) Act,[90] which was enacted some forty-five years ago.[91] The Court of Appeal disregarded social developments since the enactment of the statute, and decided that the original statutory purpose present at the time of enactment was determinative of the correct interpretation of the provisions concerned. It is clear that an approach that ignores the realities of the time the statute was drafted should not be adopted. Such danger can be seen in *WX v WW*[92] ('*WX*'), where the High Court had to interpret s 114 of the Evidence Act. Section 114 provides that a person born during the continuance of a valid marriage shall be conclusively presumed as the legitimate child of that marriage, unless it could be shown that the parties had no access to one another during the marriage. This provision was enacted at a time when DNA testing did not exist to determine the parentage of a child. On the facts of *WX*, there was a DNA test report showing that the child concerned was not the biological child of the respondent's former husband in her then-annulled marriage, but of another man with whom she had sexual relations. The question was how the DNA test report affected the application of s 114, since the child was indeed born during the marriage between the respondent and her former husband. The High Court understandably thought that the argument that the child was from the marriage 'offend[ed] both justice and common sense'[93] and that such an outcome would mean that 'the law would hold that [the respondent's former husband] is the father of the child even though the science has shown otherwise'.[94]

However, beyond this view in *WX* that this should be avoided, it is unclear exactly how far the court's statement in *AAG* that new situations can be taken into account in interpreting statutes takes us. The key point though is that the courts are at least open to the relevance of changing circumstances in the interpretation of statutes.

B CONTRACTS

It is seldom relevant to refer to changed circumstances insofar as the interpretation of contracts are concerned, since the doctrine of frustration (and *force majeure* clauses) would avoid the contract in cases of changed circumstances. However, it is, of course, trite law that subsequent conduct of the parties cannot be taken into account when interpreting contracts. But even then, when parties do act in a way completely different from their contractual obligations, the courts may find that a new contract has replaced the old. Thus, the upshot is that the courts seldom, if ever, take into account changed circumstances in the interpretation of contracts.

C The recourse to extrinsic materials

It is clear that the interpretation of the Constitution permits recourse to extrinsic materials. It appears that the scope of admissible extrinsic materials for both the interpretation of statutes and contracts follow a broadly similar approach.

1 Statutes

In so far as the circumstances in which reference to extrinsic materials is permitted in the interpretation of statutes, Rajah JA in *Low Kok Heng* emphasised that the courts may refer to extrinsic materials even where the meaning of the provision concerned is clear on its face.[95] In this regard, section 9A(2)(a) of the Interpretation Act provides for a *confirmatory* function: it provides that extrinsic material can be used to confirm that the meaning of the provision is the ordinary meaning conveyed by the text of the provision, taking into account its statutory purpose. This necessarily presupposes that the text is *not* ambiguous or obscure to begin with, and that extrinsic materials can be used to *confirm* the ordinary meaning of the text, even if no ambiguity or obscurity exists. In contrast, s 9A(2)(b) provides for an *ascertainment* function: it provides that extrinsic material can be used to *ascertain* the meaning of the text when it is ambiguous, obscure, or would be absurd in its application.

2 Contracts

For contractual interpretation, extrinsic evidence is generally inadmissible to contradict, vary, add to or subtract from the contractual terms. This is the parol evidence rule, which applies where the contract was intended by the parties to contain all the terms of their agreement.[96] The Evidence Act preserves the parol evidence rule by way of ten sections.[97] Although *Zurich Insurance* noted the decline of the rule under English law, it is also clear that relevant aspects of the rule continue to apply in Singapore under the Evidence Act.[98] It is also essential to distinguish between admitting the extrinsic evidence to establish ambiguity for the purpose of departing from the plain meaning (as conveyed by the contractual language), and admitting such evidence to establish a different meaning from the plain meaning. It is for the former purpose that extrinsic evidence can be more freely admitted. However, even here, *Zurich Insurance* has placed some restrictions on admissibility. Whether the extrinsic evidence is admissible depends on whether it is (a) relevant (ie 'it would affect the way in which the language of the document would have been understood by a reasonable man');[99] (b) 'reasonably available to all the contracting parties';[100] and (c) 'relates to a clear or obvious context'.[101] It is important to note that *Zurich Insurance* does not allow the admissibility of *all* extrinsic evidence; the limitations, both statutory and at common law, must be adhered to.[102] Furthermore, more recently, in the case of *Sembcorp Marine*, additional procedural requirements related to the pleadings were grafted into the admissible evidence.

Thus, in contrast to the interpretation of the Constitution and statutes, there is an artificial limit to the amount of extrinsic material that may be turned to for the interpretation of contracts.

D The type of extrinsic materials that can be referred to

Finally, we consider the issue of the type of referable extrinsic materials. As we have seen above, such materials must be historically related to the Constitution.

1 Statutes

This appears to be the case for the interpretation of statutes as well. Indeed, the courts take the view that section 9A(3) provides a non-exhaustive list of the types of extrinsic materials referable. This approach was confirmed in *ACS Computer Pte Ltd v Rubina Watch Co (Pte) Ltd*, where Khoo J held that the list of materials set out in s 9A(3) 'is not exhaustive' and that the 'general provision' of the section 'allows reference to any material capable of assisting in the ascertainment of the meaning of the provision in the circumstances stated in s 9A'.[103] Thus, under s 9A(3)(b), the courts have made several references to explanatory statements relating to the bill concerned.[104] As for s 9A(3)(c), which allows for reference to the Second Reading speech, the courts have made full use of this section to make the necessary reference.[105] For s 9A(3)(d), which allows for reference to 'any relevant material in any official record of debates in Parliament', the courts have mainly referred to general comments of ministers prior to the introduction of the statute being interpreted,[106] and extracts from Parliamentary Debates.[107] Applying section 9A(3)(f), read together with section 9A(3), which does not limit the extrinsic materials referable, the courts have referred to previous manifestations of the statute concerned (whether local or foreign),[108] Select Committee reports,[109] Law Revision Committees' reports,[110] case law,[111] academic commentaries,[112] and even diplomatic notes exchanged in relation to international conventions.[113] There was even an attempt to refer to a guide published by the Ministry concerned for laypersons, but this was refused on the basis that the guide was itself ambiguous.[114]

Relatedly, the Court of Appeal in *Public Prosecutor v Adnan bin Kadir*[115] regarded the 'context' referred to by section 2(1) of the Interpretation Act – which provides default meanings for certain words and expressions in written law unless there is something in the subject or context inconsistent with such meaning – as referring to 'the legislative history of that Act, the provisions of other Acts *in pari materia*, and all facts constituting or concerning the subject-matter of the Act'.[116] The court regarded this as being consistent with s 9A(2), which allows the courts to consider any extrinsic material in interpreting a statutory provision.

2 Contracts

The extent of the admissible evidence for the interpretation of contracts is very broad and is not confined to empirical facts. This involves, in appropriate cases, a consideration of the commercial purpose of the contract in question.[117] However, certain types of extrinsic evidence, such as prior negotiations and subsequent conduct, remain inadmissible even to discern an ambiguity,[118] unless being used to resolve a latent ambiguity.[119] The key question in this area, which has yet to be resolved by the Singapore courts, is whether prior negotiations and subsequent conduct should be admitted. *Zurich Insurance* departed from the present English position (embodied in *Investors Compensation* and, more recently, *Chartbrook Ltd v Persimmon Homes Ltd*[120]) by accepting the *possibility* of admitting extrinsic evidence in the form of prior negotiations and subsequent conduct.[121] However, it was also held that such evidence would likely be inadmissible for non-compliance with the requirement that the parties' intentions be objectively ascertained and the threshold requirement that the context be clear or obvious.[122] The holding that such evidence is inadmissible for being subjective in nature goes against other passages in *Zurich Insurance* (and later,

Sembcorp Marine) that the parties' subjective declarations of intention *can* be admitted in instances of latent ambiguity. On the whole, it can be said that while there is some inclination for allowing the use of prior negotiations and subsequent conduct in the interpretation of contracts, the courts have, on balance,[123] expressly left the issue open for further consideration at a later date, although it was said in *Sembcorp Marine* that even if such evidence were allowed in the future, it should be done with 'full consciousness of the concerns [relating to admissibility] ... and in compliance with the pleading requirements ... prescribed'.[124]

E Summary of key similarities and differences

From the above survey of case law, there are several similarities and differences across the interpretation of the Constitution, statutes and contracts in Singapore. Turning first to the proper interpretative approach, the key similarities and differences can be approached through several points.

First, the Singapore courts appear predisposed towards the specific purpose behind the legal document concerned, whether the Constitution, a statute or a contract. Insofar as a contract is concerned, its ambit is narrowly confined to the contractual parties, so there may not be a 'general' purpose to speak of. Indeed, preambles to contracts, which largely provide such a purpose, are routinely excluded from the interpretative process by agreement between parties. However, in so far as the Constitution and statutes are concerned, the Singapore courts have displayed strong fidelity to the specific purposes spelt out by the drafters concerned, which, in this case, would be the Government of the day. In this sense, the Singapore courts' approach is a more flexible version of Justice Antonin Scalia's 'textualist originalism',[125] which has been described to be textualist because it takes the text as the sole interpretative object, and originalist because it aims to capture the understanding of the text at the time of enactment.[126] There have, of course, been exceptions to this general approach, particularly in the interpretation of statutes, where the courts appear to pay heed at times to the more general purpose of the statute concerned.

Second, while the interpretations of the three legal documents all pay fidelity to the text, the degree to which this is done differs. It appears that the courts' adherence to the text is strongest when interpreting the Constitution, but weakest when interpreting contracts. For example, in *Sun Hongyu v Public Prosecutor*,[127] the High Court displayed 'strict textualism' in holding that while Article 9(3) protected an accused person's right to counsel, that did not extend to his right to be *informed* of his right to counsel because that did not exist in the text. More recently, in *Yong Vui Kong*, the Court of Appeal refused to read natural law rights into the Constitution and commenced its analysis of Art 9(1) with a plain reading of the provision. However, in contractual matters, the courts appear less tied to the contractual language, though of course it would be wrong to suggest that they pay no heed to it at all. Indeed, the courts have repeatedly stressed that they ought not to rewrite the contract for the parties. Nonetheless, it is equally true that the interpretation of contracts, as affected by the Evidence Act, permits the courts to depart from the plain meaning if an ambiguity of a particular type is found.

Third, as for recourse to extrinsic materials, the courts have referred freely to extrinsic materials in the interpretation of all three documents. The type of extrinsic evidence is generally restricted to those actually related to the document concerned. Thus, in interpreting the Constitution, the courts have referred mainly to historical predecessors of the Constitution, as well as the reports related to its drafting. The same might be said about statutes. As for contracts, there is a further restriction even if the evidence were linked to the contract: the Evidence Act actually prohibits recourse to extrinsic materials in certain situations. That might be regarded as a quirk of history, rather than a conscious decision by the courts to avoid recourse to such materials in the interpretation of contracts. Examples include the prohibition against prior negotiations and subsequent conduct (although the position might be changing in Singapore), as well as the prohibition of extrinsic evidence altogether if the contract were not latently ambiguous. Indeed, given that contractual interpretation in Singapore is itself premised on the interpretation of a statute, ie the Evidence Act, it might be said that the approach is not a misguided one.

In sum, while there are certainly differences across the board, it appears that, broadly speaking, the Singapore courts do interpret the Constitution, statutes and contracts from a similar starting point: they seek to give effect to the parties' intentions and do not see themselves as having the power to override that intention. Thus, any difference flows not from a different starting point, but from different degrees of applying this common starting point. The courts seem most reluctant to intervene in interpreting the Constitution, preferring to stay very true to the intention of the drafter. The same is true for the interpretation of contracts, but the courts have shown that in rare instances they may be prepared to 'override' the parties' intentions, particularly when the interpretation yields an 'illegal' result. The question for now is *should* there be any differences beyond this broad starting point? Or should there be other considerations that reveal a fundamental difference between the appropriate approach to be taken in the interpretation of the Constitution, statutes and contracts respectively?

IV Are the Singapore courts' approaches in interpreting different legal documents justified?

An evaluation of the Singapore courts' approach towards the interpretation of legal documents can be undertaken in two parts. It has been suggested above that such interpretation proceeds from a common starting point of giving effect to the drafter's intent, but differs in implementation.

A Should different legal documents be interpreted differently?

A useful account as to why different approaches should be taken in the interpretation of different legal documents is from Justice Kirby, who, writing extra-judicially, identifies three fundamental differences between contracts and statutes which he argues accounts for the differences in the interpretation rules of the documents.[128] While he does not include the interpretation of constitutions in his account, his analysis nonetheless forms a suitable framework from which we could try to explain the Singapore situation.

1 Each document is created differently

The first reason suggested by Justice Kirby is that contracts and statutes are 'created' differently. A contract is an agreement between a relatively small number of people; a statute is, however, an 'agreement' only in the broadest political sense, and one that is entered into between many more parties. It follows that there will be few available extrinsic materials that inform the meaning of contracts. By contrast, there are many public documents, such as explanatory memoranda and the ministerial Second Reading speech, which accompany the promulgation of a statute and elucidate the statutory text.[129] It is not hard to extend this reasoning to the Constitution. Indeed, it has been said that the interpretation of constitutions should not adhere to the techniques used for the interpretation of statutes and contracts. This is because, as Lord Wilberforce said in *Minister of Home Affairs v Fisher*,[130] constitutions should not be treated as Acts of Parliaments, but as *sui generis*, calling for principles of interpretation of their own.

This first reason does not tell us what the *correct* interpretative approach is, but only that the manner of interpretation of each type of document should be different because they are created differently. However, it is difficult to see why the difference in creation should result in a different interpretative approach being taken. Indeed, it could even be said that the differences that are identified – such as the varying number of parties involved or the type of extrinsic evidence available – are not actually relevant to the interpretative approach. This is because the fact remains that each type of legal document, however created, was created. The creation of each document, therefore, gives each of them a common starting point: namely, there was an initial drafter, who drafted the document with certain intentions in mind. The fact that one document involves multiple parties thereafter cannot then be used as a reason to interpret it differently.

2 Each document has a different purpose, reach and duration

To account for a different approach, the second reason provided by Justice Kirby is that a statute has a wider scope and longer (anticipated) duration than a contract. This is why statutory provisions tend to take on a broader operation and a wider meaning. This, in turn, makes it inappropriate to restrict the meaning of the statutory text to the strict 'intentions' of the original drafters,[131] a technique that might be more suited for a contract. In particular, contemporary ideas of justice and fairness might influence the interpretation of statutory provisions, and provide cause for departing from the original intention of the drafters.[132] Put another way, because each document serves a different purpose, each should be subjected to a different interpretative approach. This is known by some as the 'dynamic' interpretative approach, associated with academics such as William Eskridge and Philip Frickey. They defend the interpretation of constitutions and statutes in accordance with practical reason amounting to judicial law-making.[133] This approach has not been lost on the courts. For example, in *Yemshaw v Hounslow London Borough Council*,[134] Lady Hale said that the definition of the term 'violence' in the UK Housing Act 1996 has 'moved on' with the times, to be interpreted differently than intended during the drafting of the legislation. When applied to contracts, the conclusion presumably is that they should be interpreted more strictly since they are of a more limited duration and specific application. When applied to the Constitution, it might be thought that it should be interpreted most broadly, since it is meant to outlive even statutes.

It is suggested, however, that this reason misses an a priori question and does not accurately point to whether each legal document should be interpreted differently. It misses the question as to whether the drafter intended for the document to be interpreted so widely. And, certainly, beyond a degree of latitude, it is not clear if the line between interpretation and creation has been crossed. Thus, Lady Hale's progressive statutory interpretation in *Yemshaw v Hounslow London Borough Council* attracted trenchant criticisms,[135] and leaves one to wonder if the supposedly more 'liberal' statutory interpretation could be stated so widely, or if it is so markedly different from contractual interpretation. In the end, it is submitted that even this reason does not satisfactorily explain whether each document should be subject to a different starting point. The answer must be that it would only be so if the drafter intended it to be the case.

3 The remedies for breach of each document are different

Finally, it is said that different interpretative rules for contracts and statutes are in part necessitated by the different remedies that are available for correcting the linguistic deficiencies of the two kinds of documents. Justice Kirby observed that the courts could provide relief from contractual language via rectification or equitable remedies, but in the case of a statute, the remedies are more limited.[136] Unless the statutory language can be 'construed' to overcome the deficiency naturally, the only 'remedy' is legislative amendment or, more exceptionally, repeal, owing to the 'democratic legitimacy' of the legislative source.[137] When the argument is applied to the interpretation of constitutions, the outcome is that these should be interpreted more broadly because the remedies are even narrower than those arising from statutes.

Once again, similar to the second reason above, this reason misses the prior question of whether the drafter intended for the remedies to be different. And if the drafter so intended, that cannot account for a different interpretative approach. Indeed, it is only if the drafter intended for remedies to be similar, and if this cannot be properly effected by a 'strict' interpretation, that perhaps a different interpretative approach should be used. Moreover, the more serious remedy of striking down an unconstitutional statute must mean that the courts must be even less willing to take a broad interpretation of statutes that would result in such an outcome on a more frequent basis.

B Should all legal documents be interpreted using a common interpretative approach?

1 Fidelity to the drafter's intention is all-important

In the end, it is suggested that the Singapore courts' broad approach in interpreting the Constitution *like* the interpretation of statutes and contracts, insofar as they treat the starting point as being premised on the drafters' intention, is not wrong. Indeed, it is suggested that each document has the common starting point of a drafter with intentions that the courts should effect. This is even true where the Constitution is concerned. While the courts may have a broader power to give effect to the Constitution where unconstitutional statutes are concerned, the breadth of that power is laid down by the drafter of the Constitution and is not, as the Singapore courts have noted, inherent in the courts themselves.

This approach is also justified for the interpretation of statutes. In the first place, it rightly gives primacy to the purposive approach, as is statutorily mandated by section 9A(1) of the Interpretation Act. It gives proper respect to the statutory text. This, in turn, makes it preferable to the second view. Indeed, the view that a court possesses a general ability to rewrite statutory provisions is problematic because, taken to its logical conclusion, it effectively allows for the introduction of something not contemplated by the statutory words. The statutory language is to place proper limits to which interpretation can go. The danger of such an approach can be seen in *Knight Glenn Jeyasingam* itself. In that case, plea-bargaining in criminal cases was a concept unknown at the time the Evidence Act was enacted. Hence, to say that section 23 applied to criminal proceedings was to misconstrue the intention of Parliament and replace it with the court's own perception of the statutory purpose.[138]

The same is also true for the interpretation of contracts. Indeed, in *Sembcorp Marine*, Menon CJ noted that the common law parol evidence rule in the late nineteenth century precluded the admissibility of evidence of the subjective intention of the drafter save where there was a latent ambiguity.[139] This rule applied equally to both contracts and wills. This rule found expression in the Indian Evidence Act 1872 from which the Singapore Evidence Act was derived. Although the admissibility of evidence (governed by the Evidence Act) is different from rules of contractual construction, it is clear, as the courts have pointed out, that the rules of evidence may *affect* the application of the specific rules of contractual interpretation. Clearly, the universal approach for contractual and non-contractual documents, based on the commonality identified by Lord Neuberger, would certainly be affected by the kind of evidence that could be introduced to interpret the document in question. As such, given the common underlying rule concerning the admissibility of evidence to interpret both contracts and wills in Singapore, it is conceivable that a unified approach extends to their interpretation as well.

The accepted view today in Singapore is clearly that of separation of the legislative and judicial powers; the courts recognise this historical division between legislation and the common law and occasionally maintain that they should not act like 'mini-legislatures'. For example, in *Lim Meng Suang*, the Court of Appeal held that 'the courts are *separate and distinct from* the Legislature'.[140] More specifically, the court explained that while the courts do 'make' law, they do so only in the context of the interpretation of statutes and the development of the principles of common law and equity. The court further emphasised that it is impermissible for the courts to 'arrogate to themselves *legislative power* – to become, in other words, "*mini-legislatures*" '.[141] We shall have occasion to come back to *Lim Meng Suang*, as well as other relevant cases later on, but the point now is that Singapore courts do, broadly speaking, draw a distinction between their judicial power and the legislative power, to the point that they have no legislative power and will respect the power of the legislature 'to review its own legislation and amend legislation accordingly if it is of the view that this is necessary'.[142]

Ultimately, support for this view is firmly founded on the role of judges in interpreting a legal document, be it a Constitution, statute or a contract. As Aharon Barak puts it in his seminal work,[143] there is a difference between interpretative and non-interpretative doctrines.[144] Barak states that the authority to alter a text is one that belongs to its author, ie Parliament. The act of interpretation gives a legal text a meaning that its language (explicitly or implicitly) can bear and does not involve the express rewriting of the language.[145] Interpretation ends at the point where language ends.[146] As Lord Steyn put it:[147]

> The judge must concentrate on the different meaning which the text is capable of letting in. What falls beyond that range of possible meanings will not be a result attainable by interpretation. Principles of institutional integrity which bind all judges set those limits for judges.

Indeed, it is on the 'principles of institutional integrity' that one finds the best reason for the courts to shy away from performing non-interpretative acts such as rewriting statutory provisions in the guise of interpretative ones. The constitutional framework and the separation of powers restrict interpreters from giving the language of the statute any meaning they desire.[148] Moreover, judicial support for Rajah JA's view can be found in Andrew Phang Boon Leong J's judgment in *Nation Fittings (M) Sdn Bhd v Oystertec plc*,[149] where the learned judge said that the court's purposive interpretation should be 'consistent with, and should not either add to or take away from, or stretch unreasonably, the literal language of the statutory provision concerned'.[150]

All of these help to explain why Lord Neuberger thought in *Marley v Rawlings* that the approach 'should be the same' whichever legal document one is interpreting.[151] This is because, whatever the nature of the document, the courts' aim is to 'identify the intention of the party or parties to the document by interpreting the words used in their documentary, factual and commercial context'.[152]

The fact that a contract is agreed between multiple parties, whereas a will is a unilateral document, was not sufficiently compelling, in Lord Neuberger's view, to justify interpreting them differently. To this end, he pointed out that a patent, which is a unilateral document, is interpreted the same way as a contract.[153] The commonality of these documents is that they are intended by their drafter to convey information, which, subject to any statutory requirement to the contrary, mandates a universal approach that looks at the drafter's intention.

Whether the drafter is a testator, contracting party or Parliament, he or she entered into the relevant document with some intention. If it is accepted that the courts' duty is to uphold that intention, then it is obvious why the interpretative approach, on a general level, is largely the same. The cases are united in the view that interpretation is an effort to understand the meaning of the text and give effect to the intention within. In respect of contractual interpretation, this point is underscored by the Court of Appeal's judgment in *Sembcorp Marine*: contractual interpretation refers to the 'process of ascertaining the meaning of expressions in a contract'.[154] The same is true for statutory interpretation – the dominant interpretative approach used by the Singapore courts is the purposive approach as mandated by section 9A(1) of the Interpretation Act.[155] The value of such a general approach must not be discounted. It first informs the purpose to the whole exercise of interpretation, and this purpose then guides the more specific application of rules. Indeed, various branches of law are founded on such broad notions, with more specific guidance. For example, the law of contract could be said to be very generally based on the effecting of promises, but that general guidance is specifically applied in each area of contract law.

Whilst Justice Kirby's observations are all very well made, this does not mean that a unified approach is impossible. Perhaps unification could be approached on two levels: a general, overarching level and a more detailed and specific application level. And it is the general level that we are concerned with here, and on which we think there are sufficient commonalities to justify a unified approach. Indeed, a highly significant work by Aharon Barak, formerly president of the Supreme Court of Israel, presents such a possibility. Barak persuasively argues for a universal theory of interpretation – the purposive approach – to all legal documents.[156] The key to understanding Barak's theory is to imagine a range of 'intents' – from the 'subjective intent' (which deduces the meaning of the text from the intention of the drafter) to the 'objective intent' (which deduces the meaning of the text from fundamental principles of the legal system). A different type of legal document would, therefore, have a different starting point on this range of 'intents', with the appropriate interpretation to be taken accordingly.[157] Thus, the interpretation of statutes (especially constitutions) may have a different conception of the 'purposive approach' and may disregard the actual intent of its drafters in favour of some broader notion of policy. On the other hand, the interpretation of contracts or wills will start with another conception of the 'purposive approach' and place the intention of the drafters (as objectively determined) at the forefront of its consideration.[158]

Perhaps, even more broadly, supposed distinctions between 'broad' and 'narrow' interpretative approaches distract rather than clarify. When one considers the appropriate starting point, as already argued for above, such distinctions disappear because the only relevant question is whether the drafter's intent has been given effect to. In the end, a unified approach has several merits, the chief of which is directing the courts' focus to the overriding goal to give effect to the drafter's intention, and to appreciate that, whatever the nature of the document, language is an expression, but not necessarily the most accurate gauge, of the drafter's intent. This helps the courts to develop rules that will give effect to the overriding objective, and they will only develop different rules that are deemed necessary to take into account the differences. The general approach is then supplemented by specific guidelines particular to each type of legal document.

This general interpretative approach is then applied to each type of document with specific guidelines, taking into account the differences in the nature and purpose of the document in question. The difference is thus not with the starting point, but with *how* the starting point is *applied*. For example, even where contracts are concerned, the starting point is to discern the parties' intentions. But, from this starting point, the detailed rules might differ, for example, between a negotiated contract and a standard form contract. This is what we mean when we say that specific rules in relation to types of documents will differ, even if the general starting point should always be to discern the parties' intention. Thus, to return to our example concerning a negotiated contract and a standard form contract, the interpretation of the latter should generally be guided by restrictive examination of the context and underlined by a presumption that all the terms are contained within it. This is because the purpose of a standard form contract is to ensure expediency in payment, and to allow parties to determine their rights under the contract quickly just by looking at the contract itself. These considerations were indeed applied by the Court of Appeal in *Master Marine AS v Labroy Offshore Ltd*,[159] a case concerning a performance bond, where the Court of Appeal cautioned judicial restraint in the examination of the external context and extrinsic evidence.[160] Where statutes are concerned, the constitutional framework and the separation of powers restrict interpreters from stretching the meaning of statutory provisions. The purposive interpretation of a statute is both mandated as well as circumscribed by legislation such as Section 9A of the Interpretation Act. Thus, for example, in *AAG v Estate of AAH, deceased*,[161] the Court of Appeal disregarded social developments after the enactment of the Inheritance (Family Provision) Act and decided that the original legislative intent present at the time of enactment was determinative of the correct interpretation of the provisions concerned.

The only question that remains is whether the Singapore courts' application of a common starting point is correct in so far as each legal document is concerned. It is here that we must account for the differences in application of a common starting point.

2 Even if a common interpretative approach were justified, are the differences evident in the Singapore courts' application of this approach to different legal documents justified?

A THE DIFFERENT DEGREES OF PURPOSIVE INTERPRETATION

As we have seen above, the Singapore courts interpret the Constitution more 'narrowly' compared to other types of legal documents. This may be explained by the fact that the intention was to interpret the Constitution this way. Indeed, because it is difficult to discern a broad purpose behind a constitution, whereas it is easier to say that commercial contracts are almost always for commercial gain, it is understandable why the courts may interpret contracts more broadly than the Constitution. Moreover, given that contract is made between two parties, whereas the Constitution affects many more, a narrower interpretation is also justified so as to minimise the impact of any misinterpretation. In contrast, at the other end of the spectrum, contracts are interpreted with the broad commercial purpose in mind because that is probably what each commercial entity wants the contract to achieve. While a similar argument might be made for the Constitution, that it is meant to achieve the broad purpose of the citizens affected by it, there are myriad ways in which that purpose can be given effect to. Thus, the courts rightly state that they are not best placed to decide this, but are instead better placed to decide how commercial contracts should best be effected. This is no more than a reflection of the clear division between the legislative and judicial power, a separation that is steeped in history and recognised in Singapore.

The separation between the judicial power and legislative power as expressed in legislation only came to be in the second half of the fourteenth century.[162] By the fifteenth century, not only had the House of Commons' control over the enactment process strengthened, it had also begun to put texts of bills into the exact wording of the statutes being proposed.[163] However, even though judges were no longer significantly involved in the drafting process, they still wanted a say over the validity of a statute.[164] This followed one version of the Aristotelian argument, which held that a statute that yielded an outcome contrary to justice should be disregarded.[165] In *Bonham's Case*,[166] Sir Edward Coke said that 'when an Act of Parliament is against common right and reason, or repugnant, or impossible to be performed, the common law will control it, and adjudge such Act to be void.'[167] However, such a view lost its validity in the seventeenth century, particularly following the Revolution of 1688, which placed limitations on the power of the King and vested legislative authority in Parliament.[168] By 1765, Blackstone was able to observe that

> acts of parliament contrary to reason are void. But, if the parliament will positively enact a thing to be done which is unreasonable, I know of no power that can control it … for to set the judicial power above that of the legislature … would be subversion of all government.[169]

The predominant view, as Goldsworthy has noted, is that Parliament possessed a legally unlimited legislative authority within Britain.[170]

Judges, now no longer as involved in the enactment of legislation and faced with the prevailing thought that Parliament was representative of the people's will, considered themselves 'less informed than Parliament' and 'began to be reluctant to tread in political fields' and 'to show a greater deference to Parliament than they had shown before'.[171] It had become accepted in nineteenth-century Britain that courts could not overrule what Parliament enacted, and that judicial power was subordinate to legislative power in so far as common law must yield to legislation in areas of conflict.[172] This has remained the view in the English legal system in contemporary times. In the 1968 case of *Madzimbamuto v Lardner-Burke*,[173] Lord Reid held that if Parliament chooses to do any of those things that most people, for moral, political or other reasons, regard as improper, the courts could not hold that Act of Parliament invalid.[174]

While Singapore formally commits to the doctrine of constitutional supremacy, this deferential stance has influenced constitutional interpretation.[175] This may justify the different ways in which the courts have applied the common starting point interpretative approach to the specific interpretation of the Constitution, statutes and contracts.

B STREAMLINING THE TYPE OF EXTRINSIC MATERIALS THAT CAN BE CONSIDERED

But, perhaps one area in which the courts could reconsider their present approach is in the extrinsic materials considered. There is no problem with the courts restricting themselves to historically relevant content, because to stray outside of this might mean losing sight of the core question of discerning the drafter's intent. However, in the interpretation of contracts, the courts are unduly restricted in the consideration of extrinsic materials by the Evidence Act, which lays down antiquated distinctions between different types of ambiguity, each of which justifies or rejects the admissibility of further extrinsic evidence in the interpretative endeavour. To be fair, however, this may be a matter beyond the courts since the Evidence Act is an Act of Parliament that must be given effect to. Ironically, in giving effect to a statute (the Evidence Act in this case), the courts omit, in some sense, to give effect to the intentions of parties in a contract. This should be corrected to bring it in line with the interpretation of the Constitution, as well as statute.

V Conclusion

This chapter has sought to answer one question: should the interpretation of the Constitution in Singapore be different from the interpretation of statutes and contracts?

The arguments have shown that the differences in the Singapore courts' interpretative approaches to different legal documents result not so much from a different starting point, but from differences in applying that same starting point. This chapter has argued that the common starting point, that of giving effect to the drafter's intent, is not objectionable and should, in fact, be encouraged. This is one benefit of comparing the courts' approaches in interpreting different legal documents. And even so, the suggestion is made that the Singapore courts' different applications of that same starting point – which results in a 'narrower' interpretation of the Constitution compared to a 'broader' interpretation of contracts – can be justified. The only difference that needs to be addressed is the courts' rejection of certain extrinsic evidence when it comes to interpreting contracts, and even then, it is because they are statutorily mandated to do so.

In the end, the benefit of examining the courts' different approaches brings us back to the importance of the starting point. What is the ultimate purpose in interpreting a legal document, or any document for that matter? If the answer is, as it surely must be, to give effect to the drafter's intent and not to usurp that intention, then it must be correct that the Constitution must be interpreted similarly to statutes and contracts, with differences only in the application of that common and initial interpretative approach.

Notes

1 See *Zurich Insurance (Singapore) Pte Ltd v B-Gold Interior Design & Construction Pte Ltd* [2008] 3 SLR(R) 1029 (SGCA) [133].
2 [1980] AC 319 (PC) 329.
3 *Zurich Insurance* (n 1) [133].
4 [2014] 2 WLR 213 (UKSC).
5 Kevin M Stack, 'The Divergence of Constitutional and Statutory Interpretation' (2004) 75 University of Colorado Law Review 1.
6 See eg Thio Li-ann, 'Principled pragmatism and the "third wave" of communitarian judicial review in Singapore', Chapter 4 of this book, and Jaclyn L Neo, 'Balancing act: the balancing metaphor as deference and dialogue in constitutional adjudication', Chapter 7 of this book.
7 [2015] 2 SLR 1129 (SGCA).
8 ibid [16].
9 Magna Carta 1215. See 'English translation of Magna Carta' www.bl.uk/magna-carta/articles/magna-carta-english-translation accessed 11 August 2015.
10 *Yong Vui Kong* (n 8) [22].
11 ibid [21].
12 ibid [75].
13 ibid.
14 [2015] 1 SLR 26 (SGCA).
15 ibid [7], [77].
16 [1979–1980] SLR(R) 710 (PC).
17 ibid [26].
18 *Yong Vui Kong* (n 8) [64].
19 Thio Li-ann, *A Treatise on Singapore Constitutional Law* (Academy Publishing 2012) 548.
20 [2010] 3 SLR 489 (SGCA).
21 See Kevin YL Tan, 'Into the matrix: interpreting the Westminster model constitution', Chapter 3 of this book.
22 *Lim Meng Suang* (n 14) [48].

23 See David Tan, 'Whither the autochthonous narrative of freedom of speech? A guide to defaming politicians and scandalising judges in Singapore', Chapter 9 of this book.
24 [1994] 3 SLR(R) 209 (SGHC).
25 n 21.
26 [2012] 4 SLR 947 (SGHC).
27 Calvin Liang and Sarah Shi, 'The Constitution of Our Constitution, a Vindication of the Basic Structure Doctrine' (2014) Singapore Law Gazette (August 2014) 12 [38], [46].
28 Singapore Parliamentary Debates, Official Report (16 May 2001) vol 73, col 1726.
29 AIR 1973 SC 1461.
30 cf Tan (n 21).
31 [1995] 1 SLR(R) 803.
32 Thio (n 19) 548.
33 [2007] 4 SLR(R) 183 (SGHC).
34 ibid [41].
35 ibid [39], [41]. See also [44], where the learned judge referred to section 9A(2) of the Interpretation Act and held that the reference there to the recourse to extrinsic materials when confirming or ascertaining that the meaning of the statutory provision is the 'ordinary meaning conveyed by the text of the provision taking into account its context in the written law and the purpose or object underlying the written law' is an unequivocal rejection of the literal rule and/or any other approach suggesting that the purpose or object can be considered only when the ordinary meaning is obscure or ambiguous.
36 [2008] 2 SLR(R) 724 (SGCA).
37 ibid [10]. See also *Dorsey James Michael v World Sport Group Pte Ltd* [2013] 3 SLR 354 (SGCA) [18]; *BFC Development LLP v Comptroller of Property Tax* [2014] 2 SLR 462 (SGCA) [14].
38 [2013] 4 SLR 545 (SGHC).
39 *AXA Insurance* concerned the tort of harassment, which Parliament had legislated for from a criminal, not civil, perspective. The legislation, therefore, covered the area of law (here, harassment) generally, and not specifically, in the sense that the legislation was concerned with a criminal offence and not a civil action.
40 *Zurich Insurance* (n 1) [41], citing Neil MacCormick, *Rhetoric and the Rule of Law* (Oxford University Press 2005) 121, 122.
41 [2013] 4 SLR 193 (SGCA) [27]. See also *Precise Development Pte Ltd v Holcim (Singapore) Pte Ltd* [2010] 1 SLR 1083 (SGHC) [32].
42 ibid [125]. See also *Yamashita Tetsuo v See Hup Seng Ltd* [2009] 2 SLR(R) 265 (SGCA) [62]; *Tiger Airways Pte Ltd v Swissport Singapore Pte Ltd* [2009] 4 SLR(R) 992 (SGHC) [24]; *Straits Advisors Pte Ltd v Behringer Holdings (Pte) Ltd* [2009] SGHC 86 [14]; *Fico Sports Inc Pte Ltd v Thong Hup Gardens Pte Ltd* [2011] 1 SLR 40 (SGHC) [60]; *Shanghai Tunnel Engineering Co Ltd v Econ-NCC Joint Venture* [2011] 1 SLR 217 (SGHC) [46]; *LW Infrastructure Pte Ltd v Lim Chin San Contractors Pte Ltd* [2011] 4 SLR 477 (SGHC) [43]; *Ang Tin Yong v Ang Boon Chye* [2012] 1 SLR 447 (SGCA) [11]; *Edwards Jason Glenn v Australia and New Zealand Banking Group Ltd* [2012] SGHC 61 [33]–[35]. It is usually said that this is the meaning as would be understood by a reasonable person. However, this reasonable person is probably not always a businessperson; depending on the context, he may not be a businessperson at all: cf *Goh Eng Wah v Daikin Industries Ltd* [2008] SGHC 190 [45].
43 *Zurich Insurance* (n 1) [125].
44 ibid [127].
45 ibid [122]. See also *Yamashita Tetsuo* (n 42) [63]; *Straits Advisors* (n 42) [8]; *Van Der Laan Elisabeth Maria Everarda v Billionaires Management Worldwide (BMW)*

Pte Ltd [2010] SGHC 180 [22]; *Master Marine AS v Labroy Offshore Ltd* [2012] 3 SLR 125 (SGCA) [41].

46 *Ong Chay Tong & Sons (Pte) Ltd v Ong Hoo Eng* [2009] 1 SLR(R) 305 (SGCA) [15].

47 *Lee Chee Wei v Tan Hor Peow Victor* [2007] 3 SLR(R) 537 (SGCA) [41]. See also *Bidvest Australia v Deacons Singapore Ltd* [2010] SGHC 128 [53].

48 *Straits Advisors* (n 42) [8].

49 [2013] 1 SLR 973 (SGHC) [53], [54].

50 ibid [69].

51 *Sembcorp Marine* (n 41) [59].

52 *Zurich Insurance* (n 1) [110].

53 *Goh Eng Wah* (n 42) [45]. See also *Goh Guan Chong v AspenTech, Inc* [2009] 3 SLR(R) 590 (SGHC) [69]; *Fico Sports* (n 42) [61] (although the court phrased this as 'essence and attributes of the document', an expression which *Zurich Insurance* used to affect the range of admissible extrinsic evidence, rather than context).

54 See *Goh Eng Wah*, ibid [45]; *Yamashita Tetsuo* (n 42) [64]; *Indulge Food Pte Ltd v Torabi Marashi Bahram* [2010] 2 SLR 540 (SGHC) [9], [52]; *Soo Nam Thoong v Phang Song Hua* [2011] SGHC 159 [14]; *International Research* (n 50) [74].

55 *Tiger Airways* (n 42) [34], referring to Gerard McMeel, *The Construction of Contracts: Interpretation, Implication, and Rectification* (Oxford University Press 2007) [4.25].

56 *LW Infrastructure* (n 43) [43].

57 Thio (n 19) 548.

58 [1993] 2 SLR(R) 606 (SGHC).

59 No S 80/1967, published on 22 April 1967 pursuant to the Property Tax Ordinance 1960 (Ord 72 of 1960), now the Property Tax Act (Cap 254, 2005 Rev Ed).

60 *Raffles City* (n 58) [25].

61 ibid [23], [27].

62 [2004] 2 SLR(R) 577 (SGHC).

63 ibid [43].

64 [2012] 2 SLR 143 (SGCA).

65 ibid [30].

66 [2013] 3 SLR 380 (SGCA).

67 ibid [18].

68 [2011] 4 SLR 34 (SGHC).

69 ibid [192]–[193].

70 *Ang Tin Yong* (n 42) [12].

71 [1997] AC 749 (HL) 771.

72 *Yong Vui Kong* (n 7) [14].

73 *Low Kok Heng* (n 33) [50].

74 ibid [53].

75 *ADP* (n 65).

76 ibid [29]. By 'plain meaning', the court probably means the range of reasonable meanings capable of being borne by the text, rather than its literal meaning.

77 [1999] 1 SLR(R) 1165 (SGHC).

78 ibid [57]–[61].

79 [1996] 3 SLR(R) 390 (SGCA).

80 ibid [34].

81 *Sembcorp Marine* (n 41) [28].

82 *Zurich Insurance* (n 1) [44], citing HG Beale (ed), *Chitty on Contracts*, Volume 1 (29th edn, Sweet & Maxwell 2004) [12–117].

83 ibid.

84 [2009] 3 SLR(R) 1063 (SGHC).

85 ibid [19]. See also *Hanwha Non-Life Insurance Co Ltd v Alba Pte Ltd* [2012] 1 SLR 941 (SGHC) [32].

86 *Zurich Insurance* (n 2) [46].
87 [2013] 4 SLR 741 (SGHC), overruled by the Court of Appeal in *BFC* (n 38), but not on this particular point.
88 [2010] 1 SLR 769 (SGCA).
89 ibid [30].
90 (Cap 138, 1985 Rev Ed).
91 Singapore Parliamentary Debates, Official Report (21 April 1966) vol 25, cols 77–78 (Mr Yong Nyuk Lin, for the Minister for Law and National Development).
92 [2009] 3 SLR(R) 573 (SGHC).
93 ibid [6].
94 ibid.
95 *Low Kok Heng* (n 34) [45].
96 *Zurich Insurance* (n 2) [111]. See also *Tiger Airways* (n 43) [14]; *Anti-Corrosion Pte Ltd v Berger Paints Singapore Pte Ltd* [2012] 1 SLR 427 (SGCA) [24]. There is a live issue as to whether the parol evidence rule, encompassed within ss 93 and 94 of the Evidence Act, applies only between the contracting parties or to third parties as well. This will not be covered in this chapter, but see: *China Insurance Co (Singapore) Pte Ltd v Liberty Insurance Pte Ltd (formerly known as Liberty Citystate Insurance Pte Ltd)* [2005] 2 SLR(R) 509 (SGHC); *Lonpac Insurance Bhd v American Home Assurance Co* [2012] 1 SLR 781 (SGHC).
97 Law Reform Committee, *Report of the Law Reform Committee on the Review of the Parol Evidence Rule* (Singapore Academy of Law 2006) at para 13.
98 *Zurich Insurance* (n 2) [71], [111].
99 ibid [125].
100 ibid.
101 ibid [132]. For a more general acceptance of the three requirements, see the High Court decisions of *Goh Guan Chong* (n 54) [57], [79] and *Sheng Siong Supermarket Pte Ltd v Carilla Pte Ltd* [2011] 4 SLR 1094 (SGHC) [31].
102 *Tjong Very Sumito v Chan Sing En* [2012] 3 SLR 953 (SGHC) [97].
103 [1997] 1 SLR(R) 1006 (SGHC) [19].
104 See eg *JD Ltd v Comptroller of Income Tax* [2006] 1 SLR(R) 484 (SGCA); and *Chang Mei Wah Selena v Wiener Robert Lorenza* [2008] 4 SLR(R) 385 (SGHC).
105 See eg *Nguyen Tuong Van v PP* [2005] 1 SLR(R) 103 (SGCA); *Comptroller of Income Tax v HY* [2006] 2 SLR(R) 405 (SGCA); *Tan Chui Lian v Neo Liew Eng* [2007] 1 SLR(R) 265 (SGHC); *OpenNet Pte Ltd v Info-communications Development Authority of Singapore* [2013] 2 SLR 880 (SGCA); *Kee You Chong v S H Interdeco Pte Ltd* [2014] 1 SLR 189 (SGHC); *Public Prosecutor v Li Weiming* [2014] 2 SLR 393 (SGCA).
106 In other words, the Second Reading speeches.
107 See eg *Chang Mei Wah Selena* (n 104); *Bachoo Mohan Singh v Public Prosecutor* [2010] 1 SLR 966 (SGCA); *Re Andrews Geraldine Mary QC* [2013] 1 SLR 872 (SGHC).
108 This is especially so to trace the statutory history of a statute, on the presumption that Parliament's intention at the time of enactment endures until express parliamentary amendment: see eg *First DCS Pte Ltd v Chief Assessor* [2007] 3 SLR(R) 326 (SGHC); *Chief Assessor v First DCS Pte Ltd* (n 37); *Lee Chez Kee v Public Prosecutor* [2008] 3 SLR(R) 447 (SGCA); *ADP* (n 65); *Glengary Pte Ltd v Chief Assessor* [2012] 4 SLR 1130 (SGHC); *Tan Eng Hong v Attorney-General* [2013] 4 SLR 1059 (SGHC). However, in *The 'Seaway'* [2004] 2 SLR(R) 577 (SGHC), the High Court remarked that '[e]xcept where a statute reveals a contrary intention, every statute must always be interpreted as an "always speaking statute" ' (at [32]).
109 See eg *Lau Loon Seng v Sia Peck Eng* [1999] 2 SLR(R) 688 (SGHC). There have also been references to the Minister's Third Reading speech which took into account extracts from the Select Committee reports. Thus, while not directly referred to,

these reports were in substance referred to. See also, *Chang Mei Wah Selena* (n 104).

110 This includes foreign reports, particularly when the local statute had its origins in a foreign statute: see eg *PP v Heah Lian Khin* [2000] 2 SLR(R) 745 (SGHC) and *Lee Chez Kee* (n 108).

111 See eg *AG v Tee Kok Boon* [2008] 2 SLR(R) 412 (SGHC); *Chief Assessor* (n 37) and *Lee Chez Kee* (n 108).

112 See eg *JD Ltd* (n 105); *Ng Chin Siau v How Kim Chuan* [2007] 4 SLR(R) 809 (SGCA); and *Lee Chez Kee* (n 108).

113 *W Y Steel Construction* (n 67).

114 *Master Contract Services Pte Ltd v Sevugan Kalyanasundaram* [2005] 1 SLR(R) 475 (SGHC) [26]–[27].

115 [2013] 3 SLR 1052 (SGCA).

116 ibid [8], citing Francis Bennion, *Bennion on Statutory Interpretation* (5th edn, LexisNexis 2008) 588.

117 *Zurich Insurance* (n 1) [110]; *Yamashita Tetsuo* (n 43) [64].

118 *Zurich Insurance* (n 1) [132].

119 ibid [50].

120 [2009] 1 AC 1101 (HL).

121 *Zurich Insurance* (n 1) [132]. Although it has to be noted that, even under English law, prior negotiations may be admitted if they form part of the admissible background. However, the contours of this exception are not clear.

122 ibid For an example where prior negotiations failed the tripartite *Zurich Insurance* requirements, see *Bidvest Australia* (n 47) [53].

123 Even though *Zurich Insurance* was expressly non-committal, some courts have read *Zurich Insurance* as standing for the proposition that the admissible extrinsic evidence includes prior negotiations and subsequent conduct: see eg *Fico Sports* (n 43) [60]; *Sembcorp Marine* (n 41) [62]; *Shin Khai Construction Pte Ltd v FL Wong Construction Pte Ltd* [2013] SGHCR 4 [37].

124 *Sembcorp Marine* (n 41) [75].

125 Antonin Scalia, *A Matter of Interpretation: Federal Courts and the Law* (Princeton University Press 1997).

126 See eg Stack (n 5) 10.

127 [2005] 2 SLR 750 (SGHC). See also Scalia (n 125).

128 Michael Kirby, 'Towards a Grand Theory of Interpretation: The Case of Statutes and Contracts' (2003) 24 Statute Law Review 95.

129 ibid 108.

130 [1980] AC 319 (PC) 329.

131 ibid 106. The notion that statutory interpretation is dependent on the 'original intention' of its original drafters finds one of its strongest modern day supporters in Justice Scalia of the US Supreme Court: see Scalia (n 125).

132 Kirby (n 128) 107.

133 William N Eskridge Jr and Philip P Frickey, 'Statutory Interpretation as Practical Reasoning' (1990) 42 Stanford Law Review 321.

134 [2011] 1 WLR 433 (UKSC) [24]–[29].

135 See C Bevan, 'Interpreting Statutory Purpose – Lessons from *Yemshaw v Hounslow London Borough Council*' (2013) 76 Modern Law Review 735.

136 Kirby (n 128) 108–09.

137 ibid 109.

138 See *Law Society of Singapore v Tan Guat Neo Phyllis* [2008] 2 SLR(R) 239 (SGHC) [122], in which the High Court questioned the decision in *PP v Knight Glenn Jeyasingam* (n 77) on this basis. Also see eg *Nicholas Kenneth v PP* [2003] 1 SLR(R) 80 (SGHC) for another instance where the High Court effectively wrote into the statutory provision concerned [s 234(1) of the Criminal Procedure Code (Cap 68, 1985

Rev Ed)] a scenario which the draftsman had 'overlooked' but which was in line with the 'intention of Parliament due to the supremacy of s 9A(1) of the Interpretation Act' (at [24]). This must also be considered in light of the courts' exceptional power to read words into a statute under extraordinary circumstances: see *Kok Chong Weng v Wiener Robert Lorenz* [2009] 2 SLR(R) 709.

139 *Sembcorp Marine* (n 41) [59].

140 *Lim Meng Suang* (n 14) [77].

141 ibid.

142 ibid [82].

143 Aharon Barak, *Purposive Interpretation in Law* (Princeton University Press 2005).

144 ibid 14–15.

145 ibid 18.

146 ibid 15.

147 J Steyn, 'Interpretation: Legal Texts and Their Landscape' in B Markesinis (ed), *The Coming Together of the Common Law and the Civil Law* (Hart Publishing 2000) 81. See also J Frankfurter 'Some Reflections on the Reading of Statutes' (1947) 47 Columbia Law Review 527, 543; *Jones v Director of Public Prosecutions* [1962] AC 635 (HL) 662 (Lord Reid).

148 See also *Low Kok Heng* (n 34) [52].

149 [2006] 1 SLR(R) 712 (SGHC).

150 ibid [27]. See also *Tan Kiam Peng v PP* [2008] 1 SLR(R) 1 (SGCA) [59].

151 ibid [20].

152 ibid.

153 ibid [22].

154 *Sembcorp Marine* (n 41) [27]. See also *Precise Development* (n 41) [32].

155 *Low Kok Heng* (n 33) [39].

156 Barak (n 143). See also Gabriela Shalev, 'Interpretation in Law: Chief Justice Barak's Theory' (2002) 36 Israel Law Review 123; Thomas A Balmer 'What's a Judge To Do?' (2006) 18 Yale Journal of Law and the Humanities 139. Also see more generally a discussion on the difficulties with the concept of legislative intent: Neil Duxbury, *Elements of Legislation* (Cambridge University Press 2012) Chapter 4.

157 Shalev, ibid 123.

158 ibid.

159 *Master Marine* (n 45).

160 ibid [35]; see also *York International Pte Ltd v Voltas Limited* [2013] SGHC 124 [19].

161 *AAG* (n 88).

162 Duxbury (n 156) 22.

163 ibid 23.

164 ibid 27.

165 ibid 28.

166 (1610) 8 Co Rep 107a.

167 (1610) 8 Co Rep 107a (CP) 118a, cited in Duxbury (n 156) 29. Although Duxbury also notes that some legal historians conclude that Coke was referring to a principle of statutory interpretation and not full-scale judicial review.

168 Duxbury (n 156) 31.

169 1 Bl Comm 91, as cited in Duxbury (n 156) 30–31.

170 Jeffrey Goldsworthy, *The Sovereignty of Parliament: History and Philosophy* (Clarendon Press 1999) 233. However, there was still widespread difficulty in actually finding an official record of legislation until start of the nineteenth century, when the Record Commission published the first official collection of statutes, viz, the Statutes of the Realm: see Duxbury (n 156) 24.

171 PS Atiyah, *The Rise and Fall of Freedom of Contract* (Clarendon Press 1979) at 384, as cited in Duxbury (n 156) 33–34.

172 Duxbury (n 156) 34.
173 [1969] 1 AC 645 (PC).
174 Duxbury (n 156) 37.
175 See Jaclyn L Neo and Yvonne CL Lee, 'Constitutional Supremacy: Still a Little Dicey?' in Thio Li-ann and Kevin YL Tan (eds), *Evolution of a Revolution: Forty Years of the Singapore Constitution* (Routledge-Cavendish 2009).

Bibliography

Atiyah, PS, *The Rise and Fall of Freedom of Contract* (Clarendon Press 1979).

Balmer, Thomas A, 'What's a Judge To Do?' (2006) 18 Yale Journal of Law and the Humanities 139.

Barak, Aharon, *Purposive Interpretation in Law* (Princeton University Press 2005).

Bevan, C, 'Interpreting Statutory Purpose – Lessons from *Yemshaw v Hounslow London Borough Council*' (2013) 76 Modern Law Review 735.

Duxbury, Neil, *Elements of Legislation* (Cambridge University Press 2012).

Eskridge Jr, William N and Philip P Frickey, 'Statutory Interpretation as Practical Reasoning' (1990) 42 Stan Law Review 321.

Frankfurter, J, 'Some Reflections on the Reading of Statutes' (1947) 47 Columbia Law Review 527.

Goldsworthy, Jeffrey, *The Sovereignty of Parliament: History and Philosophy* (Clarendon Press 1999).

Kirby, Michael, 'Towards a Grand Theory of Interpretation: The Case of Statutes and Contracts' (2003) 24 Statute Law Review 95.

Liang, Calvin and Sarah Shi, 'The Constitution of Our Constitution, a Vindication of the Basic Structure Doctrine' (2014) Singapore Law Gazette (August 2014) 12.

McMeel, Gerard, *The Construction of Contracts: Interpretation, Implication, and Rectification* (Oxford University Press 2007).

Neo, Jaclyn L and Yvonne CL Lee, 'Constitutional Supremacy: Still a Little Dicey?' in Li-ann Thio and Kevin YL Tan (eds), *Evolution of a Revolution: Forty Years of the Singapore Constitution* (Routledge-Cavendish 2009).

Scalia, Antonin, *A Matter of Interpretation: Federal Courts and the Law* (Princeton University Press 1997).

Shalev, Gabriela, 'Interpretation in Law: Chief Justice Barak's Theory' (2002) 36 Israel Law Review 123.

Stack, Kevin M, 'The Divergence of Constitutional and Statutory Interpretation' (2004) 75 Colorado Law Review 1.

Steyn, J, 'Interpretation: Legal Texts and Their Landscape' in B Markesinis (ed), *The Coming Together of the Common Law and the Civil Law* (Hart Publishing 2000).

Thio, Li-ann, *A Treatise on Singapore Constitutional Law* (Academy Publishing 2012).

11 Much ado about nothing?

The enigma of engagement of foreign constitutional law in Singapore

Eugene KB Tan

On résiste à l'invasion des armées;
on ne résiste pas à l'invasion des idées.[1]

I Introduction

Students of Singapore constitutional law are familiar with the 'four walls doctrine' in constitutional interpretation. Put simply, when interpreting the Singapore Constitution and public law statutes, and in developing Singapore constitutional jurisprudence, Singapore courts should confine themselves within the four walls of the Constitution. At first blush, this suggests that legal developments outside of Singapore, especially judicial decisions of the courts of other jurisdictions facing similar constitutional issues, have little value – whether illustrative or didactic. Unlike the willingness to consider, adapt and apply foreign jurisprudence in commercial law matters, the Singapore courts have been cautious and, at times, even resistant to foreign jurisprudence in the public law sphere. This chapter examines the Singapore courts' evolving approach to and treatment of foreign law in the constitutional realm.

The use of foreign jurisprudence has been described in various ways ranging from migration,[2] importation,[3] borrowing[4] and dialogue.[5] In this chapter, I adopt Professor Vicki Jackson's use of 'constitutional engagement' in part because the terms used above to describe the use of foreign jurisprudence tend to connote a mono-dimensional, almost unthinking, utilisation of foreign jurisprudence by a domestic court.[6] This chapter is organised as follows. It begins by laying the background to the four walls doctrine, situating it within the contextual setting of Singapore's legal landscape in the 1990s. It considers the reception and application of the four walls doctrine in Singapore. The chapter then considers how the Singapore judiciary has engaged foreign constitutional jurisprudence by examining (1) the weight accorded to foreign decisions; (2) the selection of comparators and the relevance of difference in determining the use of foreign jurisprudence; and (3) the purpose of the foreign jurisprudence.

This chapter argues that the four walls doctrine has never really gained traction in Singapore. Today, with fifty years of constitutional law-making, there is less wariness of foreign constitutional jurisprudence compared to the high-water mark of the 1990s when foreign jurisprudence was effectively frowned upon as lacking relevance for a nation-state on the zealous quest for legal autochthony.[7] While Singapore is unlikely to see an easy comfort with foreign constitutional jurisprudence in the near future, such jurisprudence will take on greater importance and will have to be more robustly engaged with in the years ahead. The chapter further argues that the doctrine reinforces the need for the courts to be sensitive to the local context. Foreign jurisprudence must be carefully considered for its relevance and utility to the local context, and whether it falls within the ambit of the constitutional provisions.

Independent Singapore has thrived by being open to foreign investments, peoples and ideas. Its jurisprudence should embrace this inclusive spirit as well, particularly in an increasingly globalised world. Thus, as this chapter argues, even as Singapore seeks legal autochthony in keeping with its sovereign status, it must also look outwards if its jurisprudence is to remain relevant, authentic and authoritative. This approach promises to generate better or fairer legal solutions contextualised for Singapore's needs and interests. In turn, this will enhance the legitimacy of the legal system and the rule of law, both crucial ingredients in its long-term survival and prosperity. The supposed closing of the judicial mind to foreign constitutional jurisprudence is more apparent than real.

II History of the doctrine

The doctrine was first articulated locally in the Malaysian case of *Government of the State of Kelantan v Government of the Federation of Malaysia*.[8] Thomson LP stated that the Constitution was 'primarily to be interpreted within its own four walls and not in light of the analogies drawn from other countries'.[9] Thomson LP, however, did not elaborate on what an interpretation within a constitution's four walls meant.[10] The origins of this doctrine can be found in the Privy Council's decision of *Adegbenro v Akintola*.[11] The Privy Council put it as such:

> [W]hile it may well be useful on occasions to draw on British practice or doctrine in interpreting a doubtful phrase whose origin can be traced or to study decisions on the Constitutions of Australia or the United States where federal issues are involved, it is in the end the wording of the Constitution itself that is to be interpreted and applied, and this wording can never be overridden by the extraneous principles of other Constitutions which are not explicitly incorporated in the formulae that have been chosen as the frame of this Constitution.

Put simply, the doctrine simply stood for the proposition that 'foreign principles of law should not be applied if they cannot be accommodated by the [domestic] constitutional text'.[12] This is not surprising at all. A written constitution is after all regarded as the textual embodiment of a society's founding values.[13] Further, as Montesquieu put it, '[the political and civil laws of each nation] ... should be so closely tailored to the people for whom they are made, that it would be pure chance if the laws of one nation could meet the needs of another'.[14]

Before proceeding further, some clarification is necessary. A distinction can be drawn between the use of foreign jurisprudence in public law cases and its use in commercial cases. The issue of reference and use foreign jurisprudence in Singapore, outside of the public law realm, has been fairly uncontroversial. If anything, Singapore's reception of English commercial common law prior to the 1990s had been criticised for its overly 'slavish adherence to English law'.[15] Indeed, even as Singapore strives to develop its own autochthonous jurisprudence, it has always done so with a keen interest in how major common law jurisdictions including Malaysia, India, the United Kingdom, Australia and Canada have dealt with similar issues. In this regard, the Singapore courts recognise the promise and role of foreign jurisprudence in enriching Singapore's conscious development of its (private) common law.

In contrast, the Singapore courts' engagement with foreign constitutional jurisprudence is somewhat more restrained. In a number of post-independence cases, the courts have declined to so engage on the basis of the 'four walls doctrine'. The leading authority for this proposition is the case of *Chan Hiang Leng Colin v Public* Prosecutor,[16] a decision of the then Chief Justice Yong Pung How. This case concerned Article 15 of the Singapore Constitution, which concerns the freedom of religion fundamental liberty. The relevant portions of Yong CJ's judgment are:

> 51 It must be stated at the outset however that where the principal issue is the interpretation of the Constitution, the observations of Thomson CJ in *Government of the State of Kelantan v Government of the Federation of Malaya* [1963] MLJ 355 are pertinent:
>
> [T]he Constitution is primarily to be interpreted within its own four walls and not in the light of analogies drawn from other countries such as Great Britain, the United States of America or Australia.
>
> 52 This approach was recently affirmed by the Malaysian Supreme Court in *PP v Pung Chen Choon* [1994] 1 MLJ 566. I am clearly of the view that this would also reflect the position in Singapore.
>
> 53 In the course of the hearing of this appeal, Mr How referred me to various judicial pronouncements in the United States on the right to freedom of religion. There is a fundamental difference between the right to freedom of religion under the First Amendment to the United States Constitution and Art 15. The American provision consists of an 'establishment clause' which proscribes any preference for a particular religion (*Congress shall make no law respecting an establishment of religion*) and a 'free exercise clause' which is based on the principle of governmental non-interference with religion (*Congress shall make no law prohibiting the free exercise thereof*). Significantly, the Singapore Constitution does not prohibit the 'establishment' of any religion. The social conditions in Singapore are, of course, markedly different from those in the United States. On this basis alone, I am not influenced by the various views as enunciated in the American cases cited to me but

> instead must restrict my analysis of the issues here with reference to the local context.[17]

Oddly enough, the Chief Justice then went on to refer to the Australian High Court case of *Adelaide Co of Jehovah's Witnesses Inc v The Commonwealth*[18] in support of the need for curtailment of religious freedom on grounds of national security.

In those few paragraphs, Yong CJ had effectively raised the four walls doctrine into a standard mode of constitutional interpretation and had thrown into doubt the relevance of foreign constitutional jurisprudence in Singapore. The doctrine, in its strictest form, has been described as requiring 'a constitution to be interpreted within its four walls, and not by reference to other constitutions, thereby rendering the use of foreign judicial decisions illegitimate'.[19] This constitutional understanding dictates that foreign sources of law serve no interpretive function, either due to differences in the wording or phraseology[20] or differences in context.[21] At its core, the doctrine reflects an abiding concern that the wording of the Singapore Constitution should not be 'overridden by extraneous principles of other Constitutions'.[22]

But, it could also be said that in referring approvingly to the Australian decision, Yong CJ had implicitly demonstrated that the four walls doctrine did not require a dogmatic or wholesale rejection of foreign jurisprudence. Instead, the doctrine emphasised that a nuanced approach was needed as to which foreign cases might be accepted or rejected. The key considerations were (1) the strength of the arguments in the relevant foreign jurisprudence to be adopted, and (2) the relevance of the foreign jurisprudence to the local context. The recourse to and reliance on the 'local context' vis-à-vis the constitutional reception of foreign jurisprudence is an accompanying theme to the four walls doctrine. This local context principle functions as an additional constraint that regulates the reception of foreign constitutional law even where the arguments are persuasive. It reiterates the judicial belief that the constitutional text must operate within and be relevant to the specific context.

The context to the rise of the four walls doctrine should also be borne in mind when considering the seeming apprehension towards foreign constitutional jurisprudence. The autochthonous legal system drive that began in the early 1990s is pertinent. The 1994 Practice Statement (Judicial Precedent) is not only a significant milestone, but also aptly sums up the judicial attitude towards foreign jurisprudence:

> With the abolition of all appeals to the Judicial Committee of the Privy Council and the establishment of the Court of Appeal as the final appellate court in Singapore, we consider it desirable that we state the use of precedent in the Court of Appeal in future.
>
> We recognise the vital role that the doctrine of *stare decisis* plays in giving certainty to the law and predictability on its application to similar cases. However, we also recognize that the political, social and economic

> circumstances of Singapore have changed enormously since Singapore became an independent and sovereign republic. *The development of our law should reflect these changes and the fundamental values of Singapore society.*
>
> Accordingly, it is proper that the Court of Appeal should not hold itself bound by any previous decisions of its own or of the Privy Council, which by the rules of precedent prevailing prior to 8 April 1994 were binding on it, in any case where adherence to such prior decisions would cause injustice in a particular case or constrain the development of the law in conformity with the circumstances of Singapore.
>
> Therefore, whilst this court will continue to treat such prior decisions as normally binding, this court will, whenever it appears right to do so, depart from such prior decisions. Bearing in mind the danger of retrospectively disturbing contractual, proprietary and other legal rights, this power will be exercised sparingly.
>
> This statement is not intended to affect the use of precedent in the High Court or in any subordinate courts.[23]

In the following year (1995), Yong CJ elaborated on the legal autochthony drive:

> There has been a realisation over these years that Singapore has to develop its own legal responses to its own legal problems; Singapore has to develop a legal system that is autochthonous, that grows out of its own soil. But, autochthony does mean that we have to be willing to part ways with England, whenever necessary. To some extent we have already done so, particularly in several aspects of procedure, in legislation and case law. We must continue to evolve our own rules of procedure, suited to our own urban, multiracial, multilinguistic, Asian society. Our approaches to the law must reflect our Asian values, such as consensus and respect for authority and the group.[24]

What is clear in the legal autochthony movement, which continues in resolute fashion today, is the imperative of the law and the legal system to be suited to the local context.[25] This is particularly so in 'areas of law that are inherently contextual, for example constitutional law and human rights law'. This subtext of the constitutional jurisprudence being relevant to the local context can be seen in the four walls doctrine and in the 1994 Practice Statement (Judicial Precedent), which has a wider and more extensive remit. This brings to mind then Prime Minister Lee Kuan Yew's parliamentary remarks during the debate on the Constitution of the Republic of Singapore (Amendment) Bill in which he reiterated that for the Constitution to be effective, it must cohere with local requirements and circumstances:

> From my experience, Constitutions have to be custom-made, tailored to suit the peculiarities of the person wearing the suit. Perhaps, like shoes, the older

> they are, the better they fit. Stretch them, soften them, resole them, repair them. They are always better than a brand new pair of shoes. Our people have got used to and understand the present system.... Any fundamental change takes a long time. But most important of all, the Constitution works. Many countries have tried and gone through several Constitutions since independence ... They have not brought stability or legitimacy. I believe it is better to stretch and ease an old shoe when we know that the different shape and fit of a younger generation requires a change.[26]

Students of law are familiar with the need for a legal text to be understood and applied in the context in which it is meant to be utilised. Similarly, the four walls doctrine is not inconsistent with the imperative of constitutional autochthony, and the creation of a corpus of Singaporean constitutional jurisprudence and the moulding of a unique constitutional identity.

III Criticism of the doctrine

Colin Chan was the first of several judgments in which Singapore courts apparently utilised the four walls doctrine to 'insulate domestic cases from external influences especially when they were rights-expanding'.[27] As Thio Li-ann observes, the 'leading interpretive theory prioritises statist imperatives over civil liberties, with this "communitarianism" justified by reference to local culture'.[28] Since *Colin Chan*, the doctrine has been applied from time to time. The last explicit reference to the four walls doctrine was in the Singapore High Court decision of *Chee Siok Chin v Minister for Home Affairs*.[29] This case was a constitutional challenge premised on Article 14 on the right of freedom of assembly. VK Rajah J (as he then was) stated:

> 132 Different countries have differing thresholds for what is perceived as acceptable public conduct; differing standards have also been established when it comes to the protection of public institutions and figures from abrasive or insulting conduct. There are no clearly established immutable universal standards. Standards set down in one country cannot be blindly or slavishly adopted and/or applied without a proper appreciation of the context in another. It is of no assistance or relevance to point to practices or precedents in any one particular country and to advocate that they *must* be invoked or applied by the court in another. The margins of appreciation for public conduct vary from country to country as do their respective cultural, historical and political evolutions as well as circumstances. Standards of public order and conduct do reflect differing and at times greatly varying value judgments as to what may be tolerable or acceptable in different and diverse societies. In the final analysis, the court will not only be guided but indeed be bound by the manifest intent and purport of both the Constitution and domestic legislation, not by abstract notions of permissible conduct. In

so far as the interpretation of the Constitution is concerned, the following remarks made by Thomson CJ several decades ago in *The Government of the State of Kelantan v The Government of the Federation of Malaya and Tunku Abdul Rahman Putra Al-Haj* [1963] MLJ 355 at 358 remain most apposite:

> [T]he Constitution is primarily to be interpreted within its own four walls and not in the light of analogies drawn from other countries such as Great Britain, the United States of America or Australia.[30]

Unsurprisingly, the four walls doctrine has led to criticism that it provides a legal shelter for courts to 'cherry-pick' foreign jurisprudence, to prioritise 'statist or communal interests'[31] and thereby consolidate the status quo.[32] Such instrumental selectivity of cases is controversial given how courts disregarded the specific legal and historical contexts of the foreign jurisprudence used to buttress their position,[33] while characterising foreign cases which were unfavourable to their position as 'alien or inappropriate'.[34] In *Jeyaretnam Joshua Benjamin v Lee Kuan Yew*[35], for instance, the Singapore Court of Appeal brusquely dismissed the US Supreme Court and European Court of Human Rights decisions on the freedom of speech.[36] Instead, the court cited a different line of cases, viz, the pre-Charter Canadian cases,[37] in support of its position, but without considering the public detriment that would result from excessive self-censorship by individuals.[38]

The lack of clarity as to why one context is preferable to or more relevant than another is problematic. This is not to suggest that the judicial reasoning was unprincipled or capricious. Instead, the inadequate judicial articulation renders the four walls doctrine challenging in helping us appreciate when foreign constitutional jurisprudence can be received or not. Thus, it is not surprising if the doctrine has been understood as an effective barrier against the adoption of foreign constitutional jurisprudence.

It is submitted that this (putative or perhaps inchoate) 'walling' of Singapore constitutional jurisprudence from foreign jurisprudence might have been taken further than it should. At one level, it is certainly correct that in interpreting a constitution, a court should interpret the constitutional provisions 'within its own four walls', rather than 'in the light of analogies drawn from other countries'. This is so even if the comparators are of the same legal tradition. After all, a Singapore court is called upon to determine Singapore constitutional law, not Malaysian, Indian, English, American or Australian constitutional law, for which it has no expertise or jurisdiction. The Singapore judiciary is not an outlier in its acute awareness of its constitutional duty to adjudicate constitutional disputes in accordance with the Singapore Constitution. But, as the cases demonstrate, the four walls doctrine does not render Singapore's constitutional jurisprudence impermeable or the Singapore courts hostile to foreign constitutional jurisprudence.

Even as the four walls doctrine remains good law, the Singapore courts have continued to demonstrate their willingness and openness to considering foreign constitutional jurisprudence in resolving constitutional questions. Victor Ramraj describes the doctrine as applied in Singapore as 'legal rhetoric', observing that the use of foreign constitutional cases is 'very much the norm'.[39] This is notwithstanding the cases of *Chan Hiang Leng* and *Chee Siok Chin.* As Thio Li-ann notes:

> It appears that the 'four walls' doctrine has quietly fallen out of fashion at least in practice, as courts now regularly consider foreign cases which have only persuasive, not precedential value.... It is fair to say that the development of Singapore public law is not accomplished in a cloister sealed off from transnational models, but through a thoughtful engagement with foreign cases.[40]

What is clear is that the Singapore courts have not rejected outright foreign jurisprudence when counsel refers to them. How the Singapore court uses the foreign jurisprudence is, of course, a separate question altogether, but it has not walled itself or Singapore jurisprudence off from foreign constitutional jurisprudence.

IV A nuanced view of the doctrine

How do we then account for the cases of *Chan Hiang Leng* and *Chee Siok Chin*, and what do they stand for vis-à-vis the use of foreign jurisprudence when interpreting the Singapore Constitution? They can be understood as attempts to remind litigants and judges alike to be sensitive to the local context, especially when citing foreign jurisprudence. As Tan Lee Meng J explained of Yong CJ's decision in *Colin Chan* in a later case involving a Jehovah's Witness and Article 15:

> The learned Chief Justice rightly pointed out that when considering the Singapore position, it should be borne in mind that there are differences between the American position and the Singapore Constitution and that social conditions in Singapore are markedly different from those in the United States.[41]

Thus, whenever a question arises with respect to the effect of a provision in the Singapore Constitution, the starting point of the interpretational approach is that the Constitution is 'primarily to be interpreted within its own four walls'. Notably, Lord Diplock in the Privy Council case of *Ong Ah Chuan v Public Prosecutor*[42] had issued a similar advisory on constitutional interpretation:

> These articles are among eight articles in Pt IV of the Constitution under the heading 'Fundamental Liberties'. The eight articles are identical with similar provisions in the Constitution of Malaysia, but differ considerably in their language from and are much less compendious and detailed than those to be found in Pt III of the Constitution of India under the heading 'Fundamental

> Rights'. They differ even more widely from those amendments to the Constitution of the United States of America which are often referred to as its Bill of Rights. In view of these differences their Lordships are of the opinion that decisions of Indian courts on Pt III of the Indian Constitution should be approached with caution as guides to the interpretation of individual articles in Pt IV of the Singapore Constitution; and that decisions of the Supreme Court of the United States on that country's Bill of Rights, whose phraseology is now nearly 200 years old, are of little help in construing provisions of the Constitution of Singapore or other modern Commonwealth constitutions which follow broadly the Westminster model.

In the same judgment, Lord Diplock also presciently added:

> In a Constitution founded on the Westminster model and particularly in that part of it that purports to assure to all individual citizens the continued enjoyment of fundamental liberties or rights, references to 'law' in such contexts as 'in accordance with law', 'equality before the law', 'protection of the law' and the like, in their Lordships' view, refer to a system of law which incorporates those fundamental rules of natural justice that had formed part and parcel of the common law of England that was in operation in Singapore at the commencement of the Constitution. It would have been taken for granted by the makers of the Constitution that the 'law' to which citizens could have recourse for the protection of fundamental liberties assured to them by the Constitution would be a system of law that did not flout those fundamental rules. If it were otherwise it would be misuse of language to speak of law as something which affords 'protection' for the individual in the enjoyment of his fundamental liberties, and the purported entrenchment (by Art 5) of Arts 9(1) and 12(1) would be little better than a mockery.[43]

More pointedly, the four walls doctrine – with its accent on the domestic–foreign divide in constitutional jurisprudence – understates the importance of the judicial imperative of fidelity to the constitutional text. Where the judicial interpretation of the Constitution might seem timorous, could it be that our courts are being very conscientious that the power they wield in constitutional interpretation is significant? As the Attorney-General notes, '[S]hort of a constitutional amendment, the interpretations [the courts] lay down are final, and what they hold to be within the domain of the Constitution is thereby removed from the ordinary processes of democracy.'[44] And where the court has to go beyond the plain words of the constitutional text, the failure to justify the decision by reference to the text 'taints the court with the suspicion of preferring their own views under the guise of interpreting the Constitution, asserting judicial supremacy under the guise of upholding constitutional supremacy'.[45]

A The permeable four walls

A quick perusal of every reported constitutional law case decided post-*Colin Chan* shows that the Singapore courts regularly referred to foreign cases.[46] There was and is no evident aversion to foreign jurisprudence, even if many of these foreign cases were merely referred to rather than followed. There is no clear evidence to suggest that there was a decline in reference or citing of foreign authorities since *Colin Chan*.

Clearly, the doctrine should not be understood as a complete exclusion of foreign sources.[47] A wider interpretation of the doctrine can cover situations where the courts need not exclusively depend on domestic legal sources. The courts may examine foreign jurisprudence and learn from the experiences of their foreign counterparts insofar as the legal principles adopted do not contravene the local Constitution and can be accommodated in the local context. Such an interpretation is plausible, as reference to foreign case law was made even when the courts had steadfastly invoked the four walls doctrine.[48] In this less austere (and enlightened) form, the Privy Council noted that the doctrine permits the judiciary to 'look at other constitutions to learn from their experiences, and ... see how their progress and well-being is ensured', while bearing in mind that 'each country frames its constitution according to its genius and for the good of its own society'.[49] Such broader, more nuanced interpretation of the doctrine is preferred, given that the strict reading of the doctrine is unduly restrictive and, potentially, 'undermines the court's duty to generously interpret fundamental liberties'.[50] Also, the word 'primarily' in Thomson LP's pronouncement indicates that courts can still refer to extrinsic material as long as it predominantly considers and accords greater weight to material directly relevant to the local constitutional text and history.

To be clear, the four walls doctrine remains good law. Yet, it is evident that the doctrine never really gained traction in Singapore. This, however, does not imply that the Supreme Court judges pay lip service to the doctrine. Instead, the doctrine impresses upon the judges that in the public law realm, significant regard must be had to the local context. This entails that foreign jurisprudence must be carefully considered for its relevance and utility to the local context. In that light, one can regard the doctrine as being exhortatory rather than a prescriptive directive in constitutional interpretation.

B Manner of engagement

In considering constitutional engagement by the courts, Cheryl Saunders observes that 'how engagement occurs is a more interesting question than whether it does or should do so'. Saunders' approach seeks to make sense of the multitude of ways in which foreign legal experience contributes to judicial reasoning (in Australia) by examining (1) the weight accorded to foreign decisions; (2) the selection of comparators; (3) purpose; and (4) the relevance of difference.[51]

1 Weight

Given Singapore's constitutional history, foreign jurisprudence does feature in Singapore's jurisprudence. Singapore was part of the Federation of Malaysia between September 1963 and August 1965, and the Privy Council was Singapore's final appellate court right up to the early 1990s. The Singapore Constitution also claims lineage from the Malaysian and Indian constitutions. Barring these situations, foreign case law is not binding; it might be persuasive but even that would be putting it generously. In this regard, arguably, decisions of the Privy Council (which were not on appeal from Singapore) and the House of Lords are persuasive at best. But, this is very much less so today as Singapore is firmly charting its own constitutional destiny.

Notwithstanding the four walls doctrine, paragraphs 74(4) and (5) of the Supreme Court of Singapore's Practice Directions provide guidance on the use of judgments from foreign jurisdictions:

> (4) Judgments from other jurisdictions can, if judiciously used, provide valuable assistance to the Court. However, where there are in existence local judgments which are directly relevant to the issue, such judgments should be cited in precedence to foreign judgments. Relevant local judgments will be accorded greater weight than judgments from foreign jurisdictions. This will ensure that the Courts are not unnecessarily burdened with judgments made in jurisdictions with differing legal, social or economic contexts.
>
> (5) In addition, counsel who cite a foreign judgment must:
>
> (a) draw the attention of the Court to any local judgment that may be relevant to whether the Court should accept the proposition that the foreign judgment is said to establish; and
>
> (b) ensure that such citation will be of assistance to the development of local jurisprudence on the particular issue in question.[52]

The Practice Directions recognise and emphasise that foreign jurisprudence can provide 'valuable assistance' to the court although precedence is given to 'directly relevant' local authorities, with the latter 'accorded greater weight' than the former. The basis for this preference is not surprising at all and is practised in other jurisdictions as well. It also underlines fidelity in constitutional interpretation and the need for foreign case authorities to be relevant to the local context, especially if they were decided in 'differing legal, social or economic contexts'. This emphasis on fidelity to the constitutional text is a defining feature of the judiciary's approach to the use of foreign law.[53] The probative value of local authorities is, therefore, greater than foreign ones.

Very often, foreign authorities are distinguished or not followed primarily on the basis of the foreign constitutions being worded differently from Singapore's, and/or because the local conditions do not enable the foreign jurisprudence to be adopted or applied. In this connection, foreign authorities provide an invaluable platform by which Singapore courts can justify why Singapore's constitutional jurisprudence ought to be different.[54] How well the courts justify their position is a different question altogether but the fact that foreign constitutional jurisprudence is considered, in practice, by Singapore courts represents a significant step forward. This is in contrast to the jurisprudence during much of the 1990s to mid-2000s when inconvenient case authorities were often swept aside as being irrelevant without much substantiation, regardless of whether the four walls doctrine was specifically invoked or not.

However, it should be noted that reference to foreign precedents does not necessarily mean that courts have engaged in careful analysis of those cases and the constitutional reasoning that undergirds them. There is a tendency for Singapore courts to selectively pick arguments and propositions from foreign authorities where they are aligned with and support the local constitutional position. This self-serving tendency is challenging as it amounts to 'lite' constitutional engagement – more form than substance. This seeming reluctance to use foreign authorities as a platform to develop local jurisprudence is also observed in situations where such precedents are not aligned with how the Singapore courts see their role in constitutional adjudication.[55] In both instances, they result in the four walls doctrine being presented in a negative light.

The four walls doctrine certainly does not exclude the application of foreign jurisprudence in cases where the wording of the Singapore Constitution and the local context is the same or analogous to the wording of the foreign provision and the context in which the foreign authorities were decided. Given that judgments are subjected to increased scrutiny from academics and non-academics and the media (mainstream and social), the imperative is for the courts to deliver well-articulated judgments with sound and robust justification for their decisions in a legal culture that is increasingly accustomed to scrutinising and critiquing judgments against the backdrop of growing rights consciousness.[56]

2 Choice of jurisdictions and the relevance of difference

This methodological question concerns the choice of jurisdictions from which foreign authorities are usually drawn. Given the common law system of adversarial litigation, the choice of foreign comparators is very much dependent, inter alia, on the submissions made by the litigants (usually an individual and the state represented by the Attorney-General). It is not at all surprising if parties often elect to cite authorities from any jurisdiction, though almost exclusively common law ones, that support their arguments.[57] The party challenging the constitutional validity of a law or an administrative decision or action is more likely to feel less constrained than the state over concerns about the reception of their submissions by the court. In any case, the range of jurisdictions on which the courts typically draw is almost predictable, and is highly selective: the United Kingdom, Malaysia, India, Australia and the United States of America.[58] The preponderance of common law authorities is not surprising since similar questions about the substance, process and principle of the common law also arise in these jurisdictions.

Further, these are the jurisdictions with which both counsel and the courts are most familiar. As Cheryl Saunders notes, 'Reference to these [jurisdictions] minimises the risk of misunderstanding foreign law or the context in which it applies.'[59]

The choices of comparators also reflect the courts' institutional capacity to learn about foreign law and whether the legal system, including legal education, is conducive to comparativism.[60] Here, the four walls doctrine operates as a silent sentinel with regards to the central question of the relevance of a foreign authority. Again, paragraphs 74(4) and (5) of the Supreme Court of Singapore's Practice Directions provide useful guidance: (a) where local and foreign authorities are directly relevant to the issue, local judgments should be cited in precedence to foreign judgments; (b) relevant local judgments will be accorded greater weight than judgments from foreign jurisdictions; (c) citation of a foreign judgment will be of assistance to the development of local jurisprudence on the particular issue in question.

A perusal of constitutional law cases would show that the Singapore courts, while generally keen to engage foreign jurisprudence, have demonstrated reticence towards adopting it. For instance, in *Chee Siok Chin v Minister of Home Affairs* ('*Chee Siok Chin*')[61] VK Rajah J (as he then was) remarked:[62]

> Standards set down in one country cannot be blindly or slavishly adopted and/or applied without a proper appreciation of the context in another ... Standards of public order and conduct do reflect differing and at times greatly varying *value judgments* as to what may be tolerable or acceptable in different [societies]. [T]he court will [be] guided [and] bound by the manifest intent and purport of both the Constitution and domestic legislation.

Such a development is not surprising notwithstanding the trend towards global convergence, engaging with foreign jurisprudence, and transnational judicial dialogue.[63] The truth is that foreign precedents remain, at best, persuasive authorities in common law jurisdictions.[64] Saunders' crisp description of the relevance of difference as a methodological challenge in the use of foreign jurisprudence is apt:

> For present purposes difference might come in many forms: text, doctrine, legal context and the host of other social, political, historical and attitudinal factors that are sometimes compendiously described as culture. Identifying and making appropriate allowance for relevant difference is the challenge at the heart of comparative law, which tends to polarize comparative lawyers between the extremes of universalism on the one hand and particularism on the other.

Clearly, difference does matter. Societies are different. Fundamental liberties may well be conceived differently in different societies even where the equivalent constitutional provisions may be worded similarly. Not particularly enamoured with the universalist approach to constitutional freedoms, Singapore courts are acutely alive to difference – whether the difference relates to text, doctrine, legal context or local conditions.

'Local conditions' is a popular basis of difference adopted by the courts. Take *Colin Chan* as an example. In this case, Yong CJ asserted without further elaboration that the 'social conditions' of Singapore were 'markedly different' from America.[65] In *AG v Wain Barry J*,[66] Sinnathuray J refused to rely on contempt of court cases from other Commonwealth jurisdictions because their 'socio-political economic conditions' were different from Singapore's. Although *Wain* pre-dated *Colin Chan*, its summary dismissal of foreign jurisprudence in interpreting the Constitution is indicative of shallow comparatism, akin to the austere application of the four walls doctrine. Nonetheless, despite the high-water mark of *Colin Chan*, Singapore courts have not given short shrift to foreign jurisprudence. Even as Singapore seeks to carve its distinctive brand of constitutional law, it is diverging from its traditional comparators elsewhere in the world, even in areas where previously we took similarity for granted. This entails that new types of differences be taken into account.

The recent constitutional cases demonstrate that difference is increasingly used as a starting rather than an end point in considering the relevance of foreign jurisprudence in the case before the court. The Singapore judiciary recognises that foreign jurisprudence has its instinctive appeal to constitutional stakeholders – whether it is the litigant, the lawyer or the layman. In part, this can be attributed to legal globalisation and the growing understanding of rights as having a minimum universal core. In the commercial law domain, Singapore courts are already accustomed to accommodating difference and learning from other commercial centres like London and New York in developing Singapore private law.[67] Arguably, this mindset in the private law setting can be attributed solely to the nature of commercial law and Singapore's heavy dependence on trade and investment for its economic prosperity.

But, this judicial openness to non-indigenous legal developments and ideas in the private law arena has not conditioned the courts to reflexively use difference as the basis of engagement in the public law sphere. In dealing with the conundrum of difference, one suggested approach is that of

> understanding the multitude of purposes for which foreign law is used, the level of generality at which insights are drawn and the clarity with which the connection between foreign experience and a local constitutional problem is justified and explained.[68]

Singapore's constitutional jurisprudence has generated the 'local context' consideration as a key paradigm in constitutional interpretation. While this can be an excuse for passive or opportunistic engagement with foreign jurisprudence, the reality is that constitutions, courts and judges operate within a specific socio-political and legal context. This means that in engaging foreign jurisprudence, the courts must give greater cognisance to differences that may be relevant for the purpose for which reference is made. This does impact upon whether and where the Singapore judicial mind 'ventures' in the quest for relevant case authorities. The Court of Appeal recently reiterated that caution be exercised in relation to foreign cases, for which sufficient consideration and understanding must be given to the context of their 'unique social, political and legal circumstances'. This was in addition to the different textual formulation of a rights clause where these were 'materially different' from Singapore's Article 9(1).[69]

When this emphasis on the local context is considered together with the imperative of constitutional autochthony and a Singaporean constitutional jurisprudence and identity, then a more nuanced understanding of the choices made by the courts towards foreign jurisprudence is attained. Ran Hirschl aptly describes the identity-constructing juridical phenomenon:

> The distinctions courts make between 'pertinent' and 'irrelevant' comparators may well reflect the objective or reputational value of these sources, but more often they reflect the judicial image of the 'right' culture and 'suitable' set of values the borrowing polity ought to follow.[70]

In this regard, Singapore's constitutional jurisprudence and identity can be characterised by its focus on community interests, formalism and deference to policy choices of the executive and legislature, which connotes that the Singapore constitutional order is not rights-centric.[71] Despite commitments to law as a source of and as a means of building political community, identity and affiliation, as Judith Resnik argues, the individuated legal identity of the 'insular sovereigntist' like the USA can benefit from the consideration of non-domestic sources of law.[72]

3 *Purpose of foreign jurisprudence*

Part of the concern that courts often have with engaging foreign jurisprudence resides in the precise role of such jurisprudence in the judicial reasoning process. Broadly speaking, foreign authorities may be used as (i) a source of authority, (ii) empirical fact, (iii) a source of ideas.[73] As a precedential authority, this is rare in the Singapore context. There are not many such constitutional law cases in the first place and, where relevant, are seldom seriously questioned as they have already been incorporated into the corpus of law in Singapore. As such, these cases are often cited without fanfare. It should also be remembered that the courts are less resistant to foreign precedents when they seek to develop the common law or interpret a statute or a constitutional provision that is *in pari materia* with the Singapore equivalent. On the other hand, courts are likely to be more resistant to foreign precedents when presiding over constitutional adjudication that involves constitutional provisions that are worded differently from Singapore's and where the local conditions are different.

Nonetheless, foreign jurisprudence has much to offer as a source of constitutional ideas, possible approaches to dealing with constitutional issues, and insights into relevant reasoning. In this respect, foreign law operates as a foil for a Singapore court's ideas, judicial approach, and legal reasoning, including against universalist claims that may be proffered by a litigant. Thus, comparators can be engaged where their role is to serve as a guide to approach and/or reasoning that also seeks to clarify the constitutional ideas, principles and values that form the substratum of Singapore constitutional jurisprudence or how these should shape the development of Singapore constitutional law. Comparative constitutional law has vast potential to highlight and articulate the Singaporean context, which might not be so effectively put across without the comparison and contrasting effect of comparators.

Constitutional issues are similar across the world and the wealth of knowledge, experience, and approaches would be wasted if the rich sources of jurisprudence are not tapped. As Cheryl Saunders remarks, '... it would seem bizarre to tackle them [constitutional problems] in isolation from readily accessible experience elsewhere, whether ultimately it is applied or not'.[74] Comparative constitutional jurisprudence therefore provides a pooling of the various founts of legal knowledge, judicial experience and constitutional ideas that can be purposefully engaged for the benefit of local jurisprudence. Similarly, Attorney-General VK Rajah affirms that

> the Constitution shares many basic ideas with other written constitutions, even though its architecture and the precise wording of specific provisions may differ. It is therefore helpful to look at how the courts in other countries have interpreted their constitutions.[75]

The four walls doctrine is still good law in Singapore despite its cryptic conception two decades ago and its patchy application since then. Nonetheless, it would appear that the doctrine's relevance and applicability hinges on the degree to which the constitutional text is determinative. Singapore courts are not likely to rely on foreign decisions where the Singapore constitutional text is unambiguous. In *Nguyen Tuong Van v Public Prosecutor*,[76] the appellants argued that 'in accordance with law' under Article 9(1) of the Constitution includes a prohibition on cruel and inhuman punishment, and drew from the holding in *Reyes v The Queen*[77] to argue that the mandatory death sentence violated the supposed prohibition.[78] The Court of Appeal rejected this argument stating that that the Singapore Constitution did not contain a provision comparable to Article 7 of the Belize Constitution.[79]

It is apposite to note this, in considering the point of the extent to which the constitutional text in question is determinative. As Ronald Dworkin noted, strict textualism is either impossible or undesirable, and constitutional texts have to be interpreted against extra-constitutional considerations.[80] Even where the constitutional wording in two constitutions differs, the proper consideration is whether the principles enshrined within the text of the foreign constitution or foreign case law can help to enlighten the content of the corresponding articles in the Singapore Constitution.[81] Victor Ramraj correctly observes that the real issue then is what factors beyond the text ought to be taken into account, and not whether to look beyond the text.[82]

It does appear that Singapore courts are prepared to examine foreign jurisprudence more closely where the constitutional text is less determinative. This could, for example, relate to constitutional text where 'freedom' and 'equality' are used.[83] Ramraj uses Sujit Choudhry's framework[84] to highlight that Singapore courts have relied on foreign decisions in 'genealogical interpretations' of the Constitution. This is due to the Singapore Constitution and the foreign constitution sharing a common constitutional history.[85] For example, *Kok Hoong Tan Dennis v PP*[86] cited the Malaysian decision of *Datuk Haji bin Harun Idris v PP*,[87] which followed an earlier Indian case,[88] to hold that a legislative provision does not violate the Article 12(1) equality guarantee[89] if it passes the 'rational nexus' test.[90] Despite a minor difference in the wording of Article 12(1) and the negative phrasing of Article 14(1) of the Indian Constitution,[91] it is likely that the court in *Dennis Kok* relied on the Indian case because Singapore shares constitutional history with Malaysia, whose constitution was in turn inspired by the Indian Constitution.[92]

This 'dialogical interpretation' of the Constitution entails foreign cases as an 'interpretive foil' not so much to gain an accurate understanding of the law in the other jurisdiction, but to identify the assumptions that underpin their own arguments.[93] Yong CJ was apparently open to foreign cases in *Colin Chan* itself, where he considered the reasoning of the wartime case of *Adelaide Company of Jehovah's Witness Inc v Commonwealth of Australia*,[94] which prioritised security over liberty, as a suitable legal import to affirm the need to maintain public order in Singapore.[95]

C The rise and rise of 'local context'

Another dimension of difference in which the four walls doctrine is relevant relates to constitutional values. Foreign cases are less likely to be relevant if the constitutional provisions in question, while dealing with a specific right in question (eg freedom of speech), are undergirded by competing, if not conflicting conceptions of the constitutional values at stake in the two societies. For example, in *Jeyaretnam Joshua Benjamin v Lee Kuan Yew*[96], the need to maintain the reputational rights of Singapore's political leaders triumphs over the Article 14(1) freedom of speech guarantee where defamation was concerned.[97] Unlike the expectation and norm of political leaders being subjected to scrutiny, including otherwise defamatory statements, in Western liberal democracies,[98] the Court of Appeal opined that extending qualified privilege would deter 'sensitive and honourable men from seeking public positions of trust and responsibility'.[99] This was linked to the Confucian ideal of leaders being honourable men (or the Confucian *junzi*), whose leadership is predicated upon the trust and respect of the people, as was articulated in *Goh Chok Tong v Jeyaretnam Joshua Benjamin*.[100]

In *Review Publishing Co Ltd v Lee Hsien Loong*,[101] the Court of Appeal discussed, obiter, the applicability of the *Reynolds* privilege in Singapore. It noted that since the *Reynolds* privilege was not a pure common law development, the basis for adopting it in Singapore would have to be by way of the Article 14(1) freedom of speech guarantee,[102] which is likewise 'a right based on a constitutional or higher legal order foundation'.[103] Although the argument was unavailable to the appellants as non-citizens, the court nevertheless left the door open for Singapore citizens to make the argument,[104] implicitly raising the possibility of a shift in judicial balance from the protection of reputation in favour of protecting constitutional free speech. Here, the difference provided a segue for the courts to demonstrate the value and promise of *adapting* foreign approaches, keeping in tandem with the evolution of society and its norms and expectations. Even as the court analysed the *Reynolds* privilege,[105] it was also careful in highlighting the importance of local context in Singapore. The Court of Appeal stipulated the factors that are unique to Singapore, including the political culture[106] and the role of the media.[107] It observed that a future court, when revisiting the balance between constitutional free speech and protection of reputation, '*should* note the divergent approaches adopted by other common law courts on this issue and decide whether any of the existing approaches is relevant to our local conditions and circumstances'.[108] This attempt at being even-handed between engaging foreign jurisprudence and the four walls doctrine promises to enhance the maturing of Singapore's constitutional jurisprudence.

In a similar vein, there is also the growing judicial acknowledgement that some constitutional norms that transcend jurisdictions are incorporated within the Singapore Constitution and that the four walls doctrine does not prevent the courts from considering foreign jurisprudence. In *Nguyen*, the Court of Appeal agreed that the prohibition against cruel and inhuman treatment did amount to a rule in customary international law. However, it held that there was insufficient evidence to show that there was an international consensus as to a customary international law prohibition against the death penalty.[109] The significance of *Nguyen* is that in recognising customary international law, the Court of Appeal acknowledged that the Singapore Constitution reflects universal constitutional norms.[110]

With the growing movement for the abolition of the death penalty in recent years, Singapore courts have also been sensitive to the imperative to articulate sound justification for their ruling that the death penalty is constitutional. This can be seen in the 2010 decision of *Yong Vui Kong v Public Prosecutor*.[111] Various foreign decisions were cited to the Court of Appeal to demonstrate the unconstitutionality of the mandatory death penalty under the Misuse of Drugs Act.[112] The court did not reject these foreign decisions outright. Instead, these cases were treated with relatively detailed consideration. The court further provided substantiation for ultimately rejecting those cases.[113] For instance, in rejecting decisions from various Caribbean states, the court not only highlighted the textual differences in the Singapore Constitution but also examined the reasons for these differences by assessing the constitutional history of both Singapore and the Caribbean states.[114] The four walls doctrine was not invoked at all. In this regard, the Court of Appeal could have been seeking to engage the stakeholders rather than merely resorting to using, in a limiting manner, the interpretive device of the four walls doctrine.

The same considerations of openness to considering foreign jurisprudence and being sensitive to the local context are demonstrated in relatively novel areas of constitutional challenges in the Singapore context.[115] For instance, the growing assertiveness of the LGBT community has resulted in legal challenges mounted against section 377A of the Penal Code, which criminalises consensual sex between two men. In *Lim Meng Suang v Attorney-General*,[116] the Court of Appeal rejected American jurisprudence on due process (Fifth and Fourteenth Amendments to the Constitution of the United States) as it was '*materially different* from … Art 9(1) [of the Singapore Constitution]'.[117] However, the societal differences were not specified.

Nonetheless, whether the reasoning was relevant and useful, and the probative value that could be attached to the American jurisprudence, were not discussed. Neither was there any elaboration of what the material differences are between the Singaporean and American protection of due process. Furthermore, the court was steadfast in its view that Parliament, rather than the courts, is the proper forum to spearhead any changes in the social norms.[118] It was stressed that the Constitution did not refer to 'sex', 'sexual orientation' or 'gender' as prohibited grounds of discrimination,[119] unlike the constitutions of other jurisdictions.[120] As a result, only statutes that discriminate based on the specific grounds set out in Article 12(2)[121] will be rendered void.[122]

In the years ahead, engaging with foreign constitutional jurisprudence should not have the quality of pathos.[123] Instead, the promise of foreign law is rich. Arun Thiruvengadam argues that Singapore courts are shedding the strict adherence to the 'National Formalist' model that focuses on upholding national values in constitutional adjudication.[124] The incremental shift towards a 'Cosmopolitan Pragmatic' approach represents increased receptiveness towards foreign jurisprudence.[125] This approach can also help to ensure that the judiciary and judicial review remain effective checks and balances and the engine of rule of law respectively. At the Opening of the Legal Year 2015, Attorney-General VK Rajah SC spoke of a 'cultural change in recent years' which 'is in part due to the rise of an educated class with more awareness of their civil and constitutional rights'.[126] Against this backdrop of increasing rights consciousness, the imperative and urgency of a robust constitutional jurisprudence must mean that perfunctory judicial reasoning has no place.

Whether it is to ascertain the validity of principled normative reasoning by demonstrating consistency with foreign trends,[127] or to assist in the interpretation of the substantive content of rights,[128] or to fulfil an educative role,[129] or to fill a dearth in the law,[130] a strict and austere reading of the four walls doctrine would only stifle the autochthonous development of Singapore constitutional jurisprudence. By acknowledging that judicial interpretations of the Constitution have to 'change and evolve to changing social and national circumstances, and yet remain legitimate and faithful to the text', the Attorney-General sought to temper any expectation of interpretative exuberance. He said, '[S]uch evolution is ultimately constrained by the constitutional text. If the constitutional text does not change, there is necessarily an outer limit to its scope. A fixed constitutional text cannot have an ever-expanding meaning.'[131]

Engagement of foreign jurisprudence must still meet the requirements of probative value and of keeping faith with the Constitution. This makes the four walls doctrine still relevant as a touchstone that guides the use of foreign jurisprudence. In other words, the constitutional text is an inherent structural constraint on expansive judicial interpretation. The bottom line remains that the courts exercise prudence vis-à-vis foreign jurisprudence, rarely regarding it as authoritative. In this regard, the Singapore courts have shown an inclination towards originalism in constitutional adjudication, focusing on the 'text and intent of the constitutional founders, constructed by reference to historical materials'.[132] Originalism coupled with the four walls doctrine would ensure that inherently divisive ethical, moral, political and social issues are better dealt with by Parliament – not by the courts.[133]

V Conclusion

> I shall not mention the absurdity of wishing to draw conclusions
> about universal law from the laws of Rome....
> [T]he only way to arrange the laws and govern the state ...
> is to collect all the laws of all or the most famous commonwealths,
> to compare them and derive the best variety.[134]

The use of comparative materials in Singapore courts is not novel even in public law where the imperative that '[t]he development of our law should reflect these changes and the fundamental values of Singapore society' is arguably greatest. The four walls doctrine has a tendency to parochialism, something which Singapore can ill-afford. It is probably not inaccurate to characterise the four walls doctrine as being well on its way to being consigned to the dustbin of history in Singapore's constitutional jurisprudence and history. As Thio Li-ann and David Chong put it emphatically,

> It is now *de rigueur* for latter-day cases to comprehensively survey and weigh developments in other jurisdictions and to distinguish them, where applicable, from the Singapore context and position, or to apply them, sometimes with creative modification. This could reflect a growing trend towards a 'particularism without parochialism'.[135]

The bonds of its jurisprudence do not necessarily shackle the Singapore judiciary. This is important in enabling the courts to evaluate the strengths, weaknesses and gaps in Singapore's constitutional jurisprudence. Ran Hirschl regards comparative jurisprudence as 'a tool for understanding the political and social condition itself'.[136] Looking ahead, perhaps the Singapore courts can further develop and refine the four walls doctrine with a general theory on the use of foreign constitutional jurisprudence. This would provide further clarity and reduce perceptions that the doctrine is used defensively as a bulwark against foreign jurisprudence.

As observed above, Singapore has thrived on being open to foreign investments, peoples and ideas. This was the case during the colonial epoch and remains so in the independence era. Its jurisprudence should also embrace this inclusive spirit in an increasingly globalised world. In the Australian High Court case, *Cook v Cook*, the majority observed that

> [t]he history of this country and of the common law makes it inevitable and desirable that the courts of this country will continue to obtain assistance and guidance from the learning and reasoning of United Kingdom courts just as Australian courts benefit from the learning and reasoning of other great common law courts.... *[But] the precedents of other legal systems are not binding and are useful only to the degree of the persuasiveness of their reasoning.*[137]

Singapore's constitutional jurisprudence unequivocally demonstrates the emphasis on the centrality of the constitutional text, with proper consideration given to history, society and precedents. There is robust criticism of Singapore constitutional jurisprudence, as is evident in this volume, but we should not also confuse jurisprudential outcomes with constitutional reasoning.

The long history of constitutionalism indicates unequivocally that engagements over fundamental ideas such as fundamental liberties and national security, and how they relate, compete and even conflict with each other, show no signs of abating. These battles of ideas will persist, particularly given the evolving complexion of society and the reality that foreign developments will influence, impact and change Singapore society to varying degrees. Thus, even as Singapore assiduously entrenches legal autochthony, it must continue to look outwards if its jurisprudence is to remain relevant, authentic and authoritative. It promises to generate better or fairer legal solutions contextualised for Singapore. For a relatively young nation-state, Singapore's constitutional jurisprudence is far from being developed and settled. This, by no means, suggests that the jurisprudence does not sit on firm foundations. Are the legal actors, especially the judiciary, the Bar, and the powers that be, prepared to consider fundamentally new ways of looking at the Singapore Constitution and reshaping the constitutional reality that we inhabit if the circumstances so demand it?

Any over-exuberant sense of constitutional–jurisprudential self-sufficiency deprives us of a critical evaluative capacity and fixates us to a dogmatism of constitutional exceptionalism. Thus, foreign jurisprudence can offer relevant perspectives, including critiques and solutions, to Singapore's evolving constitutional jurisprudence. This is the promise and value of transnational judicial engagement, which reflects the dialectic of pluralism. Even then, this engagement, illustrative at its core, operates on the basis that Singapore courts only need be mindful of whether foreign jurisprudence and approaches fit the local context and circumstances.[138] Alan Watson's observations are salient: 'If courts only imported ideas that can be adapted to local circumstances, then judges can afford to be ignorant of "any real knowledge of the social, economic, geographical and political context" of the foreign rules.'[139] Or as the economist John Maynard Keynes wrote: '... the power of vested interests is vastly exaggerated compared with the gradual encroachment of ideas.... [S]oon or late, it is ideas, not vested interests, which are dangerous for good or evil.'[140]

As a facet of the engagement of fundamental ideas in organising society, the openness to foreign constitutional jurisprudence is an integral part of the story of the development of Singapore law. Pathos vis-à-vis public law need not be about the agitation of pity, sympathy and sorrow over the direction of constitutional law. Rather, the fear of pathos can function as a jurisprudential spur to persuade and convince stakeholders of a superior constitutional position not just on the strength of the legal arguments and reasoning but also from eliciting empathy and recognition for the value of adopting or adapting new principles from foreign sources. If we are not prepared to engage different ways of conceiving the fundamental ideas of constitutional law and constitutionalism, then we will not be able to reshape the constitutional reality we inhabit, especially if there is a patent need to create and shape new realities that will ensure constitutional legitimacy and robustness.

As Singapore's corpus of constitutional jurisprudence is still relatively young and limited, the need to consult how other jurisdictions have dealt with similar constitutional issues is potentially very helpful. In so doing, Singapore courts would, in Lord Diplock's much quoted phrase, 'give to Part IV of the Singapore Constitution a generous interpretation, avoiding what has been called "the austerity of tabulated legalism", suitable to give to individuals the full measure of the [fundamental liberties] referred to'.[141]

For Singapore, there are obvious limits to what constitutional interpretation by the judiciary can do as this chapter has sought to argue. The Attorney-General's conclusion to his chapter in this volume points the way forward, emphasising that constitutional change is not the sole prerogative of the judiciary. Instead, a whole-of-society approach is needed in which

> each succeeding generation must decide for itself if the Constitution continues to reflect its aspirations and our national conditions, and have the strength of conviction and boldness of spirit to make any necessary change. It is through this continuous process of refinement, stretching and easing that we work out our constitutional salvation.[142]

The dynamic balancing of values, local conditions and aspirations is inevitable. Similarly, the need to manage constitutional change (and with it the embedded contents of rights and their limits), including crafting a figurative new constitutional shoe, will benefit immensely from an enlightened comparativism that is tempered by the quest for our *sui generis* constitutional salvation.

Notes

1 'An invasion of armies can be resisted; an invasion of ideas cannot be': Victor Hugo, 'The History of a Crime: The Testimony of an Eye-Witness' (Essay on Napoleon III's 1851 coup d'état, 1878). The quote is sometimes mistranslated as 'one cannot resist an idea whose time has come'.
2 Sujit Choudhry, 'Migration as a New Metaphor in Comparative Constitutional Law' in Sujit Choudhry (ed), *The Migration of Constitutional Ideas* (Cambridge University Press 2006) 1.
3 Catherine Dupre, 'The Importation of Law: A New Comparative Perspective and the Hungarian Constitutional Court' in Andrew Harding and Esin Örücü (eds), *Comparative Law in the 21st Century* (Kluwer 2002) 267.
4 Barry Friedman and Cheryl Saunders, 'Symposium: Constitutional Borrowing – Editors' Introduction' (2003) 1 International Journal of Constitutional Law 177; Seth F Kreimer, 'Invidious Comparisons: Some Cautionary Remarks on the Process of Constitutional Borrowing' (1999) 1 University of Pennsylvania Journal of Constitutional Law 640.
5 Sarah Harding, 'Comparative Reasoning and Judicial Review' (2003) 28 Yale Journal of International Law 409.
6 Vicki Jackson, *Constitutional Engagement in a Transnational Era* (Oxford University Press 2010); cf Cheryl Saunders, 'Judicial Engagement' in Rosalind Dixon and Tom Ginsburg (eds), *Comparative Constitutional Law in Asia* (Edward Elgar 2014) 80:

> 'Engagement' is used in a neutral sense, to encompass any reference to transnational legal sources, whether positive, negative or bland. It extends to consultation of transnational sources by courts, even where this is not reflected in their published reasons.

7 Vicki Jackson describes the Singapore judiciary as '... at times inhospitable to efforts based on foreign constitutional law (or international law) to promote a less statist (or communitarian) approach to the interpretation of rights, insisting that the specificity of its constitutional provisions resist comparison': (n 6) 17.
8 [1963] 1 MLJ 355 (Federation of Malaya High Court).
9 ibid 358.
10 See also Jack Lee Tsen-Ta, 'Interpreting Bills of Rights: The Value of a Comparative Approach' (2007) 5 ICON 122, 125.
11 *Adegbenro v Akintola* [1963] AC 614 (Privy Council) 631–32.
12 Jack Lee (n 10).
13 Zaid Al-Ali and Arun K Thiruvengadam, 'The Competing Effect of National Uniqueness and Comparative Influences on Constitutional Practice' in Mark Tushnet, Thomas Fleiner and Cheryl Saunders (eds), *Routledge Handbook of Constitutional Law* (Routledge 2013) 427.
14 Charles de Secondat (Baron de Montesquieu), *The Spirit of the Laws* (1748) Book I, Chapter 3.
15 See Andrew Phang Boon Leong, *The Development of Singapore Law: Historical and Socio-Legal Perspectives* (Butterworths 1990). See also Goh Yihan and Paul Tan, 'The Growth of Local Jurisprudence' in Goh Yihan and Paul Tan (eds), *Singapore Law: 50 Years in the Making* (Academy Publishing 2015).
16 [1994] 3 SLR(R) 209 (Singapore High Court (Sing HC)). Yong CJ, interestingly, cited and followed the Malaysian case of *Government of the State of Kelantan v Government of the Federation of Malaysia* (n 8) as authority for the doctrine.
17 *Chan Hiang Leng Colin v Public Prosecutor* [1994] 3 SLR(R) 209 (Sing HC) [49], [51]–[53].
18 (1943) 67 CLR 16 (High Court of Australia (Australia HC)).
19 Arun K Thiruvengadam, 'Comparative Law and Constitutional Interpretation in Sin-

gapore: Insights from Constitutional Theory' in Thio Li-ann and Kevin YL Tan (eds), *Evolution of a Revolution: Forty Years of the Singapore Constitution* (Routledge-Cavendish 2009) 114, 121.

20 Jack Lee (n 10) 128.

21 Tan Seow Hon, 'Constitutional Jurisprudence: Beyond Supreme Law – A Law Higher Still' in Thio and Tan (n 19) 79, 83.

22 Thio Li-ann, *A Treatise on Singapore Constitutional Law* (Academy Publishing 2012) 561.

23 *Practice Statement (Judicial Precedent)* [1994] 2 SLR 689 (emphasis added). Yong CJ read the Practice Statement at the commencement of hearings of the Court of Appeal on 11 July 1994.

24 Yong Pung How, 'Speech delivered at the Singapore Academy of Law Second Annual Lecture' (Singapore, 12 September 1995). See Hoo Sheau Peng et al. (eds), *Speeches and Judgments of Chief Justice Yong Pung How* (FT Law & Tax Asia Pacific 1996) 193–94.

25 See K Shanmugam, 'Opening Address by Minister for Law, K Shanmugam, at the launch of the NUS Centre for Banking and Financial Law' (Singapore, 12 September 2014) http://law.nus.edu.sg/pdfs/cbfl/events/CBFLLaunch_OpeningAddress.pdf accessed 3 October 2015. The Minister also said that the Singapore government is 'very keen' to develop intellectual leadership and capabilities in areas such as banking and financial law. To this end, there is the need to

> build up a strong core of home-grown academics in the law faculty who are able to articulate and grow Singapore law as a law of choice for commerce in the region, and are able to help in the *development of our own jurisprudence particularly in areas of law that are inherently contextual, for example constitutional law and human rights law* (emphasis added).

26 Singapore Parliamentary Debates, Official Report (24 July 1984) vol 44, cols 1735–36. This Bill provided for the Non-Constituency Member of Parliament (NCMP) scheme, the first of a series of constitutional innovations between 1984 and 1990. On the intense and extensive constitutional engineering during this period, see Eugene KB Tan, 'Autochthonous Constitutional Design in Post-Colonial Singapore: Intimations of Confucianism and the Leviathan in Entrenching Dominant Government' (2013) 4 Yonsei Law Journal 273.

27 Thio Li-ann, 'Beyond the "Four Walls" in an Age of Transnational Judicial Conversations: Civil Liberties, Rights Theories, and Constitutional Adjudication in Malaysia and Singapore' (2006) 19 Columbia Journal of Asian Law 428, 431.

28 Thio Li-ann, 'In Search of the Singapore Constitution: Retrospect and Prospect' in Thio and Tan (n 19) 323, 338.

29 [2006] 1 SLR(R) 582 (Sing HC).

30 *Chee Siok Chin v Minister for Home Affairs* [2006] 1 SLR(R) 582 (Sing HC) [5], [86]–[87], [132].

31 Thio (n 27) 518.

32 ibid 435.

33 Victor V Ramraj, 'Comparative Constitutional Law in Singapore' (2002) 6 Singapore Journal of International and Comparative Law 302.

34 Thio Li-ann, 'An "i" for an "I"? Singapore's Communitarian Model of Constitutional Adjudication' (1997) 27 Hong Kong Law Journal 152, 177.

35 [1992] 1 SLR(R) 791 (Singapore Court of Appeal (Sing CA)).

36 ibid [56].

37 ibid [68].

38 Thio (n 27) 473.

39 Ramraj (n 33) 302, 310.

40 Thio (n 22) 566, [10.294].

41 *Peter Williams Nappalli v Institute of Technical Education* [1998] SGHC 351 (Sing HC) [42].
42 [1979–1980] SLR(R) 710 (Privy Council) [22].
43 ibid [26].
44 See VK Rajah, 'Interpreting the Singapore Constitution', Chapter 1 of this book.
45 ibid.
46 See Jack Tsen-Ta Lee, 'Foreign Precedents in Constitutional Adjudication by the Supreme Court of Singapore, 1963–2013' (2015) 24 Washington International Law Journal 253. Lee (ibid 284) concludes that

> Singapore courts have consistently referred to foreign precedent in constitutional adjudication … even during the period roughly corresponding with Chief Justice Yong Pung How's term of office (1990–2006), when the four walls doctrine held sway.

47 ibid 288.
48 Chia Huai Yuan, 'Taking Rights Seriously: 30 Years of Constitutional Adjudication' (2011) 29 Singapore Law Review 115, 125.
49 *Adegbenro* (n 11) 620.
50 Thio Li-ann, 'Protecting Rights' in Thio and Tan (n 19) 193, 214.
51 Cheryl Saunders, 'Judicial Engagement in the High Court of Australia' (A High Court of Australia Public Lecture, Australia, 20 June 2012) www.hcourt.gov.au/assets/publications/speeches/lecture-series/Lecture.pdf accessed 3 October 2015.
52 Supreme Court Practice Directions (2013) www.supremecourt.gov.sg/data/doc/ManagePage/98/ePD_PDF/ePD.pdf accessed 3 October 2015. Issued by the Supreme Court, the Practice Directions supplement the Rules of Court to regulate court practice and procedure.
53 See VK Rajah, 'Interpreting the Singapore Constitution', Chapter 1 of this book.
54 In the words of the former Chief Justice of Israel, Aharon Barak, foreign law can promote 'greater self-knowledge': Aharon Barak, 'A Judge on Judging: The Role of a Supreme Court in a Democracy' (2002) 116 Harvard Law Review 16, 110.
55 See also Yvonne Tew, 'Originalism at Home and Abroad' (2014) 52 Columbia Journal of Transnational Law 780.
56 VK Rajah, 'Speech of the Attorney-General VK Rajah SC as Delivered at the Opening of the Legal Year 2015, 5 January' (Singapore, 5 January 2015) www.agc.gov.sg/DATA/0/Docs/NewsFiles/OPENING%20OF%20LEGAL%20YEAR%202015_ATTORNEY-GENERAL%20V%20K%20RAJAH'S%20SPEECH_5%20JAN_checked%20against%20delivery.pdf accessed 3 October 2015.
57 On the influence of the choice of foreign law in constitutional adjudication, see Pradyumna Tripathi, 'Foreign Precedents and Constitutional Law' (1957) Columbia Law Review 319.
58 Other jurisdictions cited with much less frequency include the European Court of Human Rights, New Zealand and Canada. The pool of likely comparators is unlikely to change significantly.
59 Saunders (n 51).
60 See the engaging study on the use of comparative constitutional analysis by the apex/constitutional courts of Japan, Korea, Taiwan and Hong Kong: David S Law, 'Judicial Comparativism and Judicial Diplomacy' (2015) 163 University of Pennsylvania Law Review 927. Law also argues that judges engage with foreign law and foreign courts 'for reasons that have little to do with the performance of legal or adjudicative functions': ibid 1003. This is the phenomenon of judicial diplomacy.
61 *Chee Siok Chin* (n 30).
62 ibid [132] (emphasis added).
63 On the apparent convergence of national constitutional systems in the Asian context, see Cheryl Saunders, 'The Impact of Internationalisation on National Constitutions' in Albert HY Chen (ed), *Constitutionalism in Asia in the Early Twenty-First Century*

(Cambridge University Press 2014). See also Michel Rosenfeld, 'Is Global Constitutionalism Meaningful or Desirable?' (2014) 25 European Journal of International Law 177; David S Law and Mila Versteeg, 'The Evolution and Ideology of Global Constitutionalism' (2011) California Law Review 1163.

64 As Neil Duxbury reminds us (in Neil Duxbury, 'The Law of the Land' (2015) 78 Modern Law Review 26, 54):

> … it is a mistake to think that convergent foreign precedents acquire, purely by virtue of their commonality, the status of positive law. If foreign precedents are to have that status within a particular jurisdiction, the jurisdiction would have to incorporate them as part of the national law.

65 *Colin Chan* (n 17) [53].

66 *Attorney-General v Wain Barry J* [1991] 1 SLR(R) 85 (Sing HC).

67 This development is given further impetus by the Singapore Supreme Court's drive towards the harmonisation of commercial law in the Asia-Pacific region. See Sundaresh Menon, 'Transnational Commercial Law: Realities, Challenges and a Call for Meaningful Convergence' in *Core Values of an Effective Judiciary* (Academy Publishing 2015).

68 Saunders (n 51).

69 *Lim Meng Suang v Attorney-General* [2015] 1 SLR 26 (Sing CA) [48].

70 Ran Hirschl, 'In Search of an Identity: Voluntary Foreign Citations in Discordant Constitutional Settings' (2014) 62 American Journal of Comparative Law 547, 584.

71 For a recent discussion on Singapore's 'authoritarian constitutionalism', see Mark Tushnet, 'Authoritarian Constitutionalism' (2015) 100 Cornell Law Review 391.

72 Judith Resnik, 'Constructing the "Foreign": American Law's Relationship to Non-Domestic Sources' in Mads Andenas and Duncan Fairgrieve (eds), *Courts and Comparative Law* (Oxford University Press forthcoming).

73 See, further, Neil Duxbury (n 64) 29–34; Robert Reed, 'Foreign Precedents and Judicial Reasoning: The American Debate and British Practice' (2008) 124 Law Quarterly Review 253.

74 Saunders (n 51).

75 See VK Rajah, 'Interpreting the Singapore Constitution', Chapter 1 of this book.

76 [2005] 1 SLR(R) 103 (Sing CA).

77 *Reyes v The Queen* [2002] 2 AC 235 (Privy Council on appeal from Belize).

78 *Nguyen* (n 76) [79], [84].

79 ibid [84]. When the case was heard before the High Court, Kan J opined that *Reyes* would apply had there been an equivalent provision to Section 7 of the Belize Constitution in Singapore: *Nguyen Tuong Van v Public Prosecutor* [2004] 2 SLR(R) 328 (Sing HC) [90].

80 Ronald Dworkin, 'The Constitution' in Ronald Dworkin, *Law's Empire* (Harvard University Press 1986) 359–60.

81 Jack Lee (n 10) 122.

82 Ramraj (n 33) 324.

83 ibid 310.

84 Sujit Choudhry, 'Globalization in Search of Justification: Toward a Theory of Comparative Constitutional Interpretation' (1999) 74 Indiana Law Journal 819.

85 ibid 838.

86 *Kok Hoong Tan Dennis v Public Prosecutor* [1997] 1 SLR 123 (Sing HC).

87 *Datuk Haji bin Harun Idris v Public Prosecutor* [1977] 2 MLJ 155 (Federal Court of Malaysia).

88 *Shri Ram Krishna Dalmia v Shri Justice S R Tendolkar* [1958] AIR 538 (Supreme Court of India) 296–97.

89 Constitution of the Republic of Singapore (1985 Rev Ed, 1999 Reprint) ('Singapore Constitution') Art 12(1).

90 The test holds that a law that makes a classification is acceptable if it is founded on

an intelligible differentia which distinguishes persons that are grouped together from others left out of the group, and the differentia must have a rational relation to the end to be achieved by the law in question: see *Dennis Kok* (n 86) [34].

91 Singapore Constitution (n 89) Art 12(1) states: 'All persons are equal before the law and entitled to the equal protection of the law.' cf Constitution of India, 1950: Art 14(1) states: 'The State shall not deny to any person equality before the law or the equal protection of the laws within the territory of India.'

92 Ramraj (n 33) 313.

93 Jack Lee (n 10) 131.

94 *Colin Chan* (n 17) [60], citing *Adelaide* (n 18).

95 ibid [60]–[64]. See Thio Li-ann, 'Beyond the "Four Walls"' (n 27) 487.

96 *Jeyaretnam* (n 35). Although *Jeyaretnam* was decided before the 'four walls' doctrine was articulated by Yong CJ in *Colin Chan*, its cautious attitude towards the use of foreign material to interpret the Constitution reflected the same judicial attitude that is arguably representative of the four walls doctrine.

97 Singapore Constitution (n 89) Art 14(1).

98 Eugene Kheng-Boon Tan, 'Law and Values in Governance: The Singapore Way' (2000) 30 Hong Kong Law Journal 91, 107.

99 *Jeyaretnam* (n 96) [64].

100 *Goh Chok Tong v Jeyaretnam Joshua Benjamin* [1997] 3 SLR(R) 46 (Sing HC). See also *Shared Values* (White Paper, Cmd 1, 1991) para 41.

101 *Review Publishing Co Ltd v Lee Hsien Loong* [2010] 1 SLR 52 (Sing CA) ('*Review Publishing*').

102 Singapore Constitution (n 89) Art 14(1).

103 *Review Publishing* (n 101) [264].

104 ibid [267].

105 *Reynolds v Times Newspapers Ltd* [2001] 2 AC 127.

106 *Review Publishing* (n 101) [285]. The political culture of Singapore focuses on honesty and integrity in disclosing matters of public interest and not making false statements to undermine the integrity of elected politicians.

107 ibid [277]. The court noted that the role of Singapore media is distinct from that in the UK and that investigative journalism is discouraged in Singapore.

108 *Review Publishing* (n 101) [290].

109 *Nguyen* (n 76) [91]–[92].

110 Jack Lee (n 10) 139.

111 [2010] 3 SLR 489 (Sing CA).

112 ibid [34].

113 ibid [52]–[86].

114 ibid [61]–[75].

115 Other examples include the applicability of proportionality analysis in Singapore as well as the doctrine of substantive legitimate expectations.

116 *Lim Meng Suang* (n 69).

117 ibid [48]. Art 9(1) of the Singapore Constitution (n 89) provides: '[n]o person shall be deprived of his life or personal liberty save in accordance with law'. On the other hand, the due process clauses of the Fifth and Fourteenth Amendments to the US Constitution state that no person shall be deprived of 'life, liberty, or property, without due process of law'.

118 This was reiterated a few times in the judgment of *Lim Meng Suang* (n 69).

119 *Lim Meng Suang* (n 69).

120 ibid [95].

121 Singapore Constitution (n 89) Art 12(2):

> Except as expressly authorised by this Constitution, there shall be no discrimination against citizens of Singapore on the ground of religion, race, descent or place

of birth in any law or in the appointment to any office or employment under a public authority or in the administration of any law relating to the acquisition, holding or disposition of property or the establishing or carrying on of any trade, business, profession, vacation or employment.

122 See further Arun Thiruvengadam's chapter in this volume where he argues that the Chan and Menon Courts, while less absolutist than their predecessors, are nonetheless closer to the 'resistance' than the 'engagement' model in the use of foreign law. Arun K Thiruvengadam, 'The continuing resistance to foreign law in constitutional adjudication in Singapore', Chapter 12 of this book.
123 cf Chan Sek Keong, 'Judicial Review – From Angst to Empathy: A Lecture to Singapore Management University Second Year Law Students' (2010) 22 Singapore Academy of Law Journal 469.
124 Thiruvengadam (n 19) 125.
125 ibid 128–29.
126 VK Rajah (n 56) para 16.
127 Thio (n 27) 497.
128 ibid 499.
129 ibid 509.
130 ibid 510.
131 VK Rajah, 'Interpreting the Singapore Constitution', Chapter 1 of this book.
132 Thio Li-ann, '"It is a Little Known Legal Fact": Originalism, Customary Human Rights law and Constitutional Interpretation' (2010) Singapore Journal of Legal Studies 558–70, 560. On Singapore's 'prudential originalism', see Yvonne Tew (n 55) 818–29.
133 VK Rajah in his chapter puts it assertively: 'And in matters outside of the law, why should judges purport to know better than the rest of us', and 'In interpreting the Constitution, we must be guided by what the text is, not what we hope for it to be.': VK Rajah, 'Interpreting the Singapore Constitution', Chapter 1 of this book.
134 Julian H Franklin, *Jean Bodin and the Sixteenth-Century Revolution in the Methodology of Law and History* (Columbia University Press 1963) 69–70.
135 Thio Li-ann and David Chong Gek Sian SC, 'The Chan Court and Constitutional Adjudication – "A Sea Change into Something Rich and Strange?"' in Chao Hick Tin et al (eds), *The Law in His Hands: A Tribute to Chief Justice Chan Sek Keong* (Academy Publishing 2012) 87, 97.
136 Ran Hirschl, 'Remembrance of Things Past' (invited editorial) (2015) 13 ICON 1, 7. See further, Ran Hirschl, *Comparative Matters: The Renaissance of Comparative Constitutional Law* (Oxford University Press 2014).
137 (1986) 162 CLR 376 (Australia HC) 390 (Mason, Wilson, Deane and Dawson JJ) (emphasis added).
138 See eg *Practice Statement* (n 23).
139 Alan Watson, 'Legal Transplants and Law Reform' (1976) 92 Law Quarterly Review 79, 79–81. See also Basil Markesinis and Jorg Fedtke, 'The Judge as Comparatist' (2005–2006) 80 Tulane Law Review 11.
140 John Maynard Keynes, *The General Theory of Employment, Interest and Money* (Macmillan 1936) 383.
141 *Ong Ah Chuan* (n 42) [23].
142 VK Rajah, 'Interpreting the Singapore Constitution', Chapter 1 of this book.

Bibliography

Federalist Papers No. 78, The: www.constitution.org/fed/federa78.htm.

Ginsburg, Tom, *Judicial Review in New Democracies: Constitutional Courts in Asian Cases* (Cambridge University Press 2003).

Hirschl, Ran, *Comparative Matters: The Renaissance of Comparative Constitutional Law* (Oxford 2014).

Jackson, Vicki C, 'The Supreme Court, 2004 Term – Comment: Constitutional Comparisons: Convergence, Resistance, Engagement' (2005) 119 Harvard Law Review 109.

Jackson, Vicki C, *Constitutional Engagment in a Transnational Era* (Oxford 2010).

Law, David, 'Judicial Comparativism and Judicial Diplomacy' (2015) 163 University of Pennsylvania Law Review 927.

Lee, Jack, 'Foreign Precedents in Constitutional Adjudication by the Supreme Court of Singapore, 1963–2013' (2015) 24(2) Washington International Law Journal 253.

Mehta, Pratap Bhanu, 'India's Unlikely Democracy – The Rise of Judicial Sovereignty' (2007) 18(2) Journal of Democracy 70.

Shapiro, Martin and Alec Stone Sweet, *On Law, Politics, and Judicialization* (Oxford University Press 2002).

Sweet, Alec Stone, *Governing with Judges: Constitutional Politics in Europe* (Oxford University Press 2000).

Thio, Li-ann, 'The Death Penalty as Cruel and Inhuman Punishment before the Singapore High Court? Customary Human Rights Norms, Constitutional Formalism and the Supremacy of Domestic Law in PP v Nguyen Tuong Van (2004)' (2004) 4(2) Oxford University Commonwealth Law Journal 213.

Thio, Li-ann, 'Beyond the "Four Walls" in an Age of Transnational Judicial Conversations: Civil Liberties, Rights Theories and Constitutional Adjudication in Malaysia and Singapore' (2006) 19 Columbia Journal of Asian Law 428.

Thio, Li-ann, 'Reading Rights Rightly: The UDHR and its Creeping Influence on the Development of Singapore Public Law' (2008) Singapore Journal of Legal Studies 264.

Thio, Li-ann, 'Reception and Resistance: Globalisation, International Law and the Singapore Constitution' (2009) 4(3) National Taiwan University Law Review 335.

Thio, Li-ann, 'It is a Little Known Legal Fact: Originalism, Customary Human Rights Law and Constitutional Interpretation' (2010) Singapore Journal of Legal Studies 558.

Thio, Li-ann, 'Soft Constitutional Law in Non-Liberal Asian Constitutional Democracies' (2010) 8(4) International Journal of Constitutional Law.

Thio, Li-ann and David Chong, 'The Chan Court and Constitutional Adjudication: "A Sea Change into Something Rich and Strange?"' in Chao, Phang, Rajah and Yeo (eds), *The Law in his Hands: A Tribute to Chief Justice Chan Sek Keong* (Academy Publishing 2012).

Thiruvengadam, Arun K, 'Comparative Law and Constitutional Interpretation in Singapore' in Kevin YL Tan and Li-ann Thio (eds), *Evolution of a Revolution: Forty Years of the Singapore Constitution* (Routledge-Cavendish 2009).

12 The continuing resistance to foreign law in constitutional adjudication in Singapore

Arun K Thiruvengadam[1]

I Introduction

The field of constitutional law has witnessed a heated debate, lasting over a quarter-century, on the appropriate manner in which judges ought to engage with foreign cases (including both comparative and international law) while adjudicating upon constitutional disputes that invariably involve the interpretation of rights provisions in their domestic constitutions. This debate over what I term *trans-judicial influence* originally centred around the US Supreme Court and its continuing resistance to the use of foreign law in cases decided by it from the late 1980s to the early 2000s. However, in more recent years, the focus has shifted to how courts across the globe are responding to the phenomenon of trans-judicial influence. There is now substantial literature examining how judiciaries across several parts of the world, including Asia, are responding to the citation of foreign authorities before them in cases involving constitutional adjudication.[2]

In his recent work, which seeks to comprehensively analyse the contemporary state of the discipline of comparative constitutional law, Ran Hirschl argues that trans-judicial influence is a 'fast growing and proliferating area of comparative constitutional research'.[3] It is now widely recognised that focusing on this seemingly technical and trivial issue can reveal significant insights into the constitutional sensibilities of individual judges and the way in which constitutional cultures perceive their constitutional identities.

In this chapter, I focus on the views of one scholar who has, over several years, insightfully commented on the practice of trans-judicial influence. In an authoritative 2005 article, Vicki Jackson argued that the way judges have used foreign law can broadly be characterised as conforming to one of three models: convergence, resistance, or engagement.[4] The convergence model 'sees national constitutions as sites for implementation of international law or for development of transnational norms'.[5] Very few judges around the world actually adhere to this belief, but occasionally, the universalising spirit that animates such thinking can be seen as motivating particular judgments on specific issues. The resistance model, by contrast, holds that it is illegitimate (or at the very least, inappropriate) to reference foreign and comparative law while engaging in domestic constitutional adjudication. Judges such as Justice Antonin Scalia of the US Supreme Court argue that considerations of enhancing the democratic legitimacy of judicial decisions and limiting judicial discretion require that comparative law be rejected decisively. Judges who adhere to the engagement model, which Jackson endorses, do not treat foreign or international law as binding or to be presumptively followed. However, 'neither do they put on blinders that exclude foreign legal sources or experience'. Instead, they view transnational sources 'as interlocutors, offering a way of testing understanding of one's own traditions, and possibilities by examining them in the reflection of others'.[6]

There is, by now, a small but significant body of literature that has documented how courts in Singapore have engaged (or, to put it more accurately and in consonance with Jackson's terminology, resisted engaging) with foreign law in constitutional cases. In a previous work published in a volume to mark forty years of the Singapore Constitution, I documented trends in the use of foreign law across the tenures of Singapore's first three Chief Justices (Chief Justices Wee, Yong and Chan).[7] This analysis showed that while judges in Singapore have generally resisted engaging with foreign law, the trend has varied over time, with some Chief Justices advocating an absolutist position (evident in Yong CJ's adoption of the 'four walls' doctrine) while others adopted a less equivocal position (evident in Wee CJ's relatively more nuanced resistance, usually backed by a more careful distinguishing of individual foreign cases).[8]

In this essay, for a volume that marks the fiftieth year of the adoption of the Singapore Constitution, I seek to update that analysis, focusing more closely on cases decided in recent years, especially since 2009. In this period, the Singapore courts have had occasion to reference foreign law in several cases, and this has in turn generated a fair amount of scholarly literature. My principal argument is that although the more recent trend shows some marked departures from the way foreign law was engaged earlier, these changes are, ultimately, more superficial than substantial. I argue that judges and courts engaged in constitutional adjudication in Singapore continue to resist the use of foreign and comparative law, to an extent that is quite remarkable, especially given Singapore's common law heritage and the fact that in other branches of law, the traffic in comparative ideas and law has remained high. This makes the judiciary's opposition to, and rejection of, comparative law in the arena of constitutional adjudication even more exceptional and striking. To build my argument and spell out its details, I will discuss and engage with the analysis of other scholars of Singapore constitutional law.

In the next section, I analyse the more recent literature on the Singapore judiciary's use of foreign and international law in constitutional cases. While doing so, I also outline the contours of my own argument and stance. In the third section, I focus on two recent cases – *Lim Meng Suang v Attorney-General* and *Yong Vui Kong v Public Prosecutor* – where the Singapore Court of Appeal had to respond to the citation of foreign and comparative law in rights cases. These cases dealt, respectively, with a constitutional challenge to Singapore's anti-sodomy law, section 377A, and a constitutional challenge to the sentencing practice of caning in Singapore. In both these cases, the Singapore Court of Appeal ultimately resisted applying foreign and international law, showing some of the same tendencies that were on display during the height of the 'four walls' era. I argue that the record of the Chan and Menon Courts on the use of foreign law, while less absolutist than that of the Yong Court, is nevertheless closer to the 'resistance' than the 'engagement' model articulated by Jackson. In the concluding section, I offer some speculative thoughts on what might make Singapore judges consider a change in their stance towards foreign law.

II Engaging with recent scholarship on trans-judicial influence in Singapore

In this section, I describe and analyse four instances of recent scholarship on the use of foreign law by judges deciding constitutional cases in Singapore. The scholar who has written most extensively on this issue is Professor Thio Li-ann.[9] In an important 2006 article which comprehensively analysed how courts in Singapore and Malaysia had dealt with references to foreign law, Thio concluded that these courts were unlikely in the near future to either adopt robust approaches towards constitutional review or to engage earnestly with foreign and comparative law.[10] This article was published in 2006 during the tenure of Chief Justice Chan Sek Keong (2006–2012) and analysed a few decisions handed down by the early Chan Court. In my earlier work, I relied on Thio's analysis to inform my own argument and broadly endorsed her conclusions, even as I sought to focus upon underlying issues of constitutional theory.

Thio appears to have changed her view over the following six years as the Chan Court proceeded to hand down several significant constitutional decisions. In a co-authored chapter in a *festschrift* for Chan CJ published on his retirement in 2012, Thio and David Chong argue that the decisions of the Chan Court showed some departures from earlier trends. They argue that under Chan CJ, 'Singapore courts in public law decisions regularly engage with international law and foreign constitutional cases and no longer seem to refer to the "four walls" principle.' They go on to assert that

> [i]t is now *de rigueur* for latter-day cases to comprehensively survey and weigh developments in other jurisdictions and to distinguish them, where applicable, from the Singapore context and position, or to apply them, sometimes with creative modification.[11]

This leads them to conclude that '[t]his may reflect a growing trend towards a particularism without parochialism'.[12] The overall conclusion reached by the authors is:

> [T]he judicial trajectory under the Chan Court has been oriented towards greater and more nuanced engagement with academic ideas, foreign cases and international law, accompanied by more elaborated reason-giving by

way of appeal to text, original intent, local particularities, with attention to foreign and international developments and first principles.[13]

Given Thio's strident criticism of the casual and often unreasoned way in which comparative law was dismissed by courts in Singapore until 2005, this is a dramatic change, and deserves to be studied closely. What is striking about this revised view is that it appears to be based on a study that cites only two cases: the 2009 decision of the Court of Appeal in *Review Publishing Co v Lee Hsien Loong*[14] and the 2010 decision of the Court of Appeal in *Yong Vui Kong v Public Prosecutor*.[15] The former case dealt with the issue of political defamation and the scope of the right to free speech guaranteed under Article 12 of the Singapore Constitution, while the latter involved a challenge to Singapore's mandatory death penalty offences premised on the right to life guaranteed under Article 9 of the Constitution. As Thio herself notes, while *Review Publishing* extensively dealt with the UK House of Lords' decision in *Reynolds v Times Newspaper Ltd*,[16] its remarks in this respect are obiter and did not have a bearing on the actual result of the case. To describe this as more nuanced engagement with comparative law seems an odd characterisation. One has to remember that the comparative law cited did not play any role in influencing the result, which was, in line with earlier Singapore cases, quite hostile to the argument that public figures have to yield to freedom of speech considerations in a constitutional democracy by being open to more robust criticism.[17]

There is a similar problem in accepting Thio–Chong's characterisation of the *Yong Vui Kong* judgment's use of foreign law. They describe the *Yong Vui Kong* judgment's handling of international legal sources as 'deft'[18] and contrast it with the contemptuous dismissal of such sources in earlier cases, such as the 1994 High Court decision in *Colin Chan v Public Prosecutor*.[19] The *Yong Vui Kong* judgment may well have been an improvement upon earlier Singapore cases, but to assess whether it meaningfully engages with international law requires an analysis of how it actually used international law. Since that judgment eventually rejected international legal sources, and upheld the mandatory death penalty, it is not immediately clear why the use of foreign and international law has changed. Indeed, as I will show in the cases I examine in the next section, neither the substantive reasoning nor the result of the constitutional decisions has changed.

David Tan's chapter in this book suggests that more recent decisions of the Singapore courts in the area of free speech rights, all of which were delivered during the tenure of Chan CJ, show a willingness to move 'beyond four walls' and engage with decisions from common law jurisdictions. Tan also offers a normative argument to back the descriptive trend outlined in his paper. While I endorse Tan's normative argument in favour of granting more robust protection to the right to free speech in Singapore, I am sceptical of his description of the cases involving free speech as revolutionary. Tan bases his claim on his analysis of the following cases: the *Review Publishing* decision we examined briefly above, and two decisions involving the balancing of free speech and judicial contempt powers, namely, *Shadrake Alan v Attorney-General*[20] and *Attorney-General v Au Wai Pang*.[21] Tan argues that the judges who decided the three cases relied extensively upon foreign and comparative law and sought to advance free speech law within Singapore beyond its current state by making doctrinal innovations which relied upon comparative law. While this may be true, it is important to acknowledge that the doctrinal innovations did not result in a substantive change in the result in any of the three cases. The Singapore courts, which have historically been reluctant to uphold rights claims especially when pursued against state institutions, somewhat predictably found in favour of the sitting Prime Minister in the first case, and held that the individuals alleged to have committed contempt of court in the *Shadrake* and *Au* cases were, in fact, guilty.

The doctrinal innovations that Tan focuses upon may well excite academic lawyers studying these cases, but provided cold comfort to the actual claimants of rights in the three cases. One doesn't have to be a cynic to ask: if nothing changed in terms of results, was this more of a change in form than in substance? If the claim is that foreign and comparative law is being engaged with, it is fair to ask exactly what foreign and comparative law is being addressed. This is because, in many jurisdictions of the world, the law relating to defamation of public figures and that of contempt of courts has moved far beyond the current standard in Singapore, such that all three cases would have resulted in decisions against the government plaintiffs in the three cases mentioned above.

Eugene Tan's chapter makes a more complex claim about current trends of trans-judicial influence in Singapore. Tan concedes that despite its not being adhered to strictly in recent years, for the present, the 'four walls' doctrine represents good law in Singapore. Although he is of the view that the doctrine has harmful consequences, he concedes that 'Singapore is unlikely to see an easy comfort with foreign constitutional jurisprudence in the near future'.[22] He notes that this is somewhat paradoxical given that in almost every facet of its public life, Singapore exhibits forms of cosmopolitan enlightenment in being open to ideas and trends from the outside world. He emphasises that this is true for other branches of the law in Singapore, which have always displayed an openness to trends and changes in the law in the major common law jurisdictions of the world. Having laid this ground, Eugene Tan makes an impassioned appeal for a more cosmopolitan approach to the role that comparative law can play in developing Singapore public law in the future.

I agree with the broad tenor and thrust of Eugene Tan's argument, and especially with his normative sensibility on the perils of parochialism in public law, and the need for Singapore's public law to fit in with the general openness to foreign law that the rest of its legal system so amply demonstrates. However, I am less persuaded by his claim (for which he relies on the Thio–Chong piece about which I have expressed reservations) that the 'four walls' doctrine has been consigned to 'the dustbin of history' (an odd claim given his conclusion in the same piece that the four walls doctrine is still good law).[23] As my analysis in the next section will show, the sensibility behind the doctrine is very much evident in recent decisions of the Singapore Court of Appeal. It could, therefore, be premature to issue an obituary for the doctrine and the sentiments that motivate it. These sensibilities are tied up with other interpretive commitments, such as an exaggerated deference for the high authority that Parliament commands in a constitutional democracy and a disdain for non-textual forms of constitutional interpretation. As long as these tendencies persist among judges and leaders of the legal profession in Singapore, there will be significant hurdles for learning from experiences of other peoples. Eugene Tan's otherwise nuanced analysis seems to underestimate the hurdles posed by these approaches and tendencies of the Singapore judiciary.

The final work I engage with in this section is the most recent – and, in my view, the most extensive and comprehensive – analysis of trans-judicial influence in the available literature, authored by Jack Lee.[24] In an article published in 2015 but covering the period between 16 September 1963 and 31 December 2013, Lee seeks to cover every constitutional case in Singapore where foreign law was cited. Lee finds that during this fifty-year period, there were only 153 constitutional cases in all. He notes that this is low even after accounting for the small size of Singapore. After considering some other factors, he zeroes in on the fact that only in three of these 153 cases has the government's interpretation of constitutional provisions been held to be incorrect by the courts.

Although Lee does not underscore this, what is striking about the Singapore constitutional experience is that in its fifty-year history, no statute passed by Parliament has ultimately been held to be unconstitutional by its judiciary. I would argue that this is an extremely exceptional situation and may well be unique in the annals of the judicial review of legislative action. Studies of judicial review in several constitutional democracies show that judges and courts invariably wield the power of judicial review to enhance their power and authority.[25] Judges and courts in Singapore seem inured to such tendencies: the fact that the People's Action Party has been in power through all of Singapore's post-independence era and has consistently won electoral contests by huge margins, is not unrelated. As we know from the studies by Alec Stone Sweet and Tom Ginsburg of the French Constitutional Court and the newer Asian democracies of Taiwan and South Korea,[26] the possibility of a transition from a single party regime to a political culture where a genuine opposition element exists, spurs political parties to cede power and authority to courts to provide for the possibility of 'insurance' in the event of a loss at the hustings.[27] In the Singapore political landscape, the idea that an opposition grouping may form the government has so far proved illusory, leaving little scope for such illusions to be entertained by judges, nor has there been any evidence, in recent years, of judges seeking to make expansive interpretations of provisions regarding rights or judicial powers to augment their authority.

Lee proceeds to document the rate of citation of foreign cases and his data shows that both the number of constitutional cases and the foreign cases cited in them have increased incrementally across Singapore's post-independence era. He asserts that during the tenure of Chief Justice Wee (1963–1990), '[a] fairly cautious approach towards the application'[28] of foreign law was on display. During the tenure of Chief Justice Yong (1990–2006), 'the courts increasingly resisted applying foreign precedent'[29] using the infamous 'four walls' doctrine. Lee provides a close examination of a series of cases where foreign and comparative law was rejected, often while providing minimal reasons. Lee, however, notes that despite the reiteration of the 'four walls' doctrine in several cases, 'foreign cases continued to be cited' which is also the point emphasised by Eugene Tan. However, unlike Tan, who draws the conclusion that this shows that the judiciary in Singapore can be persuaded to adopt foreign law in appropriate cases, Lee draws a very different conclusion. In his analysis, such a trend shows that:

> [T]he courts' choice of which precedent to apply was driven not by a desire to engage in transjudicial dialogue, but *largely by the courts' perceived need to constrain their own power in order to maintain a deferential stance towards the executive and the legislature.*'[30]

This is an important insight that I sought to highlight in my previous work and is the template for my analysis here. Lee's discussion then turns, finally, to the tenures of Chief Justices Chan (2006–2012) and Menon (2012–present). He notes that during this phase there was a discernible difference in the way judges engaged with foreign law. Referring to some of the cases that Thio–Chong and David Tan also draw from, Lee notes that there was a departure from the tendency of the Yong Court to dismiss foreign cases on superficial grounds, and that the Chan Court typically advanced substantive reasons for rejecting foreign law. Lee emphasises, however, that even the Chan Court 'remain[ed] cautious about applying foreign [cases] on the basis of differently worded bills of rights'.[31] He cites cases where the Chan Court specifically avoided taking an activist stance when interpreting the Constitution. In his conclusion, Lee speculates about the future of trans-judicial influence in Singapore and during Chief Justice Menon's tenure. He concludes that whether the judiciary engages with foreign and comparative law will depend on whether the courts 'remain largely deferential to the policy choices of the political branches, or instead develop constitutional principles to subject [the choices of the executive and the legislature] to greater scrutiny'.[32]

Since Lee's analysis stops at the Chan Court, I will, in the next section, examine closely the use of foreign and comparative law in two significant cases decided by the Menon Court in recent years.

III Trans-judicial influence in two recent Singapore decisions

In this section, I focus on two recent decisions of the Singapore Court of Appeal that were required to respond to the citation of foreign and comparative law. Although these cases do not constitute the universe of public law cases that involved trans-judicial cases since 2013 (when Jack Lee's comprehensive survey ended), I would argue that these are significant decisions which capture the overall trend under the Menon Court. In analysing the cases, my focus will be on two issues: i) how did the courts engage with foreign, comparative and international law? and ii) what was the approach of the courts to reviewing the actions of the legislative and executive wings of government in Singapore?

A Lim Meng Suang v Attorney-General *(2014)*[33]

This long-running case involved a constitutional challenge to the anti-sodomy provision in Singapore's Penal Code, section 377A. Historically, such laws were introduced by the British colonial regime in many colonies, often in societies where same-sex relations had not been criminalised. The irony is that the UK itself abolished anti-sodomy provisions several decades ago, while these provisions continue to be in place in the former colonies. Such provisions have been the subject of constitutional challenge in many jurisdictions. Of late, courts in several jurisdictions have held that these provisions offend notions of equality, privacy and dignity.[34]

The debate over LGBT rights in Singapore has, in recent years, centred on this provision. Not surprisingly, both proponents and opponents of repealing this provision have referred to and relied upon the global context of the debate around LGBT rights, and the fact that in recent years many Commonwealth countries have decriminalised such acts and have started recognising LGBT rights more generally. In 2007, the Singapore Parliament had a spirited debate on the legality of this provision for two days, following which a majority of the House voted to retain the provision in the Penal Code.[35] Subsequently, the provision became the subject of litigation which, given the Singapore judiciary's reputation for speedy justice, took an extraordinarily long time to be finally decided by the courts, reflecting perhaps the sensitivities attached to the resolution of the issue. What is striking is that at every stage, those challenging the constitutionality of the provision relied on the extensive jurisprudence in comparative law that has evolved around anti-sodomy statutes. Comparative law on this issue was felt to be extremely relevant also because the provision incorporated by the British in Singapore (which was the predecessor to the current provision) was virtually identical to those enacted in several other jurisdictions.

The initial round of litigation in *Tan Eng Hong v Attorney-General* revolved around the issue of standing, and it took two decisions – by the High Court and the Court of Appeal – to settle this issue. Once the Court of Appeal held that the original petitioner, Tan Eng Hong, had standing to take the case forward, it was considered on its merits, ie on the substantive questions of constitutionality raised by it. What made the trajectory of the case interesting is that a second case arose which sought to challenge the provision on similar grounds, but involved different parties. *Lim Meng Suang v Attorney-General*, was, however, treated as a separate case at the High Court stage. Ultimately, Quentin Loh J heard the two cases separately and issued separate judgments, despite the fact that the cases involved essentially the same legal questions. The two separate judgments rendered by Loh J do, however, refer to each other and have similar themes and approaches. Loh J ultimately held that section 377A was constitutional and rejected the arguments of the lawyers of both cases that it violated the rights to life (guaranteed under Article 9(1) of the Constitution of Singapore) and equality (guaranteed under Article 12).[36] The losing parties took the case up on appeal before the Court of Appeal, which decided the case through a single judgment of a three-judge bench, delivered by Andrew Phang J on 28 October 2014.[37]

My focus now will be on the second round of litigation and the judgments rendered by Loh J and Phang J. Deciding the cases at the High Court in the two separately rendered judgments, Loh J devoted considerable time to analysing the comparative law cited by counsel who argued that Singapore should follow the example of other former British colonies to hold section 377A unconstitutional. Loh J also adopted a fairly nuanced position on how and when courts should intervene on social issues when Parliament has taken a stance but when constitutional rights claims are nevertheless involved. To some extent, then, Loh J's judgment falls within Jack Lee's characterisation of the approach of the Chan Court towards foreign and comparative law, of being more attentive to the persuasive authority of foreign decisions than the Yong Court.

In his judgment in *Lim Meng Suang*, Loh J refers frequently and unselfconsciously to foreign and comparative texts and case law to describe the legal terrain of the issues that confront the court. So, for instance, in discussing the fundamentals of the equality doctrine in Singapore,[38] Loh J refers to the English jurist AV Dicey's classic text, *Law of the Constitution*, the Indian jurist Durga Das Basu's much-cited *Commentary on the Constitution of India*, the US Supreme Court's decision in *Yick Wo v Hopkins* and the Indian Supreme Court's decision in *Chiranjit Lal v Union of India*. These sources are, of course, relevant because Singapore's equality jurisprudence and the 'classification' test that currently holds sway can be directly traced back to Malaysian, Indian and American authorities, a fact that is often underplayed in discussions of Singapore's equality jurisprudence.

However, Loh J's relative openness to acknowledging and discussing the impact of comparative law on domestic constitutional jurisprudence in Singapore does not lead him to adopt comparative law on the question directly at hand: the constitutionality of section 377A. Loh J held that although counsel had sought to rely upon global trends on anti-sodomy statutes, for him, the submissions were 'of no weight'.[39] His reasons are as follows:

> First and foremost, Singapore is an independent nation with its own unique history, geography, society and economy. What is adopted in other parts of the world may not be suitable for adoption in Singapore. Second, postulating examples of how the world is changing without more is unhelpful as such examples can be countered by examples of areas where there are shifts in the opposite direction. Furthermore, it can be seen that a number of former British colonies, such as Botswana, Malaysia, Sri Lanka, Sudan, Tanzania, Yemen and the Solomon Islands, have criminalised female homosexual conduct while retaining their respective equivalents of s 377A. The death penalty for male homosexual conduct is still retained in a few countries …The short – and only

> relevant – answer to this point is that our Parliament has debated the removal of s 377A and has decided against it.[40]

This passage seems to display tendencies of the 'four walls' mentality: no direct engagement with actual foreign law is cited, rather general defensive comments about suitability of foreign law in general. As Eugene Tan has argued, these differences have not prevented Singaporean judges from adopting foreign law in the context of private and commercial laws. However, it also shows a certain artfulness in countering the comparative argument by noting that foreign trends are not unidirectional, and that Singapore is not alone in keeping anti-sodomy laws on its statute books. Loh J's chief argument, however, is that the Singapore Parliament has decided the issue, suggesting that this leaves judges with no options in the matter. Further on, Loh J argues as follows:

> [I]t is not that the courts do not have any role to play in defining moral issues when such issues are at stake. However, the courts' power to intervene can only be exercised within established principles. The issue in the present case no doubt is challenging and important, but it is not one which, in my view, justifies heavy-handed judicial intervention ahead of democratic change … [T]he basis underlying s 377A's existence is, in the final analysis, an issue of morality and societal values. The views ventilated in Parliament during the October 2007 Parliamentary Debates and at the hearing of this case are without a doubt controversial and disparate among various segments of our society. What is clear, however, is that Parliament has decided that s 377A should be retained. That decision is not one which is undeniably wrong. Our courts cannot substitute their own views for that of Parliament.[41]

To support this assertion, interestingly, Loh J relies upon the views of Justice Ruth Bader Ginsburg of the US Supreme Court. Immediately after this passage, Loh J quotes at length from Justice Scalia's dissenting judgment, describing his words as 'eloquent'.

These arguments remind us of the tendency of Singapore judges to cherry-pick foreign authorities and cite them in support of their conclusions even at the height of the 'four walls' era. What is striking about Loh J's formulation of the respective roles of the courts and the legislature is his implicit suggestion that courts are justified in striking down parliamentary laws when they are 'undeniably wrong'. Whether this amounts to a clear standard is debatable, but given the clean score sheet of the Singapore judiciary when it comes to striking down parliamentary laws as unconstitutional, it appears to be a shift away from the position of extreme deference that is routinely adopted by Singapore judges in constitutional cases.

Loh J displays a similar position of (relative) nuance towards these twin issues in his second judgment on the issue, delivered a few months later in October 2013. In *Tan Eng Hong*, Loh J's judgment notes that counsel for the petitioner cited several foreign authorities for the proposition that 'homosexuality is a natural and immutable attribute'.[42] Loh J rejects this argument, but before doing so, spends eight substantive paragraphs of his judgment describing each individual judgment delivered by the UK Supreme Court, the Canadian Supreme Court, the South African Constitutional Court, the Nepalese Supreme Court, a district court in the USA and the High Court of New Delhi. What is striking is the narrow way in which Loh J formulated the question that structured his survey of foreign law. If he had adopted a broader question, arguably, he would have found it harder to reject these authorities, which take sophisticated and progressive positions on the issue of LGBT rights as a whole. Given the very narrow nature of his enquiry, Loh J is easily able to fend off the foreign cases cited before him, most of which did not take any position on the question posed by him. The seeming cosmopolitanism of Loh J's approach is thus undermined when one bears this factor in mind.

Loh J's reasons for rejecting foreign authorities at another point in the judgment are revealing when he states:

> Interesting as they are, the decisions of these foreign courts, which have adopted a more *zealous* approach [towards adopting heightened levels of scrutiny in evolving doctrines for equality jurisprudence], factor in legal and extra-legal social, economic and cultural and political considerations which are unique to their respective jurisdictions.[43]

The point being made here is trite: court decisions must always be viewed in context. However, to suggest that the courts which have adopted a heightened scrutiny towards equality claims (and not just in the context of LGBT rights) are being zealous in doing so, is odd at the very least. Many of the judges being referred to by Loh J are among the most erudite and highly regarded in the Commonwealth. This is probably an ill-chosen adjective, but it conveys the suspicion and scepticism that judges in Singapore seem to harbour in respect of judges who try to advance constitutional rights jurisprudence. This appears to downplay the fact that Singapore's Constitution has an entire chapter on 'Fundamental Liberties', which are guaranteed against the state. Traditionally, judges in many jurisdictions conceive it as part of their mandate to ensure that constitutional rights are protected from state intrusion. Instead, judges in Singapore seem to be far more concerned about safeguarding the rights and privileges of the Parliament of Singapore. It is surely a constitutional virtue to be guardians of constitutional institutions. But if this occurs at the expense of constitutional rights of individuals, for whose welfare and protection constitutional institutions are presumably erected by constitutional texts, there is certainly a great irony at work.

Although I am critical of Loh J's broad approach in these two cases, I should reiterate that they are, nevertheless, positions that are more fleshed-out than one typically encounters in constitutional cases in Singapore. This becomes clear when one reads the judgment of the Court of Appeal in these cases. As already noted, Andrew Phang J's judgment affirmed the decisions reached by Loh J in these two cases, while advancing separate grounds for the holding.

First, on the issue of comparative law, Phang J's judgment does not specifically address individual foreign cases cited at the Bar. Instead, he has this generic statement that seeks to dismiss their significance:

> [F]oreign cases that have conferred an expansive constitutional right to life and liberty should be approached with circumspection because they were decided in the context of their unique social, political and legal circumstances.[44]

This is, to put it mildly, an odd statement. Phang J seems to be expressing hostility to foreign cases that adopt an 'expansive' approach to rights interpretation, thus implying that there is something necessarily illegitimate about them. This is a puzzling statement at another level: presumably, foreign decisions adopting cabined and constrained approaches to rights interpretation are more welcome because they would be seen as fitting well with Singapore's 'social, political and legal circumstances'? However far-fetched this proposition might seem, it is a legitimate implication of the quoted statement. If there is indeed a principle being formulated here, it is a strange one. Interestingly, the only time foreign law appears in a substantive sense in Phang J's judgment is when he strays into a discussion of the law of negligence to explain a point about when courts and judges would be justified in developing the law.[45] But, there is not even a mention of the many decisions relied upon by counsel to show that courts in analogous situations acted to strike down very similar worded anti-sodomy statutes while testing them against constitutional guarantees of equality and liberty that are very similar to those guaranteed by the Singapore's Constitution.

Phang J has a similar view on the application of norms of international law within the domestic sphere. An argument raised before the court urged the judges to align Singapore's domestic law with its international obligations by eliminating discrimination on the basis of sexual orientation. It was argued that Singapore had made representations to this effect before the UN Committee on the Elimination of Discrimination Against Women (CEDAW). Phang J gave short shrift to this argument, saying that 'international law and domestic law are regarded in Singapore as separate systems of law, and the former does not form part of the latter'.[46] While this is technically true, it displays a severely restricted view of the role that international law plays in today's dynamic, interconnected world. Indeed, in several other contexts, Singapore as a small but diplomatically powerful nation has argued for the aspirational role that international law can play in pushing forward more conservative domestic legal systems on a range of issues that fit its strategic interests.[47] Singapore has played a role in shaping international law instruments such as the UNCLOS agreement that belie its small size. It is this background context that makes the presence of this strict dualist mindset towards international law in a judgment delivered in 2014 appear odd.

Phang J's judgment devotes a considerable portion of its considerable length to setting out what he considers to be the proper role of judges in constitutional adjudication. Early on, he asserts that a court 'must disregard extra-legal considerations that are uniquely within the purview of the Legislature'.[48] Phang J insists on drawing a 'line in the legal sand'; he warns that if this is not done:

> [T]he court will necessarily be sucked into and thereby descend into the political arena, which would in turn undermine (or even destroy) the very role which constitutes the raison d'etre for the court's existence in the first place – namely to furnish an independent, neutral and objective forum for deciding, on the basis of objective legal rules and principles (inter alia) what rights parties have in a given situation.[49]

This seems reasonable enough, until we study what exactly the learned judge understands by the expression 'extra-legal' considerations. Phang J's judgment has a fairly long section outlining what this expression means (paras 155–81), at the end of which one is left with more questions than answers. For instance, Phang J includes within the category of extra-legal considerations arguments asserting that since anti-sodomy laws target sexual minorities, they are an expression of the 'tyranny of the majority'. In many jurisdictions, this general argument – that laws and government policies that adversely impact non-mainstream populations – has been accepted as having force: for Phang J, this argument should be addressed to the legislature instead. In so holding, he seems to ignore the vast literature in constitutional theory which, while acknowledging the legitimacy of the legislature as a constitutional institution, also warns that it is by its very nature better designed to reflect majoritarian concerns, and is not well suited to addressing concerns that affect smaller groups that typically do not succeed in gaining popular representation in elected chambers, which is exactly what afflicts LGBT populations. What Justice Phang considers 'extra-legal' has been considered very much within the domain of the law in many other jurisdictions.

It is evident from reading Phang J's judgment that for him, judges have an extremely limited role in adjudicating disputes over controversial social and moral issues, even if they involve rights-based claims. This is reminiscent of the very similar approach to judicial deference adopted by the Yong Court in constitutional cases. It is also removed from the more moderate position adopted by Loh J, who endorsed support for the idea that if Parliament was 'undeniably wrong', courts might have space for intervention. By contrast, Phang J seems to suggest that even this concession might not be sustainable. This admonition appears towards the end of his judgment: 'The Court *cannot – and must not* – assume legislative functions which are necessarily beyond its remit.'[50] Phang J's judgment does not throw much light on how the distinction between what is a legislative and what is a properly judicial function is to be worked out. He seems to suggest that any controversial moral or social issue is automatically outside the 'remit' of the judiciary.

Once again, we see a link between a judge's approach to foreign and comparative law, and his conception of the proper role of judges vis-à-vis other branches of government in the context of constitutional adjudication. This connection comes across quite clearly in this next case.

B Yong Vui Kong v Public Prosecutor *(2015)*[51]

This case involved a constitutional challenge to the practice of caning in the criminal justice system of Singapore. The appellant, who was sentenced to life imprisonment and 15 strokes of the cane, argued that the sentence of caning violated his constitutional rights to liberty and equality under the Constitution. He argued that this was so because, among other reasons, caning was a form of torture that is prohibited by international law being a violation of the *jus cogens* norm against torture.

In its judgment issued on 4 March 2015, a three-judge bench of the Court of Appeal presided by Chief Justice Sundaresh Menon rejected the arguments raised by the appellant.

The Court first addressed the issue of international law and *jus cogens*. Menon CJ gave much weight to the fact that being a former British colony, Singapore has followed the dualist route to incorporating international law within its municipal legal system. This led him to eventually conclude that:

> [A]ssuming for the sake of argument that caning does amount to torture, the fact remains that it is expressly authorised (and in some cases mandated) by statute. The courts are bound to implement laws that have been validly passed by Parliament unless they are inconsistent with the Constitution.[52]

The Court went on to hold, eventually, that caning does not constitute torture, avoiding the possibility of any inconsistency between a *jus cogens* norm and Singapore's domestic law. However, this approach of the court is revealing of the extent to which it sees Singapore's domestic legal system as an insulated and closed space for the purposes of drawing lessons from either comparative or international law.

Responding to the argument that the court should read in a prohibition against torture and inhuman punishment into the Constitution, the court was emphatic in its rejection of such reasoning:

> [R]eading unenumerated rights into the Constitution would entail judges sitting as a super-legislature and enacting their personal views of what is just and desirable into law, which is not only undemocratic but also antithetical to the rule of law.[53]

Students of comparative constitutional law would find this assertion problematic. Courts across the world have recognised unenumerated rights within constitutional texts, especially in constitutions that were drafted one or more generations ago. In US constitutional law, the right to privacy, the substantive due process jurisprudence and even much of equality jurisprudence owes much to the creative acts of interpretation of apex court judges. Once again, the worst-case scenario for a Singapore constitutional judge is invoked: of taking over the functioning of the legislature. What is not addressed here is the powerful argument – advanced by judges in many constitutional democracies – that judges need to be equally mindful of their duty to safeguard the rights of non-mainstream groups and individuals in society. Judges in many constitutional democracies struggle to find the balance between these competing considerations: in Singapore, the attempt to strike such a balance is conspicuously absent.

On the substantive questions of law involved, the court had to resort to a number of technicalities to uphold the constitutionality of the practice of caning. This also led to somewhat forced reasoning, as is evident from the strained tone the court had to adopt in seeking to 'objectively' narrate the sequence of events in a typical caning session:

> Caning is applied on the prisoner's buttocks [...], thereby minimising the risk of any injury to the prisoner's bones and organs. It is carried out in private and out of sight of other prisoners. Before the caning, the rattan cane is soaked in water to prevent it from splitting and shearing the skin, and is also treated with antiseptic. The strokes of the cane are meted out in a measured and controlled manner at regular intervals, rather than in a haphazard and capricious fashion. There is constant medical supervision throughout the entire process, and the caning will be stopped if the medical officer is of the view that the prisoner is unfit to continue undergoing the sentence. In our judgment, these safeguards ensure that the present practice of caning does not breach the high threshold of severity and brutality that is required for it to be regarded as torture.[54]

Reading this passage, one cannot resist the sense that the court seemed eager to downplay the horrifying images that are necessarily conjured up as one reads through the sequence of events. To justify this stance, the court had to draw quite strained comparisons and distinctions. Thus, at paragraph 90, the judges argue that the practice of caning in Singapore is 'less severe' than the practice of public flogging with a cat-o'-nine tails[55] in Trinidad,[56] 'quite different' from the practice of inflicting between twenty-five and forty lashes in public on female students in Sudan, but 'more severe' than the practice of 'juvenile birching (which involves the whipping of the clothed posterior of boys with either a light cane or a birch rod)'[57] on the Isle of Man. Singapore is justifiably proud of its transformation from 'third' world to 'first' in a remarkably short span of time. It is, therefore, odd that this analysis compares Singapore, in this respect, with countries that would usually be regarded as far less 'developed'.

In the penultimate paragraph of the judgment, Menon CJ adopts a more conciliatory tone:

> We accept that the use of judicial corporal punishment is on the wane internationally, and there is a growing body of international opinion that it amounts to a form of inhuman punishment that is cruel and degrading. But there is, as yet, no international consensus that the use of caning … constitutes torture. Even if there were … this Court, operating within a domestic

> legal system, is obliged to apply domestic laws in the event of any inconsistency with international law norms.

This does not take account of the fact that some courts across the Commonwealth have taken a more pro-active stance in pushing other wings of government towards implementing norms that are accepted at the plane of international law. Leaving that aside, this statement seems reasonable enough. It is what follows which exhibits an unusually high level of deference in the realm of constitutional adjudication:

> Furthermore, it is not within the institutional competence of this Court to adjudicate on the efficacy of caning as a mode of punishment and substitute its judgment for that of the legislature. Any campaign to abolish caning is a matter that must be taken up in the legislative sphere. The courts can and will only pronounce on the *legality* of measures adopted by the legislature to punish crimes.[58]

The suggestion here is that abolishing caning cannot be a legal question, but only a political (or otherwise 'extra-legal') one. Once again, it is not clear where or how the court draws a distinction between the legal and the political. This approach is out of step with a growing trend in many jurisdictions to subject outmoded, colonial practices of punishment to the more searching standards of law that are informed by contemporary understandings of criminology, penology and sensitivity to current standards of human rights.

Both these cases exhibit common tendencies across two trends: the rejection of foreign, comparative and international law, and the adoption of extremely deferential stances towards decisions made by the Singapore Parliament. As I have suggested here and in my earlier work, there is a profound connection between these seemingly disparate trends, and anyone expecting change in one trend should also explain how the corresponding trend will be affected. This is where I disagree with scholars who are already pronouncing an end to the 'four walls' era. In my view, the increased references to foreign, comparative and international law are not yet indicative of any real shift in substance. To be meaningful, they have to be accompanied also by a shift in the self-understanding of judges and the courts about their proper role in constitutional adjudication, especially in relation to rights of non-mainstream individuals such as LGBT persons and those convicted of offences. It is for this reason that I believe that the way judges in Singapore relate to the citation of foreign authorities fits Vicki Jackson's category of 'resistance' rather than that of 'engagement'.

IV Conclusion

This section contains a short summary of the argument advanced in this chapter. Before summarising my claims, however, I need to set out my own formulation of the proper role of a judge in constitutional adjudication, given how critical I have been of the concept of the judicial role held by judges in Singapore. There is a vast amount of literature on this subject, but I rely upon what is now considered a classic statement. In the Federalist Papers No 78, thought to have been published between 1787 and 1788, Alexander Hamilton offered the following conception of and justification for the judicial role that has since gained wide following:

> It is not otherwise to be supposed, that the Constitution could intend to enable the representatives of the people to substitute their will to that of their constituents. It is far more rational to suppose, that the courts were designed to be an intermediate body between the people and the legislature, in order, among other things, to keep the latter within the limits assigned to their authority. The interpretation of the laws is the proper and peculiar province of the courts. A constitution is, in fact, and must be regarded by the judges, as a fundamental law. It therefore belongs to them to ascertain its meaning, as well as the meaning of any particular act proceeding from the legislative body. If there should happen to be an irreconcilable variance between the two, that which has the superior obligation and validity ought, of course, to be preferred; or, in other words, the Constitution ought to be preferred to the statute, the intention of the people to the intention of their agents.
>
> Nor does this conclusion by any means suppose a superiority of the judicial to the legislative power. It only supposes that the power of the people is superior to both; and that where the will of the legislature, declared in its statutes, stands in opposition to that of the people, declared in the Constitution, the judges ought to be governed by the latter rather than the former. They ought to regulate their decisions by the fundamental laws, rather than by those which are not fundamental.[59]

Judges in Singapore seem to be over-eager to ensure that they do not trample on the powers of the legislature, based on their belief that the legislature is the best-suited institution to represent the will of the people. What Hamilton urges us to consider is that more than any legislature (which only has a temporally limited mandate), the institution better suited to represent the will of the people across time and the longer history of a nation, is the text of its Constitution. Hamilton then counsels us that the institution and personnel best suited to interpret that text and its mandate over time is the judiciary and carefully chosen judges. He also reminds us that this is necessary because left to itself, the legislature can become a threat to the constitutional virtues that people naturally treasure, and it is judges who can well serve that checking function.

Not everyone will be convinced by Hamilton's logic, but it has exerted a powerful hold across many societies, and could be said to at least partially account for the fact that so many societies in the world today exhibit strong and robust judiciaries that do not hesitate to take up the cause of non-mainstream groups within their societies. Not surprisingly, many such judges and courts have conscripted earlier cases from other nations in the service of this cause. This is the connection between practices of trans-judicial influence and the robust protection of constitutional rights (especially of non-mainstream populations) that many scholars have drawn attention towards.

I have sought to engage with some recent scholarly analyses which point to a possible change in the attitude and approach of Singapore judges towards the use of comparative law in constitutional adjudication. I have argued that given the long historical entrenchment of particular approaches (both towards foreign law and in terms of the deference to be accorded to legislative choices) within the post-colonial tradition of constitutionalism in Singapore, it might be too early to either declare a new trend or to celebrate it. Relying on Jack Lee's comprehensive empirical survey and extending it to two recent cases, I have argued that many of the approaches that undergirded the thinking behind the 'four walls' doctrine are still evident in contemporary constitutional adjudication in Singapore.

What is common to the two cases I have chosen to focus upon, ie *Lim Meng Suang* and *Yong Vui Kong*, is that they involve Victorian-era colonial practices – the enactment of anti-sodomy statutes and the incorporation of the brutal and permanently defacing practice of caning. Given that Singapore has recently celebrated its fiftieth year of formal independence, it is somewhat ironic that these colonial practices continue to be defended as integral to the identity of contemporary Singapore.

I end with the following insightful comment by Ran Hirschl who draws from an analysis of trans-judicial influence in several countries in his recent work to conclude:

> [A] court's position and how it views its role with respect to socio-political struggles over the polity's collective identity is at least as significant a factor in explaining judicial choices of foreign reference as any structural, linguistic, or legal factor. Voluntary reference to foreign precedents is at least as much a political phenomenon as it is a juridical one.[60]

Thus, despite the great concern exhibited by some judges in Singapore about maintaining a strong distinction between the legal and the political, it is often the political choices of judges that help explain some of their legal choices, especially in relation to whether and which comparative law to engage with.

This book marks a significant legal, political and constitutional landmark in Singapore's history. Whether the trends – of resisting foreign law while being excessively deferential to legislative authority – analysed here will change over time will depend on both legal and political changes in the future.

Notes

1 I am grateful to Michael Hor, Ho Hock Lai, Jack Lee and Jaclyn Neo for comments and feedback that helped to improve earlier drafts. Afreen Azim assisted in the

presentation that formed the basis of this paper, while KarLuis Quek provided superb research and editorial assistance.

2 See eg David Law's recent article analysing trans-judicial influence in three relatively understudied constitutional courts in Asia: Japan, Taiwan and South Korea. David Law, 'Judicial Comparativism and Judicial Diplomacy' (2015) 163 University of Pennsylvania Law Review 927.

3 Ran Hirschl, *Comparative Matters: The Renaissance of Comparative Constitutional Law* (Oxford University Press 2014) 26.

4 Vicki Jackson, 'The Supreme Court, 2004 Term – Comment: Constitutional Comparisons: Convergence, Resistance, Engagement' (2005) 119 Harvard Law Review 109. Jackson subsequently published a book-length work elaborating on the thesis set out in the article: Vicki C Jackson, *Constitutional Engagement in a Transnational Era* (Oxford University Press 2010). However, in this chapter I rely primarily on the original article.

5 Vicki Jackson, 'The Supreme Court, 2004 Term – Comment: Constitutional Comparisons: Convergence, Resistance, Engagement' (2005) 119 Harvard Law Review 109, 112.

6 ibid 114.

7 Arun K Thiruvengadam, 'Comparative Law and Constitutional Interpretation in Singapore' in Kevin Tan and Thio Li-ann (eds), *Evolution of a Revolution: Forty Years of the Singapore Constitution* (Routledge-Cavendish 2009), 114–52.

8 A colleague questioned whether the American practice of describing apex courts based on erstwhile Chief Justices applies to judiciaries such as Singapore, which are arguably more influenced by the UK where this practice is not employed. I would argue that Singapore is a jurisdiction where Chief Justices do have significant impact on the overall judiciary during their tenure and that this nomenclature is justified. I should add the caveat that this does not rule out the possibility of individual judges and judgments that do not fit with the broad characterisation.

9 Li-ann Thio, 'It is a Little Known Legal Fact: Originalism, Customary Human Rights Law and Constitutional Interpretation' (2010) Singapore Journal of Legal Studies 558; Li-ann Thio, 'Soft Constitutional Law in Non-Liberal Asian Constitutional Democracies' (2010) 8(4) International Journal of Constitutional Law; Li-ann Thio, 'Reception and Resistance: Globalisation, International Law and the Singapore Constitution' (2009) 4(3) National Taiwan University Law Review 335; Li-ann Thio, 'Reading Rights Rightly: The UDHR and its Creeping Influence on the Development of Singapore Public Law' (2008) Singapore Journal of Legal Studies 264; Li-ann Thio, 'Beyond the "Four Walls" in an Age of Transnational Judicial Conversations: Civil Liberties, Rights Theories and Constitutional Adjudication in Malaysia and Singapore' (2006) 19 Columbia Journal of Asian Law 428; Li-ann Thio, 'The Death Penalty as Cruel and Inhuman Punishment before the Singapore High Court? Customary Human Rights Norms, Constitutional Formalism and the Supremacy of Domestic Law in PP v Nguyen Tuong Van (2004)' (2004) 4(2) Oxford University Commonwealth Law Journal 213.

10 Li-ann Thio, 'Beyond the "Four Walls"' (2006) 428.

11 Thio Li-ann and David Chong, 'The Chan Court and Constitutional Adjudication: "A Sea Change into Something Rich and Strange?"' in Chao, Phang, Rajah and Yeo (eds), *The Law in his Hands: A Tribute to Chief Justice Chan Sek Keong* (Academy Publishing 2012) 97.

12 ibid.

13 ibid 118.

14 [2010] 1 SLR 52 (Singapore Court of Appeal (Sing CA)).

15 [2010] 3 SLR 489 (Sing CA). In fact, the reference to the *Yong Vui Kong* case in the Thio–Chong piece was only in a footnote (Thio and Chong (n 11) footnote 52, 96).

16 [2001] 2 AC 127.

17 In *Lee Hsien Loong v Review Publishing Co Ltd* [2009] 1 SLR(R) 177 (Singapore High Court (Sing HC)), Woo Bih Li J granted interlocutory judgment at [232] (referred to in the Court of Appeal in *Review Publishing Co Ltd v Lee Hsien Loong* [2010] 1 SLR 52 at [15] as summary judgment) for the plaintiffs, Lee Hsien Loong and Lee Kuan Yew. At [298] of the appellate judgment, the Court of Appeal left Woo J's judgment undisturbed.
18 Thio and Chong (n 11) 96, footnote 52.
19 [1995] 1 SLR(R) 388 (Sing HC).
20 [2011] 3 SLR 778 (Sing CA).
21 [2015] 2 SLR 352 (Sing HC).
22 See Eugene Tan, 'Much ado about nothing? The enigma of engagement of foreign constitutional law in Singapore', Chapter 11 of this book.
23 ibid.
24 Jack Lee, 'Foreign Precedents in Constitutional Adjudication by the Supreme Court of Singapore, 1963–2013' (2015) 24 (2) Washington International Law Journal 253, 267.
25 This has been argued, for instance, in relation to the Supreme Court of India. See Pratap Bhanu Mehta, 'India's Unlikely Democracy – The Rise of Judicial Sovereignty' (2007) 18(2) Journal of Democracy 70.
26 See Alec Stone Sweet, *Governing with Judges: Constitutional Politics in Europe* (New York, Oxford University Press 2000); Martin Shapiro and Alec Stone Sweet, *On Law, Politics, and Judicialization* (New York, Oxford University Press 2002); Tom Ginsburg, *Judicial Review in New Democracies: Constitutional Courts in Asian Cases* (Cambridge University Press 2003).
27 Tom Ginsburg, *Judicial Review in New Democracies: Constitutional Courts in Asian Cases* (Cambridge University Press 2003) 24–25.
28 Lee (n 24) 267.
29 ibid 271–72.
30 Emphasis added. ibid 279.
31 ibid 283.
32 Lee (n 24) 288.
33 [2015] 1 SLR 26 (Sing CA).
34 In the United Kingdom, s 12 of the Sexual Offences Act 1956 provided that 'buggery' was a felony offence. It was later repealed by s 1 of the Sexual Offences Act 1967 following the Wolfenden Report. In *Naz Foundation v Government of NCT of Delhi*, the High Court of Delhi held that s 377 of the Indian Penal Code violated Art 14 (equality before the law), Art 15 (prohibition of discrimination) and Art 21 (protection of life and personal liberty). The Delhi Supreme Court later overturned the High Court's ruling in a heavily criticised judgment (this ruling is pending review by the Indian Supreme Court). In South Africa, the Witwatersrand High Court held that the common law offence of sodomy and s 20A of the Sexual Offences Act was unconstitutional. This was later confirmed by the Constitutional Court in *National Coalition for Gay and Lesbian Equality v Minister of Justice*, where the court held that sodomy laws violated s 9 (equality) of the South African Constitution and was thus unconstitutional. In Hong Kong, the Court of First Instance held that s 118C of the Crimes Ordinance (Cap 200) (which criminalised 'buggery' between two men if one [or both] of them were under 21) offended Art 25 of the Hong Kong Basic Law (equality) because the age of consent for heterosexual intercourse was 16.
35 Singapore Parliamentary Debates, Official Report (23 October 2007) vol 83, col 2354.
36 *Tan Eng Hong v Attorney-General* [2013] 4 SLR 1059 (Sing HC) (2 October 2013); *Lim Meng Suang and another v Attorney-General* [2013] 3 SLR 118 (Sing HC) (9 April 2013).
37 [2015] 1 SLR 26 (Sing CA).
38 *Lim Meng Suang (HC)* (n 36) [33]–[44].
39 ibid [133].

40 ibid.
41 ibid [144].
42 *Tan Eng Hong* (n 36) [48]–[56].
43 Emphasis added. ibid [90].
44 *Lim Meng Suang (CA)* (n 33) [48].
45 ibid [79]–[82]. Here, Phang J cites a series of well-known cases in the UK and refers to an extensive array of secondary literature. The extensive literature and case law on the central issue before the court – the constitutionality of the anti-sodomy laws – is, however, ignored.
46 ibid [188].
47 At the annual National Day Rally in 2015, Prime Minister Lee Hsien Loong underscored the critical importance for Singapore – 'a little red dot' – to be cognisant of what happens beyond Singapore's borders.
48 *Lim Meng Suang (CA)* (n 33) [6].
49 ibid [7].
50 ibid [189].
51 [2015] 2 SLR 1129 (Sing CA).
52 ibid [38].
53 ibid [75].
54 ibid [99].
55 Defined as consisting of 'a plaited rope instrument made up of nine knotted thongs of cotton cord, 30 inches long and less than one quarter of an inch in diameter each, attached to a handle': ibid [87].
56 ibid [87].
57 ibid [86].
58 ibid [121].
59 Alexander Hamilton, 'The Federalist No. 78' (*Independent Journal*, 14 June 1788) www.constitution.org/fed/federa78.htm accessed 15 September 2015.
60 Hirschl (n 3) 22.

Bibliography

Barak, Aharon, 'A Judge on Judging: The Role of a Supreme Court in a Democracy' (2002) 116 Harvard Law Review 16.

Chan, Sek Keong, 'Judicial Review – From Angst to Empathy: A Lecture to Singapore Management University Second Year Law Students' (2010) 22 Singapore Academy of Law Journal 469.

Chia, Huai Yuan, 'Taking Rights Seriously: 30 Years of Constitutional Adjudication' (2011) 29 Singapore Law Review 115.

Chong, David Gek Sian and Li-ann Thio, 'The Chan Court and Constitutional Adjudication – "A Sea Change into Something Rich and Strange?"' in Chao, Phang, Rajah and Yeo (eds), *The Law in His Hands: A Tribute to Chief Justice Chan Sek Keong* (Academy Publishing 2012).

Choudhry, Sujit, 'Globalization in Search of Justification: Toward a Theory of Comparative Constitutional Interpretation' (1999) 74 Indiana Law Journal 819.

Choudhry, Sujit, 'Migration as a New Metaphor in Comparative Constitutional Law' in Sujit Choudhry (ed), *The Migration of Constitutional Ideas* (Cambridge University Press 2006).

de Secondat, Charles (Baron de Montesquieu), *The Spirit of the Laws* (1748) Book I.

Dupre, Catherine, 'The Importation of Law: A New Comparative Perspective and the Hungarian Constitutional Court' in Andrew Harding and Esin Örücü (eds), *Comparative Law in the 21st Century* (Kluwer 2002).

Duxbury, Neil, 'The Law of the Land' (2015) 78 MLR 26.
Dworkin, Ronald, *The Constitution* in *Law's Empire* (Harvard University Press 1986).
Fedtke, Jorg and Basil Markesinis, 'The Judge as Comparatist' (2005–2006) 80 Tulane Law Review 11.
Franklin, Julian H, *Jean Bodin and the Sixteenth-Century Revolution in the Methodology of Law and History* (Columbia University Press 1963).
Friedman, Barry and Cheryl Saunders, 'Symposium: Constitutional Borrowing – Editors' Introduction' (2003) 1 ICON 177.
Harding, Sarah, 'Comparative Reasoning and Judicial Review' (2003) 28 Yale Journal of International Law 409.
Hirschl, Ran, *Comparative Matters: The Renaissance of Comparative Constitutional Law* (Oxford University Press 2014).
Hirschl, Ran, 'In Search of an Identity: Voluntary Foreign Citations in Discordant Constitutional Settings' (2014) 62 American Journal of Comparative Law 547.
Hirschl, Ran, 'Remembrance of Things Past' (invited editorial) (2015) 13 ICON 1.
Hoo, Sheau Peng, Lee Shen Dee and Phang Hsiao Chung (eds), *Speeches and Judgments of Chief Justice Yong Pung How* (FT Law & Tax Asia Pacific 1996).
Jackson, Vicki, *Constitutional Engagement in a Transnational Era* (Oxford University Press 2010).
Kreimer, Seth F, 'Invidious Comparisons: Some Cautionary Remarks on the Process of Constitutional Borrowing' (1999) 1 University of Pennsylvania Journal of Constitutional Law 640.
Law, David S, 'Judicial Comparativism and Judicial Diplomacy' (2015) 163 University of Pennsylvania Law Review 927.
Law, David S and Mila Versteeg, 'The Evolution and Ideology of Global Constitutionalism' (2011) California Law Review 1163.
Lee, Tsen-Ta Jack, 'Interpreting Bills of Rights: The Value of a Comparative Approach' (2007) 5 ICON 122.
Lee, Tsen-Ta Jack, 'Foreign Precedents in Constitutional Adjudication by the Supreme Court of Singapore, 1963–2013' (2015) 24 Washington International Law Journal 253.
Menon, Sundaresh, *Transnational Commercial Law: Realities, Challenges and a Call for Meaningful Convergence* in *Core Values of an Effective Judiciary* (Academy Publishing 2015).
Phang, Boon Leong Andrew, *The Development of Singapore Law: Historical and Socio-Legal Perspectives* (Butterworths 1990).
Ramraj, Victor V, 'Comparative Constitutional Law in Singapore' (2002) 6 Singapore Journal of International & Comparative Law 302.
Reed, Robert, 'Foreign Precedents and Judicial Reasoning: The American Debate and British Practice' (2008) 124 Law Quarterly Review 253.
Resnik, Judith, 'Constructing the 'Foreign': American Law's Relationship to Non-Domestic Sources' in Mads Andenas and Duncan Fairgrieve (eds), *Courts and Comparative Law* (Oxford University Press forthcoming).
Rosenfeld, Michel, 'Is Global Constitutionalism Meaningful or Desirable?' (2014) 25 European Journal of International Law 177.
Saunders, Cheryl, 'Judicial Engagement in the High Court of Australia', A High Court of Australia Public Lecture, 20 June 2012.
Saunders, Cheryl, 'The Impact of Internationalisation on National Constitutions' in Albert HY Chen (ed), *Constitutionalism in Asia in the Early Twenty-First Century* (Cambridge University Press 2014).

Saunders, Cheryl, 'Judicial Engagement' in Rosalind Dixon and Tom Ginsburg (eds), *Comparative Constitutional Law in Asia* (Edward Elgar 2014).

Tan, Eugene Kheng-Boon, 'Law and Values in Governance: The Singapore Way' (2000) 30 Hong Kong Law Journal 91.

Tan, Eugene Kheng-Boon, 'Autochthonous Constitutional Design in Post-Colonial Singapore: Intimations of Confucianism and the Leviathan in Entrenching Dominant Government' (2013) 4 Yonsei Law Journal 273.

Tan, Paul and Yihan Goh, 'The Growth of Local Jurisprudence' in Yihan Goh and Paul Tan (eds), *Singapore Law: 50 Years in the Making* (Academy Publishing 2015).

Tan, Seow Hon, 'Constitutional Jurisprudence: Beyond Supreme Law – A Law Higher Still' in Li-ann Thio and Kevin YL Tan (eds), *Evolution of a Revolution: Forty Years of the Singapore Constitution* (Routledge-Cavendish 2009).

Tew, Yvonne, 'Originalism at Home and Abroad' (2014) 52 Columbia Journal of Transnational Law 780.

Thio, Li-ann, 'An "i" for an "I": Singapore's Communitarian Model of Constitutional Adjudication' (1997) 27 Hong Kong Law Journal 152.

Thio, Li-ann, 'Beyond the "Four Walls" in an Age of Transnational Judicial Conversations: Civil Liberties, Rights Theories, and Constitutional Adjudication in Malaysia and Singapore' (2006) 19 Columbia Journal of Asian Law 428.

Thio, Li-ann, 'Protecting Rights' in Li-ann Thio and Kevin YL Tan (eds), *Evolution of a Revolution: Forty Years of the Singapore Constitution* (Routledge-Cavendish 2009).

Thio, Li-ann, 'It is a Little Known Legal Fact: Originalism, Customary Human Rights Law and Constitutional Interpretation' (2010) Singapore Journal of Legal Studies 558.

Thio, Li-ann, *A Treatise on Singapore Constitutional Law* (Academy Publishing 2012).

Thiruvengadam, Arun K, 'Comparative Law and Constitutional Interpretation in Singapore: Insights from Constitutional Theory' in Li-ann Thio and Kevin YL Tan (eds), *Evolution of a Revolution: Forty Years of the Singapore Constitution* (Routledge-Cavendish 2009).

Thiruvengadam, Arun K and Al-Ali Zaid, 'The Competing Effect of National Uniqueness and Comparative Influences on Constitutional Practice' in Mark Tushnet, Thomas Fleiner, and Cheryl Saunders (eds), *Routledge Handbook of Constitutional Law* (Routledge 2013).

Tripathi, Pradyumna, 'Foreign Precedents and Constitutional Law' (1957) Columbia Law Review 319.

Tushnet, Mark, 'Authoritarian Constitutionalism' (2015) 100 Cornell Law Review 391.

Watson, Alan, 'Legal Transplants and Law Reform' (1976) 92 Law Quarterly Review 79.

13 Constitutional interpretation in an age of globalisation

Challenges and prospects

Victor V Ramraj[1]

One primary goal of modern constitutionalism is to limit governmental power. In Singapore, this orthodox view – with its accompanying aspiration of limited government – was eloquently expressed by the Court of Appeal in *Chng Suan Tze*: '[T]he notion of a subjective or unfettered discretion is contrary to the rule of law. All power has legal limits and the rule of law demands that the courts should be able to examine the exercise of discretionary power.'[2] Much of the recent debate in Singapore over constitutional interpretation is concerned, directly or indirectly, with the extent to which the principle of limited government ought to apply with full vigour in Singapore, or whether it ought to be reformulated in light of the city-state's particular model of economic and political development, its emerging identity as a communitarian, Asian, and even Confucian state, or its organic political or social constitution. These are plainly important questions that will continue to occupy interpreters of Singapore's Constitution for decades to come. In contrast, this chapter addresses what might initially seem an esoteric question about constitutionalism. It is a question that is largely overlooked, but that is quickly emerging as a fundamental challenge for constitutional law, and public law more generally, in the decades ahead. The question, in short, is this: As powerful non-state actors emerge as important sources of economic and regulatory power, particularly multinational corporations and transnational private regulators, how should interpreters of domestic constitutional law respond?

In asking this question, we quickly become aware of a flaw in constitutional law's foundations. Specifically, we begin to question the assumption that the state holds the bulk of the economic and regulatory power that ought to concern constitutional lawyers, and that most other forms of power are, for their purposes, inconsequential. The purpose of this chapter is to explore the implications of the challenges posed by contemporary globalisation for Singapore over the next fifty years and to imagine how Singapore's constitutional interpreters might refashion constitutional principles and tools to achieve the higher-order goals of public law. But, in rethinking fundamental tools and principles, we must first be clear on the purpose of those tools and principles. So, we find ourselves back at the basics, revisiting first principles and, at the same time, thinking in fresh ways about the evolution of the modern state.

Singapore's unique trajectory provides the perfect laboratory for this kind of fundamental legal rethinking, because of its colonial economic history (having been founded by an entity, the British East India Company, which at the time of Singapore's founding itself defied classification as public or private), its peculiar political governance structure (as an entrepreneurial, state-capitalist, city-state), and its obvious integration with the global economy (as a key node in a network of global cities). What Singapore's experience shows us is that a new paradigm for public law – both constitutional and administrative law – must focus on moderating power whatever its source, embracing a normative and functional approach to public law rather than a rigid, formal approach. This paradigm shift will take time, but it is starting to take place.

A preliminary point of clarification is in order. Although this chapter takes constitutional law as its point of departure and acknowledges a formal and procedural distinction between constitutional and administrative law, it is nevertheless premised on the normative unity of constitutional and administrative law. Both seek to regulate and limit the exercise of power, and both typically assume that the power that concerns them is exercised by the state. This chapter questions that assumption and, as it does, the formal distinction between constitutional law and administrative law begins to fade and the need for a functional approach becomes more obvious.[3] In the meantime, this chapter begins with a focus on constitutional law as it is typically understood and will gradually expand its gaze to public law more generally, including principles usually taken as falling within the ambit of administrative law.

The chapter is divided into three parts. The first part explains more fully the challenge posed by contemporary transformations of economic and regulatory power beyond the state for the orthodox understanding of constitutional law. As will become clear in this part of the chapter, these reconfigurations of power exert pressure on orthodox legal principles, which must bend and stretch to accommodate a changing reality. The second part of the chapter highlights two developments in Singapore's legal and political order that suggest an openness to paradigmatic change. One development is largely doctrinal – a recognition in public law jurisprudence that some forms of private power are amenable to judicial review on public law principles. Another is legal and political – as demonstrated by the Singapore government's willingness to legislate extraterritorially and engage with global governance bodies, which shades into a decoupling of law and territory. The third and final part suggests how interpreters of Singapore's Constitution might use these developments to fashion a post-modern understanding of constitutionalism capable of regulating and moderating power, whatever its source.

I Contemporary global transformations as challenges to constitutional law

With its intellectual provenance in American and French revolutions of the nineteenth century, constitutional law as we understand it today is conceptually and practically congruent with the modern state. Indeed, some constitutionalist theorists see the constitution as constitutive of and co-extensive with the state, such that the state would not exist but for the constitution – what David Dyzenhaus calls Kelsen's 'Identity Thesis'.[4] According to this view, the Constitution is single-mindedly focused on the state, bringing it into existence, empowering it, and imposing limits on what it can rightfully do – captured in the ideal expressed succinctly in *Chng Suan Tze* that '[a]ll power has legal limits'.[5] The idea that the state's power is limited has been described by Dieter Grimm as part of an implicit political bargain behind the modern constitutional order.[6] In exchange for the state's monopoly on the legitimate use of force, the state's use of this power was limited to the protection of individual freedom against 'aggressors and criminals'.[7] By the same token, private persons could no longer exercise public power:

> If private persons gain a share in public power, the Constitution can no longer fulfil its claim to regulate the establishment and exercise of public power comprehensively unless the private actors submit to constitutional rules whereby they would lose their status as free members of society.[8]

The notion that private actors submit to public power on the understanding that the public power will, in turn, submit to the constitutional order is a key part of the modern constitutional law orthodoxy. But this orthodoxy rests on an assumption about the distinctive nature of public and private power, an assumption that, under conditions of modern government and contemporary globalisation, has an air of unreality.

In this part, we will see how the modern resurgence of transnational corporate power and the rise of transnational private regulation are steadily undermining the foundations of the modern constitutionalism, forcing us to take a hard look at first principles.

A States, companies, and the rise of modern constitutionalism

It is easy to overlook the significance that modern Singapore was founded in the name of a company, and a rather peculiar company at that. Before we examine the contemporary context of multinational corporations, it is instructive to take a step back and consider the historical context of modern constitutionalism and its connection to the East India Company, in whose name Singapore was established. Dieter Grimm's account of the constitutional bargain in some respects finds a concrete example in the long eighteenth century before the founding of modern Singapore. What we find in that period is the gradual erosion by Parliament of the immense economic powers wielded by the British East India Company and the rise of the modern constitutional state. The relationship between these two developments is important because, as Grimm implies, they are linked: the rise of the modern state as a consolidated constitutional entity required practically and conceptually that the East India Company's sovereign powers were legally subordinated to the state.

The East India Company's relationship to the British government was complex and often ambiguous, and it changed dramatically over the Company's 258-year history.[9] But, at the height of its power, in the early eighteenth century, the East India Company was, on a number of different measures (economic, geographic, military), possibly the most powerful and successful multinational corporation the world had ever seen.[10] To borrow a phrase that has echoed through the literature on the Company's history, it was, in essence, a company-state.[11]

At the time of Singapore's founding in 1819, the Company's monopoly on trade with Asia was gradually being eroded by Parliament and its original structure – as a trading company run autonomously by a group of wealthy London merchants – was unrecognisable. Lines of accountability to the British government had become increasingly robust. In its early days, the Company took advantage of its ambiguous status as neither 'a "mere merchant" ... [nor] an independent "sovereign"'.[12] According to Philip Stern, it found itself in a 'unique position occupying the space between England and Asia, serving as the commercial, political, and diplomatic intermediary between the two'.[13] And from this position:

> Company leaders could imagine and increasingly forge an autonomous political system, which was dependent on multiple political relationships and thus subject entirely to none – a precarious but potentially potent form of 'structural autonomy' and thus corporate sovereignty.[14]

By 1819, however, most of this autonomy had been eroded. The Company had lost its monopoly on all but the tea trade and was well on its way to becoming little more than an instrument of British imperial policy in India and beyond.[15] However, it retained its corporate form well into the nineteenth century, and Stamford Raffles was formally accountable to his superiors in the East India Company's office in Calcutta, from which the Company's operations in Asia were directed.

For our immediate purpose, three points are worthy of extraction from this brief historical excursion. First, as alluded to earlier, the gradual decline of the East India Company as what we would regard as a multinational corporation occurred in tandem with the rise of the modern (and imperial) British state. This is important because, as we shall soon see, the contemporary resurgence of multinational corporate power might well herald a correlative decline in state power (and also, perhaps, the resurgence of state capitalism). Second, in the same period in which the Company's power was being eroded, the foundations were laid for the first modern constitution, in the United States of America. There is, of course, a direct link between the Company and the new Republic: the refusal by the British Parliament to eliminate taxes on tea (which the American colonies were required to purchase through the East India Company) triggered the Boston Tea Party, which set the colonies on the path to independence.

Consistent with Grimm's bargain, the new constitution protected private economic interests, while subordinating them in turn to a limited form of government.

Finally, although it is unwise without further evidence to claim a direct causal link between Singapore's company-state foundations and its modern state-capitalist structure, we might at the very least hypothesise a weak form of path-dependency; Singapore has, through its modern history, thrived economically on government policies that have expressly sought to facilitate Singapore's strategic geographic position as a centre for regional and international trade. And, as we shall soon see, the growing power of multinational corporations, private and state-owned, poses a complex set of challenges for public law.

B The challenge of global corporate power

But even as the relationship between states and companies continues on a complex trajectory, many of the world's largest corporations are increasingly operating on a global scale, whether in terms of management structure, provision of services, manufacturing and supply chains, or distribution.[16] This complexity makes it increasingly difficult for states, acting on their own, to regulate corporations in their global operations, suggesting – for many states, if not most – a relative decline in the power of these states relative to the most powerful global companies.[17] The precise balance of power between state and company is the subject of protracted debate, often at the level of disagreement on methodology. From a legal perspective, however, it is more obvious that as companies operate across borders, it becomes increasingly difficult for all but possibly the most powerful states to regulate them. Indeed, regulating the business practices of companies on a global scale was at the heart of recent efforts, facilitated by the United Nations, to champion a set of principles, namely, the *UN Guiding Principles on Business and Human Rights*, to govern the activities of multinational corporations.[18]

Complicating matters further is the increasing presence of state-owned enterprises, including powerful national champions, in the global economy. In the first decade of the twenty-first century, some of the most powerful national economies consisted of states that, in one form or another, practised state capitalism. 'State capitalism' refers to an economic model that 'meld[s] the powers of the state with the powers of capitalism' and 'depends on government to pick winners and promote economic growth'.[19] It might use 'capitalist tools such as listing state-owned companies on the stockmarket and embrac[ing] globalization'.[20] It might also use national oil companies, privately owned national champions and sovereign wealth funds.[21] Of the largest modern economies, China, Russia and Brazil have been identified as countries that practice state capitalism.[22] So, too, Singapore. As an exceptionally wealthy state, Singapore has channelled its public reserves into a diverse portfolio of assets managed by Singapore's powerful sovereign wealth funds.[23] And it has taken the unusual step of specifying in its Constitution precisely how the institutional guardians of the state's 'accumulated reserves' are to be governed.[24]

These changes in the relationship of global corporate power to the state and the structure of the global economy challenge a basic assumption of constitutional law. The rising power of privately owned multinational corporations turns on its head the assumption that the state has a monopoly on power which allows the state alone to determine the rights and privileges of private citizens or actors within its borders, as well as the corresponding assumption that the state must, therefore, be subject to the moderating force of constitutional law. Moreover, on the state-capitalist model, a sharp distinction between state and corporate power is illusory. Even where such a line might reasonably be posited, the assumption of the state's regulatory omnipotence over corporations is exaggerated, if not entirely misplaced – not least because of a fundamental tension between state-as-regulator and state-as-owner.[25] These transformations in Singapore and the global economy suggest a greater urgency to rethink constitutionalism in a fundamental way, and to fashion legal tools that might be used to moderate power, whatever its source.

C The rise of private regulation: national and transnational, private and hybrid

In Commonwealth jurisdictions such as Canada and the United Kingdom, a trend towards 'new public management' has been identified by some scholars, which consists of the 'contracting out' of state functions to private actors.[26] Singapore's bureaucracy is, by global standards, extremely well-resourced, so it has not felt the political pressures that other developed countries have to shrink its bureaucracy or cut public services drastically. Nevertheless, Singapore has been described as 'enthusiastic' in its embrace of new public management, including the tools of privatisation, outsourcing and partnership. [27] Faced with a significant proportion of regulatory power reposed in private hands, or at least in ambiguously 'hybrid' hands, it is unsurprising that the Singapore courts have, in their public law jurisprudence, engaged with these bodies, incrementally articulating a set of principles to govern them.[28]

Even more challenging for domestic public law, however, is the rise of *transnational* private regulation – an increasingly important problem considering the sheer number of transnational regulatory bodies that claim the authority to govern a particular social or economic field, covering areas as diverse as sustainable forestry, accounting standards, capital adequacy requirements for financial institutions, and labour standards governing global supply chains. As transnational regulators become ever more pervasive, it is increasingly difficult for individuals, organisations, and in some instances states themselves, to resist the economic or reputational pressure to conform to their standards. For public lawyers, the question is whether domestic public law actors – such as the courts through judicial review – are able (legally or practically) to govern the conduct of these bodies in as much as their conduct runs foul of domestic public law principles and, if so, whether and to what extent they *should* do so.

At this juncture, it is worthwhile to offer a rough typology of transnational regulatory bodies. This chapter's interest is, first and foremost, in regulators who do not have a natural line of accountability to the state. I therefore leave aside regulators set up under formal international treaties, as these regulators are at least formally accountable to those who have created them. Most difficult for domestic mechanisms of accountability, however, are intergovernmental organisations created by informal agreements among state agencies. A body, such as the Financial Action Task Force (FATF), set up initially under the auspices of the G-7 (and later G-8) to combat money laundering and later terrorism financing, is one example of such a body. Another example is the International Organization of Security Commissions (IOSCO), consisting of regulators of securities markets from a range of jurisdictions, aimed at 'protecting investors, ensuring that markets are fair, efficient, and transparent, [and] reducing systemic risk'.[29] As Anne-Marie Slaughter has observed, the number of such bodies is legion: intergovernmental networks of bureaucrats across a range of fields is now ordinary, and such networks can be found equally in the legislative and judicial spheres.[30] Singapore is an active participant in many of these intergovernmental networks, including FATF and IOSCO (through the Monetary Authority of Singapore).

It could be argued that because these intergovernmental bodies are creatures of states, they have a claim to the legitimacy of those states and are ultimately accountable to them; where a state objects to the policies, guidelines or recommendations of an intergovernmental network, it need only withdraw. The problem, however, is two-fold. First, since intergovernmental networks operate largely through peer pressure, there is a political and reputational cost to non-cooperation. Second, and critically, the pressure to conform to the norms or regulations of the network often extends to non-member states, and individuals and organisations operating within them. For example, the FATF produced name-and-shame reports exposing non-compliance with its counter-terrorism financing guidelines in respect of states that had no role in formulating those guidelines. In this context, it is difficult to sustain the argument that intergovernmental networks necessarily have a greater claim to legitimacy because of a line of accountability to their founding states.

These concerns might not be directly relevant to Singapore, particularly when it holds a place at the table of these intergovernmental bodies. More challenging, however, and even more complex in terms of their claims to legitimacy, are hybrid and, especially, *private* regulators that operate transnationally. Hybrid regulators typically involve states and private actors working together through an institutional form to produce, monitor and enforce a set of norms or standards. These arrangements often arise on an ad hoc basis to address a specific problem. For instance, in the aftermath of the Rana Plaza factory collapse in the outskirts of Dhaka, Bangladesh in April 2013, which left more than 1,100 workers dead, two rival multi-stakeholder regimes were formed, each seeking to ensure a more rigorous and systematic approach to protecting and enforcing workplace safety standards.[31] Although the details of these mechanisms differ, the Accord provides an example of a legally binding agreement signed by garment manufacturers from twenty countries, unions and non-governmental organisations (NGOs), with the International Labour Organization serving as an independent chair with a dispute resolution mechanism drawing on the New

York Convention on the Recognition and Enforcement of Foreign Arbitral Awards.[32] Another example, in the Singapore context, is the Roundtable on Sustainable Palm Oil (RSPO), which has become particularly visible in recent years in light of its efforts to regulate, by way of a certification regime, the environmental impact of palm oil production.[33]

Transnational *private* regulators pose a challenge for public law precisely because of their private nature. These private regulators take various forms, but two in particular stand out. First, transnational private regulators might be industry bodies that purport to regulate the very industry of which they are a part. These are industry self-regulatory bodies. Industry self-regulation might consist of a company's own internal corporate code of conduct or it could be a code adopted by many firms within a particular industry.[34] The legitimacy of industry self-regulation will depend, in large measure, on the kind of enforcement mechanism that is used to ensure compliance, whether internal and confidential, or external and open to public scrutiny. A second kind of transnational private regulator is closer in structure, composition and ethos to an NGO, consisting of civil society actors and a range of stakeholders, including, in some instances, the entities that are subject to the regulations they produce.[35] The Forestry Stewardship Council is often cited as an example of a sophisticated transnational private regulator – one that has taken important steps to refine its governance structure to strengthen both its internal legitimacy (the extent of 'buy-in' among key stakeholders) and its external legitimacy (the extent to which it is perceived by those outside the organisation as having legitimate political authority to regulate).[36] More recently, many sustainability organisations have come together to establish a meta-regulatory body, the ISEAL Alliance, the goal of which is to 'strengthen sustainability standard systems'[37] within its members, thereby improving their impact, credibility, uptake and effectiveness.[38]

In many instances, transnational private regulators have emerged to fill a regulatory lacuna where states are unable or unwilling to step in.[39] Such was the case with Forestry Stewardship Council, which found its inception in the failure of states to agree on a treaty to address tropical deforestation.[40] The greater a state's interest in promoting or protecting a particular industry, the harder it is for the state to regulate the industry in a meaningful way. Other transnational private regulators operate in industries where harmonisation of standards is essential, but where states are unable or unwilling to take the lead in developing those standards, as in the case of accounting standards.[41] It is important to bear this context in mind because transnational private regulators pose both a threat and an opportunity. They pose a threat because, at least for some of these bodies, their claim to legitimacy is relatively weak (with some important exceptions, such as the International Organization for Standardization or ISO), even though they have the power to influence the conduct and, in some cases the livelihood, of many individuals. At the same time, however, they have the potential to regulate in a creative and impactful way in areas such as sustainability, labour and industrial safety standards, and other areas where the global operations of companies makes it difficult for states alone to regulate. To the extent that domestic courts are prepared to engage with transnational private regulators on the terrain of domestic law, they would be well advised to recognise the dual nature of these bodies and to articulate a set of good governance practices for transnational regulatory bodies to follow. To be in a position do so, however, the courts must be willing to rethink the traditional, statist paradigm of public law. In the next part, we explore how this might happen.

II Singapore's legal innovations

Singapore is not typically regarded as an innovative jurisdiction for public law thinking, and for understandable reasons. Singapore's constitutional law regime is often analysed through the lens of judicial review of constitutional rights, with a view to determining whether rights are interpreted in a sufficiently robust manner to uphold the values inherent in the rule of law, or to criticise or defend Singapore's 'Asian values' or 'Confucian' or 'non-Western' approach to judicial review. These important debates deserve close study, but they draw our attention away from two clusters of innovations that suggest an uncommon openness to paradigmatic change, and a creative rethinking of Singapore's constitutional order that recognises that power does not always respect formal boundaries or confine itself solely to the formal institutions of the state. As observed above, the first development is largely doctrinal and takes the form of a recognition in the public law jurisprudence that some forms of private power are amenable to judicial review. The second is legal and political, demonstrated by the growing legislative and judicial tolerance of extra-territorial legality[42] and by the willingness of the Singapore government to engage with global governance bodies. This willingness shades into a recent structural development – the decoupling of law from territory – of which the establishment of the Singapore International Commercial Court is a prime example.

A Extending public law principles to private regulators

As we have seen, one orthodox assumption of public law is the distinction between public and private. Modern (some might say 'Western') constitutional law, as it developed out of the French and American revolutions, was very much a product of a state-limiting ideology: public law, and constitutional law in particular, was the means by which state power was limited through law. At the same time, however, constitutional law tried to carve out a sphere of private activity which was largely immune from state control: the constitution, and later the principles of administrative law, governed the conduct of state power; all other activity was subject to *private* law. This sharp divide between public and private law is no longer as pervasive and many modern constitutions have demonstrated a shift away from a strict adherence to this doctrine.[43] Yet, most modern constitutions maintain some form of the 'state action doctrine', which holds that constitutional rights apply only 'vertically' to state or 'governmental' action.[44]

Singapore, too, seems largely to follow this model. Article 4 of Singapore's Constitution declares that the Constitution is 'the supreme law of the Republic of

Singapore and any law enacted by the Legislature after the commencement of this Constitution which is inconsistent with this Constitution shall, to the extent of the inconsistency, be void'. Although this particular article of the Constitution is narrowly drafted, the Singapore courts have, on occasion, articulated a broader and more purposive understanding of it as a more general limit on power consistent with the rule of law. We have already seen one example of this purposive approach in *Chng Suan Tze*: '[T]he notion of a subjective or unfettered discretion is contrary to the rule of law. All power has legal limits and the rule of law demands that the courts should be able to examine the exercise of discretionary power.'[45]

Despite the powerful grasp that this orthodox view of constitutionalism exerts on the legal imagination of public lawyers, a gradual shift is starting to take place in Singapore, particularly in the context of administrative law, with broader implications for public law thinking. The first indication of this shift concerns judicial review of the decisions of private bodies. In the common law tradition, courts have long been reluctant to intervene in the affairs of the private bodies or domestic tribunals, but a substantial and growing body of case law in Singapore and Malaysia extends public law principles to private actors. The courts have been increasingly willing to intervene in the decisions of private associations, not simply on the basis of an implied contractual term requiring compliance with natural justice,[46] but even in the absence of a contractual relationship, where serious interests are affected, such as 'the livelihood of the plaintiff … in the trade or profession controlled and regulated by the defendant and of which the plaintiff is trained or has chosen to enter'.[47] In Singapore, this trend can be seen in a line of cases that has imposed a duty to act fairly not only in cases involving disciplinary proceedings against doctors and lawyers, which have a statutory basis,[48] but also in cases involving expulsion from a political party[49] or suspension from a prestigious social club.[50]

Crucially, in the 2012 case *Yeap Wai Kong v Singapore Exchange Securities Trading Ltd*[51] the Singapore High Court took the bold step of affirming the UK case *R v Panel on Takeovers and Mergers, ex p Datafin*.[52] In *Datafin*, the Court of Appeal held that the test for whether a body is amenable to judicial review is determined not simply by the source of its power (the Panel on Takeovers and Mergers had no statutory authority), but also by considering the nature of its regulatory power. Pillai J prefaced his discussion of *Datafin* by describing, in the following terms, a transformation in the modern regulatory landscape:

> In the modern era, public policy is increasingly effected not only by government and statutory bodies but also through self-regulating entities in sectors where the domain nature and complexity of the sector requires front-line expertise coupled with back-line regulators to regulate the relevant sector.[53]

For Pillai J, *Datafin* was significant precisely because it recognised the need to control the decision-making process and to prevent abuse irrespective of the source of a decision-maker's power. To restrict judicial review to bodies that derive their powers from a statutory source would be 'to impose an artificial limit on the developing law of judicial review'.[54] It is therefore incumbent on the courts to examine a decision-maker's function, taking into consideration 'the nature of the function, the extent to which there is any statutory recognition or underpinning of the body or the function in question and the extent to which the body has been interwoven into a system of governmental regulation'.[55] Pillai J found that the Singapore Exchange, though not a statutory body, satisfied this test, and its power to reprimand was a public function that was 'subject to judicial review for minimum compliance with the standards of "legality, rationality and procedural propriety" '.[56]

The second – and seemingly unrelated – indication of a shift away from the orthodox view is encapsulated in the extra-judicial attempt, by the former Chief Justice Chan Sek Keong, to explain Singapore's administrative law jurisprudence as consistent with a facilitative 'green light' theory that 'sees public administration not as a necessary evil but as a positive attribute, and the objective of administrative law as not (primarily) to stop bad administrative law but to encourage good ones'.[57] In their famous formulation of red and green light theories, Carol Harlow and Richard Rawlings insist that green light theorists do not favour 'unrestricted or arbitrary action by the state'.[58] But, 'while red light theory looks to the model of the balanced constitution and favours strong judicial control of executive power, green light theory sees in administrative law a vehicle for political progress and welcomes the "administrative state" '.[59] On this view, as Chan Sek Keong explains, the courts play 'a supporting role by articulating clear rules and principles by which the [g]overnment may abide by and conform to the rule of law'.[60] The idea that public law has an important facilitating or enabling function is attractive in the context of state-building, where states tend to direct economic and political development. As we shall see, it might also have explanatory and normative force in other contexts, including our contemporary context of economic globalisation.

We should be cautious not to overstate the significance of these developments in Singapore. For one thing, *Yeap Wai Kong* is by no means settled law, and the idea that private power is an important concern of administrative law is controversial. Moreover, Chan Sek Keong's extra-judicial endorsement of the green light theory is still only one view of how to understand administrative law in Singapore. Nevertheless, as will soon become clear, the conceptual flexibility demonstrated both in *Yeap Wai Kong* and the green light theory opens the door to the kind of creative public law thinking that we need to respond effectively to the challenges of globalisation.

B Rethinking territorially bound conceptions of legality

A second fundamental assumption of modern constitutional law concerns the nexus between constitution and territory. If constitutional law is, according to the orthodox view, premised on the exercise of governmental power and is intended to operate as a constraint on *that* power, then in a system of territorially bound sovereign states, it seems reasonable to assume that constitutional law would operate territorially as well. Indeed, both the exercise of legislative (eg criminal law) power extraterritorially and the projection of constitutional law beyond the boundaries of the state require special legal justifications under international and domestic law.

Under principles of public international law, attempts to project state power beyond territorial boundaries are contentious precisely because of the assumption that states are sovereign within their territory. On this view, any attempt to project state power beyond territorial borders is exceptional and must find some justification in international law.[61] Public international law does, however, recognise a number of grounds for extra-territorial criminal legislation, some of which are readily acknowledged as more acceptable than others. These grounds include: nationality (passive or active);[62] territoriality (subjective or objective);[63] universality;[64] or the protective principle (regulating offences against the security, integrity, sovereignty and governmental functions of the state).[65] These grounds remain controversial, but an increase in the use of extra-territorial legislation is 'hardly surprising given the internationalization of institutions, finance and, inevitably, criminal activity'.[66] And so, attempts to justify extra-territorial legislation according to public international law principles will continue apace.[67]

Apart from the requirements of public international law, constitutional law also places limits on the state's use of extra-territorial legislative power. For example, in *Taw Cheng Kong*, the Court of Appeal held, effectively reversing on principle a decision of the High Court, that the projection of the Prevention of Corruption Act to corrupt activities taking place overseas where the offender was a Singapore citizen (but not a permanent resident or foreigner working abroad for a Singapore company) did not amount to a violation of the equality provisions in Singapore's Constitution, in part because the Singapore government had properly taken into account principles of international comity when distinguishing between the two classes of offenders.[68] In the course of its decision, the Court of Appeal reiterated a general presumption against the extra-territorial application of law.[69]

As extra-territorial legislation continues to grow – for example, in relation to the law of corruption, terrorism, human trafficking and cross-border pollution[70] – constitutional law will continue to face pressure to adapt to the projection of state power across borders. Questions will inevitably arise in relation to the extra-territorial legislation, such as the corresponding reach of procedural protections guaranteed in the Constitution.[71] Crucially, the tension between extra-territorial legislation and a territorial understanding of the constitution will continue to put pressure on a strictly territorial understanding of law, and on the assumed line between what takes place within the territory of the state and what happens beyond it.

At the same time, however, the delinking of state law and territory creates opportunities to think more creatively about the projection of public law norms beyond the state and, in particular, to non-state actors, including corporations. At an institutional and structural level, Singapore has demonstrated a distinct openness to non-territorial legal structures. Singapore's commitment to international commercial arbitration[72] affords one example; the establishment of the Singapore International Commercial Court (SICC) provides another. Established in January 2015, the SICC offers international commercial litigants 'the option of having their disputes adjudicated by a panel of experienced judges comprising specialist commercial judges from Singapore and international judges from both civil law and common law traditions'.[73]

These legal institutions might be criticised by the anti-globalisation movement for facilitating an unbridled global capitalism that undermines the regulatory power of states and exacerbates global inequality. However, they might also afford an opportunity to unleash constitutional law constraints on economic power structures beyond the state. If Singapore commercial law can journey beyond territorial boundaries, so, too, might public law principles that promote corporate social responsibility or protect citizens and others from the most flagrant abuses of economic power.

III Beyond modern constitutional orthodoxy

As we take stock of the many remarkable transformations in law and global governance in our time, we might be inclined to think that modern constitutionalism rests on a series of mistaken assumptions: on the assumption that the only power that ought to concern us is the power of the state; on the assumption that if public power is abused, it would be only by the state or, perhaps, with the acquiescence of the state; and on the assumption that if private power is a problem, the only solution is to turn to the state to resolve it. There is, I think, much to be said for questioning all of these assumptions. This is not to deny that the state retains vast swathes of power, including the coercive power of the criminal law. Nor should it be taken to mean that the core aspirations of orthodox constitutionalism, such as preventing the abuse of the state's coercive powers, should be abandoned. Far from it. It does imply, however, that an exclusive and single-minded focus on these classic state powers obscures other pervasive, but less visible, ways in which powers that we might traditionally associate with states are now exercised by bodies that are not, according to modern constitutional theory, squarely within the realm of public law. In this part of the chapter, I suggest three ways in which public law in Singapore could take the lead in adapting to a changing global economic and regulatory environment.

A The unity of public law?

A first step would be to recognise a general normative role for public law in articulating the conditions under which and purposes for which public power is exercised, and moderating that power when it fails to adhere to a discrete set of core principles, substantive and procedural. The difficulty, however, is that the courts are often preoccupied by formalistic distinctions. One example is the recent attempt by the Singapore Court of Appeal in *Yong Vui Kong*[74] to distinguish between natural justice as a constitutional law principle and as an administrative law principle.[75] Although cases such as *Yong Vui Kong* posit some common ground within public law jurisprudence as a whole, they also demonstrate a reluctance to let go of the formalistic legal thinking that prevents the creative and responsive development of public law.[76] Indeed, this chapter has moved relatively freely between constitutional and administrative law principles precisely because this distinction tends to privilege form over substance.

A search for a general unity of purpose does not mean that some finer distinctions within public law are unnecessary, for it may be that there are higher- and lower-level principles that must be distinguished according to the circumstances. For instance, Article 9(1) of the Singapore Constitution might be seen as the limiting case: where the interests at stake are of the utmost importance (life and personal liberty), the most exacting standards of procedural fairness are triggered. But, where less important interests are at stake, a different balance might be struck. The difference between natural justice in constitutional and administrative law might helpfully be understood as a matter of degree, rather than (following *Yong Vui Kong*) as a formal distinction based on the separation of powers. In an increasingly complex world, we need to move away from formalistic ways of thinking that distract us from the higher purposes of public law.

B A functional approach to power

A second adjustment to public law thinking would involve moving more deliberately toward a functional approach to power. A functional approach to power implies that *what* is being done is more important than *who* is doing it. For instance, a functional approach to power would readily acknowledge that the public interest might be *harmed* by an exercise of state power or *protected from harm* by an exercise of state power (or such exercise by other actors), according to the circumstances. In the paradigmatic public law case, a government agency decides against the interests of the public on questionable substantive or procedural grounds, and it is the role of the courts under principles of public law to hold that decision-maker to account. At the same time, however, a private actor (say, a company) might act against the interests of the public, and it might be the role of the government to take affirmative steps to address the problem, perhaps by breaking up a monopoly that is abusing its dominant position in the market or by supporting the efforts of civil society groups to work with their counterparts in the region or globally to hold a multinational corporation to account for an abuse of its power. This last example shows that private actors can be either the target of regulation (eg a monopolistic company) or regulators in their own right (eg a civil society organisation such as the RSPO). Shifting away from a 'source of power' test toward a 'nature of power' test to determine whether a decision-maker is subject to judicial review (as cases such as *Yap Wai Kong* have done) is an important first step toward a functional approach; it allows the courts to examine the reality of how power operates in order to determine whether, and on what basis, they should intervene by way of judicial review.[77]

The global resurgence of state capitalism complicates matters further. The more closely aligned the interests of industry and government are, the more difficult it is for government to regulate, with state capitalism creating the prospect of regulatory capture of the highest order. A sophisticated and enlightened state-capitalist government might, in theory, be able to regulate against its commercial interests, though a heavy evidential onus would fall on proponents of this strategy to demonstrate practically how this could be done. None of the foregoing should be read as suggesting that state capitalism is inherently problematic. For example, the history of the British East India Company and, in the United States, the federal government's support for the airline industry,[78] indicate that state support of industry has a long history even in ostensibly market-based economies. However, apart from its potential to nurture emerging industries and support economic development, state capitalism creates distinct regulatory problems and unique challenges for public law when states hold a significant economic interest in the very entities they purport to regulate.[79] As the interests of states and companies converge and the prospect of regulatory capture multiplies, transnational private regulators, at an arm's length from both states and companies, may well have to play an increasingly significant regulatory role in the years ahead.

C Transnational regulators and judicial review

Recent legal developments in Singapore make it easier to imagine a more nuanced view of public law, and a functional understanding of the kinds of entities – public, private and hybrid – that public law principles seek to regulate. More challenging, however, would be the acceptance of a new role for domestic public law actors, courts in particular, in relation to transnational regulators. So far, courts in other jurisdictions have been reluctant to review the decisions of private regulators based outside the state, even when it is not disputed that the decision had an adverse impact on constitutional rights and would have been unconstitutional had it been made by a public body.

This was essentially the situation in *Segan v Vancouver Organizing Committee (VANOC)* where a group of Canadian women ski-jumpers challenged a decision of the International Olympic Committee (a decision that was implemented by VANOC) not to stage women's ski-jumping as an event at the Vancouver Olympic Winter Games in 2010, even though men's ski-jumping was included. The women argued that the decision violated their equality rights under s 15 of the Canadian Charter of Rights and Freedoms. The trial judge had dismissed the Charter claim on the ground that, although governmental activity was involved and a substantive breach of the Charter could be established, the decision not to stage the ski-jumping event was a decision of the IOC, which, as a 'private, Swiss-based organization', was 'not itself subject to the Charter'.[80] The British Columbia Court of Appeal disagreed on this point. It held that it was unnecessary to decide whether VANOC was engaged in a governmental activity because it was 'clear on the facts that neither government nor VANOC had any authority to make or alter the decision of the IOC not to include a women's ski-jumping event in the 2010 Games'.[81] Moreover, since that decision was therefore 'not an activity to which the *Charter* applies', the women's claim of discrimination failed.[82] This was not, in the court's view, an instance of a 'governmental body attempting to circumvent the *Charter* by exercising power through contract instead of through legislation',[83] which would have attracted the scrutiny of the court. Rather, it was 'a case in which a non-governmental body is brought before the court as a result of policies which neither it nor any Canadian authority has the power to change'.[84]

The difficulty with the BC Court of Appeal's decision is that if, on these facts, a Canadian court is not prepared to assume jurisdiction to prevent a breach of the Charter (and thus the Canadian Constitution) by what is essentially a transnational private regulator, it is not clear where else a remedy might lie. It would have been open to the court, on a functional test, to find that the IOC was acting in a governmental capacity, or perhaps that different levels of Canadian government had delegated a governmental function to the IOC. Instead, the Court of Appeal chose to frame the decision as one about the *source* of the IOC's authority and in framing the decision as exclusively that of the IOC, it rendered the Canadian authority powerless. By the same measure, in denying a role for the Canadian courts in relation to the decision, it ceded to the IOC the power to violate the Charter, without an available remedy.

It is easy to dismiss a case such as *Sagen* as anomalous; it was a rare situation (the Olympics) that involved an unusual regulatory creature (the IOC). With the growth of transnational private regulation, however, this kind of situation is likely to become increasingly common, and it is worthwhile to consider how the Singapore courts might approach a similar situation. Two developments in particular bode well. First, as we have seen in cases such as *Yeap Wai Kong*,[85] the Singapore courts openly recognise the public role played by private power. The idea that a private power might exercise a public function that is amenable to judicial scrutiny under public law principles is by no means foreign to the Singapore courts. It is conceivable, especially after *Yeap Wai Kong*, that the courts might recognise a public regulatory role (with domestic impact in Singapore) played by a transnational private regulator. Moreover, the Singapore court's appreciation of 'green light theory' approaches to public administration might also be transposed into the transnational regulatory sphere. Although questions of legitimacy must be asked of any transnational private actor that purports to regulate across multiple borders in the public interest,[86] the Singapore courts might, by engaging with transnational regulators in a collaborative way, help to strengthen the governance practices by insisting on a minimum standard of procedural fairness. At the same time, the courts should be mindful that, by virtue of their operations across many jurisdictions, transnational private regulators might themselves be encumbered by multiple, inconsistent demands on their regulatory activities. Again, a facilitative, green light theory of the sort advocated by Chan Sek Keong might afford a useful starting point as domestic courts begin to engage with transnational private regulators, facilitating their regulatory activities while encouraging them to adopt best practices.

Practically speaking, however, a more pertinent question is whether an appropriate case might find its way into the Singapore courts, and for this to happen we must rely on the creativity and imagination of Singapore's lawyers. It is here that Singapore's unique history, geography and status as a city-state, with its profound engagement with the wider world, might prove an advantage, as daily life in Singapore generates the kinds of transnational disagreements and conflicts that could conceivably find their way into the legal system. But getting a case into the legal system is one thing; framing it as a public law case is another. A dispute between a transnational regulator and a regulated entity might as easily be framed as a run-of-the-mill private law dispute, perhaps over the terms of membership or requirements for certification or accreditation. It would take a legal profession attuned to the less obvious public regulatory role played by transnational private regulators to frame the case as a public law dispute. When this happens, the Singapore courts should be ready, and the stage will be set for the courts to take a decisive step toward a new paradigm of public law.

IV Conclusion

Singapore constitutional law scholarship has come a long way in a relatively short time. It is understandably preoccupied with making sense of constitutional interpretation in light of the Constitution's distinctive features and its unique approach to governance, while acknowledging the ground it shares with other jurisdictions. But, constitutional law scholarship has a statist gravitational pull, and it is difficult, in this peculiar area of law more than most others, to think beyond the state. My goal in this chapter has been to nudge constitutional law scholarship in a new direction, highlighting a largely neglected area in which Singapore might contribute to a novel understanding of constitutionalism for a world in which the relationship between state and company, public and private, local and global, are far more complex than the orthodox paradigm allows us to see. My argument in this chapter is that Singapore's unique experience – with its distinctive corporate foundations, its profound global engagement as city-state, its peculiar brand of state capitalism, and its recent legal innovations – provides Singapore constitutional law scholars with a privileged perspective on the transformation of the global economy and the transnational regulatory space and, thus, a unique opportunity to rethink constitutional law for the complex and interconnected world in which we find ourselves.

Notes

1 Professor, Faculty of Law and Chair in Asia-Pacific Legal Relations, Centre for Asia-Pacific Initiatives (CAPI), University of Victoria, Canada; Visiting Professor, NUS Law School, Singapore. I am grateful to Jaclyn Neo, Donna Greschner and the participants in the workshops at the National University of Singapore for their insightful comments on earlier versions of this chapter.

2 *Chng Suan Tze v Minister for Home Affairs* [1988] 2 SLR(R) 525 [86]. *Chng Suan Tze* is typically regarded as an administrative law case, although the principle of limited government it articulates is consistent with an orthodox modern view of public law, including constitutional law, which will be examined and questioned in this chapter.

3 Recent case law in Singapore struggles with the need for a formal distinction, oscillating between acknowledging the commonality between the basic principles of constitutional and administrative law, such as the rules of natural justice, and insisting on a distinction on the ground that they 'operate at different levels of the legal order'. See, for example, *Yong Vui Kong v AG* [2011] 2 SLR 1189 [105].

4 'The Compulsion of Legality' in Victor V Ramraj (ed), *Emergencies and the Limits of Legality* (Cambridge University Press 2008) 33–59, 36.

5 n 2.

6 Dieter Grimm, 'The Achievement of Constitutionalism and Its Prospects in a Changed World' in Petra Dobner and Martin Loughlin (eds), *The Twilight of Constitutionalism?* (Oxford University Press 2010) 3–22, 11.

7 ibid.

8 ibid.

9 See generally, Philip J Stern, *The Company-State: Corporate Sovereignty and the Early Modern Foundations of the British Empire in India* (Oxford University Press 2011); Philip Lawson, *The East India Company: A History* (Longman 1993).

10 HV Bowen, *The Business of Empire: The East India Company and Imperial Britain* (Cambridge University Press 2006); Nick Robbins, *The Corporation that Changed the World: How the East India Company Shaped the Modern Multinational* (Pluto Press 2006).

11 Stern (n 9).

12 Stern (n 9) 13.

13 ibid.

14 ibid 14.

15 Lawson (n 9). When the Company's trading and monopoly privileges (except for the tea trade with Canton) were removed in 1813, the Company 'was left with the least glamorous function of all, providing bureaucrats as agents of royal power in India' (137).

16 See, for example: Brian Roach, 'A Primer on Multinational Corporations' in Alfred D Chandler Jr and Bruce Mazlish (eds), *Leviathans: Multinational Corporations and The New Global History* (Cambridge University Press 2005), 19–44; Neil M Coe, Philip F Kelly, and Henry WC Yeung, 'The Transnational Corporation' in *Economic Geography: A Contemporary Introduction* (Blackwell 2007), 223–53.

17 On the complexities of regulating modern multinational corporations and the strategies for doing so, see Peter T Muchlinski, *Multinational Enterprises and the Law* (2nd edn, Oxford University Press 2007) Chapter 3.

18 *Guiding Principles on Business and Human Rights* HR/PUB/2011/04 (United Nations Office of the High Commissioner on Human Rights 2011).

19 Adrian Wooldridge, 'The Visible Hand' *The Economist* (21 January 2012) 3 (special report after page 48).

20 ibid.

21 Ian Bremmer, 'State Capitalism Comes of Age' *Foreign Affairs* (May/June 2009) 40, 42.

22 Wooldridge (n 19) 4.

23 The Fifth Schedule to the Constitution, Part II, lists the government companies that are subject to a constitutionally mandated appointment procedure and safeguards set out in Art 22C: Government of Singapore Investment Corporation Pte Ltd, MND Holdings Pte Ltd and Temasek Holdings Pte Ltd.

24 See Part XI: Financial Provisions, Art 22C (appointment of directors of Government companies).

25 See Wang Jiangyu, 'The Political Logic of Corporate Governance in China's State-owned Enterprises' (2014) 47 Cornell International Law Journal 631, 635 (arguing against the assumption of the Americanisation of corporate governance in China, in part because in the context of Chinese state-owned enterprises (SOEs), 'the state is both the controlling shareholder and the regulator of SOEs' making it both the judge and the most powerful shareholder and regulator of SOEs. Despite the numerous differences between China's SOEs and Singapore's government linked-companies (see Tan Cheng Han, Dan W Puchniak and Umakanth Varottil, 'State-Owned Enterprises in Singapore: Historical Insights into a Potential Model for Reform' (2015) 28 Columbia Journal of Asian Law), the tension between state-as-regulator and state-as-owner remains a fundamental conceptual challenge for public law.
26 See, for example, Felix Hoehn, 'Privatization and the Boundaries of Judicial Review' (2011) 54 Canadian Public Administration 73.
27 MS Haque, 'Public Administration in a Globalized Asia: Intellectual Identities, Challenges, and Prospects' (2013) 33 Public Administration 262, 268.
28 See Part II below.
29 IOSCO, *Objectives and Principles of Securities Regulation*: www.iosco.org/library/pubdocs/pdf/IOSCOPD323.pdf.
30 See generally, Anne-Marie Slaughter, *A New World Order* (Princeton University Press 2004).
31 The Accord on Fire & Building Safety in Bangladesh and the Alliance for Bangladesh Worker Safety.
32 See http://bangladeshaccord.org/.
33 See www.rspo.org/.
34 Colin Scott, Fabrizio Cafaggi and Linda Senden, 'The Conceptual and Constitutional Challenge of Transnational Private Regulation' (2011) 38 Journal of Law and Society 1, 7, 10–11.
35 See John Gillepsie, 'The Role of State, Non-State, and Hybrid Actors in Localizing Global Scripts in East Asia' in John Gillespie and Randall Peerenboom (eds), *Regulating in Asia: Pushing Back on Globalization* (Routledge 2009) 24–50.
36 See generally, Errol Meidinger, 'The Administrative Law of Global Private-Public Regulation: The Case of Forestry' (2006) 17 European Journal of International Law 47–87.
37 See www.isealalliance.org/about-us.
38 ibid.
39 See generally, Scott et al. (n 34).
40 Meidinger (n 36) 49–53.
41 See, for example, the standard-setting work of the International Accounting Standards Board (IASB): www.ifrs.org/About-us/IASB/Pages/Home.aspx.
42 For a recent example, see the liability provisions in Part II of the Transboundary Haze Pollution Act 2014 (No 24 of 2014).
43 See generally Victor V Ramraj, 'Beyond the Courts, Beyond the State' (2013) 88 Chicago-Kent Law Review 93; Mark Tushnet, 'The Issue of State Action/Horizontal Effect in Comparative Constitutional Law' (2003) 1 International Journal of Constitutional Law 79.
44 ibid. In Canada, see *Eldridge v British Columbia* [1997] 3 SCR 624.
45 n 2.
46 *Singapore Amateur Athletic Association v Haron Mundir* [1993] 3 SLR(R) 407 [76].
47 *Woon Kwek Cheng v HR Hochstadt* [1997] 2 MLJ 795 (High Court, Kuala Lumpur).
48 *Tan Boon Chee David v Medical Council of Singapore* [1980] 2 MLJ 116 (HC); but on the limits of judicial review in this context, depending on the stage of the proceedings, see *Manjit Singh s/o Kirpal Singh v Attorney-General* [2013] 2 SLR 844 (CA).
49 *Chiam See Tong v Singapore Democratic Party* [1993] 3 SLR(R) 774 (HC).
50 *Kay Swee Pin v Singapore Island Country Club* [2008] 2 SLR 802 (CA).
51 [2012] 3 SLR 565 (HC).

52 [1987] 2 WLR 699 (CA).
53 *Yap Wai Kong* (n 51) [9].
54 ibid [14].
55 ibid [15], citing Clive Lewis, *Judicial Remedies in Public Law* (4th edn, Sweet & Maxwell 2009) [2–003]. Following *Datafin*, however, the courts in Singapore would exclude from the scope of judicial review decision-makers in respect of which the *sole* source of their power is 'contractual or consensual': [16].
56 ibid [28].
57 Chan Sek Keong, 'Judicial Review – From Angst to Empathy' (2010) 22 Singapore Academy of Law Journal 469 [29], citing Carol Harlow and Richard Rawlings, *Law and Administration* (3rd edn, Cambridge University Press 2009).
58 Harlow and Rawlings, ibid 31.
59 ibid.
60 Chan Sek Keong (n 57) [29].
61 For an overview of the legal issues arising from the extra-territorial projection of criminal law, see Danielle Ireland-Piper, 'Extraterritorial Criminal Jurisdiction: Does the Long Arm of the Long Undermine the Rule of Law?' (2012) 13 Melbourne Journal International Law 1.
62 Respectively, where the national is a perpetrator or a victim.
63 Ireland-Piper explains: 'The territoriality principle may be invoked where conduct [takes place either] within a nation's borders (subjective territoriality) or the effects of the conduct are felt within the nation's borders (objective territoriality)' (n 61) 9.
64 These are crimes over which every state has jurisdiction, which typically include piracy, slave trading, genocide, crimes against humanity: ibid 15–16.
65 ibid 16.
66 Ireland-Piper (n 61) 6.
67 Where non-nationals are involved in activity taking place outside a state's territorial jurisdiction, it can be difficult to justify asserting extra-territorial jurisdiction: see, for example, *Kiobel v Royal Dutch Petroleum*, 569 US (2013).
68 *Public Prosecutor v Taw Cheng Kong* [1998] 2 SLR 410 (CA).
69 ibid 69, citing *R v Libman* (1985) 21 CCC (3d) 206, 228–29 (LaForest J).
70 n 42.
71 See, in Canada, *R v Cook* [1998] 2 SCR 597, confirming that the Canadian Charter of Rights and Freedoms could in 'certain rare and exceptional circumstances apply beyond Canada's territorial boundaries' – on the facts of this case, applicable to Canadian detectives interviewing a criminal suspect in the USA.
72 The Singapore International Arbitration Centre publishes on its website statistics on the number of new cases it handles each year. See: www.siac.org.sg/.
73 See www.sicc.gov.sg/About.aspx?id=21.
74 *Yong Vui Kong* (n 3).
75 In *Yong Vui Kong* the Court of Appeal sought to explain the constitutional status of the rules of nature justice articulated in *Ong Ah Chuan* [103]:

> [I]t is my view that a distinction must be made conceptually between the *Ong Ah Chuan* rules of natural justice and the administrative law rules of natural justice. This distinction stems from the difference in the juridical status of these two categories of rules of natural justice. As I have just mentioned, the *Ong Ah Chuan* rules of natural justice operate at the constitutional level in relation to the validity of legislation, whereas the administrative law rules of natural justice operate at an executive level in relation to the validity of administrative decisions.

76 See n 3.
77 A functional approach might be seen as requiring that the courts, in appropriate cases, recognise what is sometimes described as the 'horizontal effect' of constitutional law, allowing the Constitution to constrain the exercise of private power when the exercise

of that power adversely affects an individual's constitutional rights. I have made this argument at greater length elsewhere: Ramraj (n 43) 95–97. Cases such as *Yap Wai Kong*, however, justify the application of public law principles not primarily based on the outcome (the rights violation) but on the nature of the power that is exercised.

78 A recently publicised US Congressional Research Service study from 1999 reveals that 'since the dawn of American commercial aviation in 1918, the federal government had helped airlines in all sorts of ways, from direct subsidies to the building of airports and control towers, to the tune of $155 billion'; *The Economist* (25 April 2015) 14.

79 One attempt to articulate principles governing the relationship between states and state-owned enterprises can be found in the OECD's *Guidelines on Corporate Governance of State-Owned Enterprises*.

80 2009 BCSC 942 [104].

81 2009 BCCA 522 [49].

82 ibid [50].

83 ibid [65].

84 ibid [66].

85 n 51.

86 Steven Bernstein, 'When is Non-State Global Governance Really Governance?' (2010) Utah Law Review 91.

Bibliography

Bernstein, Steven, 'When is Non-State Global Governance Really Governance?' (2010) Utah Law Review 91.

Bowen, HV, *The Business of Empire: The East India Company and Imperial Britain* (Cambridge University Press 2006).

Bremmer, Ian, 'State Capitalism Comes of Age' Foreign Affairs (May/June 2009).

Chan, Sek Keong, 'Judicial Review – From Angst to Empathy' (2010) 22 Singapore Academy of Law Journal 469.

Coe, Neil M, Philip F Kelly and Henry WC Yeung, 'The Transnational Corporation' in *Economic Geography: A Contemporary Introduction* (Blackwell 2007).

Dyzenhaus, David, 'The Compulsion of Legality' in Victor V Ramraj (ed), *Emergencies and the Limits of Legality* (Cambridge University Press 2008).

Gillepsie, John, 'The Role of State, Non-State, and Hybrid Actors in Localizing Global Scripts in East Asia' in John Gillespie and Randall Peerenboom (eds), *Regulating in Asia: Pushing Back on Globalization* (Routledge 2009).

Grimm, Dieter, 'The Achievement of Constitutionalism and its Prospects in a Changed World' in Martin Loughlin and Petra Dobner (eds), *The Twilight of Constitutionalism?* (Oxford University Press 2010).

Haque, MS, 'Public Administration in a Globalized Asia: Intellectual Identities, Challenges, and Prospects' (2013) 33 Public Administration 262.

Harlow, Carol and Richard Rawlings, *Law and Administration* (3rd edn, Cambridge University Press 2009).

Hoehn, Felix, 'Privatization and the Boundaries of Judicial Review' (2011) 54 Canadian Public Administration 73.

Ireland-Piper, Danielle, 'Extraterritorial Criminal Jurisdiction: Does the Long Arm of the Law Undermine the Rule of Law?' (2012) 13 Melbourne Journal International Law 1.

Lawson, Philip, *The East India Company: A History* (Longman 1993).

Lewis, Clive, *Judicial Remedies in Public Law* (4th edn, Sweet & Maxwell 2009).

Meidinger, Errol, 'The Administrative Law of Global Private–Public Regulation: The Case of Forestry' (2006) 17 European Journal of International Law 47.

Muchlinski, Peter T, *Multinational Enterprises and the Law* (2nd edn, Oxford University Press 2007).

Ramraj, Victor V, 'Beyond the Courts, Beyond the State' (2013) 88 Chicago-Kent Law Review 79.

Roach, Brian, 'A Primer on Multinational Corporations' in Alfred D Chandler Jr. and Bruce Mazlish (eds), *Leviathans: Multinational Corporations and The New Global History* (Cambridge University Press 2005).

Robbins, Nick, *The Corporation that Changed the World: How the East India Company Shaped the Modern Multinational* (Pluto Press 2006).

Scott, Colin, Fabrizio Cafaggi and Linda Senden, 'The Conceptual and Constitutional Challenge of Transnational Private Regulation' (2011) 38 Journal of Law and Society 1.

Slaughter, Anne-Marie, *A New World Order* (Princeton University Press 2004).

Stern, Philip J, *The Company-State: Corporate Sovereignty and the Early Modern Foundations of the British Empire in India* (Oxford University Press 2011).

Tan, Cheng Han, Dan W Puchniak and Umakanth Varottil, 'State-Owned Enterprises in Singapore: Historical Insights into a Potential Model for Reform' (2015) 28 Columbia Journal Asian Law.

Tushnet, Mark, 'The Issue of State Action/Horizontal Effect in Comparative Constitutional Law' (2003) 1 International Journal of Constitutional Law 79.

Wang, Jiangyu, 'The Political Logic of Corporate Governance in China's State-Owned Enterprises' (2014) 47 Cornell International Law Journal 631.

Wooldridge, Adrian, 'The Visible Hand', *The Economist* (21 January 2012).

14 Is Singapore's Constitution Best Considered a Legal Constitution or a Political Constitution?

Michael W Dowdle and Kevin YL Tan

I Introduction

In this chapter, we discuss whether Singapore is best normatively thought of as having a 'legal constitution' or a 'political constitution'.[1] This discussion has important consequences for constitutional interpretation. A legal constitution places *ultimate* normative authority to issue constitutional interpretation in the judiciary (either in the general courts or in a particular court). A political constitution places *ultimate* normative authority to interpret the Constitution in the political system. How one conceptualises the Constitution further affects one's understanding of how interpretation takes place. Under legal constitutionalism, interpretations are as a normative matter performed using 'objective reasoning', ie teleological deductions from higher first principles leading to internally determinate right answers.[2] This is archetypically the way judges are supposed to decide the normative issues that come before them. By comparison, under political constitutionalism, interpretations are generated through processes of political balancing and bargaining. It is 'homeostatic' in the sense that the driving concern of such bargaining is one of maintaining social cohesion rather than one of finding right answers. Unlike juridical interpretations, political interpretations are not epistemically determinative: political constitutionalism involves an ongoing process of constant *re*-interpretation of the application and content of constitutional principles.

The terms of this discussion are normative, not formal or textual. In the context of Singapore, for example, it is undisputed that as a formal matter, ultimate authority to interpret the Constitution vests in the judiciary, via the confluence of Article 4 ('[t]his Constitution is the supreme law of the Republic of Singapore and any law enacted by the Legislature after the commencement of this Constitution which is inconsistent with this Constitution shall, to the extent of the inconsistency, be void') and Article 93 ('[t] he judicial power of Singapore shall be vested in a Supreme Court and in such subordinate courts as may be provided by any written law for the time being in force').[3] But, normative interpretative authority can often deviate from formal textual authority. For example, as a formal and textual matter, the United States Constitution gives *ultimate* authority to interpret the law to the American judiciary.[4] But the US

Supreme Court itself has nevertheless argued that insofar as certain kinds of governmental actions are concerned, final authority to interpret legal text actually vests in the political system rather than in the courts.[5]

We are also not debating who ultimately interprets the Constitution simply as a *factual* matter, which can be differentiated from the formal arrangement. For example, in France, as a normative matter, the Constitution grants ultimate interpretive authority to the *Conseil Constitutionnel*.[6] Nevertheless, as described by Alec Stone Sweet:

> [In France], [t]here is increasingly compelling evidence that ordinary judges are molding – by creatively interpreting – the various codes without first referring questions to the constitutional court. Judges read constitutional principles into the codes, through statutory interpretation (principled, constitutional construction of statutes), and sometimes they have gone beyond, or even contradicted, more restrictive interpretations of rights issued by the constitutional court. By foregoing constitutional referrals, ordinary judges enhance their own autonomy. In this way, both legislative intent and the alleged monopoly of the constitutional court on constitutional interpretation are subverted, enhancing the importance of the ordinary law courts as lawmakers in their own right.[7]

Furthermore, we also need to distinguish between claims about interpretive *authority* and claims about interpretive *legitimacy*. To say that normative authority deviates from formal or positivist authority is not to say that that normative authority is 'illegitimate'. In constitutional texts, normative authority frequently ends up deviating from where it is vested by the constitutional text, without impacting constitutional legitimacy. In fact, such divergences can be vital for the sustainability of the legal or constitutional system – allowing for what is sometimes referred to as a 'living' constitution.

For example, the text of the American Constitution quite clearly requires that judicial, executive and legislative powers be allocated to particular branches in particular ways. Nevertheless, by the late nineteenth century, it had become clear that the regulatory needs of the United States were simply too complex to be divided up in such a manner. The response was the invention of a new form of regulatory entity that concentrated under one institutional roof executive, legislative and judicial functions that the text of the Constitution said had to remain segregated from one another.[8] Despite its clear deviation from constitutional text,[9] the constitutionality of these 'independent regulatory agencies' – which would later be famously termed 'the fourth branch of government' – was never really called into question, and the law that governs them – aka administrative law – is often regarded as being its own kind of 'constitutional law', despite having no support in the text of the Constitution per se.[10]

II Dowdle's argument: Singapore's Constitution should be a political constitution

Despite formally vesting ultimate constitutional interpretive authority in the judiciary via its unqualified recognition of a judicial power of constitutional review,[11] I argue that Singapore's Constitution is nevertheless best *normatively* conceptualised as vesting ultimate constitutional interpretative authority in the Singaporean political system rather than in its legal system. Such a conceptualisation, it will be argued, is preferable because it better illuminates where the actual legitimacy of that system lies.

As noted above, there is nothing wrong with a constitution whose normative authority deviates from its textual authority. Not only does normative authority frequently deviate from textual authority, but some such deviation is absolutely necessary if the Constitution is to be a living one. Nor is there anything ersatz in a constitution that vests ultimate interpretative authority in the political system rather than in the judicial system. There is much literature extolling the value and desirability of a political constitution. Such constitutions, it is argued, can be more democratic and they can be more responsive.[12] They can more accurately reflect, reveal and give account to the diversity of incompatible yet valid normative perspectives that comprise the 'We the People' of the modern state.[13]

Legal constitutions, by contrast, present the state as a monolithic normative phenomenon. They are, in this sense, inherently authoritarian.[14] They have the advantage of presenting the state as if it were of a single mind, and in this way help to simplify the presentation of constitutional authority. But as a sociological matter, states are not psychologically or cognitively monolithic,[15] and the democratic robustness of the Constitution demands that the innately fuzzy and innately contested nature of state legitimacy be acknowledged rather than obscured by the constitutional system itself.[16] In this way, the conceptual clarity that is brought by a legal constitution comes at a cost to both political accuracy and constitutional accountability.[17]

It should be noted, however, that even in a political constitution courts can still play a role in the constitutional interpretive process. Courts do frequently participate in political interpretation. The key factor here is their interpretive methodology, not the interpreter as such. Under a political constitution, the courts' interpretative impact comes from their ability to convince others of the political desirability of their interpretations, not from their juridical infallibility. Elsewhere, I have referred to this particular aspect of judicial interpretation, 'constitutional poiesis'.[18] Martin Shapiro has called it, in a different aspect, 'judicial politics'.[19] Both describe a kind of judicial interpretation whose importance lies not so much in its substance per se as in the public reflections and social understandings that the interpretation provokes.

These resulting reflections and understandings can sometimes even come to rest on a particular authoritative interpretation that is very different from the one the court intended to promote. A good example of this would be the People's Republic of China's trial of Jiang Qing (Madame Mao) for treason in 1980.[20]

One might interpret the intent of the trial as showing the public that the disastrous Cultural Revolution was Jiang's fault, and not that of the ruling Communist Party (CCP). And along these lines, the court found Jiang guilty, thus indirectly confirming the CCP's 'innocence'. But the actual effect of that trial was arguably to convince China's general polity that Jiang's complicity could not be decoupled from that of the CCP: that in fact, the CCP was as responsible for the Cultural Revolution as was Jiang. In the aftermath of the trial, the CCP was forced to acknowledge that complicity and accept changes in China's constitutional structure that forced it to begin sharing constitutional authority with other constitutional actors.[21]

Furthermore, whether a constitutional system is better conceptualised as a political constitution or as a legal constitution primarily depends on how that system derives its legitimacy. Different constitutional systems found their legitimacy on different conceptual grounds. In general, we might distinguish between two broad kinds of foundations for constitutional legitimacy, what we might call static foundations and dynamic foundations. Static foundations see constitutional legitimacy as vesting in contiguity with particular historical (or pre-historical) benchmarks or conditions – such as founding events, founding ideologies, or simply eternal, natural orders. Dynamic foundations see constitutional legitimacy as deriving from the constitution's responsiveness to changes in an evolving world. Performance legitimacy is a good example of a dynamic foundation for constitutional legitimacy, as are popular sovereignty and other conceptualisations of constitutional responsiveness to a general will.

At least in the common law world, legal constitutionalism tends to correspond with static measures of constitutional legitimacy. This is because the normative role that consistency with historical precedent plays in establishing juridical legitimacy under the common law parallels and reifies the normative role that consistency with historical benchmarks plays in establishing constitutional legitimacy under what we call static foundations of constitutional legitimacy. Relatedly, we might also note that legal understandings of constitutionalism tend to be associated with more mature and more stable constitutional systems.[22] Such longevity and/or stability give experiential meaning to the very permanence and stability that static foundations of constitutional legitimacy work to highlight and emphasise. Political constitutionalism, by contrast, is better suited for constitutions founded on more dynamic conceptualisations of constitutional legitimacy. Politics is by its very nature driven by and thus responsive to human needs and interests, and it is in changes in these needs and interests that changes in the larger constitutional environment are most likely to be initially felt.[23]

Constitutional systems can also evince different foundations of legitimacy at different times in their history and can oscillate between static and dynamic foundations in response to larger evolutions in their socio-economic environment. For example, Bruce Ackerman's notion of 'constitutional moments' can be seen as describing punctuated periods of political constitutionalism dividing longer phases of legal constitutionalism in the context of American constitutional history. This reflects the fact that while the American socio-economic environment has been distinctly and perhaps unprecedentedly stable through most of it post-revolutionary history[24] (hence the long-term predominance of legal constitutionalism), it has nevertheless experienced occasional episodes of dramatic and dynamic socio-evolutionary change, for example, the 1860–1865 Civil War, industrial transformation in the 1890s, global economic collapse in the 1930s, and the egalitarian revolution in the 1950s, episodes that, because they demanded a more responsive constitutional reaction, ended up provoking a distinctly political form of constitutional regulation.

Some might argue that the political vision of constitutionalism requires a strongly and robustly liberal political environment in order to be effective. Politics is an innately highly pluralist phenomenon and, this being the case, political constitutionalism might only work in a polity that is able to accommodate and give meaningful voice to a wide diversity of pluralist perspectives. But, while it is true that the term derives from John Griffith's germinal article, 'The Political Constitution,'[25] which develops this idea to describe the British constitutional system, I have argued elsewhere that the same general dynamic can be identified in the constitutions of non-liberal states, and, perhaps more interestingly, can actually be seen as contributing to the development of a more open, pluralist political–constitutional environment. I termed this dynamic 'discursive benchmarking' in the context of my own work as I was trying to understand China's constitutional evolution during the 1990s (now in abeyance, unfortunately).[26]

Similarly, EP Thompson's magisterial study on early-industrial England, *The Making of the English Working Class*, shows a similar political–constitutional dynamic underlying the transformation of the English constitution from a strongly aristocratic–authoritarian constitutionalism into a much more liberal and democratic constitutionalism during the early part of the nineteenth century.[27]

A Political constitutionalism in Singapore

Given the above, I would argue that Singapore is best served by a political rather than legal constitutionalism, for three reasons. First, Singapore's constitutional environment is particularly dynamic at present, and a political constitutionalism system thus better suits its constitutional needs at present. Second, Singapore's actual constitutional environment much more resembles a political constitutionalism as a practical or sociological matter, and normative acknowledgement of that fact would enhance both the legitimacy and the effectiveness of its actual constitutional system. Third, and perhaps ironically, a political constitution could actually work to strengthen the judiciary's role in the process of constitutional interpretation.

B Singapore as a dynamic constitutional environment

Singapore's is a particularly dynamic constitutional environment at present. This is not simply the product of economic growth – Singapore's economic growth has been relatively constant over the past 120 years.[28] That has something to do with it, but so also do changes in the industrial system and in the regional environment. The foundational concerns that Singapore's constitutional system was originally designed to address are fast becoming irrelevant. Singapore no longer faces particular military threat, nor does it face existential threat from militant ideologies. It has, in the words of Lee Kuan Yew himself, transited 'from third world to first' and, as many studies have shown, such a transition also involved a transition in the polity's particular concerns and interests.[29]

This rapid transformation of concerns and interests requires constant negotiation and renegotiation of constitutional balances. The legal model of constitutionalism does not well accommodate such a process.[30] Authoritative judicial resolution of disputes arising from the environmental changes provoked by this dynamism are not subject to easy renegotiation as the environment continues to evolve, often in unforeseen directions. The political environment, in contrast, is constructed precisely out of such a need. In sum, a political constitution provides a much more responsive constitutional–regulatory system than does a legal constitutionalism – and responsiveness is an important quality in a rapidly changing constitutional environment.

C Singapore's constitutional system is 'political' in fact

Viewed from my own perspective as an outsider, it appears that regardless of its normative construction, Singapore's actual constitutional system is a political one. Despite having formal constitutional authority to do so, the courts do not appear willing to issue authoritative constitution interpretations that deviate from those issuing from the government or Parliament. Again, this is not a bad thing. As discussed above, actual authority often deviates from textual authority in a constitutional system, as is frequently the case when the constitutional system is dynamically evolving in response to changes in its environment (see discussion immediately above).

But, if Singapore's constitutional system is indeed political in fact, if not in text, then its constitutional ideology would do well to acknowledge that fact. A legal constitutionalism advises that constitutional disputes should be resolved by the courts. It focuses one's constitutional attentions on judicial matters and processes. But, to the extent that Singapore's is a political constitution in fact, this would mean that one's understanding of and navigation of that system would be best served by focusing one's constitutional attentions on political rather than judicial processes. A normatively political understanding of Singapore's constitutional system would encourage such a focus, and thus promote the effectiveness and responsiveness of that system.

D Political constitutionalism allows the judiciary to better contribute to constitutional interpretation in Singapore

As described above, political constitutionalism does not remove the judiciary entirely from the process of constitutional interpretation, but it does change the courts' role. The courts are no longer authoritative constitutional interpreters. Instead, they are suggestive constitutional interpreters – in the sense that the effectiveness of their interpretations does not come from their status as courts, but from their capacity to introduce new and significant insight into the political–constitutional process.

There is good evidence that Singaporean courts see themselves in such a light. Two recent cases show the courts issuing decisions that appeal directly to the political–constitutional process, as opposed to simply asserting legal–constitutional authority. One of these is the judgement of the Court of Appeal in *Vellama d/o Marie Muthu v Attorney-General*, also known as 'the Hougang by-election case'.[31] Despite holding that the appellant ultimately lacked standing to sue the Government, the court nevertheless found it worthwhile to issue a reminder to the Government that:

> Art 49 does not give the Prime Minister an unfettered discretion in the calling of an election to fill a casual vacancy of an elected MP. He must do so within a reasonable time and in that regard, the Prime Minister is entitled to take into account all relevant circumstances and only in clear cases can there be judicial intervention.[32]

Such obiter has no juridical standing. Its inclusion in the judgment thus only makes sense if one is approaching Singapore's constitutional environment from the perspective of political constitutionalism, its import stemming not from the court's constitutional status as ultimate interpreter, but from the intellectual strength and political persuasiveness of its reasoning.

A similar observation attaches to Andrew Phang JA's opinion in the already widely discussed section 377A case of *Lim Meng Suang and another v Attorney-General*.[33] Viewed from the perspective of legal constitutionalism, Justice Phang's opinion is curious. *Lim Meng Suang* is not a particularly hard case: the legal doctrine on which the decision ultimately rests is quite well established, and the facts of the case seem to fall well within that doctrine. Nevertheless, Justice Phang's judgment runs over 30,000 words. Most of his argument is devoted to showing why the petitioner's various claims should properly be addressed to Parliament rather than to the court – citing, in the process, a wide range of literary as well as juridical sources. From a juridical perspective, one wonders why Justice Phang would devote such incredible effort to what in fact appears to be quite an easy case.

But the case acquires a much more sophisticated meaning from the perspective of the political constitution. To recap, the case involves the question of whether the anti-sodomy provision in the Penal Code (ie section 377A) comports with the guarantees of 'liberty of the person' and 'equal protection' under Articles 9 and 12(1) respectively of the Singapore Constitution. The court's opinion emphasises, over and over, that a simple demonstration that section 377A might be offensive, absurd or illegitimate are not considerations that the court should take into account. But after showing and emphasising again and again how none of the appellant's arguments are of legal merit, the court then devotes 35 out of its 190 paragraphs to evaluating their persuasiveness *as extra-legal arguments*:

> We turn now to consider the status and role of the aforementioned extra-legal arguments, a number of which were made by the parties in both their written as well as their oral submissions before this court. In our view, these arguments are (as already mentioned) clearly neither relevant nor material in so far as the application of the 'reasonable classification' test is concerned. Neither are they relevant in so far as the application of Art 12(2) is concerned. What, then, would be the relevance (if any) of these arguments? In order to answer this more general question, it would be useful, in our view, to consider the specific extra-legal arguments which were made in the context of the present appeals. We should, however, emphasise that in doing so, we are not in any way taking these extra-legal arguments into account for the purposes of our decision on the legal issues set out above at [41] vis-à-vis the constitutionality of s 377A.[34]

In fact, the court notes that it finds a number of the appellants' extra-legal arguments at least somewhat compelling:

> In our view, whilst many of the Appellants' extra-legal arguments are valid (or, at least, plausible) ones, they are not arguments that maybe appropriately considered by the court and are thus legally irrelevant. Put simply, the court is not the appropriate forum in which to canvass such arguments; the appropriate forum in this regard is, instead, the legislature.[35]

Furthermore, the court found the appellants' arguments similarity to the Devlin–Hart debate and JS Mill's notion of the 'harm principle' particularly worthy of note, observing that the Devlin–Hart debate ultimately led to the repeal of the UK's anti-sodomy law:

> The Appellants' argument based on the absence of harm was that their sexual conduct caused no harm to others. This particular argument was, of course, part of the broader jurisprudential debate on the enforcement of morals between Lord Devlin on the one hand … and Prof H L A Hart on the other.[36]
>
> …
>
> Turning, first, to the general debate between Lord Devlin and Prof Hart, the arguments on each side of the philosophical divide are, as mentioned above at [166], weighty ones.… In particular, the Appellants' reliance in these proceedings on the 'harm principle' enunciated by Mill raises the very pertinent issue of what constitutes 'harm' in the first place.… Hence, the Appellants' argument based on the absence of harm, when examined more

> closely, reveals itself to be, in substance if not in form, one which ought (if at all) to be considered by the legislature.[37]
>
> ...
>
> Indeed (and consistent with the observations just made), it is also highly significant, in our view, to note that the Wolfenden Report, which (as we mentioned above at [163]) was the effective catalyst of the jurisprudential debate between Lord Devlin and Prof Hart, ultimately led (albeit only a decade later) to legislative action on the part of the UK Parliament (in the form of the Sexual Offences Act 1967 (c 60) (UK), which, inter alia, abolished the UK equivalent of s 377A).[38]

It is also notable that in numerous places, Justice Phang seems to be almost imploring the appellants to take their arguments to Parliament:

> The underlying thread of our discussion at [157]–[177] above is clear and may be stated simply: all the arguments referred to in those paragraphs are extra-legal arguments that, whilst not necessarily unpersuasive, ought nevertheless to be raised in the appropriate forum, which is the legislature.... It is also important to emphasise that the Appellants are not thereby deprived of the opportunity to proffer the extra-legal arguments they have raised, but they have to do so at a different forum, *viz*, before the legislature.[39]
>
> ...
>
> Indeed, our legislature can, apart from actually abolishing s 377A, also effect solutions which are clearly beyond the powers of the court. For example, Ms Barker strongly urged this court (as a possible alternative) to at least delete the words ‘or private’ in s 377A, hence ‘reading down’ s 377A to that extent (see the paragraphs of Lim and Chee’s Appellants’ Case which we referred to above at [19]). However, consistent with the analysis set out above, this proposed solution is clearly outside the powers of this court, although it is an approach which can be taken by our Parliament (if it is so persuaded).[40]
>
> ...
>
> The present appeals were argued by both Ms Barker as well as Mr Ravi with great passion on behalf of their respective clients. This is not surprising, especially when one takes into account the intensely controversial (and even emotional) nature of the arguments surrounding the nature and function of s 377A which have been canvassed by proponents on either side of the extra-legal divide. Indeed, many of the arguments tendered to this court, whilst valid (or, at least, plausible) in their own right, involved extra-legal considerations and matters of social policy which were outside the remit of the court, and should, instead, have been canvassed in the legislative sphere. It is entirely appropriate, at this juncture, to reiterate a point we have already made several times in the course of this judgment, not least because it is an extremely important and fundamental one: the court can only consider legal (as opposed to extra-legal) arguments.[41]

All of this obiter is not relevant from the perspective of a legal constitution. If the appellants' arguments do not raise justiciable issues, then they can be summarily dismissed without evaluation of their argumentative merits. But it can be seen as making sense from the perspective of political constitutionalism. Is Justice Phang's obiter not possibly saying, not simply that this is an issue for the political process, but that this is an *important* issue for the political process, one that the political process really should revisit? Is his extensive discussion about how even reasonable moral objectionability does not make a statute amenable to judicial nullification really a discussion about the very possible – probable? – reasonableness of the petitioners' moral objections? Is this a subtle – but, at the same time, very visible – suggestion that due to the *reasonableness* of the petitioners' moral objections, the 'constitutionality' of this statute should in fact be revisited by the political process?

If this is the court's point, then the extensive space it devotes to the jurisprudential limits of the doctrines of legality and rationality seems logical. Such a discussion serves to highlight the actual reasonableness of the petitioners' objections. It thereby demands that while these objections might not resonate in the realm of legal constitutionalism, they should resonate very strongly in the realm of political constitutionalism. And for this reason, this is a matter that very much demands and deserves constitutional revisiting and reconsideration. The court might be saying that even if the constitutionality of this statute is not problematic from a juridical perspective, it does clearly appear very problematic from a political–constitutional perspective. The length of obiter might have been intended to compel political–constitutional reconsideration, even if legal–constitutional reconsideration is inappropriate.

III Tan's riposte: Singapore's Constitution should be a legal constitution

Dowdle argues strongly that Singapore is *best normatively thought of as* having a political constitution rather than a legal one. This is because 'it better illuminates where the actual legitimacy of that system really lies'. Whether a constitution is seen as a 'political' or 'legal' one, says Dowdle, depends on where *ultimate* authority for interpreting the Constitution lies. Thus, in a 'political constitution', it is politics rather than the courts that determine the ultimate meaning of the Constitution. As Dowdle says, 'ultimate interpretative authority *should* and should properly be seen as lying in the political system'. Furthermore, political constitutions 'do not recognise, as a normative matter, that *ultimate* interpretive authority should or can be vested in any particular institutions' because in such constitutions, courts do not 'sit above the political process' but are instead part of it.

What is the basis for the legitimacy of Singapore's Constitution such that it should be seen as a political constitution? Dowdle argues that there are two 'broad kinds of foundations for constitutional legitimacy': *static* foundations and *dynamic* foundations. Static foundations –found mostly in common law countries and mature polities – vest legitimacy 'in contiguity with particular historical (or pre-historical) benchmarks or conditions' such as 'founding events, founding ideologies, or simply eternal, natural orders'. Dynamic foundations vest legitimacy in the 'constitution's responsiveness to one or more particular aspects of an evolving world', as such, factors such as performance legitimacy, popular sovereignty and 'other conceptualisations of constitutional responsiveness to a general democratic will'.

Singapore, says Dowdle, is a 'particularly dynamic constitutional environment' because its rapid transformation from 'third world to first' requires the constitutional balance between its citizens' concerns and interests to be constantly negotiated and renegotiated. This dynamic environment cannot be accommodated by a legal model of constitutionalism, whereas a political constitution 'provides a much more responsive constitutional–regulatory system'.

A Is a responsive constitution necessarily political?

Dowdle's entire argument hinges on his typology wherein constitutional legitimacy rests on either static or dynamic foundations. This typology is interesting but unrealistic because elements that make up a constitution's legitimacy are not so easily bifurcated. Is it not possible that Singapore's constitutional legitimacy rests on both static and dynamic elements? More importantly, such a typology ignores the fact that courts and politics play different but complementary roles in shaping the Constitution. This is as it should be in a constitutional supremacy where the roles of the courts and other branches of government are clearly demarcated. Parliament has, for the most part, the power to amend the Constitution, but this process is regulated by the Constitution, and if there is a dispute as to whether the proper processes and procedures are adhered to, it is the courts that make the final determination.

When the political branch responds to a need to balance competing interests by amending the Constitution, it is performing its constitutionally prescribed and defined role and not undertaking any form of interpretation as *ultimate* authority. Dynamism and responsiveness alone do not make Singapore's Constitution a political one. Not every major political debate or dispute is a constitutional question or dispute, but if a constitutional question has arisen, the courts have not shied away from responding. If a court is unable to respond because the dispute or controversy is not a legal one, its legitimacy is not in any way diminished. For example, the question as to whether the Government should nationalise the public transport services is a matter of great political and practical import, but is not one which any court of law can decide since it is purely a matter of policy. No issue of constitutional interpretation will arise in such a case, even in a dynamic setting.

B Constitutionalism, constitutional supremacy and the separation of powers

By requiring the courts to be the *ultimate* authority on all things political and policy matters, Dowdle pays scant attention to the fact that: (a) we operate under a constitutional supremacy; and (b) under the Constitution, the doctrine of the separation of powers requires each branch of government to respond to issues and disputes in different ways. It is for this reason that courts have developed the 'political question doctrine' alongside the 'judicial power' doctrine. Each branch of government is co-equal but functions differently. As the High Court declared in *Law Society of Singapore v Tan Guat Neo Phyllis* (2007):

> In Singapore, the Constitution establishes a form of parliamentary government (based on the Westminster model) based on the separation of the legislative, executive and judicial powers. Each arm of the government operates independently of the other and each should not interfere with the functions of the other. As each of them is limited in its authority and power by the Constitution itself, it is necessary that there should exist a means whereby each arm may be prevented from acting beyond its constitutional powers. Under the Constitution, the means adopted and recognised by all three arms of government is the judicial power of the court to review the legality of legislative and executive acts and declare them unconstitutional and of no legal effect if they contravene the provisions of the Constitution.[42]

By expecting the courts to resolve every major issue, Dowdle is putting an unrealistic burden on the judiciary. This is not only unrealistic, but it ignores what Alexander Bickel in *The Least Dangerous Branch* calls 'the counter-majoritarian difficulty'. Judges are appointed and not elected and thus do not carry anyone's mandate to decide policy. If judges venture into political territory, they lose credibility and legitimacy.

It seems to me that Dowdle's puzzle is whether courts are the ultimate authority to decide all matters of constitutional import rather than whether courts are the ultimate authority to interpret the Constitution. These are quite different questions. There are a great many issues that touch on our constitutional rights, some fairly minor and others of great import. And if this is Dowdle's main concern, then it is fair to say that the ultimate authority for deciding these matters is more likely to be in the political than the legal sphere. That is because debates about rights issues emanate from the polity itself. These debates may or may not manifest in laws and contests may or may not end up in court. It is only when a constitutional dispute arrives at the doorstep of the courts that the second question kicks in. Who then is the ultimate interpreter of the Constitution? The judiciary, of course.

Let me end by addressing the two cases Dowdle cites as being instances that show Singapore to be operating under political constitutionalism. The first case he cites is the Court of Appeal's decision in *Lim Meng Suang v Attorney-General*

(2014)[43] where he reads Andrew Phang JA as 'endorsing political constitutionalism' because the judgment 'implies that responsibility for interpreting the constitution, at least insofar as public law jurisprudence is concerned, ultimately vests in the political process'.

This case involved a constitutional challenge to section 377A of the Penal Code. In sum, the argument raised in this case was that section 377A violated Article 12(1) of the Constitution in that it discriminated against male homosexuals. The Court of Appeal held, applying the long-standing reasonable classification test, that it was constitutional. The object of the section was clear; it was intended to criminalise male homosexual conduct by outlawing sodomy. If the parliamentary object was so clear, and since the court refused to deviate from the reasonable classification test, the provision must, *ipso facto*, be constitutional. In the course of his judgment, Phang JA remarked – several times – that the court was not and should not act as a 'mini legislature' thus suggesting that reform of this law – which is seen by a substantial segment of the public as being unfair – can only come from the law-makers in Parliament.[44] This is an acknowledgement of the boundaries of what the judiciary can do under the Constitution and not evidence of political constitutionalism at work.

The second case Dowdle cites is another Court of Appeal decision – *Vellama d/o Marie Muthu v Attorney-General* (2013).[45] Dowdle argues that we can read the court's obiter dicta as encouraging the executive 'to engage in extra-legal – and, therefore, possibly political – deliberation as to what the proper constitutional demands are for calling by-elections'. I do not see it in this light. Both the High Court and Court of Appeal rightly allowed the matter to proceed even though the issue was moot by the time it went for hearing – a by-election in Hougang constituency had already been called – because the matter was of grave constitutional and legal import. The key concern in this case was the interpretation of Article 49 of the Constitution. A proper and authoritative interpretation of this provision – hitherto not litigated upon – is well and clearly within the province of the judiciary. The fact that the Court of Appeal left it to the executive branch to decide what was a 'reasonable time' was not a politicisation of this decision. The court still has ultimate authority to determine if the Prime Minister exercised his discretion reasonably.

We live under a constitutional supremacy. This means that the Constitution is our highest law. The interpretation of that law is functionally the responsibility of the judiciary. The idea of 'political constitutionalism', at least as popularised by John Griffiths, is a realist's critique of the British judiciary and a brutal acknowledgement of its powerlessness in a system where Parliament is sovereign.[46] Ultimate sovereignty in any democracy lies with the people as a constituent body and, in a parliamentary supremacy, the two bodies become synonymous. That is not the case in a constitutional supremacy. Singapore's Constitution recognises – as a matter of law, not politics – that in selected matters, the decision of a mobilised electorate is required. So, Article 6 of the Constitution mandates that there shall be 'no surrender or transfer … of the sovereignty of the Republic of Singapore as an independent nation' without a referendum that is carried by at least two-thirds of all electors. In such a major constitutional issue, the people are called upon to make a choice but this does not mean that the courts have in this instance been sacrificed at the altar of the political. That is what the supreme law of the land requires. And *ultimate* authority to determine what that means remains with the court. Singapore's is, both empirically and normatively, a legal constitution.

Notes

1 See generally John AG Griffith, 'The Political Constitution' (1979) 42 The Modern Law Review.
2 See Ronald Dworkin, *Law's Empire* (Harvard University Press 1986).
3 See also Li-ann Thio, *A Treatise in Singapore Constitutional Law* (Academic Publishers 2012), 252–57, 556–70.
4 See US Constitution, Art 3 (1789).
5 See eg *Marbury v Madison*, 5 US 137 (1803); *Chevron US, Inc. v Natural Resources Defense Council, Inc*, 467 US 837 (1984).
6 See French Constitution, Art 62, § 2 (1958).
7 Alec Stone Sweet, 'The Politics of Constitutional Review in France and Europe' (2007) 5 International Journal of Constitutional Law 69.
8 See generally Stephen Skowronek, *Building a New American State: The Expansion of National Administrative Capacities, 1877–1920* (Cambridge University Press 1982).
9 Harold H Bruff, 'On the Constitutional Status of the Administrative Agencies' (1986) 36 American University Law Review 491.
10 Alan B Morrison, 'The Administrative Procedure Act: A Living and Responsive Law' (1986) 72 Virginia Law Review 253.
11 See Thio (n 3) 252–57, 556–70.
12 See Richard Bellamy, *Political Constitutionalism: A Republican Defence of the Constitutionality of Democracy* (Cambridge University Press 2007).
13 See also Martin Loughlin, *The Idea of Public Law* (Oxford University Press 2003) 52.
14 See also Michael A Wilkinson, 'The Reconstitution of Postwar Europe: Liberal Excesses, Democratic Deficiencies' in Michael W Dowdle and Michael A Wilkinson (eds), *Constitutionalism Beyond Liberalism* (Cambridge University Press 2016).
15 See eg James Q Wilson, *Bureaucracy: What Government Agencies Do and Why They Do It* (Basic Books 1989) 31–112.
16 See Loughlin (n 13) 52.
17 See eg Wilkinson (n 14).
18 Michael W Dowdle, 'Beyond "Judicial Power": Courts and Constitutionalism in Modern China' in Stéphanie Balme and Michael W Dowdle (eds), *Building Constitutionalism in China* (Palgrave Macmillan 2009).
19 Martin Shapiro, 'Public Law and Judicial Politics' in Ada W Finifter (ed), *Political Science: The State of the Discipline* (The American Political Science Association 1993).
20 See generally Dowdle (n 18) 204–10.
21 ibid 210.
22 See Michael W Dowdle, 'Of Parliaments, Pragmatism and the Dynamics of Constitutional Development: The Curious Case of China' (2002) 35 NYU Journal of International Law and Politics 1, 22–30.
23 See Loughlin (n 13) 52.
24 Bruce Ackerman, *We, The People*, Vol 1: *Foundations* (Belknap Press 1993). Cf Akhil Reed Amar, 'Some New World Lessons for the Old World' (1991) 58 University of Chicago Law Review 483.

25 Griffith (n 1).
26 See generally Dowdle (n 22).
27 EP Thompson, *The Making of the English Working Class* (Penguin New Edn 1991).
28 See Gregg Huff, *Economic Growth of Singapore: Trade and Development in the Twentieth Century* (Cambridge University Press 1994).
29 Lee Kuan Yew, *From Third World to First – The Singapore Story: 1965–2000* (Harper 2000).
30 See also Michael W Dowdle, 'On the Public-Law Character of Competition Law: A Lesson from Asian Capitalism' (2015) 38 Fordham International Law Journal 301, 355–60.
31 [2013] SGCA 39.
32 ibid 92.
33 [2014] SGCA 53.
34 ibid 155.
35 ibid 156.
36 ibid 162.
37 ibid 169.
38 ibid 174.
39 ibid 178.
40 ibid 180.
41 ibid 189.
42 [2008] 2 SLR(R) 239, 310.
43 [2015] 1 SLR 26.
44 ibid 28, 52, 54, 56, 57, 61, 61, 88 and 94.
45 [2013] 4 SLR 1.
46 See Griffiths (n 1).

Bibliography

Ackerman, Bruce, *We the People: Foundations* (Belknap Harvard 1991).
Amar, Akhil Reed, 'Some New World Lessons for the Old World' (1991) 58 University of Chicago Law Review 483.
Bellamy, Richard, *Political Constitutionalism: A Republican Defence of the Constitutionality of Democracy* (Cambridge University Press 2007).
Bruff, Harold H, 'On the Constitutional Status of the Administrative Agencies' (1986) 36 American University Law Review 491.
Dowdle, Michael W, 'Of Parliaments, Pragmatism and the Dynamics of Constitutional Development: The Curious Case of China' (2002) 35 NYU Journal of International Law and Politics 1.
Dowdle, Michael W, 'Beyond "Judicial Power": Courts and Constitutionalism in Modern China' in Stéphanie Balme and Michael W Dowdle (eds), *Building Constitutionalism in China* (Palgrave Macmillan 2009).
Dowdle, Michael W, 'On the Public-Law Character of Competition Law: A Lesson from Asian Capitalism' (2015) 38 Fordham International Law Journal 301.
Dworkin, Ronald, *Law's Empire* (Harvard University Press 1986).
Griffith, John AG, 'The Political Constitution' (1979) 42 Modern Law Review 1.
Huff, Gregg, *Economic Growth of Singapore: Trade and Development in the Twentieth Century* (Cambridge University Press 1994).
Lee, Kuan Yew, *From Third World to First –The Singapore Story: 1965–2000* (Harper 2000).
Loughlin, Martin, *The Idea of Public Law* (Oxford University Press 2003).

Morrison, Alan B, 'The Administrative Procedure Act: A Living and Responsive Law' (1986) 72 Virginia Law Review 253.
Shapiro, Martin, 'Public Law and Judicial Politics' in Ada W Finifter (ed), *Political Science: The State of the Discipline* (The American Political Science Association 1993).
Skowronek, Stephen, *Building a New American State: The Expansion of National Administrative Capacities, 1877–1920* (Cambridge University Press 1982).
Sweet, Alec Stone, 'The Politics of Constitutional Review in France and Europe' (2007) 5 International Journal Constitutional Law 69.
Thio, Li-ann, *A Treatise in Singapore Constitutional Law* (Academic Publishers 2012).
Thompson, EP, *The Making of the English Working Class* (Penguin New Edn 1991).
Wilkinson, Michael A, 'The Reconstitution of Postwar Europe: Liberal Excesses, Democratic Deficiencies' in Michael W Dowdle and Michael A Wilkinson (eds), *Constitutionalism Beyond Liberalism* (Cambridge University Press 2016).
Wilson, James Q, *Bureaucracy: What Government Agencies Do and Why They Do It* (Basic Books 1989).

Index

For Product Safety Concerns and Information please contact our EU
representative GPSR@taylorandfrancis.com
Taylor & Francis Verlag GmbH, Kaufingerstraße 24, 80331 München, Germany

www.ingramcontent.com/pod-product-compliance
Ingram Content Group UK Ltd.
Pitfield, Milton Keynes, MK11 3LW, UK
UKHW020023200926
475702UK00014B/2032

* 9 7 8 1 1 3 8 4 7 7 7 5 9 *